D0406966

WILLIAM FAULKNER AND SOUTHERN HISTORY

WILLIAM FAULKNER AND SOUTHERN HISTORY

Joel Williamson

New York Oxford
OXFORD UNIVERSITY PRESS
1993

Oxford University Press

Oxford New York Toronto
Delhi Bombay Calcutta Madras Karachi
Kuala Lumpur Singapore Hong Kong Tokyo
Nairobi Dar es Salaam Cape Town
Melbourne Auckland Madrid

and associated companies in
Berlin Ibadan

Published by Oxford University Press, Inc.,
200 Madison Avenue, New York, New York 10016

Oxford is a registered trademark of Oxford University Press

Library of Congress Cataloging-in-Publication Data
Williamson, Joel.
William Faulkner and southern history /
Joel Williamson.
p. cm. Includes bibliographical references and index.
ISBN 0-19-507404-1
1. Faulkner, William, 1897–1962—Knowledge—Southern States.
2. Faulkner, William, 1897–1962—Biography.
3. Novelists, American—20th century—Biography
4. Southern States in literature.
5. Southern States—Civilization.
6. Southern States—Biography. I. Title.
PS3511.A86Z98574 1993
813'.52—dc20 [b] 92-22780

Permissions are listed on p vi.

1 3 5 7 9 8 6 4 2

Printed in the United States of America
on acid-free paper

For Anna

I am grateful to the following writers and publishers for permission to reprint selections from previously published works and to use selections from previously unpublished works:

Random House, Inc. For excerpts from:

Light in August by William Faulkner. Copyright 1932 and renewed 1960 by William Faulkner. Reprinted by permission of Random House, Inc.

The Hamlet by William Faulkner. Copyright 1940 by William Faulkner and renewed 1968 by Estelle Faulkner and Jill Faulkner Summers. Reprinted by permission of Random House, Inc.

Go Down, Moses by William Faulkner. Copyright 1942 by William Faulkner and renewed 1969 by Jill Faulkner Summers. Reprinted by permission of Random House, Inc.

Selected Letters of William Faulkner, ed. Joseph Blotner. Copyright 1977 by Joseph Blotner. Reprinted by permission of Random House, Inc.

The Sound and the Fury by William Faulkner. Copyright 1946. Reprinted by permission of Random House, Inc.

The Reivers by William Faulkner. Copyright 1962. Reprinted by permission of Random House, Inc.

The Mansion by William Faulkner. Copyright 1959. Reprinted by permission of Randon House, Inc.

Absalom, Absalom! by William Faulkner. Copyright 1936. Reprinted by permission of Random House, Inc.

Intruder in the Dust by William Faulkner. Copyright 1948. Reprinted by permission of Random House, Inc.

The Town by William Faulkner. Copyright 1957. Reprinted by permission of Random House, Inc.

Faulkner: A Biography by Joseph Blotner. Copyright 1974, 1984. Reprinted by permission of Random House, Inc.

University Press of Mississippi. For excerpts from:

William Faulkner: A Life on Paper, script by A.I. Bezzerides, introduction by Carvel Collins, adapted and edited by Ann Abadie. Copyright © 1980.

Count No-Count, Flashbacks to Faulkner by Ben Wasson. Copyright © 1983.

University of Tennessee Press. For excerpts from:

Sherwood Anderson: Selected Letters, ed. Charles E. Modlin. Copyright © 1984.

University of Texas Press. For excerpts from:

William Faulkner: Life Glimpses by Louis Daniel Brodsky. Copyright © 1990. By permission of the author and the University of Texas.

Seajay Press. For excerpts from:

William Faulkner: His Tippah County Heritage by Jane Isbell Haynes. Copyright © 1985.

The Letters of Sherwood Anderson, ed. Howard Mumford Jones. Copyright 1953 by Eleanor Anderson. Copyright renewed 1981 by Eleanor Copenhaver Anderson.

The Viking Press. For excerpts from:

Writers at Work: The Paris Interviews, ed. Malcolm Cowley. Copyright 1958.

Dun and Bradstreet and the Baker Library of the Harvard University Graduate School of Business Administration. For excerpts from:

The R. G. Dun & Co. Collection.

Writer to writer, I am also grateful to the following:

Ann Abadie
Joseph Blotner
Louis Daniel Brodsky
Robert Hamblin
James Meriwether
Michael Millgate
Joan Williams

Contents

WILLIAM FAULKNER AND SOUTHERN HISTORY

Out of the Garden

Himself

"Born?" he said, repeating the question.

"Yes. I was born male and single at an early age in Mississippi. I am still alive but not single."

William Faulkner, in 1931, was being flip and fighting for his privacy as he answered the questions of Marshall Smith, a reporter from the Memphis *Press-Scimitar*. Faulkner had leapt suddenly into the popular eye with the publication of his book *Sanctuary*. In writing that story, he later said, he had deliberately set out to create not a great novel, but merely a lucrative one. His goal, at age thirty-three, was to publish a book that would sell 10,000 copies. None of his several earlier works had sold more than 2,000. By his own account, *Sanctuary* did not represent a heavy investment of time; he wrote the manuscript, he sometimes boasted, in three weeks. In reality, it was written in several months over a two-year period.[1] The story featured sex and violence—the two meeting most memorably when a gangster-bootlegger-villain named Popeye raped a seventeen-year-old University of Mississippi co-ed, Temple Drake, with a corncob and subsequently held her a not entirely unwilling captive in a Memphis brothel.

Sanctuary won instant attention, including some significant acclaim as a work of genius and general condemnation as a dirty book. Ironically, critics at large had only grudgingly noticed Faulkner's *The Sound and the Fury*, published in 1929, a work that many literary scholars eventually came to see as America's greatest twentieth-century experiment in the art of the novel, one that compared favorably with James Joyce's highly celebrated *Ulysses,* published in 1922. Neither were they impressed, at first, with another masterpiece, *As I Lay Dying,* published in 1930.

William Faulkner's writings abound in paradox, and so too does his life. He craved fame and fortune, but he hated the scrutiny that success brought to his personal life. Usually mannerly, sometimes engaging, even warm and easy with children, some relatives, and a few friends, he grew reticent and ultimately surly and insulting when he felt that his own life was under inspection. When forced to emerge into public view against his will, he often stood behind a shield of impeccably correct manners and a reticence that approached taciturnity. At other times, he exhibited a Faulkner manqué, a persona, a Faulkner that was neither appealing nor, objectively considered, very real.

The Memphis reporter had traveled the seventy-five miles southeast to Oxford, Mississippi, to visit Faulkner at Rowan Oak, his home on the southern edge of the village. It was summer and Sunday in the midst of the Great Depression. The interview began with Faulkner, unshaven, casual, a small, slight, dark man, squatting on the kitchen floor, siphoning homebrew into used ginger ale bottles out of a cracked churn. A neighbor, a black man, was helping him. Another black man came to the back door. Standing barefooted on the porch, he mumbled something about "two bits" and needing some "cawn meal." He left, flipping a quarter into the air, catching it, flipping it again. Faulkner and the reporter carried cool pitchers of beer out into the yard and sat under cedars planted for the pleasure of Rowan Oak's antebellum mistress. Faulkner had bought the house a year before. It was built in the 1840s, the landscaping of magnolias, cedars, and crape myrtle designed and executed, tradition insisted, by an English architect specially imported for the task. Once considered a grand mansion for its time and place, with a portico and four two-story columns, it was now gray and decaying. Faulkner was bringing Rowan Oak to life again, doing much of the work himself, installing support beams, plumbing, heating, and wiring day by day after he had finished a morning of writing.

The interview ran through one pitcher of beer and into another. The reporter asked Faulkner what he thought about education. The writer confessed to having spent five years in the seventh grade (metaphorically true in that Faulkner had very little interest in school beyond his seventh year). He continued his biography. "Quit school and went to work in Grandfather's bank," he said, dropping to a style of omitting the personal pronoun. It could have been an outline of a story, or a parody of the clipped language of entries in *Who's Who in America.* "Learned the medicinal value of his liquor. Grandfather thought it was the janitor. Hard on the janitor." World War I saved Faulkner from the bank and brought him out of Mississippi. "Liked British uniform. Got commission R.F.C. pilot. Crashed. Cost British government 2000 pounds. Was still pilot. Crashed. Cost British government 2000 pounds. Quit. Cost British government $84.30. King said, 'Well done!' Returned to Mississippi."[2]

The persona that Faulkner offered the reporter was one of a highly talented and unpretentious writer, cosmopolitan in experience but still a country man, a farmer, hunter, and fisher—and a naturally good storyteller. Nothing of the "Smart Set" about William Faulkner, no lacing of language with French phrases, no hint of racing sports cars or smooth-legged flappers, no Hemingway or Fitzgerald here. Indeed, he was unique. Perhaps no American writer between the World Wars wrote so well without leaving home, and probably none was so deeply unknowable. Over the next twenty years particularly, Faulkner would remain very much a man of mystery. When pressed, he offered stories that were, in effect, deceptive, and made statements that contradicted themselves or were so elliptical as to be nearly meaningless. Virtually no one, it seems, ever knew the real Faulkner. But they certainly knew his work.

His Work

In the year 1931 Faulkner was in the second of three major phases of his life as a publishing writer. The first began in 1924 when he produced a book of poems entitled *The Marble Faun.* It is often alleged that Faulkner changed the spelling of his family name at that point from the traditional "Falkner" by simply accepting and adopting an error in printing. It is much more likely that Faulkner, himself, deliberately chose to change the spelling in 1918 when he was posing as an Englishman and plotting to join the Royal Air Force. For several years thereafter, sometimes his name would be spelled with a "u" and sometimes not. Whenever and however the switch occurred, Faulkner afterward embraced a change that set him slightly and subtly apart from his family, and through his writing he brought high honor and global fame to that chosen name.

In 1925, at the instigation of his friend, the writer Sherwood Anderson, Faulkner authored, in six weeks, the original draft for his first novel, *Soldier's Pay* (1926). This story was a relatively shallow reflection of the mood of the writers of the "lost generation," people such as Ernest Hemingway and F. Scott Fitzgerald who were disillusioned with the fruits of World War I. In 1927 he ended this first phase with *Mosquitoes,* a parody rather bitterly attacking the superficiality of New Orleans society and its pretensions to cultural sophistication. Within these two novels, there were suggestions of genius, but no one could have guessed what was to come.

In 1929, when he was barely thirty-two, Faulkner published *The Sound and the Fury.* Most of his early works were written in a matter of months, and sometimes with very little or no rewriting. *The Sound and the Fury* took three years, so he said, from inception to completion.[3] In reality, it was less than a year. But he rewrote it five times, and he certainly labored at it with an intensity and a concentration he had not previously achieved. It was a labor of love; he never expected the story to be published successfully, and by the time he finished the manuscript he had even surrendered hope of earning his living as a writer. Later, he prized that book above his other works, and declared that it was the most painful of all to write. Its appearance marked a high point in the ten-year period between 1926 and 1936 in which Faulkner enjoyed a productivity unmatched, perhaps, in brilliance in American literature. Out of that labor came three of America's great novels: *The Sound and the Fury* (1929), *Light in August* (1932), and *Absalom, Absalom!* (1936); and seven monumental characters: Thomas Sutpen, Joe Christmas, Dilsey Gibson, and the Compson children: Benjy, Jason, Candace, and Quentin.

In these three novels, Faulkner accomplished a remarkable array of literary achievements. Most importantly, he laid out the natural and human geography of the mythical Mississippi county, Yoknapatawpha, that was at the core of his work. Fourteen of his nineteen novels centered on the people and culture of Yoknapatawpha. It was the "little postage stamp," as he said, of native soil that he knew so well and which he peopled with men, women, and children who seemed to have lives of their own, independent of the author. It was as if he had only to look in upon them from time to time to see what they were doing and thinking, often himself to be amazed, amused, or appalled by what he saw. He listened well to them, and they told him all—or nearly all—in a multitude of voices. Appropriate to that mood, he often said that he never named his characters. They told him what their names were, and if they did not, he did not give them names. Obviously, he was a superb listener; if told, he got the names right; if not told, the characters were no less true.

The stage happened to be the South, the subject was the human condition, and the play was on-going and without end. For Faulkner, his literary world was a theater in the round of humanity, visible to him from every point of view, true from every point of view, at once divisible into individual lives and indivisible as a social organism. Stories could never be totally told from a single perspective, or by a single person, and sometimes perhaps they could not be fully told at all. In the effort of telling, however, he was fantastically adventurous, almost suicidal in his willingness to cast aside traditional modes of writing. He was boldly innovative in structure and style. Like Joyce, Eliot, and Pound, he rode full tilt and heedless of hazard, furiously inventing language to capture the plenitude of life.

The genius as artist faded after 1936, but the craftsman lived on in the third and final phase of his life as a writer. In 1938 he published *The Unvanquished,* a series of stories in which the child Bayard Sartoris grew from youth to manhood during the Civil War and Reconstruction, and in 1939 *The Wild Palms,* two stories woven together counterpunctually to explore the implications of choosing a life that presses at the limits of either human freedom on one side or human order on the other.

In 1940 with the publication of the first novel in the Snopes trilogy, *The Hamlet,* Faulkner, at age forty-three, exhibited the qualities of a mature, practiced, and superbly controlled writer. He continued the saga of the transplantation of Southern dirt farmers physically to the towns and culturally into modernity in *The Town* (1957) and *The Mansion* (1959). At the same time, he turned to address the race question powerfully and pointedly in *Go Down Moses* (1942), *Intruder in the Dust* (1948), and *Requiem for a Nun* (1951). Race was central, integral, and vital in the three great novels of the earlier phase of his work. Indeed, in the characters Dilsey Gibson, Joe Christmas, and Charles Bon these works remain, probably, the ultimate indictment not merely of the injustice of the racial establishment in the South in and after slavery, but of its capacity for the often subtle, always brutal reduction of humanity, both black and white. Simultaneously, however, these novels offer the contrary capacity of humanity at large to survive and transcend the most devastating afflictions. Criticism of race relations is implicit in the early novels; in the later novels it is explicit.

In this last phase, Faulkner recapitulated the essence of his writing in two superb stories. In 1942 the master was at work in a quiet and sober mood in "The Bear." This is the story of a boy, Isaac McCaslin, becoming a man in the post-Civil War South. It is a beautifully crafted, tight, crystalline story, one clear, smooth face, touching another at angle after angle to form a flawless gem that one can turn in one's hand. In the year preceding his death in 1962, Faulkner wrote *The Reivers* in a very different mood. It is profoundly humorous, yet deeply serious, and perhaps the most appealing of all his tales. It, too, is about a young boy, Lucius Quintus Cincinnatus Priest, coming of age in the modern world, but the mood has shifted dramatically. Whereas "The Bear" ends with death and despair, *The Reivers* ends with birth and a new life. "The Bear" longs for a return to nature, to the Garden of Eden, while *The Reivers* faces the reality that we are now and forever out of the Garden and manifests a faith that we will, indeed, endure and prevail.

PART ONE

Ancestry

ONE

The Falkners

The Land

Faulkner's Yoknapatawpha County was, of course, his own Lafayette County, Mississippi, and the surrounding counties. Like Mississippi, Yoknapatawpha had regions. In the river bottoms the land was flat, dark, and rich, made rich over the ages by the rushing waters that tore away topsoil from the undefended flanks of hills and mountains, flooded over the banks and levees, spreading, slowing, and as it slowed gently dropping a rain of fresh soil onto those broad acres soon to be filled with black people and white cotton—dropping, as it were, money into the pockets of the cotton aristocracy, the Compsons, Sartorises, Sutpens, and McCaslins of Faulkner's fictional world. In the hill country, the soil was red and thin. It bled easily and profusely at the touch of the plow, and ran eventually to gullies, to farm houses unpainted and weathering, and to the plain folk of the Old South and the New—the lean and tendon-tough Gowries, Quicks, Workits, Bundrens, and McCallums.

Yoknapatawpha was Mississippi, and it was also all of the South. The black belts, those areas where the black population stood near a majority or more, extended up and down the vast level lands alongside the Mississippi River and its major tributaries, skipped to form a jagged-edged belt across central Alabama and Georgia, then skipped again to run generally along the eastern coastal plain from northern Florida through low country Georgia, South Carolina, North Carolina, Virginia, and Maryland. The black belts were heavily peopled by African Americans because slavery had commanded the best lands, and these lands were, each in its time at least, the best. For the most part, large slaveowners were successful business people who would not work a thousand-dollar slave on fifty-cent land. Slavery also seized upon and moved with the most profitable crops, first in the colonial era with tobacco in the Chesapeake Bay area and rice and indigo along the Carolina and Georgia coasts, then, after the 1790s, with cotton in the upcountry of the Carolinas and Georgia, spreading westward over the decades and, by the 1850s, filling eastern Texas and Arkansas. Broadly speaking, from the beginning of slavery in the South to its end, valuable slaves worked valuable lands to turn maximum profits. Even emancipation did not change the congruence of rich soil and dark people in Dixie—nor has it yet. What the demise of slavery did do, paradoxically, was turn the richest counties in America in 1860, those most slave, to the poorest in 1870, and that result, too, has persisted.

Relatively less rich lands in the South—those in the piedmont, the mountains, the "pine barrens" and the "wire grass country" of the coastal plains—tended to be populated by white majorities. Most of these people owned no slaves, lived on farms, worked hard, raised families, and went to church. Roughly two-thirds of all Southern whites belonged to this element. There were great slaveholders in the white belts just as there were yeoman farmers in the black belts. But wherever they were, the great slaveholders tended to dominate economics, politics, and society generally.

On the wastelands of the South, down in the swamps and high in the mountains, lived the so-called poor whites, a third element that probably constituted less than a hundredth of the total white population. Usually they were squatters living on land that they did not own, and usually the women tended small gardens and raised animals while the men fished and hunted.

~

The structure of antebellum Southern society was complex, but, taken as a whole, it was pyramidal with slaves and free blacks constituting a caste and forming a base. At the bottom of the white caste were the poor whites who were generally despised by both blacks and other whites and sometimes referred to by them as "poor white trash." The great mass of white Southerners were yeoman farmers who might, indeed, own one or more slaves but who turned their hands to the very same tasks as their slaves. At the top stood the large slaveholders (often identified as those owning fifty slaves or more) whose work was management and who were somehow able, usually, to enlist the support of other whites in the defense of the system from which they derived great power and wealth. In the last years of slavery, there were, perhaps, 50,000 people belonging to some 10,000 families that constituted the slaveholding elite. A surprisingly large number of leading ministers, lawyers, politicians, physicians, businessmen, and intellectuals were members of these families, even though they might, themselves, own few or no slaves. There was among these people a generalized sense of superiority—manifested most signally in a reluctance to marry beneath their station. But they did not often boast publicly of their elevation over others. On the contrary, usually they were very adept at running a rhetorical line that preached democracy for whites and slavery for blacks as an ideal for Southern society.

The war and the loss of the war brought the great slaveholders rudely down. Some lost out in wealth and power altogether, and their lands and places in the social hierarchy were sometimes taken by the more ambitious, able, and fortunate members of the postwar yeomanry, whom Faulkner called "The Peasants." Others persisted, reduced in wealth and power but still palpably the local "quality." These, if they stayed in the South, were doomed perpetually to be major players in the minor leagues. The truth is that military defeat for the rebels in the Civil War led inexorably to the reduction of their political and economic power in the nation, and so, too, that of their children and their children's children. Over the two generations after Appomattox, the South became imperial America's first colony. The reduction was effected by discriminatory tariffs and railroad freight charges, by high interest rates and low wages, and by holding the South to the production of low-priced raw materials and the consumption of relatively costly finished goods produced in the North.

The decline began with the loss of political power in the nation. It is perfectly symbolic that eight of the first twelve presidents of the United States were Southerners, and that all eight were not just slaveholders, but very large slaveholders. Moreover, their collective tenure was long while that of Northern-bred presidents—two Adamses, Van Buren, and Harrison—was short, comprising all together only slightly more than twelve of the sixty-one presidential years between 1789 and 1850. After the Civil War, more than a hundred years would elapse before a "true" Southerner would occupy the White House again. Andrew Johnson (1865–69) was a Tennessean who chose the Northern side during the war. Two generations later, Woodrow Wilson was president. He was born in Staunton, Virginia, and reared in the South, but he was president of Princeton and governor of New Jersey before he was president of the United States. Harry S. Truman was from Independence, Missouri, but Kansas City was his metropolis and he was more Midwestern than Southern. Lyndon B. Johnson was born and reared on the southwestern-most edge of the South, so far in that direction in fact that his second language was Spanish. Finally, it was Jimmy Carter who brought the South again to the presidency, but he, like the two Adamses and Van Buren, enjoyed only a short tenure. In sum, the South was vastly reduced after the war, and only recently—five generations later—are there signs that it might rise again to some parity in national power.

If there has been anything like a thoroughly Southern state in these United States in the last hundred and fifty years, Mississippi is it. This is true, in large part, because Mississippi drew upon the older areas of the South for its peopling and its culture. For example, in the nineteenth century very few South Carolinians migrated to Virginia and vice versa, but both centers of eastern culture sent their representatives to Mississippi in great numbers. On the eve of the Civil War, Mississippi was filled with the descendants of the primal stock that had first settled the South Atlantic seaboard. Sometimes those migrants came the distance in one generation, sometimes in two or three, and often they came west and south by way of Tennessee and Alabama. Mississippi could be thus representative because it was new. It filled with people and formed its collective identity only in the last generation before the Civil War when the civilization of the Old South was maturing and coming to full bloom. As late as the 1830s the northeastern two-thirds of the state was still a raw frontier. Indians, roving whites, and blacks had mixed in the area even before the American Revolution, but it was only in the 1790s that the first permanent settlers came, and later still the flood.

In the days of the early republic, much of northern Mississippi was Indian territory. In 1830, in the Treaty of Dancing Rabbit Creek, the Choctaws signed over claim to their lands in middle Mississippi in return for lands in Oklahoma and money. They acted reluctantly upon advice given by one of their chiefs, Greenwood Leflore, a man who was himself the son of an Indian mother and a white father and who received gifts from the United States government for his work. Two years later, King Ishtahotapa of the Chickasaws led his people to yield their lands in northern Mississippi in the Treaty of Pontotoc.[1]

It was cotton, of course, that brought both whites and blacks to Mississippi, cotton to feed the burgeoning textile mills of New England, England, and Europe. Pioneering settlers poured into the state in the early and middle 1830s as the price of cotton rose and land remained relatively abundant. The panic of 1837 and the depression that followed gave pause. But recovery in the mid-1840s brought a new and greater influx from the slave-rich, land-poor upper South and Southeast. With cotton selling fairly steadily at ten to twelve cents a pound in the local markets, the 1850s were high times in Mississippi, and it seemed as if the bubble would never burst. In the spring of 1860, the future looked so sanguine to the clerk of court of Lafayette County sitting in Oxford that he could not refrain from opening the March term of court with a celebratory entry in one of his record books:

> . . . good Times in our County   Cotton worth 10¾   Corn one dollar per bushel Bacon 15 cents per lb. Negroe men 1500 to 2000-hundred dollars and woman [sic] from 1300 to 1800 and times Still looking up   So press up Boys[2]

The First Mississippi Falkner

Family tradition says that William C. Falkner, the first Mississippi Falkner, walked into Pontotoc, a village some thirty miles east of Oxford, about 1842.[3] He was a penniless teenager, his family having fallen upon hard times in Ste. Genevieve, Missouri, and he was searching for his uncle by marriage, John Wesley Thompson. William had left home, the story goes, because of a fight in which he had cut his brother Joe's scalp with the blade of a hoe and been punished.[4]

William Falkner was born in 1825 near Knoxville, Tennessee, the first child of Joseph Falkner and Caroline Word. His parents had married in 1816 and had come west from their home in Surry County, North Carolina, on the eastern slopes of the Appalachian Mountains. The spelling of family names often varied and drifted in these times; Falkner sometimes became Forkner or Faulkner, and in North Carolina members of the clan usually called themselves Forkner. Given names in the family, however, did not vary greatly. For males, William and John were highly favored, while Henry, James, and Thomas were frequent.[5] Census and other records indicate that the Falkners continued to live in Tennessee into the year 1837, when William would have been twelve, and then moved to Missouri.[6]

John Wesley Thompson, the uncle whom William sought in Mississippi, had married Justianna Dickinson Word, William's mother's sister, in 1834. Their father, Thomas Adams Word, had been the sheriff of Surry County, a justice of the peace, a lieutenant colonel in the militia, and a substantial landowner near the village of Mt. Airy. His father, Charles, had joined Colonel George Washington's Virginia Blues as "a mere boy" and barely survived Braddock's defeat (1755) in western Pennsylvania during the French and Indian War. Charles Word, however, did not survive the Battle of King's Mountain (1780) during the American Revolution. Charles's youngest brother, Cuthbert, also met his end in that struggle. He was captured by the Tories and British and died as a prisoner of war aboard the ship *New Jersey.* Charles and Cuthbert's father, also named Charles Word, had come to Virginia from the city of Landaff in Glenmorgonshire in Wales before the French and Indian War, and probably settled in Pittsylvania County on the southwestern frontier.[7]

After the War of 1812, Thomas Adams Word moved with some of his family to Clarkesville in Habersham County in northern Georgia. There, in the fall of 1834, John Wesley Thompson, his son-in-law, got into a fight and killed a man with a knife. From surviving family papers, we catch first-hand impressions of that drama. In the October term, 1834, the Habersham County grand jury found that John Wesley Thompson, aged twenty-five, had indeed thrust "a certain Knife of the value of one dollar" into the belly of Calvin J. Hanks inflicting a mortal wound two inches wide and six inches deep. "Aiding, abetting and assisting" Thompson were three other men, including Cuthbert Word, Thompson's brother-in-law.[8]

Justianna, then nineteen, visited her husband in jail once and wanted to return but was prevented from doing so by his desire to spare her the pain of again witnessing his incarceration. Instead she sent a letter, urging him to allow her to provide him with bed clothes and "a cloke" because there was no fire in the jail. Apparently "Wesley," as she addressed him, persisted in playing a proud role and scorned creature comforts. "Mother wanted Cuthbert to carry . . . a cloke to you and he said you did not want it," Justianna wrote. Wesley replied on the same sheet of paper, brushing past matters of logistics and asking her to save some of his recent letters to her "as a fond Memento of him who found but one on Earth whom he loved without alloy and you are She." He went on to declare his undying love for Justianna in the grand and flowing language of the Romantic era. "The mighty Globe on which we live and move will in its destined round wane, and sink and disappear;" he wrote, "but we Shall Survive its break; and live in immortal youth; twined together by the Silken Cords of mortal love; such bonds as can not be broken."[9] Justianna was hardly less romantic than her husband. A decade before she had written a poem entitled "A Nosegay" for a gentleman friend:

> I'll pull a bunch of buds and flowers,
> And tie a ribbon round them,
> If you'll but think (in your lone hours)
> Of the little Girl that bound them.[10]

John Wesley Thompson was acquitted by the Georgia court and subsequently moved to the village of Ripley in Tippah County, in northeastern Mississippi. In 1838, John and Justianna were joined in Tippah County by Justianna's sister Elizabeth and her husband Charles W. Humphreys.[11] According to one version of the family legend, in 1842 John was away from home teaching school in Plenitude in Pontotoc County when he fell into an affray and killed yet another man. When William arrived in the village of Pontotoc, the county seat, he found his uncle in jail awaiting trial for murder, and, of course, not well situated to help his nephew. Young William, tired, ragged, and barefooted, sat down on the steps of the local hotel, dropped his head into his hands, and began to cry. A little girl named Elizabeth Vance befriended him, and the next day she and her mother arranged for him to journey by stage to Ripley to stay with his aunt Justianna. Eventually, Lizzie Vance became William's second wife. The legend says that John Wesley Thompson studied law while in jail and successfully defended himself against the charge of murder. Once free, he returned to Ripley, became a lawyer, and prospered.

The court record indicates that John Wesley Thompson was never even charged with—much less jailed for—murder or any other crime in Pontotoc County. On the other hand, he was indeed an early settler in Tippah County. He was listed on the very first tax roll in 1837 as owing a tax bill of 37½¢[12]. He was also listed for taxes in the county in 1838, 1839, and 1840 and was carried in the federal census of 1840 as the head of a household in which there lived one slave, two adult females, and two adult males.[13] The state censuses of 1841 and

1845 show that John Wesley Thompson continued to reside in the county in those years. In 1841 his household consisted of one adult female and two adult males, and he owned two lots in town worth the sizable sum of $1,400. In 1845 another adult male, probably William, had been added.[14] By 1850 Thompson was the district attorney for the state's 7th Judicial District, and a decade later he was the district judge.[15]

In Ripley, as the protégé of his uncle John, William C. Falkner proved to be an exceedingly ambitious lad. While he read law with John Wesley Thompson and other attorneys, he earned his living working in the county jail. In June, 1845, an ax murderer named McCannon escaped from the jail. He had befriended a family that was migrating westward with all their possessions. One night in camp, he had decapitated them all with an ax while they slept, then fled with their valuables. It was a usual frontier horror story in which the community was alerted when hogs uncovered the shallow grave of one of the children.

William joined a pursuit that led the posse well up into Tennessee before they brought the fugitive to bay. Almost twenty-one, William was in the front ranks of those who faced McCannon's "cocked guns." Having returned to Ripley with their prisoner, a crowd "wrestled him out of the hands of the guards who were bringing him to jail."[16] McCannon was about to be lynched when he talked his captors into saving him for the proper process of law in exchange for his telling them the whole story of his life and how he came to commit this awful crime. It was young William who wrote down the account and had it printed: "The Life and Confession of A.J. McCannon, Murderer of the Adcock Family."

Half a century later, a longtime friend of Falkner's reported that William had deposited a stack of pamphlets containing the story on the gallows on the day of the execution and commenced to sell them to the gathering citizens at $1 each. By the end of the day, after McCannon had died "spinning like a top," he had renewed his stock several times and was never again without money in his pockets.[17] Not everyone would think that William's use of McCannon's end was seemly, but it revealed a character trait that marked his life. He recognized opportunities for self-advancement when he saw them, he acted quickly and boldly to make the most of every advantage, and in doing so he was seldom deterred by possibilities of moral condemnation from the community in which he lived.

In 1846 the Mexican War broke out, and early in 1847 William joined the invasion of northern Mexico as a first lieutenant in the Second Mississippi Volunteers. In his company was Private Cuthbert Word, aged thirty-four, the same Cuthbert Word who had assisted John Wesley Thompson in the killing of Calvin Hanks in Georgia in 1834. Also present were two other Falkners, Thomas and Joseph, aged nineteen and eighteen, whose names were identical with two of William's brothers. Both Falkners enlisted as privates at Spring Hill in the northwestern part of Tippah County on December 29, 1846. Thomas died in the General Hospital in New Orleans in January as the regiment moved south. Joseph was discharged for disability by the regimental surgeon at Matamoros, Mexico, in March, 1847. Cuthbert, who had enrolled in Ripley on December 4, 1846, was discharged at Matamoros on the same date and for the same reason. Cuthbert died on his way home and was buried on the west bank of the Mississippi about three miles upriver from Baton Rouge.[18]

On April 14, within weeks of his arrival in Mexico, William rode away from his camp near Monterrey, venturing beyond the limits set by the commanding general. On that day, he was acting as the commander of his company, the captain being ill. Perhaps he felt that he had a special license to scout beyond the lines. About a mile and a half distant from camp, he was ambushed by, as he later claimed, a band of "guerillios." His horse, wounded and dying, sank beneath him. Falkner himself was hit in the sudden fusillade. One shot shattered his left foot and another took away the first joint of three fingers of his left hand. He returned fire and his assailants retired. Falkner attempted to walk back to camp, but, weakened by the loss of blood, he realized that he was about to faint. Wisely he hid himself in the bushes before losing consciousness. Perhaps later that day, more probably the next, his fellow soldiers found him. Back in camp on April 18, Surgeon Thomas Love wrote that Lieutenant Falkner had been severely wounded in the left foot by a rifle shot, "the ball passing between the first and second metatarsal bones." Another rifle shot had taken off "the first phalanges of three fingers."

Within weeks Falkner was home again, recovering from his wounds. In July, he married Holland Pearce, an affluent young woman newly arrived in Ripley from Tennessee. At the end of summer he returned to Mexico where an army surgeon certified his disabilities. His resignation was accepted in October, 1847. Home again, he settled in Ripley, entered the bar, and in September, 1848, Holland bore him a son. At age twenty-three, it seemed that fortune had, indeed, chosen William Falkner as her own.[19]

Holland Pearce did not come at all empty handed to her marriage. Along with several siblings, she was an orphan who was in the process of collecting a substantial inheritance when she met William. Also, she was in some way connected to Simon R. Spight and his family. Both the Pearces and the Spights were originally from Jones County, North Carolina, a region of wealthy planters and slaveholders in the eastern part of the state. Simon Spight was primarily a merchant and hotel owner in Ripley; but he also owned land and slaves and would become one of the several richest men in the county during the 1850s. Very early in 1847, he became the guardian for Holland and her four brothers and sisters. Holland's father had died without a will in Weakley County, in northwestern Tennessee, "leaving a large estate" that included twenty-eight slaves.

Simon Spight undertook the complicated business of settling affairs in Tennessee and moving the Pearce children to Ripley. He bought and sold slaves during the division of property in Tennessee, in one case making a purchase to keep Jim and Rachel and their one-year-old daughter together as a family. Also, he hired people and transportation to move the Pearces, their effects, and their slaves to Ripley, a twenty-seven-day journey by wagon and carriage. In January, 1847, he leased out for the year the employable slaves for $1,088, keeping the unemployables in his own household. During that year, at a cost that exceeded their income, he maintained the Pearce children and saw to their education.[20]

In September, 1848, the same month in which Holland gave birth to their son John Wesley Thompson Falkner, the young couple joined with Holland's newly married sister, Mary, and her husband to petition the court to divide the estate among the heirs. Simon Spight had already anticipated that event. In the spring he had totaled his numbers and submitted his accounts to the court as the "Guardian's final Settlement" for both women.[21] Obviously the transfer was soon made because in February, 1849, William and Holland sold one of the slaves, Phillis, aged 32, and her three sons, John aged 5, Joe, 3, and Peter, 1, for $1,200.[22] In 1847 Simon Spight had rented out Phillis and four children for $20.[23] Specifically, William and Holland sold Phillis and her sons to William and Martha Edgerton, and on the same date they bought 320 acres of land from that couple for $2,200.[24] Apparently, the Falkners were going into the farming business in a modest way. In addition to Phillis and her children, other Pearce slaves came to Holland through inheritance, and two came to William as collateral for a loan. In January, 1850, with his uncle John taking a trustee's role in the transaction, William bought Patsey and her child Benjamin, about sixteen months old, from Holland's brother Lazarus for $256. The bill of sale indicated that, in effect, the family was using these slaves to finance young Lazarus's migration to California, no doubt to join the gold rush already begun by the "Forty-niners."[25]

In 1849, Falkner's luck ran out. In Tippah County one of the leading families was the Hindmans. The Hindmans were great slaveholders who had moved west very early and settled in the vicinity of Knoxville, Tennessee. Thomas Hindman, Sr., had actually been born in Tennessee before it became a state in 1796. As a young man he served as a lieutenant with Andrew Jackson in his wars against the Indians and against the British in the Battle of New Orleans in 1815. In 1832, he floated his family, his slaves, and their effects down the Tennessee River on rafts to northeastern Alabama where he became a planter with extensive holdings. He also engaged in a highly lucrative trade with the Indians.

It was characteristic of the melting of cultural lines on the frontier that his wife's sister married the brother of the leading chief of the Cherokees, both of whom were themselves half-Indian and half-white. In the middle 1830s, Thomas Hindman and his brother-in-law were commissioned by the U.S. Government to organize the logistics and manage the actual physical removal of a large body of Cherokee Indians to southwestern Oklahoma. This involved the purchase and use of vast quantities of supplies. Apparently, both men emerged from the operation considerably richer. In 1841, Hindman moved his family west again, this time to Tippah County where he developed a large plantation and built an impressive house one mile east of Ripley.[26]

The Hindman family included two brothers who were relatively close to William's age. Thomas, Jr., three years younger than his brother Robert, was the more impressive of the two. In the spring of 1846, he completed six years of study at the Lawrenceville Classical Institute near Princeton, New Jersey, and returned home. The Hindman brothers soldiered with William in the same company in Mexico, a company that Thomas had been instrumental in raising. Like Falkner, both men enrolled in Company E in Ripley in early December, 1846. Robert became the second sergeant, and Thomas, at age eighteen, became the second lieutenant. Robert was discharged by the surgeon near Monterrey in April, 1847, with the rank of private. Thomas remained, spending the summer months "In Arrest," then during the spring of 1848 he was on detached duty as the acting adjutant to the commander of his post. Finally, he was discharged, still a second lieutenant.[27]

By the end of 1848 everyone was home from Mexico, and in 1849 Robert Hindman wanted very much to join the local chapter of the Sons of Temperance to which both William and Thomas belonged. William supported Robert's admission, but his candidacy was rejected in a process in which votes were cast secretly. Robert understood that William had voted against him and swore to kill him. William confronted Hindman and denied the charge.

"You're a damned liar," Robert declared and pulled his revolver. The two men struggled with the pistol between them. It misfired—once, twice, a third time, before William drew his knife and stabbed Robert through the heart. The Hindmans buried Robert in the family cemetery, under a gravestone that declared, bitterly and boldly, that he had been "Killed at Ripley Miss by Wm. C. Falkner May 8, 1849." Allegedly, the stone had at first declared that Robert had been "Murdered" rather than "Killed" by William Falkner.[28]

In the trial, Falkner was acquitted, but two years later he shot and killed a friend of the Hindman family, Erasmus W. Morris. Several months before the shooting, William and Erasmus were at least friendly enough to gamble at cards together. In September, 1850, they were in a group of nine hauled into court, charged with "playing cards for money," convicted, and fined $20 each.[29] On February 28, 1851, the two men had been arguing over the rental of a house when Falkner pulled his pistol and fired directly at Morris' head, killing him instantly. The grand jury indicted Falkner for murder, finding that he had inflicted upon "the left side of the face of the said Erasmus W. Morris one mortal wound of the depth of six inches and of the breadth of three inches." On trial in March, Falkner faced as one of the lawyers for the prosecution Thomas C. Hindman, Jr., the brother of the man he had killed two years before. On March 12, he was again acquitted.[30] Soon afterward, as he entered the dining room of a nearby hotel, Thomas C. Hindman, Sr., rose from his table, pistol in hand, obviously intending to shoot Falkner. Somehow, Hindman fumbled the pistol. It fell to the floor and fired, shattering plaster off the ceiling. Falkner drew his own pistol and avoided further violence.[31]

The feud, however, continued. Falkner and Thomas Hindman, Jr., drew up an agreement to fight a duel on April 1, 1851 (1857 by one account). The site, "the field of honor," was to be in Arkansas just across the Mississippi River from Memphis, thus making it difficult for the authorities to prosecute the survivor for murder. Each man was to have two revolvers, take stands fifty yards apart, and advance and fire as he pleased. Happily, a mutual friend, Matthew C. Galloway, later the founder of the *Memphis Avalanche,* intervened to settle the immediate difficulty.[32] Afterward Thomas Hindman continued to prosper in his usual style. In 1852 he won a seat in the state legislature, and in 1853 moved to Helena, Arkansas, a thriving town on the Mississippi River some fifty miles below Memphis. In 1858 he was elected to a seat in the U.S. Congress.[33]

The enmity between Falkner and the Hindmans did not end with the avoidance of the duel. A long-running conflict between them revolved around Falkner's attempts to claim benefits as a result of the wounds he had received during his Mexican service. In 1849 Congress decided that disabled veterans from the Mexican War should get a pension and a grant of 160 acres of federal land. Falkner lost no time making his application and shortly began to receive his pension of $204 yearly. Learning of this, Thomas Hindman, Sr., challenged Falkner's claim, asserting that his wounds came not in the line of duty as he said, but rather—as Robert Hindman would testify were he alive—of his having "made some indecent and improper advances upon a Mexican female, which was resented by some male Mexicans." Furthermore, Falkner had declared that his wounds prevented his doing manual labor. Yet the previous winter in Ripley, the senior Hindman had seen "him engaged for several hours in breaking wild horses to run in a sleigh." It was cold, he asserted, yet Falkner wore no gloves, and used both hands equally well. Also, "he wears either a tight fashionable boot or shoe" with no discernible discomfort to his injured foot. Hindman declared that everyone knew of Falkner's fraud against the government, but no one would complain because of "the known character of Falkner for violence—His Bowie Knife and Pistols are constantly about his person."[34]

Hindman succeeded through Congressman Jacob Thompson in getting

Falkner's pension suspended. However, Falkner soon visited Washington personally and secured its reinstatement for six months—using the fact that Hindman himself had penned some of the documents filed in his service record stressing the severity of his wounds and had thus virtually endorsed his claim to a pension. Hindman had, indeed, helped Falkner secure his discharge on account of his wounds, perhaps to promote his son Thomas in the military hierarchy by removing an officer immediately senior to him. The result here, however, was to nullify his influence, and Falkner's pension was restored and continued until the Civil War began.[35]

Domestic Relations

A SHADOW FAMILY IN THE FALKNER YARD

On May 31, 1849, within four weeks of the killing of Robert Hindman, William suffered the death of his wife Holland, probably from tuberculosis.[36] For two years and several months thereafter he lived as a bachelor. In September, 1850, when the census taker (who happened to be Thomas Hindman, Jr.) came to his door in the village of Ripley, he found Falkner living with his two-year-old son in a household that included five slaves. Sometime later Falkner gave over the rearing of his infant son to his aunt Justianna and her husband, John Wesley Thompson. They were childless, and the sickly youngster needed the kind of attention that they could give him. The transfer was made on the promise that William would never attempt to reclaim the child.[37]

Falkner kept his promise, and soon began another family. He was prominent in meetings of veterans of the Mexican War, and at a reunion of veterans he met Elizabeth Houston Vance, the little girl who had allegedly helped him a decade before. It was later said that her parents opposed the proposed marriage, perhaps because of her youth, perhaps for other reasons. Whatever the circumstances, the records do indicate that they were married, apparently secretly, in Pontotoc on October 14, 1851.[38] Lizzie was eighteen, Falkner twenty-six. Lizzie's history as now known demolishes much of the legend surrounding her early relationship with William Falkner.

On September 10, 1850, the census indicated that Lizzie was living in a hamlet containing a store and a blacksmith shop somewhere in Tippah County. She lived in a household with Isaac and Mary Jane Buchanan, a married couple, both of whom were school teachers. Isaac was forty-five and owned no real estate; Mary Jane was thirty-one. Mary Jane was, in fact, Lizzie's older sister. She was born in 1819 in Knoxville, Tennessee. She had graduated with honors from the Tuscaloosa Female Institute in 1836 and remained there as a teacher. Tuscaloosa, Alabama, was the site of the state's university, and the Female Institute no doubt reflected that pedagogical eminence. In the fall of the same year, Mary Jane's mother, Elizabeth Allen Vance, died, leaving her to support herself and four younger siblings, including Lizzie. She did so, initially, by becoming the governess in the Walter Glover household, and in the next year by becoming the first teacher in the newly formed Female Seminary in Marion, Alabama. There she married a man named James H. Rutledge and commenced a family of her own. Even though her father survived her mother by four years, dying in Mobile in 1840, there is no indication that he supported his children. Indeed, Mary Jane named her first born child Walter Glover Rutledge, in honor of the man who had helped her maintain the family after the death of her mother. In the middle 1840s, Mary Jane moved to Holly Springs to teach, and then in 1849 to Tippah County where she opened her own school, the Ripley Female Academy. Meanwhile, James had died and Mary Jane had married Isaac Buchanan.[39]

It seems highly improbable, then, that Lizzie at age nine back in 1842 was in Pontotoc, Mississippi, to meet William Falkner for the first time as alleged. Certainly, she had no mother to manage bed and board for William and subsequently his dispatch to Ripley. That story, recalled so vividly by Falkner in May, 1886, was part of a talk he gave in Pontotoc in an attempt to rally the natives to support one of his very ambitious railroad ventures.[40] It simply was not true. He married Lizzie in Pontotoc, this much the record shows, but that is one grain of truth in an otherwise apocryphal tale.

In 1849, the year in which Lizzie came to Tippah County, William's wife Holland Pearce died, and afterward he lived in the town with his infant son. In 1851, he was in the midst of his frightful feud with the Hindmans, and it was then, apparently, that he met Lizzie. She had no parents living to disapprove of a marriage. It was probably Mary Jane who objected, and for good reason. Hence, the journey to the neighboring town of Pontotoc to marry secretly.

The couple's first child, William Henry, was born in August, 1853. Willie Medora came in 1856, Thomas Vance in 1859, and Lizzie Manassah in 1861, after the Battle of Manassas in Virginia. The Falkner household in Ripley in the decade after 1851 was slightly unusual in that the mother and father at first conceived and bore children less frequently than was common. But the household was very unusual in another respect. In 1850 all of the slaves in the yard were black; in 1860 they were all mulatto.

~

In 1850 William Falkner owned five slaves, and these lived on his lot in Ripley. Two were adults, two were in their teens, and one was a two-year-old boy. One of the adults was male and thirty years old, the other female and twenty-one. The two year old was almost certainly the child of the woman. One teenager, age thirteen, was a girl, the other, age fifteen, a boy. All five were listed by the census taker as "black" as opposed to "mulatto"—this being a matter that was left to the census taker's perception.[41] Local tradition and contemporary documents indicate that these slaves came to Falkner through his marriage to Holland Pearce.[42] Obviously, they formed a set as was usual in divisions made for heirs in a relatively large holding when the master or mistress died. This particular set was carefully designed for long term profitability in the slaveholding world. In effect, between four slaves the young white couple had two prospective families in the making and could reasonably expect a child to appear every year. Assuming good health, each child would become marginally profitable at about age six, profitable with adolescence, and marvelously profitable in his or her early twenties. More immediately, they had one prime male worker, were about to get another, and had the labor of the two women when they were not engaged in the even more profitable task of bearing children. In the 1850s an ambitious young couple could hardly have chosen a more likely group of slaves for combining—to use the parlance of the modern stock market—both income and growth.

The census indicates that in 1860 William had six slaves living in the house in his yard, and its occupants were radically different from those in 1850. All six were mulattoes. This meant that they were easily identifiable by the census taker as people of mixed blood. Four of the slaves were children, whose ages were given as eight, six, four, and one. Two were adults—a woman age twenty-seven and a man age twenty-one. Their ages and the ages of the children strongly suggest that the adults were not man and wife. The woman appears to be the mother of the children. The age pattern was perfectly normal for the time. No other Ripley household of comparable size had servants that were all mulatto. Most had all black slaves, and many had a mixture of blacks and mulattoes. For example, William's uncle John had in his yard five black and two mulatto adults, along with a single black infant. That child was probably the offspring of one of the two mulatto females among his slaves, one of whom was nineteen and the other twenty-one. The father was probably one of John's three male slaves, all of whom were black and whose ages were given as twenty-three, twenty-five, and forty-five.[43] Rather obviously, John Wesley Thompson had bought at least some of his slaves with an eye to balancing current productivity, increasing numbers, and future profitability. Indeed, we know that in January, 1852, he promoted that end by buying from F.T. Leak, one of the several large slaveholders in the county, "Emily a mulatto girl slave."[44] William Falkner's holding, in contrast to that of his uncle—and his own in 1850—was not very well cast for a combination of current utility and future profit, a situation that was definitely not consistent with his character in material matters. The circumstances suggest that William Falkner in 1860 was working some special agenda with his slaves. We now know what that agenda was.

The mulatto woman in Falkner's yard was involved in a perpetual union, in effect a quasi-marriage with a white man. That situation was, apparently, unusual for Ripley, but it was not at all unusual in the slaveholding South at large. In virtually every community there was at least one white man, or sometimes an entire family of white men, who mixed. Almost invariably, these men chose young women who were mulatto rather than black, and household servants rather than field hands. Some of these men, such as Booker T. Washington's probable father, were promiscuous and went from woman to woman. More often they stayed with the same woman year after year, having one child after another by that woman. Such connections frequently began with what was in fact rape, but often over time the men showed by some extraordinary behavior signs of caring for these children and their mother. If the mother and her children remained in slavery, they might be trained to be domestic servants and skilled artisans. Often measures were taken to keep ownership within the family. If freed, as many were, they might be resettled in a free state or territory in the northwest, the children provided an education, and given a start in life. In and after the 1830s, Ohio was a preferred state for such a process and, in fact, became the "most mulatto" of the free states. With amazing frequency, white men of property recognized their mulatto children as beneficiaries in their wills. Sometimes white kinspeople, scandalized and outraged, moved aggressively to break such wills—occasionally, by having the man declared incompetent or, more bluntly, insane.

White men of the master class who created mulatto families tended to fit one of three basic models. One model, the bachelor, posited a male of the slaveholding class (usually the owner himself but occasionally his son, brother, father, uncle, nephew, or a male in-law) who never married but rather took as his de facto wife a mulatto slave and by her conceived a sequence of children. This was the case with writer and poet Langston Hughes's great grandfather who was a Virginia planter, large slaveholder, and Revolutionary War soldier.

A second model offered a man who lost his wife by death and then took in her stead one of his slaves, sometimes his wife's maid and thus a woman uniquely well prepared for the position. It has been alleged that Thomas Jefferson fit this "widower" model, supposedly taking as lover his slave Sally Hemmings after Mrs. Jefferson had died in childbirth. Sally was, indeed, a likely substitute; she was Mrs. Jefferson's half sister as well as her maid. Jefferson did not remarry though still in the prime of life, and Sally gave birth at Monticello to a steady sequence of light-skinned children. Some observers noted a distinct physical resemblance between these children and the master of Monticello and sometime President of the United States. Jefferson's defenders argue plausibly that actually Jefferson's nephews were the fathers.

The third model involved a man who reared a mulatto family in the servant's quarters at the very same time that he maintained a white family in the main house, in effect, having two wives simultaneously. Ironically, the mulatto family sometimes mirrored the white family not only woman for woman, but child for child, and, because it lived in the very shadow of the white family, might well be called the "shadow family."[45]

As a way of getting a feel for the fabric of miscegenation in Southern culture, a theme that writer William Faulkner wove brilliantly into his stories, it is useful to speculate who might have fathered the mulatto children in his great grandfather's yard. One candidate was James Word Falkner, William's youngest brother. James was twenty-three in 1860. He was a bachelor and lived in the village with his uncle, John Wesley Thompson. Probably, he had come down from Missouri in the 1850s with other members of the family to resettle in Ripley. In fact, James was the first Falkner to attend the University of Mississippi, taking his degree in law there in July, 1860.[46] Immediately thereafter, he entered practice with William, and remained in Ripley until he went off to war in March, 1862. At the time of his enlistment, James declared that he had been born in Knox County, Tennessee. He was described as 5 feet 8 inches tall, with hazel eyes, dark hair, and dark skin.[47]

For the white male, miscegenation imposed at least two requirements. The man who mixed needed both access to the woman and an inclination to have sex with her. Surely there were dozens of men in the vicinity of Ripley who might have had the inclination. Some were bachelors, such as the seven young men who lived in 1860 in the Simon Spight household (a sort of boardinghouse as well as a hotel and home) and were overseers, stage drivers, and ditch diggers. Others were young widowers such as John Y. Murry, physician and for a time sheriff too, who lost his wife after the birth of their third child, or Dr. William D. Carter, thirty-seven, who had also lost his wife in childbirth.[48] Yet, it is unlikely that William Falkner would have allowed just anyone to visit his lot—or his servant to visit freely off the lot. James Word Falkner would probably have been a welcomed visitor to Falkner's house, and his bachelorhood argues for inclination. His age, however, argues against his fathering of the older children. James would have been only about thirteen when the first child was conceived, and the evidence definitely indicates that the vast majority of mixers were very mature men, not boys. Also, very often the white man involved was the most powerful person in this woman's life, namely, her master.

We know that William Falkner, himself, was an emotional, highly romantic, willful man who insisted on getting what he wanted. Usually, in one way or another, he succeeded. The years from 1848 through 1851 were especially turbulent and stressful for him. He killed two men and twice faced trial and possible death on the gallows. He established a bitter and deadly enmity with one of the wealthiest and most influential families in the county and to that extent at least had alienated himself from the community. His wife had died suddenly, leaving him with a sickly infant and a set of slaves that came with his marriage. Never one to yield without a fight, he battled with the Hindmans to preserve his honor, immersed himself in legal and business affairs to make money, and maintained his associations with his fellow veterans of the Mexican War. He gambled and kept "his Bowie Knife and Pistols . . . about his person." In matters of love and sex, as in everything else, it is unlikely that William Falkner was passive. Perhaps he took a lover or lovers in those early years of widowhood. Then, he met Elizabeth Vance, a budding young woman in her teens. Clearly, he was passionate about Lizzie. Taking refuge from his conflict with the Hindmans by visiting in Cincinnati in the middle months of 1851, he wrote a would-be epic poem entitled "The Seige of Monterey." In that work he raved, almost in the same breath, about having seen a nearly nude dancer in a theater in the city and about his "angelic Lizzie." He concluded that marriage was a fine institution because it made "copulation" "lawful," while the other state was "awful."[49]

Perhaps, William was true to Lizzie in the 1850s, perhaps not. It is possible that he had two loves. In the late 1950s, Donald Duclos, a scholar whose work still stands as the most thoroughly researched biography of the first Mississippi Falkner, discovered a story that asserted "that in addition to his immediate family buried in the Ripley cemetery one may also find the grave of the woman who for many years was his mistress." Professor Duclos pronounced this one of the "complete absurdities" among the many legends that persisted after Falkner's death.[50]

Having come to him through his first wife, Falkner managed his black slaves of 1850 for the benefit of his son. A local agent for a credit rating company reported in September, 1853, that "he has the int. [interest, meaning income] of some slaves that belonged to his wife now dead, which really under our laws belongs to his child a son aged 5 years."[51] Taking color, sex, and age as rendered in the census into account, it is clear that none of Falkner's slaves in 1850 were his slaves in 1860. One, and only one, of those might have passed to his uncle before 1860, and that switch was effected by outright sale. In March, 1857, he sold "my boy Wash" (a nickname for Washington) to John Wesley Thompson for $1,350.[52] It is almost certain that Wash was both the fifteen-year-old black male in Falkner's household in 1850 and the twenty-five-year-old black male in John's household in 1860. He was very probably the same "Washington a Boy" whom Simon Spight brought down from Tennessee in 1847 with the Pearce slaves and rented out for the year at $40.[53] And he was certainly the "Negro Boy Wash" that Falkner, in reporting his administration of his wife's estate for the benefit of his son to the court in January, 1856, declared as "now in my possession" and valued at $1,000. Wash would have been about twenty years old at that time.

In the same report, Falkner declared that he had sold out of his wife's estate a half section of land for $4,200 (including his own cotton gin and mill for which he sought a reimbursement of $800), and two slaves, a "negro girl Betsey" and a "negro boy Charles," age about forty-two, for $1,000 each.[54] Both names appeared among those of the Pearce slaves in 1847. Rather clearly, Falkner was shrewdly holding Betsey, Charles, and Wash until the market seemed right. The half section of land was the 320 acres that he and Holland had bought in 1849 for $2,200.[55] William Falkner managed his son's estate very well, as he did his own. In January, 1858, Falkner also sold his uncle "a negro woman named Livy" for $640 guaranteeing "the title clear & that she is a slave for life."[56] These four sales and other records indicate that Falkner was selling some slaves and keeping others.[57] There were reasons for this certain pattern.

It is beyond belief that the situation in Falkner's yard could have arisen without his knowledge and, in some degree, approval. It is certain, too, that the community was aware of such situations, and looked askance at the owner. In the South in the 1850s, pressures against miscegenation increased dramatically as tensions between the North and the South over slavery and race escalated. It was an embarrassment to the white South in its running battle with the North that mulatto children with a white parent, especially a slaveholder, were being born constantly into slavery. More and more in that decade, white male miscegenators were punished by their communities. However, the punishments for mixers in the white elite were social, often subtle, and definitely not economic or political. Indeed, a white man could mix and still prosper in important spheres in the white world. At least one leading Southern senator in the 1850s had mulatto children who were also his slaves, as did numerous eminent planters and businessmen. It is not too much to say that there were well-known generals in the Confederate Army who had mulatto children at home. In a large way, elite white men who mixed were protected in their sins by the very fact that the South could not admit to the world that the sin existed.

A slave society had to be a tight society, with roles very clearly prescribed and stringently enforced as to race, sex, and place in the social hierarchy. Any deviation became a horrendous problem, and Southerners were often driven to explaining away difficulties in ways that might have seemed strange to a candid world. Slaves were by definition black, thus the fact that many very light mulattoes were being held in slavery came to be covered by a novel concoction called "the one drop rule." This rule declared that anyone possessing a single drop of black blood was all black, regardless of whiteness of skin and the appearance of Caucasian features.

Most of all, a shadow family was an insult to the white womanhood of the South. Women were supposed to be ladies, and for them the role prescribed piety, purity, domesticity, and submissiveness. First among these was piety—a closeness to God—and the achievement of piety was tightly linked to purity. A true woman was pure in mind as well as body. She had no lustful thoughts, was a virgin before marriage, and faithful to her husband thereafter. All over the Western world in the nineteenth century, standards of sexual purity for women of the elite were extraordinarily high, their freedoms consequently greatly restricted, and a system of rewards and punishments constructed sufficient to maintain the order. In the South, because of the necessities of slavery, feminine roles were prescribed in double strength. Ideally, men should also be pure, but in reality certain transgressions were tolerated. There, and elsewhere, brothels flourished and their patrons not penalized. But to rear a mulatto family in the very shadow of the white family was another matter. It was the ultimate in masculine cheating.

Episodical evidence indicates that where there was a shadow family, the wife usually responded in one of three ways. Either she never allowed herself to see the truth before her eyes, or she saw the truth and remained silent, or she saw it and resented it bitterly and more or less openly. Whatever the cause, there were signs that Lizzie Vance was not always worshipful of her husband. The couple was a bit tardy and sporadic in producing children. When William went off to Europe for travels in 1883, Lizzie did not go with him. Instead he took his fifteen-year-old daughter. In the end Lizzie went to Memphis to live, leaving William wifeless and alone in his house in Ripley.[58] Finally, the mulatto family in Falkner's yard in 1860 was, as we shall see, of bizarre provenance and did not dissolve with emancipation in 1865. Indeed, it persisted, and with an intimacy to the late master not matched even during its years in slavery.

The World Slaveholding Made

Mississippi in the 1850s was not Massachusetts, nor even Abe Lincoln's Illinois, a northern state that was settled in roughly the same time period. Mississippi was a slaveholding culture. White people owned black people, and from that single fact flowed a whole broad stream that permeated life in Mississippi and made it qualitatively different from that in the nonslaveholding states. In Mississippi in the 1850s more than half of the people were slaves (in 1850, 435,000 or 57 percent), and they were legally owned by about one quarter of the white families. In that decade approximately two-thirds of all the people in the state were directly involved in slavery, either as slaves or members of slaveholding families. The economic effects of this have often been calculated, but the psychological consequences—as suggested by the whole issue of miscegenation and the shadow family—are beyond reckoning.

Slavery also involved the majority of whites who owned no slaves. One vital connection was through governments, state and local, that were dedicated to maintaining the order. The police, the courts, the penal system all found a large part of their work in enforcing the "peculiar institution." The state militia, to which every able-bodied white man belonged, was the ultimate weapon to enforce slavery. Closely associated with the militia was the "patrol," a sort of standing *posse comitatus* that rode the roads at night to keep slaves and free blacks—and such whites as might deal with slaves illicitly—in check. In effect, every white person, in uniform or out, was a policeman in the face of every black person. Such was the necessity of the slave system because a rebel slave was a rebel black, and rebel blacks saw all whites—men, women, and children, nonslaveholders as well as slaveholders—as enemies. The indiscriminate killing that occurred during Nat Turner's rebellion in Virginia in 1831 had established that fact undeniably, and only fools would ignore the lesson.

Slavery was a hard system and, in the Western world, of increasingly dubious morality as the nineteenth century progressed. The churches of the South strove to meliorate the plight of the slave and the anxiety of the owner. During the last generation before the war, missionaries of every major denomination moved among slaves with an intensity not matched before or since. White people labored not only to make Christians of blacks, but also to make them culturally white like themselves—always, of course, within strict limits. The Southern church worked vigorously to impress upon black people the necessity of striving for Victorian morality and familyhood and upon masters the necessity of promoting and honoring such efforts among their slaves. It was a peculiar performance, this support of slavery in a certain soft style; in effect, another reform movement in America's "Age of Reform."

It was, nevertheless, an effort that did not prevent the alienation of Southern Protestants from their co-religionists in the North. In the 1840s Southern Methodists and Baptists (some 90 percent of all the Christians in Mississippi) seceded totally from their Northern brothers and sisters to form separate denominations. Among Baptists, that separation persists today. Already in the 1830s some Southern Presbyterians had withdrawn, and in the 1850s the remainder would follow. Thus, well before political secession and the actual coming of the war, Southern society in the pursuit of prosperity through slavery was already well along the road toward defining itself as a cultural nation distinctly different from the North and, indeed, from any other major cultural group in the Western world. It was not unlike nationalist movements under way in the same decades in Italy, Germany, and elsewhere.

Slavery in the South was a whole system woven into the fabric of a broader culture. Inevitably, it tied all slaves and all whites together. That connection was very clear in the courts in which William Falkner practiced. Consider, for example, the case of "Dave a Slave" who was tried in Ripley in the Tippah County courthouse in March, 1853, for having stabbed to death another slave, John, who belonged to another master. Dave was found guilty of manslaughter by a jury of twelve white men, selected regardless of their slaveholding status. The record book indicated that the court ordered that "Dave be burned in the hand by the Sheriff which was immediately done in open court and it is further considered by the Court that for said offense the said defendant shall receive Two Hundred and fifty lashes upon the bare back to be inflicted by the Sheriff of the County One Hundred of which shall be inflicted tomorrow, One Hundred the day following and the remainder the day following."[59] The hand that was to be marked by burning was, no doubt, the hand that had wielded the knife that killed John. Probably, the sheriff burned an "M" on Dave's hand to signify to all that he was a murderer and a danger to society. In the North in the 1850s no one could have witnessed the branding of a man in open court, and even in the South in that decade no white man would have received a single lash, much less two hundred and fifty lashes.

Branding, lashing, notching ears, and otherwise marking were punishments reserved for slaves and, sometimes, free blacks. By design, they were excruciatingly painful and the body itself carried for life visible evidence of conviction for wrongdoing, but they did not long separate the slave from his labor. Legal justice for black people was always administered by white people, and it was not and could not be blind. There were two systems of justice, and everything began and ended with the color of the accused.

Slavery, of necessity, was a violent institution and the violence went both ways. Masters raped and flogged their slaves. Slaves assaulted their masters and sometimes, too, women of the ruling race. In September, 1851, John Wesley Thompson, as the District Attorney for the 7th Judicial District, prosecuted Abe, "a Negro man slave," for assaulting Mary Harris, "a free white woman." The state charged that Abe intended "to ravish and carnally know" Mary. The all-white, all-male jury found the slave guilty, and the judge ordered the sheriff on October 17, at some time between the hours of noon and six o'clock, to take Abe to an "enclosed yard" and "hang him by the neck until his body is dead."[60] Mississippi law, to ensure that justice was truly done and society protected, wisely compensated owners whose slaves were thus executed. Accordingly, all the whites of Tippah County sometimes found it necessary to buy slaves with their tax money. In this strange way, they were all slaveholders.

In the interest of peace and good order in the commonwealth, the courts also enforced discipline upon both slaveholding and nonslaveholding whites in their relations with slaves. In September, 1860, Willis K. Embry was indicted by the Tippah County grand jury for the "Cruel Treatment of [a] Slave," an outrage to the decency of the community but more vitally a threat to its safety because slaves cruelly treated were liable to become dangerous to all whites.[61] The record is silent on the outcome of Embry's case, but in March, 1859, William Falkner himself successfully defended James W. Whitten against a charge of "Trading with [a] Slave."[62] A year later Whitten was charged with several counts of the same offense. He was convicted, fined $100, and sentenced to ten days in jail.[63] Trading with a slave without the master's express consent encouraged slaves to steal, and, worse, it promoted freedoms and ambitions best denied. Trading with slaves might draw a fine of $50 and imprisonment for a month for each count. Also, there was a continuous parade of men charged with "Stealing a Negro," "Stealing a Slave," or "Harboring a Negro." Often, the latter meant hiding a runaway slave, which might, in turn, lead to stealing and selling the runaway. The court records of Tippah and other Mississippi counties are full of charges, trials, convictions, and the sentencing of white people accused of tampering with the system.

Justice for black people in Mississippi was not evenhanded, but conviction did not come automatically with an accusing white finger. In Oxford, in November, 1855, "Charley a Slave" was charged with arson, one of the most feared of slave crimes because of the ease and secrecy with which it could be initiated and the awful result that might follow—death in the night by fire for the slaveholding family as their house burnt down around them. Charley was tried a year later and found not guilty.

Isolated violence by individual slaves was fearful, but organized violence by a number of slaves was the worst of all. Even here, apparently, the courts demanded evidence for a conviction. In October, 1857, a slave named Wash was brought into court in Oxford accused of "Conspiracy." He was tried immediately and found not guilty.[64] The process was complicated and meanings not always clear, but court records suggest that what might have been the situation in these two cases was always a relevant factor: When a slave was brought to the bar and tried, so too was his master.

Man on the Make

LAWYER, SPECULATOR, BUSINESSMAN, POLITICIAN

In 1860, the census taker recorded that William Falkner's occupation was "atty at Law." During the 1850s Falkner probably spent most of his time working in that pursuit. Sometimes he practiced with his uncle, sometimes alone. Law could be a "starving profession," as one young lawyer complained, or it could be a fairly lucrative activity. For William and, to a lesser extent, for his uncle, it seemed to be the latter. Both men worked regularly at the bar. Court records indicate that a major part of William's business involved suits for relatively minor debts—seldom more than a few hundred dollars and often less than a hundred.

The courthouse, apparently, was virtually a clearing house for business accounts that became very complex as people frequently gave and took credit, and even loaned their borrowing capacity to others by endorsing their notes. A successful lawyer was constantly in court, suing for debts, defending against suits for debts, and settling accounts. Friends, relatives, acquaintances, and total strangers sued each other frequently, routinely, sometimes over great distances, and seemingly with no great acrimony. It was no disgrace at all, it appears, to be sued for debt, and individuals went blithely along creating new knots of debts even as they left their lawyers tediously unravelling or simply cutting away the old by forced sales and settlements.

Matters of property were tried in a civil court, in Mississippi called the "Chancery Court," in which the judge carried the title "Chancellor." Criminal cases were tried in "Circuit Court." The docket of the Circuit Court in Tippah shows Falkner steadily at work there, too, defending citizens against charges of having committed the usual array of crimes against persons: assault and battery, manslaughter, rape, and murder; and against property: trespass, misrepresentation, and larceny great and small. He was also engaged in cases alleging crimes against the peace and good order of the community: fighting, riot, affray, disturbing worship, swearing in public, swearing in front of ladies, card playing, public drunkenness, and, very often, "retailing"—selling liquor in an illegal fashion.[65]

In addition to practicing law, Falkner bought and sold slaves and speculated in land. A very close student of land dealing in Tippah County found that in the years before the war he bought 2,697 acres in the county and three whole blocks plus thirteen and one-half lots in Ripley. Of these holdings, he sold 2,000 acres for an average price of $8.53 an acre, realizing a profit of $3,990.70. These operations put him in the middling range of land dealers in the county.[66] Falkner speculated, too, in land elsewhere in the Indian cession. In 1854 in Lafayette County he acquired three widely separated plots of 160 acres for $200 each. Within a year, he had sold one of these, located near the Yocona River (sometimes called Yoknapatawpha by Native Americans) for $40, thus closing out a not very successful venture.[67]

Falkner also engaged in business in the town of Ripley, at which, apparently, he enjoyed considerable success. We know this from the records of R.G. Dun & Co., a company that specialized in researching the credit worthiness of businessmen all over America and making that information available to its subscribers. Often a local lawyer would become the company's part-time agent, providing both detailed information and generalized opinions about local businessmen and also advice about reliable lawyers who might be employed by persons elsewhere to sue for specific debts. These records are now housed in the Baker Library of the Harvard Business School, and William Falkner is easily visible in them. In 1853 R.G. Dun & Co.'s man in Ripley reported that Falkner "is marrd has some means say 3 improved houses / lots in Town to rent out. His income from this source is some 4 $ 5c$ [four to five hundred dollars] per annum." One of his investments was in a small store run by E.B. Word, probably one of his kinsmen. Word was described as unmarried, young, sometimes intemperate, but mostly not very able. Early in 1855 the business failed but left no debts unpaid. By the middle of the year, the reporter declared of Word: "Not worth one cent nor ever will be." A year later he concluded, "This gent. has gone to Texas."[68] During this and later generations, Texas was often the resort of restless, failed, or fugitive Mississippians. Not a few accounts were simply closed out with "G.T.T.," meaning "Gone To Texas."

In 1855 Falkner went into business in a much more aggressive way with L.C. Norvell, a highly enterprising young man of twenty-six who had, inauspiciously, just gone broke after two years of doing business by himself. Even so, the reporter pronounced him "one of the best business men we have but last yr he over traded," meaning he bought too much and sold too much on credit or not at all. The same reporter described Falkner as a married man with good habits and a fair business capacity. He had about $7,000 in capital and some good property in town, including two brick stores worth about $4,000. There were no judgments against Falkner for debt. Within the year, however, Norvell and Falkner had discontinued business and Falkner was overseeing a settlement of accounts. Norvell, reputedly, had gone to Memphis to enter business with the son of a rich man, and Falkner "has gone into the practice of law."[69]

Indeed, William Falkner is also in R.G. Dun & Co.'s reports on lawyers. In partnership with his Uncle John, he practiced in all of the counties around Tippah as well as at home. These reports vary somewhat in their assessment of the young man—even as they are uniformly complimentary of his uncle, who they said had been the prosecuting attorney for the District for twelve years before 1855. In that year, the reporter from Pontotoc County indicated that Falkner had been in practice for about five years. So far as he could discover, Falkner was responsible but "has been a little wild in his hab[its]." In Marshall County, where Holly Springs was the county seat, the reporter thought him a young man of fair ability, honorable, and worthy of confidence. Interestingly, he was under the impression that Falkner was not married. Strangely, the reporter for Ripley seemed to confuse William with his uncle. He erroneously asserted that Falkner was the oldest attorney in the village and had won a seat in the legislature in the recent election without seeking the office. "He does not desire to be in politics," declared the reporter, "& says he will not be after this." More accurately he wrote that Falkner owned a section of land, had a small farm near town, and "has 3 slaves." At the end of 1858, the current reporter announced to his employers that both he and John Wesley Thompson had been elevated to the bench. William Falkner had bought his law office and, he thought, might be a good choice to attend to R.G. Dun & Co.'s business locally in the future.[70]

R.G. Dun & Co. did, indeed, make Falkner their local agent. The supervisor in these matters reported that he was thirty to thirty-five years old (actually he was 33) and possessed no property. Curiously, he too was under the impression that Falkner was unmarried. Falkner had assured him that he was fully posted on all the merchants in "any part of North Miss as he is well acq. with nearly all of them." Among his references he had listed Jacob Thompson, then Secretary of the Interior, and Col. Matthew C. Galloway of Memphis, the founder of *The Memphis Avalanche*. Early in 1859, the supervisor declared that William C. Falkner had been appointed company agent as of November 24, 1858. He regarded him as a reliable collector, perfectly solvent, and safe "in money matters but not a profound lawy[er]." Falkner's talents were sufficient, he believed, for all collection purposes. Later that year, after he had met Falkner in person, he upgraded his estimation substantially. Falkner was then described as a very good man of some property, "high toned," and honorable. In March of 1861, on the very eve of the Civil War, R.G. Dun & Co. still thought well of William Falkner.[71]

~

In the middle 1850s, Falkner also sortied into politics, not as a Democrat, the party to which his uncle steadfastly adhered and from which he received both honors and offices, but as a "Know-Nothing." Nationally, the Know-Nothings were breakaway Whigs who sought to smother the controversy over slavery under a thick blanket of patriotism. Officially named the American Party, the party in the North shouted alarm at the flood of new immigrants, primarily Irish and German, coming into the country. When members were asked what their organization was about, they took up the mask of secrecy. They were instructed to reply: "I know nothing," hence the interesting sobriquet for the name of their party. In the South, where immigrants were not nearly so numerous, Know-Nothings were essentially Whiggish and more likely to rally to the idea of promoting material progress through government aid to internal improvements—especially railroads. Unsurprisingly, Know-Nothingism in the cotton belt often found its vanguard in cities and towns. Every town was avid for a railroad and wisely so.

Falkner's material interests were town centered, and his politics served his economics very well. In any event, he was prominent enough in the ephemeral Know-Nothing movement to become a frequent contributor to, if not indeed sometimes the editor of its local organ, *Uncle Sam.* Much later, when he wrote himself up for the publication *Men of Mark in Mississippi,* he was proud enough of that journalistic activity to give it a prominent place in his list of achievements. In the election in 1855, Falkner was the leading and vigorous spirit in an unsuccessful attempt to deliver Tippah County to the Whig candidate for Congress, D.F. Fontaine. In the same year, he himself ran for the legislature as a Know-Nothing candidate only to suffer defeat, ironically, at the hands of his Democratic uncle. On July 7, 1856, Falkner wisely announced his return to the Democratic fold.[72]

In the early 1850s William Falkner was an active member of one of the most ardently evangelical organizations of the time—The Sons of Temperance. Judging from an extensive set of minutes of the order held in the Ripley Public Library, the Sons seemed to be dedicated primarily to catching one another in the act of drinking alcoholic beverages. In 1852 there were more than forty men in the Ripley chapter, mostly young men but ranging up into middle age. William, characteristically, was one of the very first to be caught. On August 14,

1852, C.A. Brougham brought William to trial. "I charge Bro. W.C. Falkner for violating Article 2 of the constitution by drinking cider in my presence," he declared. Before the month was out, Brother Falkner, again in character, made a formal motion "that the word 'cider' be stricken out of the pledge."[73]

The recording secretary and, seemingly, the prime spirit in the local Sons was the ubiquitous Thomas C. Hindman, Jr. Apparently, Hindman himself had something of the mentality of a policeman. He soon improved considerably on Brougham's performance by simultaneously bringing three of his brothers up on charges of tippling.

William C. Falkner, contrary to popular myth, was never a great slaveholding planter. Indeed, he was not a planter at all and never held more than several adult slaves. He had a substantial amount of money to invest in the 1850s, but obviously he chose not to do so in plantations and slaves. On the contrary, during that decade he seemed to disengage himself from the minor involvement in those areas that had come to him through his marriage to Holland Pearce. In that time and place, Falkner's was a curious abstinence that marked him as different. No Sartoris or even a Thomas Sutpen of fictional fame here. He was a town dweller and a town lawyer and businessman who took advantage of such opportunities as came his way and grew to affluence without the benefit of slaves and a plantation.

Indeed, over the generations the most ambitious Falkner men seemed to operate in this mode. The original Falkner, John, came to America from England in 1665. His father William was a "draper"; that is, he bought and sold cloth. Successful in commerce, however, William was able to marry Elizabeth Filmer, the daughter of a gentleman, Sir Edward Filmer. John's grandson William was one of those peripatetic frontier types who, in 1794 and late in life, simply left his estate in western North Carolina to his son William, Jr., and slipped away, probably across the mountains, to begin again. William, Jr., the uncle of Ripley's William C. Falkner, settled down and thrived in a variety of simultaneous business ventures in and around Mt. Airy (Surry County), including operations along what is still known as Faulkner Creek.[74]

In Ripley, William Falkner was both in and strangely out of social life in the community, unlike his uncle John, who obviously was well integrated and highly acceptable. For example, religion was a large and vital part of local life; yet Falkner, in spite of his presumptive Methodism, was not a church member and seemed not much concerned with religion in any form. His wife, Lizzie Falkner, on the other hand, staunchly maintained her Presbyterian connection and so engaged her children.

With, for examples, Falkner's Mexican experience, the incident with the Sons of Temperance, and his venture into politics, a pattern seems to emerge in the life of the young man. Apparently, he was able initially to fall into line with other people in his community and engage in various common pursuits; however, once he was in he was not able to stay. He conformed enough to win admission into various communions, then turned maverick and did what he wanted without great regard for the opinions of his erstwhile fellows. The result was a measure of alienation from the ruling elite of Tippah County and the town of Ripley.

The Ruling Elite

From local records one can easily pick out the dozen or so clans that form the elite, the "aristocracy," of Tippah County and the town of Ripley. In the county, the elite were the great slaveholders, men such as Francis Leak, who held ninety-seven slaves in 1850, and Moses Collins with eighty-six in the same year. Invariably the wealthiest of these came into the county with a large slave force already made. Some came early, like Epsey Moody who was there with fifty slaves even before the county was organized in 1837. Others like the Hindmans, who came in 1842 with about sixty-five slaves, arrived only slightly later. Some families, such as the Hamers, Grays, Cheairs, and Collinses, had several branches and each had a plantation with a dozen or more slaves.[75]

The children in these families had a distinct headstart in life. Thomas Hindman, Jr., for instance, in 1850 at age twenty-two already had his own plantation with sixteen slaves to work it for him. None of his slaves was older than thirty-four, and apparently three of the women were in the prime of child-bearing life.[76] Rather clearly, his slaves were carefully selected out of the larger clan holding to insure his prosperity. Thomas's sister Mildred, in November, 1847, at not quite seventeen, married into the Doxey clan in Pontotoc County. The senior Doxey reputedly had several plantations and scores of slaves. Doxey gave the couple a farm, a house, and slaves. The Hindmans also sent along four slaves to the newlyweds, "a man, woman, girl, baby."[77] As with many other sons of the planter elite, Thomas, Jr., became a lawyer. Like some of those, he seldom went to court but rather took a leading role in civic activities such as the militia and in social organizations such as the Sons of Temperance.

The ruling elite in the town of Ripley had a somewhat different character. Some clans, such as the Spights, maintained both plantations in the country and impressive households in town, and their sons might become lawyers and doctors.[78] However, most of the leaders in Ripley arrived early, possessed a significant degree of formal education, and, usually, owned strikingly few slaves. They were primarily trade oriented rather than agriculturally oriented. By far the most eminent of the early leaders in Ripley was Charles P. Miller, a Methodist minister who came in 1836, a year before the town was formally organized. The Millers at first lived in a tent and later in a log cabin. Reverend

Miller organized a congregation and, while he ministered to his church, he also managed several businesses. In 1840 he built the first hotel. Two of his daughters married rising young men. One of these, Richard J. Thurmond, born in North Carolina in 1831, came with his parents as a first settler. In the early 1850s he was the deputy clerk of court, and later in the decade rose to be clerk. He, too, was involved in several businesses, primarily as an investor.[79] Over the decades, Dick Thurmond's life would become intimately entwined with that of William C. Falkner. Charles Miller's second son-in-law, Dr. John Young Murry, would become one of writer William Faulkner's great grandfathers.

John Y. Murry was born in 1829 and came to Ripley as a small child. In 1850 he married Emily Holcombe, who soon bore a daughter, Sallie, and died. Afterward he married Charles Miller's daughter Mary. John went east to take a degree from Jefferson Medical College in Philadelphia in 1855. When he returned, he became not only a practicing physician but the sheriff of the county, a post he held from 1856 to 1860. During the Civil War he attained the rank of captain and commanded Company A of the 34th Mississippi Regiment in the Army of Tennessee. Afterward, he resumed his practice, became the Grand Master of Mississippi Masons, and served one term in the legislature before his death in 1915.[80]

~

William C. Falkner was not a member of the slaveholding aristocracy nor even an early comer to the village of Ripley. In the 1880s, looking back from the heights of his success, he liked to picture his arrival in Mississippi as that of a "barefooted and penniless youth." In truth, of all the leading men in Ripley and Tippah County in the first half century of its existence, he was the one who began—in a purely material sense—furthest back. Even so, he did have advantages beyond his considerable natural talents. He was the protégé of his well-respected uncle, he had made an advantageous first marriage, and he had somehow acquired a good education and an engaging public manner even before his arrival in Mississippi. The education and manner might well have come to him through his mother and the traditional cultural expectations of the Word family.

The Words were clearly well educated, influential, and ambitious people. Yet they are curiously slighted in Falkner family tradition. Thomas Jefferson Word, William Falkner's maternal uncle, is a case in point. He was born about 1809 in Surry County, North Carolina, where his father was deeply and successfully engaged in politics. Thomas served in the North Carolina legislature in the 1832–1833 session before moving to Mississippi, probably in 1834. He continued to be active in politics, taking up the cause of the Whiggish anti-Jacksonians. He not only served as a lawyer or a litigant in several of the first cases tried in Pontotoc County in 1836 and 1837, he also made the first entries in the record book for the district court. In 1838 Thomas was elected to Congress as one of Mississippi's two representatives and served in Washington through the winter session of 1839. He first lived in Pontotoc, gained eminence as a leading lawyer, and won popularity as an orator, an amateur violinist, and "a remarkably fine looking man."[81]

"Jeff" Word was living in Pontotoc in 1842 when William Falkner arrived in Mississippi. Why the "penniless youth" and ambitious young man did not settle in with his prestigious Uncle Thomas Jefferson Word on his arrival in Mississippi and make effective use of that important connection remains a mystery. Instead Falkner later concocted a story about his salvation in Pontotoc by little Lizzie Vance.

The absence of T.J. Word from Falkner family tradition is even more striking in view of the decades of support given to each clan by the other. In fact, the Words and the Falkners intermarried through several couples. William Falkner was a part of that highly supportive network and must have known his Uncle Thomas very well. During the late 1840s and early 1850s when they lived in Holly Springs, Thomas Word and his wife Mary bought and sold land in Tippah County, including a $400 purchase from their brother-in-law, John Wesley Thompson.[82] During the sectional crisis of 1849 and 1850, Colonel Word (as he was then called, reflecting his eminence) was often quoted—and highly lauded—as a leading defender of Southern rights against Northern intrusions against slavery. Indeed, in 1850, he served conspicuously, a Whig among Democrats, as one of Mississippi's delegates to a convention in Nashville called for that purpose.[83] More locally, in September, 1854, he made a celebrated speech to the Sons of Temperance in Ripley.[84]

Over the decade of the 1850s, William Falkner enjoyed an extraordinary prosperity. In truth, it sprang primarily from his own exertions. His style in financial affairs seems to have been very much like his style elsewhere. He combined orthodoxy with unorthodoxy. He was always solvent and, in that highly litigious age, seemed to have practically no judgments for debt lodged against him. He could make a daring venture in business, as with the Norvell partnership, but when it failed manage a dissolution that left his credit rating unimpaired. In 1855, the rating company thought that Falkner's capital might amount to something over $8,000. In the next year, William indicated to the tax collector that he had $2,000 out on loan. He had no pistols at all, but he had retained his "Bowie knife," perhaps the instrument with which he had done in Robert Hindman. John Wesley Thompson and several other men in Ripley each had a "Bowie knife," and almost everyone had one or two pistols.[85] Clearly, William Falkner was turning his considerable energy into business pursuits. In 1860, Falkner himself declared in the census that he possessed $10,000 in real estate and an astounding $40,200 in personal property. Personal property is defined as moveable property, and included slaves. Falkner's slaves just then might have been valued at about $5,000. If he simply was not boasting to the census taker, which seems unlikely, he had an unusually large amount of his assets in liquid form.[86] At a more intimate level, state tax rolls in 1861 indicated that William Falkner rode a saddle horse valued at $200, drove his family about in a "pleasure" carriage worth $100, and told time from a $75 gold watch.[87] He was not the richest man in Tippah County, but he was well off.

The affluence of William and his Uncle John helps account for the substantial changes over the decade in the white membership in the households of each. By 1860 William had brought to live with him, probably from Missouri, his mother Caroline Word Falkner, aged sixty-two, and a twenty-two-year-old sister Frances (called "Frank" but described accurately as female in the census). Uncle John had taken in not only William's young son, John, and William's younger brother, James Word Falkner, but also the grandmother of the Word clan, Justianna, aged eighty-four.[88] Seemingly the Falkner family—and the Words—had at last found a home in the West, and it was in Ripley, Mississippi. It was about to find its patriarch and most significant personage in William.

TWO

The Colonel

If there was a watershed in William Falkner's adult life, the Civil War was it. Before the war, he was one of a score of ambitious, rising young men vying for leadership in the town of Ripley and the surrounding countryside. Soon after the war, he was one of the top few. It was perfectly symbolic of his rise in the social hierarchy that he began the war as a captain, ended it as a colonel, and aspired to be a general.

The War

At the outbreak of the Civil War, William C. Falkner helped organize the Magnolia Rifles, a company composed of Tippah County men of which he became captain. That company joined with other Mississippi companies to form the Second Mississippi Volunteer Regiment, and Falkner won election as its colonel. In May, 1861, soon after it arrived in Virginia, the inspector general visited the Second Mississippi and found it sadly lacking. "The officers are entirely without military knowledge of any description," he reported, "and the men have a slovenly and unsoldier-like appearance." He described the Mississippians as badly clothed, poorly armed, and careless of their military equipment.[1] Even so, in July, in the Battle of Bull Run, or Manassas as the Confederates called it, Colonel Falkner and his men acquitted themselves well. They formed up with four other regiments around Henry House to meet a jolting attack by a force of 16,000 Union troops. For an hour they stood against a withering fire, holding the line until General T.J. "Stonewall" Jackson could bring his men up to the front and turn the battle into a thumping Southern victory. In the fray, however, the Second Mississippi lost 25 men killed and 82 wounded, a heavy toll in a regiment that mustered altogether only 500 men.[2] In the months after the battle, the Colonel drilled his troops vigorously.

One result of Falkner's boldness in action and dedication to drill, family legend maintains, was that in the election of officers in the spring of 1862 he lost his colonelcy to John M. Stone. The diary of a member of the Second Mississippi, A.L.P. Vairin, tells the story of the election first hand. In the initial balloting Stone received 250 votes, Falkner 240, and Captain Miller 129. Miller withdrew, and Stone, Falkner, Vairin, and others made speeches. On the next round Stone was elected, and "much dissatisfaction was manifested by Col. F's friends." Predictably, Falkner had again built up a cadre of ardent loyalists and an array of equally ardent enemies. Again true to his nature, he contested the result of the election, but lost. The legend implies that Stone was more popular than professional. In reality Stone was at least equal if not superior to Falkner in martial talent and capacity for leadership. He was several times wounded while leading his men, promoted to brigadier general, and later twice elected governor of Mississippi.[3] Deprived of his colonelcy, Falkner returned to Mississippi where, by the summer of 1862, there was plenty of fighting to be done—literally at the front door of his home in Ripley.[4]

In its initial phase, the war in northern Mississippi was related to the plan of Union generals to splinter the Confederacy by seizing control of the major rivers in the West. In April, 1862, General Ulysses S. Grant, the master in the "riverine war," had advanced as far south as Pittsburg Landing on the Tennessee River near Corinth, a town in northeastern-most Mississippi. There a Confederate army under the joint command of Generals Albert Sydney Johnston and P.G.T. Beauregard suddenly attacked. In the battle, which the Southerners called Shiloh after a nearby church, Grant barely managed a standoff. Nobody really won at Shiloh, but each side paid dearly in casualties, and each was brought soberly and sadly to the realization that this would be a desperate and bloody war. In Mississippi, after Shiloh, husbands and fathers, middle-aged men and callow youths all went into the Confederate regiments in large numbers. For a time after the battle, while Grant reorganized and made preparations for continuing the river war, Union forces moved forward and maintained a loose occupation of the northeastern edge of Mississippi. Their backs were to the Tennessee River, which was their major supply line; their headquarters was in Corinth; and the countryside that lay on both sides of the thirty-mile road southwest to Ripley provided the ground for continuous and bloody skirmishing.

At home again, Colonel Falkner lost no time getting into the fray. In July, he recruited a special force of about six hundred mounted men, designated the First Mississippi Partisan Rangers. His object, apparently, was to harass the enemy and, simultaneously, use them as a source of supplies. Furthermore, the Rangers were organized under a law that allowed them to be paid for munitions captured from the enemy. They were to be, ideally, land-roving privateers, out for profit as well as martial glory. Seemingly, it was a universe constructed specifically for the talents and ambitions of William Falkner.[5]

Hardly had Colonel Falkner's Rangers been mustered into service before he led them, in August, on a sortie into Tennessee. During that venture he fought with General Dodge some five miles east of Dyersburg and returned home with fifty-five of the enemy's horses but lost thirty-one men killed.[6] Shortly thereafter, in late August, he decided to surprise cavalry General Phil Sheridan at his camp at Rienzi near Corinth. He achieved the surprise, but the redoubtable West Pointer quickly rallied his troopers to drive the assailants off and then give hot pursuit. Falkner's men attempted twice to make a stand, but broke quickly under fire from the galloping Yankees and fled in great disorder. Union troopers chased them to within five miles of the Rangers' home base in Ripley before their horses gave out and they were forced to break off contact. General Sheridan reported the event to his superiors. "Colonel Falkner, commanding this rebel force, was so hard pushed that he separated from his command on one of the little by-paths and made his escape," he said. "He left us his hat, however, as did nearly the whole of his command." It was a "complete rout," the Yankee general declared, "the road was strewn with shot guns, hats, coats, blankets, dead horses, &c."[7]

Falkner continued his operations into the fall of 1862 with steady losses and no signal success. In late November, the Union cavalry seized Ripley itself, and they almost caught the colonel of the First Mississippi Partisan Rangers. "Falkner with about 100 men escaped by dint of the hardest running" wrote the attacking cavalry commander. He concluded: "I consider Colonel Falkner's regiment now broken beyond any hope of reorganization, and a great source of petty annoyance to our forces entirely removed."[8] Colonel Falkner's regiment was badly bent but not broken, and he would have been outraged to hear his command classed as "a great source of petty annoyance." Nevertheless, thereafter it seemed to ride from one disaster to another.

So, too, the Confederacy at large. On July 4, 1863, Grant took Vicksburg even as Lee in the East was losing at Gettysburg. By the end of the year, Union forces practically controlled Tennessee and were moving on Georgia. During 1864 a Union army under William Tecumseh Sherman fought its way to Atlanta and then marched across Georgia to reach the Atlantic Ocean at Savannah by Christmas, finally turning north to cut a wide swath of destruction through the Carolinas.

Meanwhile, northern Mississippi became, relatively speaking, a martial backwater. For Southern soldiers still operating in that area, it was often a loose, ride-and-shoot war, the kind in which the ex-slave-trader, planter, and Confederate cavalry general Nathan Bedford Forrest excelled. His putative motto, "git thar fustest with the mostest," fit the circumstances perfectly. It was a war in which a rag-tag group of men and boys could romantically call themselves Partisan Rangers, individuals might do daring deeds with horse and pistol, and a bold and wily Bedford Forrest could dodge bullets even when his name was written on them. But it was also one in which, increasingly, the numerous, powerful, and exasperated Yankees could sortie out of their Memphis stronghold and march, ride, and sit wherever they wanted. Forrest might get there first, but he could never stay long. In April, 1863, near Hernando, a dozen miles south of Memphis, during one of those stout Yankee raids in force, the First Mississippi Partisan Rangers in one quick firefight with the Twelfth Wisconsin Cavalry lost forty-two men killed and seventy-two captured.[9]

As the Confederacy declined, Colonel Falkner, it seems, simply faded away. In the fall of 1863 he resigned his command, pleading "ill health." His regimental surgeon and Ripley neighbor, William D. Carter, ascribed Falkner's condition to "indigestion and internal hemorrhoids."[10] The Colonel, apparently, had ulcers.

During 1862 and 1863, Falkner had spent considerable energy and a small river of ink attempting to secure a brigadier general's commission. He had been one of eight brigadier generals in the Mississippi militia at the outbreak of war and, with wonted ambition, had tried to enter the Confederate Army at that rank but had been bested by other candidates. Allegedly, later in Virginia he had been offered a generalship, but chose to stay with his regiment out of consideration for his men. Then, back in Mississippi and belatedly, he had drawn upon every source of support he could imagine to achieve the rank of brigadier, and all to no avail. It must have galled Falkner no end that his longtime rival, Thomas Hindman, entering the Confederate army from his new home in Helena, Arkansas, became a brigadier in September, 1861, and then a major general in April, 1862, and that he earned those promotions by his effectiveness in the field and his "gallant conduct in the Battle of Shiloh."[11]

Bitter, frustrated, and feeling vastly undervalued, William Falkner disappeared from view for almost two years. It seems probable that he spent the duration of the war running cotton across the ever-shifting borders of the Confederacy into Union occupied territory, perhaps to Memphis or Helena (on the Arkansas shore of the Mississippi River), and bringing in Yankee goods that were in critically short supply—such as medicines, salt, and footwear. His partner in this enterprise might have been the erstwhile clerk of court in Ripley, Richard J. Thurmond. Thurmond joined the war late. In April, 1864, he was a private in a home guard unit, Lieutenant Stricklin's "Unattached" company of State Troops. That unit, on May 2, merged into Ashcroft's Battalion of State Cavalry in which Thurmond became captain of a company. Two days later this unit mustered into Confederate service as a part of the Eleventh Mississippi Cavalry.[12] At that point, however, Thurmond disappeared from Confederate records, and the Eleventh Cavalry went on to bloody battles in the Atlanta campaign and final surrender with General Johnston in North Carolina.

Almost surely after leaving the service, Falkner based himself in Pontotoc, close enough to Memphis and Helena for commerce, yet rarely visited by the Yankees. Yankee traders in Memphis let it be known that they would buy cotton there at $2.50 a pound, and we know that Pontotoc County soon supported a large trade in contraband, some of it done by older women and boys fifteen or sixteen, that is, boys large enough to drive two oxen pulling a cart with one bale of cotton several score miles and just young enough to avoid conscription by either army if caught. From time to time the civilian "grapevine" would announce that "the lines were open," and the carts would roll out in groups of five or six and return a week or so later laden with supplies.[13]

Such commerce was dangerous and illegal, of course and illegal on both sides—but it was also exceedingly profitable. The Civil War blockade runner, like the fictional Rhett Butler created years later, could be regarded as either patriot or traitor just as one chose.

Reconstruction

Colonel Falkner came out of the war neither vanquished nor impoverished. He lived in a land, however, that had been severely ravaged. Railroads were destroyed, bridges burned, whole cities, towns, and villages, including Ripley, had been put to the torch and burned virtually to the ground. Most of all, slavery was ended, and some two billion dollars in Southern capital, a vast amount for that time, evaporated. With the loss of forced labor, the land lost value too. Confederate money and bonds were worth nothing, and the great majority of large slaveholders found themselves without the capital necessary to turn their plantations into working farms.

In radically altered circumstances, William Falkner was uniquely well situated. He had no great slaveholding to lose and no great plantation to plunge in value. Furthermore, he somehow came out of the war with a lot of hard cash in his pocket. It is not at all surprising after the war to see him first in Pontotoc. On April 26, 1865, even before all of the Confederate armies had surrendered, he put down $2,500 in cash for lot #137 in that village. It is not clear whether this was a lot with a house or a lot for business use. In any event, it was prime real estate (roughly two acres located just off the town square), and the purchase price represented a serious commitment by Falkner to a future of some kind in that area. Some three months later, however, it became clear that he would resettle in Tippah County not Pontotoc. On July 27, 1865, he was in Ripley buying twenty feet of business frontage on the south side of the town square. His house had been burned along with those of other leading citizens in Ripley, but he did not rebuild on that site. Instead, on August 7, he bought for $800 an entire block of land just off the square on North Main Street from his enterprising associate Richard Thurmond. There, he built a rather simple one story house along with one small detached building that served as his office, and another that served as a kitchen, also detached in case of fire. No large house was needed; two of his children (Thomas Vance and Lizzie Manassah) had perished in the war, leaving only Henry, age twelve, and Willie Medora, age nine. Furthermore, his mother had died early in the war, and his grandmother near its end.[14]

Three days after he bought his home lot, Falkner acquired another lot from Simon R. Spight for $250, and several days later still another. Over the next couple of years he bought more lots in town and acreage in the country, loaned out money at ten percent interest, taking as security land, cotton, and, in one case, a printing press and, in another, a 1,620 acre plantation in Pontotoc County. He also began the practice of advancing provisions to tenant farmers against their expected crops.[15]

Falkner was instrumental, too, in raising another significant structure in Ripley. Mary Jane Buchanan, Lizzie's sister, had lost her school building in the burning of Ripley. In the summer of 1866, the trustees gave her a ninety-nine year lease on the land upon which the building had stood. Falkner donated more land to increase the size of the campus and helped signally in a community effort to raise a new school. It was opened as Stonewall College in 1867 and flourished until 1882, when it was again consumed by fire.[16]

Even while the Colonel was fighting in Virginia in July, 1861, the law firm of Falkner and Falkner continued to operate in Ripley in the person of his brother James. Indeed, for some months there was no guarantee that the war would not end shortly and business as usual would resume. Eventually, however, the judicial process in Tippah County ground to a halt.[17] During the winter of 1862, Colonel Falkner came home to gather recruits and raise a new company for his regiment. James enrolled in the company and was soon elected a lieutenant. His military career was even more sporadic than the Colonel's, who returned to Ripley not long after James arrived in Virginia to join the Second Mississippi. James Falkner participated in the Battle of Seven Pines near Richmond, May 31 to June 1, but thereafter missed a sequence of important engagements by being ill. One entry in his record declared that he had been left "sick at Richmond" while the army marched northward into Maryland and fought the Battle of Antietam in September. The record stated also that he had been furloughed for thirty days from September 3, but concluded that he was "not heard of since and from declaration made to several men, not likely ever to return." In October the official record indicated that he had been "dropped from the rolls as a deserter."

In fact, James had returned to Ripley and joined his brother's regiment of cavalry. In May, 1863, he was captured at Holly Springs. For a year he was a prisoner of war in Illinois and Maryland. He suffered such severe "chronic diarrhea" that in the spring of 1864 he was paroled and exchanged.[18] For a time after the war, James practiced law in Ripley, then married and moved away. He had several children, one of whom followed Falkner family tradition by becoming a student at Ole Miss in the 1890s. James eventually died of consumption contracted, so his great-great-grandson thought, when he was a prisoner during the war.[19]

William and James Falkner quit the war in the East. But a large majority of their Confederate friends and relatives remained in the Second Mississippi and in the Army of Northern Virginia. Some of these survived, others did not. Among those who did not was Lazarus Pearce, the brother of William's first wife, Holland Pearce. It was he who had pawned his slaves to William in order to venture forth to California during the Gold Rush. Lazarus, having become a farmer and a married man, had enlisted in the Second in March, 1862, well after the war began. He was thirty-four, 5'11", blue-eyed, light haired, and fair of skin. He had been wounded at Gaines Mill on June 27, 1862, and left at Richmond to recover while his regiment marched into Maryland and back. In the lines again, he was captured at Gettysburg on July 3. A year later he died of disease as a prisoner of war in Fort Delaware.[20]

Another of William's marital relations had better luck. Lizzie's nephew, Walter Glover Rutledge, at age eighteen in 1860 had described his occupation to the census taker as "Gentleman." In the next year when he enrolled in the Second Mississippi, he was a nineteen-year-old mail carrier. In November, 1861, Colonel Falkner brought Walter onto his staff as regimental sergeant-major. Glover campaigned all during the war, fought in all the great battles, and almost escaped unmarked. On March 9, 1865, however, a month before the surrender at Appomattox, he was shot through the hand and admitted to a military hospital in Richmond. For Walter, the war was over.[21]

Two of William's cousins also enlisted in the Second Mississippi. David W. and Charles W. Humphreys, Jr., had grown up on a farm in Tippah County. Their mother, Elizabeth Word, and her South Carolina-born husband, Charles, had come to Tippah in 1838. In January, 1842, they bought 168 acres a few miles northeast of Ripley from Thomas Jefferson and Mary Word for $1,200. In 1850 the Humphreys worked their farm with two sons, three daughters, and four slaves, apparently a family. In 1860, the Humphreys family still lived on the farm as in 1850. With real estate valued at $4,000, they were comfortable but not rich.[22] David, age thirty-one and unmarried, enlisted in William Falkner's company in March, 1861, more than a month before the war commenced. He began as the second lieutenant in Company B of the Second Mississippi and quickly rose to command a battalion as major. In the elections of April, 1862, he was chosen lieutenant-colonel "by a large majority over all opponents," as diarist Sergeant A.L.P. Vairin recorded. David, obviously an able and respected officer, took command of the regiment from his cousin William "until protest of [the] election question is settled."[23]

In October, 1861, David's brother Charles also joined the regiment as a member of Company B. His service record described him as twenty years old and a "farmer living near Guntown." He was 5'11" and red haired, with grey eyes and a "ruddy" complexion. He was in every major battle from Seven Pines on.[24]

During the Civil War, it was the battles that killed men, and so too with the Second Mississippi. At its peak in June, 1862, the Second mustered about 1,200 soldiers. As it marched into Pennsylvania in the summer of 1863 in this "Second Invasion of the North," (the battle of Antietam having ended the first), the regiment numbered barely 300 men. On July 1, the Second Mississippi was in the vanguard that probed toward the village of Gettysburg when it suddenly encountered stiff resistance from a New York regiment. Veteran soldiers, the Second responded aggressively. They rushed forward and quickly overwhelmed the New Yorkers only to find themselves almost surrounded by a much larger force. Under heavy fire, many of the Mississippians sought refuge in a railroad cut. Shortly, however, the Northerners got into position to fire into the ditch from one end and commenced a slaughter. Recognizing the inevitable, the senior officer present surrendered 232 men, including the greater part of the Second Mississippi. Among those surrendered was Private Charles Humphreys, who spent the remainder of the war as a prisoner in Fort Delaware. Even so, Charles was one of nineteen soldiers in the regiment whose names were placed on the roll of honor for valor shown in battle.[25]

Sergeant Vairin and several score others recognized the trap in the railroad cut and veered off. Colonel Stone was disabled by a shell fragment and command passed to David Humphreys. On July 2 the remnant of the Second Mississippi moved to the right end of the line facing the Union forces arrayed on Cemetery Ridge. On the afternoon of the third—that fateful day for the South that writer William Faulkner so loved to ponder—the regiment, "60 guns strong" as Vairin said, joined in Pickett's famous and fatal charge. Vairin himself was badly wounded. He was captured, nursed back to health by Yankees in a New York hospital, and exchanged at Richmond in November, 1863. He recuperated at home for a year, then rejoined the regiment in the lines at Petersburg.[26]

Lieutenant-Colonel David Humphreys was "killed in battle" valiantly leading his men in Pickett's charge. Altogether the Second at Gettysburg lost 40 men killed, 183 wounded, and scores missing in action. Only one soldier in the entire regiment came out both unscathed and uncaptured. Thereafter the Second Mississippi, much diminished, joined in every major battle, but only a few of the men made it as far as Appomattox.[27]

William Falkner's briefly shining moment in the Civil War was at the Battle of First Manassas. Thereafter, nothing in his record would mark him as a military chieftain of formidable talent. On the contrary, the soldier inside him, like some mechanical toy, seemed to wind down and stop in the middle of the war. But even when he was active, he did not compare well with his cousin David Humphreys. If we can believe the report of General Sheridan, in the summer of 1862 Colonel Falkner saved himself by separating from his men and dodging away on a side path. In sharp contrast, Lieutenant-Colonel Humphreys died at Gettysburg facing the enemy and leading his men in a last brave charge. Indeed, if we could have stopped the clock of history in April, 1865, it would be men of the Word connection rather than of the Falkner connection who would seem truly heroic.

In Ripley after the war, William Falkner lived among men—and the ghosts of men—who were undeniably superbly courageous and heroic, and he must have suffered somewhat by comparison. It is interesting indeed that before his death in 1889, we hear much of his service in, and wounds from, the Mexican War but very little about his Civil War experience.[28] It seems to be left to his eldest son in the turn of the century years to celebrate Colonel Falkner's Confederate service and still later generations to raise that service to legendary heights. William C. Falkner, himself, after Appomattox, seemed not unlike the fictional Scarlett O'Hara. He was very willing to let the war go, and turn his considerable intelligence to the business of making money.

~

During Reconstruction Falkner emerged as one of the several richest and most influential men in Tippah County. The richest of all, probably, was his associate Richard Thurmond. At least in the persons of these two men, the town came to dominate the country after the war, to turn the tables of hegemony from agriculture in the plantation slaveholding mode to commerce and finance. Neither man had invested directly in plantation slavery, and yet both were highly astute and aggressive businessmen who carefully built up and conserved impressive amounts of capital that they obviously did not invest in the Confederate war effort. When the plantation-slave system collapsed, each apparently made the most of a once in a lifetime opportunity to catapult himself out of the middling ranks to the forefront of wealth and power. For his part, Thurmond signaled his postwar arrival by buying the Cole House (built in 1845) on "Quality Ridge" in Ripley. It was an elegant residence with a detached kitchen and a small house in the rear for servants. Curiously, visitors would later recall that doors inside the house had "iron drops" to cover key holes and insure privacy.[29]

After the war, both Falkner and Thurmond were among the most active and successful speculators in land in the county. Thurmond kept enough of his holdings to become the largest landowner in the area. Falkner kept enough of his to develop, by the 1880s, a 2,000 acre "farm" several miles northwest of Ripley. Situated on Ishatubby Creek, it was a beautiful site. Much of the acreage was bottom land—flat, rich, and walled in by suddenly rising hills. Falkner called it Ishatubby Farm, most people called it Falkner Farm, but some black people called it Damascus after the church they created there. The Colonel did not live on his farm, rather it was a business that he ran using a manager, hired labor, and tenants.[30] Like his contemporary John D. Rockefeller, Falkner paid close attention to details and drove his employees hard. "Put Mart Stanford to work and make him work like hell," he instructed his overseer, Ira South, in 1887, giving explicit, detailed directions about making water barrels tight and putting the cotton gin in good running order. "Hire hands at 60 cents a day if need be," he urged. "Move things ahead as fast as you can."[31]

By the fall of 1865, William Falkner was also picking up his law cases where he had left them and gathering others as he entered what would be a very lucrative postwar practice.[32] Further, he engaged in business in Ripley. Soon after the war, R.G. Dun & Co. began again to keep track of his affairs. On New Year's Day, 1867, they found that he had a dry goods store in town containing some six to seven thousand dollars' worth of goods all bought for cash. "Pays punctually and is never sued on mercantile a/c [account], and very little in any way," the reporter noted. "No liens on his property, nor encumbrances of any kind." The agent estimated his worth at ten to fifteen thousand dollars and gave him an excellent credit rating, concluding, however, that he "is not in the habit of asking for credit." In the middle of 1868, the rating company declared that Colonel Falkner "is a practicing lawyer of good standing & engaged in trade." He was worth $30,000, they thought. Six years later, R.G. Dun & Co.'s man put Falkner's net worth at over $100,000.[33]

It was totally fitting with Falkner's antebellum Whiggery and Know-Nothingism that he should become one of the leaders in the building of a railroad to connect Ripley with Middleton, Tennessee, twenty-five miles to the north. There it would join the Memphis and Charleston (South Carolina) line, and thus the markets of the world. A Ripley railroad company had been incorporated in 1856 but never got beyond the planning stage. In 1871 a new company was formed with Falkner as president and Thurmond as secretary-treasurer, and in 1872 the first train ran the length of the track. As was so often the case with the building of shortline railroads in this era, it was a community venture in which local people donated enthusiasm, goods, and, most vitally, labor. Falkner later explained that at one time he had 1,500 volunteers working on the road, including the sheriff and all his deputies, the clerks of the two courts, and a battery of ministers, while the "ladies" along the line provided food taken from their own larders. It was, as he said, "a universal combination here among all classes, both black and white." It is easy to imagine Falkner as a sort of "Music Man," galvanizing the whole community symphonically to produce a splendid little railroad in which it could take pride—and profit, since land values along the line increased dramatically.[34]

In spite of its auspicious beginnings, the road soon fell into the hands of its creditors and from them passed to four local citizens, two of whom were Falkner and Thurmond. Falkner, still president, wanted to extend the road further south. The others were not so ambitious. Falkner persisted. Previously, he had enlisted 1,500 volunteers to do the work. Early in 1886, he leased 100 convicts from the state of Mississippi to extend the line. Disagreement culminated in April with Falkner buying out Thurmond's interest for some $20,000.[35] Thurmond probably demanded payment in gold, in effect an insult to Falkner, whose credit was certainly excellent.[36] Falkner paid Thurmond off and using convict labor pushed the road on to New Albany. There it made a critical juncture with the Tupelo and Memphis line, originally projected by General Nathan Bedford Forrest, and became significantly less dependent on the Memphis and Charleston at its other end. Furthermore, General Forrest's line ran through Holly Springs, and from there a road ran southward through central Mississippi to Oxford and Jackson. By the time the Ripley railroad reached New Albany, Falkner was virtually the sole owner. Near New Albany, he bridged the Tallahatchie River, a major obstacle, and pressed further south toward Pontotoc.

In building his railroad, Falkner continued to lease convicts at the rate of fifty dollars a year each plus keep and guards. There were charges that the convicts were ill used. Colonel Falkner admitted that one foreman had abused the men. But that man had been dismissed, he said, and insisted that the convicts generally were fed, clothed, housed, and treated "as well as any poor."[37] One of those convicts, romantically depicted as a Frenchman falsely imprisoned, was shot and killed while attempting to escape, allegedly to join his wife, who had fallen ill. He was buried alongside the railroad, a white picket fence erected around his grave, and the site kept neat over the years by the railroad men.

The railroad reached Pontotoc in the summer of 1888. Always ambitious, Colonel Falkner called his road the Ship Island, Ripley, and Kentucky, though it touched neither Kentucky nor Ship Island, a terminal point on the Mississippi coast. Eventually, Falkner's railroad did connect with another railroad to reach Hattiesburg, which had a line to the Gulf.[38] The grand design was, ultimately, to connect the Gulf with the Great Lakes at Chicago by a single line via Ripley, a feat that was expected to create a route 100 miles shorter than all its competitors. Clearly, the Colonel was a clever, hard-driving entrepreneur; he was bringing his talent into the railroad business, and he was succeeding.

The local press in 1886 and 1887 offered glimpses of Colonel Falkner busily traveling about organizing his road. He was off to Memphis in April, 1886, apparently to get the gold to pay Thurmond. Then he was off to the capitol in Jackson to lease convicts, later to the northeast to raise cash and buy equipment for the railroad, and then to Washington where he called on President Cleveland at the White House. One of his vital Washington contacts was Senator

Edward C. Walthall, a Confederate major-general, fellow veteran, and Holly Springs native. The senator had worked diligently to secure a grant of nearly one million acres of federal land in return for the timely completion of the road. Early in 1887 Falkner journeyed down to Gulfport on the coast where he took time out from business to pay his respects to the Jefferson Davis family at their handsome estate, "Beauvoir." Within a week he had moved on to Memphis where he stayed at the beautifully ornate Peabody Hotel. His wife, Lizzie, had moved to Memphis with daughters Effie and Alabama the previous October, presumably to enable the girls to go to school there.[39]

~

By 1880 the Falkner household had metamorphosed yet again. Like many returning soldiers, Falkner began another family after the war. Effie (Stephanie) Deane was born in 1868, a set of twins (who died within two weeks of birth) in 1870, and the last child, Alabama Leroy, in 1874. The census of 1870 revealed that Colonel Falkner's sister, Francis, had already disappeared from his household, and daughter Willie Medora would soon marry. In 1878 his son Henry was allegedly shot dead at age twenty-four by a Ripley jeweler who objected to Henry's attentions to his wife.[40]

Henry as a young man had, indeed, led a tempestuous life. The Colonel had first sent him off to Washington and Lee College in Lexington, Virginia. One evening in the fall of 1873, Henry was in the town and so drunk that he could hardly stand on his feet. He made a remark to another student, Phillip Pendleton Dandridge, who happened to pass by. Dandridge did not answer, and Henry cursed him. All during the next day, rumors of an impending duel flew among the young men at the school. After dinner, Henry and Phillip confronted one another on the porch of the boarding house they both patronized. They scuffled and Phillip fell over the porch rail some ten feet to the ground. Regaining the porch, he approached Henry with fists raised. Henry stabbed him in the stomach with his pocket knife. Officials intervened, heard the case in a lower court, and because of Phillip's rapid recovery and generous nature did not punish Henry. Even so, Henry left school and returned to Ripley. Next, his father sent him to college in Texas. This time Henry gambled away the money allocated for his education and again came home.[41]

In 1869 Henry, at age fifteen, had been admitted to the recently reorganized Sons of Temperance, the same association in which his father had possessed such troublesome membership a generation earlier. By this time the "Sons" had opened their club to females. They seemed to attract the more vibrant young women about town, including "Sister Sallie Murry" who, within the year, would marry Henry's half-brother John.[42] The club lapsed into inactivity within a few months but was revitalized in the spring of 1874. By February, 1874, Henry had returned to Ripley and during the summer was once more a member of the organization, apparently a totally appropriate activity for this young man. In February, 1875, he became marshal of the Sons of Temperance and in June, treasurer.[43]

In October, 1875, Colonel Falkner, apparently impressed with Henry's new-found sobriety and sense of responsibility, set him up in a grocery store with some $3,000 in stock. Shortly thereafter, however, the Colonel announced publicly his refusal to be responsible for his son's debts—or his actions. As Henry's supplies rapidly dwindled, R.G. Dun & Co.'s agent pronounced him intemperate and declared that he "has no stdg here pecuniarily morally socially or politically." Within several months Henry was out of business.[44] Thereafter his life spiralled rapidly down, and his end seems strangely connected to his associates in the Temperance Club.

A moving spirit in the reorganization of the club was "Brother" Joseph E. Rogers, a longtime and exceedingly loyal supporter of William Falkner. An early settler in Ripley, he was president of the town board in 1849. In 1855 he and Falkner were the leading spirits in a rather chimerical attempt to turn Tippah County to Whiggery and hence seize political dominance in that domain. Sometimes farmer, deputy sheriff, unsuccessful candidate for office, and minister of the gospel, Joe Rogers also sired a large family, including one daughter charmingly named Pocahontas and another named Charly. During the war, he served briefly as the Colonel's quartermaster captain in the Partisan Rangers. He seemed the kind of man who popped up wherever the excitement was—a romantic, a dreamer. After the war, Joe retreated to farming, attempting to support his sizeable family on a small farm. By 1880, however, at age sixty-one, he was in the vanguard of progress again, living in town, and working for the Colonel's railroad as depot agent in Ripley. It was a position he held for eighteen years.[45]

One of the "charter petitioners" in the reorganization of the Temperance Club in 1874 was Joe's attractive and very vital fifteen-year-old daughter Charly. Well into the twentieth century a rumor persisted that Charly was Colonel Falkner's lover. Moreover, the rumor maintained that she bore a child by him, a daughter named Noverta. Like her father, Charly was a mover and shaker. Shortly after the revival of the club, she was elected "Recording Secretary pro tem." Within weeks Charly's future husband, John Lawrence Walker, age twenty-one, also enrolled and soon became the "Recording Secretary." Charly, John, and Henry were associates and officers in what was clearly an intensely emotional gathering of young men and women.[46] In November, 1876, the circle of intimacy widened when John's teenage sister, Nannie, married the jeweler James A. Plummer, the man who allegedly shot and killed Henry in January, 1878.[47]

Charly and John Walker lived out their lives, essentially, in Ripley. Yet, they married in another county in 1879 and on January 20, 1880, Charly gave birth to Noverta. Charly and John were not recorded as living in Tippah County in the census of 1880, taken during the summer and fall. However, they must have returned to the village in good season, bringing with them their infant daughter. In October, 1882, Charly bore her second child, a son whom she named Henry. For many years, John Walker, like his father-in-law Joe Rogers, worked for the Colonel. He was the conductor on the Ripley railroad, replacing in that office Walter Rutledge, late sergeant-major of the Second Mississippi and Colonel Falkner's nephew. In 1900 both Charly and her daughter Noverta were carried in the census as dressmakers. John was then described as a farmer. When Charly's parents died, they were buried in the older portion of the Ripley Town Cemetery close to the Colonel. Her mother's stone—she died in 1905—bears the inscription: "Her Children Arise Up and Call Her Blessed." Charly herself passed away in 1931. Noverta died unmarried in 1957 and was buried in the town cemetery alongside her mother. She left a scrapbook gathered over the years and full of local lore, now held by the Ripley Public Library.[48]

The exact circumstances of Henry's death remain a mystery. The favored story is that the "crippled" (and presumably unattractive) jeweler James Plummer shot him for paying too much attention to his wife. Yet, the details of the story have floated about over decades and generations in such a way as to make it unclear which wife or woman was involved and which male Falkner was accused of sexual transgressions. In 1964, Sallie Burns, a Falkner kinswoman who grew up in Ripley, recalled that her mother told her that Henry "was a handsome, likable, rather wild fellow who was shot in a quarrel about a woman."[49] Most curiously, some of the Falkners understood that Plummer killed Henry over his wife just as tradition said, but they also understood that Henry argued with Plummer because he had been talking about the Colonel in some slanderous way.[50] It is possible to read into this version a scenario in which the old Colonel was trifling with some young woman's affections and poor Henry, the dissolute and disowned son, was killed in a pitiful and unappreciated attempt to defend his father's name.

Henry's baby sister, Alabama Leroy Falkner, who was three years old in 1878, had her own story concerning her brother's death. Little Bama, among other women and children, adored Henry. "I remember, though I was just a little girl then, looking up to him as the handsomest young man I'd ever seen," she told an interviewer in 1959. Bama always stoutly maintained that Henry was a perfect gentleman and that he died, simply, of a ruptured appendix.[51]

Ironically, the last word in the traditional Henry story was attributed to the Colonel himself. In this rendition—which has the ring of essential if not literal truth—the jeweler came to Falkner in fine manly fashion just after the event, declared that he had been compelled to shoot Henry, and apologized. "That's all right," replied the Colonel, adding that otherwise "I guess I'd have had to shoot him myself someday."[52]

Before 1886, William Falkner was not all business. He had been an avid poet and writer from young manhood, often arranging for the printing and selling of his own work. After the war he resumed that career simultaneously with his professional and business pursuits. In 1881 he published his most successful story, a highly romantic novel titled after the name of a Mississippi riverboat, *The White Rose of Memphis.* Eventually the book went through thirty-five editions and sold 160,000 copies. The story had been serialized in the Ripley *Advertiser* beginning in the fall of 1880.[53]

In the early 1880s, before Falkner bought out Thurmond's interest in the railroad and turned massive energies in that direction, he seemed to delight in the company of his daughters. In August, 1882, he took his family to a local resort for a vacation. In June, 1883, with his teenage daughter Effie as companion, he sailed from New York for Europe aboard the luxury liner *City of Berlin.* All during the summer and fall, he and Effie saw the traditional sights. Clearly the Colonel liked it all, but he loved Italy. As they traveled, Falkner wrote letters home for publication in the *Advertiser.* Back in Ripley, he gathered these into a book entitled *Rapid Ramblings in Europe.*[54]

When Falkner returned from Europe he decided to rebuild the family seat in a style he had seen in Italy.[55] The result was a striking square structure of three stories, the second story having large gables on each of its four sides, and the third story consisting of one large square room with four windows. The house was crowned with a sort of widow's walk. The building arrested the eye and was unique in that part of the country. It came to be called "The Italian Villa."

Even as Falkner was constructing his villa in 1884, he was also building a large house on North Main Street for his daughter Willie Medora. Willie had married Ripley physician Nathaniel G. Carter, the son of the Colonel's regimental surgeon.[56] In February, 1885, he went to New Orleans for a four-day visit to the World's Exposition staged by the city that year. In the spring he returned for a twelve-day stay bringing Effie and Bama. He had hardly returned from New Orleans before he took Effie, now seventeen, to the races in Memphis. During the ensuing summer, the Colonel treated himself to a vacation at White Sulphur Springs, the elitist spa in West Virginia. This was a very expensive resort frequented almost exclusively by the rich and famous.[57] Early in 1886, however, Colonel Falkner began to turn his interest— almost single-mindedly it seems — to the railroad.

In all of this, there appeared to be a rising separation between William Falkner and his wife. One manifestation, perhaps, was frequent visits by the Colonel to Memphis. "He was a stockholder in the Gayoso Hotel," his great granddaughter later declared, "lived there a lot," and "was unhappy with his second wife, Lizzie Vance."[58] The family felt, sometimes, that he had married beneath himself on this second occasion. Certainly Holland Pearce brought considerable wealth to his first marriage while Lizzie brought none to the second. In the fall of 1886, "Mrs. Colonel William C. Falkner," took Effie and Bama to Memphis and remained there until the following spring. In the fall of 1887, Bama moved to Memphis for schooling at the Clara Conway Institute. A year later Effie married businessman Edwin Campbell and moved to the city to live. In August, 1889, the Ripley *Advertiser* noted that "Mrs. Falkner and daughter Effie Campbell left today for Memphis." It declared flatly that "Mrs. Falkner will reside permanently in Memphis."[59] Bereft of wife, daughters, and sons (save one, John Wesley Thompson Falkner, who had been reared by his uncle and aunt and had moved to Oxford in 1885), the Colonel was seemingly alone in his Italian villa.

It appears, however, that Falkner was not lonely and certainly he was not idle. He had dreams of empire, a railroad empire that he would begin by organizing a "short route" from the Gulf of Mexico to Chicago. The enterprise would require cooperation from the Mississippi legislature. Pursuant to gaining that end, in August, 1889, he secured quite easily the Democratic nomination for a seat in the state's House of Representatives.[60] His victory in the general elections in November was assured. Obviously that honor had long been within his grasp. He wanted it now, some said, so that he could lobby for his railroad from inside the legislature.

Simultaneously, Falkner brought to a successful end another phase in his railroad scheme that he had begun two and a half years before. Acting as the chief bondholder of the railroad company, he demanded immediate payment of amounts due him but beyond the current capacity of the company to pay. Thus, he threw his own company into bankruptcy. He then himself bought the whole thing at the public sale on the courthouse steps in Ripley. On October 25, 1889, the chancellor of the chancery court officially declared Falkner the owner—the sole owner—of the railroad.[61] Colonel Falkner was showing every sign that he was about to attempt entry into the ranks of what some would call the "Robber Barons"—the Rockefellers, Morgans, and Guggenheims of the turn-of-the-century decades. He had always been, primarily, a man of business, and it was a logical progression.

Rather clearly, William Falkner was consumed with a new and dazzling ambition—one that might well have resulted in his ending the century with wealth of national scope, with a seat in the United States Senate if he so chose, and with real place and power in what was about to become imperial America on a global scale.

Demise

About five o'clock on the afternoon of Tuesday, November 5, 1889, Colonel Falkner's ambition was cut suddenly short. He was shot down on the square in

Ripley by Richard Thurmond, his erstwhile partner in business. A Ripley newspaper, *The Southern Sentinel,* reported that Thurmond used a .44 caliber pistol to do the work.[62]

Over the years various accounts of the causes of the shooting evolved. All seem to agree that the two men had been feuding bitterly for some time. The conflict was exacerbated by their differences over how to run the railroad, culminating with Falkner buying Thurmond out in 1886. For several years the feud continued, Falkner often declaring in public that Thurmond made his money by foreclosing on widows and orphans while Thurmond referred to Falkner as the murderer of Robert Hindman and Erasmus Morris. On November 1, 1886, three years before the shooting, both men were hauled into court, convicted of "swearing and cursing," and fined.[63] On another occasion, Falkner approached Thurmond among a group of men on the courthouse grounds. Facing Thurmond squarely, he struck a self-confident pose by looping his thumbs through the armholes of his vest. "Well, here I am, Dick," he declared and demanded defiantly, "What do you want of me?" Thurmond answered with his fist, flattening the Colonel with one blow. But Falkner quickly rose and launched into a tirade against Thurmond. Finally, Thurmond walked away from the still taunting Falkner. One of the Colonel's grandsons, a child of seven in 1889, later declared that Falkner deliberately created conditions that forced Thurmond to shoot him.[64]

There are numerous conflicting accounts of the crucial event. A pro-Falkner version has him simply standing on the sidewalk in front of Thurmond's office on the west side of the square talking to his friend Thomas Rucker when Thurmond emerged from the building and pointed a pistol at Falkner's face. "What do you mean, Dick?" he exclaimed. Then seeing Thurmond's intention, he cried "Don't shoot!" Thurmond fired. The bullet shattered the Colonel's jaw, knocked out teeth, and came to rest partly embedded in the carotid artery. Lying on the pavement before he lost consciousness, Falkner seemed incredulous. "Why did you do it?" he asked Thurmond.[65]

A pro-Thurmond version of the scene had Thurmond sitting at his desk at a window open to the sidewalk. Falkner approached the window and stopped, each man in full view of the other. Falkner said something to Thurmond. The Colonel was exhilarated by the results of the general elections held that day. He had just won a seat in the legislature. Even though he ran behind every other Democratic candidate on the ticket, his victory signaled another step toward the achievement of his ambitions for his railroad.[66] Falkner had been drinking and was behaving in a way that threatened Thurmond physically. Thurmond's supporters alleged that he might reasonably have concluded that Falkner was carrying a gun concealed in his clothes and was making gestures indicating his willingness to use it.[67]

The first report to come out of Ripley concerning the shooting was telegraphed to the Memphis *Avalanche* and tended to support the pro-Thurmond version. It was written on the evening after the shooting by a local man named J. Brown who sometimes supplied news to the *Avalanche*. The copy that comes to us was recently found in the railroad station in New Albany, shortly before the building was demolished. It was the copy that the telegrapher made before he put the message on the wire. Apparently, there was no telegraph office in Ripley; messages were carried by train or handcar down the tracks to New Albany and wired out by the operator at the depot. Brown reported that the shooting was "the result, as we learn, of demonstration made by Falkner, he being intoxicated." Brown put the shooting in the context of state and local elections held that Tuesday following heated campaigns. He indicated that there had been a number of minor fights during the polling, and that there had been "more drinking than usual at our elections."[68]

Unconscious and bleeding, Falkner was lifted and carried up North Main Street past his own house to the home of his daughter Willie Medora. There was no wife, daughter, or son at the Villa to care for him, and, in the emergency, the Colonel's friends acted sensibly. Willie's husband, of course, was a physician, Nathaniel G. Carter. Medically, it was a delicate situation. The wound was leaking blood into Falkner's lungs. Removal of the bullet might cause a hemorrhage, flooding the lungs. A specialist, rushed in from Memphis, confirmed local medical judgment that the risk of removing the bullet was too great.

By custom, primary responsibility for managing the crisis fell to William Falkner's eldest child and only surviving son, John Wesley Thompson Falkner. Like his father and his great uncle, for whom he was named and by whom he was reared, he was a highly respected and very prosperous lawyer. In 1885 he had moved his practice from Ripley to Oxford. John was no stranger to Oxford, having taken his law degree from the university in 1869. About nine o'clock on the night of the shooting, he received a telegram from New Albany. "Thurmond shot Col Falkner this evening," it read. "Badly shot. Come. Walker here with hand car."[69] John Falkner made his way to New Albany, then rode the hand car some twenty miles to Ripley. The Colonel continued to lose blood all during the night. He died Wednesday morning, in effect, suffocated by his own blood. John telegraphed to his wife in Oxford that his father had "died 2 hours after we got here. Don't know when I will be home." About the same time he sent a telegram to Memphis to Colonel M.C. Galloway, family friend and publisher of the *Avalanche*. The message was brief: "Send metallic case for Col Falkner size 6 feet 2 inch."[70]

On Thursday, Falkner's funeral service was held in Ripley's Presbyterian Church, the congregation to which his wife belonged, the Colonel never having joined a church. He was laid to rest with full Masonic rites in the town cemetery, located on a rise just north and east of Ripley. A correspondent of the *Avalanche* reported that he was survived by his wife, three daughters, and a son, and had left an estate valued at half a million dollars. One local newspaper described him in Horatio Alger fashion as "a man who has arose from the bottom to the top by his own exertions."[71]

~

Colonel Falkner was barely settled in his casket before John Falkner sent an urgent wire to Ira D. Ogelsby of Senatobia, Mississippi, perhaps the best criminal lawyer in the state. "Will you accept fee to prosecute the murderer of Col Falkner?" he asked. "If so come to Ripley at once. Answer immediately."[72] John chose the right man, but fast as he was he was not fast enough. Ira Ogelsby became the leading lawyer in Richard Thurmond's talented team of defenders. When the grand jury met in February, 1890, the defense secured an early and crucial victory—an indictment for manslaughter rather than murder. Thurmond would not be hung no matter what the trial judge or jury might want.[73]

Shortly after the indictment was handed down, Thurmond was brought from the jail and arraigned in court. He pleaded not guilty, posted a bail of $10,000, and was released on his own recognizance and that of other leading citizens of the town.[74]

A usual ploy in the defense of all serious cases was to secure a continuance—that is, a postponement of the trial for the obvious purpose of allowing the tempers of the aggrieved to cool. Thurmond's case was continued for an entire year. But when the trial began on Wednesday, February 18, 1891, District Attorney Thomas Spight labored diligently to secure a conviction. The trial lasted all through Thursday and Friday, and the courthouse was, as the Ripley *Sentinel* reported, "jammed with interested spectators." Curiously, one person who deliberately put distance between herself and the courtroom was Charly Rogers Walker. She went to New Albany to visit relatives, and returned three days after the trial was over. Presumably, she took her daughter, Noverta, age eleven, with her. On Saturday arguments were closed, and the judge instructed the jury. After brief deliberation, the jury brought in its verdict. For most people it was a surprise. For the Falkners it was an outrage. The jury declared Thurmond "Not guilty."[75]

That verdict by twelve men "good and true" of Tippah County constituted either a miscarriage of justice or a recognition that Colonel Falkner was not quite the total innocent that tradition has often depicted. The more detailed records of the trial have disappeared from the courthouse, but Thurmond's lawyers probably argued self-defense. They would have insisted that Thurmond had good reason from previous and present circumstances to believe that his life was in jeopardy at Falkner's hand. Elements in such a defense, legally, were that the defendant's life was in imminent danger and that there was no safe retreat. Under the circumstances, it seems that such would have been a very difficult case for Thurmond's lawyers to make. But whether or not there was lethal danger and no safe retreat was a matter for the jury to decide. In this case, the jury closed the gap that the defense lawyers had astutely narrowed.

The community generated various explanations for this result. Will Tieir was twenty years old in 1889 and had lived next door to the Thurmonds on "Quality Ridge" since he was nine. Mrs. Thurmond was "a wonderful woman," he said, "and very attentive to mother who was sick all the time we were there." Will declared in 1967 that "the regret was" that the defense lawyers had seated jurors who owed Thurmond money.[76] Sallie Burns, whose aunt Sallie was John Falkner's wife, understood that Thurmond's lawyers had spent money freely to determine the attitude toward the case of virtually every prospective juror in the county. One story declared that they had sent a well-known lamp salesman through the countryside to gather this intelligence and used it to pack the jury. "He was as sure of acquittal as every white man in Mississippi who kills a negro has always been," Sallie Burns concluded in an interesting analogy.[77]

Thurmond's lawyers were among the best in the state, but there are signs that less able counsel might have achieved the same outcome. The quick and unanimous verdict suggests a high level of sentiment for Thurmond's acquittal in the jury and, probably, in the community. The reporter for the *Sentinel* sensed a curious mood in the courtroom during the proceedings. There was "no excitement and not a single 'scene' during the trial," he declared, "and even the verdict was silently received by all."[78] Those persons present seemingly felt that sufficient justice was done.

Dick Thurmond's wealth might work for him, but his personality did not. He was sharp and successful at the business of making money. Will Tieir identified him as "the moneyed man." Like Colonel Falkner, he usually got what he wanted. Generations later, there was a rumor in the Falkner family that every night between November 5, 1889, and February 7, 1890, while Thurmond was in jail, "a negro woman" was allowed to visit his cell. Further, the woman produced a son whom she named "Dick Thurmond." One summer night about 1910, young Dick attempted to rape the daughter of Judge Stephens, one of Thurmond's lawyers, and was lynched.[79] The implication was that one reaps as one sows. Sallie Burns, who knew Ripley well during these decades, denied the lynching of any Dick Thurmond in Ripley, but declared that the white Dick Thurmond "was a dissolute, selfish, unloved man."[80]

Probably, Thurmond was saved, finally, not so much by the brilliance of his lawyers as by Falkner's personality. Recurrently, Falkner alienated himself from his community by his independence, his willfulness, and his egoism. In 1889, perhaps, he played the role his character dictated one time too many, and the jury seemed to say that he got what he deserved. He got it, of course, not at the hands of some drunken, pistol-wielding ruffian, but rather from a man who was wealthy, socially well-placed, and sober. Very few people in Tippah County would have killed Falkner as Thurmond did, but once it was done by him, many could approve the action.

Judgment

Thus, Falkner ended as he had so often lived, a man alienated by his own acts from the community of which he was undeniably a part. William Falkner, apparently, could not understand that the world did not value him as he valued himself. This was the golden thread that joined together the beads of his life. It accounts for the persistent boldness that brought him successes and raised him high in the hierarchy of the community—his antebellum rise as a lawyer, as the colonel of the Second Mississippi, and as the sole owner and manager of the railroad.

Falkner had no doubt about his own great talents, but he was proud not so much of his talents as of his accomplishments, and as he matured his mind dwelt less on what he had done and more on what he intended to do next. He was not an egotist. He was rather, to make that exceedingly useful distinction, an egoist—a person who believes that the world revolves around himself and works for the ends he desires. He simply could not imagine that other people had other agendas, could legitimately want things other than what he wanted. Because he so often gained power in key areas of his life, he was sometimes able to require other people to move around himself in orbits that he prescribed—in the army, in the courtroom, in business, and on the railroad—and thus lend verisimilitude to a little universe where he stood at the center. But there came a time in each arena when the people closest to him were the very people who cast him out. Hence his flight from his family in Missouri as a teenager, hence his dis-election as colonel of the Second Mississippi, hence the blatantly rebellious behavior of his son Henry, and hence his wife Lizzie's departure to Memphis. Finally, as he lay stricken on the sidewalk on the square in Ripley, it would have been perfectly fitting for him to be genuinely surprised and unable to understand why Dick Thurmond had shot him, to respond as if he could not believe what had happened. This capacity for alienating himself—innocently enough—from community, friends, and even family marked his life from the time he left Missouri to come to Mississippi until the day of his death. Ironically, it followed him to the grave . . . and beyond.

Colonel Falkner, in spite of his surprise at the shooting, had prepared for his passing, and—as befitted a man who lived in an "Italian Villa" in Ripley, Mississippi—the preparations were very unusual. Some months before his death, he had told a friend that Thurmond was going to kill him. On October 25, 1889, two weeks before the shooting, he was in Memphis writing his first, as well as his last, will and testament. It is amazing that he had filed no will in Ripley before. Why he chose to file this will in Memphis instead of Ripley is a question. Lizzie and both daughters lived in the city by then, and perhaps the Colonel had some idea of eventually settling there himself as his railroad ventures grew.[81] For some time he had rented a lock box at the Union and Planters Bank in the city, and one of his closest friends was Colonel M.C. Galloway, publisher of the Memphis *Avalanche*.

In the will, Falkner made elaborate arrangements for a board of trustees headed by his son John to manage his estate so as to keep the capital intact and distribute net income annually. Also, he gave specific instructions that he be put away with Masonic rites, a common desire, and that his body be placed in a "metallic case" and the case be placed in a "Vault" constructed "on the Surface of the earth."[82] The latter was very unusual in a culture in which one's earthly remains commonly ended six feet under.

After his death, a story circulated that Falkner had commissioned a marble statue of himself during his Italian travels. It seems more likely that he conveyed his wish for such a monument to his heirs in the same mood in which he wrote his will. He wanted some symbol of his life and work to remain clearly visible in the community. In any event, an artist somehow affiliated with a marble works in Grand Junction, Tennessee, made an image of the Colonel in either wax or plaster, using pictures, drawings, a suit of his clothes, and a local man of striking resemblance as a model. The image, properly treated and perhaps accompanied by helpful materials and instructions, was sent to Italy to be fashioned in Carrara marble by a sculptor. Eventually, the finished statue arrived in Ripley. The Colonel and his heirs perhaps thought the town and county would honor him by erecting the figure on the square in the center of Ripley. There seemed to be virtually no demand for such a consummation.[83] Falkner had, of course, again misread the sentiments of the community in which he had lived during the last forty-five years of his life. The monument to Colonel Falkner, conceived, executed, and paid for ($2,022) by Colonel Falkner and his heirs, brought to Ripley no doubt on the Colonel's train, ended on Colonel Falkner's plot in the town cemetery.[84]

It stands there today, eight feet in height and one quarter larger than life. It rests atop a fourteen-foot pedestal, too high to be comfortably viewed from the ground, indeed, not seeming to have much to do with the ground. The marble man on the pedestal is about sixty years old, bearded and mustached but without sideburns. The long wavy hair is brushed loosely back, showing his ears. He has a high forehead; but perhaps his hair is simply thinning with age. He wears a frock coat, the kind that falls easily away in front but reaches almost to knee level behind. On his vest, a heavy chain drapes ponderously, gracefully, from pocket to button hole to pocket again. Most of his weight is supported on his left leg. The knee of the right leg is bent forward slightly, *contraposto* style, not as if walking, but rather as if standing and speaking, declaiming, tilting toward his audience to engage their attention more persuasively. At and behind his left foot, eight books are stacked, reminding the observer that Colonel Falkner was a literary man. The leg is buttressed by the stacked books, perhaps to favor the foot crippled in the Mexican War. The right forearm thrusts forward from the elbow, hand open, palm up, explaining earnestly, patiently, things that can be made clear to thoughtful persons. The left hand is tucked, seemingly casually, into the pocket in the front of his trousers. The thumb and forefinger are on the outside; the index, third, and little fingers are partially hidden in the pocket. The hand in the pocket, of course, hides the fingers shot away in Mexico.

The eyes of the marble man gaze forward toward the western horizon. These days, a century after the burial, if the eyes could see, they would catch a glimpse of the tracks of his railroad that still run along the edge of the cemetery less than a hundred yards away. If they could glance to the left, they would see the red roof of the Pizza Hut and a Walmart megastore in Ripley's new shopping center.

The pedestal carries no praiseful paeans for William Falkner, though there are large sheets of marble clean and ready—begging, if stone could beg—for the predictable laudatory words. On three sides the tablets are totally blank, and on the fourth, the north side next to his grave, it simply declares:

COL. WILLIAM FALKNER

BORN

JULY 6, 1825

DIED

NOV. 6, 1889

The statue is on a sizable plot of ground surrounded by a waist-high iron fence topped with spikes in a tasteful and then common design. In one corner, in a brick and stucco vault raised several feet from the ground and covered by a concrete slab, lie the remains of William C. Falkner, presumably in the metallic case he wanted. A modest sized marble stone atop the vault bears his three initials: "WCF." In another corner lies his son Henry, shot dead, we hear, by some woman's husband. The plain concrete slab that covers his remains bears only one word, "Henry." In a third corner, huddled together like anxious lambs, are his children Vance and Lizzie who died during the Civil War and two grandchildren. All four died in infancy or early childhood. There is abundant space for other family members in the plot, but there seemed to be no volunteers. Even his wife Lizzie is buried elsewhere—in Hollywood Cemetery in Richmond, Virginia, where she died in 1910 while visiting her daughter Effie.[85]

In death William Falkner is strikingly alone, strangely alone, his statued self in the center of a still, small universe that holds only the remains of his derelict son and four tiny children. It is almost as if these were the ones who could not escape him. The final rejection, the ultimate denial came some time after the body was buried and the statue erected. An unknown person or persons in the community came to the graveyard and rather deliberately shot away the other fingers, the marble fingers of the explaining hand.

The Other Mississippi Falkners

In the Ripley Cemetery there are other Falkners to whom the Colonel seemingly never publicly claimed blood kin. Less than fifty yards distant, to the right and slightly to the rear of the marble man, are the remains of three members of the slave family, "the shadow family" that lived in his yard in 1860. They lie buried in a row—Emeline Falkner, the mother; Delia, the oldest daughter; and Hellen, the second daughter.

Emeline Falkner's grave lies between those of her two daughters. Emeline is at the center, also, of an amazing story—actually the saga of a slave woman and her children, fathered by the white men who owned her, and how they passed out of slavery and beyond into the broad stream of black life in America. It is a story that resonates marvelously with William Faulkner's depiction in his fiction of that same vast and vital phenomenon in Southern—and American—culture. The kinship between fact and fiction is not coincidental. Through Emeline and her children, Faulkner was personally intimate with a real story, a historical happening, fully as powerful as any that he ever conceived in his imagination. It is a story worth a close and careful telling.

The writing on Emeline's tombstone has become indecipherable to the eye over the decades. Initially, using my fingers to spell out the words, I imagined that it said "Samuel Long." Later, after I had definitely identified the people in the graves on either side, I made a "rubbing." This is what emerged:

SACRED TO THE
MEMORY OF OUR MOTHER
MRS EMELINE LACY
FALKNER
BORN
FEB 1837
DIED
OCT 17 1898
BLESSED ARE THE PURE IN HEART
FOR THEY SHALL SEE GOD

We now know that Emeline was indeed born a slave about 1837. Her family was centered on the Washington plantations in Caroline County, Virginia, about fifty miles south of the nation's capital. Emeline's mother, Hellen—who, in 1870 at age forty-nine, still lived in Caroline County—was light complexioned, and Emeline herself was very "white" in her appearance. So, too, were her children. For some unknown reason Emeline alone among her siblings was sold away from the very wealthy Washington family connection to a man named Benjamin E.W. Harris, a man who described himself in 1860 as a carpenter.[86] Delia and Hellen always knew that Ben Harris was their father. Delia, the oldest, might well have been conceived late in 1852, when Emeline was approaching her sixteenth birthday and Harris was forty-two. Hellen came some two years later.

Harris had a white family as well as a family by Emeline. By early 1855, he had moved with both families from Virginia into north-central Tennessee and had settled in the vicinity of the village of Waverly. Seemingly, he brought white children in the move west, but no wife. His taxable wealth in the spring of 1855 consisted only of one slave, surely Emeline, valued at $800. Slave children were not taxed, hence Emeline's girls do not appear in local records.[87]

Ben Harris was described by his uncle as "a poor and unfortunate man." In Tennessee and Mississippi, it soon became apparent that he was in fact a man who did not flourish in a land that was prospering as never before. Recurrently without funds, Harris fell into the habit of using his slaves, Emeline and his children by Emeline, as collateral for loans. In effect, he "pawned" his mistress and his children for cash. He would borrow money from one man to pay his debt to another, always adding some surplus for himself, and thus pass Emeline and the little girls from one household to another as the amount of the debt increased. It was a game that worked well on the cotton frontier where the value of slaves in the 1850s was high and rising.[88] As Harris moved south and west the last lender in his continuing stream of creditors was William C. Falkner. In September, 1858, Falkner advanced Harris $900 and brought Emeline, Delia, and Hellen into his yard to live. In November, Emeline bore her third surviving child, Arthur. The other two slaves listed in the Falkner household in the census of 1860 were not related to Emeline. They were, simply, the flotsam and jetsam that might appear in the holding of any affluent person who bought and sold slaves for profit.[89]

For several years after Arthur's arrival, Emeline apparently bore no child who survived. However, at some point between mid-1864 and April, 1866, she gave birth to a baby girl, Fannie Forrest Falkner. Emeline's descendants have always maintained that Colonel Falkner—not Ben Harris—was Fannie's father.[90]

An abundance of evidence supports this claim, beginning with the circumstances of the child's birth. It is virtually certain that the Colonel gave Fannie Forrest Falkner her name. Fannie, an affectionate form for Frances, was derived from the name of Falkner's favorite sister, and Forrest came from his favorite Confederate general, Nathan Bedford Forrest, the commander who soundly trounced the Yankees at the Battle of Brice's Crossroads in June, 1864. If specific information given in the censuses of 1870 and 1880 is correct, Fannie was born in or about July, 1864.[91]

Thus, it seems that Fannie was conceived about the time Colonel Falkner resigned from his command, distressed spiritually by the frustration of his martial ambitions and physically by something that looked like bleeding ulcers. Possibly, he found solace in Emeline's arms. It is highly relevant that we have absolutely no trace of the Colonel between the time of his resignation in the fall of 1863 and April 26, 1865, when he bought a lot in the town of Pontotoc. During this interval, as suggested previously, he probably became a "blockade runner" in the daring fashion of Rhett Butler, basing himself behind the lines in Pontotoc, smuggling cotton out of rebel territory in violation of Confederate law, and bringing in goods that were in short supply and extremely expensive. However acquired, he ended the war with an abundance of cash in his pocket, a resource that he immediately began to turn into real estate.

It is probable, too, that Emeline was in Pontotoc with the Colonel during this period while Mrs. Falkner remained in Tippah County. Furthermore, Fannie was most likely born in Pontotoc and spent her early years there. Fannie's biographers and some of her descendants—as well as the descendants of Ben E.W. Harris—always understood that she was born in that village. This assertion has relevance to the broader family history because Fannie's husband-to-be was Matthew W. Dogan, and Dogan family tradition asserts that Matthew and Fannie were childhood sweethearts in Pontotoc. Matthew, born in 1863, was the son of a local barber who had bought himself out of slavery eight years before general emancipation. The Dogans remained in Pontotoc until 1869 when William relocated his business and his family in the much more important town of Holly Springs. In the same year Colonel Falkner sold his lot in Pontotoc, and it was then, perhaps, that Emeline and Fannie returned to Ripley.[92]

Whatever might have been the case in Pontotoc, it is clear from the national census that in August, 1870, Emeline and Fannie Falkner were living in an affluent neighborhood in Ripley and "keeping house" together. At the same time, Delia and Hellen worked and lived as domestic servants in the homes of eminent families in the village, and Arthur was attached to the household of a well-to-do farmer. Ben Harris, as a father to his children, seems simply to have faded away, and Colonel Falkner definitely emerged as their protector and sponsor.[93]

Ten years later, Emeline and Fannie ("Frances" in the census) were still living together in Ripley but had changed situations in an astonishing fashion. In 1880, they worked as "Servant" and "House Maid," respectively, in the household of Richard J. Thurmond, the man who would kill Emeline's erstwhile master and the probable father of her daughter. Also, Emeline and Fannie lived on Thurmond's lot.[94] Apparently Emeline was comfortable in her relations with Richard Thurmond as employer, but in the next year she made a distinct move toward independence. In July, 1881, she bought a town lot from Thurmond for $195. The lot was large, about one and a quarter acres, and roughly one block west of Thurmond's house on Quality Ridge. It adjoined a lot previously "sold to the African church," and thus lay close to the center of the rising black community on the west side of Ripley. Emeline built her house in the middle of the lot and settled there for the remainder of her life, just north of the church.[95]

In 1880 the census listed only one servant living in Colonel Falkner's household on Main Street, but she was a Falkner too. Her name was Lena Falkner. She was thirteen years old and mulatto.[96] It is possible that Lena was also Emeline's daughter, born about 1867, perhaps in Pontotoc, and that Colonel Falkner was her father.

Lamentably, we know very little about Lena Falkner, either before or after this provocative sighting in the Colonel's house in 1880. But we do know that Lizzie Falkner took her two teenage daughters to school in Memphis in 1886 and during the school year stayed in the city with them. In August, 1889, when Lena Falkner would have been twenty-two, Mrs. Lizzie Falkner announced in no uncertain terms, that she had left Ripley and the Italian Villa forever. Certainly, the Colonel did not remain there alone. He would have had one or more servants doing the considerable labor involved in running the household, and there were buildings detached from the main house that could have been used as quarters for servants. It is possible that the situation in his house created a scandal that Lizzie would not tolerate. It is also possible that the situations in both Falkner's and Thurmond's households had something to do with the obvious hatred of Thurmond for the Colonel, and that, after all, he did not kill him in the way that he did solely over the falling out that had occurred between the two men in the matter of the railroad, and, finally, that the failure of the jury to convict Thurmond was not simply a matter of money spent overtly and covertly in his defense, but was also a fair reflection of the judgment of the community as to what was true justice in this case.

In the fall of 1885, Fannie went off to Rust College in Holly Springs. Rust was the most prestigious black school in northern Mississippi. It was sponsored by the Northern Methodist Church and offered its students an education of high quality. One of its recent graduates was Ida Wells, a young woman whose roots, like Fannie's, went back to an interracial liaison in Tippah County. In the 1890s she became nationally famous as Ida Wells-Barnett, a very influential writer and activist in the cause of social justice for black people. At Rust, Fannie began to move into the top social strata of black life in America. Her life-style became that of a young lady of color, and it was not cost-free. Family tradition asserts that Colonel Falkner paid the bills. It also says that frequently he came to see his daughter in Holly Springs, and that when he did so he brought her flowers.[97]

The family has preserved Fannie's autograph book from 1885 and 1886.

Playing-card size, made for the feminine hand, it bears highly complimentary inscriptions—sometimes cast in poetry—written by friends on delicately colored pages with flowered borders. Through this girlish treasure we catch intimate glimpses of Fannie on occasional excursions to Memphis, moving about in a social whirl with children of the affluent—often mulatto—elite of the mid-South metropolis. One young man who autographed Fannie's book on Sunday, May 30, 1886, was Matthew Dogan, another Rust College student, one who stood at the top of his class.[98]

In the same month and year that Matthew wrote in Fannie's book, Colonel Falkner gave a public talk in Pontotoc, presumably the place of her birth. He was there to rally support for his railroad, but he fell into telling a story, subsequently a family legend, about how he first came to the village. He painted a picture of himself as "a poor, sick, ragged, barefoot, penniless boy" whose "cup of sorrow was filled to the brim" after trudging from Memphis to Pontotoc in search of his uncle only to find him gone. He wept "bitterly," but was saved by "the little girl," "the little Samaritan"—presumably Lizzie Vance—whom he married years afterward. A local journalist reported that, as he told the story of the little girl who saved him, "Col. Falkner became so affected that utterance failed him, and he had to pause until his emotions had subsided."[99]

Falkner did marry Lizzie in Pontotoc in 1851 in the aftermath of his bitter feud with the Hindmans, and his speech in 1886 came in the midst of his exceedingly acrimonious feud with Dick Thurmond, his rising obsession with the railroad, the impending departure of his wife and daughters for Memphis, and the already accomplished and permanent departure of his only surviving son for Oxford. Furthermore, Fannie Falkner had left Ripley for Holly Springs and Rust College. We now know that whoever saved William Falkner in Pontotoc in 1842, it was not Lizzie. Perhaps the real salvation came some twenty years later and the savior was Emeline. One can only wonder what was in the mind of this complex and difficult man as he spoke that day, and then, overcome with emotion—and perhaps genuine confusion—fell silent. Fannie graduated from Rust in 1888. According to the graduation program she was featured as the student speaker of the day. Her topic was "Women in History." Near the end of the ceremony she also sang a solo: "On the Heights."[100] She had voice training at Rust, one granddaughter later recalled, and a catalogue published by Rust in the mid-1890s indicated that she had finished in the academic department.[101] On July 21, 1888, immediately after graduation, Fannie married Matthew Dogan.[102]

In 1889, Fannie and Matthew moved to Nashville where he became a professor of mathematics at Central Tennessee College. He also did work in science that led to his constructing an exhibit in the "Colored" section of the 1895 Atlanta Exposition, the event that raised Booker T. Washington to the pinnacle among black leaders in America. His exhibit at the exposition, apparently, earned young Matthew Dogan the presidency of Wiley College in Marshall, Texas. He headed this Northern Methodist institution until 1942, and his granddaughter, Forrest Luther, lives there still, just off campus.[103]

Forrest has a photograph from about 1910. President Dogan and his family are seated on the front steps of the president's house on campus. Matthew wears a dark suit and a bowler hat set levelly on his head. He is poised, self-possessed, almost arrogant in his pose. Like Frederick Douglass and Booker T. Washington in their mid-forties, he appears a ready, self-conscious, practiced leader of his people. Fannie, plump in the Victorian fashion of the day, is dressed in rich and flowing black. Surely, somewhere in the house there is a broad-brimmed matching hat, perhaps with a sightful feather. Five children surviving. Two others had died in infancy. Emma Lucile, (with one "l"), born in 1893. Clara, who had no children, taught school and died in 1931. Ruth, born in 1900, married young, and bore Forrest in 1921. Then there was Blanche, the youngest girl, who had three daughters and lived in Baltimore. In the photograph, Fannie's daughters are long-skirted, starched white shirts, high-necked. The son, Matthew Winfred, Jr., who arrived in 1906, slated to be his father. Decidedly, this is an American family in the age of J.P. Morgan and Theodore Roosevelt.

Five children and six grandchildren. Forrest is the oldest grandchild. Lucile married Joseph H. Teycer and had a son, Joseph, Jr. She divorced in 1930 and came home.[104] After her mother's death, Lucile became the hostess at the presidential residence on campus. Blanche married W.A.C. Hughes, Jr., the son of a Methodist bishop and a lawyer. She was active in the Baltimore chapter of "Jack and Jill of America," an organization dedicated to raising the self-esteem of black children and young adults. Her three daughters participated in the Me-De-So Cotillion of 1955 and one daughter, Faulkner (spelled with a "u") Hughes, was Queen of the 1956 Cotillion.[105] Faulkner died young; Miriam and Alfreda continue to live in the Washington-Baltimore area.

Fannie, herself, lived until 1929. We know she returned home to Ripley at least once in the twenties. She had wanted to come home when Emeline died in 1898, but a yellow fever epidemic and a quarantine kept her away. When she did come, Hellen's granddaughter, Elizabeth Rogers, was at Hellen's house and saw her first. Elizabeth was a little girl then and remembers the occasion vividly. She saw the big car pull up in front of the house, the lady in the back seat, the driver, and ran to tell her grandmother. "Mama . . .!"

Fannie was sick, even then. Her stay with Hellen nourished and restored her. Hellen was an excellent cook. "Hellen," she said, "if I could just stay with you, I would be well again." Back in Texas, Fannie suffered a lingering illness, and died in 1929.[106]

Emeline Falkner had died in October, 1898, perhaps in the midst of a yellow fever epidemic. The *Ripley Standard,* which seldom mentioned deaths in the black community, noticed her passing:

> 'Aunt' Emeline Falkner, one of the good old ante-bellum colored women of Ripley, died Monday at the home of Sam Edgerton, her son-in-law.[107]

In Ripley black people were buried in the northeastern quarter of the town cemetery, marked off from the graves of the whites by driveways and a waist-high iron fence. Emeline's was the first grave to be dug in a row that came to include two of her daughters, one daughter's husband, and three grandsons. Clearly, this was a family that saw itself as a family in perpetuity. Emeline's gravestone stands there now, rectangular, modest in size, unique and tasteful, the engraving almost unreadable under the fine grey-green moss.[108]

Emeline's gravestone is a powerful statement of selfhood. She might well have approved the emblem on the stone that depicts a teenage angel. Approved, too, the wording that identified her as "Mrs. Emeline Lacy Falkner." There is in the records prior to her death no trace of the "Lacy" association, and nothing in the rather full and well-preserved marriage records of Tippah and other counties to indicate that she was ever officially married. One gathers, however, that Emeline in the end was insistent in an extraordinary degree that she was a married woman. Graveyards in the South are full of tombstones of married women next to those of their husbands. Occasionally, the stone declares explicitly "Wife of . . ." Emeline, of course, could not describe herself as the wife of Colonel William C. Falkner, but she did establish firmly the fact—indeed had it written in stone—that she was "Mrs. Falkner." She is, in truth, the only Mrs. Falkner in the cemetery where *his* marble self rises above all.

Emeline's Children

At first, Emeline and her children in their proximity to the elite and to whiteness had a unique history in Ripley, but, as postwar generations came and went, they tended increasingly to share experiences common to the black population. The continuing family virtually personified the rising separation of the races that followed emancipation. The first generation, so white themselves, moved out of the white folks' yards and came to settle in the all-black western portion of the village. Hellen and Delia, in time, moved their work out of the white folks' houses by becoming washerwomen and working at home. Beyond family and clan, the social center of their lives became the Second Baptist Church, a loyalty that has passed down through three and four generations and continues today. Recurrently, there are homecomings and reunions at the Second Baptist Church—the First Baptist Church being all white—bringing back the scattered children. One Sabbath in the summer of 1991, Elizabeth Rogers, at sixty-nine, stood in for the absent musician to play the piano and pace the singing, apologetic because her fingers were not as nimble as they used to be. Any Sunday, still, some of Emeline's children will be there at the church.

Delia, Hellen, and Arthur married people who were sometimes described as "black," and census takers sometimes saw some of Emeline's grandchildren as "black." When the family petitioned the court for a division of Emeline's land in 1919, they declared in a preamble, perhaps not entirely gratuitously, that "we are colored people." Within the black community there was always a consciousness of how dark or light an individual was, but with the physical and cultural separation of the races and with intermarriage and a melting together of mulattoes and blacks, such distinctions, relatively speaking, lost value. After 1920, the U.S. Census ceased to make such judgments; everyone became either Indian, white, or, simply, black.

The third generation of Emeline's children, in particular, shared in "the Great Migration" of black people to the larger cities both in and out of the South. In 1919, of Delia's seven surviving offspring, only two still lived in Tippah County. Tom Prince, the eldest, had moved to Tunica, in the Delta near Memphis. John Prince, a carpenter, was in Nashville. Arthur Prince had moved to Beloit, Wisconsin; Henry to Flint, Michigan, an automobile city; and Eugene, to State Street in Chicago. Delia's other child, George, had died, perhaps was murdered, over in Arkansas. He left three daughters—the fourth generation—of whom it had to be said to the court, "address unknown."[109]

But, again typically, a goodly proportion of Emeline's grandchildren came home to be buried. Eugene returned and was laid to rest in 1980 alongside his mother Delia. Robert died in 1963 and lies in a nearby plot. Hellen's sons Matthew and Sam lie close to their mother, while Falkner Edgerton, apparently the youngest grandchild, lies close to Emeline. Falkner Edgerton was born in 1897, the same year in which the most famous Falkner, William, was born, and he died in 1965, three years after the writer died.

Fannie Forrest Falkner's progeny had a different history within that rapidly separating black world. They were born into a post-slavery mulatto elite. Most of all, they had the advantage of higher education. All five of her children graduated from Wiley College, and other institutions as well. As the children and grandchildren of one of the most prominent (and definitely the longest tenured) presidents of a black college in America, they moved among the most eminent African Americans in the country. It was a life highly tangential to the lives of Colonel Falkner's white children, grandchildren, and great grandchildren, and it was one, of course, that the cousins on the white side of the line hardly knew, much less understood.

The Second Mississippi Falkner

John Wesley Thompson Falkner, the second Mississippi Falkner after his father, achieved an acceptance in Mississippi society that was nearly total. Having been reared by his uncle, the well-respected Judge Thompson, and probably being related through his mother, Holland Pearce, to the well-to-do and locally eminent Spights, he had a good start. After the war, John went to the university in Oxford and in July, 1869, took his degree in law.[110] Shortly thereafter, on his twenty-first birthday, he married Sallie Murry, the eldest child of Dr. John Young Murry, the founder of one of the several most prominent families in Ripley. For John Falkner the marriage signaled a social arrival. It connected him by marriage not only to the Murrys, but to the Millers and through the Millers, ironically, to the Thurmonds. It meant, too, that his offspring, children who carried the Falkner name, would be connected by blood, not merely marriage, with the first families of Ripley. There were three of these children: Murry Cuthbert, born in 1870, Mary Holland, born in 1872, and John W.T., Jr., born in 1882. Another child, also named John, died in infancy in 1876.[111]

Initially in practice with his father, John W.T. Falkner soon took to the law on his own and did very well. When the census taker came in 1870 (on the day that Murry was born), John and his bride lived very near his uncle John Wesley Thompson, owned their house, and possessed some $1,800 in real and personal property.[112]

Ten years later, in 1880, they were still in Ripley. Murry and Mary Holland were ten and eight and must have often seen the adolescent mulatto maid Lena Falkner in their grandfather's house around the corner on Main Street—along with Effie and their "baby aunt," Alabama, then age five. Grandfather Murry lived in a fine large house on Jackson Street, the elegant residential avenue in Ripley that ran parallel to Main Street and three blocks west. Dick Thurmond also lived on Jackson. His home was three blocks south of Dr. Murry's and was served by a large staff that included Emeline and Fannie Falkner. Fannie, it appears, was John's half-sister, and if it were so he could not have been unaware of that fact.[113]

John Falkner practiced law in Lafayette County as well as in Tippah, and in 1885—the same year in which Fannie went to school in Holly Springs—he moved both his family and his law office to Oxford, the county seat.[114] Oxford was larger than Ripley, and it was also the site of the state university, which made it a center, cultural, social, commercial, and otherwise, for the whole of Mississippi. Definitely, the move put some distance between himself and his father.

In Oxford, the Falkners first rented a house on North Street (now North Lamar) and later settled into a modest home on a very large lot several blocks southwest of the town square. Murry and Mary Holland, by then teenagers, entered the newly formed public school in the town. John practiced law with Charles Bowen Howry, the son of Virginia-born James M. Howry, the earliest and most eminent judge in the county.[115] Later, in 1903, he took another partner who would become famous. Lee Russell was a poor boy from the vicinity of a hamlet called Varner in Beat Five in Lafayette County. He worked his way through the University of Mississippi and in 1919 won election as governor. In that post he earned Democratic if dubious fame by attempting to close down the fraternities on the campus of Ole Miss—including the one to which all of the Falkner men had belonged and from which the future governor had been excluded while he was a student. Soon afterward Russell won more unfavorable notice by being sued, unsuccessfully as it happened, by his female secretary for seduction and breach of promise.

In addition to pursuing the law, John Falkner engaged in a variety of businesses, and with fully as much success. By 1890 he and another partner, merchant Samuel W. Howry, had erected an elegant two-story brick building in the northeast corner of the square—one door west of the office of the *Eagle*—and rented out the first floor as a store.[116] After his father's death, John picked up the management of the Colonel's very considerable business interests for the benefit of the widow, himself, and his three half-sisters, Willie Carter, Effie Campbell, and Bama McLean. Apparently the railroad did extremely well all during the 1890s. Making his report to the court as the executor of his father's estate, John indicated that in the year before November 1, 1899, the road had earned $20,227.50, a very large amount of money for that time even when divided five ways.[117] On his own account John invested in land, started the first phone company in Oxford, operated a livery stable, an oil company, and the Opera House.[118] In 1910, he organized and subsequently ran the First National Bank of Oxford.

He was also very active in civic affairs. He was the organizing commander of the Lamar Chapter of the Sons of Confederate Veterans in 1901, and played leading roles in establishing the town's water works, sewerage system, and electric light company. Finally, he was active in politics, serving as chairman for the Democratic party in Lafayette County, winning election to the state House of Representatives in 1891, representing the county in the state senate, and becoming a staunch loyalist in the James K. Vardaman faction of the Democratic party in Mississippi. In 1896, he was appointed to the board of trustees of the university.[119]

In the late 1890s John Falkner signaled his eminence by building a home, which the family came to call the "Big Place," on the southwest corner of South Street and University Avenue just below the square.[120] In the same vein, his political affiliations brought him titles, probably derived from gubernatorial appointments in the state militia. In the 1880s he was sometimes referred to as Captain Falkner, and in the 1890s he was elevated to colonel, apparently having leapt over the ranks of major and lieutenant colonel. There was no sign that he had the slightest military experience, nor even any special interest in such—other than through reliving the Civil War.

In the 1890s with John Wesley Thompson Falkner in Oxford, the Falkners had undeniably arrived in Mississippi society. The social columns of the local presses recorded with high fidelity the comings and goings of the Falkners, their friends, and kinfolk. Dr. John Y. Murry, by then the leading Mason in all Mississippi, was a frequent visitor in his daughter's house in Oxford, and the whole family often visited him in Ripley. John Falkner's daughter, Mary Holland, was one of the local belles and a very social creature. In January, 1896, she attended the governor's inaugural ball in Jackson, and in July had the entire local military company to a party at her home.[121]

In 1898 Mary Holland eloped and married James Porter Wilkins, the son of Washington Porter Wilkins, who in 1860 was described in the census as a "Negro trader," at that time not at all necessarily a pejorative term. Wash Wilkins, indeed, was the son of the minister of the local Cumberland Presbyterian Church and totally respectable.[122] He entered the livery stable business shortly before the war and in March, 1862, at age twenty-seven, joined the Lafayette Rebels—which became Company A of the Twenty-ninth Mississippi Regiment—as its third lieutenant.

Wash proved to be an able and valiant soldier. During the battle of Murfreesboro in middle Tennessee, his regiment was severely damaged in the fierce fighting in "The Cornfield" on December 31, 1862. In May, 1863, he became the first lieutenant of his company. Meanwhile his fellow townsman, Charles Bowen Howry, son of Judge Howry and later law partner with John Falkner, rose through the ranks to become the second lieutenant at age eighteen. In the hard fought and victorious battle of Chickamauga in September, 1863, the regiment lost 194 men killed, wounded, or missing out of the 368 who were engaged. On New Year's Eve, 1863, Lieutenant Wilkins was at Dalton, Georgia, and in February, as the Army of the Tennessee retreated, he led a select platoon of sharpshooters detailed to pick off unwary bluecoats. All spring and into the summer, the army fought and retreated, keeping Atlanta at its back. On August 8, the captain of Company A was killed at New Hope Church, and on August 11 Wash Wilkins reported only two officers (himself and Charles Howry) and seventy-four men present for duty. On August 23 Wash was promoted to captain, and on August 31 the company joined in a last ditch and desperate attack on encircling Federal forces at Jonesboro, twenty miles southeast of Atlanta. The regiment lost fifty-five killed or wounded in that fateful battle. Atlanta fell, and in September the army fought its way back into Tennessee. In October, Wash went into the Confederate Army military hospital in Jackson, Mississippi, with "Rheumatism." On November 29, 1864, however, he was with his regiment again, and both he and Charles Howry were wounded in a hopeless and bloody assault against a numerically superior and entrenched Federal force at Franklin, Tennessee, just south of Nashville. The impetuous Confederate General John B. Hood ordered the attack to discipline his own troops, whom he considered laggardly. It was a foolish order by an inept and not very bright commander, and it broke the back of his army. There was nothing for the army in the west to do now but "to walk backward slow and stubborn and to endure musketry and shelling"—to borrow a line from William Faulkner's novel *Absalom, Absalom!* (347).

Pulling back to Montgomery, Alabama, by February 28, 1865, the company consisted of Captain Wilkins, Lieutenant Howry, one sergeant, and seven privates available for duty. Twenty-five privates were sick. Finally, in May, mercifully, came the surrender.[123] This was the real stuff out of which William Faulkner made his mythical Civil War; these were the real veterans among whom he came of age. By the 1890s, Wash Wilkins ran a number of successful businesses in Oxford, including some that were major suppliers for the university with its several hundred students. The marriage of his son added to his blessings.

James Wilkins and Mary Holland Falkner went to San Francisco for their honeymoon and then lived across the bay in Oakland while John pursued medical studies. They returned to Oxford with a child, Sallie Murry, but, lamentably, Dr. Wilkins died of consumption within a few years. Mary Holland came with her daughter to live at the Big Place, and, after her mother's death in 1907, served as housekeeper for her father.

John W.T. Falkner, Jr., (1882–1962) was a half-generation younger than his siblings. He went through the University of Mississippi as an undergraduate and then in his mid-twenties took his law degree there. In 1909 he was admitted to the bar and entered practice with his father.[124]

Murry

John and Sallie Falkner's oldest son was named Murry Cuthbert. The name Murry, of course, was the family name of his mother and in itself connected him with the leading families in Ripley. Cuthbert possibly came from the Murry side, though there was a Cuthbert Word, as we have seen, not very far up in the maternal family tree. Indeed, Cuthbert was a name that ran in the Word family, whose primal ancestor in America came from Wales. It seems probable that the "C" in the Colonel's name actually stood for Cuthbert not Clark, as the later Falkners understood, there being no Clarks visible anywhere in the line. John Falkner had grown up in the house with Cuthbert's mother and the sister, Justianna, to whom Cuthbert was closest in age. It is likely that John wanted to continue that name in the family, the name of a favored bachelor uncle, the "baby brother," who had died as a soldier in the Mexican War.[125]

Murry entered the university in due course in the fall of 1887.[126] By the summer of 1889, however, he had practically ceased to be a student. He was in love with his grandfather's railroad. Before and after the Colonel's death, he worked for the road. He rose through the ranks from fireman to brakeman, to engineer, and conductor. While living in Pontotoc, at the south end of the line, he courted Miss Patricia Fontaine, the rather belleish daughter of a prominent physician. In an overly aggressive attempt to defend her honor against possible slander, he got into a fight with a local man with a dangerous reputation named Elias Walker. Murry won the fight, having knocked Elias down with his fist, but the next day, while he was sitting at a drugstore counter, the man entered. First he shot Murry from behind with a twelve-gauge shotgun, leaving a "fist-sized hole in his back." Then, while Murry lay on the floor, Walker pointed a pistol at his face.

> "Don't shoot me anymore," Murry said. "You've already killed me."
> "I want to be damned sure," Elias declared and shot Murry in the mouth.[127]

Badly wounded and bleeding, it was feared that Murry was dying. John and Sallie Falkner rushed to Pontotoc. John, drinking copiously, found the assailant, aimed his pistol at him, but somehow was unable to fire. Perhaps, in the excitement, he had his finger on the trigger guard rather than the trigger. Elias drew his pistol, fired once, and fled, leaving John with a bleeding hand. Meanwhile, Sallie was nursing Murry, whose condition, with a bullet lodged in his mouth against a bone, was critical in much the same fashion as his grandfather's had been. The doctors were despairing of his life when Sallie tried a desperate resort. She induced vomiting, and as her son threw up into a basin, the bullet fell with a welcomed clink, and the crisis was passed.[128]

Thereafter, Murry continued to work on the railroad, and, seemingly, gave up amorous adventures. Instead, he took to the big woods, hunting and camping with his male friends. One hears of his love for dogs and horses, but women, as his son William Faulkner might have written, "ain't in it." Decades later, Murry's ten-year-old grandson saw him slip a pistol into his pocket as they were about to go to the circus. "Big Daddy, why are you doing that?" he asked. "I might see that fellow," Murry replied.[129]

Over the years, Murry was a frequent visitor in his parents' home in Oxford. It began to seem that they were family enough for him, and he would live his life as a bachelor. But then, during a visit in Oxford in the fall of 1896, he encountered a young woman named Maud Butler. After a brief courtship, they married with no prior announcement. Within a year William Cuthbert Falkner was born.

THREE

The Butlers

Even in early infancy, knowing persons observed that William was more Butler than Falkner. In Oxford and Lafayette County this was a statement fraught with meaning because Butler family history was intimately linked to both town and country. Some of the associations were highly complimentary to the Butlers, others were not. The latter was especially the case with Maud's father, Charles Edward Butler.

The First Mississippi Butlers

The Butlers were among the very earliest settlers in Lafayette County and in the town that became Oxford. Maud's paternal grandfather was Charles George Butler. He was the first sheriff of the county and the man who surveyed the land and laid out the town. Charles was born in North Carolina in 1805.[1] Charles's wife, Burlina W. Butler, was born in the Tarheel state in 1811. Possibly the couple married in North Carolina while Burlina was still seventeen and then moved west. Certainly, the first of their six surviving children was born in Henry County in northwestern Tennessee, probably about 1828.[2] The second child, Emily, was born in Tennessee about 1832, and the third, Henry S., in Mississippi in 1834.[3] Apparently, sometime between 1832 and 1834, when the Chickasaw cession opened up a vast new land for settlement, the Butlers, like so many others, moved south to take advantage of the abundant opportunities thus afforded.

In 1832, by the Treaty of Pontotoc, the Chickasaws ceded six million acres in north-central Mississippi to the United States government. The Chickasaws as a nation were allowed to sell these lands to whoever might buy them, purchase new land for themselves from other Indian nations in the Oklahoma Territory, and relocate there under the auspices of the United States Army. Ostensibly, the role of the government was simply that of intermediary. In reality, Native Americans were pressed out of the area by the army, and the government undertook to hasten its settlement by whites. Federal officials surveyed the land, opened up an office in the village of Pontotoc on the eastern edge of the cession, and proceeded systematically to sell tracts to the highest bidder. Receipts from the sales went into a special fund reserved for the use of the Chickasaw nation.

The government made its survey in the checkerboard fashion usual in the western territories since the 1780s. It measured off six-mile squares called townships. These, in turn, were laid out in thirty-six one-mile squares called sections. A section contained 640 acres and was the basic unit of sale. After the initial sale, half sections, quarter sections, and smaller divisions frequently changed hands.

The Butlers settled in Mississippi even before the Indians left in 1837 and 1838, and they were among the first to buy land in Lafayette County. Among other purchases, Charles bought lots in Wyatt, a projected town in the northwestern portion of the county. Located on the north side of the Tallahatchie River, Wyatt was thought to have two significant advantages. First, shallow draft steamboats that plied the rivers of the Mississippi River basin could navigate up the Tallahatchie as far as Wyatt. Second, it was at a point on the river suitable for either a ferry or bridge that might link the county to northwestern Mississippi and, most important, to the thriving river port city of Memphis. Wyatt faded even as it was formed, but already Charles and Burlina Butler had found a better alternative.[4]

Happily for their future prosperity, the Butlers tied their fortunes to the incipient town of Oxford, the place that would become the county seat and, in a dozen years, the site of the state's university. Early in 1836 the state legislature created nine counties out of the Chickasaw cession, including Lafayette. On March 21, 1836, the governing body of the county, which was called the board of police, held its inaugural meeting. One of the first things the board did was to draw lines establishing four political subdivisions.[5] In Mississippi counties these were called "beats," probably because the state was virtually conceived in slavery and the policing of slaves by jurisdictions labeled beats was the most important single function of government at the local level. This police function was carried out by the "patrol," a sort of *posse comitatus* to which every adult white male of military capacity was required to belong. In Mississippi, the patrol in each beat was organized by county officers, and it was the duty of these citizen-policemen to enforce the slave laws. For the most part, this meant riding the roads at night to insure that slaves stayed in their place. Generally in the South, the patrol had the power to arrest, try, convict, and punish slaves on the spot. In

Lafayette County, the patrol was recalled vividly by a black woman, Polly Comer, in an interview in the 1930s. Polly had been a slave in the Woodson's Ridge community in northern Lafayette County, and she stated succinctly the role of the patrol. "Dat's what dey keep de patrollers fur," she said, "to keep de niggers frum runnin' 'round at nite an' from runnin' away."[6] The real, if sporadic, threat to black people posed by the patrol was caught, folklore-style, by blacks who sang a popular ditty that declared:

> Run, nigger, run,
> Or the pater-r-olle will get you.[7]

Ultimately, the patrol was the first line of defense in the event of a slave insurrection. In some counties of Mississippi where the slave population amounted to 70, 80, and even 90 percent of the total, this was a vital function. In Lafayette County, where the slave population soon rose to about 45 percent, the patrol was very important, tying non-slaveholders to the institution of slavery and heightening the significance of race. In Lafayette, Beat One occupied the center of the county and included Oxford. Beats Two (to the northeast), Three, and Four, (and, later, Five, created by dividing Beat Four), were ranged around Beat One in counter-clockwise order.

On April 2, 1836, Charles George Butler, at age thirty, became the first sheriff of Lafayette County.[8] Hardly had he been sworn into office before he won another important commission. He became the surveyor who laid out the town that was to be the county seat. Under the Treaty of Pontotoc, some influential individuals in the Chickasaw nation were allowed to keep certain specified lands as their personal holdings. These could be sold directly to incoming whites. Such was the case with Ho-Ka, an Indian woman who, on June 6, 1836, sold a section of 640 acres to three white men for $800. Shrewdly, the new owners immediately offered to donate 50 acres of the tract for the site of the county seat. Because the land offered was pleasing to the eye and very near the center of Lafayette County, the county board agreed, and Charles Butler was employed to lay out the town into a grid of streets, a central square, and lots.[9] The main street ran north and south through the middle of the grid, feeding into the square at the mid-point. Now called North Lamar and South Lamar, for several generations the two parts of the main thoroughfare were known simply as North Street and South Street. Butler himself came to own 125 of the 160 acres that made up the northeastern quarter of what had been Ho-Ka's section. More importantly, he acquired lots on the town square and there he built the hotel that became the centerpiece of the Butler family's prosperity.

Charles Butler is very visible in the early records of the town. Sometime between 1835 and 1837 he obtained a license for the operation of an inn and liquor shop.[10] Between 1836 and 1838 he paid a tax on at least one slave.[11] Obviously of a vigorous entrepreneurial spirit, in and after 1837 he was also one of the leaders in promoting a railroad through the village. Some twenty years later, on the eve of the Civil War, the dream came true as a line running north and south through the county passed half a mile west of the square.[12] The depot is still there at the bottom of a long hill. South of the depot is a deep cut in the earth first dug by slaves and through which the railroad line yet runs. In 1838 Charles was still sheriff of the county, and in that year Oxford won its charter as a town. The name was chosen amid hopes that the projected state university would be located there, an issue that was decided favorably in 1839. In that year, Charles Butler owned eleven lots in town valued together at $5,550 and seven taxable slaves.[13]

In 1840 Butler was no longer sheriff, but it was he who took the United States Census in Oxford. At that time Charles and Burlina owned and operated the Oxford Inn, one of the two leading hotels in the town.[14] The Butler hotel occupied a large building on the north side of the square on the corner immediately west of the main street, rebuilt after the Civil War as the Thompson House. The inn was not simply a hotel, it was also a social center and a boarding house for various adults—usually single, male, and young—who had come to the new land to make a life for themselves. Charles listed the people in his hotel as a census household and counted there sixteen adults and five children. All of the children were his own. Of the sixteen adults, fourteen were in their twenties and twelve were males. Of these, ten fit the census category as being either artisans, engineers, or persons in commerce or the learned professions. There were also six slaves in the household. Of these, three were over twenty-four years of age and three under. No slaves were older than thirty-six, and only two of the white men, one of whom was Charles himself, were in their thirties.[15] The demographics were typical of a frontier community. The great majority of whites were male and nearly everyone was young.

Almost certainly, some of Burlina's family had joined her in Oxford. Her mother and father were probably Nancy and Sherwood Henry House. Sherwood House died in Oxford in 1841, and Charles Butler became the administrator of his estate. In 1860 Nancy, aged seventy-one, still lived with Burlina. She died in 1868 and was buried in the Butler family plot alongside her husband Henry. It is highly probable that the Houses came from Raleigh and the community of House's Creek in Wake County, North Carolina.[16]

The decade of the 1840s saw rapid growth in Lafayette County, punctuated by high excitement in 1846 as young men marched off to fight the Mexicans. During that period Charles George Butler served at least one more term as sheriff.[17] The census of 1850, much more detailed than any previous census, indicated that the Butlers were spending their energies and gaining wealth not as planters and slaveholders, but rather as townspeople and hotel keepers. Their rural land holdings came to only 230 acres valued at $1,000 and produced corn but no cotton at all. Their slave holdings had actually shrunk over the decade from six to four, all of whom were seen as black rather than mulatto and included a man and woman in their twenties, a two-year-old boy, and a fifty-year-old man. On the other side, the Butler's real estate, taken altogether, was valued at $12,000, placing them comfortably among the well-to-do people in the county. The white male population in the hotel had doubled in ten years to thirty-three, ranging in age from seventeen to forty and including lawyers, merchants, professors, and physicians.[18]

On May 23, 1855, four days before he died, Charles Butler made out his will. He seemed to be moved by two primary concerns. One was that his youngest child, Charles Edward Butler, then about six, start school during the next year and be educated. Charles, Sr., apparently, believed in the education of his sons. Perennially, he was a trustee and moving spirit in Oxford's private academy for the education of young males.[19] The eldest son, William R. Butler, entered the University of Mississippi in November, 1848, with the Class of 1852, the first full four-year class to begin at the school. Indeed, he was among the very first students who enrolled in "Ole Miss," being the tenth among seventy-four students who matriculated that inaugural fall.[20] Eleven members of the class of 1852 graduated, thirty-nine did not and William was among the latter.[21] Instead, he dropped out of school to enter business and marry, in July, 1850, Anna Elizabeth Bowen, the sister of a classmate in the university, William Bolivar Bowen. Bowen, the ninth student to enroll in the university, also dropped out, and in the same year, married William Butler's sister, Emily.[22]

The Bowens were planters and slaveholders of very substantial proportions, having brought their wealth with them when they migrated from upcountry South Carolina. Also, they were early comers. In 1836, they had a plantation in Tallahatchie County, in the Delta southwest of Oxford, and soon established a residence in Oxford. The father died in 1842, leaving thirty-nine slaves on the plantation and twelve in domestic service in town.[23] Bolivar Bowen came to be known as one of the most charming, laziest, and luckiest young men in the county. An only son with six sisters and a widowed mother, he was thought to be spoiled. Seventy years afterward, he was the boy in their childhood school that the girls as women all remembered. Usually they brought buttermilk to school to drink with their lunch, and in 1908 one of these women "specially"—and fondly—recalled "the many fights that we girls used to have with Bolivar Bowen because he would try to drink our buttermilk, he was so full of pranks and fun."[24] Pressed into labor hoeing the family rose garden, Bolivar chopped down the rose plants, possibly out of sheer awkwardness, and thus spared himself subsequent such assignments. At Ole Miss he led a group of students that hired a carpenter to build a scaffold alongside a building so that they could lead a bull to the roof during the night. The next morning the authorities found the bull on the roof but no scaffold.

Bolivar Bowen became a planter, then joined the Confederate army early, in May, 1861. For a time he served as a sergeant and as a scout. On one occasion he had his stirrup shot cleanly away, leaving his foot untouched. In January, 1862, however, he received a medical discharge for rheumatism. At that time he was described as six feet tall, fair-haired and complected, with "hazel" eyes. Emily Butler Bowen died in 1874, leaving five children, the last of whom was named Charles Butler Bowen (1862–1909), after her father. Bolivar, "Bolly," himself lived to a ripe and, characteristically, happy old age, dying a generation later. Still more generations later, a member of the Bowen family would write that "William and Emily came from different social backgrounds as well as different religious backgrounds." "The Bowens were aristocrats," he explained, "and the Butlers were business, in that they owned one of the first inns in Oxford."[25]

Actually, the Bowens had married into the elite in both town and country. The eldest daughter, Narcissa Bowen, married Judge James M. Howry, the second married a United States senator, and the third married William S. Neilson, the founder in 1837 of what is now Neilson's Department Store in Oxford.[26] It was Narcissa's son, Charles Bowen Howry, who fought all through the war in the Twenty-ninth Mississippi Volunteer Regiment and in 1885 went into law practice with John W.T. Falkner. In William Faulkner's fiction, Bowen might have become Benbow. Two of his more interesting characters were Narcissa Benbow and her aristocratic, bright, ineffectual brother Horace.

The second Butler son, Henry S. (probably Sherwood), entered the university in the class of 1856. Henry also did not graduate.[27] He went into business and married Jarusha Vermelle Boone, the daughter of one of his partners.[28]

As indicated in his will, Charles Butler wanted most of all after his death that his wife Burlina keep the hotel running. She was to have possession of the slaves and the "Hotel, Stable & all lots necessary for use of same." The hotel was to be sold only if Burlina and the coexecutor of the will, Charles's very good friend and business associate William H. Smither, agreed that such was advisable.[29]

In regard to the hotel, Charles could, indeed, rest in peace. Burlina was a woman of impressive managerial skills. In 1842 she had been one of the founders of the Baptist Church in Oxford. After her husband's death she not only executed the intent of his will to preserve the family holding, she improved upon it impressively. Charles's estate, immediately after his death in 1855, was appraised at $21,341.55. In October, 1860, when the census taker called at the hotel, he found that Burlina was a "Hotel Keeper" whose real estate was worth some $40,000 and whose personal property was valued at about $10,000. Burlina had more than doubled the value of her husband's estate in five years, and she was, by local standards, a woman of property.[30]

Moreover, Burlina had become a slaveholder of significant proportions. Where there had been four slaves in 1850, there were twelve in 1860. Eight of these were between eleven and twenty-four years old, and six of these eight were female. If slavery continued, she was well positioned to profit in the near future.[31]

Burlina was an excellent manager, and so were her two first-born sons. In 1860 Burlina's oldest son, William, lived with her. At age thirty-two, he had already acquired $13,000 in real estate and a very healthy $20,000 in personal property. The census taker did not give us William's occupation, but the figures suggest that he was in business in some fashion and carrying on operations that required a considerable investment in personal property in the form of slaves. Possibly he owned a plantation and slaves in another county. His personal property in Lafayette County included only two female slaves, probably a mother and daughter.

Burlina's second son, Henry, was listed as the head of a household very near to Burlina's. He was described as a "l[ivery] Stable Keeper" possessing $1,600 in real estate and $10,000 in personal property. Henry also claimed two slaves, including a thirty-year-old black man who probably worked in his business.[32] Henry's livery stable, surely, was closely associated with his mother's hotel. In fact, it was probably located on North Street immediately behind the hotel. Altogether, in 1860, Burlina, William, and Henry owned property worth some $95,000. Even allowing for the tendency of people to be more generous in estimating the value of their property with the census taker than with the tax collector, the Butlers were well-to-do people in their community.

The Butlers might have been, as a Bowen descendant declared, merely business people, but they were very good at their business. Land records in the courthouse indicate that, on the eve of the Civil War they owned the northwest corner of the town square, an entire block just north of that and a dozen or more lots in the northeastern part of the town. On South Street (later South Lamar), they owned at least eleven of the eighteen residential lots between University Avenue and what became Garfield Street at the town's southern edge. These included Lot No. 1 upon which John Falkner later situated the Big Place. In addition, they owned a goodly number of less valuable lots scattered all over town.[33] During this time, "the Butler homestead," as it was called in 1893, was at the northeast corner of Jefferson and 14th Streets—located by recent landmarks as just across 14th Street from the swimming pool at the Holiday Inn.[34] In material matters, then, the Butlers in Oxford were not vastly unlike the Falkners in Ripley. Indeed, Burlina's wealth matched that of William C. Falkner in Ripley, and with that of her two sons nearly doubled the Falkner family fortune.

In part the affluence of the Butlers was simply a reflection of the general rise in the value of property in the Cotton Kingdom in the decade of the 1850s. These were high times in Lafayette County and in Mississippi. Oxford shared specially in that prosperity as the county seat and as the site of the University of Mississippi, to which the wealthy planters so often sent their sons. Located on the western edge of Oxford, the state university commenced operations in the late 1840s and soon flourished. Its longtime president, Georgia-born Augustus

Baldwin Longstreet, was one of the community's most prominent citizens. His daughter married Lucius Quintus Cincinnatus Lamar, who in 1850 was the university's twenty-five-year-old professor of mathematics and who, after the war, would become Mississippi's most famous statesman.[35] It is clear enough that the Butlers, on the eve of the Civil War, had chosen to seek their fortunes, not primarily as planters and slaveholders in the countryside, but rather as leaders in the commercial life of Oxford, and in that pursuit they were, indeed, doing very well.

~

The war produced a dramatic reduction in the wealth of the Butlers, effected most directly by the depredations of marauding armies. In December, 1862, General Ulysses S. Grant marched into Oxford as he began maneuvers to take Vicksburg—the last major stronghold of the Confederates on the Mississippi River. An attack on his supply base at Holly Springs forced Grant's withdrawal, but two years later, in 1864, the Yankees were back again. This time they were under the command of General A.J. "Whiskey" Smith. The general was in an especially vengeful mood, perhaps because a Confederate force had recently burned Chambersburg, Pennsylvania, or perhaps because a leading citizen of Oxford, Jacob Thompson, was rumored to have conceived the idea of attacking Grant's base at Holly Springs in 1862 as a way of halting his advance on Vicksburg. Whatever the reason, under Smith's orders Union soldiers set fire to the town. The courthouse and all of the buildings on the square save one were burned to the ground, and many of the houses in the village were destroyed. Tradition relates that Burlina Butler, herself, barely escaped her burning hotel with her life, and that she came away with only the clothes on her back. Thereafter, until the end of the war, many Oxfordians were forced to rely for shelter on the hospitality of friends and relatives in the countryside.

Both of the older Butler brothers went off to war. William, the oldest, joined the Twenty-eighth Mississippi Cavalry as a private in February, 1862. He was in his early thirties, well-educated, accustomed to leading, and soon became a sergeant. But William was not a healthy man. In November, after four months of illness at "University Gen'l Hospital" in Oxford, he was certified as unfit "for duty in six months if ever." His certificate described him as born in Henry County in northwestern Tennessee, "5 feet 10 inches, light complexion, *Blue* eyes, *light* hair, and by occupation when enlisted *A Planter.*" It is possible that William took some of the fifteen slaves that still belonged to his father's estate in 1857 and operated a plantation in another county while living in Oxford. It is also possible that he was operating a Bowen plantation with Bowen slaves for the benefit of his children by Elizabeth Bowen. William's military physicians, Thomas D. Isom and H.R. Branham, thought he was suffering from tuberculosis.[36]

In November, 1858, Henry S. Butler had married Vermelle Boone. Soon he was the father of two sons, Willie and Ernest. In May, 1862, shortly after the battle of Shiloh, he left his family and livery business to join the Twenty-ninth Mississippi Volunteer Regiment as a private. Within a few months the army, taking advantage of his experience in the livery business, made him a wagon master in the supply train. In that capacity he served under his fellow townsman, William G. Beanland, Captain and Quartermaster for the brigade. All during 1862, 1863, and 1864, he and Beanland campaigned together with the Army of Tennessee and suffered its desperate battles and declining fortunes as it fell back through Tennessee and northwestern Georgia toward Atlanta. Henry was near Jonesboro, Georgia, on the night of August 31, 1864, when the Confederates, striving to hold open the last railroad line into the city, launched a frontal attack on the encroaching Union force. Henry joined the assault with Washington Wilkins, Charles Howry, and the men of the Twenty-ninth Mississippi. It was a futile effort in which the already depleted regiment lost fifty-five men killed and wounded. One of the wounded was Henry. In the fray, he was shot through both the right knee and the left shoulder. Eight hours passed before his wounds received, as his service record noted, a "Simple Dressing."[37] It was a scene vividly out of *Gone With the Wind.* At the very time that Henry, twice wounded and bleeding, was struggling for his life, the fictional Scarlett O'Hara, was fleeing from burning Atlanta, driving the spavined horse to pull the sagging, creaking wagon carrying Melanie, Melanie's newborn infant, and herself, trying to reach Tara near Jonesboro.

After the fall of Atlanta, the Confederate Army retreated toward Tennessee, and Henry was left behind, the usual fate of the severely wounded among Confederate soldiers. On September 8, he was admitted to a military hospital in Macon. A week later, Henry died. A handful of effects and $1.50 in Confederate money were sent to his widow, Vermelle.[38] Henry could not have known, but Oxford had burned only days before Atlanta fell. His livery stable and his mother's hotel were no more. His wife would appear frequently in town and county records in and after 1865. Usually, she was suing people, and one gets the image of a perpetually bitter and angry woman, a ghost of Confederate failure. Early in the twentieth century she applied for a pension as an indigent Confederate widow.[39]

For a time, after the war, the Butlers continued in their usual enterprising spirit in the person of the eldest son, William R. Butler. On September 25, 1865, William was a member of the town board as Oxford began the process of rebuilding. Interestingly, he participated in the decision of the board not to revitalize the "patrol" in the town. In Oxford, the patrol had consisted of five men and a "Captain," and its duty, of course, was to keep slaves, free blacks, and such whites as might tamper with either element under tight rein. However, with the end of the war, blacks had been freed, and the town quickly turned to recognize that fact by abolishing the patrol and creating a separate roll of sixty-two "Freedmen" resident in Oxford who would be taxed at the rate of $5 each (a "poll" or head tax) just as were white men.[40] Other Southern communities were not so wise. They reactivated the patrol only to suffer rude reminders from the occupying Union Army that there were no longer any slaves to be patrolled.

William Butler was not only an alderman, he was also active in the physical rebuilding of the town. The board explicitly thanked him and paid him for work done on Oxford's streets, even though it denied his claim for pay for some improvements completed before the war. In September, 1865, William paid $25 for a license to do business in the town, the highest fee in the scale. The third son, Charles Edward Butler, entered the university in November, 1866, with the class of 1870. Like his older brothers, "Charlie," as he was called, would also terminate his education before taking his degree.[41]

William died early in 1868. He was buried in the town cemetery next to the wife of his youth, Anna Elizabeth Bowen, who had passed away a decade before.[42] Possibly, William had married again—to a young woman named Penelope H. Butler, who lived with the Butlers in the hotel when the census was taken in October, 1860. In November, 1866, Penelope bought lots 140 and 141 (just north of the Butler homestead) for $495 from Ole Miss President Augustus Baldwin Longstreet, who, as evidenced by courthouse records, was also a private banker of no mean proportions. Mrs. W.R. Butler was carried in the census of 1870 as the head of a household, a widow, the owner of $1,500 each of real and personal property, the mother of two sons ages eight and six, and the employer of a black woman as cook and a young black man as laborer.[43]

Burlina had lost her hotel and, probably, most of her supporting buildings in the burning of Oxford in 1864. In December, 1865, she made a momentous decision for the Butler family fortunes. She sold for $2,800 the land on the square upon which the hotel had stood, another whole block near where the jail now stands, and several lots.[44] In 1867 she sold off nine prime residential lots on South Street for an additional $1,800.[45] In 1874, she rented out some of her farm land—probably a farm she had retreated to during and after the Union occupation—to Fancy Hurt for "two bales of cotton of 500 lbs. each" and $52 payable to her son Charles.[46]

Simultaneously, Burlina was disposing of lands belonging to her husband's estate for the benefit of her children, each of whom was due some $1,500. In June, 1866, daughter Mary Ann Edwards got five lots along South Street. In 1872, she turned over three lots of ten acres each to Charles as his share. She retained, however, gardening rights on one plot for "as long as she lives." Burlina died in December, 1877. Meanwhile, her hotel had been rebuilt as "The Thompson House." In August, 1869, the *Oxford Falcon* bragged that a "magnificent three story Hotel is now rapidly rising upon the former ruins of the Old Butler Hotel . . ."[47]

Charlie Butler

After William's death, male leadership in the Butler family passed to Charles, the third son, not yet twenty.[48] During the war, he was in his early teens and too young—just barely too young by the end—to enter the fray. Though he is not listed as living in the hotel with his mother in 1860, he must have been in or near Oxford during the war and felt the impact of marauding armies and the burning of his hometown, much as did his nearly exact contemporary John W.T. Falkner in Ripley. Charlie's brother William R. Butler was at least eighteen years older than he, and probably William had comfortably supplanted their father after his death in 1855. William's own death at forty in 1868 must have represented a shocking loss to the Butlers materially and psychologically, and so too to Charlie who now found himself the "man" in the family. William died in February, and early in August Charlie married nineteen-year-old "Miss Leila Swift."[49]

Falkner family tradition has it that Leila was "an Arkansas girl" and a cousin of the founder of the meat packing company, Gustavus F. Swift. There is no clear relation between Leila and that particular Swift family, the latter having sprung from Cape Cod, Massachusetts, and having left no visible record of any connection with the southwest. Leila was born on March 5, 1849. In 1880 the census taker understood that she was born in Mississippi and that both of her parents had been born in Tennessee.[50] Actually, there were Swifts in Lafayette County in 1850, including one J.T. Swift, a farmer who held nine slaves.[51] But Leila does not appear among Lafayette County Swifts. It is possible that her relatives were among the early settlers in the county before moving to Arkansas.

Later, Leila often used her middle name, Dean. At her death in 1907, someone, possibly her children, chose to put that name instead of Swift on her gravestone in St. Peter's Cemetery. Thus, her memorial read "Leila Dean Butler" instead of "Leila Swift Butler," which would have been the case had a more usual form been used. The name Dean persisted in the family, whereas Swift did not. Leila's daughter, Maud, named her fourth child, a son, Dean. His only child, a girl born after his death, continued the line. It might be that Dean was the maiden name of Leila's mother. It does not appear to have been a Lafayette County name at all.

Exhaustive searches in the censuses of 1850, 1860, and 1870 for Mississippi, Arkansas, and Tennessee have not found Leila. Other than the Arkansas and meat-packing-Swift stories and her representations to the census taker in 1880 that her parents were born in Tennessee and she in Mississippi, Leila's background and ancestry remain mysteries. All we really know of her beginnings is that she was there in Oxford on July 31, 1868, to take out a license to marry

Charlie Butler. She bore her first child, Sherwood Tate Butler, on May 20, 1869, and her second, Maud (William Faulkner's mother), more than two years later, on November 27, 1871.[52] At some point after her marriage, it became clear that Leila had had artistic training in painting and sculpting and had developed talents that she frequently exercized, often to the admiration and wonder of her neighbors. Toward the end of her life she was a staunch Southern Baptist.

Charlie, on the other hand, is easily traceable in local newspapers and in town, county, census, and other official records. He first appeared in county records after his marriage. In January, 1869, Burlina transferred to one James Kimes a tract, possibly a farm, of about one hundred acres for two notes amounting to $1,000 due a year later. Shortly, probably early in 1869, Charles acquired these notes from his mother for "a valuable consideration." Possibly, this asset came to him as a portion of his share of his father's estate. By the middle of 1869 Kimes had paid in only $160 toward satisfying his obligations and resort to the courts brought no further payments. More than a year after the notes were due, Kimes still had not paid, and Charles presented the papers to him for settlement. Kimes did not and probably could not pay. Charles then brought his case to court and secured a ruling that Kimes should pay him $960 plus interest on or before the fourth Monday in July, 1871, or face the consequences.[53]

R.G. Dun & Co. reporters picked Charlie up in September, 1873, after he had become a partner in a confectionary store operated by William G. Beanland. Beanland, of course, was the Quartermaster Captain with whom Charlie's brother Henry had soldiered before his death in Georgia in 1864. Beanland had come to Oxford as a young man in the late 1850s. He was an unusually likeable and very enterprising person, a man who obviously loved to serve his community by providing folks with goods and services. In 1860, at age twenty-three, he was a merchant with $21,000 in property. After the war he tried several business ventures, usually in association with men with more capital than he. One of his associates, for instance, might well have been Jacob Thompson, Oxford's leading citizen before the war. In 1870, Beanland (pronounced Binland) ran a hotel (in reality, probably better described as a boarding house) just off the square in Oxford. William's guests at one point during Reconstruction included nine Southerners, five Northerners (one of whom was the town marshal), two Germans, and one Irishman. Two of his boarders were young men on the rise—W.E. Andrews, a grocery clerk who would become the clerk of court for many years, and Francis Marion Stowers, who had entered the university in 1867, but dropped out to pursue a career in business. In 1870, Stowers kept accounts for a local grocer. In the 1880s, he became a prosperous dry goods merchant, and in 1887 won election to the town board. Francis was the son of Robert M. Stowers who was a slave overseer associated with the Jacob Thompson family before and during the Civil War. It is possible that Charlie Butler also had some connection with William Beanland's hotel. It was the business, of course, to which he was born.

In 1873, R.G. Dun & Co. recognized William Beanland as a good businessman in spite of his previous involvement in several ventures that failed. In regard to Charlie, the rating company's agent reported in 1873 that "Butler is a yng man of 25 marrd gd char + habits + ordinary bus capacity has lived in LaFayette Co. all his life has a small ppy. consisting of a tract of land near Oxford." In the following year the reporter entered a "no comment" on his record, but the state tax rolls suggest that he was comfortably equipped with a $50 carriage, a $25 horse, a $25 watch, and a $7 pistol. In September, 1875, in the depth of a great world-wide depression, R.G. Dun & Co. declared tersely that Charlie's confectionary business had closed.[54]

There were other signs that Charlie was not prospering in these early years of his marriage. As we have seen, in 1872 his mother had signed over to him three lots as his share of the residue of his father's legacy. Two of these were on the northwestern edge of the town and the third two blocks south of the square. Altogether, they were valued at $500. In January and February, 1875, he mortgaged the first two lots and a mule to the merchant firm of Isom and Kendal for $373.78. It appears that Charlie was borrowing money to maintain his household, which then included two children—his son Sherwood, age five, and Maud, age three.[55]

On April 25, 1876, Charles's professional life took a new and very important turn, one that brought his small family to financial stability, if not, indeed, to a modest prosperity. He was elected marshal for the Town of Oxford and "duly qualified and installed in office."[56] This was an office to which he would be reelected by the mayor and six aldermen every two years and hold for almost a dozen years—until he tendered his resignation in an indirect but very dramatic and decisive manner.

It is easy to follow closely Charlie's career in the minutes of the meetings of town officials still preserved in the Town Hall. The character of the marshal's office evolved over time, and there are signs that Charlie himself, as Oxford grew in size and affluence in the 1880s, improved upon the importance and power of his position. In the beginning, the marshal served two primary functions. First, he was the town's policeman, instructed by the board to arrest anyone "drunk or committing a nuisance, or exhibiting a deadly weapon or using profane or obscene language or acting disorderly or violating any ordinance of this town or the criminal law of the State within the corporate limits of Oxford." For performing his police duties Charles was paid $50 a month. Second, the marshal was also the tax collector. For this work he was paid 5 percent of the taxes collected. In 1876 tax collections amounted to some $3,000 annually, yielding the marshal a commission of about $150, an amount that more than quadrupled over the next several years.[57]

Apparently, during the year before Charles took office, the town had difficulty collecting all taxes due. Possibly Charles's election represented a determination by the board to improve the sweep by taking a new broom to the task.

Within a week of his election, the new marshal was handed a list of delinquent taxpayers and ordered either to collect the taxes or report the delinquents to the mayor who would begin a process of "distress" (that is, legally forced) sales to do so.[58]

The marshal also carried out the directives of the town board concerning the health of the town, ranging from the heavy responsibility of enforcing quarantine regulations during recurring epidemics down through overseeing the destruction, construction, and "liming" (disinfecting with lime) of privies. Further, he enforced various ordinances governing loose livestock, especially pigs that perpetually escaped into the streets and other people's lots. There was extra money for the marshal in enforcing the stock laws, though the board shifted the specific amounts from time to time. In 1879, for example, the marshal was ordered to seize pigs loose in the streets and hold them until the owners appeared to claim their property. For the seizure, he would be paid 50 cents, and for keeping the animal 25 cents a day. In 1882 keep was reduced to 20 cents a day. Some of Charlie Butler's early labor was rather ignominious. For instance, in July, 1876, he was given 25 cents for "removing [a] dead dog." Finally, some of his work was less than glorious but not without its perquisites—for many years he boarded the "corporation mule" for $10 a month while the cost of keeping the animal was probably something less than $8.[59]

The minutes of the meetings of the town board indicate that Charles Butler's managerial function grew rapidly during his tenure as marshal. Early in 1878 he was directed by the board to inspect the streets once a week and report their condition to a standing committee of aldermen. When a prolonged and terrifying yellow fever epidemic struck the entire Mississippi River basin in the following summer and continued to rage into the fall, Marshal Butler hired and headed a platoon of "quarantine guards" that sealed off the town—even to the point of allowing no trains to stop at the depot and intercepting and, prior to delivery, sanitizing the mails cast from the moving train. The seriousness with which the town took these matters was indicated by the fact that C.W. Petrie, a local businessman who was away when the fever hit Oxford, was hauled into mayor's court and fined $50 for slipping into town through the quarantine lines to join his family.[60]

In reality, the marshal filled an office that would later be identified by the title "town manager." The structure of town government in Oxford made it inevitable that such would be the case. All during the 1870s and 1880s, the town had only two full-time employees. There was a marshal and a lesser officer, at first a jailor, and later, after the county assumed responsibility for that function, a night watchman. The mayor, secretary, and treasurer were each paid for part-time work only. The jailor or night watchman, obviously, could not be a rival for Charlie Butler's managerial function. Most significantly, the marshal was the person who collected the taxes, and, in a large measure, spent them. It was in the nature of the growing town that the marshal should manage more and more of its business. Finally, one gets the image of Charlie Butler as, innately, a volunteer and a "joiner," a rather energetic and engaging young man in his late twenties and early thirties who moved about town doing its business effectively and efficiently. It was, it seems, in Charlie's nature, perhaps in the traditional Butler male character, that he should do the community's work with steady, dependable competence.

In the late 1870s and early 1880s Charlie Butler's place in the Oxford community seemed very secure. His mother died in December, 1877, and it was probably in her house on the northeast corner of Jefferson and 14th streets that he and Leila lived with their two children. In 1878, he commenced to gather a series of important community credits. On July 16, 1878, he applied for membership in Masonic Lodge #1063 in Oxford. It was fully appropriate that he do so. In the 1840s his father had been a pioneering member and an officer in the local Masonic Lodge. After the usual careful investigation into his character by a committee of the lodge, he was admitted.[61]

Thereafter, through the minutes of the lodge, one sees a very active Charles E. Butler. Frequently, he joined others in signing a letter (in the form prescribed by rather elaborate Masonic protocol) addressed to the presiding officer, the "Dictator," asking him for a "called meeting" of the membership. In both 1879 and 1880 he was appointed to the committee on arrangements for the spring celebration of the anniversary of the establishment of the lodge, events that included processions, speeches in and about the courthouse, and prodigious quantities of lemonade and food (e.g., fifty pounds of cake and fifteen gallons of ice cream). Along with Charlie on the committee were his friends, thirty-year-old Clerk of Court W.E. Andrews and the German-born, Civil War cavalryman and blacksmith Herman Wohlleben.

The criteria for membership in the Masonic lodge in Oxford are not given to us. Still, the characters of all applicants for membership were carefully scrutinized by committees appointed specifically for each individual and not all who applied were admitted. For example, rather surprisingly, William V. Sullivan, Vanderbilt University graduate, rising young lawyer, and a future United States senator from Mississippi, was refused membership during the winter of 1879. However it came to be, as a Mason Charlie Butler was leagued with some two dozen men representing very respectable families in the town. One of his fellow Masons, for example, was young Samuel M. Howry, soon to become a business partner of J.W.T. Falkner. Oxford's Masons were an earnest crew and dedicated to the work of the Order. Sometimes the membership met twice a week, usually for the purpose of instructing junior members in the lore associated with three levels of Masonic achievement: "Infancy," "Youth," and "Manhood." Occasionally they met for such business matters as buying a hall and, later, for keeping it in repair. In July, 1879, Charlie Butler was installed as the "Sentinel" of the lodge, a task obviously congruent with his capacities as a police officer. The Sentinel was the lowest in a hierarchy of eight officers in the lodge. In September, 1880, however, Charlie was elected "Guardian," seemingly the next highest office in rank.[62]

Town Marshal

In January, 1880, Charles Butler was again elected town marshal. On June 7 of that year, the census taker found the family of four settled in their house several hundred feet northeast of the courthouse. It was a good neighborhood, where Charlie's daughter, Maud, age eight, sometimes played with the daughters of Lucius Quintus Cincinnatus Lamar, the Mississippi senator whose house, a block or so further away from the courthouse, was modest in size but nevertheless as beautifully classical as the name of its owner. Charlie's son Sherwood was then eleven and in school.[63]

Other members of the Butler clan also lived in Oxford. Charlie's oldest sister Mattie Nelson, widowed two years before, headed a household in which two of her nephews, Henry and Walter Butler, ages eighteen and fifteen, lived. Both of these young men were store clerks. Also in Mattie's house was her seventy-six-year-old father-in-law, a widower. In Oxford and single was Charlie's niece, Anna Bowen, aged twenty-five, and other relatives in the Bowen connection.[64]

In the census of 1880, Charlie's occupation was given as "Police." Well might one have been impressed with the police side of his duties that summer. Oxford was growing and the city fathers obviously felt that vice was on the rise and controls needed to be instituted. In August, the board ordered the marshal to take action on two particular problems. "Street Walkers" were becoming more obtrusive and disturbing the good order of the town. Corruption in a novel and more virulent form had sprung from, as the board declared, "that class of boys know[n] as 'Mackerel' who congregate upon the streets and by whistling, dancing, singing and harp playing greatly disturb the peace of our city." The marshal was directed to take up all such for "disorderly conduct." Apparently, however, some vices were more acceptable than others. The women were to be arrested only after eight in the evenings while the Mackerel, the boys, were to be hauled in "day or night," whenever and wherever found.[65]

In the early 1880s there were occasional signs that there was something less than perfect trust between the town board and its marshal. But there were also signs that when there was a difference the board moved easily to accommodate its principle executive officer. In January, 1882, the board passed an ordinance ordering the marshal to stay in town at all times unless his absence was approved by the mayor. Violations would be fined at the rate of $10 each. At its February meeting, the board rescinded that ordinance. At the March meeting the board had a much more serious bone to pick with the marshal in his capacity as tax collector. They found that he had collected taxes for the years 1880 and 1881 to the amount of $10,285.74, but had paid in to the treasurer only $8,284.81, leaving almost exactly $2,000 missing. However, as they worked out the figures in their meeting, they concluded that his 5 percent commission reduced the deficit by $514.28. They further found that he had paid "street hands" $535.40 in 1880 and $751.92 in 1881, and that $61.28 in taxes had actually never been collected. Thus, the marshal owed the town only $138.05. This relatively modest debt was quickly settled, but the whole affair made obvious the need for closer accounting in the future. In April, 1882, the board ordered that "from and after this date the City Marshal make settlement with the treasurer monthly and that the latter report to the board the cumulative results every July and January."[66]

The large and recurring item in the marshal's account was labelled "amt pd street hands by him." There was much work to be done on the streets, as well as on drains, plank sidewalks, and other facilities supplied by the town. Further, there was a tradition that allowed taxpayers, if they chose, to perform "street work" to pay their taxes. In return for such work, indeed for all labor done on these public facilities, Charlie gave out "Street Tickets"—usually at the rate of ten cents for every hour worked. He also accepted street tickets as money when he collected taxes. In the course of a year, perhaps dozens of men would work on the streets. Some were taxpayers, some not, and many of them worked for very short periods of time. Thus, every year Charlie created a stream of paper money that passed out to a large and relatively indeterminant group of men who worked on the streets, then passed through his pocket as a part of tax collections, and ended in the town treasury.

The bookkeeping was also in Charlie's pocket. It was up to him to declare how much in street tickets he had given out, and up to him, too, to say which taxes had been paid. If he chose to do so, he could dishonestly inflate the total amount of street tickets given out, and convert the excess into cash for himself as taxes were paid. Fraud could be proved conclusively only by polling all the men who had worked on the streets, the time of whose work might go back as much as two and a half years, who kept no records, and some of whom could not have said exactly how much they had been paid. Further, Charlie might have insured that the poll could never be completed by including men recently deceased in his list or by creating some men who never existed and hence could never be found.

If the board had been nervous on this matter before, it had no good reason to be at ease after the reform of April, 1882. Charlie himself still paid out large amounts of money to men who could be thoroughly polled only with great difficulty as to hours worked and wages received. Moreover, as Oxford grew in size and affluence, the amount paid out for labor on public works became larger. On January 1, 1883, under the new system, the board allowed the marshal $751.40 for "street tickets" taken in for taxes for the year 1882. In February the committee appointed to oversee the treasury reported that the marshal had collected taxes for 1882 in the amount of $6,762.62 and that his commissions were $337.29. The marshal owed the town only $13.48, and just prior to the meeting he had shown the committee a receipt from the treasurer for that amount.[67]

As Charlie's fortunes improved he revealed an interest in and capacity for the traditional Butler business of dealing in real estate. In August, 1878, he bought from Sallie Fox Thompson for $300 cash and a note for $350 due in two years a prime piece of property on North Street three blocks away from the town square. It was virtually an entire block, very suitable for a number of businesses, and, in modern times, recently occupied by a branch of the Mississippi food stores that trade under the fascinating name "The Jitney Jungle." This land had been acquired by his older brothers before the war and was sold to W.F. Avent and Sallie Thompson by William R. Butler for $1,200 on December 9, 1865, the same date on which these two bought the old hotel site from Burlina.[68]

Two years later, in 1880, Charlie continued in a venturesome vein when he borrowed $700 against the "Butler homestead" from family friends Mrs. Ida Campbell and Miss Kate Carothers. His friend Deputy Sheriff John B. Roach acted as referee in the transaction.[69] In view of Oxford's rising prosperity, increasing land values, and his income as marshal and tax collector, it does not seem that Charlie acted imprudently.

The Killing of Sam Thompson

It was at this point that Charlie's work as a peace officer seriously jeopardized his future career as town manager and business person. On May 17, 1883, the *Oxford Eagle* reported that on Tuesday, May 8, "Mr. S.M. Thompson, editor of the *Oxford Eagle* was shot and killed by Chas. Butler."

Elizabeth A. Thompson, wife of the dead man and author of the article, charged that her husband was killed by an officer who had him in custody "in a state of intoxication, unarmed, and under arrest," leaving her a widow and her daughter fatherless. The man killed was the owner as well as the editor of the stoutly Democratic *Eagle,* Samuel Moore Thompson. Before the war, while still in his teens, Thompson was the junior partner in the *Oxford Sentinel.*[70] During the war he had enlisted in the Confederate cavalry. For a dozen years after the war, he had edited the *Oxford Falcon,* and in 1877 launched his own paper, the *Eagle,* as a rival to the *Falcon.*[71]

The *Eagle* admitted "Captain" Thompson's intoxication on the streets and his use of "abusive language" to a passing citizen. However, it insisted that after he was arrested by Butler he went along peacefully until "goading" by the officer caused him to refuse to go farther, "flushed as he was with strong drink."

It was broad daylight on the square in Oxford, and the scene played before an audience of scores of men because court was then in session on the second floor of the courthouse. The *Eagle* declared that "fair minded" people concluded "that the officer clothed in a little 'brief authority,' killed Capt. Thompson, not because he resisted, nor because it was necessary; but did so on account of malice, arising from previous grudge, and that in doing so he was encouraged by persons of vastly more respectable standing in society than himself." The *Eagle* headed this story: "A Brave Man Will Not Take the Mean Advantage."[72]

After this early and vigorous assault on Charles Butler, the *Eagle* appears not to have mentioned the matter again. However, Eliza Thompson, who had been trained by her husband in the newspaper business from printer's devil on up, resolved to continue the paper and run it herself. Thirty-two years later, she was still running it.[73]

Two weeks after the killing of Sam Thompson, both the Vicksburg *Post* and the Jackson *Clarion* printed a carefully assembled and apparently balanced account of the event drawn from interviews with numerous eye witnesses. In this version, Capt. Thompson was sitting on the sidewalk in front of the Thompson Hotel on the north side of the square when Butler, who served as bailiff of the state district court as well as town marshal (and who, incidentally, as marshal also held an appointment as a deputy sheriff), came onto the balcony of the second story of the courthouse across the street to call H.M. Sullivan to appear before the court then in session. He had called several times in the usual stentorian voice of bailiffs before Thompson, very drunk and in full view of Butler, answered "here" in "a tone corresponding to the call." Then Thompson began calling out his own name in the same style, as if he were himself the bailiff. Sullivan, the man being called to court, passed near Thompson on his way into the building. Thompson spoke to him in a familiar manner. When Sullivan did not reply, Thompson cursed him. Sullivan stopped, turned, and made some remark to Thompson. Thompson then stood up, moved to the edge of the sidewalk facing Sullivan, and said "see me now" in a very challenging tone, "applying to him at the same time a very gross epithet."

Sullivan did not answer, but went on into the courthouse. Thompson then turned, walking westward, crossed over to the sidewalk on the west side of the square, and headed south. The marshal now emerged from the courthouse and followed him. Coming up behind Thompson, he slid his left hand under Thompson's right arm and said, "Sam, I arrest you." Thompson looked at Butler and a few words passed between them. The exchange was "of an apparently inoffensive character which ended by the deceased saying all right, and they walked on together, Butler still having his left arm locked in Thompson's right, and talking to him." They had gone some twenty steps when Thompson suddenly stopped, declaring he would go no further. A scuffle followed, Butler still holding Thompson's right arm, while Thompson with his left hand grabbed either Butler's coat sleeve, lapel, or throat—as the various accounts went.

Butler stated subsequently in an affidavit that there were seventy-five to a hundred onlookers. He called on one of these by name, William O. Beanland, to "come help me take this man." Beanland, a young man in his early twenties, came up promptly and seized Thompson's left hand. The three men stood for a few moments thus locked together. Then Butler reached into his hip pocket with his right hand, drew his revolver, placed the muzzle against Thompson's breast, and said, "Thompson, if you don't let me go, I'll kill you." Thompson held fast. Butler lowered his pistol until the muzzle pointed to the ground and the three men held their positions for a few moments. Butler then again raised the pistol to Thompson's breast and said, "Turn me loose or I will kill you." At that point Beanland let go of Thompson's hand because, as he later said, "I saw that Butler was going to shoot him."

Thompson was adamant. "Shoot, you ______," he challenged. Immediately Butler fired, the ball passing through "the lower region of Thompson's heart." Still grasping onto and facing Butler, Thompson seemed incredulous at the turn of events. "Charlie, you have killed me?" he cried. Butler, holding his pistol in his right hand, slowly lowered the dying man to the pavement with his left hand. Much sobered now, Thompson uttered prayers for his soul, his wife, and his child. Then he died.[74]

Butler immediately surrendered himself to a fellow police officer, Deputy Sheriff John B. Roach. The next morning, Wednesday, May 9, he was indicted for manslaughter by the Lafayette County grand jury then in session and was released the next day on a bail of $2,500. The court ordered a continuance of the matter until its next term in November.[75]

Why Charlie Shot Sam

Why Charles Butler should thus shoot and kill the drunken editor of a local newspaper seems, at first sight, beyond comprehension. It would be more understandable if Thompson had been armed. Rather pathetically, turning out the dead man's pockets produced only a few dollars, a pipe, some tobacco, keys, and a small pocket knife.[76] Why did Charlie call upon only one man to assist him when, presumably, he could have summoned as many as he needed to help him, as he phrased it, "take this man"? Apparently, he had arrested Sam several times before for being drunk on the streets; why this time did he feel that he had to kill him?

We shall never know the full answer, but the explanation of the killing begins with the fact that Sam Thompson was himself facing trial in the criminal court then in session, and his case was slated to be called at 10 A.M. the next day. He was charged with "abduction of [a] female and unlawful cohabitation." In addition, in the same session, he was appealing a conviction by a lower court on

February 4, 1882, of "unlawful disturbance of a family," for which he had been fined $250 and sentenced to ninety days in the county jail.[77] Behind the conviction was a complaint by William Watkins that on January 22, 1882, Thompson had disturbed the peace of himself and his family by "tumultuous and offensive conduct," especially by pointing a pistol at him and his wife Louisa. Watkins swore that Thompson on that day did "exhibit said pistol in a rude angry & threatening manner." Behind this event was an exceedingly involved relationship between Captain Sam Thompson and Eudora Watkins, William Watkins' teenage daughter. On January 23, 1882, Eudora herself took out a warrant for Samuel Thompson and Julia Avent charging that they did on November 1, 1881, "unlawfully & against affidvits [sic] will & by force menace & strategem and duress compel affiant to be then and there by him the said SM Thompson defiled."[78] Julia Avent was a black woman who worked as a servant in the Thompson household. In 1880 she was forty years old and described herself as a washerwoman. The court found that Julia, indeed, "did unlawfully and feloniously abduct [and] decoy away and imprison one Eudora Watkins."[79] Thompson's bond of $500 for "disturbance of a family" was posted by himself and his wife Elizabeth. His bond for abduction and defilement was set at $1,000 and supplied by himself, Elizabeth, and his lawyer, C.M. Phipps.[80]

The most prominent police officer in the case was, apparently, Charlie Butler. Acting in his dual capacity as town marshal and as a deputy sheriff, it was he who organized the process by which all concerned parties were brought to court.[81] It was also he who acted upon Eudora's complaint and put Julia Avent in the county jail. Presumably, he would have lodged Sam Thompson in the same place except that Thompson posted bond to stand while his appeal went forward. Shortly, Sam also posted a $500 bond for Julia.[82]

The court that found Sam and Julia guilty was actually that of the mayor of Oxford, Patton B. Murry, who acted ex-officio as a justice of the peace for the county and the state. His police officer for mayor's court was Charles Butler, and, in addition, Butler probably served as his officer when Murry acted as a justice of the peace. Murry was also editor of the *Oxford Falcon,* the rival newspaper to Thompson's *Eagle.*[83]

From the census of 1880, we know that in June, 1880, Eudora Watkins was seventeen years old and that she was born in Tennessee of a Tennessee-born mother. She had a brother, age three, also born in Tennessee of a Tennessee-born mother. Her father, William, was age fifty-six and born in England. William offered no entry for his occupation. His current wife was Louisa, age forty, Georgia-born, and "Keeping House." Presumably, within the preceding few years, Eudora and her three-year-old brother had lost their natural mother, their father had remarried, and all had moved to Oxford. Living in the household with them, probably as roomers, were two white men, unmarried and in their twenties. One was an Alabamian who clerked in a store, the other was a

German who was a blacksmith. They lived in a house near the university, which is to say on the west side of town, close to the railroad tracks and the train station. It was not an affluent neighborhood. Indeed, Oxfordians sometimes called this area "Hashtown."[84]

In February, 1882, Sam was found guilty of violating the peace of the Watkins home by the mayor's court; on May 3, 1882, his difficulties escalated as the grand jury of the circuit court indicted him for the "abduction of [a] female and unlawful cohabitation." The grand jury found that on May 1, Sam "with force and arms" took Eudora and "against her will and by force menace fraud deceit and Stratagem did induce her the Said Eudora Watkins to be defiled." In another specification of the charge, the grand jury declared that Thompson, "a man with force and arms on the first day of May, AD 1882 in said County of Lafayette then & there unlawfully did Cohabit in Adultery" with Eudora. This new charge and escalation sprang from Sam's actions on the eve of the hearing of his appeal. On Monday, May 1, on the first day of court during the spring term, Sam, with tremendous unwisdom, did what he had done before, and again with disastrous results. Anticipating trouble from Eudora in the impending proceedings, he took his pistol and went calling. He ended, it appears, by carrying Eudora away to Julia Avent's house, where persuasion failed and he quickly slid into the use of force to have sex with her.

Prior to May 1, 1882, Sam Thompson was in trouble primarily with the Watkins family. Things might have been negotiated between them, and the law subsequently mollified. But now he had acted "against the peace and dignity of the State of Mississippi," and state authorities seemed determined to bring him to account. In truth, Sam was becoming outrageous to the community. Indicting him for "Unlawful Cohabitation" apparently was based upon the premise that he took Eudora to Julia Avent's house for sexual purposes and forced her to live there. Obviously, it was a charge that District Attorney James T. Fant felt would be effective in prosecuting the malefactor.[85]

Perusal of court records in Lafayette and Tippah Counties over the decades from the 1830s reveals shifts over time in the primary concerns of the civic mind in regard to peace and good order. In the 1850s, of course, the courts were dedicated to the cause of slave control. In the 1880s there was a distinct rise in litigation between local citizens and corporate entities in the North and abroad (e.g., in Lafayette County, the British American Mortgage Co. Ltd). There was also a shift in the sexual realm. There had always been a readiness to punish rape, fornication, adultery, and bigamy, but in the 1880s the charges became more subtle and included such things as "Cursing" or "Profane swearing in [the] presence of [a] female," "unnatural intercourse," "Seduction," "paternity" (fathering a child out of wedlock), attempt or intent "to commit rape," and "unlawful cohabitation." Now, Sam Thompson faced this latter charge in Oxford.[86] The movement of the town fathers in Oxford to eliminate male "Mackerel" totally and limit female "Street Walkers" also seems to reflect this rising sentiment.

Episodic evidence suggests that all over the South in the 1880s men were policing men—not women—in sexual matters. It is as if men, even the "best" men, did not trust other men—or themselves—to behave responsibly in this realm. It appears, ironically, that, as a modicum of affluence returned to the South in the 1880s, as growth and modernity began to bestow benefits upon communities, anxieties about sexual matters also grew and with that a determination to enforce a new orthodoxy. It might be, even, that the shooting of Colonel Falkner in Ripley and the exoneration of his killer was the denouement of such an episode.

This broad-gauged emphasis on sex in the courts does not appear to have continued into the 1890s. However, there was one charge that seemed to increase in frequency in the 1890s and continued as prominent into the early twentieth century. That was incest. Charges of incest were not usually leveled at persons having sex with an adult relative, male or female, though such cases occurred—often when people, seemingly innocently, married near cousins or other close blood kin. Most incest seemed to involve men having sex with girls to whom they were connected by blood or marriage—stepdaughters, their own daughters, or nieces. A desire to punish bizarre or perverse sex also continued into the twentieth century. In Ripley, Jeffrey Long was secretly indicted by a grand jury that concluded that on January 13, 1906, he "did commit that detestable and abominable crime against nature by then and there having sexual intercourse with a certain beast, to wit, a cow."[87]

In Oxford in 1882, it seems that the general turbulence and ad hoc violence that had characterized the Civil War, Reconstruction, and Redemption, and in which Sam Thompson had thrived, would no longer be tolerated. Clearly, Sam was now in serious difficulty with the law. He was charged by the state with a criminal offense that bore weighty moral implications, and District Attorney Fant was determined to bring him to justice. If he were convicted he faced an active and demeaning prison term. Behind him staunchly stood his wife Elizabeth. At home with her was his daughter, Maggie, a girl only a year younger than Eudora. Most of all, by his repeated acts of violence and sex in his relations with Eudora and by his not being at all secretive in the process, there were plenty of witnesses to establish his guilt. Charlie Butler himself was among those witnesses and had been summoned to appear in court in the appeal process.[88] Without doubt, in early May, 1882, as well as on May 8, 1883, the day of the shooting, Charlie was very visible to Sam in and about the courthouse as a part of the public proceeding that would inexorably bring him to answer for his outrageous behavior.

As his crisis mounted in May, 1882, Sam Thompson shrewdly sought delay, and he got it. The court allowed him a "continuation" in both cases until the fall term, 1882, an indulgence granted "on account of sickness in the family of his sole counsel."[89] Sam seemed to do a lot of his own legal thinking and he did it well. In the fall, his strategy was to win still another postponement by pleading the absence of a large number of his key witnesses. The prosecution had a long list of witnesses, but Sam added significantly to the length of the whole list with his own. Somehow it happened during the fall when court was in session that many of his witnesses were absent and scattered in foreign parts. Repeatedly, the sheriff's deputies returned summonses to court with the endorsement "not found in my county after diligent search." Indeed, getting all of these people to court at the same time would have been a marvelous accomplishment in the orchestration of human behavior—even had they all been eager to be there. The witnesses included people both high and low. Among them were L.Q.C. Lamar, Jr., the son of the famous senator; various officers of the law; William Isom who had been indicted for forgery; Henry Vinegum, who had been indicted for assault and battery; and Mike O'Brien, the Irish-born, sometimes jailor who had been indicted, tried, and found not guilty of forgery; and half a dozen of the more racy young men about town.[90]

In November, 1882, Charles E. Butler was again summoned to court as a witness in Thompson's trial, but again a continuation was allowed on Thompson's affidavit that he could not yet secure the presence of his most important witnesses. These witnesses, he insisted, would "make his defense absolutely impregnable and overwhelming." This time, however, the judge pointedly declared that Thompson would come to trial at 10 A.M., Wednesday, May 9, 1883.[91]

One set of witnesses did show up for the scheduled November trial, and their appearance must have caused Sam Thompson some anxiety. Eudora, Louisa, and William Watkins were each paid $13.70 to travel 107 miles to Oxford, where they remained for two days until the motion to continue was granted. The current residence of the Watkins family was not recorded, but Jackson, Tennessee, was almost exactly 107 miles north of Oxford on the Illinois Central line. The Watkins family, however, did not appear for the May, 1883, term of court nor could they be found. A subpoena for the trio issued in March, 1883, for May 9 was endorsed by Deputy Sheriff John B. Roach in the usual way for absentees, "not found in my county after diligent search."[92] Meanwhile, the sheriff had been directed by the judge to take up and hold—that is, jail—Eudora Watkins should her whereabouts come to be known to him. One might well suspect that Sam had been cleverly at work again, and a bit more deftly than before, that dire threats had been made on the one side and that, on the other, money had been held out to convince the rather rootless Watkinses that prosperity for them lay elsewhere. But there was an even better reason for the disappearance of the Watkins family. It was that Eudora was herself under indictment.

On May 1, 1882, the same date of her last legally noticed abduction by Sam, Eudora was arrested for "carrying [a] deadly weapon—to wit—a Pistol." One can easily guess the use Eudora intended for her pistol, and one imagines that there was some public flourishing of that weapon by her on May Day, 1882, the date that Sam abducted her for the last time. Four days later the young woman was formally indicted by the grand jury for carrying a "concealed weapon" and a "deadly weapon."[93] With little to gain and much to lose by staying in touch with the authorities, the Watkins family probably took flight again, on this occasion leaving no forwarding address. Sam might, indeed, have encouraged Eudora's departure by threats and bribes, but even if he had, he had no assurance that the high-spirited and volatile Eudora would not be back—suddenly appearing in court to tell of her seduction and defilement by a man old enough to be her father. It was easily conceivable that Eudora might decide to avenge herself, and that no amount of persuasion or force could stop her.

Eve and the Apple

Thus, when Sam Thompson sat on the sidewalk on Tuesday afternoon, May 8, 1883, he was not uninterested in the fact that criminal court was in session in the building across the street and that at 10 o'clock the following morning his own name would be called. He was drinking heavily, and when Charlie Butler came out on the balcony to call H.M. Sullivan into court, it was not totally inappropriate that Sam should answer, perhaps at first with a sense of irony; and then, catching the bitter humor in his life at this juncture, begin to call himself to court in the ringing, sing-song style that ritual required. Perhaps he felt the weight of his failings, infidelity to an obviously fine and faithful wife with a girl only a year older than his teenage daughter Maggie. He had flaunted the community that had given him a home and a livelihood since the end of the war almost twenty years before. Perhaps, too, there was in his mind some sense that justice was about to be done to him by that community and that he deserved punishment. But as a rough and ready man, a Confederate cavalry trooper and Redeemer Democrat who most often had his way, he hated his feelings of powerlessness in the circumstances. It was understandable, too, that he should begin to lose humor at being ignored by a member of a family, the Sullivans, that had offered a steady opposition to his political power and influence, and that he turned suddenly surly, abusive, and violent.

Some insight into Sam's apprehension concerning his own vulnerability vis-à-vis the mercurial and redoubtable Eudora might be gained by looking closely at an affidavit filed by him with the court on November 14, 1882, as a part of his plea for a continuance. In this remarkable document he cast back to tell, with supposed candor, the whole story of his relationship with this young woman. Also he argued his innocence and demonstrated that the malefactor was really not himself but Eudora. In essence, it was she who seduced him.

It had all begun, he swore, in late February, 1881, when he, the "affiant" (as he referred to himself in the affidavit), "had only a slight acquaintance and no intimacy whatsoever" with Eudora. She was brought to his office one day by potential witness William Bracely. She had remained there after Bracely left and "immediately made herself at home and familiar." She told him "about having just returned from a visit to a lady who had prayed for her and expressed her wonder and curiosity to know if the lady knew what a wicked little soul she, said Watkins, was at that very time, and had been always before, and [what] she would think and say if she had known it at the time she was praying & singing for her."

Sam was busy during Eudora's visit, but he showed the girl the type, press, and other effects of his business at which she seemed pleased. She followed him into the back room, still talking with great animation and telling Sam that she was badly treated at home. Sam came out for a few minutes, working in front of the shop and leaving Eudora in the back room. Returning, he shut the door.

Telling the story well, almost cinematically, Sam shifted the camera eye, dissolving one scene, pausing, and bringing up another. When the witness Bracely "next saw them, Eudora had her arms around his neck and her head resting on his shoulder and breast, her eyes closed and she standing on some books and her back against the wall." Subsequently, Bracely saw Eudora "coming and going at her pleasure and on terms of intimacy and familiarity with him and always apparently in a gay and pleasant humor." Sam was angry with Bracely "for discovering him & said Eudora in said back room and threatened him with death if witness should ever tell of it." Bracely would also testify in court that soon after their first encounter Eudora went with Sam to the Mardi Gras in Memphis, in company with a party that included Bracely.

After Memphis, the affidavit continued, Eudora went on to Kentucky. Returning by train to Oxford in the fall (some nine months later), she had telegraphed Sam to meet her at the depot on November 2 at 9 P.M. A second missing witness, James ("Jimmie") Gillespie had gotten the telegram but failed to deliver it for several days. Meanwhile, Eudora arrived. Not finding Sam at the train station, she went to a private house, not her father's. Eudora was offended by Sam's not meeting her and sent word for him "to meet her alone next morning at a certain bridge." Sam was apprehensive about such a meeting and, instead of going to the rendezvous himself, sent his servant, Julia Avent, to tell Eudora to come to the newspaper office. Before they arrived, Sam, still worried about being discovered, had gone out to find the two women. Failing, he returned to his office and was seen about the streets of the town for several hours. Actually, Julia and Eudora had gone to Julia's house. Soon, however, Sam and Eudora managed to meet, and witness Jimmie Gillespie would testify that subsequently Eudora often came to the office and remained about him "at various times and places," that "she was always free to go away and stay away from him if she had chosen to do so, and that her conduct was uniformly that of a loose woman."

At this point Sam's story took a new and surprising turn. He began to depict himself as a veritable saint in his efforts to reform the wayward Eudora. Frequently, she had said that she "would not stay with her parents, said she would cut her own throat first, and gave as her reason that her step mother, Mrs. Louisa Watkins had sexual intercourse with other men, both black and white." Sam—as savior—spared no effort in his attempts to relocate Eudora in a proper moral environment. Jimmie Gillespie would testify that he went with Sam when Sam succeeded in placing Eudora in "a respectable house in the country." Eudora, however, refused the reform and soon returned to town to be with Sam. Presumably, she stayed at Julia's upon her return.

Still another witness was Austin Bramlett—young, male, and also absent. Whenever he could be found, he would testify that Eudora stayed at Julia's entirely of her own free will and would "fully corroborate said Gillespie as to said Eudora's loose manners." Austin would also swear that Sam had often begged Eudora to leave him, "reform and abandon her evil ways, and have nothing to do with him or any other man until she should be lawfully and honorably married." It was his ambition for Eudora, Sam swore, that she should become a school teacher in some place "where she was not known."

Two other absentee witnesses, Winter and Moore, would testify that "instead of attempting to mislead or abduct a virtuous woman," Sam "had rather become interested in a bad one, and tried to induce her to abandon her evil course and reform and become a decent and useful woman." Sam insisted that he had done "all that was in his power to aid her in a total and complete reform." Indeed, he had made Moore promise to "travel through the country and get up a school for said Eudora to teach small children in a neighborhood where she could be respected and properly cared for by good people, and be useful."

Sam argued that "the manifest honesty and integrity" of his witnesses on the stand would prove his innocence. He expected "to have them all present" at the next term of court "if continuance be allowed."[94] On Monday, May 8, 1883, the next court began its session, and it is reasonable to doubt both that Sam Thompson himself believed his own story and that his witnesses would in fact appear and prove creditable. Indeed, William Bracely, the young man who had originally introduced him to Eudora, was then under indictment for murder and his usefulness to the defense substantially impaired.[95] Sam's was an old and venerable story, of course, as old as the Garden of Eden, but in this case the judge and jury might well ask who, after all, fed whom the apple.

Out of the Garden

On Tuesday, the second day of the first week of court in May, 1883, Sam Thompson sat drunk and musing on the sidewalk in front of the hotel (ironically the site of the old Butler Hotel) on the north side of the square facing the courthouse. Tradition required that the bailiff, now Charlie Butler, appear from time to time on the second story balcony to call citizens into the building to have justice done. Charlie, in Sam's mind, was rightly identified with the opposition who, Elizabeth would soon say, were using a personal difficulty to gain political advantage.

Oxford mayor Patton B. Murry was, indeed, a leader in a group opposed to Sam Thompson, and as mayor he was Charlie's immediate supervisor. On Monday evening, May 7, Charlie had attended the regular monthly meeting of the town board that received the "melancholy intelligence of the death of Patton B [.] Murry, mayor of the City of Oxford."[96] The mayor, apparently, had died of natural causes the previous week. Patton Murry, of course, had first sentenced Thompson. He owned and edited the rival paper, the *Oxford Falcon,* and Charlie Butler was the police officer for his court. In that capacity, Charlie had acted in the Watkins case. One month before he stood on the balcony and watched Sam on the square below, Charlie had been served a summons by Deputy Sheriff John B. Roach to appear in court on Wednesday, May 9, as a prosecution witness in the Sam Thompson trial. Charlie had arrested Sam several times before, arrests that Sam had not accepted at all gracefully. Sam's proclivity for public drunkenness, pistol wielding, and loose and violent language was notorious. But Sam saw his arrests as harassment motivated by politics.

Compared with many parts of America, Mississippi in the late 1800s was a very violent place and Oxford was no exception to the rule. Even so, the official record of Sam's transgressions in this respect leaves him outstanding among the town's citizens. The docket of the circuit court exhibits a clear trail. His violation of the public peace gained judicial notice at least as early as 1867. In the last half of the next decade, however, he seemed to be steadily at odds with the law. In the October term of court in 1875 Sam was charged with the unlawful exhibition of a weapon. The case was "nolle prossed" (canceled by the prosecution) on the condition that he pay court costs. In the November term of 1876 he was charged with "assault with intent to kill and murder." That case was continued to the May term, 1877, and again to the November term of that year when the charge was reduced to "Exhibition of a deadly weapon." In the trial, the jury found a verdict of "not guilty," despite the efforts of District Attorney James Fant. Meanwhile, in the May term, 1877, he was charged with another instance of assault and battery and exhibition of a weapon. This case was "dismissed on payment of costs." In November, 1878, Sam was in court yet again, charged now with "Shooting at with intent to kill and carrying concealed weapons." The case was continued until the May term, 1879, when he was again found "not guilty."[97] Thereafter, Sam seems to have retired from the legal lists until, in January, 1882, he reentered the fray at full tilt. This time he met Eudora Watkins.

Sam's violence stood out because of its continuous nature. But sometimes he was in good company, including, interestingly, the mayor himself, Patton B. Murry. Murry was charged in November, 1878, with "Shooting with intent to kill and carrying concealed weapons." In May of 1880 he was indicted for carrying concealed weapons and exhibiting a weapon in a "rude, angry, and threatening manner." All charges against Murry were dismissed, but it is likely that the object of the mayor's bellicosity was Sam Thompson.[98]

Murry's lawyer in these cases was William V. Sullivan, who would also become Charlie Butler's lawyer. William Van Amberg Sullivan, mentioned previously as rejected for membership by the Masons, was a young attorney in the firm of Sullivan and Sullivan. He had entered the University of Mississippi as a new student in 1872 and proceeded to Vanderbilt University to take his degree in law. In 1880 he was twenty-four, and he and his wife Belle lived as boarders in someone else's house. He was on the rise and would become one of the leading lawyers in the county. Later, in 1896, he was elected to the United States House of Representatives and thereafter by appointment of the governor and a subsequent election served in the U.S. Senate until 1901. In the end, the monument of his wife, who died in 1895, would stand high in the town cemetery—rivaling, for examples, those of Augustus B. Longstreet and J.W.T. Falkner.[99] At the time of the shooting of Sam Thompson, William Sullivan was in the courthouse working to defend a man named William Turnage against a murder charge. He had just caused H.M. Sullivan to be called as a witness.[100]

When Eliza Thompson asserted that Charles E. Butler "was encouraged by persons of vastly more respectable standing in society than himself," she was referring to a faction that had considerable local power and included Murry and the Sullivans. On the other side, the Thompsons promoted an opposition. In the *Eagle,* on May 3, Sam endorsed Captain William Thompson (no relation to himself) for mayor, taking prompt advantage of Murry's sudden and unexpected death. William Thompson was a sixty-five-year-old businessman and the younger brother of Jacob Thompson, the leading citizen of the town in the antebellum era. In by-gone years, Sam had been a political supporter and a personal favorite of Jacob.[101] On the day of his killing, Sam had chosen to be drunk on the sidewalk in front of the hotel at least partly owned by the Thompsons and known as the Thompson House.

Sam and Eliza Thompson were also very closely allied with the Phipps family. The Phippses were wealthy planters, ex-slaveholders, and lawyers. In 1870, the elder Phipps was a "farmer" with vast holdings ($62,000 worth of real estate), and both of his sons were middle-aged lawyers. One son, J.M. Phipps, was Sam's attorney, and after Sam's death Eliza made the other son, Colonel Richard W. Phipps, the political editor of the *Eagle.* Richard Phipps had begun the war early as the first lieutenant of the Avant Southerners. He fought all through the war with the Army of Northern Virginia in the Nineteenth Mississippi Infantry, for a time under L.Q.C. Lamar as its colonel. "Dick" Phipps, himself, ended the war as the colonel of the Nineteenth. In Reconstruction he was an ardent opponent of the Republican regime and head of the Ku Klux Klan in Lafayette County. The Klan in Lafayette carried out a well concerted and very effective campaign of intimidation and violence—primarily whippings. Sam Thompson seems to have been a particular leader in these, as well as in editorial assaults against the Republicans. Interestingly, and revealingly, his journalistic opponent on the Republican side was his brother, Victor Thompson, sometimes editor of the *Ricochette* and thus a "scalawag."[102] To some extent, the division after 1875 seemed to be between "Red-hot" Redeemers and those Democrats who had been more moderate.

In the contest between factions in the town, Charlie Butler was indeed on the Murry-Sullivan side, but Eliza exaggerated. In arresting Sam, Charlie was not acting solely as a political partisan and on a grudge. He was bound to arrest Sam or himself face charges of dereliction of duty. The law made him liable to criminal action if he failed to make an attempt to arrest a man blatantly drunk on the streets. He had seen enough and heard enough on the square below to excuse himself from the court room, seek out, and arrest Sam. He had arrested Sam a number of times before. What was different this time was that the Eudora Watkins case was coming to a crucial juncture. No longer were men simply playing at the masculine game of pointing guns at one another and, now and again, letting a bullet fly. Thus far, no wound had been inflicted in a game of manly challenge and response—no male body had been penetrated. Rather, Sam's extravagance, his boisterous and bullying behavior now involved a young woman to whom he was not married. The state of Mississippi could *nol-pros* and dismiss cases involving only men and pistols, and juries could render verdicts of not guilty in affrays that involved, after all, consenting adult males. But the repeated abduction, seduction, and "defiling" of a teenage girl—sometimes in the home of a black woman—could not be forgiven. It mattered not that Eudora apparently had a large sexual appetite, that she was flirtatious, and even meretricious. Indeed, her weaknesses made matters worse because Sam's responsibility in the case was thus increased—if he were in fact truly a man and a gentleman.

Sam sensed the depth of his new difficulty, and hence the desperate, outrageous, even ridiculous statement he had given to the court, and, consequently, for the public record. According to his own account, he had had sex repeatedly with the wild and often willing, always provocative, even exotic Eudora. He had thus not only taken advantage of an obviously disturbed, distressed, and vulnerable young woman not yet out of her teens, he had also defiled his own house where dwelt a wife so faithful that she stood by him even in this crisis—which was in itself an insult to her fidelity to him and to her own ladyhood as well as to the younger lady who was his own daughter. All of this from a man who had been a soldier in the Confederate States Army and the owner and editor of a prominent newspaper. On one level, he had refused to be bridled by the reins at which other men strained. On another, he must be punished by them for doing what they had abstained from doing. If there was any man who "needed killing" in Lafayette County on May 8, 1883, it was Sam Thompson.

Upstairs in the courthouse, the murderer Turnage would get off with two years in the state penitentiary.[103] On the square below, Sam would get a bullet through the heart. The crisis would be reached, and he would die with scores of men looking on. His executioner would be a thirty-three-year-old town marshal with a half dozen years of experience as a police officer and the eldest surviving male of a founding family in the community. Interestingly, Sam Thompson, a Confederate veteran, was killed by a man who had been—just barely too young to be a soldier in the war. More interestingly, Charlie Butler in this case—in enforcing the law in the name of the community—was defending a young woman who had not herself asked to be defended, had perhaps not even wanted to be defended, and, indeed, was no longer there in her person to be defended. Taking account of the fact that on May 1, 1882, Eudora Watkins was carrying her own gun, it seems that this spirited young woman felt fully prepared to defend herself. Yet, after all is said and done, it might be that Charlie Butler killed a man who was asking to be killed.

During and after Reconstruction, Sam was usually referred to as "Captain Sam Thompson," and it was understood that he was a cavalry officer, presumably a rather daring and dashing one. A search through records of veterans of Confederate cavalry from Mississippi reveals no Captain Sam M. Thompson. Indeed, there appears to have been only one Mississippi veteran in any branch named S.M. Thompson. This one enlisted in Company B of the First Mississippi Cavalry at Purdy, Tennessee, on April 15, 1862—just after the battle of Shiloh. Company B had, indeed, been organized in Oxford by Oxfordian Andrew J. Bowles on April 24, 1861, two weeks after the first shots of the war had been fired on Fort Sumter in Charleston Harbor. It was filled with Lafayette County men, including such staunch warriors as Herman Wohlleben who had distinguished himself for heroism in Forrest's raid on Holly Springs in 1862, whose record indicated that he was "Wounded severely" in the leg in the fall of 1864, and who finally laid down his weapons at Citronella, Alabama, on May 4, 1865. Private S.M. Thompson, in contrast, lasted hardly a year before being dropped from the roll by General Van Dorn "for absence without leave."[104]

If Sam had gone to jail, either quietly or noisily, there would have been no shooting. If he had not grabbed Charlie somewhere—sleeve, lapel, or throat—and refused to let go, there would have been no shooting. If he had not been so large a man with the clear potential of overpowering the arresting officer, again there would have been no shooting. But he did resist, and he did grab hold of the officer. He had sworn never to be arrested by Charlie again, and he was known to carry concealed weapons and subsequently exhibit those in a "rude and threatening" manner. In truth, anyone who knew the history would agree that there was grave danger that Sam might take his left hand from Charlie's person and pull a gun out of his pocket before Charlie could secure his own gun. From all appearances, Charlie was *in extremis.*

Later, in his trial, Charlie attempted to establish that he had called on the several score watching men generally for help and no one had stepped forward. Then he called William O. Beanland by name. Probably, he singled out William because he was a strong young man in his early twenties, and possibly because he was a Mason. William's father, William Garner Beanland, had soldiered with Charlie's brother, Henry, during the war, had been Charlie's business partner a decade before, and was a fellow Mason. Indeed, W.G. Beanland was a member of the committee appointed to investigate Charlie's character when he was admitted to the Order. Later, Beanland was Vice Dictator of the Lodge while Charlie was Sentinel.[105] It might well be that one Mason in distress called upon another for assistance and the assistance could not be refused. Undeniably, Charlie called by name upon the son of his friend and fellow Mason for assistance, and the son responded promptly and effectively when scores of other men present would not.

Given the fact that Sam's arrest was an event fraught with danger, Charlie showed amazing restraint. Assuming that Sam had a gun in his pocket as usual, Charlie was admirably cool in circumstances in which his life was in jeopardy. He hoped, probably, that Sam would come along quietly. He had first raised his gun to Sam's heart and then lowered it when the act had no effect. He seemed almost sad at the duty that then rose before him. He raised the gun again, and the line was drawn. When Sam cried—as trial records indicate—so that all could hear him, "Shoot you house-burning son-of-a-bitch," it might have been that Charlie Butler, a man among men, felt that he had no choice. He did what had to be done. He pulled the trigger.

Why Sam Thompson should have accused Charlie of house burning remains a mystery. Regardless of specifics, it was a highly insulting charge for one man to make against another. Arson—house burning, and barn burning too—was particularly the crime of the powerless, of slaves, "niggers," and poor whites, of sneaks and cowards. Arson was, indeed, a "mean advantage" that "a brave man" would not take.

Charlie's Trial

On the day following the shooting, Charles Butler was indicted for manslaughter.[106] His bond, posted on May 10, virtually constituted a poll of eminent men in his favor. Set at $2,500 it was supplied by more than a score of prominent persons in the community, including John Kimmons, the new mayor; Washington

Porter Wilkins, Confederate captain, livery stable owner, and one of the most respected businessmen in town (whose son would marry William Faulkner's aunt); Charles Bowen Howry, son of a leading jurist, Confederate officer, and lawyer; both of the lawyers Sullivan; Francis Marion Stowers, the rising young dry goods merchant and future alderman; and Charlie's fellow deputy sheriff, John B. Roach.[107] A goodly portion of the respectable manhood of Oxford was supporting Charlie's defense. Further, Charlie had friends in the courthouse. Fellow Mason, W.E. Andrews had been a young grocery clerk in 1870, but in 1883 he was clerk of court, a position he ably filled for many years.[108] On May 11, Charles Butler asked for a continuance to prepare his defense and it was granted.[109]

The town minutes indicate that Charles Butler continued to perform his duties as town marshal without interruption after the shooting of Sam Thompson. A day before the shooting the board had allowed him credit for some $220 for paying street hands and keeping the town mule. In September, 1883, he commenced building a plank walk from "Miss Eades' residence to the plank walk in front of W.L. Archebald's residence." In November, the circuit court granted him a second continuance on the ground that his key witness, W.O. Beanland, was away and could not be reached. Beanland was a "drummer" (a traveling salesman) for a business house based in St. Louis. If present, it was argued that Beanland would testify that "Thompson was resisting and choking affiant and after affiant had called for help and assistance and no one would come to his assistance he called specially for said Beanland."[110] Later, Beanland swore that he was sick in bed in an Alabama town in November and hence missed that court date. Meanwhile, in December, 1883, Kimmons was reelected mayor, and Charlie's friends W.E. Andrews and W.V. Sullivan were elected to the town board. On January 7, 1884, Charles was reelected by the board for another two-year term as town marshal.[111]

In May, 1884, a jury was impaneled and Charles Butler's case came to trial. We do not have a verbatim record of the trial, but we can surmise the character of his defense from documents filed with the clerk of court by his lawyers. Procedures allowed lawyers for both the defense and prosecution to submit to the court drafts of "charges," that is, instructions as to the limits of the law to be given by the judge to the jury just before it retired to deliberate. The judge might use one of these or write his own. Charlie's lawyer, again William V. Sullivan, submitted several such statements, attempting to find one that was acceptable to the judge and would combine facts and law in a way to promote a verdict of not guilty for his client. In these, the lawyer stressed that Butler was an officer of the law bound to do his duty or face charges himself, that Thompson was resisting arrest, and that he had previously threatened to kill Butler if Butler ever tried to arrest him again. In one charge drafted by Sullivan, he would have the judge say to the jury that "Thompson was physically a large strong man and at the time of the killing was seizing Butler by his throat." The judge refused to give any of these charges, and, apparently, himself wrote one that gave the marshal no favors.[112] Even so, the defense was successful. On the back of the indictment itself, wrapped around all relevant documents and bound with a string was written the foreman's conclusion: "We the Jury find the Defendant Not Guilty."[113] A year before, in the docket book, the clerk of court made a final entry in the case of *The State* vs. *Samuel M. Thompson* regarding Eudora Watkins. "Abated by death of defendant," he wrote.[114] Abated, indeed.

FOUR

Flight

After his trial, life quickened for both Charlie and Oxford. In the middle 1880s the town grew apace, established its own school system, and provided more and more material amenities to improve the quality of life of its citizens. The federal government decided to construct a large new building on the square to house its post office and the headquarters of its district court for northern Mississippi. Charlie Butler, as *de facto* town manager, would have important roles to play in all these things.

Such improvements reflected the general prosperity of the period, the happiest time, really, since the Civil War, not only for Oxford, but for the South as a whole. The economic outlook was sanguine, and there were clear signs that the South was again joining the Union. In November, 1884, Grover Cleveland was elected president and took office in March, 1885, the first Democrat in the White House since 1861. Cleveland was anxious to signal the reengagement of the South in the nation, and his eagerness led his thoughts straight to Oxford, Mississippi. He offered the post of secretary of interior in his cabinet to Lucius Quintus Cincinnatus Lamar.

During Reconstruction and after, Lamar was Oxford's most eminent citizen. He had come to the town as a young man, taught in the university, and practiced law. He married the daughter of the president of the university, Augustus Baldwin Longstreet, and in the late 1850s was tapped by Jacob Thompson to represent the district in Congress. He was a Confederate colonel and diplomat, and the Redemption senator from Mississippi at the close of Reconstruction.[1] Conservative, learned in the classical style, and gentlemanly, he came to be in the eyes of many Americans the personification of a safe and sane South—beyond rebellion.

Ironically, in the early 1880s Lamar had seen himself at the end of his political life. In Washington, he felt intense animosity from such Republicans as Senator Henry W. Blair of New Hampshire, whom he called a "South-hater" and a "half crazy old man."[2] All during the decade, Blair menaced the South with a very strong bill that promised to improve the educational opportunities of black children and enhance their competitive capacities in economic and political life. In May, 1882, Lamar confided to a Vicksburg friend that he felt ill and tired. His wife was seriously ill. He had often absented himself from the Senate to be with her and seldom spoke when he was on the floor, derelictions that he feared would "excite comments." His wife, Virginia, he declared, "wants me all the time, (I am writing this in the intervals of her fitful and troubled sleep.) and cannot bear for me to leave her." Mrs. Lamar, apparently, had tuberculosis. "Dr. Isom says he is sure the tubercles which once were upon her lungs have formed upon her brain." Lamar disagreed with the diagnosis, but despaired of her life and his political future.[3]

While Senator Lamar nursed his wife on North Fourteenth Street in May, 1882, Charlie Butler was buying such things as axle grease and horse collars for the town, Eudora Watkins was packing a pistol, court was getting under way on the square, and Sam Thompson was busy trying to delay trial for his multiple transgressions. Virginia was still ill when Charlie shot Sam downtown on the square a year later, and she died in the year of Charlie's trial, 1884. Lamar's spirits rose rapidly in early March, 1885, when he learned with genuine surprise of his nomination for a cabinet post, and soared in the middle of the month with his quick confirmation by the Senate.[4] Interestingly, the previous Southern Democrat to hold cabinet rank was his fellow townsman in earlier years, Jacob Thompson, who had also been secretary of the interior. Lamar would end his political life in the 1890s as an associate justice of the Supreme Court.[5] Decades later, Oxford would honor him by taking his name for its main street. The town was fond of Lamar, at once a man among men but given to romantic sentiments. The Daughters of the American Revolution in their 1922 history of the county recalled that one might see him leaning on his fence, "his face long, massive, and sallow; bareheaded, his long brown hair stirred up by the breeze; his deep mysterious eyes fixed on the yellowing western sky."[6]

In the 1880s, Oxford's leading industry, the university, was also rising and flourishing. Town and gown got along well together in Oxford. The dozen or so faculty members at the university could not be very aloof, either from the town or from their several hundred very active students. The classical curriculum was still in vogue and oratory in the style of the Greeks and Romans was highly valued. One of the most prestigious student organizations on the campus was the Hermaean, a debating society. In October, 1887, student Dunbar Rowland, later the organizing genius of the state archives, was elected president. One of the duties of his office was to declare the winner of debates on such questions as: "Resolved that the laboring classes are justifiable in combining themselves into secret organizations to protect their interests against capital," and "Resolved that the North American Indians have been treated unfairly." In both cases, President Rowland announced victory for the negative. Lamentably, the debaters were not always prepared. On one such occasion, student Eddie Cross Gilliland, later a successful merchant in Memphis, supplied the deficiency by debating both sides of a question—extemporaneously. On December 17, 1887, just as the Hermaeans at Ole Miss were deciding that the Native Americans had nothing substantial to complain about, Charlie Butler in town was about to announce his complaint about the course of his life in a very dramatic way.[7]

Charlie After Acquittal

Shortly after his acquittal in criminal court in the spring of 1884, Charles Butler by his own initiative came into civil court in connection with the settlement of the estates left by his father and mother. In 1879, more than a year after his mother died, it seems that there was real property still remaining in his father's estate that needed to be sold off. In April, Charlie appeared in court asking for "letters of administration" to sell those lands and divide the proceeds. The chancellor of the civil court granted the letters. John W. McLeod, then sheriff, and Washington Porter Wilkins agreed to go bond for Charlie in these proceedings to the extent of $350 each. In the November term, 1884, Charlie was cited to appear in court to show cause as to why he had not made annual reports of his trust. In court during the following April, he testified that there were "no assets whatever" to administer and hence no annual report. The chancellor thereupon accepted the surrender of his letters of administration.[8]

In reality, there were assets to administer, but Charlie had not sold the land. Apparently moved by the summons to court, he now acted to settle the estates of both his mother and father. On December 14, 1884, he had his lawyers, Sullivan and Sullivan, draw up a document, a "bill for partition," that would put in motion a legal process by which the estates of his father, consisting of 125 acres immediately northeast of Oxford, and of his mother, consisting of 23 acres in or very close to the northeastern portion of town, would be sold and the proceeds divided among thirteen surviving heirs. The real difficulty was that five of the heirs were either in Texas or other parts of Mississippi and a process had to be commenced to secure their legal, if not bodily, presence in court. On the 19th, his lawyers filed the proper document (technically a "complaint" against the absent parties) pursuant to the sale of property belonging to the two estates. On January 2, 1885, Butler certified to the court the truth of the statements in the document. At least one of the statements he made was not true—that his father did not "make any will." Actually, his father's will, made in 1855, was on file in the chancery clerk's office. Indeed, in his petition for letters of administration sworn to and filed in 1879, Charles Butler had mentioned his father's "leaving a last will and testament." In January, 1885, the clerk of the chancery court ran advertisements in four successive weekly editions of the *Oxford Falcon* summoning the absent parties to the March term of court. In the April term those persons, though still absent, were deemed as if in court, and the judge ordered the public sale of these lands and division of the proceeds by a commissioner, to which office he appointed the clerk, J.F. Brown. Early in 1886 Commissioner Brown advertised his intent to sell the land at the courthouse door and did so on September 27. He made that sale for $150, the purchaser "paying his bid in full in cash." The buyer was Charles E. Butler.

Thus, Charlie acquired the 148 acres remaining in his parents' estates for about $1 an acre. There could be no argument that the sale was not legal, but Charlie had made a noble bargain for himself—perhaps at the expense of his relatives. The 125 acres belonging to his father had been valued, apparently, at six to seven hundred dollars seven years before. In October, Chancellor B.F. Kimbrough ruled that "the property sold for a fair & reasonable price" and ordered execution of a deed of conveyance to the buyer, after paying costs and a "reasonable attorney's fee to W.V. Sullivan."

In the packet of papers in the clerk's office relating to this case, there is a receipt written by C.E. Butler on August 23, 1887, for $85 for the payment in full of the burial expenses of his mother. The receipt is signed by M.J. Nelson, his sister "Mattie" (Martha), who had probably advanced money for the burial a decade before. Also in the packet is a receipt for $25.40 given on September 3, 1887, by Butler himself to the estates of his parents for partial payment of the amount the estates owed to him. Having paid $85 for the burial of Burlina, and probably having paid $29.60 for the cost of selling the land and attorney's fees, that $25.40 was nearly all that was left of the $150 for which the land was sold. The relevant papers were filed with the clerk of chancery court by Charlie on September 3, 1887. Thus, on that date the estate was settled, and the business concluded with Charlie in possession of 148 acres of land north and east of the town square.[9]

~

In pursuit of his duties as town marshal Charlie Butler's heart hardly skipped a beat in the aftermath of the killing of Sam Thompson. Indeed, in the mid-1880s his work as town manager escalated considerably. In October, 1883, he rented an office for a year from which he administered his increasingly important duties. In addition to his work as tax collector, he was purchasing agent, engineer, disbursing officer, and general manager for a host of other town functions. In 1884 Oxford began preparations to enter the public school business, taking responsibility for that activity away from the county. The town secured permission from the legislature to issue bonds up to $10,000 in amount for the construction of educational facilities and levied a substantial school tax on property holders that was earmarked specially for education. Thereafter, Charlie collected the school tax along with the regular tax, a considerable addition to the amount of money that passed through his hands. In November, 1884, he was designated the town's agent to pay the builders of the new public schoolhouse $1,500 directly out of school taxes collected by him when he judged portions of the work properly completed. In December, $750 was added to that amount. By this time, apparently, the accounts of the marshal were becoming so complicated that he was allowed $86 for the hire of a bookkeeper for the first ten months of 1884. In 1885, he was the officer assigned by the town to negotiate with the supervisor of construction of the new three-story, red-brick federal building going up on the northeast corner of the square—the building that now serves as Town Hall. In September he was empowered to borrow $190 in the name of the town, in this case to purchase bricks probably to be used for paving. In the same month, he was one of the five trustees of the Oxford White Male Academy empowered to sell the land upon which the town's black school was located as a part of the process of creating a general public school system.[10]

In January, 1886, Charles Butler was the only candidate for marshal and was unanimously reelected. Of the six aldermen chosen in the elections in the previous December, only his lawyer, W.V. Sullivan, was reelected. But also joining the board was fellow Mason Henry Herman Wohlleben, now a man of about fifty. By the mid-1880s, Henry was no longer a blacksmith. He was a traveling agent for a wire manufacturer, the Hedge Fence Company, doing well financially, and, judging by the notices the local press gave his five daughters, socially too.[11]

All officers in Mississippi who handled public funds had to have bonds covering the amount of money handled. Charles Butler's bond as marshal was fixed at $5,000 and made. The marshal's salary was set at $600 a year, where it had been since he took office, but his commission for collecting taxes was reduced from 5 to 3 percent, probably because the school tax had been added, and the dollar amount of collections was expected to increase considerably with no significant increase of effort on the part of the collector. Still, the adjustment should have left the collector even because the school tax was put at 4 mills out of a total of 10 mills (1 percent) assessed by the town.[12]

Apparently, the board was slowly coming to the realization that a much closer accounting of funds was needed. In April, 1886, it accepted a committee report reviewing and approving the accounts of the marshal and treasurer for 1884 and 1885, and in May the board approved $755 paid out by Butler for street work. However, in the next month they ordered the marshal to "render unto this board a monthly account showing the number of hands employed by the corporation in the streets and for any purpose whatever with the amount paid to each accompanied with the voucher therefor." Those accounts would be referred to a special committee that would report to the full board the results of its review the following month.[13]

In September, 1886, the month in which Charlie Butler bought the family estates, the marshal-as-town-manager drew down a very responsible assignment. William Jenkins had finished construction of the new school, but demanded more money than the board thought reasonable. The board refused to pay, and Jenkins refused to give up the keys to the building. Finally, the board directed the marshal and the town treasurer to make up a package of $2,000 in cash and take it to Jenkins as an offer of final settlement. If he failed to accept the money and surrender the keys, the marshal was to proceed to the school, force the locks, install new locks, and take possession of the building. Apparently Jenkins refused the offer, the marshal seized the building, and the town shortly found itself in court facing suit by Jenkins. The town retained lawyer Charles Howry and his new partner, J.W.T. Falkner, to represent their case at the cost of some $500.[14]

The year 1887 was to be critical in Charlie Butler's life, but it began in almost humdrum style. Every month he was paid his $50 salary, plus $10 for keeping the corporation mule. In February he was ordered to effect the removal of all "backhouses and privies" in the alley north of the square as nuisances. Things stirred a bit in April when the town of Oxford was sued for "trespass" by Vermelle J. Butler, the widow of Charlie's brother, Henry. So important was this case that the board again felt compelled to hire Howry and Falkner to represent their interest at the cost of another $500. The case would continue for three years before the town emerged victorious. Ole Miss law professor Edward Mayes, who had married a daughter of L.Q.C. Lamar, represented Vermelle. In the same meeting, the board showed some sort of pique by declaring that the marshal and others paid by the board held office "only at the pleasure of the board."[15] All during the summer Charlie was working on the streets and sidewalks, buying pipe for drains, erecting lamp posts and burners for lighting the town at night. At its meeting on September 2, the board voted to levy a 10 mill tax (1 percent) for the year and ordered the marshal to collect all taxes by November 1, 1887, or else commence the process of collecting by "distress." Toward the end of each month the marshal, as usual, took his salary and fee for boarding the town mule. In a November 25 meeting, the board ordered town elections for the first Monday in December. These were held in the usual fashion with the usual results, that is, the turning out of most or all of the old aldermen and the installation of a new set. When the aldermen next convened on Friday, December 30, 1887, they "ordered that H.H. Walton & Charles Roberts be appointed a committee to examine and report on the condition of the books of C.E. Butler City Marshall [sic]."[16] When the board met again on Monday,

January 2, it decided to "proceed at once" to elect a town marshal. They chose J.J. Quarles, not Charles E. Butler.[17]

At 3:00 P.M. on January 12, when the board assembled for a "called" meeting, it became clear why it had suddenly decided to look at the marshal's books and promptly elected a new man to that office. That meeting was summoned, as the town secretary recorded in his usual abbreviated style, "for the purpose of hearing report of committee to audit Books of C.E. Butler absconding marshall."[18] The key word was "absconding." Charlie Butler was gone, and with him a substantial amount of the town's money.

~

The committee of two appointed to examine the marshal's accounts was blue ribbon and signified the board's belief that the marshal in his flight had taken much of Oxford's money with him. Probably, he had left town about Christmas, 1887. His timing was very nearly perfect to maximize the amount of cash he could take and the amount of time he would have to make good his escape before the authorities rallied. During November and December he had been completing the collection of town taxes for the year 1887. With the new school tax now added to the regular tax, the total amount of money passing into the marshal's hands in this season probably came to something more than $5,000. Small wonder that the new board should be agitated, and that they should now commission two practiced accountants to audit the marshal's books. One of these, Charles Roberts, was the owner of the local bookstore and a number of other enterprises. An Englishman by birth and a prewar settler, he had married a local girl, had two children, then enlisted as a private in the Confederate army where he exhibited such logistical and accounting genius that supply officers would pay him out of their own pockets to put their accounts in order. After the war, he became not only one of the most successful businessmen in town, but also one of the wealthiest and most respected. Appointed with Roberts was thirty-seven-year-old Bem Price, the cashier of the Bank of Oxford.[19] Price was the son of one of the richest men in Lafayette County before the war, and already Bem himself was becoming the richest man in postwar Oxford. Soon he would buy "Edgemont," an impressive estate on the northern edge of the village, and develop the mansion for himself and the grounds for the construction of saleable houses. The mansion still stands on North Lamar.

For about two weeks, the town board exuded an air of disbelief at Marshal Butler's defection. By January 12, however, they had accepted Charlie's departure as final, and, apparently, turned to an attempt to establish how much money went with him. Butler was, of course, bonded, and the board at first proceeded in a spirit of cooperation with the bondsmen. In the January 2 meeting they had even agreed to allow the bondsmen until January 20 to collect as much as they could of taxes still unpaid. The assumption at this point seemed to be that the bondsmen were simply responsible for the whole amount of taxes owed the town, not merely the part taken by the "absconding" marshal. However, it did occur to the board that the marshal might also have stolen money from the tax collections of the previous year. In the January 12 meeting, a bondsman of Butler's was voted permission to hold the marshal's books "for a period sufficient to review the record of 86."[20]

Gradually, it became clear that the real difficulty lay in determining just how much of the town's money Charlie had carried away. The problem, again, sprang from the hip-pocket style in which the marshal conducted the town's finances. In relation to taxes, auditors would simply have to call on each taxpayer to determine who had paid and how much. Presumably those who had paid would have been wise enough to get a receipt and careful enough to have preserved it. The town board itself, rather belatedly, on February 6, ordered the new marshal to make the rounds of persons doing business in Oxford and collect license fees (another source of revenue for the town) from those who could not show a receipt for having previously paid. At the same meeting, the board voted specially to credit one citizen with having paid $5 to Marshal Butler for which, apparently, he possessed no receipt.[21] There was no way, ultimately, to account totally for the dollars that the marshal might or might not have spent in paying workers and buying materials.

Recognizing the depth of their problem more fully now, the board paid Roberts and Price $50 for a thorough audit of Butler's books. In addition, they asked that the auditors confer with Butler's bondsmen "to determine the amount, if any, that is due the corporation and report to the board at its next meeting to be held February 9, 1888 at 7 P.M."[22] "If any" was probably simply a circumspect use of language. As time passed, it became increasingly clear that the bondsmen were not eager to honor their obligation, and their reluctance seemed to arise from the fact that the auditors were concluding that Charlie had departed Oxford with a shockingly large amount of town money. The report was not ready for the meeting of the 9th, nor for another on the 13th, nor for two more sessions on February 14 and March 7. In the latter session, the mayor himself was requested "to invite surities and committee to meet with board at its next meeting for the purpose of adjusting the deficit as might be agreed upon between contending parties." The cautious "if any" was now gone. On the next day, still trying to bring the bondsmen to the negotiating table, the board agreed to certify to them amounts that had been paid to the town by taxpayers according to town records.[23]

In return, the bondsmen were not at all cooperative. Apparently, one of the bondsmen was Charlie's friend, the clerk of the circuit court, W.E. Andrews. Asked by the board for a copy of Butler's "time books" (listings by him of the amount of time individual workers had labored for the town and amounts paid), the lawyer for the bondsmen, who was, again, Charlie's attorney William V. Sullivan, refused. It was then decided that the town, more aggressive now, would hire its own lawyer to deal with the case.[24] Matters proceeded slowly until June when the board determined how much tax money had been paid to Butler and moved to "charge the amount to Butler's bondsmen." The amount was $2,890.[25]

Finally, on June 11, the board and the bondsmen met. However, they "proceeded to investigate the questions at issue without coming to any conclusion as to the actual deficit in the official records of Butler." Still another committee of two, this time two aldermen, was appointed to study the matter. This committee cast back to look at Butler's accounts for street work in 1884 and 1885. They found that he had claimed $1,625 for money paid workers in those two years, and they seemed to suggest that there was less than a full accounting for that sum.[26]

An attempt to get Lawyer Sullivan to the mayor's office on June 18 failed, but on the 22nd, at a called meeting in the office of Mayor John H. Kimmons, the board at last met Butler's bondsmen and the amount of the "deficit after much argument and calculation was agreed upon by way of compromise." The board agreed to settle for $874.83 if the bondsmen paid that amount within thirty days. Further the bondsmen were to honor and pay all "street tickets" for work done in 1886 and 1887 that were belatedly offered.[27] Rather clearly, the bondsmen had taken advantage of the looseness in Oxford's fiscal system in a degree hardly less costly to the town than that of the "absconding marshal."

Why Charlie Left Home

Tradition holds that Charlie Butler went "bankrupt" before he left Oxford. There is absolutely no indication of this in the official records. He was not being sued for money at any time before his departure. Indeed, his name is notably absent from the long list of his friends and neighbors in the chancery court records who were sued for debts. In the mid-1880s Charlie Butler seemed to be entirely solvent and prospering materially. At one point the town increased its assessment of the value of his home property by $150 for purposes of taxation. In 1885 his house was assessed at $1,800 when the Bank of Oxford on the square, for comparison, was rated at $10,000.[28] Further, his admission to membership in the Masonic Lodge and rise to office in that fraternity suggests that he was regarded as a worthy, materially responsible young man. Finally, he paid $150 in cash to buy the family estates in September, 1886, and he still owned at least those lands and some others at the time of his departure. Both facts are good evidence of his solvency.

There is every indication that Charles Butler labored steadily and faithfully, and that his work was regularly rewarded. In addition to the monthly $50 he had received for twelve years, he received commissions for collecting town taxes. That came to $535 for 1880, $752 for 1881, $514 for 1882, $337 for 1883, and $252 for 1884. We do not have the figures for 1885 and 1886, but his income from tax collecting must have averaged several hundred dollars annually. For the five years for which we have hard figures, 1880–1884, Butler earned an average of $1,080 a year in salary as marshal and commissions as tax collector. In addition, he drew extra income from his services as a bailiff for the court and deputy sheriff. Finally, his fees—including serving legal papers, taking up and keeping loose stock, and boarding the town mule—surely brought his income over the $1,200 mark. In the deflating 1880s, a cash income of this amount meant considerable security and definitely put the Charlie Butler family comfortably in the middle of Oxford society.

By way of comparison, on December 31, 1887, at the very time that Charlie was taking flight from Oxford with at least $3,000 in his pocket, the head of the faculty at the University of Mississippi, Professor of Law Edward Mayes, made a checklist for himself to insure that he paid the quarterly salaries of each of the thirteen professors. Nine of these were paid $2,000 yearly; Mayes himself received $2,800, and the only woman on the faculty, Sally McGee Isom, drew $700. Sally Isom was the unmarried daughter of Thomas D. Isom, an early settler and a leading local physician who had begun his life in Lafayette County as clerk for a merchant who traded with the Indians. Former governor James L. Alcorn pronounced Sally Isom the premier professor of "elocution" in the South, an honor that was rewarded more with words than dollars. Obviously, Isom suffered the loss of salary because of her gender. Further down the salary scale, Professor Mayes recorded that several laborers on campus, probably black, received $20 a month each, while their white supervisor got $41.66.[29]

Charlie's acceptance in the community, doubtless, had something to do with the excellent reputation built by his family. He was the son of a first family of Oxford and Lafayette County. As we have seen, his father, "Captain" Charles Butler, had surveyed the town and was the county's first sheriff. His mother had been a founder of the Baptist Church and had carried the family bravely and beautifully after her husband's death in 1855. His two older brothers had been among the first students to enter the university and had served honorably as Confederate soldiers, Henry dying of wounds received in battle. William had returned from the war to become a prominent businessman and a leading alderman in Oxford before his untimely death. His older sister, Mattie, was recognized locally as something of a Baptist saint.[30] Charlie himself had entered the postwar university, and while his business venture with Beanland failed, it did so debt-free—that is, with mercantile honor.

Charles Butler earned a good living, and there is no indication that he spent his money in riotous living. If he drank there is no sign that he drank excessively. Indeed, he seems to have been a "duty" man, one who strove earnestly—as had his father and older brother before him—to do his work as it ought to be done. Judging by the town minutes, which are both very matter-of-fact in tone and full of complaints against others, no one ever accused him of being a poor police officer; no one complained of shoddy work on the streets or sidewalks; and no one charged him with stealing the town's money before his flight—though the "street ticket" process was itself inefficient, an invitation to dishonesty, and bound to raise suspicions. Charlie maintained a home in one of the best neighborhoods in that part of the state, and he sent his children to school with the children of the local elite. Their later full reception into the social life of the community and their marriages testify eloquently to the attainment by the family of material, social, and moral orthodoxy. Finally, Charles Butler was a Mason, active in arranging the social events of the Order, and an officer in his lodge.

Charlie's unsolvable problem, one is led to think, was not financial and it was not downtown. Primarily, it was emotional, and it was at home. He and Leila, one surmises, did not get along. The evidence for this is circumstantial, but there is a fair amount of it, and it is fairly strong.

Leila and Charlie were married on August 2, 1868. We do not know Charlie's exact age, but probably Leila was only some months younger than he in a culture where the groom was almost always distinctly older than the bride, usually by several years. However, Southern marital patterns were generally and profoundly disrupted by the war. For several years after 1865, there was a severe shortage of marriageable men. The experience in Mississippi would not have been vastly different from that in Orange County, North Carolina, where scholar Robert Charles Kenzer has very carefully calculated that about 90 percent of the men between ages fifteen and thirty-five in 1860 went off to war in and after 1861, and a quarter to a third of these never returned. The result was that the ratio of marriageable men to marriageable women which had been 89 to 100 in 1860 fell to 69 to 100 in 1870. In that decade statistics declared that three out of every ten women would not marry at all.[31] In the crisis, some young women like Leila married young men; some married older men like the fictional Scarlett O'Hara who stole her sister's would-be husband Frank Kennedy; some married beneath their social rank like Scarlett's sister Sue Ellen who took cracker Will Benteen to wed; and some even married black. Others, of course, never married at all.

Leila was eighteen and a half when she married, and Charles was perhaps a bit older. For a male, he was young to marry. But he came from a family that had been affluent and showed a progressive and enterprising spirit, and Leila might well have anticipated a life with Charlie that would bring her material comfort and considerable respect in the social order of the town. Their early married life followed the usual pattern. Nine months and twenty-six days into the marriage, the first child, Sherwood Tate Butler, was born. Sherwood was probably named for Burlina's father.[32] Two and one-half years later Leila gave birth to a baby girl, Maud. It was not unusual in that time for a first child to follow so quickly upon marriage, nor for a second to follow some two years later. What was unusual was for physically able parents to stop there. Charles and Leila were apparently healthy, vigorous people. Charles had been one of six children. His sister Emily had five offspring. Three others had smaller families, but in each of these a spouse died. Leila lost no child by death, and there were no stillbirths. Such things have to be highly speculative and hence dangerous ground to tread, but one is tempted to take the next step. One might consider the possibility that, after Maud's birth, the Butlers abstained from sexual relations during times in which Leila might have conceived. Given the high level of ignorance about birth control at that time, it seems more likely that they abstained over the next sixteen years during which they lived together.

In their published accounts, Leila's grandsons remembered her as a gentle woman, but tradition also asserts that Leila had a sharp tongue.[33] She was a mystery woman, and the mystery might have been deliberately preserved by her. A grandson, who was about seven when she died, remembered her fondly. He wrote a book about the family, but could not even supply the names of Leila's father and mother to a Falkner biographer in the 1970s.[34] She simply did not talk about her past and neither did her daughter Maud.

Clearly Leila was an intelligent, talented woman. She developed a reputation in the community as an artist—she would carve ice into interesting shapes for parties, draw a lion in fresh butter, paint, sew, and form soap into dolls. It was sometimes said that in 1890 she was offered a scholarship to study sculpture in Rome but could not accept because she had to care for Maud.[35] Possibly Leila was a bright, sensitive woman who wanted very much to enter the higher life of art, who, early in marriage thought that all things were possible, then realized that she had tied her future to a man who would not have the success that his father, mother, and older brothers had achieved. In 1871 she stopped having children. By 1876 she might have been relieved to see Charles become the town marshal at a steady and respectable salary.

Seen from the outside, the Butlers were doing well in the 1880s. The wife was artistic, and the two attractive, healthy children played and went to school with the children of the leading families in the village. As town marshal, Charles Butler's duties sometimes involved unpleasant tasks ranging down to arresting drunks and runaway hogs. But he was also the town tax collector whom every citizen had to meet every year on or before November 1 with money in hand or else beg indulgence. As the town grew with streets, sidewalks, streetlights, paving, and drains, and especially schools, he became very much the town manager.

Charlie's flight in December, 1887, was perfectly timed, and its causes, surely, were deeply rooted in the life he had led in the community. Yet, there are indications that he decided to act only within several weeks of the event. In January, 1887, he had bought for $250 the Anderson Chelton homestead on the south side of town. It was a bargain price occasioned by the previous removal of the Cheltons to Texas. In August and September, 1887, as we have seen, he finalized his purchase of the Butler lands for $150 in cash. These do not seem to be the acts of a man about to flee. In September, however, he also sold a fraction of a lot for $50, and then, more signally, on November 12 sold the Chelton homestead to well-to-do Miss Kate Brown for $275. The papers of the sale were filed on the same date of the sale, a haste not usual in such transactions.[36]

Thus, into the year 1887, Charlie Butler seemed to be a responsible citizen in the community and a good father and husband at home. Events that occurred at the end of that year belied previous appearance. His desertion of his wife and two teenage children and his absconding with a large fraction of the town's income for the year indicts him solidly on one side, and a rumor about his love life that was circulating well into the twentieth century indicts him by innuendo on the other.

The Jacob Thompsons

The tradition said that Charlie Butler not only went bankrupt, but also that he ran away with the "beautiful octoroon" companion of Mrs. Jacob Thompson. What we now know of the circumstances makes plausible the truth of the latter half of the rumor.

First, the story comes down to us through interested parties who were likely to know the facts in the case. Joseph Blotner included the story in a detailed biography of William Faulkner published in 1974. He got it from an interview with Faulkner's wife Estelle.[37] Very possibly Estelle got it most authoritatively from her sister Dorothy Zollicoffer Oldham. Dorothy was born in Oxford in 1905 and lived there until her death in 1968. In 1930 she took her master's degree from the University of Mississippi. The subject of her thesis was, amazingly, the life of Jacob Thompson.

The footnotes in Dorothy's thesis indicate that she drew most of her information from interviews with a woman named Mamie Slate. Mamie Slate was born Mamie Lewis, the daughter of Abner Lewis and Sarah Thompson. Sarah was Jacob's sister. Abner and Jacob had been schoolmates in the University of North Carolina about 1830. Sarah and Abner had met, married, and come to Mississippi, all with Jacob's encouragement.[38]

In the antebellum period, Jacob Thompson was the leading citizen in Lafayette County and the town of Oxford. After the Civil War, Jacob and his wife Catharine moved to Memphis. Over the years before his death, Jacob brought several young people—youthful relatives and children of friends—up to Memphis to live in his large and comfortable house while they attended schools in the city. One of these was Mamie Lewis. As a teenage girl in the

1870s, Mamie wrote out her uncle's memoirs while he talked, and she knew the family stories very well. By 1930 Mamie Lewis Slate lived on a plantation on the Tallahatchie River, roughly a dozen miles north of Oxford, and talked a number of times with Dorothy Oldham as the young woman prepared her thesis.[39] Almost surely, Mamie had known personally the "beautiful octoroon" in question.

Even if the story of Charlie's flight with Mrs. Thompson's companion is not true, it is still useful to study Jacob and Catharine Thompson and the world in which they lived because it brings us more deeply into the culture of the cotton frontier in the southern United States before, during, and after the Civil War. It gets us, so to speak, into a truly historical Yoknapatawpha County. This is not the world that William Faulkner created; it is, rather, the world that created William Faulkner, and it encompasses the universe of race, class, sex, and violence, of family, clan, and community that affected him so profoundly and about which he wrote with such telling effect. Moreover, with the Thompsons, we become intimate with the ruling elite of the South. Indeed, if there was an "aristocracy" in the slaveholding South in the last generation before the Civil War, Jacob and Catharine are its personification.

Jacob Thompson comes very close to representing the model of the cotton frontier aristocrat who came west with material advantages already well in place. Historically, this was by far the usual case. It is opposed to the model of the poor boy who rose by his own efforts and made good, the case alleged of himself by the original Falkner in Mississippi and generated by William Faulkner for most of his fictional aristocrats. Jacob's father, Nicholas, had himself begun somewhere near the middle. He had learned the tanner's trade in 18th-century Virginia. His work brought him down into the vicinity of Leasburg in Caswell County in north-central North Carolina where he made money, bought a slave, made a tanner of him, made more money, bought more slaves and land and so on. In the process he married Lucretia Van Hook, a Quaker and, significantly for the Thompson family fortunes, the only child of parents rich in land and slaves.[40]

Nicholas had great ambitions for his sons. Each in turn was sent to an eminent preparatory school operated in the military style in Hillsborough, and thence ten miles south to the state university in Chapel Hill. The third son, born in 1810, was Jacob. His father slated him for eminence as a Presbyterian minister. Jacob was not really a good candidate for the ministry, but he was very reluctant to disappoint his father. In Chapel Hill, he blossomed in a different style. He matured so well that after he graduated with first honors in 1831, his professors kept him on as a tutor. During his stay in the university, he won a grudging independence from his father and developed a remarkable sense of self-confidence. After serving some time as a tutor, he went to Greensboro, read law, and was admitted to the bar. In 1835, he headed west, riding a fine horse, stopping at inns enroute, and having his luggage freighted separately. His destination was Natchez where he had heard, correctly, that opportunity was golden for a bright, well-positioned young lawyer.

Some weeks after his departure, Jacob arrived at Columbus, Mississippi. Columbus sat next to the Tombigbee River, which ran through a high, relatively flat plateau in northeastern Mississippi immediately west of the Alabama border. This land rivaled the Delta, not in size, but in the richness of its soil. It was a cotton frontier already in blossom, having been ceded to the whites by the Chickasaws early in the century. Columbus was already wealthy in 1835, and it became very wealthy during the next generation—as anyone can still see simply by touring the antebellum houses in the town. To the west of Columbus, the Chickasaw cession of 1834 was just opening to whites, and Jacob decided to spy out that land instead of proceeding to Natchez. As he was riding away through the outskirts of Columbus, he heard someone behind calling his name. Astonished that anyone in this land of strangers should speak to him so familiarly, he stopped and turned his horse to see his brother Young Thompson galloping up. Young had become a physician after leaving Chapel Hill, and he too was moving west to seek his fortune. Hearing that his brother was heading for northern Mississippi and dreadfully afraid that he had been weakened by recent hard study and might succumb to the fevers of the Chickasaw Territory, he had chased after Jacob to persuade his brother to travel elsewhere with him. Instead, while they talked in the road, Jacob persuaded Young to go with him into the cession.

The two young men settled in Pontotoc, a sort of advanced base from which settlers launched themselves into the Indian cession. Pontotoc was like a village in a gold rush. In this case, however, the gold was land. It was the focal point for trades in land because it was there that the federal government operated its office for selling lands in the cession. In the boomtown setting, the two brothers rapidly acquired wealth. Young as a physician dealt with the rather bloody results of physical combat between pioneers, while Jacob handled the legal aspects of combat, both criminal and material.[41]

Jacob's work often took him out of Pontotoc and through the cession. Frequently he spent the night with a client. One of these was John Peyton Jones who had settled very early in an area called Woodson's Ridge, in the northern part of what would become Lafayette County. John P. Jones had been born in Virginia in 1787, and his wife Tabitha Whatley in Georgia in 1799.[42] They had come west from Georgia, bringing much of their wealth with them. John Jones was one of the four commissioners appointed to organize the county and the inaugural meeting of the board of police was held in his home.[43]

When Jacob came visiting he found the Joneses living in a large one-story log house. The mud between the logs had been mixed with white clay for decoration. The Joneses had brought slaves to the frontier, and the slave cabins were made of logs also. Jacob later recalled that the slaves ate from troughs hollowed out of logs, sometimes separated into individual bowls by wooden dividers. In time, the older slaves were issued tin plates and cutlery, but children continued to use the troughs.[44] In 1850 the Joneses had $90,000 in property, two overseers, and ninety-three slaves (none of whom, interestingly, were recorded as mulattoes), ranking them among the several largest slaveholders in Lafayette County.[45] With a 3,400-acre plantation, they were the fourth largest among over a thousand landowners in the county.[46]

Jacob found in the Joneses' daughter Catharine the love of his life. Kate was born in December, 1822, and was only thirteen when Jacob first saw her in 1836, but she was already well known as a beauty.[47] She was a bit too young yet for Jacob to marry. While he thought of Kate, Jacob continued to practice law, bought land and slaves, and, predictably, moved into politics. He entered the race for attorney general of Mississippi. He lost the race, but during the campaign he developed friendships throughout the state. He was nominated for Congress in 1839, won the seat, and became the congressman from the Chickasaw cession. It was the seat, in essence, that William C. Falkner's maternal uncle, Thomas Jefferson Word, had occupied only months earlier. Fearful that Kate would marry someone else during his absence in Washington attending a session of Congress—she was not only beautiful, but potentially very wealthy—Jacob married her. In October, 1839, several weeks before her seventeenth birthday, she gave birth to a son, Caswell Macon, the only child they would have.[48] Kate was, as yet, unlettered. She was not ready, Jacob felt, for the sophistication of the nation's capital. He did an extraordinary thing. He took Kate to France, and put her into school where she remained, reportedly, for some time. When she was twenty, he brought her home to live in the Washington of Presidents Tyler, Polk, and Taylor, where her continental education and her natural beauty made her one of the brightest stars in the social sky.[49]

In 1851, during a Whiggish upsurge in Mississippi, Jacob was defeated in his race for Congress, but he gladly retired to manage his substantial property holdings—including a 2,400 acre plantation in the slave-rich Woodson's Ridge community.[50] He chose to live in Oxford where he had already persuaded two of his brothers from the East, Dr. John Thompson and William Thompson, to settle. He had also convinced his sisters, Sarah and Anna, and their husbands Abner Lewis and Yancy Wiley to locate in the county.[51] By 1850, both the Lewises and the Wileys were well established and prospering as planters and slaveholders.[52] Jacob owned considerable property in and about Oxford, and he chose to build his house on Taylor Road just south of town. As it happened, he built next door to the Bowens and directly across the road from Colonel Sheegog's residence, later restored by William Faulkner and called Rowan Oak. Jacob erected a grand twenty-room mansion, using bricks made by his slaves and lumber specially imported from Memphis. In the early decades of the twentieth century, the house was still vividly remembered in the community for its tastefully designed verandas, hand-carved furniture, and an art gallery full of "rare and costly painting."[53] Jacob was a leading patron of the local Episcopal Church, St. Peter's, and Kate, in November 1851, was one of the first two people brought into the communion at that site.[54] In 1856 he gave the land east of North 16th Street for St. Peter's Cemetery. He reserved a central plot for his own family and fenced it in with cedars, iron posts, and heavy chains. William Thompson and his wife are buried there, so too are John Peyton Jones, his wife Tabitha, and their only son Thomas. In July, 1846, at age twenty-five, Thomas died of fever in Vicksburg on his way to the Mexican War with Colonel Jefferson Davis's First Mississippi Volunteers. His death left Kate sole heir to the Jones properties.[55]

Meanwhile Jacob, himself, was becoming one of the wealthiest men in northeastern Mississippi. In 1860, at age fifty, he possessed some $500,000 in real estate and another $400,000 in personal property, mostly slaves. Oxford was home to several families of great wealth. Planter James Brown, sixty, lived on South Street and claimed assets worth $674,000. William F. Avent was a planter and at age thirty-four in 1860 valued his holdings at $486,000. Avent (sometimes spelled Avant) was born to a very ambitious family of Virginians who had come into the area at the beginning and bought large amounts of land, some of it directly from the Indians. In 1851, William Avent had married one of the Brown daughters.[56] It was he and Jacob Thompson's daughter-in-law, Sallie Fox Thompson, who, after the Civil War, bought the Butler Hotel site from Burlina and built the Thompson House, a structure that still stands. With Avents from Virginia, Thompsons from North Carolina, Pegueses ("Piggies") from low-country South Carolina, Joneses from Georgia, and Sheegogs from Ireland, Oxford on the eve of the Civil War was a very wealthy town. Married as it was to the University of Mississippi, it is proper to think of it as the epitome and the apotheosis of cotton culture in the new Southwest.

In 1856, Jacob Thompson reentered active politics as a Buchanan Democrat, and in 1857 was rewarded by the new president with appointment to the office of secretary of the interior. He and Catharine again moved to Washington, leaving their son Macon a student at the university in the class of 1858. In 1861, Macon emulated his father in taking a teenage wife, Sarah Francis Fox. Meanwhile, in Washington, Kate became close friends with President Buchanan and Miss Harriet Lane, Buchanan's niece who served as White House hostess for the wifeless president. In contemporary records, one gets glimpses of them moving easily and genially in and out of each other's houses—including the White House—for lunches, dinners, and informal visits.[57] In the secession crisis, Jacob resigned his post, but not soon enough to avoid charges that he used his office to spy on the Union government.

During the war, Jacob was a staunch and prominent rebel, a fact that made him, his family, and his property a special target for punishment by the North. When Union troops entered Oxford in 1864, Jacob was in Canada on a secret mission for the Confederate government. In his absence the Yankees wreaked vengeance on his family and his property. General Edward Hatch first took a wagon to Jacob's house and carried away a load of his possessions. A week later General Andrew J. "Whiskey" Smith went there and looted the place entirely. Macon's wife Sallie had just given birth to her first child, Kate. General Smith ordered his men to bring mother, bed, and baby into the yard. Then he set fire to the house and burned it to the ground. Catharine subsequently took everyone and all she could salvage to her mother's house in the country.[58]

After the war Jacob and Catharine lived abroad for several years, fearing that Jacob would be prosecuted and his property confiscated if he returned home. In the late 1860s, however, they did return, built a modest house for Macon on the site of the antebellum mansion in Oxford, and themselves settled in Memphis. Jacob maintained an office downtown, but did not practice law. Instead, he managed his considerable investments, bought plantation land in the Delta at depressed prices, and dealt in timber. He was a wise investor, a capacity implied in the fact that in 1885 he willed $100,000 of stock in the "Bell Telephone Company of Washington City" to the University of the South at Sewanee, Tennessee.[59] In summers, Jacob took Catharine abroad for her health. They visited the most expensive spas in Europe and traveled to Cuba, Bermuda, and Canada. Jacob seemed especially responsive to the needs of friends, family, and his ex-slaves. Family tradition asserted that he practically supported Jefferson Davis during Davis's Memphis years and that Davis was a frequent visitor in the Thompson house. Clearly, Jacob brought young folks from Mississippi into his circle in Memphis for their care and education. In particular, he took in the orphans of his favored brother, Young Thompson. Also, Joseph McDonald, his gardener in Oxford, was brought as head coachman and butler. MacDonald, eighty-five in 1870 and a native Nova Scotian, had landscaped the grounds in the antebellum period for what became Faulkner's Rowan Oak. Finally, according to Mamie Slate, most of the ex-slaves who had been house servants in Lafayette County before the war went to Memphis with the Thompsons.[60]

~

It is entirely possible, of course, that Catharine's octoroon companion had been a Thompson slave, born and reared in the Thompson household in Oxford. It happens that we do know something about the history of slaves and servants in the Thompson family. One of the things we know is that Jacob Thompson's proclivity for association with beautiful women extended to at least one of his slaves. The story comes to us from Joanna Thompson Isom, the daughter of that slave. Joanna was born into the Jacob Thompson household in Oxford shortly before the Civil War. She was among the many thousands of ex-slaves interviewed in the mid-1930s as one of the programs of the Works Projects Administration of the New Deal. In 1936 Joanna's interviewer found her in a small, neat house, bought by her forty years before on the edge of Oxford's

"Freedmantown." She was "a tall, slender, and very intelligent mulatto woman," the interviewer observed, and "her features are almost classical in their regularity." Joanna's mother and grandmother had been bought by Jacob in Georgia before the war, apparently as house servants. Her mother, Amy, was a "Madagascan," and her grandmother later told Joanna about her mother, who died giving birth to Joanna in the late 1850s:

> She said she wuz jus' too butiful; she wuz jet black, but her skin wuz as smooth as mole skin; her hair wuz perfectly straight an' hung down below her knees; she had large limbs, and little han's an' feet—de men jus' fell on dere faces for her. I don't know nuttin' 'bout my father, but dey tells me I has indian blood . . .[61]

Joanna's father must have been very light in color, and she seems to suggest that her lightness related to her Indian heritage. Possibly, this was a tradition created to avoid disturbing speculations about the true source of Joanna's light skin and nearly "classical" features.

Joanna was reared "rite up in de house wid Miss Sallie— dey wuz de riches' white folks in town an' dey had lots ev slaves. Mister Macon giv' me to Miss Sallie when I wuzn't but three hours ole." Joanna was a premature baby; she was delivered by Dr. McEwen with great difficulty and with Macon himself in the room. As her mother was dying, she gave Joanna to Macon "to raise rite." Joanna continued the tale she must have heard many times as a child and herself often retold. Macon "wropped me up in a towel, an' put me in hiz overcoat pocket an' tuk me to Miss Sallie's room where she wuz sick in bed an' he said to her: 'I bro't you sumthin' that I bet you ain't never seen befo'; hit is a seven month's [sic] baby jus' three hours ole.' I hasn't never had no toe nails to speak of."

Joanna was five years old in 1864 when the blue-coated soldiers burned the Thompson mansion. Her grandmother helped raise her until she married Henry Isom at fifteen. She was married in Macon Thompson's parlor, not long before his death in 1873. Thereafter, she bore ten children by Henry who died in 1917. At the time of the interview Joanna lived alone in the clean, tiny house on the outskirts of town, and she collected rocks that were so remarkable that they drew a visit from Professor Alexander L. Bondurant of Ole Miss who declared, to her delight, that she ought to become a professor in the university.[62]

Joanna would have been in and about the Thompson house on Taylor Road when Jacob came home from Washington in 1861, when Grant came in 1862, and when Jacob left for Canada in 1864. Probably, she also took refuge with Catharine Thompson in the country. It might well be that Catharine took her household into the country even before the house was burned in 1864. The reason for doing so was that in that household there was another slave girl who was, it seems, irresistably attractive to men. This story, presumably, came to

Dorothy Oldham from Mamie Slate, and Mamie probably got it from the Thompsons themselves. After Jacob left for Canada, the overseer on the Thompson estate, a man named Stowers, was very cruel to the slaves. Moreover, he embezzled money, he insulted Catharine, and he became infatuated with Kate's personal maid, a young woman still in her teens. The maid repulsed his advances, and the affair ended with his allegedly beating the poor girl to death. Catharine then took the house servants and went to her mother's place in the country. Apparently, she returned to town to assist in the delivery of baby Kate, Macon and Sallie's firstborn child, and that event coincided with the coming of the Yankees. Catharine was there for the burning, and indeed a servant rescued Macon's portrait from the house for her just before the burning. When the Union troops left Oxford, so too did the great mass of Thompson slaves, not out of disloyalty to the Thompsons, but, as Catharine later explained, because of the great cruelty of the overseer Stowers.[63]

Stowers is in the census of 1850. Judging from the listing, he was an overseer on either the Jones plantation with its ninety-three slaves or the adjacent Thompson plantation with its eighty-three slaves. In that year, none of either the Jones or Thompson plantation slaves was recorded as mulatto. This was often the case when planters, such as the Joneses, came into Mississippi early and directly from Georgia or South Carolina bringing large groups of slaves. Robert M. Stowers was twenty-eight and, like the Joneses, from Georgia. He had a twenty-eight-year-old wife and six children ranging from eight years down to two months.[64]

In 1860, Stowers was still an overseer, but he had also become a slaveholder. He had acquired a young black woman and she had given birth to three children, the youngest of whom was mulatto. He had acquired, too, an eleven-year-old mulatto girl. Mulattoes had also appeared among the Thompson and Jones slaves during the decade. Jacob now had ninety-seven slaves living in twenty "slave houses." Three of these were mulattoes. One was six months old, another was eighteen months, and the third, a man age twenty-five, was a "runaway." This slave appeared first on the list and, by the ordering of men, women, and children, was apparently the companion to a nineteen-year-old black woman and father of her six-month-old mulatto child.[65] In contrast, the 150 slaves on a neighboring plantation owned by the Pegues family and originally derived from low-country South Carolina remained all black in 1860, as did L.Q.C. Lamar's thirty-one slaves who were probably mostly Georgia born.[66] After the war, Stowers appeared briefly in the circuit court record, charged with and found guilty of "Assault and Battery."[67] His son Francis Marion Stowers entered Ole Miss in the Class of 1871. Soon, however, he left school to become a successful merchant in Oxford. He was the alderman who made the motion early in 1888 to elect a successor to Marshal Butler.[68]

Thus, a generation before Charlie Bulter's unannounced departure, Mrs.

Jacob Thompson had one beautiful female servant whom at least one white man could not resist and another, an exotic Madagascan, who, her mulatto daughter declared, no man could refuse.

Maybe

It was unusually and bitterly cold in the mid-South that Christmas season of 1887 when Charlie Butler took flight. On Christmas Eve four inches of snow fell on northern Mississippi.[69] One can easily imagine Charlie Butler bundled up and hunkered down in his seat as the train pulls out of the station in Memphis, heading west. The train moves onto the bridge, high above the Mississippi River. The heavy timbers of the bridge strain and creak, the passenger car swings ponderously from one side to the other and back, the steel wheels clack in slow rhythm as they roll across the gap from one section of rail to another. Charlie gazes down at the gray-black water, slow-flowing and freezing. In his pocket, a large sheaf of paper money, bulky because of the small bills with which most Oxfordians paid their taxes. Perhaps he strikes a match and lights a cigar; he looks westward, across the river where the earth lies flat and rich and open as far as the eye can see. Elsewhere in the train, perhaps, there sits an elegant, well-dressed, light-skinned woman, an octoroon, she too watching the glazing river, dark mirror beneath a somber sky.

People who fled usually did not change occupations. The chances are that wherever Charlie went he either became a police officer or rued the loss of his profession. His father had been the original sheriff of Lafayette County and he had been a marshal and a deputy sheriff for most of his mature life. Possibly, somewhere in west Texas, Charlie Butler wore a badge again, a star perhaps. Also Charlie left town with a fair amount of capital in his possession. It might be that in a new land he could do what his parents and older brothers had done—he might succeed in investing in town lots and running a hotel, perhaps with livery stable attached. Given his proven managerial skills, the chances are that his material fortunes did not run downhill. Probably, he did well enough wherever he was.

Charlie was thirty-eight or thirty-nine when he ran away. If there was an octoroon, she was probably younger. It is likely that they married, or offered themselves as married, and she "passed for white," as the phrase went then. It might be that before Charlie she had never married, never had a black lover, never had a child, and never even had a lover of any kind to have a child with. Given Charlie's and the octoroon's ages, given a considerably high level of emotional and physical attraction, it seems likely that the couple had children—perhaps three or four before the woman passed the child-bearing age. These children would have been half-brothers and half-sisters to Sherwood and

Maud. If the woman was really an "octoroon," that is one-eighth black, the children would have been only one-sixteenth black—like Charles Bon in the novel *Absalom, Absalom!*—and probably their blackness would have been all but indistinguishable to the eye. The ensuing generation—who would have been William Faulkner's cousins—would have very nearly lost even the memory, the certain knowledge of their black heritage.

Oxford After Charlie

In the decade after Charlie Butler left town, Oxford underwent a profound change. In 1893 the agricultural depression that had been deepening since the late 1880s suddenly gave way to a worldwide depression, the most devastating and shocking yet seen in the industrial age. Well into the late 1880s Lafayette County farmers brought their wagonloads of cotton to the square in Oxford, and they sold it for eight to ten cents a pound to merchants and dealers who came out of their stores onto the street to buy.[70] In 1894, the price had dropped to six cents. For many farmers this was less than it cost them to grow the fleecy staple. "You can't afford to buy corn to raise six cent cotton. Can you?" challenged the editor of the *Globe* in the spring of that year.[71] In effect, Lafayette County's farmers answered with a resounding yes. The county that had expected to ship 9,000 to 10,000 bales from the 1890 crop was expecting to deliver 12,000 bales from the crop of 1894.[72] Distressingly low prices continued through the middle 1890s.

These were hard times for farmers of all kinds, but it was especially hard on tenants who rented their farms for a share of the crop. Sharecropping might be fair enough when the price paid for the crop exceeded the cost. The assumption was that roughly a third of the cotton crop would pay the landlord for the use of the land, a third for the supplies required to raise the crop (seed, fertilizer, mules), and another third would go to the tenant for his labor. The system often faltered on the fact that the tenant did not bring to the arrangement a year of support for himself and family. Consequently he had to get "furnish" from a country store, often owned by the landlord himself. In the best years rent and supplies for farm and family would be paid for out of the sale of the harvested crop, and there would be something left over for the tenant and his family. In bad years, the rent would be paid, and perhaps farm supplies might be paid for, but the furnish bill went wanting and the tenant got nothing. The tenant and landlord might contract again for the next year and hope to do better. But several bad years meant that the landlord, often enough a debtor himself, was squeezed. When times were bad for a number of years, these farms were not available for rent under any terms. It was under such circumstances that tenant farmers loaded up their meager belongings on mule-drawn wagons—if they had access to such—and went looking for other places to live. In some parts of the South they found homes in the cotton mill villages where the hours were long and the pay was slight, but at least it was certain and company housing was not only available but mandatory. Others came into the towns and villages seeking work of any kind, and still others—the poorest of the poor—simply existed on the land as best they could, usually as exceedingly poorly paid farm laborers. It was from this element that William Faulkner would draw the Snopes clan.

There is a paradox involved in the economics of the South in the 1890s. At the very time that agricultural depression was devastating the land, some people were finding capital enough to build factories, especially textile factories, expand businesses, and generally launch themselves into the industrial age and its technological and commercial concomitants. In 1894, the same year that cotton sank to six cents a pound, the mechanical age hit Oxford with renewed vigor. In the spring there was a bicycle craze and the village was filled with big wheels, small wheels, and even one wheels. In the same season a wholesale dealer in sewing machines advertised for a local man with a suitable rig of horse and wagon to become his traveling agent in the countryside around Oxford.[73] Oxford journalists thought that it might be better to join the industrial revolution rather than to fight it. One editor rather wistfully quoted the *Manufacturer's Record* of Baltimore as saying that large textile mills in the South were paying about 10 percent on investments and small ones from 18 to 20 percent.[74] Even so, Oxford got no textile mill, and the town remained in the thrall of the white staple in its raw form. The town, like the country, watched its price with great interest, and like the farmers, townspeople were perennially optimistic. "Cotton will hardly go lower," the editor of the *Globe* whistled into the wind as the year's crop poured into town in the fall of 1895 and the price fell yet again.[75]

Cotton was down in Lafayette County, but somehow modernity was up. In December, 1895, telephones began to ring for the first time in Oxford homes, and a year later a water tower rose to dominate the skyline.[76] The town had contracted with a Chicago company to put a 60,000-gallon tank on the top of a 140-foot steel tower.[77] Finished, the water tower meant water lines running through the town, indoor plumbing, and a sewerage system, but another result highly valued by the citizens was that fires in Oxford would be far less liable to destroy people's homes. Some folks with large houses now felt safe enough to move their kitchens from outbuildings into the big house. The water tower was also a point of pride for Oxfordians, a beacon signal to the world that Oxford was in the vanguard of municipal progress.

Butlers Without Charlie

When Charlie left home, he left a wife and two children. Leila was thirty-eight, Sherwood eighteen, and Maud had just turned sixteen. Sherwood wasted no time entering the job market. In April, 1888, the town paid him $8.35 for eighty-three and one-half hours of work on the streets—under the supervision of the man who had replaced his father. Sherwood had labored more hours than all three of the other men working on the streets combined during the same period of time. In June, he was paid $13.75 for an additional thirteen and three-fourths days of street work.[78]

A few months later Sherwood worked for the town in a different capacity. In September, 1888, Oxford had something very serious to worry about. Yellow fever was rampant again and the board quickly resolved that "the Town is hereby strictly quarenteened [sic] against the world." Trains were not allowed to stop nor even to slow below a speed of six miles an hour when passing through Oxford. Special "quarantine guards" were hired to block the roads and patrol the boundaries of the town, stopping all ingress. The guards, as is obvious from their family names, were respectable young men of the town, hired to serve for $1.25 a day. Among the two dozen people hired were Sherwood Butler and Murry Falkner, the man who would marry Sherwood's sister. Murry was eighteen then and the eldest son of the rising thirty-nine-year-old lawyer John Wesley Thompson Falkner.[79]

Maud turned sixteen in the month before her father disappeared. We have a photograph of her, perhaps made within a year after Charlie's departure, taken with her good friend Holland Falkner, Murry's sister. The two young women are posing self-consciously, talking over a table, both dressed to the throat with hair upswept, Maud looking gaily shy and pretty. Holland is acting for the camera, smiling ruefully and shaking a finger at Maud who smiles gently, hands and arms relaxed, as she looks at and listens to straight talk from her friend.

Charlie Butler stole the town's money and ran away; but, strangely, he left some value in property even as he stole in cash. He left the house in which the family lived, the land that had belonged to his father's and his mother's estates, and a scattering of lots and parts of lots in town. Charlie did leave some debts, but these do not appear to have been especially large or onerous. Apparently, the house was in Leila's name, a common arrangement in those litigious times when a man might lose all that he owned, but his wife might still hold the home. Probably the largest debt, however, did spring from the $700 Charlie had borrowed on his house back in 1880. Moving to satisfy the obligation, the trustee in the affair offered the house for sale on January 30, 1888. Led by W. Harvey Carothers, several citizens stepped in and paid off the debt, and clear title was registered to "Mrs. Leila Dean Butler" on the following day. The Carothers family had been loyal friends of the Butlers from pioneer days in Oxford.[80] Later that year, in September, Leila, "Mrs. Charles Butler," petitioned the town to reduce the evaluation of her real estate in Oxford, probably her house, for taxes from $1,800 to $1,500, and the board responded positively.[81]

In the end, four businessmen joined to bring successful suit against Charles Butler's estate for other bills owed. One of these was bookstore owner and dry goods dealer Charles Roberts who had audited the marshal's books. Another was Charles Meyer, a merchant, who won a judgment for $203.02.[82] Finally, to satisfy those judgments, Sheriff P.E. Mathews advertised that on May 6, 1889, at the courthouse door he would sell those lands, 148 acres, that Butler had acquired from the estates of his parents.[83]

In September, 1889, Maud Butler was an entering student in the Industrial Institute and College for the Education of White Girls of Mississippi in Columbus—now the Mississippi University for Women. The *Oxford Globe* on the 19th duly noted her departure by announcing that "Miss Maud Butler left Monday night for Columbus, Miss., to attend the I.I. & C."[84] Interestingly, the school featured a two-year business course in a mood that accentuated material advancement not vastly different from that of Booker T. Washington's all-black Tuskegee Institute a hundred miles to the east. It was a popular program. Indeed, there were twice as many girls in the business curriculum as in the traditional liberal arts program in the college, and "Maude" (as her name was spelled in the catalogue) was one of them. Tuition was free, and room and board on campus cost less than $10 a month, largely because every girl had housekeeping duties. A student needed only a $30 deposit to begin, and once enrolled might earn 6 cents an hour doing work assigned by the school.

From information published by the college, we can surmise something of what life for Maud in Columbus might have been like. There was little room for personal displays of wealth. On dress occasions in the fall and spring, such as opening ceremonies on Wednesday, September 18, 1889, which Maud must have attended in proper attire, all the girls wore skirts and blouses of "blue sateen" modestly outfitted with "smoked pearl buttons." Each student was equipped with a hat of "navy blue straw." On work days, the girls wore clothes of any material, but the color was always navy blue. Students pursued a busy regime that ran from 6 A.M.. to 10 P.M. In the first year, they took courses in arithmetic, English, free hand drawing, penmanship, and "Industrial Art." Ultimately, young women might earn certificates in "Phonography" (shorthand), Telegraphy, Book Keeping, Dress Making, and Water Color, Crayon, and Free Hand Drawing.[85]

A year later, Maud was not among the students listed in the catalogue, and clearly she never graduated from the college. Therefore, her name does not appear among the graduates whose progress was so faithfully reported in annual catalogues year after year as students became teachers, stenographers, book keepers, cashiers, and in one case a student in the Philadelphia Medical College for Women and, subsequently, a practicing physician in Mississippi.[86]

One tradition has it that in 1890 Leila had to give up a scholarship for studying sculpting in Rome in order to care for her daughter.[87] One wonders about the facts in that case, because with very little money Maud could have remained in school for the year 1890–1891 and completed work for her certificate. In truth, it might have been eighteen-year-old Maud who gave up school to care for her mother. Certainly, family lore asserts that in 1896 Maud was working as a secretary in Texarkana, Arkansas, and supporting both herself and her mother.

The personal columns of the Oxford press reveal that by the summer of 1891 Leila and Maud had settled in Jackson, Tennessee, a sizeable city and railroad center about a hundred miles north of Oxford. Sherwood was also there, working for a railroad company. From time to time family members visited Oxford where the children had been born and reared and still had friends and relatives, including their father's sisters Mattie Nelson and Mary Ann Edwards and several cousins. In July, 1891, the *Globe* noted that "Mrs. L. V. [sic] Butler and her charming daughter, Miss Maude, of Jackson, Tenn., are now in the city visiting friends."[88]

Sherwood, apparently, was an even more frequent visitor, and soon returned to stay. By the summer of 1893 he was clerking in Buffaloe's confectionary store. George W. Buffaloe, the owner, was a very popular merchant who sold everything from ice cream to fresh oysters in his downtown store and associated restaurant. He was also a clever businessman, liberally advertising his goods in the press, including, in January, 1891, a special 5 cent cigar that he had had made to his order and labeled "Farmer's Alliance."[89] Seemingly, Sherwood did well at the store. When he was ill briefly in 1893, the editor of the *Globe* cheerfully predicted that he would return to work "in a day or so, pleasing every one by his presence."[90]

During that summer, 1893, apparently Leila and Maud had also returned to Oxford. By the end of the season, however, they made a highly significant move toward breaking with their Oxford past. On August 29, Leila borrowed $750 on the Butler homestead from E.H. and Mary Kimmons. On the next day, Leila and Maud signed a document in Memphis that allowed family friend J.B. Roach to give title of the property to the Kimmonses on August 31 for $1,000. Sherwood also signed to signify his assent to the proceedings.[91] On this occasion, perhaps, Leila and Maud had taken care of business in Oxford and immediately entrained to build a new life for themselves in Arkansas.

Back in Oxford, one person Sherwood especially pleased was Addie Buffaloe, the boss's twenty-two-year-old daughter. He so pleased her, in truth, that in the summer of 1894 she married him. "Last night at the Methodist Church Mr. S.T. Butler and Miss Addie Buffaloe were married," reported the *Oxford Globe* on July 12. "Sherwood and his sweet and blushing bride left on the North bound train on their bridal tour." The church had filled to overflowing with well wishers, the paper declared brightly, a fact that bespoke, in part, the community's appreciation of Sherwood's in-laws. Mrs. Buffaloe often welcomed out-of-town visitors into her University Avenue home, while George's comings and goings were fondly mentioned in the press. Genial, gregarious, the Buffaloes were clearly in the social swim in Oxford, and they were affluent. In September, 1893, in the midst of the great depression, George and Mrs. Buffaloe traveled to Chicago to witness the wonders of the World's Fair, and next April they went with leading local lawyer William V. Sullivan and others to the races in Memphis.[92] Within nine months of marriage Addie gave birth to a boy and, said the newspaper, "Grandpa Buffaloe is just beaming with smiles."[93] The smiles, lamentably, soon turned to tears. That child died, and before the turn of the century, two more infants came and went in that household.[94]

Meanwhile, Sherwood was becoming a merchant. In 1896 advertisements appeared in the local press for "Baird & Butler" whose store featured, at various times, chewing tobacco, pickles, salad dressing, and horse radish.[95] Probably, Sherwood had gone into business with George Buffaloe's encouragement and assistance. When the census taker came in 1900, he found Sherwood and Addie, age thirty-one and twenty-nine, childless and living in a rented house. Sherwood described himself as a "Confectioner," as did his father-in-law.[96] In November of that year, "the boys of the city" gave their "annual 'Possum Feast' at Buffaloe & Butler's Cafe."[97]

Maud

Maud was not far behind her brother in her travel to the marriage altar, and she, too, came home to Oxford to find her mate. In late 1892 or early 1893 when Sherwood ceased working for the railroad in Tennessee and moved back to Oxford, Maud and Leila perhaps went to stay with relatives in Arkansas. In time, Maud found work as a secretary, and Leila kept house for the pair. Probably Leila and Maud attended Sherwood's wedding in July, 1894, and, subsequently, visits occurred back and forth. Leila and Maud returned to Oxford for the summer of 1896, and it is possible that they had some idea of resettling there.[98] Perhaps Leila stayed with Sherwood and Addie, where sickness, pregnancy, and child death seemed to abound in those middle years of the 1890s and where she could feel useful. Apparently, it was agreed that Maud would spend some time in the home of her friend Holland Falkner. During that summer, Murry was home too, managing his father's business while John was in St. Louis fighting the claims of Native Americans to Mississippi lands.[99]

Holland Pearce Falkner was J.W.T. Falkner's only daughter and was named for the mother he had never known. The newspapers leave us without doubt that Holland was a very social young woman. She often entertained friends and relatives from out of town, and she visited friends and relatives elsewhere.[100] It is not surprising that on into the fall of 1896 she had her longtime friend Maud Butler as a house guest.

Murry Falkner, of course, was recurrently at home. He was twenty-six, still a bachelor, and now worked as depot agent for the family railroad in New Albany.[101] The Falkners were not at all strangers to the Butlers. Murry and

Maud, and Sherwood and Holland had all been teenagers together in Oxford, and they had moved in the same social circles. In fact, when the Falkners first came to Oxford in 1885, they took a house on North Street near the Butlers. Maud later recalled how she could stand on her back porch—at the Butler homestead—and call over to Holland on her back porch, just to the north, and over to the Lamar sisters on their porch, to the northeast, to organize a rendezvous downtown. Now adult and alone, Murry was obviously attracted to Maud and, for a time at least, she rivaled the railroad for his attention. On October 29, Murry was again in Oxford for a visit and ten days later he and Maud were married. Having gone out for a walk on Sunday night, November 8, they stopped at the Methodist parsonage for an impromptu ceremony, then returned home to announce the news.[102] The next morning, skipping a honeymoon to any romantic spot, they traveled to New Albany to commence their life together. Neither was inexperienced in the world, and, while each might later rue the act, neither could have argued very convincingly that he or she did not know what they were doing.

PART TWO

Biography

FIVE

Youth
1897–1918

Childhood

Seemingly, William Faulkner had a storybook childhood. He grew up in the country villages of New Albany and Ripley, and—after the age of five when his father's change in business relations made a family move necessary—the town of Oxford. One could almost illustrate his life in those turn-of-the-century years with Winslow Homer paintings. Barefoot boys in overalls with trouser legs rolled up a notch or two, baseballs, fishing poles, and shaggy-haired Shetland ponies fit the picture perfectly. "Willie," as he was first called, had plenty of games, plenty of play, and plenty of friends with names like Buck, Buddy, and Tochie. Yet, somewhere, something went wrong.

The Falkners lived where Murry's job took them. At first, this meant the village of New Albany, where Murry worked for the family railroad.[1] It was there, in a modest frame house, that William Falkner was born on September 25, 1897. Leila Butler rushed over from Oxford for the event. Almost certainly, Leila had been staying with Sherwood and his wife Addie in Oxford where she could be very useful as Addie gave birth in quick succession to three infants after March, 1895. Sadly, each of the three would sicken and die before June, 1900. Probably, the first of these was born prematurely.[2] Possibly, Addie had continuing difficulty bringing any of her babies to full term. With the threat of infant death rampant in the family, Leila and Maud could hardly have felt secure with little William who, indeed, was a baby much given to colic during the first year of his life. Virtually every night, Maud rocked him through the darkest hours in a straight chair in the kitchen, stiff wooden legs thumping the floor while Murry slept.

In November, 1898, Murry was promoted to auditor and treasurer of the road and made supervisor of the Traffic and Freight Claim Departments, duties that required his presence in Ripley. Soon, the family moved to Ripley and settled into a house on the northwestern corner of Jackson and Cooper Streets. Early in May, 1899, Leila Butler arrived, and in June Maud gave birth to her second son. He was named Murry Charles but called "Jack." Charles, of course, was the name of Maud's father, now eleven years gone. Leila stayed through the summer. Then, early in 1900, she was back again.[3]

The move to Ripley was, to a significant degree, a homecoming for Murry. He had been born and reared in the village, and he was fifteen the year his family moved to Oxford. His maternal grandfather, Dr. John Young Murry, lived two doors south, and his aunt, Willie Medora, lived with her husband, Dr. Nathaniel G. Carter, three blocks east on North Main Street in the fine house built for them by Colonel Falkner.[4] One of William Faulkner's earliest memories was of a time when he was about three years old and visiting his great aunt Willie Medora Carter and her two daughters Natalie and Vance. He had gone there to spend the night, but, as he later recalled, he experienced "one of those spells of loneliness and nameless sorrow that children suffer." His cousins bundled up the boy and took him home by lamplight, across the railroad tracks that divided the town. "I remember how Vanny's hair looked in the light—like honey. Vanny was impersonal, quite aloof, she was holding the lamp. Natalie was quick and dark. She was touching me. She must have carried me."[5] It was a poignant memory and one that he carried to the end of his life. He carried another powerful memory also. He felt that there remained bitter feelings in the community against his great grandfather, which he somehow associated with Richard Thurmond's killing of Colonel Falkner. "I can remember myself," he said, "when I was a boy in Ripley, there were some people who would pass on the other side of the street to avoid speaking—that sort of thing."[6]

Meanwhile, Murry's business prospects continued to improve. Soon after the family moved to Ripley, his father, John Falkner, out of the "affection" he had for his son, deeded over to him a lot and a half on the southwestern corner of the square. Six months later, in June, 1901, John transferred to Murry a 560-acre farm immediately southwest of the village. The Colonel had acquired this acreage in 1867 when cash was scarce and land cheap. This bucolic connection cognated well with Murry's interest in horses, bird dogs, and hunting—an interest that he pursued eagerly at this time in his life.[7] Thus, as he approached age thirty, Murry held one of the top management positions in the very prosperous local railroad company, he operated a farm of considerable size, and he also bought an interest in a drug company in Ripley.

By the spring of 1901, Maud was pregnant with her third child and not feeling well. Early in the summer Leila came again to stay for some months before the baby, John, was born.[8] "Johncy," as the family dubbed him, arrived on the day before William's fourth birthday and proved to be the healthiest infant of all. However, shortly after his birth, Willie and Jack both came down with scarlet fever, a killing disease that they survived with careful nursing.[9] These were the usual hazards of a child born in the turn-of-the-century years. Still, the statistics argued that if such diseases didn't get you in the first few years, they didn't get you at all, and this proved to be the case with the Falkner boys. Once past early childhood, they were all very healthy and ready for the apparently beautiful childhood the family could afford. When Willie recovered from his bout with scarlet fever, his grandfather celebrated by giving him a Shetland pony, for which his great grandfather, John Y. Murry, ordered made a special saddle. At Christmas time, "Master William Falkner," age four and fully recovered, returned to Ripley with his grandmother Sallie after visiting at the "Big Place" in Oxford.[10] In March, 1902, William was in Oxford again, and in May, Maud brought all three boys over from Ripley for a stay.[11]

The critical turn in the life of the Murry Falkner family came in 1902 when John Falkner decided to sell the railroad. In the depressed 1890s, railroad companies all over America suffered severe financial problems and were gobbled up into great combinations that dominated the transportation industry well into the twentieth century. The Gulf and Chicago, as the railroad was now called, had no such problems. Indeed, in the 1900–1901 fiscal year, it paid each of the five heirs some $4,000.[12] Why John would sell such a profitable business to the Illinois Central for only $75,000 remains an open question. Perhaps, he simply tired of the responsibility he bore as the administrator of his father's estate. Family harmony, as he saw it, might have been promoted by translating everything into cash and making a division.

John's convenience, if such it was, was Murry's distress. The railroad was the centerpiece of his life and the foundation of his self-respect. Uncertainly, falteringly, he sought to save it. One of his sons later wrote that Murry went to talk to a banker in Corinth about financing to buy the road himself. The banker simply could not imagine that anyone would sell such a prosperous railroad and began by treating the matter as a joke. Murry, never adept at handling new situations, grew flustered and abruptly departed. The road was sold in May, 1902.[13]

John Falkner wanted Murry to move to Oxford. Murry resisted the idea and talked about going to Texas as his idolized Uncle Henry had once done. On New Year's Eve, 1888, he had attended a masquerade party dressed as a "cowboy," and he never quite gave up the dream of heading west and running a cattle ranch. Texas was still something of a frontier where a man could make a fresh start—perhaps in the cattle business. Maud vetoed Texas, however, and the family made preparations for the move to Oxford. Murry hired wagons, teams, and men to help him freight the household furnishings the fifty miles overland to Oxford while Maud and the three boys went by train, first south to New Albany, then northwest to Holly Springs, and finally south again to Oxford. They stepped down from the train in the early evening of September 24, 1902, the day before Willie reached his fifth birthday. They were met at the station by their grandfather and grandmother, loaded into a carriage, and driven the half-mile uphill to the town square and south down the main street to the Big Place.[14]

Jack Falkner, the second son, described in his book of reminiscences how he and William looked wide-eyed at the arc lamps and board walkways as they drove to and through the square on the first night of their permanent residence in Oxford.[15] Neither he nor his brother Johncy, who wrote a similar book, mentioned that some of the posts that supported those lights and some of those boardwalks were put into place by their mother's father, Charlie Butler, nor, more vitally, that they passed within a few yards of the spot upon which their grandfather had shot Sam Thompson to death. They failed to mention that the very pattern of streets and square upon which they rode was laid out by their great grandfather, and that they passed the site of the old Butler Hotel in which Burlina had flourished in spite of her widowhood. Indeed, family tradition as published seems to paint a picture in which the affluent Falkners found an unfortunate half-orphaned working girl, Maud, and brought her into the family. "She married 'Big Dad,' that was it," one of her grandsons declared flatly to a prospective biographer of William Faulkner in 1972.[16] The history behind Maud Butler appeared to be barely worth mentioning, especially in comparison with that of old Colonel Falkner and his son John Wesley Thompson Falkner.

In 1902 John Falkner was, indeed, doing well in Oxford. Certainly, he was relatively wealthy; he was also a town alderman, had twice been state senator from the county, and was a prosperous lawyer and businessman. He was a Knight of Pythias, one of the leaders in founding the local chapter of the Sons of Confederate Veterans, and his wife and children moved comfortably enough in the highest social circles of the town. Yet he, himself, was resented at some times and in some places for his bluff and blustery manner. John's father had come to Oxford to visit him now and again in the late 1880s and was known in the town. Sometimes he was recognized as "Colonel Falkner," but also sometimes as "that man." One trouble with the Colonel was that he himself had no visible father, no great plantation left over from slave times, no grand eastern seaboard associations that anyone had ever heard about, and no college or university in his past. This could not be said of the Thompsons, the Lamars, Howrys, or Pegueses, the people whose burial plots, significantly enough, would be located on the highest ground in the Town Cemetery—along with the Butlers—while the Falkners would be buried just a little lower on a second circle of that red clay necropolis. The Falkners, after all, were latecomers to Oxford and Lafayette County, and it was in the nature of Southern society that they would not be admitted to full and unqualified membership in the community either early or easily—regardless of money, manner, or ostensible power.[17]

John Falkner was not all work. He was a social person, who belonged to an array of men's clubs. He was also a heavy drinker, and sometimes had to go away for the cure. In November, 1902, within weeks of Willie Falkner's arrival in Oxford to live, his grandfather checked into Crawford's Sanitarium in Memphis "for treatment." By mid-December, he was home again, "much improved," as the *Oxford Eagle* declared.[18]

The Murry Falkner family moved into the modest house on Second South Street that had been occupied by the John Falkners during some fifteen years of their early residence in Oxford.[19] Murry, in fact, had lived there in his late teens. The house sat on an entire block, 400-feet wide and 1,000-feet deep. It was six blocks south of the square and one block west of the main street. The whole property was surrounded by a picket fence while another fence divided the lot into two parts. The back part, sloping off down hill to the west toward the railroad cut, contained the barn and pasture. In the front part sat the one-story wooden frame house. For those times, it was a comfortable place, raised about three feet from the ground in front, with latticework between the supporting pillars to keep the larger animals out. There was a wide hall down the middle with high ceilinged rooms opening on either side, each with a fireplace for heating in winter and windows that reached down toward the floor for cooling during the often torrid Mississippi summer. A porch decorated with wooden gingerbread stretched across the front of the house. The boys could play there, or spill easily down the few steps into the ample front yard.

When the Falkners moved into their new home, Leila Butler moved in with them. Leila and Maud, it seems, shared a bedroom while, presumably, Murry slept alone—as he had during much of Willie's first year of life. Probably, Leila had previously spent some considerable time with Sherwood and Addie. Addie had at last given birth to a child, Edwin Ross Butler, who survived. For five years, apparently, Leila had shuffled between Oxford and Ripley. On one occasion she stayed with her bitter and impoverished sister-in-law, the Confederate widow Vermelle Butler. On another she stayed with the affluent George W. Buffaloes in their University Avenue house, a switch probably caused by the fact that Sherwood had taken a job with Western Union in Memphis and moved to the city with Addie and their infant son.[20]

Leila made herself useful in the Falkner household. Especially, she catered to the sons, who called her "Damuddy." She prepared special foods for Jack's finicky taste, nursed the boys through minor illnesses, and, somewhere between Leila and Maud, William Faulkner gained an intimate knowledge of the Bible. The Butlers were staunch and pioneering Baptists in Oxford, and every Sunday Leila Butler would dress in black, presumably to claim widowhood from Charlie Butler, gone now more than a dozen years, and make her way to the First Baptist Church. Sometimes she took Willie with her—the small, sensitive, bright boy sitting on a bench in the church that his great grandmother Burlina Butler had helped to create.

Leila had taught Maud to draw, and when she moved into the house with the Falkners she brought her easel. In September, 1904, Leila filled the window of J.N. Gipson's store, "fancy groceries," with pictures and other work that revealed, according to the *Eagle*, "talent of a high order." It was a panorama entitled "The Presidential Race" and displayed, according to the local newspaper, "both creative genius and artistic taste."[21] Leila's and Maud's artistic talents were interesting, but not at all unusual. In those days, Southern ladies were supposed to have some accomplishment in music, writing, reading, conversation, or the arts. Both women took care to pass on whatever they could of their knowledge to the Falkner boys.

Probably William's most salient memory of his grandmother's artistic skill came not from her painting, but from a doll that she made for him. Remarkably, the doll was a policeman, about nine inches tall, uniformed in the 19th-century style with swallowtail coat, bell-shaped cap, and bright buttons. Perhaps his name should have been Charlie Butler, or perhaps he should have had the name of the policeman who ought to have arrested Charlie wherever he was and brought him home to his wife, his children, and his duty. Willie chose to call him Patrick O'Leary. Charlie Butler's absence amounted almost to a perpetual—and painful—presence in the household in which William Faulkner grew up. Sallie Murry Wilkins understood that John Falkner, among others, didn't blame Charlie for running away. Charlie couldn't stand living with Leila. Now Murry Falkner was living with her, and she was making his life miserable.[22]

~

Sometimes Willie would take Patrick to the Big Place where he would play dolls with his cousin Sallie Murry and a little girl who had recently moved onto South Street with her family. Her name was Lida Estelle Oldham, and she would become the woman that William Faulkner, in 1929, would marry. Faulkner's life and writings were profoundly affected by his virtually perpetual intimacy not only with Estelle but with the whole of the Oldham family.

Estelle's father, Lemuel, "Lem," Earle Oldham, entered the University of Mississippi in 1886 as a new student, but did not graduate. Rather, he read law in Oxford with Henry Clay Niles. In 1895, he married Niles's stepdaughter Lida Corinne Allen. Their first child, Lida Estelle, was born in Texas on February 19, 1897. Estelle was the name of Lem's younger sister. Their second child, Melvina Victoria, was born in Mississippi in May, 1899. Melvina—or Millie—was the name of Lem's mother; Victoria was the name of Lida Corinne's mother.[23]

The census taker in 1900 found Lem and Lida living next door to her mother Victoria in the town of Kosciusko in central Mississippi. Lem was then thirty years old, a traveling shoe salesman, and routine questions from the census taker elicited the fact that he had been unemployed for one month during the preceding year. Lida was twenty-five. Lida's mother, Victoria Swanson Allen, lost her first husband, John Wilburn Allen, a teenage Confederate soldier and later a physician, by his early death. In 1885, she had married Henry C. Niles and in 1887 gave birth to twins, James and Jason, their only children. Niles had been born in Mississippi in 1850 of a Vermont father and a Tennessee mother. He was a Republican and, by 1900, had become the judge for the Northern District of the federal court in Mississippi, a very important and lifetime position that he held by dint of the fact that a Republican president sat in the White House. In Kosciusko the Nileses and the Oldhams lived in a neighborhood among families headed by a deputy sheriff, a dry goods merchant, a day laborer, and an agent for a "Patent Window."[24]

Kosciusko was Lemuel's home town. In 1880, he was ten and lived there with his sister Estelle, age eight, and his mother, Millie, age twenty-six. Millie was a mother at sixteen and, obviously, had been a child bride. She was also an early widow, in 1880 living in the same house with her mother Ophelia Doty, forty-nine, also a widow, and her brother Lemuel Doty. Lem's father was Everett Charles Oldham, another teenage Confederate soldier who became fifth sergeant in his brother's company in the Twentieth Mississippi Volunteer Regiment. Everett, according to military records, was "captured by the enemy in skirmish on July 28, 1864" in front of Atlanta, and sent to a prisoner of war camp in Ohio before being exchanged at City Point in Virginia in March, 1865, probably because his health had failed. Everett died in 1873 and Millie, sometime after 1880, remarried. Lem grew up in Kosciusko and attended the public school and the local "institute" that prepared children for college.[25]

In 1903, Lem Oldham moved to Oxford to become the clerk of the federal court for northern Mississippi, the court over which his father-in-law presided. At $6,000 a year, it was an astonishingly well-paying job, considerably more than the governor of the state made for his labors.[26] The rub was that, at this particular time, one had to be a Republican to get it, and among the white people in Mississippi becoming a Republican was still generally associated with becoming a turncoat, selling out the South to the Yankees, and consorting with black people. However, in and after 1901 President Theodore Roosevelt worked assiduously to revitalize the Republican party in the South and make it respectable. He began to use a considerable portion of the presidential power of appointment not to reward political hacks among blacks and scurrilous white scalawags (as white Southerners saw most Southern white Republicans), but rather to enlist socially respectable Southern whites under the Republican banner. It was a persistent Republican strategy that finally triumphed in the 1960s during the Civil Rights movement when the Democrats clearly identified themselves as pro-black, and such powerful Southern politicians as South Carolina's J. Strom Thurmond moved their political organizations eagerly and openly into the Republican camp.

Even so, white people in Oxford looked askance at Lem as the only white Republican in town, and they understood that Perry Howard, a black lawyer who ran the Republican party in the state, approved appointments and got a kickback of two to five percent on every federal salary. "Which means that Oldham had to pay a Negro (or people thought he had) for his job," an Oxford native later recalled. In the racial and social order of those times, a white man who put himself in the power and at the pleasure of a black man in this way severely demeaned himself. "People were quiet about the Oldhams," the Oxfordian continued, "but they didn't think much of Lem."[27] The key to success in this maneuver was to insist upon one's membership in the social elite—to become la crème de la crème.

The Oldhams certainly qualified as a respectable family. Lemuel Earle Oldham was descended from pioneer settlers, and his grandfather Bayless Earle Oldham had represented Attala County in the legislature during the antebellum period. Even though he had not graduated, Lem Oldham, himself, had been a student in the University of Mississippi and eventually was titled "Major" Oldham. His wife Lida was a Southern lady who claimed kinship with an eminent Mississippi family that included at least one Confederate general, Felix Zollicoffer. Such titles and claims were common in the South in those times. Usually, however, the military titles came from service in the state militia, sometimes, especially in the higher ranks such as colonel or major, by appointment to the military staff of the reigning governor. Rarely did it come from actual military service. Claims of kinship, also, were easily made. Local marriage was the norm, but occasionally someone married into a neighboring circle with the result that everyone was related more or less to everyone else—if he or she felt the need of asserting the relationship. Ambitious Southerners were almost always able to connect themselves vaguely to some well-known governor, senator, general, or colonel, some first family of America, or, all else failing, to an "eminent" legislator, minister, doctor, lawyer, landowner, or businessman. Over time, claimed eminence became plausible and usually stood unchallenged.

The Oldhams eventually claimed kinship to the Bowdens of Maine, an emigrant named Doty who had arrived on the *Mayflower*, and Swiss Baron de Graffenreid, founder of New Bern, North Carolina.[28] After settling in Oxford, Lem and Lida had two more children, and each child would register such claims in their given names. Dorothy Zollicoffer would appear in 1905, and Edward de Graffenreid in 1907.

It was almost as if the Oldhams felt a need to declare familial antiquity and social eminence to match Lem's sudden rise to a position in the federal judiciary and a high salary. The ploy, if such it was, succeeded because of the particular way in which Southern society worked. Even being a Republican was permissible if one's father and uncles were Confederate veterans, if one went to Ole Miss, was admitted to Sigma Alpha Epsilon fraternity, and was a staunch Presbyterian. In the South everyone, it seems, was—and is—allowed one and only one great aberration. A man could even safely be a Communist as long as he was also, for example, a good family man, a Sunday-go-to-meeting Southern Baptist, and paid his dues on time at the country club. Major Oldham later took much of the sting out of his party affiliation by declaring that he was a "life long Republican," thereby implying that he had not converted to the then despised party to secure a lucrative appointment in his father-in-law's court.[29]

Thus it was that Major Oldham was not rich, but the Major's salary allowed the Oldhams to live in Oxford as if they were rich, and they made the most of it.[30] In 1903 they rented a large two-story house on South Street. Soon, with the births of Dorothy and Ned, the arrival of Lem's half-sister Maude Mabry (a young music teacher), and the hiring of Magnolia Cottrell as cook and Lindie Mise as nurse, the Oldham household became a substantial establishment.[31]

It was a comfortable life for the Oldhams. The tale was often told of how, soon after their arrival in Oxford, Estelle was sitting in a front room of the house having her hair curled by the maid, "Nolia" Cottrell, when she saw little Willie Falkner riding his pony up the street toward town in the company of his brothers. "See that boy, Nolia?" she said. "The one in front?—the one riding the pony by himself? That's the one I'm going to marry." And Nolia said, "Hush yo mouf, Chile. Folks what say they're going to get married while they're little grows up to be old maids."[32] In this case, Nolia was wrong. Later evidence suggests that Estelle might have said the same about several boys, but, definitely, she was not fated to be an old maid.

~

Lida's mother, Victoria, had, indeed, made a fortunate second marriage, and it might have saved her from financial difficulties arising from "a false statement" made by one of the Allen men after her husband's death.[33] Henry Clay Niles's Vermont-born father, Jason, had come to Mississippi as a school teacher, then flourished at law, represented Mississippi in the United States Congress from 1873–1875, and in the 1880s was a well-to-do local financier. Henry had followed his father into law. He became a town alderman in 1885, the same year he married Victoria, and by 1891 was the United States district attorney for the court that operated in and out of Oxford. Henry C. Niles was very much liked and highly respected in Oxford. People understood that he did not have to be a Republican to make a living. He looked down on both blacks and "rednecks"—including among the latter, by his lights, the Vardamans, the gubernatorial family in Mississippi after 1903. Deeply Presbyterian, the Nileses saw themselves as a few saints in a world full of sinners and, on the bench, Henry did his part by meting out just punishments to them all. A superior gentleman with a talent for clothing his condemnations in flowing and erudite language, Henry Niles was soon adopted and dearly held as one of their own by the Oxford elite.[34] "Papa Niles"—and sons Jason and James—were often at the Oldham home on South Lamar. Estelle, for instance, later recalled that he was teaching her Voltaire when she was twelve in 1909.[35]

Judge Niles lent maximum possible prestige to the Lem Oldham family in Oxford, and they certainly made the most of that and other opportunities as well. For nearly two decades, their home positively glittered as a social and cultural center. Probably no one was more impressed than the small boy, Billy Falkner, who, after 1906, lived up the street only two houses away from the Oldham residence.

Two years after arriving in Oxford, the Oldhams solidified their gains in a very significant fashion. In 1905, they put down $400 in cash and bought for $6,800 a large and elegant house on the southeast corner of South and Fillmore Streets, two blocks down and across South Street from John Falkner's "Big Place." That fall, Lida hosted in her new home the Twentieth Century Book Club one week and the Card Club the next. On Christmas morning the Oldhams had all their friends in for eggnog by the fireplace and gifts under the Christmas tree.[36]

Lida was thirty-two in 1905 and she was beautiful. Like her mother she was a superb pianist, and in the evenings she would play for hours in the high-ceilinged music room in the large house on South Street while her husband sat and listened. Lem, it was said, was "high-strung" and proud. "He wore a Chesterfield," one Oxfordian recalled, "even when he had no money for groceries." Estelle remembered as a little girl looking up at her father and seeing "a large expanse of shirt front" topped by a string tie. Fastidious, Lem would fix a napkin about his neck at mealtime to protect that broad front. After dinner he liked to dip English walnuts in port and savor the result. Lida would then have to soak the napkin in lemon juice and water to clear the stains.[37]

~

The life style of the Murry Falkners was very different from that of the Oldhams. Murry's very first job in Oxford was supervising the grading of the main street north of the square. Soon, however, he acquired a livery stable, and for some years that was his primary business. His stable was tied to the Falkner Transfer Company, a business that he managed for his father. He also ran his father's Oxford Oil Mill Company, a fairly simple operation that ground up surplus cotton seed to produce a saleable oil and a final residue, a "mash," that could be used for animal feed or fertilizer. Murry's office was also an all-male social center where, in the winter months, he and his cronies could sit around a sizzling, crackling pot-bellied stove and tell stories about horses and dogs, hunting and guns. Murry's managerial duties were light. He had several black men to take care of the fifty or so horses, other animals, and equipment and two white men to drive the hacks.[38] Hack drivers had to be white, of course, because white ladies alone could not be driven by a possibly strange black man.

Thus there were always people about the stable to do the physical labor of lifting and carrying, grooming and feeding, and Murry had a great deal of freedom. He was able, for example, to take advantage of the hunting camp that his father had created in the Tallahatchie bottom some miles north and west of Oxford. Later, when the boys were bigger, he took them with him. Sometimes Maud came too, perhaps at her own insistence because "Buddy" was increasingly given to spells of drinking and, occasionally, to fighting. He was a relatively large, stout man who fared well in combat as long as no weapons were introduced. Once he threw the constable of Beat One, Dick Oliver, through a downtown store window with a great showering of glass. That event was not nearly so damaging to Dick's body—and perhaps his pride too—as when his pistol somehow fell out of his pocket, fired as it hit the ground, and shot him in the thigh.[39]

Finally, the drinking became a serious problem and Murry, like his father, occasionally had to visit the Keely Institute near Memphis for the "cure." It was a family affair in which everyone took the train up to the big city and lived in quarters provided by the Institute while Buddy dried out. The boys loved the excursion because their mother would allow them to take long rides on the streetcars by themselves. They explored the city from this safe and mobile base, and it was on one such occasion that Billy Falkner first saw the mighty Mississippi, truly the "Father of Waters," rolling south.[40]

In all of this Maud was the anchor person, of course, and she was sorely tried. Shortly before Christmas in 1906 grandmother Sallie Murry Falkner died.[41] William, age nine, his younger brothers, and cousin Sallie Murry Wilkins attended the solemn service in the parlor of the Big Place, then made the sad trek to the family plot in St. Peter's Cemetery. Holland Wilkins, John's widowed daughter, continued to live in her father's house with Sallie Murry, her only child. Holland was strong in mind but, unfortunately, not in body. Maud, always her close friend as well as her sister-in-law, worked to hold both that household and her own together.

John Wesley Thompson Falkner was much depressed by the death of his wife. He was sometimes seen, quiet and morose, writing Sallie's name in the air with his finger. Now and again, he would walk the few blocks to the cemetery where he had raised a handsome monument of marble at the foot of Sallie's grave. On the south side of the obelisk a bust of Sallie was carved, framed, cameo-like, in an oval wreath. The west face, nearest her grave, bore his final tribute to her: "The heart of her husband doth safely trust in her. Her children arise and call her blessed. Her husband also, and he praiseth her." That fall, Sallie's father, Dr. John Y. Murry, came over from Ripley to Oxford to visit for several days. Each day he walked to the cemetery and brought flowers to place on Sallie's grave.[42]

In the spring of 1907, Leila Butler also fell ill, and it was soon learned that she was suffering from cancer—"one of those female cancers with a horrible odor," Sallie Murry Wilkins recalled. Maud carried that burden too, sometimes relieved as nurse by her brother Sherwood and his wife Addie, and always by the liberal doses of morphine that doctors then prescribed in such cases. One Saturday evening in June, Leila Butler died. The funeral was held Sunday afternoon in the parlor, the children present again, and she was buried in St. Peter's alongside her mother-in-law, Burlina Butler. Next to her was a space not yet filled where, presumably, Charlie Butler's body had been expected to find rest.[43] Billy Falkner, age nine, would never forget that day.

In the very weeks in which Murry's mother was dying, Maud became pregnant for the last time. The child was born in August, 1907, soon after Leila's death. It was another boy. Murry and his father wanted to call him Henry, after John

Falkner's wastrel half brother whom Murry had known and admired when he was a child in Ripley. Maud would have no part of it. She named him Dean Swift after her mother's family.[44] Seemingly, she had had enough of Falkner men.

In October, 1906, before his mother died in June, 1907, Murry Falkner bought the large and handsome John R. Brown House on South Street. The Browns had been among the very rich in antebellum Oxford. Located on the southeast corner of Taylor and South Streets, the house was one block down and across the street from the Big Place. Again, the Falkner boys had a spacious lot in which to play, with out-buildings (including a new barn), separate enclosures for animals, and a pasture that stretched down the eastern slope behind the house to include a ditch and a small creek at the bottom. The house, wooden and painted white, was two storied with a cellar and full attic. The porch ran all the way across the front and around the right side, where a portion was screened against insects for summer lounging. Inside, off the wide central hall to the right, sliding doors led to the parlor, then other doors back to the dining room and kitchen. To the left off the hall was the master bedroom and a bath. Front and back stairs led to an upstairs hall and four bedrooms. White plaster walls lined all the rooms, which were filled with oak, walnut, and mahogany furniture—dark, heavy, and Victorian. Already Oxford had telephones, piped water, and sewerage, and the house was soon to be electrified.[45]

Next door to the Falkners, on one side, the Cumberland Presbyterian minister lived with his three young children, and on the other a druggist, whose wife gave dramatic "readings" on stage. The Oldhams lived two doors south. It was an interesting neighborhood that included Circuit Court Judge William Arthur Roane (Ole Miss, Class of 1876); merchant George Buffaloe, Jr. (who was Sherwood Butler's brother-in-law); a town-dwelling farmer and businessman named G.R. Hightower who had soundly defeated John W.T. Falkner in his bid for a seat in the state senate in 1903 and would become the founding president of Mississippi State University; eighty-six-year-old Charles Word, who was probably a cousin to old Colonel Falkner; and a Russian Jewish family with two girls, Rosie and Florrie Friedman, who were almost identical in age to and close friends with Estelle and Victoria "Tochie" Oldham. Estelle remembered the parents vividly. Mr. Friedman was blond, blue-eyed, and handsome; Mrs. Friedman was elegant and perhaps, Estelle thought, of noble blood. Almost every house in the neighborhood had one or two servants, many of whom lived in small dwellings on the backside of the lots.[46]

This was the seemingly superbly comfortable world in which Billy Falkner lived from 1906, when he was nine years old, until 1912, when he turned fifteen. In a sense it was a golden age for the Murry Falkner family before Murry's material fortunes began visibly to decline. It was a time when Billy passed from boyhood into adolescence, and he and his brothers were especially intimate with the Oldham household. This was the beginning of a very special intimacy between the two families that would persist for generations. Particularly and profoundly, it would mark the life of William Faulkner.

Race

When the Falkners had moved into their house on Second South Street in 1902, they were joined by Caroline Barr, a black woman who was born a slave in 1855. Caroline also came to South Street with the Falkners. There the household added a cook, a black woman in her mid-thirties named Sara Beaver.[47]

Caroline had grown up on the Barr plantation a few miles outside of Oxford and by the turn of the century was working for John Falkner. She was known among black people as Callie "Watermellon" Brown.[48] She would be known to the Falkner boys as "Mammy" Callie. She lived on the lot and served steadily as a lieutenant to Miss Maud in running the household. Taken away from time to time by a romantic interlude, Mammy Callie always returned to her place among the Falkners. She cooked, she cleaned, and she cared for them, but most of all the boys liked her stories—of animals in the woods, ghosts, and the "Old Days" of slavery. The boys loved her dearly, but they were casual in honoring her orders and they seemed to be totally unmoved by her threats of discipline. In truth, there was no commanding black mammy in the Falkner household, nor could there be. Maud was the woman in the house, and she never yielded one iota of her dominance in that sphere to anyone. Perhaps, her trials as a young woman with a fugitive father had forged within her personality a vein of iron.[49]

Mammy Callie represented a black population that was somewhat more numerous and visible in Lafayette County than in Tippah. In Lafayette black people were about 45 percent of the total. Mostly they were sharecroppers out in the countryside, renting plots of land of forty acres or so for a third of the year's crop. In bad years, of course, the tenant did not "pay out." Black folklore caught this phenomenon in a ditty that described the accounting process at the end of the year:

> Naught's a naught
> And five's a figger
> All for the white man
> And none for the nigger.

In a sequence of bad years, either the landlord simply closed up some of his farms, or he didn't pay out. It was a hard school, it presented problems that had no solutions at the local level, and it bred feelings of powerlessness among all of its students. The great majority of blacks were tenant farmers, and so too were increasing numbers of whites.

Some whites had been tenant farmers before the war; after the war the numbers of white tenants swelled. More and more, they came into competition with blacks for tenancy on the best farms. Often white landlords preferred black tenants to white, and in very bad years in Mississippi and elsewhere in the South, white farmers organized to drive black tenants off the land by violence. Sometimes they did this work in disguises fashioned from bedsheets for robes and pillowcases for hoods and thus came to be called "whitecappers." In Mississippi in the turn-of-the-century years there grew up a strange species of warfare in which white landlords fought poorer whites with Pinkerton detectives and the power of the state while blacks who had been tenant farmers fled for their lives. Not a few of these went upriver and ended in Memphis, St. Louis, and Chicago. Among other things, they carried their music with them.

Mammy Callie belonged to the small percentage of ex-slaves who left the farms for the towns and cities of the South soon after emancipation. Black people lived all over Oxford, some in small houses in the yards behind the big houses where they worked. Most of the newcomers, however, concentrated along the railroad line north and west of the town's center. "Freedmantown" that still-visible community was called, using the word invented by whites to describe the status of ex-slaves. Freedmantown evolved its own exclusively black institutions—businesses, schools, and churches. By the turn of the century, the second generation had thrust up a cadre of leaders—the more substantial landowning farmers, ministers, school principals, teachers, and entrepreneurs in stores, barber shops, funeral parlors, insurance, and hip-pocket banking.

Among these, ministers were central. Increasingly after emancipation, the local church became the focal point of black life, social and cultural as well as religious. It was no mere coincidence that Emeline Falkner in Ripley in 1881 bought land just north of the "African church" and soon moved out of Richard Thurmond's lot and onto her own in the black neighborhood west of Quality Ridge, and that she and her family developed an intimacy with the Second Baptist Church in Ripley that has lasted for more than a century. The black church gave birth to a unique, vital, and ongoing music, and to a style of preaching that spoke the message clearly, passionately, and persuasively. William Faulkner, in his novel *The Sound and the Fury* (1929), caught something of that essence when he had Dilsey Gibson take Benjy to her church on Easter Sunday, 1928.

Wherever there were black people there was certain to be a church nearby. At least once every seven days there was a meeting in the church that moved the body and exhalted the spirit. The black church was local, but it also transcended the local in that black ministers belonged to denominational organizations that were national, and it was usual for black ministers, like white, to move from church to church over the years. Probably the most powerful black denominations were the African Methodist Episcopal Church and its sister the AME Zion Church, both of which came out of secessions of black Methodists from white-dominated churches in Philadelphia and Baltimore in the 1790s. Probably black Baptists were always more numerous, and they had their associations too, as did the relatively few Presbyterians and Episcopalians, but the Methodists had both numbers and a central organization.

To be black in the South was always to be not-white, and black people created a culture that was perpetually evolving and never white. Sometimes elements in black culture were deliberate borrowings from whites, sometimes they were deliberate rejections of whiteness, most often they evolved from perceptions by black people of their own needs without a focused regard to color. Most of all, black people simply struggled, as everyone does, to create meaningful lives for themselves. White people, however, saw black culture as a more or less crude imitation of their own. Blacks might sing and dance differently, but most whites could not imagine that black people could have a life that was not complimentary in some way to their own. They flattered themselves further that they knew all they needed to know about blacks and their lives. In their view, black people—with the exception of the talented few—were white children with black skins, and like children they could either be charming and very useful in their simplicity and innocence, or they could be appalling and bestial. As most whites saw it, the problem with blacks was that when a black adult male was bad, he was endowed with a physical strength that made him very bad indeed.

White people had not always lumped black folks together in this fashion. In the colonial period, white Southerners did not think that all blacks looked alike. Instead they tended to identify black people according to the African ethnic group from which they came. Mandingoes, for instance, were large people and they were supposed to be fierce and proud. Mandingoes made very dangerous slaves until broken, until strength and pride was turned to the master's service, and then they were among the best of slaves. Other groups would be recognized by a yellow tinge in the eye, by a tendency to smile (Yorubas), or by "blue gums" (dark patches on mucus membrane). In the last generation of slavery, however, white people strove desperately to see all black people alike. All blacks were "Sambo," and those who failed in that role were, in one way or another, erased.

During Reconstruction, the child-like Sambo image was replaced by a confusion of images, but with the end of Reconstruction in the 1870s (1875 in Mississippi), he came to the white mind again in altered form. In this revived racial conservatism, it was almost as if Sambo were allowed to add a dozen or so years to his life before he froze into a stereotype again. He—and she—could, after all, exist separately as functional adults with a home and family. When in their place, black people were fine. Blacks could tenant a farm or pursue a trade, and a few, perhaps with some white blood in their veins, could preach, teach, and lead. Whites need exercise only the mildest form of supervision. Northerners had gone home, and ruling whites in the South were very ready to agree that they were, indeed, God's chosen people to take care of Southern blacks, ninety percent of the nation's total. In effect, in the 1880s an unwritten contract was made in which the South exchanged "home rule" in social matters for the surrender of economic and political power in the nation. One of the prime architects in effecting the arrangement was the Oxfordian L.Q.C. Lamar. Indeed, for many Northerners and Southerners too, he came to personify a South that could be trusted.

156

During the turn-of-the-century decades, the very years in which William Faulkner was born and came of age, the racial picture in the South changed radically. Never before or since have so many white people believed for so long and so deeply that black people were becoming bestial. The essence of the thinking of racial radicals in these years can be succinctly stated. Before the Civil War, the naturally savage potential of the African in America had been held in check only by the very tight reins of slavery. Freed from slavery for a full generation, black people in the 1890s—especially young black people—were falling over the edge of civilization and, hence, must eventually disappear from the American scene. The retrogression was everywhere apparent—in the dissolution of the black family, the degradation of the black church, and the rise of crime, disease (venereal and otherwise), idleness, and improvidence in the black community. Nowhere was it more clear or threatening than in the alarming increase of rapes and attempted rapes by black men upon white women. It was here, in this crucible, as it were, that a profound confusion of race, sex, and violence occurred in the South. It was a confusion that worked with tremendous power in William Faulkner's fiction, that was exported to the North in the early decades of the twentieth century, and that subtly permeates white thinking in America today.

Phillip Alexander Bruce, Virginia aristocrat, writer, and intellectual, caught the image of the "black beast rapist" at its very beginning in 1889. "There is something strangely alluring and seductive to them in the appearance of a white woman," he wrote:

> They are aroused and stimulated by its foreignness to their experience of sexual pleasure, and it moves them to gratify their lust at any cost and in spite of every obstacle. This proneness of the negro is so well understood that the white women of every class, from the highest to the lowest are afraid to venture to any distance alone, or even to wander unprotected in the immediate vicinity of their homes; their appreciation of the danger being keen, and their apprehension of corporal injury as vivid, as if the country were in arms. [Whites were outraged by such assaults] and not unnaturally, for rape, indescribably beastly and loathesome always, is marked, in the instance of its perpetration by a negro, by a diabolical persistence and a malignant atrocity of detail that have no reflection in the whole extent of the natural history of the most bestial and ferocious animals.[50]

Radicalism was especially a black belt phenomenon, and Mississippi was the darkest state in the nation. In Mississippi, no single name is better associated with radicalism than that of James K. Vardaman, first in journalism and later in politics. In 1903, after a decade of struggle, Vardaman won the governorship and shortly led his state into a phase of racial extremism that has, perhaps, never been equaled in the American experience. In Mississippi, conservative racism suffered a nearly total eclipse. Vardaman voiced almost perfectly the radical racist mind. "Six thousand years ago," he declared in one speech, "the Negro was the same in his native jungle that he is today."[51] The Negro freed from slavery was rapidly retrogressing to that savage state, Vardaman thought, and no amount of sympathy or help on the part of whites would save him. Education simply empowered his immoral tendencies and led him to seek social equality and amalgamation by more subtle, more insidious, and more effective means. In 1904, a prestigious Northern journal printed a statement of Governor Vardaman's views. The Negro was "one-third more criminal in 1890 than he was in 1880," the governor declared. Black male assault on white women was especially high. "You can scarcely pick up a newspaper whose pages are not blackened with the account of an unmentionable crime committed by a negro brute, and this crime, I want to impress upon you, is but the manifestation of the negro's aspiration for social equality, encouraged largely by the character of free education in vogue."[52] Shortly after taking office the governor closed down completely the state's normal school for blacks in Holly Springs, literally chaining and padlocking the doors and metaphorically throwing away the keys. Whatever education black people required, he said, could be gained while laboring in the fields.[53]

Most of all, the retrograding black male was after white women, and that not only legitimated the lynching of black men, it made such summary, horrible, and highly visible punishments mandatory. Rebecca Latimer Felton, very nearly the first lady of Georgia in these decades and the first woman ever, in 1921, to occupy a seat in the United States Senate, caught that mood perfectly in a speech she delivered to the Georgia Agricultural Society at its annual meeting in the summer of 1897—on the eve, virtually, of William Faulkner's birth. A year later, she recalled that there had been seven lynchings for rape in Georgia in the week before she spoke. "A crime nearly unknown before and during the war had become an almost daily occurrence and mob law had also become omnipotent," she said. In her speech, Rebecca Felton had no qualms about calling upon white men to do their duty. ". . . if it takes lynching to protect woman's dearest possession from drunken, ravening human beasts," she cried, "then I say lynch a thousand a week if it becomes necessary."[54] Felton might have been gratified by the performance of white men in Mississippi. In the twenty years from 1889 to 1909, at least 293 blacks were lynched there, more than in any other state in the nation.[55]

The Nelse Patton Lynching

Radical racism—this conjunction of race, sex, and violence—came vividly home to Oxford in 1908 in the lynching of Nelse Patton.[56] Patton was a black convict lodged in the county jail, but he was also a "trusty" who was allowed to move about town on various errands. Mattie McMillan, white, was the wife of a man who had been jailed. About noon on Tuesday, September 8, McMillan sent Patton to his wife with a message. When Patton arrived at the McMillan house, about a mile south of town, he had been drinking. He delivered the message to Mrs. McMillan, but then, the story goes, refused to leave. Mattie attempted to get a pistol from a drawer in her bureau, but Patton grabbed her. As they struggled, Patton forced her head back with one hand, and drew a razor blade across Mattie's throat with the other, almost severing her head from her body. The wounded woman ran screaming into the yard and collapsed. At that point her seventeen-year-old daughter appeared on the scene. Patton "attempted to assault" the daughter, but she managed to escape and spread the alarm.

Patton fled and white men scrambled to organize a pursuit. Among the hunters were the teenage sons of Deputy Sheriff Linburn Cullen, John and Jencks. A third son, Hal, was a classmate of Willie Falkner's in the town's graded school. The Cullen brothers correctly guessed the path the fleeing murderer would take and met him with shotguns. John halted Patton with two loads of squirrel shot, and the boys held him at gunpoint until the officers came up. Badly wounded, Patton was jailed, and the jail was put under heavy guard.

In the initial Associated Press report, Mattie McMillan was simply "a white woman." In a "fuller account" sent to a Jackson paper an hour or so later, she was "a highly respected young white woman," and "a white lady." In the first account she was "killed"; in the second she was "assaulted and killed."

The townspeople, in "a frenzy of excitement," gathered around the jail, just north and east of the town square. As night came on, "great crowds came in from the country" until some 2,000 people had assembled. One paper declared that "the entire population of the city and half the county of Lafayette was crowded about the jail and the courthouse." Judge Roane (the Falkners' neighbor), a minister, and others addressed the crowd from the porch of the jail, pleading with them to let the law take its course. Suddenly, lawyer William V. Sullivan, recently a United States senator from Mississippi and Charlie Butler's attorney in the 1880s, leapt to the porch and urged the mob to lynch Patton. Handing his revolver to a deputy sheriff, he ordered the officer to "shoot Patton and shoot to kill."

Soon, the mob, led by Sullivan, moved into action. They overpowered the sheriff, but wisely he had locked Patton in the jail building from the outside and hidden the key. Bravely, he refused to reveal its location, and the crowd turned its attention to forcing its way into the jail. The building proved to be a veritable Bastille. At first, scores of men worked at the large steel doors that barred the front entrance. For more than three hours they battered at the doors with sledge hammers and used heavy timbers as rams—all to no avail.

After midnight, they started working on the steel-shuttered windows using hammers, saws, and cold chisels. Finally, some minutes after 1:00 A.M. they managed to open holes through which they could see the inside of the jail.

Sticking the muzzles of their guns into the holes, they sprayed the interior with bullets. A few minutes later they gained bodily entrance and found Patton, bleeding badly and almost dead, slumped on the stairs leading to the second floor. Putting ropes around his neck, they dragged him through the crowd to the square, strung him up naked on a telephone pole, and riddled his body with bullets. Finally, they "dispersed, and Oxford was quiet again." Nelse Patton's body swung through the night—suspended from a "telephone pole" that probably also carried the electrical wires that had lighted the homes of the city for the first time only four days before.[57]

William Falkner was almost eleven on the night of the lynching, and his bed was not more than a thousand yards from both the jail and the square. Knowing William Faulkner as man and boy as we now do, it is impossible to imagine that he failed to record and retain every detail of the drama that came to his senses. Possibly, he saw it all. Surely he heard the first volley fired into the jail, then the fusillade that riddled the swinging body, heard too the fevered noise of the crowd as it rammed at the steel doors and came to successive crescendos in the shootings. Two houses down the street, in her bed, Estelle Oldham, too, must have heard.

In 1935, Faulkner would reject abruptly a suggestion from a national magazine that he do a lynch story, saying that he had never witnessed a lynching and hence could not write about one. It was a curious performance. He had indeed published a lynch story called "Dry September" in *Scribner's* in 1931. In that story a middle-aging, frustrated belle accused an innocent, unsuspecting, hard-working black man of rape, and eight white men of the lower social orders did him in, quietly and secretly.[58] This was a lynching in the style that prevailed in the middle decades of the twentieth century. They were secret and small and a far cry from the public and massive events that occurred with appalling regularity in the turn-of-the-century decades. In 1932, in telling the story of Joe Christmas in his novel *Light in August*, the author tried again, and he succeeded brilliantly. Though set in contemporary time, he wove together powerful themes of race, sex, and violence to capture the essence of lynching at its apex in the turn-of-the-century South. Clearly, in that writing, he recalled the Patton affair.

The details of the Patton lynching were specific to Lafayette County, but the pattern was general. The justification was rape or attempted rape, the crowd numbered hundreds and thousands, an active cadre of several dozen men did the actual work, and the body would be mutilated, castrated, and displayed in a public, ritualistic, and dramatic way. Afterward, white people would feel a significant measure of relief. The Patton lynching was also true to the general pattern in that it was done not only by "rednecks," the lower orders of whites. It was done by everybody, and the white community found release in the event.

In the Patton lynching the prime leader was William Van Amberg Sullivan, a man we have met before and who was certainly no redneck. He attended Ole Miss, graduated from Vanderbilt University in 1875 at age eighteen, and read law. In 1880, he and his wife Belle lived in modest material circumstances, but over the years his law practice grew steadily and he rose to the ranks of the well-to-do. In time, the couple had four children and joined the social elite of Oxford. In 1894, we catch a glimpse of William going off to the races in Memphis with the George W. Buffaloes and other prominent Oxfordians. In 1895, Belle died, and William continued to move upward in prestige and power. In 1897, he won a seat in the United States House of Representatives, the seat that had been occupied by Jacob Thompson and L.Q.C. Lamar. The death of Mississippi senator Edward C. Walthall resulted in his elevation in 1898 to the Senate by appointment of the governor and his election subsequently to fill out the term until March, 1901.[59] Sullivan was very busy at the law after his return from Washington, and one of his regular clients was—amazingly—Nelse Patton.

"Nelse" (for Nelson) was a bootlegger. He was well known to the Oxford community long before his lynching, particularly to officers of the law and to those who patronized his apparently flourishing business.[60] He carried in his name the names of two eminent Lafayette County families, but he seems to have been notorious as a denizen of the netherworld of Oxford and environs. In the mid-1890s he was brought into court and indicted for "Assault and Battery with intent to kill." He was a frequent visitor to the courts in the middle years of the first decade of the century, invariably for "retailing," that is, for selling liquor contrary to law. In Oxford, selling liquor was a special crime because it was illegal to sell spirits within five miles of the university, a law obviously—and futiley—designed to preserve youthful students in their innocence of alcohol.

Apparently, Nelse was plying his trade against a flooding tide of opposition from respectable citizens in the community. In 1906 the *Eagle* published an impassioned appeal to the men of Oxford to rid the town of "the blind tiger in our midst." A "blind tiger" was a drinking place. In the next year the authorities even closed down Bramlett's Drug Store, having found liquor there.[61] It seemed that a war against alcohol was on. Between September, 1906, and March, 1908, Nelse was repeatedly hauled into court and finally indicted on five separate counts of retailing. After a great deal of hassling between officers, the courts, and lawyer Sullivan, Nelse pled guilty to two counts. He was then fined a total of $150 and sentenced to 90 days in jail.[62] He had served time in the county jail before, and he had been out on bond while awaiting a decision in these most recent cases. It is not surprising that he should have been treated as a "trustee" in Lafayette County's penal system. Nor would it be vastly surprising to find that Nelse had been well acquainted with both Mr. and Mrs. McMillan before they all gained such signal public attention and that their familiarity was not unrelated to the reasons for Mr. McMillan's incarceration. In brief, it is likely that the whole affair was not so coincidental, and that white parties of both sexes were not as innocent as they might, at first blush, seem.

Somehow in the Patton case the community found itself confronting the alarming results of a commingling of race and sex with the disinhibiting effects of alcohol. This was a theme that profoundly disturbed whites in the black belt South in the early years of the twentieth century, a theme that contributed to an horrendous race riot in Atlanta in 1906 and was soon woven into that very telling film, *The Birth of a Nation* (1915). White society seemingly felt itself being drawn into a tangled knot of venereal corruption, and its solution was to blame the black man and cut the knot away in one quick, dramatic, and furious slice. If Patton's behavior over the years had suggested that white people were losing control, that the moral order was dissolving and damnation was imminent, his execution by the communal efforts of some 2,000 white men—"the entire population of the city and half the county"—spurred to action by Senator Sullivan symbolized that the crisis was bravely met and safely passed by those very persons. In Lafayette County, clearly white people would rule, and order would be achieved.

During the day following the lynching, Senator Sullivan gave an interview to a reporter. "When I heard of the horrible crime I started to work immediately to get a mob," he declared candidly. "I led the mob which lynched Nelse Patton," he boasted, "and I am proud of it." He had viewed with satisfaction the results hanging on the square that morning, he said. He would gladly stand the consequences of his actions, and he would eagerly do it again if the need arose. For him, as for Joe Christmas's executioner in *Light in August*, Percy Grimm, it was perfect justice. "Cut a white woman's throat and a negro?" Sullivan exclaimed. "Of course I wanted him lynched."[63]

~

There is a mountain of ignorance, myth, and outright misunderstanding layered over the reality of interracial happenings in the South in the turn-of-the-century years. One of the omissions is that there was a flood of horrendous lynchings in the region beginning essentially in 1889. Indeed, between 1889 and 1909, there were at least 2,000 such events, a sort of temporary and localized insanity. The tendency has been to see lynchings as sporadic episodes, as brief and isolated events. This in spite of the fact that the NAACP in 1919 published a count and catalogue of these gory occurrences. In the early years of the new century, when some leading and thoughtful Southerners occasionally took the rash of lynchings as a whole and as a phenomenon with social significance, they often described them as the work of the lower orders of whites, "rednecks," "crackers," and "grits." What we now see is that lynchings were part of a whole broad cloth. They were community efforts, made for profoundly cogent reasons, both conscious and unconscious, incited, encouraged, virtually programmed by a respectable element in local leadership for higher ends of social stability. After a lynching, clearly the white community felt relieved. God was in his heaven and life on earth was manageable after all.

In retrospect, it appears that the broad history of the South was, indeed, simply writ small in Lafayette County. In the decades after the Civil War, modernity began to invade the region with railway and industrial expansion, an influx of the very visible products of technological innovation, and a reorganization of money, banking, and credit. In the 1880s, in particular, Southern whites seemed concerned about their own loss of sexual civility—as the killing of Sam Thompson by Charlie Butler clearly suggests. In the same years, civil awareness of the evils of alcohol commenced a distinct rise. In the turn-of-the-century decades, great numbers of Southern whites combined the two failings, and imputed them specially to black people—as the lynching of Nelse Patton signifies.

William Faulkner spent the formative years of his life in the very midst of the radical racist hysteria. It was in the social air, and a child could no more escape the miasma than he could escape breathing. Racism was, of course, institutionalized in the segregated, all-white Oxford graded school. William and all of the Falkner boys began school at the then customary age of eight, Maud having taught them to read at home. In September, 1905, Billy began the first grade in the two-story brick building on Jackson Street that his grandfather Charlie Butler had helped bring into being twenty years before. Billy's first teacher was Miss Annie Chandler. Her father, Josiah, had married into the Jacob Thompson–Peyton Jones connection. He had been a surgeon and eventually the captain of Company B of the First Mississippi Cavalry, the unit to which Herman Wholleben and other Oxfordians belonged. Her brother Edwin, born in 1893, was retarded. She and her sisters kept Edwin at home, where he could sometimes be seen moving about in the yard behind a high fence.[64] Miss Annie was unmarried and deeply fond of the children she taught.

Somehow Miss Annie's copy of Thomas Dixon's *The Clansman* (1905) found its way into Faulkner's personal library. This was a book that painted blacks generally as retrogressing to a savage state and black men in particular as ravaging, raping beasts. The book sold more than a million copies, and Dixon turned it into a play. Soon, he organized several companies that took the show on the road throughout America. By 1908, more than four million people had seen the performance. Two weeks after the lynching of Nelse Patton, the *Eagle* advertised the coming of "The Clansman" to Oxford, and a month later the play opened at the Opera House, owned by Billy's grandfather. Without doubt, the performance included the usual superbly dramatic and climactic scene in which white-sheeted, spiked-hooded klansmen sat on live horses on stage, also white-sheeted, witnessing an actually burning cross after having lynched Gus, a black man who had attempted the rape of a virginal white girl.[65] It is highly probable that Billy and his brothers had their usual choice seats from which to view this spectacular production.[66] Both the book and the play explained why Nelse Patton had to be lynched. *The Clansman*, interestingly, provided the basic story line for the film *The Birth of a Nation*.

Radical racism required lynching, but only enough to keep black people under control as they passed on to their general demise. Ironically, even the worst radicals saw themselves as paternalistic—as did the best conservatives. Sometimes, as the logic went, the parent had to be cruel to be kind. The best a radical white could do was to let black people know that they had to stay in their place until they died, and, if they stayed in their place, that radical could be generous to individual blacks. Thus Nelse Patton could be lynched while Mammy Callie was cared for, and the Falkner boys could consort with black playmates such as Joby and Durwue, the cook's sons, and even with such adult males as Chess Carothers, a "freckled, mocha-colored man" who acted as valet and chauffeur to their grandfather. Chess, incidentally, had his own special terminal encounter with modernity. He struck a match to find a leak in the gas line of an automobile and burned to death.

Eventually, the radical image faded. In the South during the second decade of the twentieth century, the fear that had been projected upon the black beast was transferred in large measure to alien Jews and Catholics, and after the Russian Revolution in 1917 especially to the Communists—who often came in the guise of labor organizers, preferably Jewish, stirring up otherwise complacent blacks. Indeed, in Mississippi in the decade after 1909, the number of blacks lynched averaged six a year as opposed to fifteen a year in the previous decade.[67] By the 1920s the ubiquitous black beast rapist was virtually lost to the white mind, and certainly to the history books. Our blacks were good blacks, Southern whites declared stoutly, and we were good to them. Previous unpleasant events were treated as curious and isolated episodes, largely the result of the particularly benighted racism of the poor whites.

Adolescence

During the summer and fall of 1909, just as he turned twelve and entered the sixth grade, Billy Falkner began to change in ways that would make him very different both from his brothers and other young men of the leading families of Oxford. He began to skip school, dodge work, and perpetrate practical jokes. "I never did like school," he later recalled. There is abundant evidence of the truth of this statement.[68] At one level, no doubt Billy was experiencing the "growing pains," as they were then called, that all young people suffer as they approach adulthood. Nevertheless, the course he steered to make that passage was decidedly different from those usual among his contemporaries. At least five individuals played crucial roles in this particular transition—his mother, his father, his grandfather, Estelle Oldham, and a young Oxfordian several years his senior named Phil Stone.

"I escaped my mother's influence pretty easy," Faulkner once declared, revealing an amazing lack of self-understanding.[69] In truth, taking the whole of his life into account, no other individual influenced him so profoundly. Faulkner outlived his mother by only two years, he lived in her home during a large portion of his adult life, and even after his marriage he dropped by her house for a visit almost every day whenever he was in Oxford. The connection was perfectly understandable. Maud's faith in "Billy," as she always called him, was total and absolutely unshakeable. When so many others easily and confidently pronounced him a failure, she insisted that he was a genius and that the world would come to recognize that fact.

There were many ways in which mother and son were different, but they shared one vital characteristic—an unswerving commitment to individualism. Maud's independence might well have sprung primarily from her father's desertion of her and her family, and that quality put her at variance with a community that made deference to the communal order almost a religion. "Don't Complain, Don't Explain" was the motto that she painted on a board and hung in her kitchen. Neither she nor her mother Leila seemed to give out freely the story of Charlie Butler's defection. Yet his defection was felt—even after Damuddy's death. There was always that unfilled space alongside Leila Butler's grave under the cedars in the Butler plot in St. Peter's Cemetery.

There is no indication that Maud ever bemoaned, publicly or privately, her unjust fate. On the other hand, Billy never seemed to cease his multi-parted laments over his fate. Through most of his life, he railed against a world that seemed not to value fairly either him or his work. Publishers, editors, agents, employers, wife, children (when they became adults), lovers, kin, neighbors, men and women, blacks and whites, patricians and plebians—all failed him. But, like Maud again, he would not die. Instead, he worked about as hard and long as anyone could, but only at the labor of his choice—writing.

Maud Butler had more in her past than met the eye, and an even more vital reminder of that fact than the empty space next to her mother's grave was the presence of her brother Sherwood in the town. Estelle Faulkner later remembered him when he was a jeweler in Oxford and said that he looked like Miss Maud and Billy. She also recalled that "Sherwood Butler was charming and outgoing," and he "had everything Miss Maud, his sister, didn't." Maud's grandson, Jimmy, said that they all called him Uncle Sherwood "and everybody that knew him said he was a gentleman in every sense of the word."[70]

In 1910 Sherwood was, indeed, a jeweler with his own store in Oxford. He and Addie lived with her father on University Avenue, just around the corner from Maud. By now George Buffaloe, Sr., was rich and retired. He was, in age, almost exactly a contemporary of Sherwood's father and, back in 1883, had in fact served on the coroner's jury that found that Charlie Butler had shot Sam Thompson to death. Mrs. Buffaloe, before her death, would often entertain the Ladies' Literary Society in her home, just down the avenue from John Falkner's "Big Place" on the corner at South Street. Addie Buffaloe Butler, like her mother before her, was very much in the social swim. In December, 1917, the local press noticed that "Mrs. Sherwood Butler and Miss Flora Buffaloe will leave Friday for Greenwood to spend Christmas with their sister, Mrs. Dr. Rains," and later that winter recorded that "The Twentieth Century Book Club met with Mrs. Sherwood Butler Wednesday evening."[71]

Sherwood and the Buffaloe connection are strangely slighted in published Falkner family accounts, though William Faulkner used the Buffaloe name for an attractive—and minor—character in his writings. Perhaps most striking is the omission from the family history of William's only Butler cousin, Sherwood's son Edwin Ross Butler. In 1910 Edwin was eight years old, lived close-by, and seemingly was well qualified as a playmate for the Falkner boys within whose age cohort he clearly fitted. Yet, there is no mention, ever, of their first cousin Edwin in the published reminiscences of the Falkners, while their cousin on the Falkner side, Sallie Murry, gets abundant and laudatory attention.

The Sherwood Butlers and their Buffaloe relations were not at all lost to the community of Oxford. During World War I and afterward, Sherwood worked and lived in Monroe, Louisiana, and Greenwood, Mississippi, and the local press often reported family visiting back and forth between these places and Oxford.[72] When Sherwood died in 1930, he was buried two or three spaces north of his mother in the Butler plot in St. Peter's, apparently by Edwin, who caused a handsome marble copse to be put around his grave with the word "Dad" carved into a stone scroll at the foot. In 1949, Addie died and was buried alongside her husband. It is inconceivable that Maud and her son William were not standing by both graves as the bodies were laid to rest. Yet, William in all his writings apparently made no clear reference to Sherwood, Addie, or Edwin Butler.

Somewhat more understandable is the omission of written mention of the previous Butler generation. When William was a teenager, Maud Butler's aunts Mary Ann Edwards and Mattie Nelson still lived in Oxford. In 1910, Mattie kept house with her unmarried daughter Ella, age forty-four, and her unmarried son, Joe, a carpenter age thirty-six. With them also lived her married daughter Nettie Sims and Nettie's husband Will, another carpenter. Mattie's obscurity is emphasized by her grave. Even though she was lauded by the DAR in their 1922 history of the county as a "missionary" for the Baptist cause, her last resting place is marked by a very inexpensive, very plain concrete oval bearing her name but no dates or fond inscription.[73]

When Faulkner declared that he escaped his mother's influence easily, he seemed to have in mind especially the period during 1908 and 1909 when he began to help out at his father's livery stable. Indeed, every Saturday it was eleven-year-old Billy's job to circulate around Oxford collecting bills for jobs done during the week. Obviously, Billy loved the all-male world at the livery stable, and surely it was there that he began to gain the intimate knowledge of horses and horse-trading that he later used so well in his fiction. After a time, however, his father manifested a measure of dislike for his oldest son. Perhaps with a touch of malice, certainly with cruel effect, he called the boy "Snake Lips."[74] Possibly, this was a loose reference to a physical attribute—thin lips—that Billy had inherited with his Butler genes. Making matters infinitely worse, Murry apparently turned special favor upon his second son Jack.

This fate between father and sons might have been fixed at conception when some genetic predestination ruled that Billy would inherit mostly the physical characteristics of Butlers rather than Falkners. Only his relatively long and slightly hooked nose was Falknerian. In childhood the difference between Willie's physical attributes and those traditionally associated with Falkner men were noticeable but not striking. In adolescence, the difference rapidly became not only striking, it was glaring. Billy's great-grandfather, grandfather, and father, at nearly six feet, were tall men for those times. They were also large and substantially fleshed. In an age when the average American male stood at about 5'7" and weighed about 145 pounds, they were conspicuous simply by dint of their size. William grew finally to a height of 5'5" and a fraction. Moreover, until middle age, he was relatively slight in build, probably weighing about 125 pounds during most of his young adult years.[75] As a man, William Faulkner was very likely to be lost in a crowd, or, worse, to be noticed as especially small and slight. Even as a youth, people thought of him as "small," and he also seemed shy, particularly at school. For a time, his brother Jack, two years younger, seemed to be his best friend, and at school he tended to stay close to Jack whenever he could. But in 1909, when Jack was about ten, he began to grow rapidly and it soon became obvious that he would reach the relatively Olympian proportions of Falkner men.

Seemingly, Billy responded to paternal rejection by rushing to perfect his alienation from home and family—always excepting his mother. Previously, he had performed well in school. In the fall of 1909 he entered the sixth grade. His teacher, Miss Minnie Porter, had a "nervous breakdown" and was replaced by Miss Essie Eades. Almost sixty years later "Miss Essie" would remember Billy as a quiet, normal boy who loved to read. His classmates, however, had a different opinion. One conceded that he was nice, soft-spoken, and "smart as he could be," but declared that he was not a "friendly kind of boy."[76] One classmate asserted that he never did any work, in school or out. He just sat there, he said, and behaved.[77] The records are not perfectly clear, but, possibly, he spent two years in the sixth grade and hence lost back the time that he had gained by skipping the second.[78] Asked questions by his teacher, he would simply respond, "I don't know." At one point, Maud attempted to establish regular study hours at home and lectured Billy on his truancy. Defiant toward his father, Billy quietly absorbed chastisement from his mother. Finally, he went to Ripley for a prolonged visit where it was hoped, apparently, that his Presbyterian great-grandfather, Dr. John Y. Murry, would command Billy's respect and set him again on the path to proper manhood. But, alas, nothing seemed to work.[79]

Billy next turned to his father's father. It was as if he had decided that if he could not pattern himself upon his father at the livery stable, he would do better, he would model himself on his father's very successful father. Deeply lonely after Sallie's death, John Falkner welcomed Billy's company and appreciated the emulation. He bought Billy a vest and watch fob just like his own. In particular, Billy liked to elicit Civil War stories from his grandfather who, as a teenager, had seen firsthand a lot of the action in Tippah County and environs.

In 1910 John Falkner, after having sole or part ownership of a dozen profitable businesses in town in addition to his very prosperous law practice, established the First National Bank of Oxford. By this time, he was in his early sixties and the perfect picture of the Southern colonel. In summers, he dressed in white and wore a "Panama" hat such as Teddy Roosevelt had made popular during a visit to the Canal Zone during the digging of the "big ditch."[80] John was hard of hearing, almost deaf, but otherwise hale and hardy, a cigar smoker and a lusty drinker. He was irascible, gruff, and blustering—a style that amused even as it offended. Weather permitting, it was his daily habit to sit in a straight-back chair in front of his bank, leaning the chair against the building, watching life as it moved about the town square. One revealing story has a farmer approach him to borrow money. The deal is made, John Falkner scribbles out a note on a piece of paper and pokes it at the man.

"Here, sign this," he says gruffly. The farmer looks at the note, studies it.

"I can't sign this, Colonel," he says.

"You can't?" exclaims the Colonel, taken aback. "Why not?"

"I can't read it," says the farmer.

Falkner takes the note, looks at it for a moment and says, "Damn, I can't either. Come in here." They go into the bank, presumably to get someone with a better hand to write out the document.

John Wesley Thompson Falkner's famous independence was perhaps best revealed by yet another well-known story that has to do with his bank. One warm evening he was cruising about with some of his friends in his large Buick touring car, the canvas top folded back. Riding around the town square, he ordered the driver to stop in front of his bank and get him a brick. Standing up in the car, he took deliberate aim and heaved the brick through the large front window, creating a tremendous crash followed by the dying tinkle of shattering glass. When one of his friends suggested that he shouldn't have done it, he replied in his characteristic mock-fierce style, "Dammit! It's my brick and my bank, I can do what I want to!"[81]

~

Even as Billy turned toward his grandfather, he began a life-long and deeply intimate relationship with Lida Estelle Oldham. Estelle, as she was always called, perhaps to distinguish her from her mother Lida, was from the very beginning a little girl's little girl. In grade school she stood out as "remarkably beautiful." One of her classmates, Taylor McElroy, later a district judge, recalled that the other children looked at her "goggle-eyed." The move to South Street in 1906, of course, brought the Falkners and the Oldhams into close proximity. At first, it was Estelle's younger sister Victoria, a notorious tomboy whose nickname was "Tochie," who fell in with the Falkner boys and their cousin Sallie Murry. The games sometimes approached the unisexual as the children played dolls and climbed trees together at the Big Place, did combat in a kind of bruising stick hockey in the middle of South Street, and generally engaged in rough and tumble action.[82]

However, during that summer and fall of 1909 when he turned twelve, Billy also turned to Estelle. Sallie Murry later declared that Billy had loved Estelle from the time he was old enough to have a girl. In 1965, Estelle herself recalled that in those early adolescent years they were together every day, sometimes out in the field watching clouds and interpreting their shapes, fantasizing about being married and having a chicken farm. Like Estelle, Billy became fastidious about his appearance, "almost a dandy," this small, slight boy in knickers, with light brown hair bearing a trace of red, deep brown eyes, and solemn face. In May, 1910, the Falkner boys and the Oldham girls shared a special, once-in-a-lifetime treat. For three or four weeks Estelle and Victoria would rise at 4:00 A.M. and join the Falkner boys in their eastward-sloping pasture to watch Halley's Comet.[83]

About this time, Estelle also made a transition. She came of age as a young woman. Sallie Murry remembered her as like "a little partridge" with a beautiful figure, teeth, and hair. People generally thought that Victoria was even more attractive, and they admired her as "a smart little cookie, afraid of nothing," in part because in her eighth and ninth grade years she traveled alone by train regularly to Memphis and back to have her teeth straightened.[84] But Estelle had somehow developed a style, a high style of manners, dress, and tone that made her unique as a young woman in that place and time.[85]

Everyone also agreed that Estelle blossomed early. One of the grade school teachers, Miss Essie Eades, always thought Estelle was two years older than William when the gap was actually only seven months.[86] Indeed, even Sallie Murry declared late in life that, "William was small in build and nearly two years younger than Estelle." Also, Estelle developed a reputation for being "fast," which meant highly flirtatious. Sallie Murry said she was "boy crazy" from the age of thirteen and cited the fact that Jeff Hamm, an older boy, would drive her home from school in his "jitney," a sort of homemade car.[87] In truth, Estelle was precocious, dating boys at the university when she was still in high school.[88]

At the end of the school year in 1910, Billy probably failed to be promoted to the seventh grade.[89] The following fall, at thirteen and perhaps repeating the sixth grade, he dropped the more strenuous physical sports and began to dress in high fashion. Furthermore, like his cousin Sallie Murry, he began to wear a shoulder brace under his clothes.[90] The device held one's shoulders rigidly back and promised to do wonders for the posture and, hence, appearance to the world. But it was a perfect marvel of discomfort to the wearer. Billy wore the brace for more than a year, and, whether or not it was the cause, for the rest of his life people would remark on the peculiarly stiff and "rared-back" way in which he walked. He was almost a real-life Charlie Chaplin figure strolling about before Charlie Chaplin appeared on film. Later, Billy maintained his trim physique by taking only toast and coffee for breakfast and displaying the results by having his mother resew his ready-made trousers to make them tighter. Other boys in Oxford began to tease Billy by calling him "quair," meaning "queer."[91]

Meanwhile, he and Estelle devoted themselves to the arts—to music, drawing, and poetry. He and she wrote poems and shared them. Often they met in the reading room of a local jewelry and bookstore, Billy browsing through books of poetry while Estelle read the latest fashion magazines.[92] They also loved dancing. Billy was especially fond of drawing an elegant couple in evening clothes, dancing toe to toe, cool and close. These were images that young people might take from the more pretentious British and American magazines of the day—things that did not have much relevance to an as yet rather rustic Mississippi, even to the acknowledged capital of its culture, the state university in Oxford. Obviously, Billy and Estelle worked hard at being different in Oxford, at standing out like an island of smartness in a flat and somber sea.

In September, 1911, when he became fourteen, Billy entered the seventh grade, in Oxford the first year of high school. It was then that he had one last good experience in school. He was blessed with an especially gifted, much loved, and rather Junoesque young teacher named Ella Wright. "Miss Ella" offered her students a rich array of Civil War and Mississippi history. Billy absorbed that lore thirstily, perhaps in part because of the source from which it sprang. Soon he did an appealing sketch of Ella Wright for the high school annual. It was a tactic he later used repeatedly in campaigns of courtship and seduction. After Miss Ella, however, Billy lost virtually all interest in regular school work.[93]

The year 1912 was very difficult for the Falkner clan and highly successful for the Lem Oldham family. In January, John Falkner, at sixty-three, married again. His bride was the widow of a ship's cabinetmaker from San Jose, California, whom he had met on a trip to the west coast. John realized his error even before the wedding, but Mrs. Mary Kennedy had been advised by her friends to marry "one of those Southern colonels." Now she had one, and she threatened to sue for breach of promise if he reneged. The result was that John married Mary in San Jose on January 10, and arrived with her at what had been "his," and suddenly was "their" Oxford home on Saturday the 13th. The following Tuesday afternoon cousins Sallie Murry Wilkins and Billy Falkner found themselves serving punch at a reception at the Big Place as Oxfordians welcomed the new Mrs. Falkner to "her house in the sunny South."[94] John, apparently, used his legal expertise to save as much as he could of his wealth from the rapacious widow. He set up a separate estate for his new wife; then, on March 23, he made a will noting that fact, leaving the remainder of his estate to his three children, and making them the executors. The latter should pay all debts and place "a medallion of myself on my monument in St. Peter's Cemetery Oxford, Miss."[95] In death, at least, he would rejoin Sally Murry.

John Falkner's marriage came to a rocky end that summer when Mary returned from a visit to California bringing with her a grown daughter, a son, his wife, and a grandchild, all intent, apparently, on making their permanent home not only in the sunny South, but in the Big Place with John, Mary Holland, and Sallie Murry. As Sallie Murry later said, "This was too much."[96] John secured his divorce, but the settlement probably cost him about $30,000, a minor fortune at the time.[97]

More deeply damaging to young Billy Falkner was the failure of his father's livery stable business. It was killed, of course, by the rather sudden appearance of the factory-made car in Oxford. Characteristically, the ambitious lawyer Lee Russell did the town proud by buying its first truly elegant touring car in October, 1909. During the next summer he improved on that with a seven-passenger, sixty-horsepower Thomas Flier, "the highest class car built in America," bragged the *Eagle*. By the fall of 1911, Lem Oldham had bought "one of the prettiest automobiles ever seen on our streets," and during the next summer John Falkner, taking G.E. Sisk and Sherwood Butler on the trip, daringly "motored through" to Memphis in his new automobile.[98] Within a few years the whole town would be awash with Model T Fords.

Sponsored by his father, Murry made what appeared to be a good move—he dissolved his livery stable operation and went into the hardware business. In doing so, however, in November, 1912, he sold the beautiful house on South Street to banker Relbue Price for $4,500 and bought from him a downtown hardware store already well established and running.[99] After some months of moving about—during a part of which they lived in "the old Beanland Residence"—Murry reestablished his family in a less expensive house at the far end of North Street.[100]

The Falkner star in Oxford appeared to be setting, but the Oldham star was definitely rising. In January, 1912, Lem was made a major on the governor's staff. By May, "the Major" had acquired and was remodeling the Thompson House—on the square on the site of the old Butler Hotel—into a modern hotel. He had bought the property for $8,000 in 1910 from absentee owners, after having made a quick $2,500 profit by buying two stores on the square from other absentee owners and selling them within three months. In August, 1913, Lem also invested in a gravel pit near Iuka, seemingly a wise move in the time of rapid road building and cement construction.[101]

The social rise of the Oldhams kept pace with their material advance. In August, 1912, Major and Mrs. Oldham and "their beautiful daughter Miss Estelle," now fifteen, enjoyed a delightful week at the encampment of the Mississippi National Guard at Columbus. In September, the *Eagle* published a photograph of the Major in his regimentals with a very flattering write-up that described him as popular, conscientious, efficient, and an enterprising businessman.[102] In December, Estelle, almost sixteen, ended the social year brilliantly by attending a weekend party at the Vardamans' home in Jackson. Accompanying her was her friend Katrina Carter, the granddaughter of Confederate cavalryman and successful businessman Herman Wohlleben.

On the train coming home the girls encountered Estelle's grandfather by marriage, crusty old Judge Henry Clay Niles. Unfortunately for Estelle, she introduced him to Vardaman's son who happened to be traveling with the two young women. Judge Niles refused to shake Vardaman's hand and turned to Estelle. "Do you mean your parents let you visit these god-damned people?" he roared. Young Vardaman vanished and Estelle dissolved into tears. Instead of de-training at Kosciusko, his home town, Judge Niles went on to Oxford where he proceeded to "take off Lem's head" for allowing Estelle to socialize with the Vardamans, whom he considered lower class.[103] Judge Niles maintained his position as a Republican without apology and with dignity. He was able to do so in large measure because he was such a thorough, uncompromising elitist. It was a lesson that the Oldhams in Oxford struggled hard to learn.

For nearly a generation, the Oldham house on South Street was a significant social center in Oxford. Oldham celebrations of holidays—Halloween masquerades and eggnog on Christmas morning—became famous, conspicuous, and very exclusive events. The Oldhams also advertised in various ways their commitment to high culture. There were two pianos in the house and both might be played simultaneously in duets by Lida and one of her accomplished daughters, marvelous harmonies knelling out across the broad yards and into the street for the uninvited to hear.[104] In time there was a tennis court in the yard, with tea or lemonade served by a maid on the side gallery between sets. All this was presided over by the beautiful Lida who, after seven years of no additions to the family, gave birth to a girl and a boy in quick succession and ceased. As noted before, the girl, born in 1905, was named Dorothy Zollicoffer. The latter name was taken from the family tree several steps removed from the child, but one of the Zollicoffers was a Confederate brigadier killed in the war. The boy, born in 1907, was named Edward de Graffenreid, and living kinship was thus established with Swiss nobility in the person of Baron de Graffenreid who founded New Bern, North Carolina. Earlier, Estelle and Tochie (Victoria), of course, had been named for more immediate and less famous connections.

The Oldhams worked hard at maintaining their position in the social hierarchy, and a part of their energy was spent attempting to enforce a measure of social exclusivity on their neighbors. Later in life, a woman who knew Lida in those years remembered her as very proper and very snobbish. Robert Farley, an Ole Miss student who became mayor of Oxford and a professor in the school of law, recalled that she was sweet but strange. She had notions about conventions, he said, that were out of this world. Sallie Murry, up the street in the Big Place, was also a famous party-giver, but she invited everybody she knew. The Bogarts, for instance, were always at the Falkner house but never at the Oldhams. Eventually, Mrs. Oldham would not let Estelle and Victoria go to Sallie Murry's parties because of the "democratic selection of guests."[105]

Clearly, Oldham children emerged into adulthood with a sense of social superiority ingrained in their characters. In the 1960s when a Faulkner biographer told Estelle that classmate Taylor McElroy said he had helped her with her homework, she replied that he could not have because he came from the wrong "background." Later, in the early 1970s, Estelle commented in the same vein on President Richard Nixon's meeting with China's Chairman Mao. She had lived in Shanghai for several years in the 1920s and thus had a basis for judgment. "I can't understand why the President would take a long trip to China to talk to a peasant like Mao," she declared in an interview with a reporter. "I wouldn't have let him into my house."[106]

Murry and Maud and the residents at the Big Place never deferred to the Oldhams socially. On the other hand, the four Falkner boys seemed to have been deeply impressed by the Oldham style of life and sense of class. Jack Falkner, the second son, always held them in high regard, and declared that he and his brothers saw a lot of the Oldhams because they were of the "same class." In particular, Billy Falkner was impressed. One of his contemporaries thought that Lida was especially influential in Billy's young life. Mrs. Oldham brought out the best in him, she said. She had a way of reproving people most gently, and yet achieving a favorable response.[107]

Perhaps it happened in 1912 and 1913 as Billy was passing through adolescence that he found a home away from home at the Oldhams. Sartorial elegance, a superior posture, an understanding of highly refined social etiquette, and a sense of aesthetics offered a counter-weight to what appeared to be and, in fact, was a relative decline if not a dissolution of the Falkner family fortunes. Billy's father—the livery stable man who insisted on silence at the dinner table, who smoked cigars and drank alcohol in its raw form, who sang "Glow Worm" beautifully but little else, who seemed to have rejected him in favor of his brother Jack—might well be answered by Billy's adoption of the attitudes, manners, and modes of the Oldhams.

In the fall of 1913, when Billy turned sixteen, Estelle went away to Mary Baldwin College, a school for young women in the very Presbyterian town of Staunton, Virginia. Near the end of that year, Murry finally settled his family in an ample but plain two-story house at the end of North Street.[108] One explanation for the move was that he had given up the livery stable, gone into the hardware business, and no longer needed the barn, outhouses, and lots behind the house on South Street. In reality, the change in houses was tied directly to financing the purchase of the hardware store, and it was a very visible manifestation of Murry's plight. Billy's friends noted that he became silent and withdrawn that fall after Estelle's departure. During the following spring, however, he pitched baseball, played pick-up football, wrote, drew, and read. One of his friends remembered his "don't give a damn attitude" and his physical daring. He always played football with the bigger boys, and during these years never weighed more than 120 pounds.[109]

Estelle did well during her first year at Mary Baldwin. Predictably, she excelled in piano, improved steadily in English grammar and composition, and had only minor difficulties with mathematics. However, she found the Presbyterian atmosphere dull and oppressive. President Woodrow Wilson, then in the White House, upright, austere, and unsmiling, had been born in Staunton and accurately reflected its character. Furthermore, Estelle later declared, she could not stand being shut in with a lot of females.[110] In 1915, she persuaded her father to let her remain in Oxford and enroll as a special student in the university.

Home again, Estelle had no difficulty at all in finding male companionship. Indeed, she recalled, she never dated the same boy two nights in a row, and never finished a turn on the dance floor without being cut in on by another worshipful young man. There were also house parties in the homes of her friends in other towns. One of her admirers called her "the butterfly of the Delta." Another, a woman, remembered that she was delightful, the essence of "it." All of the college boys were crazy for her, this woman said. Indeed, Estelle's major complaint now was that she was "violently chaperoned." The chaperone, often, was Lida Oldham, who never missed a dance at Ole Miss, and would ride with Estelle and her date in the hansom cab from the Oldhams' to the campus and back. Sometimes Lida invited a dozen or so boys and girls, including Billy, to breakfast at dawn in her South Street house. Estelle would also have private dances at home, bringing in a small band of black musicians led by Lucius Pegues—often a trio of guitar, banjo, and drum.[111]

Billy Falkner would come to the dances at the university too, and there he might hear W.C. Handy's band play the "Memphis Blues" (1912) and his even more famous "St. Louis Blues" (1914). By the end of 1915 Billy had dropped out of school and was working as a bookkeeper in the back room of his grandfather's bank. Estelle visualized him at his post with his feet on the desk, hating the job and reading a book instead of working.[112]

Soon Billy was making trips to Memphis, where he became friends with Arthur A. Halle, a young man who owned a men's clothing store. Arthur's mother would see him there, sitting all day in a comfortable chair—one of which was "a gold loveseat"—in the back of the store, and sometimes slipping upstairs to nap in Arthur's bed. At Ole Miss dances, one of his contemporaries remembered that Billy was always impeccably dressed—"a fashion plate"—

perhaps the fruit of his visits to Memphis.[113] Maud once sold a diamond ring privately to pay his bill at Halle's.[114] Billy did indeed wear a "Style-Plus" suit, the height of ready-made fashion, but young women thought he was a poor dancer, and one of these unkindly compared him to a little "hopping toad."[115] Estelle liked his dressing up, but also downgraded his dancing. Now and again he cut in on her partner and "pushed her around," as she described his performance. But mostly he stood on the sidelines, and Estelle would sometimes sit with him and talk. They had an "understanding," she later said.[116]

During the spring of 1915, while home on vacation from Mary Baldwin, Estelle had become engaged to marry Cornell Franklin, a man from Columbus, Mississippi, some seven years her senior. Cornell had been an Ole Miss undergraduate (as had his father before him), and he had also finished in law. When Cornell first graduated in 1913, sixteen-year-old Estelle's picture appeared in the annual as his "Sponsor." Still in high school, she was already a belle on the university campus. Cornell took his law degree in June, 1914, and soon joined his Uncle Malcolm Franklin in Hawaii, where he was Collector of the Port of Honolulu, a highly lucrative political appointment. Physically, Cornell was a small, solid man with dark hair and eyes, charming and strikingly handsome. He was well-to-do and already marked for success in politics and law. During a visit home, Cornell proposed marriage, and Estelle accepted, as she later declared, "lightly."[117] Afterward, with Cornell's prolonged absence, the engagement did not seem very firm.

Indeed, Estelle considered another marriage proposal in the fall of 1917, some two and a half years after having accepted one from Cornell. This man was also a student at Ole Miss. He was attractive, charming, dark, and from the Delta. Estelle thought his darkness sprang from Creole (French or Spanish) blood. Major Oldham knew better. When she told her father of her possible engagement, he exploded. "You can't marry him," he shouted. "Don't you realize he has Negro blood?"[118] That affair ended abruptly, but in the spring of 1918 Estelle's mother and Cornell's mother (divorced from his father and now Mrs. Hugh S. Hairston) decided that Estelle and Cornell would make the perfect couple. Cornell apparently agreed.

Estelle did not feel ready for marriage and took evasive action. When Mrs. Hairston sent Estelle her own engagement ring, double diamonds and very expensive, Estelle hid it at the bottom of a drawer of her bureau and said that John Henry, "the colored boy," had stolen it.[119] John Henry was jailed. Mrs. Oldham grew suspicious and confronted Estelle, who confessed. John Henry was released, but, understandably, he refused to work for the Oldhams again . . . ever.[120] In 1964, late in life, Estelle asserted that she had told Billy she would elope with him if he said yes. Billy, age twenty, with no money, an uncertain future, and knowing that the Oldhams were fond of him but did not want him to marry their daughter, could not bring himself to that point. According to Estelle's memory, he put the matter to each father and each "blew up."[121]

Meanwhile, the marital juggernaut rolled forward. On Thursday, April 11, 1918, the *Eagle* announced that "Mr. Cornell Franklin will arrive in Oxford Friday and will be the guest of friends." Cornell arrived as advertised, proposed marriage to Estelle yet again, and she accepted. Already, on March 30, Billy Falkner had himself as bookkeeper closed out his account at his grandfather's bank and boarded a train, heading for New Haven where he had a close friend, Phil Stone, studying in the School of Law at Yale.[122] He was pursuing a strategy to get into the war then raging in Europe by joining not the American but an allied army. Back in Oxford, arrangements for the wedding between Estelle and Cornell went forward with amazing rapidity. Family and friends rallied from near and far to celebrate the event in splendid style. Miss Florence, "Florrie," Friedman organized a bridge party for the bride and her guests. Miss Nena Somerville hosted a breakfast and another bridge party.[123]

At 7:30 on the evening of the 18th, Estelle and Cornell were married in the First Presbyterian Church. However, the ceremony was conducted in the Episcopal style by the Reverend W.A. Dakin of Clarksdale, a priest who had previously served the parish in Columbus, the groom's home town. (Interestingly, the Rev. Mr. Dakin was Tennessee Williams's grandfather, and seven-year-old Tom—as he was then called—was living in the rectory in Clarksdale at the time.) The Oldhams were Presbyterians, but seldom at church. From this time forward Estelle and her immediate family would be Episcopalians. In the South, this affiliation carried aristocratic implications. Cornell's mother, Mrs. Hairston, was present at the ceremony as matron of honor. Victoria, the "pretty sister" of the bride, was maid of honor. A bevy of bridesmaids "wore gowns of pink georgette crepe" and carried bouquets of roses. Probably no one at the wedding was more brilliantly attired than the groom. Cornell had secured a commission as a major in the Hawaiian Territorial Forces by dint of his appointment as judge advocate of that martially virgin group. He was a lawyer by profession and had received his office at the hand of the territorial governor of Hawaii with whom his family had some influence. He chose to wed in full dress whites with "insignia of gold braid" and wearing his ceremonial saber.

The reception was held in the large two-story residence of the Oldhams on South Street, "ablaze with color" and decorated for the occasion in pink, white, and green. The couple rode from the church to the house in the Oldhams' car, proudly chauffered by Johncy Falkner, Billy's sixteen-year-old brother.[124] Three years earlier, a similar scene had occurred at the same place when the Oldhams gave a masquerade ball and Billy Falkner, then seventeen, was very much in evidence. "In the receiving line," reported a local paper, "were Maj. and Mrs. Oldham and Mr. William Falkner who bid the guests welcome." Estelle's sister Dorothy, then age nine and her brother Ned, age seven, served the punch.

Estelle appeared at the party as the "Pink Lady," and her sister Victoria as the "French Maid."[125]

William Falkner, of course, was not in the wedding party in 1918, and one hopes that he did not see the issue of the *Eagle* published the following week. The front page carried a full description of the wedding and the reception, noting especially the high point of the event when the bride, her hand no doubt steadied by that of the groom, cut the wedding cake with his sword.[126] It was exactly the kind of high style romance and heady symbolism that William Falkner adored, and it was truly a shame that he could not have been the groom in the piece, at least a lieutenant if not a major, and his the saber that Estelle held.

After the wedding, Cornell and Estelle left for a short bridal trip, announcing that after June 1 they would be at home in Honolulu. The announcement of Estelle's departure was premature. Actually, late in May she was back in Oxford visiting her parents before going off to Columbus to rejoin her husband.[127] At last the newlyweds headed west, but had to reverse directions in El Paso, Texas. Melvina Victoria, home after two years in a convent school in Washington, D.C., was marrying Paul F. Allen, a young army officer just back from France. Pete had played baseball at Ole Miss and was the son of a successful lumberman in Hattiesburg. According to Sallie Murry, Lida did not approve of the rather torrid courtship. She had opened Victoria's mail from Pete, concluded that the affair was proceeding much too rapidly, and wanted to kick him out. Always independent, Victoria defied her mother, and Estelle had to return to Oxford to serve as maid of honor in the proceedings. Already, Estelle was pregnant.[128] Presumably not too long after Victoria's wedding, Estelle and Cornell began again the long journey to Hawaii, first by train to San Francisco, and then by ship to Honolulu.

Even while Estelle was marrying Cornell, Billy was turning his energies into efforts to enter the great war in Europe. For many young men, it offered a chance to prove their courage. Fathers, grandfathers, and great-grandfathers had fought in the Civil War and, in 1898, in that short and splendid war against Spain. By 1917 a new generation emerged that had been reared on stories of martial courage—who in fact could not stroll through the square in a Southern town without gazing upon the marble Confederate soldier atop the pedestal.

We do not know exactly when and how William Falkner first tried to enter the military. There was a draft to sweep up all the able-bodied young men at twenty-one, and William, at nineteen and twenty, was precisely the age that was counted as ripe and ready for cannon fodder. Tradition says that in the spring of 1918, as he approached twenty-one, he attempted to join the Aviation Section of the Army's Signal Corps. He was fascinated by airplanes. As a boy, he had led his little brothers and their friends in the building of an airplane, following directions supplied by a magazine called *Popular Mechanics*. Using bean poles and newspapers, they constructed the craft in the barn, laboriously wheeled it to the edge of a great ditch in the pasture, and with Billy all set to fly, pushed it over the edge. It flew straight down, of course, leaving Billy unhurt but considerably crestfallen in the midst of the debris in the bottom of the ditch. When Billy attempted to join the incipient American flying force early in 1918, he was ruled too short and too light in weight. He stuffed himself with bananas and water before the next try, only to suffer rejection again.[129] Then he began to develop a scheme to get into the flying service of an allied country.

The pivotal person in getting William into the war was Phil Stone, the young man who would become central in his life as Estelle faded. Like the Falkners, the Stones were another prominent, if late-coming, Oxford family. However, unlike both Falkners and Butlers, the Stones came out of the planter elite. One great-grandfather had come into the area as a planter well before the Civil War. Phil's grandfather had been a major on the staff of General Nathan Bedford Forrest. Phil's father, James Stone, an only child, became a lawyer in Batesville as well as a Delta planter. In 1879, he married Rosamond Alston, "Miss Rosa," of Memphis and Lafayette County. In the 1890s he moved the seat of his practice to Oxford and added banking to his professional activities. He became a general on the staff of the governor, having prepared himself for that position by spending his high school years in a prestigious military academy in Kentucky. Phil Stone's ancestors, like the Hindmans in Tippah and the Thompsons and the Joneses in Lafayette, began life in Mississippi at or near the top.[130]

The Stones of the early twentieth century, the father and his sons, manifested that ideal combination of large planters and eminent lawyers in the Deep South that William Alexander Percy of Greenville came to personify. Phil's father acquired a mansion for his family on the northwestern edge of Oxford. Originally built by the Avents, the house had passed to the son-in-law of L.Q.C. Lamar, and then to the Stones. Phil was born there in 1893. He was a precocious youngster, learning to read at three. But he was also a sickly child. He had to learn to walk three times because of prolonged stays in bed, a peculiar redundancy that he almost matched academically by taking two bachelor's degrees, one at Ole Miss and another at Yale, and then two law degrees from the same institutions.[131] Phil first graduated from Yale in 1914, and in that summer, at age twenty-one, he was back in Oxford, waiting to begin as a student in the university's School of Law. Introduced to Billy Falkner by Katrina Carter, he was deeply impressed by the young man's intelligence and by his talent, both manifest and latent, as a writer and poet. For some ten years he was more than a friend to Billy. He was an academic mentor and a social model, both of which Billy sorely needed. Urbane, cosmopolitan, intensely and eagerly engaged in the world, he was a man vastly different in style from William's father, grandfather, and younger brothers.

Perhaps the need for the help of someone like Phil Stone had become critical for Billy during the fall of 1909 when he entered his twelfth year. It was as if he had somehow fallen out of the family nest, a fledgling not yet able to fly. He had missed some turn in the road that would have made him undeniably a Falkner. The Butler body worked against that end, but clearly Murry was not helpful in the crisis. Maud was there, and grandfather John Falkner was there also, but neither could supply Billy with what he needed. Apparently, for a time, he found relief with Estelle—and with the socially and culturally pretentious Oldhams who somehow gave him a shelter and refuge for difference. However, in the fall of 1913 Estelle went off to Mary Baldwin, and Billy was left in Oxford, drifting downstream through another school year without rudder or power.

In 1914, in Billy's sixteenth summer, Phil Stone appeared. For two years he lived in Oxford and proved himself a steady ally and faithful friend to Billy who responded fully, hungrily to the attention of the aristocratic, Ivy League-educated, and voluble young man. They were together virtually daily, and for hours at a time. Phil became Billy's tutor in literature, grammar, and music. Moreover, it was with Phil and other men in the Stone family—not Murry Falkner—that Billy went hunting in the Delta in the big woods along the Tallahatchie River. Like Phil, he affected a pipe, and, like the Stones, a generally lusty and genteel attitude toward alcohol. It was almost as if Billy had decided, at last, that if he could not be a Falkner like his father or grandfather, he would be a Stone like Phil.

Family tradition boasts that Billy quarterbacked the high school football team during the fall of 1915, his senior year, and got his nose broken in the annual game with Holly Springs. One local newspaper gave the line-up for Oxford High when it played Holly Springs in September, 1915. There was no mention of William Falkner among the players. Another paper gave his name and described him as quarterback, but made no mention of his performance, spectacular or otherwise.[132] Billy dropped out of school some time that year and went to work as a bookkeeper in his grandfather's bank. He hated the job. He drank, he cultivated a "smallish mustache," and sometimes dressed like a small town dandy.

During the next school year, 1916–1917, while Phil Stone was attending law school at Yale, Billy, then nineteen, himself befriended a young student, Ben Wasson, recently arrived at the university from the Delta town of Greenville. Ben was sixteen, small, bright, and blond. Fellow student Robert Farley remembered him as a sweet kid—"seraphic"—who was fondly adopted by upperclassmen. "He was as pretty as could be," Farley said.[133] In 1962, Ben himself recalled his first meeting with Falkner. He was crossing "The Grove," the wooded center of campus, with a new friend, a senior, when they encountered "a small, slight fellow . . . wearing a pair of baggy, gray flannel trousers, a rather shabby tweed jacket, and heavy, brown, brogans."

Ben's friend said, "This is Bill Falkner."

Falkner nodded quickly, eyes brown, penetrating, almond shaped. His nose was aquiline, above a thin, neatly trimmed moustache. As he talked—soft-spoken words from the narrow, straight mouth—Falkner intermittently pulled a handkerchief from his sleeve, used it, and stuffed it in again. Ben was fascinated by the performance and Bill explained. "The British wear handkerchiefs in their jacket sleeves," he said. "I prefer the sartorial usage, also." Turning, he continued a discussion of Housman's poetry with the senior.

As they parted Ben made his manners with a flourish. "Ah," Falkner said, "we seem to have a young Sir Galahad on a rocking horse come to our college campus." Leaving, Falkner paused to light a straight-stemmed pipe he had been holding, then strolled on.

Soon, Bill sought Ben out, loaned him books, and often took him to the Stones' house, having access even while Phil was away in New Haven. He would take Ben into the library, light a fire but not the lamp, and start up the Victrola with classical music. Settling in a chair he once explained to Ben that "even light can be too much distraction when music is being played." It was mostly Beethoven. "Listen to those horns of triumph and joy crying their golden sounds in a great twilight of sorrow," Bill would exclaim.[134] In the spring of 1917, Ben recalled, Bill lent him a book of poems with a studiously casual remark that it was something he might enjoy.

Decades later Wasson recalled an event that happened during his sophomore year. One night he was upstairs in his room in the dormitory studying when Bill came to get him. He had been listening to the alluring strains of the orchestra for the "Red and Blue Dance," he said, and Ben had to come hear. They stood outside the window of the hall, listening to the music, the excited talking and laughing, the sound no doubt of leather-soled shoes moving on the polished wood, watching the gliding bodies, male and female entwined. Soon, Wasson went back to his room and his work, leaving Bill standing at the window looking in.[135] It was almost as if Falkner were attempting to pass along to young Ben the magic key to aesthetics that Phil had given him. Wasson later recalled that Bill possessed an "innate kindness and gentleness and a rare ability to dramatize himself interestingly."[136] It was a friendship that lasted a lifetime, at least in Ben's eyes.

By now, Billy's father was predicting no good end for his son. Jack had displaced Billy in the livery stable earlier, and Murry and Jack grew especially close. Billy was excluded, an exclusion that he seemed not only to accept but to embrace by adopting high fashion dress, or the opposite, and conspicuously reading and talking the Romantic poets—Byron, Shelley, Keats, Housman, and Swinburne. Estelle remained in the midst of the social whirl at the university—interspersed with dazzling visits to Jackson and the Delta. Billy, it seemed to his family, was at sea. From the outside, one would assume that he was deeply miserable. And yet, one feels that miserable only begins to describe his situation—that there is also a sort of glory in his misery and a fierce joy in pushing out from the conventional world. Behind that still, almost unmoving face, behind those level-gazing dark brown and seemingly brooding eyes, within that small slight stiff body, there is a jumping, leaping, grinning imp of a boy, delighted by the almost violent responses he evoked in striking such poses.

Rejected by the American military, William Falkner in the spring of 1918 was maturing a plan to get into the war by enlisting in the flying service of an allied nation. He succeeded. On June 27, 1918, the *Oxford Eagle* ran a note in its "Personal and Local" column: "Mr. William Falkner who has been spending a few months in New York is visiting his parents Mr. and Mrs. Murry Falkner. He has joined the English Royal Flying Corps and leaves the eighth of July for Toronto, Canada, where he will train."[137]

Actually, Billy had enlisted in the Royal Air Force, not the Royal Flying Corps. The name had recently been changed, but Billy preferred to give out the earlier, more romantic sounding version.[138] Also, he had not spent a few months in New York. Apparently, he had gone to New Haven in early April. Thirty years later Phil recalled that he got Bill a job in a Winchester arms factory while they both attempted, futilely, to join the allied armies by passing themselves off as Canadians. Then an English friend who dined with them at the Commons at Yale taught them to "talk like Englishmen" while they plotted to pass as citizens of that nation. In late June, Bill went down to New York and succeeded in enlisting in the Royal Air Force.[139] Probably it was in this phase of his life that Bill began to develop for himself a full-blown British, perhaps even an Oxonian persona. He somehow managed to convey the impression to some people that he was an Englishman who had been studying in the United States and now wanted to enlist in the cause of his country. He was in the process of creating that character, perhaps, when he first added a "u" to the spelling of his family name. Later, he would insist that the alteration meant nothing, but rather clearly the "u" gave him significant distance from his family and from his own previous self. Certainly he used it while in the service in Canada. Out of Mississippi, it seems, he could begin anew.[140] Even though he relished the role of Englishman, such elaborate ruses were probably not really necessary. With the life expectancy of a novice British flyer on the Western Front at about three weeks, Billy apparently had no real difficulty getting into the military as a pilot candidate.

Just before Billy Falkner went off to war, the family had an outing. "Mr. and Mrs. Murry Falkner and sons motored through and spent a few days in Muscle Shoals, Ala.," the *Eagle* reported brightly on July 4. The same issue ran another article, one in a very persuasive series in favor of the war effort entitled "Why We Fight." It also published a long list of draftees from Lafayette County. Elizabeth Thompson, the widow of the man whom Charlie Butler had killed on the town square, was in her seventies and still publishing the *Oxford Eagle*. That newspaper was clearly doing its part in the war effort. Early in February, it had printed a piece on "The Training of an Airman" that described the three stages in the process: ground school, flying in America, and, finally, flying behind the lines in Europe before launching the airman into combat. After the candidate had flown thirty miles across country and up to 10,000 feet, he won the "coveted wings and shield of Uncle Sam," it said.[141] Shortly thereafter the paper began to publish a series of articles entitled "Over the Top," ostensibly written by an American machine gunner serving in France.[142] All about Billy's head, the bugles blew, and he responded eagerly to the call.

The real war news in the Falkner family, however, came from Jack, not William. In May, 1918, at the age of eighteen, Jack had enlisted in the United States Marine Corps. After basic training in America, he was shipped to Europe on the *Von Steuben*, a ship that the Germans had outfitted as a commerce raider but which was captured by the allies. He landed in France on August 27, 1918, and was assigned to a unit that provided replacements for soldiers killed or wounded at the front.[143] Actually, Americans had arrived in force in Europe only several months before. On the very day that Estelle was married, the *Oxford Independent* carried news of the first major American engagement against the Germans with banner lines that read: "Americans Acquit Themselves Nobly" and "All Night Battle Raging on the Neuve Eglise Wulvergen Line." Americans did acquit themselves fully as nobly as the French, Germans, and British had before. Eagerly enough, they leapt out of the trenches and charged into the same awful slaughter that both sides had attended faithfully during the three previous years.[144]

Jack Falkner moved up to the front lines on September 11 and was enrolled in a unit. On the 12th he went over the top, taking part in the all-American St. Mihiel offensive.[145] After the event he wrote to his father, addressing him as "My Dear Pardner." "Gosh," he exulted, "I wish you could have seen those Dutchmen run."[146] Soon his company was pulled out of the lines. On November 1 they went in again, this time to take part in a drive in the Argonne Forest in the Verdun sector. The battle had hardly gotten under way when Jack's unit came under heavy shelling. While he was lying in the mud, a fragment from a shell ripped through his helmet and across his skull. He was also hit in the leg. Badly wounded, he was taken to the rear.[147] It was December before his family heard from Jack. By that time he was in a hospital in France slowly recovering from his wounds. He wrote to his father, declaring that he would tell him all about it when he got home. "And believe me, Dad, I can talk for two years." Jack Falkner's letter was printed in the *Eagle* under the heading: "Jack Falkner Writes from Front Line," "Oxford Boy is Improving of Scalp Wound Received While in Action."[148] On March 11, 1919, Jack finally landed at Hampton Roads, Virginia, and was hospitalized there.[149] A large, comfortable, modest man, he always joked that the marines taught him everything except how to duck. He went through the university and on through law school. He joined J. Edgar Hoover's recently organized Federal Bureau of Investigation, and Oxfordians subsequently understood that he was involved in the successful culmination of some of the FBI's most exciting ventures in the 1920s and 1930s.[150]

While Jack was winning honors as a young marine in Europe, Billy Falkner went north to Canada to search for glory as a flying officer. During the summer and into fall, he was in ground school near Toronto, along with some 2,000 other young men, learning the very basics of military life and flight.[151] Other cadets later remembered him. J.M. Hinchley, a Canadian, recalled that he stood out for his "diminutive physique, his feeble mustache, his rich Southern drawl," which another cadet took to be an English accent.[152] Hinchley, who spent two days alone with Falkner on assigned duties, thought that he had been a student at Yale. Hinchley did, however, correctly identify Falkner as a Southerner by his drawl and by the fact that he appeared in camp on the first day with a large suitcase labelled, as Hinchley recalled, "Wm. Faulkner, Oxford, Mississippi."[153] Late in August, Billy wrote Maud that he was "trying to learn to walk and salute nasty, like a British officer."[154] Sometimes, he received money from home and bought a bottle of bootleg whiskey which he might share with his friends. On one such occasion, Faulkner performed a one-man drill on the sidewalk next to their quarters, shouting out orders to himself, marching to and fro, and turning about briskly.[155] As usual, Billy was less than brilliant as a student. He took meticulous notes in class, but he achieved only fair grades on examinations.

On November 11, 1918, the war came to an end. It was distressingly early for a young man desperate to get into the fray and prove his manhood. Shortly, Billy's imagination took flight as his body had not. He wrote a letter to Phil Stone in which he jauntily described how he had celebrated the armistice by having a few drinks and taking a plane up only to crash upside down into the roof of a hangar.[156] Billy wrote his mother that he had finished ground school on November 13, two days after the cease fire. In a series of letters, he said that he had begun to fly back in August, and by the end of November had four hours of solo flying.[157]

But, of course, all of this could not have been. The authorities began dissolving the ground school within days of the armistice.[158] No one in Billy's cohort completed the course. Further, the nearest military aircraft were at a flight school fifty miles away, and there is no shred of evidence that his dramatic crash ever occurred. Furthermore, different people understood different stories. Jack thought that he had crashed a Spad upside down into a hangar roof while on a drinking spree. Johncy understood that the plane was a Sopwith Camel. Phil Stone thought there were two in the plane, and they had tried to drink from a bottle while hanging upside down among the rafters.[159] In all of the stories he had suffered injury, but declared bravely that he was alive and cheerful. Also, he was coming home.

One morning early in December, William Faulkner stepped down from a train at the Oxford depot. He was smartly attired in the uniform of an officer in the Royal Air Force—slacks, hip-length jacket, belted at the waist and flared, with his officer's signs near the cuff at each wrist. On his chest were the wings of a flying officer. His hat was the billed kind, the crown unwired and floppy in the fashion allowed only to veteran flyers. He wore it jauntily, tipped to one side. Billy had matured a mustache that functioned, at least in part, to hide his upper lip. For several weeks, he wore the uniform in and around the town, sometimes heightening the effect by carrying a swagger stick and taking salutes from returning soldiers who had not achieved officer status. Sometimes his brother Dean, age eleven, proudly accompanied him in his Boy Scout uniform. On Christmas eve, Billy still wore the uniform, carrying leather gloves and walking with a rattan cane.[160]

It is virtually certain that Faulkner crashed no planes, and probably he never even flew as a passenger in an airplane in Canada. The documents definitely indicate that he never finished ground school and was not an officer when discharged. The fact is that his class was aborted within days of the signing of the armistice on November 11, and everyone was discharged with startling rapidity and a lack of ceremony that seems almost rude. Indeed, among Faulkner's papers at the University of Virginia there are instructions handed out to the cadets on the eve of discharge explicitly ordering them not to consider themselves officers and to wear their cadet uniforms only until "permanent discharge." These documents do indicate, however, that at some future date they would be made "honorary" lieutenants in the Royal Air Force, a promise that was realized a year after Billy's return to Oxford.[161] If called to the service again, Billy would have been a second lieutenant and that gave the barest trace of legitimacy to his wearing an officer's uniform. However, there was no legitimacy at all in his wearing the wings of a flying officer. Moreover, taking salutes from soldiers below officer rank, some of whom perhaps had been in the lines in France, was distinctly less than honorable behavior on his part. In all of this charade, however, William Faulkner's salient talent, an amazing capacity for creating convincing fiction, had made its first striking appearance.

SIX

The Artist as a Young Man

1918–1929

In less than a dozen years, the young man who descended from the train that day would write a book that many literary scholars would acclaim as the best yet in twentieth-century American letters.[1] How did this come to be? William Faulkner was not always consistent in answering questions about his work, but he repeatedly declared that his writing came from "imagination, observation, and experience." The greatest of these, he might have said, was imagination. He would see or read about something, put himself in the midst of it, and breath it all to life in a story. Always the story worked to make William Faulkner, himself, more whole as a person. The power of the artist sprang from the terrific tension that lay at the base of his psyche: always he was an outsider observing critically the social universe to which he was born, which he knew marvelously well, and which, paradoxically, gave him both sustenance and pain. Surely his alienation began at conception and birth, but in and after 1909, it rapidly became a way of life.

Personae

"It got so that when Billy told you something, you never knew if it was the truth or just something he had made up," his cousin Sallie Murry complained thinking back to that fall of 1909 in which Faulkner turned twelve. In later years, family and friends commented again and again that he seemed to have a "private world" as an adolescent. They felt that he "drifted" and sometimes suffered a "brooding melancholy." Faulkner didn't see himself this way at all. At first, ably abetted by Estelle who happily joined the game, he saw himself as smart and stylish far beyond poor Oxford's capacity for comprehension. Later, when Phil

Stone came home in and after 1914, Billy joined the literati. He read poetry with a passion, smoked a pipe, affected an intimate knowledge of English manners, and pursued high culture. As an adolescent, Billy was becoming, it seemed, such a person as few Falkners had ever aspired to be and no Falkner had ever been. Tentatively, he was building an answer both to an earthy, manly Murry and to his high-achieving, community-serving, brick-throwing grandfather.

In 1918, when Bill Faulkner descended from the train in his splendid uniform, he also had an answer to the examples posed by the Old Colonel of Civil War fame and by Jack, his hero brother, the wounded marine. He was a new model officer in the flying service, not a foot soldier, and while he was not wounded in combat, he had flown his plane with such daredevil verve—by his own account—as to establish that he would have been valorous in battle and, ultimately, either victorious or dead. Moreover, he had been truly cosmopolitan in his military career, transcending provincial Mississippi, the South, and even America. He had been a soldier in the service of the fully matured, superbly cultured, world-beating British Empire. He had not been simply another American "doughboy" in a rough cut, ready-to-wear, ill-fitting uniform, a member of the relatively late-coming and often naive American military. Kings and knights, cavaliers and dawn patrols were his images, gentleman jousting gentleman in mile-high skies, not mud and blood and millions of men torn apart by cannon never seen or mowed down by machine guns like so many lambs pressed to uncelebrated slaughter.

Faulkner was amazingly persistent in offering himself as a flying officer, and credibility ran amazingly high. A. Wigfall Green, Oxfordian and professor at Ole Miss, published an intimate description of the rising young author in the *Sewanee Review* in the summer of 1932. Bill Faulkner was modest about his RAF service, Green declared, "although he has two enemy planes to his credit and several times barely escaped death."[2] Until very late in life his close friend Ben Wasson believed the flyer story. It would have been difficult to do otherwise with Faulkner playing his role with such consummate skill. "I miss flying," he said sadly to Wasson in the autumn of 1919.[3] Faulkner was fully conscious of his deception, and he attempted at least a partial repair. Robert R. "Baby" Buntin, a student at the university soon after the war and a flyer, revealed many years later that Faulkner had asked him for flying lessons. "Everybody thinks I can fly," Faulkner explained, "but I can't." He proposed that they "sneak off" to the airfield so that Buntin could instruct him secretly. Faulkner and Buntin took to the air, but it soon became clear that Faulkner had little talent for landing an airplane and the lessons ended. In the early 1930s, however, Faulkner did earn his pilot's license with a professional instructor in Memphis, but his tendency to botch the most vital element in flying, coming smoothly to earth again, made him notorious in the flying fraternity.[4]

The persona of the flying officer was most likely to appear when Faulkner met a stranger, and that, of course, happened most often when he was away from Oxford. Also, the image shifted considerably as it traveled through time and space. Occasionally it would have attained the heights of hilarity had Faulkner not seemed so deadly in earnest about it. In New York in 1921 he managed to give the impression that he was a pilot returning from France, wounded in combat, and just out of a military hospital with "a metal disc close to his hip."[5] In New Orleans in 1925, he improved considerably on the performance by affecting a slight English accent and including in his story a plane shot down in France, a silver plate in his head, and a persisting pain that explained his heavy drinking.[6] Publishing one of Faulkner's first pieces in 1925, the editor of a New Orleans magazine described him as a lost generation poet and very much a war hero. "During the war he was with the British Air Force and made a brilliant record," the editor declared. "He was severely wounded. To date his literary interest has been chiefly in poetry."[7]

William Faulkner's genius as a writer was, of course, directly related to his tremendous capacity for withdrawing from the immediate world and creating others in which he seemed truly to live. Getting out appeared less difficult for him than for other people. As he often said, he really didn't care about "facts." Of necessity, he declared, a writer was a "liar." In this sense, Faulkner was a superb liar. He had a marvelous talent for abstracting facts and creating myth. In his own life, it was as if he were, indeed, the wounded hero; it was a truth higher, more true, than the apparent facts. He was the hero he played, and details—such as not actually having been wounded in the war—were not vitally important. So, too, with the characters he created. The reason they seemed so real, Oxford lawyer Bob Farley would say, was because they were real.[8]

Faulkner was not limited to the elegant flying officer persona. Soon after his return to Mississippi from Canada, he developed another and very different image. Sometimes he became the bohemian writer, artist, and poet. This persona accorded well with his penchant for heavy drinking, lack of money, and disdain for regular work on one side, and the very real artistic talents that he was quietly developing on the other. Some two years after he stepped down from the train in Oxford in such sartorial splendor, Katrina Carter saw him at the railroad station in Holly Springs in quite different garb. He was wearing shabby, threadbare clothes and no shoes at all.[9] Barefooted and hungover, he had spent the weekend on a drinking spree in the Delta with Phil Stone, Phil's brother Jack, and Jack's wife Myrtle. Now he sometimes offered himself as the incipient town drunk and prospective bum, the aristocrat fallen and of "no account," as the oft-used Southern expression for "useless" went. With slightly malicious glee, some people in Oxford mocked him as "Count No-Count," catching, as they saw it, the incongruity of his arrogant manner and poor prospects.[10]

As with his wounded aviator role, Faulkner elaborated on this persona as time passed and he traveled about. One of the elaborations was to identify himself with the denizens of the underworld, and in this Phil Stone was again his mentor. Often he would go with Phil to Clarksdale in the Delta to visit Phil's friends Reno De Vaux and Eula Dorothy Wilcox. Reno ran a roadhouse there and Dot a beauty parlor. Prohibition was in, but at Reno's bootleg liquor ran freely, as did gambling. Phil loved to gamble, and he was good enough at it to take on the professional gamblers that Reno often had at his place, especially when the law and order people in Memphis, seventy-five miles to the north, were on the attack and sinners had to flee the city. Reno had friends who were bootleggers and prostitutes, and Faulkner came to know well one representative of each profession in Clarksdale.

Through the prostitute, who ran a house in the town, he learned something about life in a brothel. Also, Phil Stone would sometimes take him to the houses in Memphis. Phil was a bundle of nerves. He was brilliant, voluble, and electric with feelings of insecurity. He was a bachelor then and for a time had sworn off drinking. He was balding and so sensitive about it that he wore his hat when playing tennis and occasionally indoors.[11] In the brothel, with his hat cocked to one side, he was at ease. Madams, prostitutes, and whorehouse maids knew him well. They accepted him, and they accepted his friend Billy. Thus Faulkner came to know intimately the nether life in small town Clarksdale and the more ample sins of Gayoso and Mulberry streets in Memphis. He relished that atmosphere and later translated it into his fiction. In these quarters he heard about a young woman in one of the houses being horribly raped with an instrument of some kind. He also learned of a mobster in his mid-twenties named "Popeye" Pumfrey, a handsome man who was reputedly impotent but "a dead shot" with a pistol. Eventually, he would use these stories in his novel *Sanctuary*.

True to his pattern, Faulkner observed and imagined, but he did not experience. On one occasion when he and Phil were in a house in Memphis, a friendly madam teased him about going upstairs with her. One of the "girls," as they were called, joined in and was persistent until Billy said firmly: "No thank you, ma'am, I'm on my vacation." The suggestion, of course, was that he had an abundant sex life outside of the brothel.[12] Probably nothing could have been further from the truth. On another occasion while Faulkner, Phil, Lem Oldham, and an unnamed Oxford lawyer waited for a train at the Memphis railroad station, the lawyer decided to treat everyone to a drink at a nearby bordello. After a time the lawyer decided to go upstairs with one of the women in the house. As he went, he asked in a cruelly teasing style if any of the women ever "had a good time with little Billy."[13] In the mid-1920s, Faulkner's bragging about his sexuality included boasting about fathering a bastard child. He never mentioned the child's sex, nor made any reference to the condition of the mother. It seems likely that this was another of those events appropriated from the experience of someone else.

Later, after Faulkner had lived in New Orleans, he developed yet another netherworld tale about himself. He had hired out as a deckhand on a trawler that went out into the Gulf of Mexico where the real mission involved smuggling-in bootleg whiskey. But there was a hijacking and a killing as rival gangs vied for control of the bootleg business in New Orleans. The bohemian here shaded into a tough guy, one who was aware of evil in the world, even intimate with evil, and cynical—a semi-saint, semi-sinner who was somehow still a good man. He just happened to live close to hijacking and murder. He knew both crimes well from being there, but himself did neither. He was "all man and not always legal," but still he was a moral man. This persona was akin to the one played by Humphrey Bogart in *To Have and Have Not*, a film with which Faulkner was closely associated during his years as a Hollywood scriptwriter.

Searching

Faulkner resisted the real world with his imagination, but the real world would not leave him alone. It insisted that he find a place, including a job, and get in it. Given his massive revulsion against working regular hours at conventional tasks, he made at least three valiant attempts during the years from 1919 to 1924. First he was a student, then a clerk in a New York bookstore, and, for much too long by his lights, the master of the university post office on the campus of Ole Miss.

On the very day, November 11, 1918, that the armistice was signed in France, the chancellor of the University of Mississippi appointed Murry Falkner assistant secretary for that institution. This was an administrative post, probably secured for him through his father, a trustee of the university. The place paid $1,500 a year and was not taxing. A letter from the chancellor to Murry gave the hours as 8 to 12 and 1:30 to 4:00, unless there was a crush, such as start-up time in the fall, in which event there was "no limit" on the hours. A few months later, writing on stationery from his then defunct hardware business, Murry asked the chancellor for the use of Ross House on the campus as his residence.[14] It was not, merely, that he wanted to live close to his work.

With the failure of his hardware business, Murry was forced to sell the house on North Street. John Falkner then brought the whole family (Maud, Murry, and all four sons, ages 22, 20, 18, and 12) to live at the Big Place. Soon, Maud insisted that they find a home of their own and they rented a small, very unlovely house on Van Buren Street. It was painted yellow and they called it, derisively, "The Bird Cage." Before Christmas, 1919, however, the Murry Falkners were comfortably settled in a house on campus.[15] It was a large, three-story structure previously occupied by the Delta Psi fraternity. In that house, for ten years on and off, William came to occupy a room on the second floor.[16] Most often it was the room in the turret of that rather castellated building. In the same decade, the spelling of his name drifted. Sometimes he was a Falkner, and sometimes he was, uniquely, William Faulkner.

In September, 1919, both Bill and Jack enrolled as students in the university, taking advantage of special concessions made to veterans concerning entrance requirements. Jack took a full load in a pre-law program. Bill signed up for classes in Spanish, French, and Shakespeare. In the French course he studied the Symbolists very much on his own and did well. In all of his courses, however, he was reluctant to take examinations and probably his survival depended on the considerable respect that the faculty had for his father. One day in the literature class, the professor asked him what he thought Shakespeare meant by a certain passage. After a pause, Faulkner responded, "How should I know? That was nearly four hundred years ago, and I was not there."[17] Clearly, Bill Faulkner had no good future in the classroom.

Yet he was not at all idle. He was writing and drawing—which was exactly what he wanted to do and nothing else—and he was very productive. A month before school started he had published a poem in the highly prestigious national magazine *New Republic*. Entitled "L'Apres-Midi d'un Faune," it depicted the faun in a pastoral setting in pursuit of a passionate nymph, delighting in the flight and the chase, then alone, sad, and yearning, watching dancers in the moonlight. In November the *Oxford Eagle* printed what was most likely his first commercially published short story. (It had been printed days before in the student newspaper, the *Mississippian*.) It was a war story called "Landing in Luck." It concerned air cadet Thompson in the RAF who had great difficulty learning to fly, but concluded his first solo flight with a relatively successful crash landing. In the same issue he published a poem entitled "Sapphics."[18] Within the university, William Faulkner was very visible in student publications. He had five drawings in the yearbook for 1920, but more importantly he supplied a steady stream of writings to the *Mississippian*. He began in October with a slightly altered version of his "Faun" poem, and followed in the spring term with nine other poems. In addition, during that semester, he offered a sequence of stories, essays, and book reviews.[19]

In the spring, however, other students began to tax him for his supercilious ways. They excluded him from the writers' club, commented unfavorably in print on his writings, and soon fell to vicious attacks not only on the work but on the author himself.[20] He was referred to, often anonymously as the "mushroom poet," "a peculiar person who calls himself William Faulkner," and "the beau-u-tiful man with cane." In May, the *Mississippian* printed a parody of his "Faun" poem as "Une Ballade d'une Vache Perdue" in which the maiden pursued was a cow.[21] At first, Faulkner responded with humor, then he turned bitter and lashed back with vitriolic wit.[22]

One can easily understand how Faulkner's critics could come to such cutting attacks. In the university—as he had elsewhere—Billy Faulkner cultivated and flaunted his difference from those around him. He was voted into the SAE fraternity as all the Falkner men had been, but when the group had its picture taken in the fall of 1919, he stood on the back row and wore casual clothes while every other brother save one was formally suited. After he had been initiated along with Ben Wasson, he responded to Ben's enthusiasm for the beauty of the ritual with a disparaging reference to "all that hash."[23] Again, when the A.E.F. Club, an organization of veterans, stood for their photograph for the yearbook, he looked steadily away from the camera while all the other men looked steadily into it. Furthermore, he improved on the image of difference and indifference by posing with a cigarette in a very long holder held nonchalantly in his mouth. His manner seemed to say that Billy Faulkner was in this world, but he was not of it.

Interestingly, at the very same time that he was separating himself from most of his adult male contemporaries by affecting airs of superiority, Billy was playing games with his brother Dean, age twelve, and the sons of Professor Calvin Brown, thirteen-year-old Robert and Calvin, Jr., age eleven. With these boys he would go off into the woods and play "paper chase," "hound and hare," and "capture the flag"—mock war and hunting games that stressed endurance and cunning. These lads developed a great respect for Bill Faulkner, and later recalled nothing in his attitude that suggested that he was anything other than a superb companion a bit older than themselves.[24] Not everyone could have performed so well in these events. On one occasion, Faulkner induced Stone to join them on a chase. Exhausted by the play, Stone declared that he would never again participate.

In the fall of 1920, Governor Lee Russell, in his ambition to democratize the university, began to enforce stringently the rule against fraternities on campus. The students burned him in effigy, and he came to campus to preside personally over the punishment of the culprits. Faulkner, it seems, used the occasion to withdraw formally from the university and to characterize his withdrawal as a protest. But he did not withdraw at all from extracurricular activities. The *Mississippian* soon published his review of William Alexander Percy's book of poems, *In April Once*. It was beautiful verse, he thought, but sadly out of time. It was poetry for Victorian England or Swinburne's Italy and would not win much notice in the modern world, he said.[25]

During the fall and winter of 1920–1921, Faulkner was much taken up with the Dramatic Club that Ben Wasson, by then a student in the School of Law, and a friend of his, Lucy Somerville, also a law student and also from Greenville, had been instrumental in forming. He wrote a play for the group (never performed) starring a liberated young woman who rejected a domineering suitor for a man who at first seemed submissive but later turned out to be a fine, strong character. Meanwhile, Lucy had circulated a book among club members that described an exceedingly avant-garde form of drama resembling that of marionettes. The club decided to call itself the Marionettes, and

Faulkner took it upon himself to write a play in the appropriate style. When he gave the fifty-five pages to Ben Wasson toward the end of the year, Ben saw immediately that the club could not enact this "vision of beauty undone by betrayal and time." As consolation, he persuaded Faulkner to make several copies of the book by hand which he then sold for $5 each.[26] The Marionettes offered their first play in January, and Bill Faulkner helped with the staging. In March they did another for which he served as property manager. "He loved it," Ben Wasson declared. "He got whips and the like when they needed that kind of thing."[27]

During that winter he also published a review of Conrad Aiken's book of poems, *Turns and Movies* (1916). His review signaled an ongoing literary love affair. Aiken, a Georgia gentleman by birth and rearing, had become his ideal poet. Faulkner described a string of famous poets as "British nightingales" and dismissed Amy Lowell's verse as "merely literary flatulency," while Aiken compassed the French Symbolists and reached all the way back to the Greeks for his proper company. In a decade and a half, he thought, Aiken might emerge as "our first great poet."[28] Meanwhile, Faulkner continued his work as an artist. When the yearbook came out that spring, he was very much present in his drawings.

All during this academic year, Billy continued to live with Maud and Murry on campus. He earned a little money by taking odd jobs, some of them coming from the university through his father. Billy was small, but he was strong and surefooted, and he would do painting in high places where others would not dare to go.[29] When school started in the fall of 1921, he did not enroll. He needed a change, and a change was offered by Stark Young, then thirty-six and the son of a local physician. Stark had won considerable success as a writer and lived in New York. In 1914, Phil Stone had introduced Billy to Young as a talented youth. Indeed, Young had been a mentor to Phil during summer vacations in Oxford much as Phil was later to Billy.

Stark Young had first become a professor, teaching in elite schools in the East. Then he quit academics to become a writer and critic, basing himself in New York. He was well known and still rising in the 1920s. In 1934 he would publish *So Red the Rose*, an exceedingly romantic novel about the deep South that would bring him briefly to heightened national fame. Oxfordians were proud of Stark as their literary eminence, and they praised his every move. Estelle Oldham knew and liked Stark, even though she took pause from his wearing sandals while otherwise dressing fastidiously. Billy liked Stark too, and Stark liked him.[30]

On September 15, 1921, the *Eagle* announced that Stark Young would be in Oxford for a visit before training on to New York. He had just returned from another of his repeated trips to Italy where he was much taken with the kind of high romance personified by the super-masculine poet Gabriele d'Annunzio. Soon, both he and d'Annunzio would become ardent admirers of the dictator

Benito Mussolini. Young pronounced Faulkner "bruised and wasted" in Oxford, and, to encourage a move, offered him the use of his couch in New York. Urged by Phil Stone, Bill accepted the invitation.[31]

Faulkner arrived in Manhattan only to find that Young was out of the city. His money began to evaporate rapidly, but then Stark returned and Bill moved in. Perhaps in defense of his couch and his privacy, Young asked a friend, Elizabeth Prall, to give Bill a job in the up-scale bookshop that she managed in Lord and Taylor's department store at the corner of 38th Street and Fifth Avenue. With $11 a week in salary, Faulkner could now afford $2.50 a week for a room in Greenwich Village. Thus, he became a store clerk by day, and an adventurer, writer, artist, and student by night. He also amazed everyone by his capacity for alcohol. He was a good clerk, according to his employer, so helpful that even the most difficult customers, especially older women, liked him.[32] In his free time, Faulkner drew and wrote fiction and verse. He also read broadly—proceeding with that remarkable self-education that would later produce in his fiction such amazing insights into the Western Civilization to which he was born.

~

Several weeks passed before Bill Faulkner and the bookstore came to a comfortable parting. Faulkner did have a tendency to give gratuitous advice to customers. "Don't read that trash," he advised one potential customer, and he might say to another, "read this," and thrust a book into his or her hands.[33] Meanwhile, back in Oxford both his mother and Phil Stone were getting anxious about him. Stone feared that he might go totally bohemian and never write the great work. He bestirred himself to perform a minor miracle. With help from Republican Lem Oldham and other friends, he secured Bill's appointment as master of the university post office, the school having its own fourth class establishment in that line. In December, 1921, Faulkner, very reluctantly took the place, and he made, as Phil well said, "the damndest postmaster the world has ever seen."[34]

Faulkner promptly hired two friends as his assistants and turned the post office into a private club in which they played cards, talked, and delayed delivery of the latest magazines to the addressees, sometimes for days, while they read them.[35] Occasionally, the staff would close the post office entirely while they went over to the university's "golfing pasture" to play a few holes. Often customers would come to the window to find Faulkner sitting in a rocking chair, to one arm of which he had fixed a wide board for writing. The postmaster would continue to write while they waited, perhaps tapping a coin on the counter. Finally, grudgingly, he would rise to serve them with a minimum of conversation or none at all. One of the professors later remembered a confrontation between the postmaster and a freshman.

"What do you want?" Faulkner demanded.

"A book of stamps," the student answered.

The postmaster flung the book of stamps across the counter at the boy, and the boy flung a quarter across the counter at the postmaster.[36] Mail came and went, usually slowly and sometimes not at all. One patron found his mail in the trash can behind the building. Amazingly, Faulkner held this job for almost three years.[37]

In reality, Faulkner was doing what he had been doing since at least the spring of 1919—he was writing and rewriting, steadily, purposefully, even furiously.[38] "All I want to do is write," he once told his friend Dot Wilcox when she got after him for his ragged dress, mismatched shoes, heavy drinking, and seeming idleness. "Don't you want to make something out of yourself?" she had demanded.[39] In June, 1922, he sent off a manuscript entitled *Orpheus and Other Poems* to the Four Seas publishing house in Boston, a company that had printed a number of Conrad Aiken's books. Ironically, the reply was one of the many letters lost in Mississippi that year, and it was November before the author read a copy. The editors indicated that they could not afford to publish a book of poetry just then, but if Faulkner would supply the cost of printing a first edition, they would pay him a royalty on copies sold. He decided he couldn't afford the several hundred dollars required and told the Bostonians that it was not worth the money anyway.[40] He said something quite different to a friend at the post office. "It's beautiful but not what they're reading," he declared, and his face reddened. "Dammit," he said, "I'll write a book they'll read. If they want a book to remember, by God I'll write it."[41]

There were other things in Faulkner's life in these years. He had put together a car by buying a racer body and having it fixed onto a Ford chassis. The vehicle signified the fact that, for a time, Faulkner enjoyed a mild material prosperity. Early in 1924, he was able to loan $103 to his brother Johncy, recently married and already with an infant son.[42] When his father decided to buy a new Buick convertible, Billy persuaded him to trade in his homemade car while he took his father's roadster. Thus well-mobilized, he frequently threw his golf bag into the rear and took off for Charleston and a weekend of partying with the Stones. Briefly, he attempted romance there with a very attractive young woman, Gertrude Stegbauer, who worked in the Stones' law office. When she cooled toward him, he erased her image, as he said to Phil, "by deliberately developing mental pictures of that otherwise idealized person in the least romantic regularly repeated acts of our species."[43]

He used the car also to transport boys belonging to the local scout troop to their various rendezvous. Soon, he himself became the scoutmaster, and thereafter he would lead the boys on various ventures, sometimes wearing his uniform, including the wide-brimmed campaign hat that regulations prescribed. One of his scouts was a country-bred lad who first knew Faulkner when he operated a refreshment stand at the first tee of the golf course. The boy would find lost golf balls and exchange them for Nehi sodas and Baby Ruth candy bars. Scouting was a high point in the boy's young life, and he remembered

Faulkner as totally different from other men. He was "right forward, knew what he was talking about," he said, and described him as "outgoing" in his attitude toward the boys.[44] Faulkner's tenure as scoutmaster earned him nothing but praise from his scouts. One night, however, during a camping trip, he might have had some complaint to make against the boys. He bedded down by the fire in what they considered his overly comfortable bed roll. Soon he stirred, then started violently and jumped out of the roll, uttering a string of curses. After him came a sizeable but harmless snake, put there by his fellow campers. Still not understanding their part in the play, he apologized both for himself and the snake. "I'm sorry, boys," he said. "That snake must have wanted a warm place out of the cold."[45]

While Billy was in the post office, the Falkner clan entered a new phase in its history. John Wesley Thompson Falkner had grown increasingly deaf and irascible. In 1920, other trustees had forced him out of control of the bank he had founded. In March, 1922, the old man died. They all made the journey to St. Peter's Cemetery again. Billy Faulkner stood by the open grave and watched Joe Parks, the leader in the move to squeeze John out of control of his own bank only two years before, throw the ceremonial shovelful of dirt on the casket.[46] Parks, always acquisitive in troubled situations had also bought the Murry Falkner house on North Street in which Billy had spent a significant part of his youth.[47] In Billy's eyes, this man represented the avaricious "redneck" who had come to town to displace his betters.

After grandfather Falkner's death, the mantle of leadership in the clan bypassed Murry, the eldest son, and went to the younger son, also named John Wesley Thompson Falkner. "Uncle John" was aggressive, successful, opinionated, and brutally outspoken. He passed through the School of Law at Ole Miss making Cs and Ds. In court, however, he was known as a "strong pleader" and had more business than any other lawyer in Oxford. His nephew later declared that he won 99 out of 102 murder cases he tried.[48] Sallie Murry, who was fully equal to her cousin John in strong opinions and candid expression, declared that John "was crooked as a barrel of snakes."[49] He was, indeed, more than a match for any ambitious redneck—any "Snopes"—that William would later invent in his fiction. John Falkner carried on the family law practice, kept his hand in at the bank after the ouster of his father, dealt in real estate, and was the most effective political organizer in Lafayette County—and perhaps in that whole northeastern part of Mississippi. He was known as an ardent supporter of sometimes Governor Theodore Bilbo and thus followed one of the most unscrupulous and demagogic politicians ever produced in America. John's advice to candidates on the campaign trail was: "Be vague and indefinite as hell."[50] It seemed, however, that he could get anyone elected but himself and for official honors had to settle for an appointive position as a judge.

Billy loyally drove his Uncle John around during political campaigns, but

John did not think much of Billy. Standing on the square in front of the First National Bank surrounded by a group of men, he declared that "that damn Billy is not worth a Mississippi goddamn—and never will be." He hated talking about a Falkner and his own nephew that way, he said, but every family had a black sheep and Billy was the Falkners'. Phil Stone happened by and stopped to challenge that statement. "No sir, Judge Falkner," he said. "You're wrong about Bill. I'll make you a prediction. There'll be people coming to Oxford on account of Bill who would never have heard of the place except for Bill and what he writes." The judge was not convinced. "Ah, hell!" he swore. "That goddamn tripe Billy writes!"[51]

By May, 1924, Faulkner had another book of poems ready for publication, and this time Phil Stone undertook to provide the $400 necessary to finance the printing. Excitement ran high as surety of publication became clear. Ben Wasson arranged for a professional photographer near Greenville to provide highly romantic photographs of the young poet—suggestive of portraits of Byron, Shelley, and Keats that might have been produced a century before.[52] Stone began to organize a vigorous sales campaign among friends and acquaintances—including those from his years at Yale—and the author himself typed out a brief biographical sketch. "Born in Mississippi in 1897," it began. "Great-grandson of Col. W.C. Faulkner, C.S.A., author of 'The White Rose of Memphis,' 'Rapid Ramblings in Europe,' etc." Thereafter, he numbered out most of the things he had done and closed with the line: "Present temporary address, Oxford, Miss."[53]

Interestingly, Faulkner had added a "u" to the spelling of the name that marked his great-grandfather's grave in Ripley, and the indication that his address was temporary was perfectly prophetic. Already, the postal inspector in Corinth was alerted to the fact that not all was well in the university post office. He had written to the postmaster and received no response. One day as Faulkner and his friends were playing a hand of bridge in the rear, there came a loud and insistent knock at the general delivery window. Faulkner went to the window to see Postal Inspector Mark Webster standing there silently holding up his identification for the postmaster to read. Faulkner and his assistants got a lecture on the sacred character of the U.S. mails, followed by an investigation of how the office had handled incoming mail.[54] Faulkner later said he was happy that Webster had not asked about the outgoing mail.[55] When it was over, Faulkner and his friends left, fully understanding that happy days at the university post office were at an end. "Skeet" Kincannon, one of Faulkner's friends and a fellow card player, asked Faulkner how he felt about this ending. Faulkner thought a minute, and replied, "I reckon I'll be at the beck and call of folks with money all my life," he declared, "but thank God I won't ever again have to be at the beck and call of every son of a bitch who's got two cents to buy a stamp."[56] About the same time that Faulkner was fired as postmaster, he was also dismissed as scoutmaster. One of the local ministers objected that he drank.

Flight

NEW ORLEANS

For some years, Faulkner had been restless in Oxford. Now, he and Stone decided that it was time for the young writer to have his European tour. Initially, the plan was that he would go to New Orleans and find a ship that would take him to Europe in exchange for his labor. In Europe he would write travel pieces for newspapers back home, as his great-grandfather had done, and thus finance his stay abroad.

Bill Faulkner, of course, was no stranger to New Orleans. After the war, he had sometimes taken jaunts to the Crescent City—at least once with Phil, Dot Wilcox, and Reno de Vaux when a joyous celebration in their Roosevelt Hotel room brought a visit from the police. In the winter of 1922, he went to pay his respects to the editors of the *Double Dealer*, a magazine recently begun by several of the city's most talented and ambitious writers and intellectuals. He ended up one Saturday afternoon in the *Dealer*'s offices, sitting in a corner listening to a group of writers arguing about great writing while he pulled at his bottle of whiskey. Finally they came to Shakespeare and *Hamlet*. "I could write a play like *Hamlet* if I wanted to," Faulkner suddenly asserted, and then fell silent.[57] In its June, 1922, issue, the *Double Dealer* published a poem by Faulkner, and on the same page a shorter one by another young writer, Ernest Hemingway.[58]

Faulkner had not completed the final accounting for turning over the post office to his successor before, in the fall of 1924, he was in New Orleans again. He called on Elizabeth Prall, his erstwhile employer in New York, who had since married writer Sherwood Anderson. In 1919 Anderson had leapt to literary fame with the publication of his book *Winesburg, Ohio*, a series of interrelated stories that centered on a midwestern community. Faulkner very much admired Anderson's work and had talked about it with Ben Wasson while they sat on the levee overlooking the Mississippi River near Greenville. When he called on Elizabeth, he met Anderson, and the two men quickly became friends—as well as master and apprentice.[59] Anderson was a short-legged, barrel-chested man with a booming voice, large face, and midwestern drawl.[60] He was a nonstop talker with definite opinions about everything. He was already into his middle years and saw himself as an avuncular mentor to young American writers. Among the people that Faulkner met through Anderson during this visit was Hamilton Basso. "Ham" Basso would make his hit in 1954 with a novel entitled *The View from Pompey's Head*, and he was then a reporter for the *Times-Picayune*. Basso was doing a story on a "flying circus" and invited Faulkner to come to the airport with him. They met pilots, parachutists, and "wingwalkers" and were treated to several rides in the shaky aircraft.[61]

Faulkner had to return to Oxford to effect the final surrender of the post office, and also to receive his ten free copies of *The Marble Faun*, just printed. The very first he gave to his mother. Another went to the Oldhams, Lem and Lida, and a third to Estelle, who was home again on a visit.[62] Bill enjoyed Christmas and New Year's in Oxford, including the traditional eggnog at the Oldham house on Christmas morning.

On January 4, 1925, Faulkner and Phil Stone journeyed to New Orleans where they checked into the elegant Lafayette Hotel. On the next day they went calling on Sherwood Anderson at his apartment in the Pontalba building on the south side of Jackson Square in the Vieux Carré—the oldest part of the city. Elizabeth welcomed them, but Anderson would be gone for weeks on a lecture tour.[63] It was decided that Faulkner would use their spare room while he tried to find a ship that would give him passage to Europe in return for work. William soon discovered that there was no demand at all for his labor as a seaman, but he did find that through the founders of the *Double Dealer* and his New Orleans friends he could sell his writings to the local press. The pay was not great, but it was enough to live on.

It was then, at age twenty-seven, that William Faulkner began his ascent to a new, high plateau as a writer. In this year and the next, he would write almost continuously and come of age in his profession.[64] When Anderson came home, Faulkner moved in with another acquaintance, William Spratling, a twenty-four-year-old architect, painter, writer, and an all around hell raiser. He was also an organizer, a mover and shaker who would eventually head an artist colony across the border in Taxco, Mexico, for centuries a center for high art in silver working.[65] Spratling lived just off Jackson Square, north and west of St. Louis Cathedral. Friends soon noticed that whenever they passed that way they heard the tapping of Bill Faulkner's typewriter—mornings, afternoons, and on into the night.[66]

William Faulkner seemed to be taking stock of himself, and the result was coming out in his writing. Retrospectively, he looked at his life as a poet in an essay published in the *Double Dealer* entitled "Verse Old and Nascent: A Pilgrimage." Much of his early work, he said, was to promote "various philanderings" or "to complete a youthful gesture . . . of being 'different' in a small town." He had missed the importance of Shelley and Keats on the first try, he admitted, because of a "youthful morbidity." He had really begun to move with Swinburne and then read his way up to the moderns who left him hungry for what he finally found in Housman. Then he went back to Shakespeare, Spenser, the Elizabethans, and at last up to Shelley and Keats again. Keats now moved him most deeply, and he called for a revival. "Is there nowhere among us a Keats in embryo?" he cried.[67] It was too late to fill the void himself, he thought. He was passing out of the youth necessary for poetry.

Indeed, he was writing a lot of prose now—sketches and short stories welling up and containing many elements that would later appear in his most powerful works.[68] In the "Kingdom of God," for example, he created a young man with the body of an adult and the mind of a child, an idiot whose eyes were as "clear and blue as cornflowers" and utterly vacant of thought. The idiot was given a flower, a narcissus, to hold in his hands to keep him quiet while he accompanied his brother on his rounds in New Orleans delivering bootleg whiskey. In another story, a youthful gangster, soon to die, met a strange young girl in the street. He almost mistook her for the lover he had just left, but she held his hand and declared herself to be "Little Sister Death."[69] Both characters would rise powerfully in *The Sound and the Fury*, the first as Benjy, the second as the little Italian girl whom Quentin would meet on the day of his death. Most revealing of his own life was an unfinished piece that told about a boy whose great-grandfather had walked into a Mississippi village from the mountains of Tennessee where he had killed a man, about the boy's father who ran a livery stable, and finally about the boy's feelings of social inferiority and shame from his father's low status in the community. Further, the lad suffered from the usual sexual longings, and had an unusual penchant for alcohol.[70]

Faulkner was learning things in cosmopolitan New Orleans that he could never have learned in conservative Oxford. Thirty years later, for example, he recalled that everyone in the city was then talking about Freud—whose writings, he said, he never read. But neither, he observed wryly, had Shakespeare, Melville, or Moby Dick.[71] Clearly, Faulkner understood Freud well enough. He was also doing things with friends and acquaintances that would later breed stories. He joined Sherwood and Elizabeth Anderson and a group of their friends in renting a boat for an excursion across Lake Pontchartrain. The engine failed and they drifted for a time. The heat, humidity, and mosquitoes were terrible, and everyone was glad to get home after a miserable day. The experience became the setting for Faulkner's second novel, *Mosquitoes*.[72]

Bill also wandered about the city with Sherwood. One night, he went with Sherwood to visit his friend "Aunt Rose" Arnold. Rose had been one of the more famous madams in the city's red light district, Storyville, before the military closed the houses down in 1917. The two men had downed a number of drinks before Anderson decided to take Bill to meet Aunt Rose. On the way he had to walk slowly because Faulkner was limping. Anderson and other New Orleans friends understood that the limp—like the silver plate in his head—was but another sad consequence of wounds Faulkner incurred from being shot down in France during the World War.[73] After they arrived at Aunt Rose's, Faulkner had some more drinks, curled up, and went to sleep while Rose and Sherwood talked on into the night. Anderson soon fictionalized the episode in a short piece he entitled "A Meeting South."[74]

Sherwood and Bill were at Rose's often, sitting in a small patio beside a banana tree exchanging stories. Rose had begun as a telegrapher for a news service in Chicago. Then she had owned several houses of prostitution in New Orleans. In the 1920s she still had albums with photographs of call girls from the 1880s and 1890s. Rose was more than six feet tall, buxom, and red-haired. She had a specially made copper tub in which she was bathed and massaged by her German butler. Allegedly, he had been rendered impotent by doses of salt-peter administered to him as a soldier during the war. Neighbors would hear her shout for him, her palace eunuch, whenever she needed something. Rose had lost her adopted son during the war. He had been in a Scotch regiment, and they had sent his kilts to her. She tried to get Faulkner to wear them, but he refused.[75]

While Faulkner was staying at the Andersons, the writer Anita Loos was also a house guest. She was, in fact, writing the French portion of her most famous book, *Gentlemen Prefer Blondes,* and used New Orleans names for some of her characters. She later remembered a thin, unkempt, quiet young man coming down to breakfast with a glass of corn whiskey in his hand. Bill's friends explained him, she recalled later, by saying, "you can't expect much of Bill because he has that plate in his head and he isn't very smart."[76] Indeed, Faulkner seemed constantly to stoke the fires of mystery around himself. One of his friends thought that he had not only been shot down in France, but that he was English. The friend insisted that he had a real British accent and walked around like a British colonel.[77] Another friend would see him come slouching out of an alley in his dirty trenchcoat with the collar turned up, hands in the pockets, looking "fox-faced" and furtive. Still another witness was Hodding Carter, Sr., then a college undergraduate and later the publisher and editor of the Greenville, Mississippi, *Times-Democrat.* He saw Faulkner one night in the French Quarter. "He was a frail and handsome little man," Carter recalled, "and he looked silly because he was barefooted and wore what seemed like a cloak."[78]

It was Prohibition but everybody drank. Sherwood Anderson had an interesting bootlegger, whom he shared with Anita and Bill. He was a young priest who conducted his business in the belfry of St. Louis Cathedral overlooking Jackson Square. They would climb the stairs to meet him there and place their orders for later delivery. Often there was a girl with the priest, very young and stunningly beautiful. Anita understood that she was from an aristocratic family and wanted to be an actress. Faulkner, in particular, appreciated the girl.[79]

Sometimes Sherwood and Bill would sit in Jackson Square in front of the cathedral and talk. On one of these occasions, Faulkner told Anderson that mulattoes were effete and that they could not breed beyond the third generation, a strangely vital myth in Southern white thinking.[80] He and Anderson began to tell exaggerated stories to each other. They decided to put one sequence into the form of an exchange of letters. One character was an early arrival in the watery lower Mississippi landscape who soon evolved into half-alligator and half-man. There were other mutations for other characters, such as webbed feet, that Bill thought were absolutely hilarious.[81] All this soon ended. Sherwood began a book of his own and simply withdrew, leaving Elizabeth to do his talking for him.

In the spring of 1925, even while he was producing a stream of stories and sketches for the *Picayune,* Faulkner began a work that would signal a major turn in his literary life. He was writing a novel. He called it "Mayday," but it would be published as *Soldier's Pay.* The hero was a flyer wounded in the war. He returned home to Georgia to find rejection, disillusion, and dying love—finally himself to die. In late May, Faulkner was finishing that manuscript when he met Elizabeth Anderson on the street. According to one of several appealing versions of the encounter, they exchanged news and she told Faulkner that Anderson said to tell him that he would recommend the manuscript to his publisher provided that he did not have to read it. "I'll do anything for him," Anderson allegedly said, "so long as I don't have to read his damn manuscript."[82] These were terms to which Faulkner could readily agree. Actually, Anderson was warmly supportive. He wrote his publisher, Horace Liveright, on June 1 telling him about "Mayday" and including an estimate of the author's talent. "I think he is going to be a real writer," Anderson said.[83]

Liveright was distinctly the rising man in the publishing business in America just then. He had already published Anderson, Pound, and O'Neill, and he was about to do Hemingway and Dreiser. Scion of the Philadelphia Jewish elite, Liveright had scorned completing his high school education, declined to continue managing a toilet paper factory for his wealthy father-in-law, and entered publishing. His firm Boni and Liveright "stood for something lonely and brooding in American life," one of his editors later recalled, "and unruly and defiant."[84] He was interested in the theater and in women, and actresses occasionally got a higher priority in visits to his private office than writers, editors, and other staffers. Liveright seemed a perfect publisher for William Faulkner. Encouraged by Anderson's endorsement, Faulkner made a quick visit home to Oxford while his friends pitched in to retype the whole manuscript for submission to Liveright and company.

At this point, Phil Stone decided that Bill needed a vacation, so he arranged for him to join his sister-in-law and her children at their beach house in Pascagoula on the Gulf. Again, this was the beginning of an intimate and lifelong association—the beach at Pascagoula. The Stones gave Bill a side porch to sleep on, and he staked out work places for himself on the grounds. In the yard, there were "wild palms" that grew close to the earth and whipped and rasped crazily in high winds. Faulkner worked on the final draft of the novel, but he also began to write more stories. Two of these were tales about the country folk at home. Already, he was capturing the accent, diction, and syntax of the rural people of northern Mississippi.

There was a lot more than writing going on in Faulkner's life that summer at the beach. At Spratling's he had met a young reporter named James R. "Pete" Baird and his twenty-one-year-old sister, Helen. She was an "elfin" girl, a "Gypsy," slim-hipped, shapely, and barely five feet tall. She would come to Spratling's place for parties and Faulkner later recalled how she looked. "I remember a sullen-jawed yellow-eyed belligerent gal in a linen dress and sunburned bare legs sitting on Spratling's balcony and not thinking even a hell of a little bit of me that afternoon, maybe already decided not to."[85] Helen's mother was a well-to-do widow who had a house in Pascagoula, and Helen was there with her mother and her younger brother Kenneth who was also called "Josh" or "Gus."

Helen was an aspiring sculptor and very different from any woman that Faulkner had ever known. She had been a Nashville debutante, but she was no mere Southern belle. She was well-educated, witty, and very serious about her work as an artist. Often her paint-splotched clothing directly reflected her current labors. She hardly cared about her clothes, and seemed to take no pains to adorn her slim body. She was as straightforward in her talk as in her attire. She had suffered a gasoline burn as a child that left her badly scarred from waist to upper arm, yet she wore a bathing suit that showed the scar. "I was burned," she would say simply. Helen was still a young woman when Faulkner first knew her, and some would describe her as child-like. Her whole manner seemed to declare, "take me as I am or not at all."[86]

William Faulkner definitely took her as she was. Indeed, he adored her as she was. Every day he was busy writing, playing with the Stone children, and sailing with friends, but he still managed to put himself in her sight much of the time. On her side, Helen seemed merely to tolerate Faulkner. Years later, in a letter, he reminded Helen of that summer in Pascagoula. "Do you remember one evening, the first evening," he asked, "I seemed to have had (or been under the apprehension or delusion that I had) an engagement with you and so you sent me word not to come and so I came and we stopped outside the nigger church and listened to the singing?" They also went sailing. The boom knocked Helen overboard, "and you bawled me out for not saving you."[87]

Helen called Bill "just one of my screwballs," like Spratling, and thought of him, hirsute as he was, as "a fuzzy little animal."[88] Her mother, Mrs. Baird, was even less complimentary. When a friend commented that Bill was very talented, she replied curtly: "He smells."[89] The Bairds as a family were not themselves at all conventional. The brothers delighted in dressing the black servants as "Ubangis" and filming them with a movie camera in the head-high grass behind the beach house as if they were in Africa.[90]

Bill Faulkner certainly fit the screwball description. He loved going barefooted. He used a rope for a belt and was often unshaven. On the other hand, he wore neat white ducks, a white shirt, and smoked a meerschaum pipe. Helen was casual about their relationship, almost to the point of rudeness.[91] Once when she missed a date with him, she returned home some four hours later to find him sitting on the front steps waiting. He had sat there the whole time. When she made something of an apology, Faulkner said it was all right. He had been working—that is, thinking about his writing—while waiting. That was when she first learned that he was a writer.[92] Beginning that summer, he would compose fifteen sonnets for Helen. Months later he presented them to her as a homemade book, hand bound, with the title: "Helen: A Courtship." He wanted to marry Helen, and he said so to her aunt.[93] Helen could not have missed his intention, yet she gave him no encouragement at all.

Faulkner still intended to go to Europe. Preparations went forward rapidly after Spratling found passage for them both on an outbound freighter.[94] Bill returned to Oxford to put a final draft of "Mayday" together and mail it off to New York. He made his goodbyes in Oxford and went over to Memphis to say farewell to his great-aunt Alabama who, in a rare fit of generosity, gave him $20 to speed him along his way. Saying farewell to Dot Wilcox, he confided he had already put together the words he would use to explain himself in Europe. "*Je suis un poete,*" he would say.

On July 7, he and Spratling stood on the deck of their freighter as it cleared New Orleans, bound first for Savannah, Georgia, where Faulkner copied inscriptions off tombstones, and then out into the Atlantic. Faulkner and Spratling had rented a cabin, and they traveled to Europe as favored passengers—eating at the captain's table and having full leisure to enjoy the trip. Off Majorca, Faulkner wrote another sonnet to Helen. This one, he called "Virginity."[95]

Europe

Faulkner and Spratling landed in Genoa on August 2, 1925. They went immediately to a bar with some of the ship's officers. Spratling, drinking lustily, got into a difficulty with a group of prostitutes and their pimps. The police came and he spent the night in jail. Faulkner met him as he emerged from his incarceration the next day. "You no longer look so vulgarly healthy," he declared. Spratling accused him of sounding irritated. "What the hell," Faulkner replied. "Why shouldn't I be? Missing an experience like that."[96] Apparently, Spratling told Faulkner that while he was in jail, he participated in a homosexual act. Later, when Bill told Ben Wasson about the incident, he said that it was he who got into difficulty and was thrown into jail. Presumably, however, Bill did not tell Ben about a sexual encounter.[97]

On August 3, Spratling headed for Rome while, apparently, Faulkner made his way along the coast. He paused in Rapallo, where the poet Ezra Pound, Idaho-born and educated at the University of Pennsylvania, lived and worked on his *Cantos*. Pound was very well known for the encouragement he gave talented young writers, especially those whose gifts, like his own, did not run in a conventional vein. Faulkner very much admired Pound and had a letter of introduction from Phil Stone who, of course, did not know Pound but had faith in Pound's sympathy. Phil later remembered the essence of his message. "Here's a comer," it said, "Do see him."[98] Faulkner, however, was much too shy to go knocking on Pound's door, and after a day or so moved on up the coast, through Switzerland, and on to Paris, frequently relating tales of high adventure in letters to his relatives and friends back home.

Faulkner delighted in Paris. He moved into a cheap room on the left bank and began writing. As in New Orleans, he was highly productive, and again one of the most striking products was autobiographical and never published. It began as a short story called "Growing Pains" about a fourth grader named Elmer Hodge. Elmer's family moved often and, in his search for security, he came to adore his older sister, J'Addie or Jo Addie, a strong young woman who was "Dianalike" and with whom he shared a bed.

Soon, the story grew into a novel of more than 30,000 words. The third chapter picked up Elmer Hodge in the fourth grade, at a point in his life not vastly different from where Billy Falkner had been in the summer of 1909. Elmer—shy, silent, almost dumb with yearning—was enthralled with another boy who was handsome, slender, and exceedingly cruel to him. He was fascinated with phallic symbols, standing "in a dull trance staring at a factory smokestack" and later fondling cylindrical tubes of paint. Growing up, entering the army, and shipped overseas, he wounded himself accidentally with a hand grenade and returned to an unsympathetic America, literally and figuratively limping on through life. He fell in love with Ethel, who got pregnant by him but married another man. In 1921, he met Myrtle Monson in Houston. She too became pregnant by him, and bore his bastard son. He wanted to marry Myrtle, but her snobbish mother took her off to Europe. Elmer went to Europe too, and in Italy had generally the experience with the authorities that Spratling had in reality. Finally, Elmer, a would-be painter, was in Paris with a companion with whom he had been in jail in Italy.[99]

Faulkner used his time well. In the mornings he wrote. In the afternoons he would stroll and sit in the Luxembourg Gardens, talk with strangers and acquaintances, and visit the Louvre and other galleries. Most of all he studied the paintings. He appreciated them all, he liked some, and he loved the light colors and pastoral scenes of others. "And Cezanne!" he exclaimed to Maud in a letter. "That man dipped his brush in light like Tobe Caruthers [an Oxford house painter] would dip his in red to paint a lamp-post."[100] In art, Cezanne had given answer to the Impressionists. Instead of attempting to catch the fleeting moment, he was after the lasting underlying structure, which he was sure had a natural affinity for the cylinder, the sphere, and the cone. For Cezanne, and eventually for Faulkner too, the mission was to take the seemingly disorganized images we see before us and gradually, subtly reveal the essential unity within it all. Faulkner wove the art world into Elmer's story as he brought the young man to Paris, "that merry sophisticated cold blooded dying city to which

Cezanne was dragged by his friends like a reluctant cow, where Degas and Monet fought obscure points of color and life and love, cursing Bougereau and his curved pink female flesh, where Matisse and Picasso yet painted."[101]

The author of *The Marble Faun* must have seen Bougereau's paintings, and he would have liked one in particular in which four curvaceous, believable, and very self-confident nymphs lay purposeful hands on an apprehensive satyr. He is resistant, back-pulling on cloven hooves, but one might imagine that they will carry him off to their secret place and have their way with him to the exhaustion of desire.

Faulkner went to the Moulin Rouge, a night spot where he observed real-life female flesh in poses nowhere available in America. As he told Maud, it was a "music hall, a vaudeville, where ladies come out clothed principally in lipstick. Lots of bare beef but that is only secondary." He was particularly delighted by one performance in which "a man stained brown like a faun and a lady who had on at least 20 beads, I'll bet money, performed a short tone poem of the Scandinavian composer Sibelius. It was beautiful." He concluded that Americans did not do well with sex. "All our painting, our novels, our music, is concerned with it, sort of leering and winking and rubbing hands on it. But Latin people keep it where it belongs, in a secondary place." All of this from a man who boasted that he once spent his vacation in a whorehouse and bragged that he had a bastard child. He finished his comments to Maud with astonishing hyperbole. "Their painting and music and literature had nothing to do with sex," he declared.[102]

In Paris, Faulkner also visited with his Aunt Vannye and her daughter Willie, then touring Europe. Vannye was actually his father's cousin. She had, with her sister, carried him home that night when he was a frightened tot back in Ripley. In Paris, he departed from one meeting with a birthday present of a thousand francs in his pocket and the conviction that the two Mississippi ladies were simply doing Europe without Europe making the slightest impression on them. "They make you think of two people in a picture show who are busy talking to each other all the time," he said.[103] Billy gave Maud a vivid account of his dinner in a Paris restaurant with Vannye. She wanted all courses served at the same time and refused any wine at all. The staff was confounded.

> The waitress said to me: "What will Madam drink?" I say coffee. She says "Pardon me?" I say coffee. She says "But—coffee?" "Of a truth," I say, "but certainly. Is it not so?" "But yes," she says, "It is so. But—coffee. It is perhaps the wine of Anjou to which mister refers?" "No no one thousand," I say. "Madam does not admire the wine. Madam would but of the coffee. This makes himself is it not so?" "Yes, yes." I say, "Let to arrange himself for Madam the coffee." "Madam would that the coffee arrange himself during the march of the meal?" "Yes yes, if one permit him." "Yes yes, mister. One permits him. But——coffee. It is perhaps———" So Vannye got her coffee.[104]

Bill also called on Helen Baird and Mrs. Baird at their hotel in Paris. Helen, like Elmer's Myrtle Monson, had been whisked off to Europe by her mother, in part, perhaps, to avoid a Faulkner courtship. Faulkner arrived at the hotel coatless and tieless, and the Baird women thought it strange that he planned a walking tour of Europe. "He was an oddball," Helen said. "Others traveled in autos, he on foot. He knew he was a genius." Mrs. Baird still did not like Faulkner. "She thought he was a screwball," Helen declared flatly.[105]

In Paris in 1925, Faulkner was at the very center of artistic creativity in Western Civilization. He went to Gertrude Stein's salon a few times, but apparently made no lasting connection.[106] He and Spratling would go to a certain cafe near Place d'Oden where James Joyce would come in for his apertif. They would see him, but only at a distance.[107]

Faulkner also fell in with young American artists and recited risqué poems at studio parties in Montparnasse. He amused his friends with a demonstration of how RAF flyers in World War I walked to their planes carrying stovetop lids under their arms. They used the lids to protect themselves from German bullets fired from below. He also told them he had flown planes for New Orleans bootleggers, bringing in liquid goods from the Caribbean islands.[108] Bill Spratling introduced Faulkner to William Odiorne, a highly talented photographer and mysterious person from New Orleans who did indeed catch some marvelous images of the budding writer. Everyone called Odiorne "Cicero," and he and Faulkner became good friends. Odiorne was homosexual, and, sadly, limped because he had a club foot.[109]

At one point, Faulkner broke off working on Elmer to do a 2,000-word story ending with a young American woman sitting quietly in the Luxembourg Gardens after having suffered a devastating tragedy. It was poetry in prose, and he had worked on it "for two whole days," he told Maud. A few days later he was still in love with his creation. "I have finished the most beautiful story in the world," he wrote to his Aunt Alabama. "So beautiful that when I finished it I went to look at myself in a mirror. And I thought, did that ugly, ratty-looking face, that mixture of childishness and unreliability and sublime vanity, imagine that? But I did. And the hand doesn't hold blood to improve on it."[110]

On September 21, Faulkner took a train to Rennes, and soon began a walking tour to the north and east, hiking through the heart of the war zone. Seven years after the armistice, the land was still marked by devastation. Along the roadside there were lengths of barbed wire, unexploded shells, and shell casings unearthed by farmers as they tilled their fields. These they piled along hedgerows, much like New England farmers took stones plowed up year after year to the edge of their fields to make walls. Occasionally, he saw a tank rusting in a farmyard.[111]

In October, Faulkner took another significant journey—this time to the England that he had sought to serve as a soldier and so much admired. He had planned to stay a month and began with London and the usual sights. He went to a tailor and bought himself an expensive Harris tweed jacket, but he complained of London prices and moved southeast into the Kentish countryside. Prices were still too high, and he returned to France to learn for certain that Liveright had accepted his novel.[112]

Faulkner continued working in Paris for a few weeks, and on December 9 left for home. Phil Stone had told Liveright that Faulkner would be in Europe at least two or three years. The young author had shortened that to 129 days. He had "done" Europe too, but few Americans had ever done so much in Europe in so short a time. Not only had he seen the sights and absorbed the culture, he had continued to write and think, and he had ripened as an artist.

Home

In 1925, the year in which he became twenty-eight, Faulkner moved from seeing himself as a poet who must always struggle simply to survive to a person who could write prose for money. Then, with the acceptance of his book by Liveright, he caught an exhilarating vision of himself as a fully professional writer. All of this happened as Faulkner moved away from home and Oxford. He had not made it with Murry, and he had not made it with his grandfather, nor with the University of Mississippi or the United States Post Office. However, he had succeeded with Phil Stone, particularly in the postwar years. Stone, like Maud, had been a staunch defender both of his talent and his future. Maud was mother forever, but Phil was an overbearing friend—not pointedly toward Bill, but simply by nature. He pushed wherever he was and whoever was near. Faulkner needed somehow to stand free of Stone.

New Orleans began the process. Bill survived there on his own and with no special thanks to any single person. Even so, Sherwood Anderson was vital in the transition. He was a famous author who said that Bill Faulkner could write, and guaranteed him a careful reading by a top flight publishing house. Then Sherwood did better. He deserted Bill. He had a book to write, he said, and he was not even going to talk to his friend, much less would he read his manuscript. By example, he prescribed a ruthless but salutary independence for writers. When the book was running, friends and family were out. It was a hard line for those excluded, and there are signs that Faulkner was hurt by the rejection. Anderson reported to Liveright that Faulkner later was "so nasty to me personally that I don't want to write him."[113] Faulkner soon joined with other friends and protégés of Anderson to write a cutting parody of his life in New Orleans entitled "Sherwood Anderson and Other Creoles." If Anderson had been a surrogate father, there were several men in New Orleans who had struck a blow to become father free.

Faulkner's ship landed across the Hudson River from New York on Saturday, December 19. There was not much business one could do in the city on that day, but, before he got on the train for home, he made two significant visits. Playing the part of the young writer calling on his publishers, he dropped by the offices of Boni and Liveright, then housed in a fine old nineteenth-century brownstone mansion on Forty-eighth Street near Madison Avenue. Unfortunately, the publishers were out, and the single editor present had not read the author's novel. However, the editor did assure him that they would gladly read Faulkner's next manuscript. Faulkner also called on Helen Baird, then working in New York as an artist. Now he could offer her more than passionate expressions of love and a homebound book of poems. Lamentably, Helen seemed even less impressed than before. Later, she remembered of the occasion simply that he looked more unkempt than usual. Probably Bill went to the meeting with high hopes and departed in deep disappointment.[114]

Faulkner took the train for Oxford, where he was met by his entire family in Murry's large touring car. Maud made a wry comment about his lengthy beard, and they had hardly stepped through the front door of the house on the campus at Ole Miss before his mother said, "For Heaven's sake, Billy, take a bath."[115] Back in his room in the turret, a presumably sweet-smelling Faulkner went straight to work.

He finished a manuscript book for Helen that he called "Mayday." It was a fairy tale in which a young knight, Sir Galwyn, had a vision of a perfect woman and set out to find her. He explored the passions with three princesses only to discover each lacking in some way. Continuing his search, he encountered St. Francis who told him that his vision was only that of "Little Sister Death." Continuing still, the knight waded into the River of Oblivion and drowned, thus ending his frustration with life in an imperfect world.[116] Faulkner inscribed his gift:

to thee
O wise and lovely
this: a fumbling in darkness

He datelined the entry: "Oxford Mississippi, 27 January, 1926."[117]

Probably at this time he also wrote a short story entitled "Divorce in Naples" in which he explored aspects of male homosexuality. The story involved two sailors. George was large, dark, and Greek. Carl was slight, blond, American, and only eighteen. Ashore in Italy after a month at sea, Carl betrayed his lover by going with a prostitute. They reconciled, but the ending hinted that Carl would fall again.[118] Once more, Faulkner echoed elements of Spratling's experience in Genoa.

New Orleans had worked for Faulkner before, and it would work again.

Bill Spratling had already returned and taken a loft at 632 St. Peter Street near Cabildo Alley in the Vieux Carré. He gladly shared it with his friend.[119] Faulkner quickly finished a 268-page novel that he called "Once Aboard the Lugger," a story about bootlegging in the Gulf of Mexico.[120] He began another called *Mosquitoes* about the social world and the intelligentsia of New Orleans. The first was never published, but the second proved more viable. In the summer, the Stones invited him to Pascagoula, and he went. Throughout the season, he worked on his novel.

What was missing at Pascagoula was Helen Baird. She had gone to Europe, then traveled about visiting friends in America. In an unmailed letter, written on the back side of a sheet of his *Mosquitoes* manuscript, Faulkner begged her to come to the beach. He said that he had made her "another book." "It's sonnets I made you, all bound," he declared plaintively. This one, he called "Helen: A Courtship."[121]

Possibly, what Faulkner could not work out with Helen on the beaches of Pascagoula, he worked out in his writing of *Mosquitoes.* The action occurred during a weekend yachting party on Lake Pontchartrain. In the novel he created Patricia Robyn, an eighteen-year-old woman of adolescent character and almost boyish figure. There was "something masculine" about Pat's jaw. Her older brother Josh called her "Gus." Pat crawled into Josh's bunk, and, incestuously, bit his ear and kissed his neck. He threw her out. Josh barely tolerated his sister's presence on the boat, and turned his interest toward a "voluptuous shopgirl," Jenny, whom Pat had impulsively invited to the party.

Also in the party was a sculptor, Gordon, seemingly the character most approximately Faulkner himself. Gordon had just sculpted a piece. It was "the virginal breastless torso of a girl, headless, armless, legless, in marble temporarily caught and hushed yet still passionate for escape."(11) When Patricia appeared in the story, her body looked as if the girl in stone had taken flesh and life.(24) Patricia finally turned her attention to the yacht's steward David, a young man struck dumb with his love and longing for Pat. The engine failed, and the boat was immobilized. Patricia induced David to go to the deserted shore with her, anticipating perhaps a passionate consummation. They got lost among the bushes and brambles on the hot, flat, sandy beach and wandered into a swamp where they were almost devoured by mosquitoes. The physical world off the luxurious yacht was so uncomfortable, so ignominiously and relentlessly painful that making love became impossible. The virgin, against her will, remained virginal.

Faulkner finished the typescript for *Mosquitoes* on September 1, 1926, and returned to Oxford. Phil Stone helped him produce the smooth draft that he mailed off to Liveright. In the fall, Faulkner was in New Orleans again, living with Spratling in the attic apartment. He was heartsick about Helen, and he might have hoped to see her there in the city. Bill's good friend Ben Wasson ultimately concluded that it was Helen who was Bill's great love—the love of his life.[122]

In New Orleans Bill renewed his acquaintance with an attractive young woman named Marjorie Gumbel. She was an unhappy, restless person, married to a stockbroker. Later she became a rough model for Charlotte Rittenmeyer in *The Wild Palms*. Some of their friends thought that Bill was in love with Marjorie. Once she visited Spratling and Bill in the apartment. Bill read her a story he had recently written while Spratling sketched her. Another time he met Marjorie at a party. "I want to talk to you," he said. They went onto a porch, and Faulkner told her he was in love with a girl. It was Helen. He talked on and on, giving Marjorie all of the details. Then they joined the party again.[123]

William Faulkner was suffering great distress from unrequited love at the very time that he was entering a ten-year period in which he would produce at least three masterworks in American literature and lay the foundation for a lifetime of superb writing. That fall in New Orleans, he began working on two stories. One dealt with the dirt farmers of rural northern Mississippi, and the other with the established elite of the towns. In the first, he created three characters who would become literary immortals—Flem Snopes, Eula Varner, and V.K. Ratliff (at first called V.K. Surratt). On page twenty-five of that manuscript he faltered and stopped. The other story had drawn his attention.

In late 1926 or early 1927, he began to write about the town-dwelling elite. Ultimately, this element came to be symbolized by the Sartoris family. The love story included four people—all of that social milieu. Horace Benbow was highly educated (Harvard and Oxford universities), very intellectual, and a small town lawyer. Narcissa was the sister that Horace loved, that he wanted in his heart of hearts to possess in every way, feelings that Narcissa mirrored. Benbow, as noted earlier, was suggestive of the name Bowen, the "aristocratic" family into which William's maternal ancestors had married, and in which, in fact, there was a female named Narcissa. Bayard Sartoris was the returned hero flyer, psychologically devastated by having witnessed his twin brother, John, shot down in flames in France. Belle Mitchell was the tremendously sexual, ripe, totally womanly woman that Faulkner had groped toward with the character Jenny in *Mosquitoes*. In the end, Narcissa would marry Bayard and give birth to his child on the same day that he rather deliberately killed himself test-flying an airplane. Horace had married Belle when Narcissa married Bayard and thereby embraced perpetual misery. Faulkner worked on the story all during that winter and the following spring. It grew to prodigious length. This was the visible beginning of Yoknapatawpha County, that "postage stamp of native soil" (as he said) that he was to re-create in his imagination and proudly claim as sole proprietor.

Probably during that winter, 1927, he wrote to Helen the last letter in his courtship. "Broke since Jan. 1," he declared, hence he did not have the $25 to come to Baton Rouge. "I wanted to marry you," he said, "because I am working well now. actually am." And then a cryptic passage. "What have you been in hospital for? You would not have been sick: you can never be sick to me any-more than you can ever get old. It must be something else. Is it anoth[er] child. Helen Helen Helen Helen."[124]

In April, 1927, *Mosquitoes* was published. It was dedicated "To Helen." Originally, the dedication had been much more elaborate: "To Helen, Beautiful and Wise." But Helen was married now, to an ambitious, well-placed young lawyer in New Orleans. She never even read the book. Nor did she read "May-day," the fairy tale book that he had created for her. Later she sold to a collector the letters and other manuscripts he had sent to her.[125]

With Helen beyond his reach, Faulkner focused even more intensely upon his manuscript. He went to Pascagoula again during the summer of 1927, and this time he stayed to finish his novel after the Stones left. He had been ecstatic with his Luxembourg Gardens piece two years before, but now he was feeling calm solid power as a writer. "I believe that at last I have learned to control the stuff and fix it on something like rational truth," he declared.[126] Near the end of September, just as he turned thirty, he completed smooth typing the manu-script—at 563 pages, his longest yet. In mid-October, he sent it off to Liveright with a letter that declared, "I have written THE book, of which those other things were but foals. I believe it is the damdest best book you'll look at this year, and any other publisher."[127] By now he was once more living in Oxford—upstairs in the turret room in his parents' house on the Ole Miss campus. He would never live in New Orleans again.

Late in November, Faulkner received a letter from Liveright rejecting his manuscript, then titled "Flags in the Dust." Essentially, the publisher and his staff saw no growth in the author since his earlier efforts. The story was diffused and, they concluded, "didn't get anywhere." Indeed, Liveright himself confessed his impression that "you don't seem to have any story to tell." The company would not publish it, and they thought that Faulkner ought not to offer it for publication elsewhere. The work was beneath his talent, they declared.[128]

With this letter, Faulkner's world really did fall apart—probably for the first and last time. Phil Stone always remembered Faulkner's mood just then. "We were standing on the walk by Bill's house," he recalled, "and he said, 'I think I not only never will make any money, I never will get recognition either!'"[129] His disappointment was understandable. All Faulkner wanted to do was write, and he had said he was convinced that he could write the great novel—a *Hamlet* in prose. But here he had labored all during winter, spring, and summer, and one of the most progressive publishers in America told him to stop, think, and start again. For a time he responded with blind denial. He retrieved his manuscript, apparently with the intention of immediately sending it to another publisher. Then he thought again, and began, sporadically, to revise.[130]

Sometime later in New York, Liveright's junior editor Louis Kronenberger attempted to persuade Faulkner to drop "Flags" and accept an advance on a new book. Almost forty years afterward the editor recalled the scene. He also captured beautifully Faulkner's talent for silence. Cloistered together in his tiny office, Kronenberger talked on and on with less and less force as Faulkner sat in absolute silence. He stopped, and still Faulkner said nothing. Kronenberger tried to make small talk, then fell silent himself, and, totally embarrassed, began to read a manuscript. Still Faulkner sat there and said nothing. Finally he rose, said goodbye courteously, and left.[131]

Faulkner had learned in New Orleans that he could write short pieces for money, and now he turned to writing short stories. Perhaps he needed to prove to himself that he could indeed write and earn his living as a writer. It was a kind of healing from the hurt that the rejection of "Flags" had caused. Early in 1928 he began a story called "Twilight." It was about a little girl named Caddy Compson and her three brothers, Quentin, Jason, and Benjy. It was, of course, the beginning of *The Sound and the Fury*. Several years later he tried to recall what had happened. "One day I seemed to shut a door" to all that world of competitive writing and publishing, he remembered. "Now I can write," he told himself.[132]

The story began with the children being sent away from the house while the funeral of their grandmother, called "Damuddy" like Leila Butler, took place in the parlor. The children went down into the pasture behind the house to play. The geography in the piece was very much like that of the Murry Falkner house and lots on South Street. They got into a water fight in the small stream that ran through the pasture and Caddy slipped and sat in the water. They returned to the house. Caddy climbed a tree to look into the parlor window. The other children watched her climb, their sight fixed like a camera eye on her muddy drawers.

Then Faulkner saw another image. During the water fight, the smallest brother, frightened and confused, sat down and started crying. Caddy came to comfort him. "When she quit the water fight and stooped in her wet garments above him," Faulkner later recalled, "the whole story seemed to explode on the paper before me." It was more like a series of explosions. First he told the story through the experience of Benjy, an idiot and truly innocent. When he finished, he found the story incomprehensible, and so he told the story again through the person of Quentin. That was not enough either, and he wrote the Jason section, he said, as "counterpoint." Finally he saw that he would "have to get completely out of the book." So he wrote the fourth section that focused on Dilsey Gibson, the black woman who held the Compson family together as best she could, standing in the stead of the ever-complaining, demanding, hypochondriacal wife and mother and the disillusioned, nihilistic, semi-alcoholic father, even as she struggled to rear her own family.[133] All around him in 1928, in fact and in fiction, William Faulkner was intimate with declining fortunes and failing families.

Marriage

It is from Ben Wasson's recollections, published in 1983 shortly before his death, that we have the most striking evidence that, even early on, Estelle was not totally fulfilled in her marriage to Cornell Franklin. Ben knew Estelle almost before he knew Billy Faulkner. He had hardly arrived on campus as a freshman in 1916 before a group of his SAE fraternity friends took him to call on Sallie Murry Wilkins, Billy's seventeen-year-old cousin. The only other girl present on that occasion was Estelle Oldham, "whose popularity had become a legend," and, Ben said, not only in Oxford. Sallie Murry was pretty, but Estelle was "alluring." She was thin to the point of frailty, and very feminine. Ben thought her least attractive feature was her mouth. When "pursed up," as it often was, it made her appear selfish. She rarely stopped her "chatter," and occasionally her talk was "mildly malicious." Estelle seemed to prefer talking to men. "She was always thoroughly absorbed in whatever a man was saying to her," Ben recalled. "One would have thought watching her as she listened to a man, that he was the most fascinating and brilliant creature in the world." She flirted a lot, and women generally were not fond of her, nor she of them.[134]

Thereafter Ben was often among the gentleman callers at the Oldham house on South Street, recurrently the gathering place for young men from the university and the town. Rarely did they find coeds from Ole Miss or other girls from town there. Always, they found Estelle and perhaps one or two of her closest friends.[135] Katrina Carter, the granddaughter of Herman Wohlleben, and Ella Somerville were Estelle's special friends. Everyone considered the three girls "fast" because they smoked cigarettes.[136] Estelle's mother, Lida, was a very social creature, of course, and she relished the visits of acceptable young men. Indeed, she and Ben composed an Ole Miss alma mater, he providing the words and she, a fine pianist, supplying the music. Major Oldham, on the other hand, made his manners on such occasions and retired.[137]

Probably during the late summer of 1921 while Estelle was visiting home with her daughter Victoria, nicknamed Cho Cho, Ben was in Oxford visiting Bill and his family in their house on the campus. One afternoon, he went calling on Estelle while Bill worked on a poem in his room. He found her at home with many other callers. Some were playing tennis on the Oldham court; others were sitting on the side porch drinking tea served by the Japanese servant Estelle had brought with her from the Orient. Bill had prepared Ben for the presence of the serving woman. He said that a couple of local swains had made "oafish" attempts to seduce her, and went on to mention the current American male idea that Oriental women were "made on the bias." Estelle welcomed Ben with her usual effervescence, and he was so enjoying himself that he lingered after the others had left. Cho Cho and the nurse had gone upstairs, leaving Estelle and Ben alone. Estelle declared that she wanted to play the piano, and took Ben into the music room. She played several popular tunes, then stopped and rose. She put her arms around Ben's shoulders, and they kissed. As they stood holding one another and kissing, Cho Cho slipped into the room. She called out to her mother and the startled couple quickly separated. Cho Cho held up her arms and Estelle swept her up. Ben left and walked around town for a while in the twilight, greatly distressed by his lack of discretion. Finally, he went back to the Falkner house and found Bill in his room.

"Get lost in the great metropolis, did you?" Bill said in a welcoming tone. No, he had not been lost, Ben mumbled. He had heard the gossip that Estelle's marriage to Cornell Franklin had been pressed by Estelle's parents and that she really loved Bill. But in several years of knowing Bill, he did not have the impression that Bill loved Estelle. Obviously with no fear of hurting his friend and host, Ben told Bill in detail what had happened, and confessed he was afraid of the consequences. He feared that Cho Cho, who would be three in February, might "prattle."

Bill was silent for a time after Ben finished. Then he said: "Watch out and remember, Bud, that Eve wasn't the only woman who handed out an apple, just the first one." Then he handed Ben the poem he had written. Ben read it and they talked poetry. Bill never mentioned the event again.[138] Within days, Ben secured his license to practice law from the Lafayette County chancellor and left town, while Estelle took Cho Cho to visit her grandmother in Columbus.[139]

Most likely the poem that Bill showed Ben was included in the book that he gave to Estelle before she left for the Far East that fall of 1921. Eighty-eight typescript pages, handsomely bound by himself, it was called "Vision in Spring," and the title page simply proclaimed "Manuscript Edition, 1921."[140] Originally, it was said, there was an inscription for Estelle in the book, but it was so torrid that she tore it out before taking it home where Cornell Franklin might see it.

~

Estelle was having trouble with marriage; Billy was having trouble with gender at more elementary levels. It was a persisting problem. Ella Somerville, a fellow student at Ole Miss after the war, recalled that "he wasn't a ladies' man, didn't go with girls very much." One coed, who later married a Delta planter, told her that "Bill would ask me for a date and I would make some excuse." He wrote out some verses for this young woman and tied them with a blue ribbon. All to no avail. Somehow, she lost them.[141]

Billy looked for love in other places. He became well known in the bordellos of Memphis. Phil Stone made the introductions. Phil also introduced him to Eula Dorothy Wilcox in Clarksdale. Dot was born in Oklahoma, orphaned at twelve, sold her inheritance at sixteen, and put herself through beautician's school. In the twenties she had her own shop in Clarksdale, also her own house with a high solid wooden fence to insure her privacy. She was very much a bachelor girl, almost one of the boys, in a time when girls of traditional families would not dare such a life, and she was a favored companion to some of the more rakish men of the local elite. At first Bill would come over with Phil. Later, when he had his own car, he showed up every few weeks alone. "Put on your best bib and tucker," he would say, "I'm gonna take you up to Moon Lake Club." To its patrons, the Club was a refuge from the ordinary, stilted life of middle Mississippi. One Sunday morning about eight o'clock, Bill was at Dot's house having coffee. She was still in her nightgown and housecoat. The doorbell rang. It was County Commissioner Hooks and Judge Talbert determined to kidnap Dot as she was and take her off to Moon Lake. Faulkner declared that he and Dot were twins, so he must be taken, too. So off they went, in spite of it being the Sabbath, and didn't return until three in the afternoon.[142]

Desperate searches and still Bill had no lover. Within three days in September, 1922, both Jack and Johncy Falkner married local girls, and within a year Johncy had a son, Jimmy. Billy, the oldest brother, had not even succeeded at courtship. Ben Wasson later declared Faulkner "a randy little man," and thought that he probably did go upstairs with prostitutes when he was with Phil Stone on Mulberry Street. Interestingly, other close friends did not see him in that way at all. Dot Wilcox, riding the fast lane of social life in the Delta, never saw him put hands on a woman or even say "that's a beautiful woman." Bill Spratling, with whom Faulkner lived on and off for two years, declared that Bill simply "didn't seem highly sexed."[143]

Faulkner was, indeed, deeply troubled by what he perceived as his deficiencies. He was much bothered by his diminutive size. "He detested his height," Dot remembered. He admired tall people. "Dot," he once asked, "do you know anything that would make me grow tall?" She: "What do you want to get in that mess for?" He: "I think it would be a pretty good life for a while." In a culture in which, supposedly, "men were men and women were glad of it," Faulkner was sometimes seen as less than manly. Sallie Crane, another student at the university, remembered vividly that he had a "high pitched, almost effeminate voice." Still another contemporary, Branham Hume, thought him slightly effeminate. He seemed shy and withdrawn, Branham said. In the post office he didn't enter into conversations, but he didn't miss a word either—or a drink.[144] It is not surprising that Branham should associate sexuality and drink; so too did mainline Southern culture. Indulgence in alcohol lent excitement to life. Liquor gave license to disinhibition; a sort of bootleg Mardi Gras everywhere available.

The Vieux Carré in the Roaring Twenties was, itself, indeed a sort of perpetual Mardi Gras for the inland Southerner, an easily accessible exotica.

Faulkner discovered that island of delight, and he could not soon let it go. Everyone drank there and sex was unleashed. In New Orleans there were houses where not only heterosexual men and women might mix, but where homosexual men and women, too, were welcomed. One of those was Celeste's, a house conspicuously located, just across the street from a police station.[145] The Vieux Carré was very un-Mississippi, very un-Calvinist and un-Protestant, defiant of marriage, family, clan, and community—perhaps even of love. It seemed to be exactly what Faulkner needed at this point in his life, better for him than Greenwich Village or even Paris.

In Oxford, the community was hardly conscious of the homosexual possibility. It seemed not to cross its mind that its first literary lion, Stark Young, was gay. In the 1960s, Estelle recalled that Stark had "courted Ella Somerville to death." Gently queried about his public and candid display of his sexual preferences in other times and places, Estelle replied that she did not think Stark was homosexual.[146] Indeed, Southern communities danced gingerly around gayness. In private conversation some males might be sometimes called "pretty boys" by women and "queers" by men, and there was no word at all for women who wore slacks, cut their hair too short, and eschewed make-up. People simply did not long dwell upon these subjects.

In New Orleans, Faulkner stumbled into a realm of dim, fading, and sometimes even lost sexual horizons. Bill Spratling was in the boating party on Lake Pontchartrain that later made the setting for Faulkner's novel *Mosquitoes*. Spratling and one of the men were sitting in chairs in the darkness on the forward deck of the boat when Spratling felt himself "groped." The man's hand was on his leg. Spratling indicated that he wasn't interested. The man responded frankly, "I'm sorry but I just like boys and that's all there is to it." The same man came to Pascagoula in the summer of 1925 to visit one of Helen Baird's brothers. Faulkner took him sailing, but between the two of them sailing skills were such that they only went around and around in tight circles.[147]

Europe was more of the same. There was the Spratling episode in the Genoese jail. And in Paris, Spratling introduced Bill to his friend "Cicero" Odiorne, the talented photographer who produced some marvelous images of the writer. Odiorne and Bill were very good friends; Bill allowed Odiorne to read some of his current work, always a sign of respect and affection on his part.[148]

In New Orleans again, Bill resumed his extraordinary pursuit of Helen Baird. He moved to put himself before her eyes, always a bit shabby, always needy. Estelle called it "that helpless look," and thought that any woman except herself would "fall for it."[149] Helen did not. In fact, she claimed never even to have read the book of sonnets he made for her and entitled, marvelously, "Helen: A Courtship."

In the spring of 1927, the hope of a consummation with Helen faded. Soon she was married, and actually spent some of the summer at Pascagoula next door to the house in which Faulkner was losing himself in what he thought would be his best novel yet, *Flags in the Dust.*[150] That fall, apparently, he did not return to live in New Orleans. Instead, at age thirty, he moved back into the house of his parents, into the turret room again, where he worked furiously at his writing. Why Faulkner chose Oxford over New Orleans at this point in his life remains a question without answer. Perhaps it was a lack of money. Perhaps it was because Helen was in New Orleans. A decade or so later, when she was married and had two children, he was comfortable with both Helen and her husband—and also New Orleans. "I don't hate it," he replied when she chided him about not visiting the city. "I don't come back much because I had more fun there than I ever had and ever will have again anywhere now."[151] Whatever brought Bill Faulkner home, it was a move that determined the shape of his personal life for its duration because Estelle Oldham had come home too.

~

Estelle had cried all night before her wedding to Cornell Franklin and not from happiness.[152] Katrina Carter, who was one of her bridesmaids, was standing near Estelle as the wedding ceremony began. When they started playing "Here Comes the Bride," Estelle said to Katrina, "I don't know if I love Cornell or if I want to marry him."[153] A year later, in June, 1919, Estelle returned home in part because her sister Victoria had died in October, 1918, during the great influenza epidemic.[154] Victoria's unborn child died with her. It was a crushing blow to the Oldhams, who had also lost their only son Ned, age nine, two years before. Ned had rheumatic fever. He had gone 'possum hunting with Dean Falkner, also nine, and the exertion left him too weak to fight off a virus.[155]

Now two places were filled in the Oldham plot in St. Peter's Cemetery. Edward de Graffenreid Oldham's was marked by a large monument at the head that called him "Little Major Ned" and a small one at the foot that said, "Auf Wiedersehen Little Boy." Victoria's headstone omitted her first name Melvina and declared her the "Wife of Capt. Paul F. Allen, USA." A stone at the foot called her "Tochie."[156]

Estelle's first child was born in February, 1919, and named Victoria de Graffenreid, thus carrying on the names of both her deceased sister and brother.[157] Home again, Estelle attempted to persuade her mother to go with her to visit a friend down-state, Mary Vic Mills, but Lida was still grieving and reluctant to go into the world. "Oh, she is so heart broken!" Estelle exclaimed to Mary Vic. At the same time, however, Estelle seemed to pick up her social life where she had left it barely a year before—undiminished and undaunted by her now-married state. She had gone to Memphis for a round of parties. She had hurt her ankle and couldn't dance, she said, and her clothes were still in a mess from the trip. But repairs were soon made. "I have embroidered some awfully pretty linen and before long will start on my 'undies,'" she wrote to Mary Vic. She thought a mutual friend, Louise, should marry someone's cousin, and "John Kimbro is up here to see me now! *He* doesn't know yet." Seemingly, John was an old beau who had not yet heard that Estelle was married; perhaps he had been off to war. In spite of her marriage, Estelle, apparently, had maintained her capacity for keeping more than one young man busy at the same time, including a husband. Her attitude toward marriage to Cornell, however, had changed dramatically. "I'm very fortunate for Corny is a *love* positively," she gushed to her friend.[158]

In October, Estelle returned to Honolulu, and in the next year Cornell moved his professional interests and his family to Shanghai.[159] Physically, Shanghai was literally a world away from Oxford, but in May, 1921, Estelle was home yet again, bringing Cho Cho and her exotic servant. Soon, she went to Memphis with Katrina Carter, then over to Columbus to see her mother-in-law. Estelle summered in Oxford, and in the fall Cornell came for a brief visit before they all returned to China.[160]

Just before Estelle and Cornell moved to China, Lida and Dot had visited them in Honolulu. At home, Lem had moved into his hotel on the square, but the very next day he moved back into the house on South Street. Billy Faulkner joined him for a month while the women were gone.[161] That summer, Lem sold the hotel property to the ubiquitous banker Joe Parks.[162] He also attended the Republican national convention in Chicago where he probably supported the winner, Warren Gamaliel Harding. In the summer of 1921, Lem was appointed United States district attorney for northern Mississippi, a choice patronage plum. He named as his assistant district attorney the youthful lawyer, Phillip Avery Stone.[163] Between the two of them, in the fall of 1921, they persuaded the Republican administration to make William Faulkner a postmaster.[164]

William was just leaving that post in December, 1924, as Estelle came home again after a three-year absence. On this visit, she brought her one-year-old son, Malcolm, and her Chinese Amah, as well as Cho Cho, now almost six.[165] Faulkner gave Estelle a copy of his *Marble Faun,* just off the press, but not before he had given the first one to his mother. He was at the Oldhams on Christmas morning for the traditional eggnog, but already he was thinking of Europe and heading for New Orleans. In March, 1925, during a brief visit home, he saw Estelle again, but he was writing steadily now and his thoughts filled with other matters. He and Phil Stone had "motored through" to Memphis over the weekend, and he left for New Orleans right after his return.[166]

In fact, Oxford and all that leaden past seemed to be falling rapidly away from Faulkner's life; now it was New Orleans and Pascagoula and, increasingly, Helen Baird. When Bill saw Estelle again in the spring of 1926, he had been to Europe and published his first novel.[167] During the summer he was at the beach writing *Mosquitoes* while Estelle and her children were in the Tennessee mountains at Monteagle.[168] Estelle returned to Shanghai that fall, but just before Christmas she surprised everyone when she arrived back in San Francisco with her children, without a maid and not enough cash to take the train on to Mississippi. She wired her father for money to come home.[169] In January she entertained the bridge club at the Oldham house on South Street.[170] To outsiders it seemed to be simply another of Estelle's visits home. The family soon knew better. There came a phone call for Estelle from Columbus. It was her mother-in-law. "Do you know Cornell is in the country?" Mrs. Hairston asked. He was in Memphis, apparently talking to a lawyer, Hurd Hudson, whom they all knew. "If you want to save your marriage," she said, "you'd better go up to Memphis and see him."[171] Cornell was seeking a divorce.

Estelle met Cornell in the lawyer's office in Memphis. Cornell charged that Malcolm was not his child. "Cornell, you know he's your child," Estelle responded.[172] Later, Estelle explained Cornell's desire for a divorce. Everyone had a lover in Shanghai, she said, and he had to have one too.[173] In truth, Cornell had fallen in love with another woman, Dallas Lee, the wife of an American naval officer, and he wanted to marry her.[174]

Estelle, apparently, had no place to stand to resist divorce. Possibly she was being very frank much later in life when she said to a friend: "While Cornell had his lovers in China, you don't think I was sitting at home do you?" Estelle reputedly gambled at Mah Jong for high stakes—as did Cornell—and drank. Cornell complained to his mother of another of her alleged sins. "Mother," he said, "if you could only tell when she's telling the truth. She lies all the time."[175]

Estelle did not want people to think that Cornell was leaving her. She insisted that he take her back to Shanghai where she would leave him, then he could start divorce proceedings there. Together, they soon departed for Shanghai, she, as announced, to take care of some "legal matters."[176] By mid-March, 1927, she was back again, giving a tea for her old friend Florrie Friedman, by then Mrs. David Levy of Freeport, New York.[177]

Briefly, Estelle and Mrs. Oldham explored the idea of Estelle suing Cornell for divorce. They went to see Bob Farley, a local lawyer and a friend. Estelle showed Bob two letters from Cornell. They were sympathetic in tone, warm and kind. Bob started the legal process, but later stopped it, all agreeing that Cornell could end things more easily in Shanghai and without a local fallout of embarrassing rumors.[178]

Bill Faulkner was supportive of Estelle in her crisis, but he was also a bit distant. In the fall of 1926, he bound a number of his New Orleans sketches together into another homemade book and sent it to her. The inscription read:

To Estelle, a
Lady, with
Respectful Admiration:
This.

He was grieving over Helen's indifference to him, but he was also busy writing, creating Flem Snopes and Eula Varner. Early in 1927, Bill, too, was home in

Oxford. This time he made a book, not for Estelle, but for Cho Cho on the eighth anniversary of her birth. It was a charming forty-seven-page story about a little girl's birthday.

Estelle had written a book too, "White Beeches," and Bill sent it off to Liveright. When the publisher turned it down, Estelle allegedly burned the manuscript.[179] However, a copy of another story by Estelle does survive in the archives of the University of Virginia. Set in Shanghai, it is an interesting and probably revealing tale of a young woman from Toledo, Ohio, named Emma Jane. In Shanghai, Emma began a flirtation with a young and elegant Chinese aristocrat named Chang. Like Estelle, Emma Jane was thin, and loved to dance. She was also blonde. Provocatively, she kissed Chang, her "little body wriggling closer." In bed with Chang, Emma Jane heard noises in the yard. "Young good-looking men were probably fighting over her again," she thought. Indeed, they were fighting, and they were her Western would-be lovers. Simultaneously with the violence, she relished the moment of lovemaking with Chang, blue-eyes and black, bodies the colors of "white jade and moonstone," and decided "never to tell it at home."[180]

By this time Faulkner was writing *Flags,* and in the summer he went off to Pascagoula again while Estelle went to Columbus to visit Mrs. Hairston.[181] Probably before the end of September he was back in Oxford. He had just completed the long labor on *Flags,* and he was euphoric. He wrote to his great aunt Alabama about a woman he wanted her to meet. He hoped Bama would be "taken with her utter charm, and intrigued by her utter shallowness." She was "like a lovely vase," he said, not "even empty," but filled with "a yeast cake in water." The affair sounded highly romantic, and also ultimately sad. "I hate this place," he declared near the end of the letter, meaning Oxford. "She gets the days past for me, though," he said, and concluded, "Thank God, I've no money, or I'd marry her."[182]

In mid-October Faulkner wrote to his publisher in a very different mode. He asked Liveright for money to finance a lusty adventure across the sex line. "I am going on an expedition with a lady friend, for purposes of biological research," he said, "so if by any means you can let me have the rest of the advance on this mss., for the love of Priapus do so." Horace Liveright approved the request, but redefined the object as "gynecological research."[183]

Again Billy was playing the dirt road casanova. All evidence up to this point indicates that women had defended themselves very well against Faulkner's seductive stratagems. It was as if nothing worked for him. He could be bad in a brothel, and he could be good in the parlor, and still, heretofore, no woman seemed to throw herself into his open and willing, indeed his hungry, arms. Neither woman was named in his letters to his aunt and his publisher, but surely it was Estelle who gave him comfort as he sat in his tower room brooding over his labor lost when *Flags* was rejected late in November. Early in 1928 when he "closed the door" on all that mean world of commercial publishing and turned to discover Caddy, Quentin, Jason, Benjy, and Dilsey, she was just down the street and around the corner. Feminine and fairy as she was, Estelle was someone who might save him, take him and make him whole in a way that neither mother Maud nor any man could.

It is highly relevant that Faulkner by the end of 1927 had come home to Oxford. He would not live again in New Orleans nor ever envision permanent residence in New York, California, or abroad. He was one of the few great writers of his time who continued to live and write in the very locale in which he was born and reared. During 1928 and on into 1929 not only was he living in Oxford, he was still living in his father's house, eating at his mother's table, and it all seemed comfortable enough in spite of his protests. Somehow, Bill Faulkner was at ease in Zion, somehow more whole with this woman, Estelle, with whom he had shared a deeply troubled adolescence. It is also highly relevant that, in this ambience, his writing took root and life again as he caught first the image of "a beautiful and tragic little girl" with muddy drawers climbing a tree to look into a house to see a forbidden sight. Then, as he said, another image pressed out the first, and "the entire story . . . seemed to explode on the paper before me."[184] It was the same little girl bending over to comfort her tearful brother. What had been exhilaration with *Flags* became creative ecstasy with *The Sound and the Fury.* What had been excellent work before literally exploded into brilliance. At last Faulkner was writing an Oxford story set in present time. In one sense, he had mustered the strength to come home and stay. In another, perhaps he had lost the strength to leave.

All during the spring of 1928, Bill was often at the Oldhams'. When Estelle would go to Columbus with the children to visit Mrs. Hairston, he would follow. Interestingly, he was probably with Estelle, either in Columbus or Oxford, on Easter Sunday, April 8, 1928, the date he gave to the Dilsey section that ended his novel. Certainly, on Saturday afternoon, April 14, Estelle was in Oxford entertaining her bridge club.[185] Thereafter for about a year, Estelle appears not to have been active socially. Much of her time, and that of her children—Vickie now nine and Malcolm four—was spent with Faulkner. Estelle seemed to do a lot more for Bill than simply get the days past for him. By 1928, he and Estelle had probably become lovers. As he moved into the fourth decade of his life, seemingly Estelle had given him his manhood—not only in a physical sense. In a way, with Estelle he had discovered himself across the sex and gender line, found at last the woman he yearned for but never had, his feminine twin, his sister-self. When circumstances were right, Estelle's attention was a gift that she could bestow superbly—that total listening to the nearest male that Ben Wasson had seen. If she had not, indeed, been born for such a task, she was certainly bred for it and Billy Faulkner was exceedingly needy. Estelle was needy too. And exceedingly vulnerable.

Brought together in this way, there might have occurred a serious complication in the affair between Bill and Estelle. Later, there was a rumor that Faulkner had caused a woman in Oxford to become pregnant, and the couple sought out a person who could procure an abortion for them. Awareness of the pregnancy, the ensuing anxiety, and effecting termination came at the very time that Faulkner was shutting himself up in his tower room and pouring his life into the story that was becoming *The Sound and the Fury.* Thirty years later Faulkner told Joseph Blotner that he had got Estelle pregnant before she was divorced from Cornell. He procured an abortion for her, he explained, and felt he had to marry her.[186] But, of course, all of this might have been the Faulkner imagination running wild again.

If there was a pregnancy and an abortion, it did not long separate Estelle and Bill. He continued to visit the Oldham household, walking along streets finally paved by crews brought in from outside for that work.[187] In particular, he paid attention to the child Victoria. Vickie's first memories of Bill were from this time when she came back to Oxford to live. They would walk in the woods together, sharing a five-cent box of vanilla wafers, he making up fairy tales for her.[188] Her schoolmates remembered that Faulkner would come to the school to see Vickie at recess, bringing candy. Vickie and Malcolm were always better dressed than the other children, Malcolm in "sissy-type" clothes. To the children, Estelle was glamorous, like "a visiting movie star," and Faulkner had been a pilot during the World War. They were "not tied down like others."[189]

Then came a signal professional achievement. Ben Wasson, living in New York and acting both as Bill's editor and agent, chopped *Flags* down to size and secured a publisher, Alfred Harcourt, who would issue the book under the title *Sartoris.*[190] Faulkner trained up to New York where he moved into the Greenwich Village studio of aspiring artist Owen Crump, whom he had met through New Orleans friends. Owen later remembered Faulkner working day after day, immaculate in tweed suit and tie, sitting cross-legged in stocking feet in the middle of the bed. He would buy a supply of tiny ruled notebooks, write each one full and drop it into a valise by the bed, and now and again take the valise up to his publisher's. Probably, he was improving on Ben's editing of *Flags.* At the same time, he was drinking, eating, and enjoying life in the Village. In October he also finished the writing of *The Sound and the Fury.* Entering Ben Wasson's room, he threw the manuscript on the bed. "Read this, Bud," he said, "it's a real son-of-a-bitch."[191] Soon he launched into a tremendous drinking bout, recovered, and, in early December, headed home.[192]

As he entered the new year in 1929, Faulkner knew that he was winning as a writer. He had four novels either in print or (with *Sound*'s acceptance in February) on the way to print, and he could feel better about himself professionally than he had ever felt before. But still the world was slow to respond to his talent. Other writers in his cohort were getting recognition and money. Clearly, he hungered for the same. Early in 1929, he began to write *Sanctuary* to compel attention. He wrote the first draft of this fifth novel, he said, quickly and easily.[193] "It's horrible," Estelle declared when she read the manuscript. "It's meant to be," he replied. Then added, "But it will sell."[194] Other people read it as a story about sexual perversion and violence, or the corruption of the aristocratic Horace Benbow. Faulkner said that it was about how "completely impervious" women are "to evil."[195]

On April 29, Estelle was divorced. So frequent by then were Bill's visits to South Street that the local wits referred to him as "Major Oldham's yard boy." Sallie Murry remembered that "there was a lot of talk" about it. Bill and Estelle were becoming a scandal to the community.[196] Seemingly, the person most scandalized was Estelle's twenty-three-year-old sister, Dot. There were heated arguments in the Oldham household. By Victorian rules, the Major should have acted vigorously in these circumstances to preserve the reputation of his daughter for purity and the honor of his family. Lida, the very soul of social propriety, seemed driven almost to a catatonic state. After one particularly bitter family discussion, Dot told Bill in no uncertain terms that it was time he married her sister.[197] Estelle, meanwhile, was going through desperate emotional straits. She seemed not to appear in the social column of the *Eagle* as before, and, at one time, she had bandages on both wrists.

Faulkner soon arrived at the conclusion that marriage was indeed a necessity. "I am going to get married," he wrote to his new publisher, Harrison Smith. "Both want to and have to," he said, "for my honor and the sanity—I believe life—of a woman." He was not being "sucked in," he said. "We grew up together and I don't think she could fool me in this way; that is, make me believe her mental condition, her nerves, are this far gone." It was not a matter, either, of her being pregnant. "That would hardly move me; no one can face his own bastard with more equanimity than I, having had some practice." He would explain more fully later, he said, but for now "it's a situation that I engendered and permitted to ripen which has become unbearable, and I am tired of running from devilment I bring about." He asked for a $500 loan, saying that it would be his last request for money because "from now on I'll have to work." He promised Smith another novel within nine months. He worked well under pressure, he said, "and a wife will be pressure enough for me."[198] Miraculously, now it was he who would stand next to Estelle in Ben Wasson's place when the music ceased, and he who would taste the apple.

Marriage was distinctly a new page and crucial juncture in William Faulkner's life. It related directly to his taking up dreaded conventional labor and earning regular money. Estelle recalled that Phil Stone was "violent" in his opposition and said that it would be Bill's ruination.[199] Faulkner, himself, later said that he had been tricked into marriage, and resented it bitterly as hobbling his creativity. But, in 1929, it appeared to Bill that his writing would itself earn money enough, and he could have his art, his honor, and his love too.

On the morning of Thursday, June 20, Bill Faulkner borrowed his mother's Chevrolet coupe (a sort of one-seater, then in vogue) and drove to the Oldham house on South Street. Estelle and Dot squeezed into the single seat with him, and they drove to the square. In the courthouse they took out a marriage license. Back in the car, they headed away from the square, but suddenly Faulkner turned around. He drove to the square again and parked near Lemuel Oldham's office. He marched into the Major's presence. "Mr. Lem," he said, "'Stelle and I are going to be married." The Major expressed both his fondness for Faulkner and his opposition to the marriage. But he would not try to stop them, he said.[200] The trio then drove to the parsonage at the College Hill Presbyterian Church, several miles northwest of Oxford. Estelle had become an Episcopalian when she married Cornell, and her church frowned upon divorce. The pastor at College Hill was a kindly, elderly man, and also a professor in the university. He received them cordially, brought his wife in from the kitchen with flour still on her hands from making bread to join Dot as a witness, and conducted the ceremony.[201]

Back in town, they exchanged Maud's car for Murry's more capacious sedan, picked up five-year-old Malcolm—who had run up and down South Street declaring to the world, "Goody, goody! Mama and Mr. Bill got married"—and headed for Columbus, where Cho Cho was staying with her grandmother, Mrs. Hairston. Leaving Malcolm with Mrs. Hairston, they spent their bridal night in the neighboring town of Aberdeen. The next day they returned to Columbus to pick up Malcolm before heading for Pascagoula. Mrs. Hairston, who seemed indefatigable in pressing Estelle to marriage either with her son or with Bill Faulkner, insisted that they take some of her silver as well as her maid Emma to Pascagoula with them.[202] At the beach, they had rented a run-down two-story house with a yard full of grass head-high tall, but they brought into it the maid, the silver, and Estelle's still stunning array of oriental dresses. The neighbors soon came to suspect that the Faulkners even dressed for dinner. One noted that Faulkner had beautiful manners, and observed that Estelle, elegantly attired, gave teas in the high grass.[203]

Three weeks after their arrival at the beach, Mrs. Hairston came with Cho Cho. Bill took the children swimming and crabbing daily. By now Bill had bought one of those long, open "touring" cars, and sometimes the family would cruise along the beach, top-down, taking the air. It was an idyllic time for Cho Cho and Malcolm. After a week's visit, Mrs. Hairston went back to Columbus, carrying the children with her. By now Faulkner was working on the page proofs for *The Sound and the Fury,* but he took time out to take Estelle to New Orleans, where they stayed a few days at the fine old Monteleone Hotel and Estelle met some of Bill's New Orleans friends. Then they returned to Pascagoula.[204]

The marriage seemed beautifully launched. There were signs, however, that not all was well. One neighbor came to make a social call. She found the children downstairs but no parents. She suspected they were somewhere in the house drinking.[205] Another neighbor would sometimes hear Estelle shouting, a private performance that seriously detracted from her very lady-like public demeanor. A physician friend and neighbor, Tom Kell, saw irritation on both sides and attempted to effect relief by entertaining Bill and Estelle separately. Once, Faulkner said to him, "They don't think that we're going to stick, but it's going to stick."[206]

Martin Shepherd and his wife were close neighbors to the Faulkners at the beach. One evening while they were sitting on their porch, they heard Bill excitedly calling to Martin. "She's going to drown herself," he shouted. Martin rushed out to find Estelle wading out into the Gulf of Mexico, wearing one of those marvelous silk dresses. Running and stumbling out into the water nearly the length of a football field, Martin finally caught Estelle just before she would have plunged into the depths of a ship channel. She fought him, but he managed to bring her back to shore. The Faulkners, apparently, had been drinking heavily that evening.[207] If the incident had been a scene in a film, the appropriate background music would have been Faulkner's favorite song, sadly rendered:

Yes sir, that's my baby,
No sir, don't mean maybe,
Yes sir, that's my baby,
N - o - o - w.[208]

In the late 1960s a newswoman interviewed Estelle in Charlottesville, Virginia, where she then lived. Estelle had taken up painting and had begun to exhibit her work. "I love to dance," she said, explaining her appreciation of the arts. "I probably know every night club in Europe, Asia, and everywhere else." The reporter saw her in a size five miniskirt, smoking a cigarette, full of energy and enthusiasm. Estelle declared that both her mother and grandmother had graduated from conservatories of music, and that her grandmother had also painted. The reporter commented on the fact that Estelle did underwater scenes. "Yes," Mrs. Faulkner replied, "I don't know why, but I am deathly afraid of the water; yet the sea fascinates me. I keep wondering what can be under the sea . . ."[209]

SEVEN

The Middle Years
1929–1950

The watershed year in William Faulkner's life was 1929. It was the year in which the first of his great novels, *The Sound and The Fury,* was published. It was also the year in which he married Estelle Oldham and thereby reentered Oxford's tight little world. Both events marked the beginning of a phase of his life that culminated with his taking the Nobel Prize for Literature in 1950.

Family

In the Southern social universe to which Faulkner was born, as one became an adult there was a clear progression in relations with the opposite sex. In the first order came love, marriage, and sex. With sex, ordinarily, came children and the second order—an intensification of bonds to family, clan, and community. Training for the progression started early. One thinks immediately of a land filled with little girls skipping rope in country yards and on village sidewalks, sing-songing out the words in a rhyme that everyone knew. Estelle, for example, might have done it on South Street:

> First comes love,
> Then comes marriage,
> Then comes Estelle
> With a baby carriage.
>
> How many babies
> Will she have?
> One (skip),
> Two (skip),
> Three (skip) . . .

The move from marriage to first birth was often rapid. Estelle's first child, Cho Cho, arrived within ten months of her appearance at the altar with Cornell Franklin.

For the male, marriage meant that he became—among other things—a provider. Before marriage, Faulkner might well throw away his post office job, he might live in a room in his father's house, eat at his mother's table, and earn five dollars by odd jobs when he felt the need. After marriage there had to be a house to live in and a steady income. Marriage also brought in-laws, and in-laws of in-laws, all of whom were counted in the familial firmament. When Bill married Estelle, he also married the Oldhams, and when his first child came, he married Oxford and the community.

Returning to Oxford in the fall, Faulkner moved his ready-made family of four into an ample, high-ceilinged, first floor apartment in a large house belonging to Miss Elma Meek at 803 University Avenue. The family needed money immediately, and Bill took a job as the night supervisor at the university's power plant. At six every evening during the working week he would leave home dressed in clean, starched khakis, taking a dinner pail packed by Estelle and his writing materials. Later he let people believe that he had laboriously shoveled coal into the hot furnace beneath the boiler.[1] Actually, his primary duty was to oversee the work of the two black men who fed the furnace while he watched the gauges and kept the records. It was not a very demanding job, but it was a responsible one. Occasionally, boilers did explode, and the carnage was often horrendous. Late in the evening, as people began to retire, the need for power dwindled rapidly and the fires could be banked—that is semi-smothered—until people began to wake the next morning. During the wee hours of the night Faulkner was writing his new novel *As I Lay Dying.* At six, he would be relieved to go home to breakfast and a nap. Every day, Faulkner would walk the short distance to visit his mother on campus. They would drink coffee in the kitchen and talk. Daily maternal visits was a practice that he continued for thirty years whenever he was in Oxford.[2]

For her part, Estelle quickly settled into the life of the young matron. In October, just after *The Sound and the Fury* was released, Mrs. J.W.T. Falkner III, Bill's sister-in-law, hosted the Bridge Club at her home on University Avenue. Mrs. Bob Farley, whose husband was then a professor in the School of Law, got the prize for high score, "while Mrs. Bill Faulkner received low score prize, a dainty piece of lingerie."[3]

A significant break in the routine came when Cornell Franklin brought his new wife, Dallas Lee, for a visit. Malcolm reported to the neighborhood that his mother and father talked in the parlor while Bill and Dallas talked in the garden. Cornell, no doubt, had brought Dallas to meet his friends and relatives in Mississippi, and in Oxford he wanted to see his children again before leaving for Shanghai. The signs indicate that Cornell loved Cho Cho and Malcolm, and he did as well as he could by them in the circumstances. Cornell had money, and he arranged to send sums for their support to Major Oldham, whom he made their custodian. Before the visitors left Oxford, however, Faulkner began to drink and felt a sudden need to visit Memphis. He did not return until they had gone.[4]

One can understand William's desire for distance from Estelle's first husband, but another family connection that all the Falkners curiously seemed to persist in slighting was that of William's uncle, Sherwood Butler. Sherwood's only child, Edwin Ross Butler, had been a fellow student with the Falkner boys at Ole Miss in the early 1920s.[5] Sherwood had settled in Greenwood soon after World War I and had prospered.[6] He had married Addie Buffaloe in the 1890s, and Addie's sister and her physician husband had settled in Greenwood also. All during the 1920s and into the 1930s, members of the Sherwood Butler family frequently visited at George Buffaloe Jr.'s home on South Street—finally renamed Lamar Street. The Buffaloes were still as fondly regarded in the community as they had been in the 1890s, and they too hosted book club meetings and bridge parties—one of the latter honoring Edwin's wife.[7] By the time William moved his newly formed family onto University Avenue, his cousin Edwin Butler was living in Memphis and bringing his little daughter to Oxford to visit the Buffaloes on South Lamar.[8]

On October 7, Cape and Smith published *The Sound and the Fury,* and on the 25th Faulkner began to write *As I Lay Dying.* Now he showed Estelle, not Phil Stone, what he was writing. Predictably, after Bill's marriage, Phil was becoming vastly less important in his life.[9]

October was a signal month for Faulkner, but it was also a signal month in America and the world. On October 29, 1929, "Black Tuesday," the New York stock market crashed, preluding a worldwide economic collapse and a decade of want and fear that extremists on all sides would exploit with disastrous effect. It was ironic that Faulkner's great genius first manifested itself to the world in the very month in the twentieth century in which no one should have committed himself to earning a living for his family as a professional writer. Still, it seems that Faulkner never yielded either in his life or in his writing to the crash on Wall Street or to the Great Depression that followed. He seldom mentioned the depression explicitly in his stories, and yet those stories were undergirded by a keen awareness of the long history of poverty in the South, one that really began with the Civil War and, in effect, put the South as a region in the position usual among the underdeveloped regions of the world. He well understood that the economy of the South was marked by low wages and high interest rates, and by the production of basic commodities, such as cotton and lumber, that supplied the industrialized portions of the North and the world, making some people outside the region vastly wealthy.

In 1930, however, Faulkner may have come to see himself as able to buck the trend. Over the past few years he had sent out his short stories to national magazines scores of times and received scores of rejections. He once told an aspiring but discouraged young writer that you had to have about 200 rejections before you were even up to zero.[10] Early in 1930, he received his first acceptance. *Forum* would print "A Rose for Emily" in its April issue.[11] Much encouraged, Faulkner sent out eight stories each in February and March and six more in April. In February the very well paying *Saturday Evening Post* took "Thrift," a story that was set in Scotland but peopled by characters very similar to those in his Yoknapatawpha County.[12] Soon he sold another story, "Honor," to *The American Mercury.*[13] He now had evidence that possibly he could earn a living by selling stories to leading national magazines. It must have been some such feeling that led him to buy a house—or, rather, the remains of a house.

It was called the "old Bailey place," and before that, the Sheegog place. It had been built about 1848 by Colonel Robert R. Sheegog for his wife under the supervision of an English-born architect named William Turner. As we have seen, the grounds were probably laid out subsequently by Joseph MacDonald, the Nova Scotian gardener of the very rich Jacob Thompson who lived just across the road. In 1930, it was a relatively modest structure in size and undistinguished, even awkward, in design. But when it was built, the county was hardly a decade old, and it was a suitably imposing structure for one of the town's leading merchants—who happened, incidentally, to be a close associate of William's "other" great-grandfather, Charles George Butler, hotel man and sometimes sheriff. In 1855 when Butler's estate was evaluated at his death, Robert Sheegog, along with another prominent merchant, W.S. Neilson, served as appraisers.[14]

On April 12, William Faulkner, for $6,000 to be paid in monthly installments of $75 each, took possession of a house on the verge of dissolution.[15] The roof had been leaking and the supporting timbers were rotting with depressing results all in between. There was neither electricity nor plumbing. Surveying her future home, Estelle sat down on the front porch and cried, but the children were delighted. The family moved in during the summer and went to work, sometimes bringing in local workmen for special tasks.[16] Bill fell into a routine in which he wrote in the mornings and worked on the house for the rest of the day. He himself undertook to replace the rotting timbers upon which the entire structure sat. This involved jacking up the house, prying out the old pieces and fitting in the new. Often he had help, but mostly it was his own work. When his brother Jack complimented him on his Herculean effort, Faulkner replied: "Well, as big as you are, you can march anywhere you want, but when you are little you have to push."[17] His house had to have a name, and he chose Rowan Oak. In Scottish folklore a rowan oak was a tree that stood for good fortune.

Falkner men had a history of unusual houses. William C. Falkner had belatedly turned his modest house in Ripley into a replica of an Italian villa. In the 1890s J.W.T. Falkner had built the Big Place on South Street in Oxford. In the 1920s, however, the eminence of that house faded rapidly under the hand of Faulkner's "Uncle John." J.W.T. Falkner, Jr., administered his father's estate after his death in 1922. At first, he rented out the Big Place to his father-in-law, who made it into a boardinghouse. When that and other attempts to make the property profitable failed, he managed a deal of which Flem Snopes would have been proud. He gave Murry a note for Murry's third interest in the property and bought his sister Mary Holland's share with money borrowed from Murry, again for a note. Murry emerged from the deal with no house, less cash, and more paper than he had before. However, he did salvage from the arrangement a building lot on the south side of the property on Oxford's main street. Uncle John moved the house back from the corner and cut it up into apartments. He then sold the vacant corner lot to the Standard Oil Company for a filling station for $5,000.[18] But now again, in 1930 with Rowan Oak, someone born with the Falkner name had a "mansion." Interestingly, the deed was made out to William Falkner without a "u"[19]

Murry soon had need of his lot on South Lamar. In 1930 he refused to contribute a substantial portion ($500) of his year's $3,000 salary to Governor Theodore Bilbo's political machine and was forced out of his job. This, in spite of the fact that his brother John, a politician as well as a lawyer and businessman, was notorious as "a red hot Bilbo man."[20] For public consumption, Murry explained blandly that he had become too old for the work.[21] Rapidly failing in health and forbidden to drink, he was withdrawing more and more while Maud was becoming increasingly assertive. It was she who managed the building of a small house for them on their lot on South Lamar, to which they moved after surrendering their quarters on campus.

On the domestic front, Bill Faulkner had much more than his house and his parents to think about during the summer of 1930. Estelle was pregnant—probably as of the end of June and during their first month of living in their new house. In his thirty-third year he was becoming a father. Life was looking better in August as *Post* bought another of his stories for $750, and during the next month even the *Oxford Eagle* bragged about him when "Thrift" appeared in the September 6 issue of *Post*. Inevitably, William Faulkner as family man was also moving into the community. For three nights in mid-September he appeared as a World War I Jewish soldier of comic dimensions in a benefit play staged in the local grammar school auditorium. People were surprised that he played at all; they were amazed that he was very sociable with cast and crew during the proceedings and that he performed very well.[22] They forgot, perhaps, that a decade before he had been deeply involved with The Marionettes in the same mood. Faulkner also performed well at the Halloween party at Rowan Oak to which Cho Cho, age eleven, invited all her friends. It was a chance to be with children again, and to tell ghost stories as he had to his boy scouts several years before.[23]

On January 11, 1931, Estelle gave birth prematurely to a baby girl, whom they named Alabama after William's favorite great-aunt. Faulkner telegraphed his Aunt Bama indicating that they had named the child "Alabama Falkner." Curiously, the "u" was omitted again.[24] Estelle was anemic, frail, and it is very possible that she should not have attempted to carry a baby at all. After a week of bearing the expense of keeping mother and child in the hospital, Bill brought them home. The baby was suffering from an in-growth of the intestines—"locked bowels" as Sallie Murry worded it—and losing strength rapidly. Years later, Victoria remembered seeing the tiny child very ill in an upstairs bedroom, perhaps Faulkner's.[25] In one version of the story, while Bill and Dean were off to Memphis to bring back an incubator for her, the child died.[26] Bill rode to the cemetery in the back seat of a car, sitting stony faced and staring ahead, holding the tiny casket across his knees.[27] Murry Falkner said the prayer at graveside, rising above his usually inarticulate self.[28]

Apparently, in his grief Faulkner's imagination ran wild again. There were rumors in Oxford that Faulkner had shot Dr. Culley in the shoulder, or that he had wanted to shoot him.[29] Later that year in New York, he gave Ben Wasson his own version of the story. He said that he had been hard pressed for money, and, desperate, he had taken Estelle and the baby out of the hospital, thinking that he and Mammy Callie could care for them at home. One morning just at dawn Mammy Callie had awakened him. They looked at the baby in the crib and saw her labored breathing. He telephoned the doctor who said there was nothing he or anyone could do and abruptly closed the conversation. Sending Mammy Callie to take care of Estelle, Faulkner took his pistol and drove to the doctor's house. When Dr. Culley answered the door, he shot him in the shoulder. The doctor fell to the floor, and Faulkner left. "The bastard deserved to die," Bill concluded. There were no charges because the town agreed with him, he said.[30]

Faulkner told other people different stories. In one, he had taken the baby into the bed with him. She was bubbling at the mouth, and he knew she was dying. When he woke, she was dead. He wanted some tobacco for a smoke. He rose, put on his pants, came downstairs, and saw Dr. Culley at the door. He shot at him but missed.[31] About the same time, he told writer Paul Green that the baby turned blue. Again, the story included his needing tobacco. He went into town, saw Culley on the sidewalk, put a pistol to his stomach, and pulled the trigger. It clicked but didn't fire.[32]

No such thing ever happened, of course. It was simply William Faulkner working out in fiction what he had not worked out in real life—and the story, as usual, made him a hero in his own eyes.[33]

First Fame

Faulkner began his life in 1931 with personal tragedy; he ended it with professional triumph. The decisive factor in his success, of course, was that he never stopped writing. He calculated that in the last half of 1930 his stories had brought him an income of $1,700. In February, 1931, he sold a story he called "Spotted Horses" to *Scribners* for $400.[34] Then there came a dry spell for short stories, but *Sanctuary,* his novel, came out on February 9. People with limited vision were horrified, but those who knew more saw its power. Ernest Hemingway, who could hardly bear the idea that any writer approached his own excellence, read *Sanctuary* and said that Faulkner was "damned good when good."[35]

Faulkner had written *Sanctuary* to get attention and money, and it worked; it especially won attention for him as veteran reviewers compared him to Dostoevsky and Euripides and used phrases such as "prodigious genius."[36] In the writing he created an Ole Miss coed named Temple Drake who saw a man murdered by a pistol shot to the head right before her eyes. She was then raped by the murderer with a corn cob, and subsequently held prisoner by him in a Memphis brothel. The murderer, a bootlegger and gangster named "Popeye," was impotent and used one of his men, Red, to rape Temple while he watched from the foot of the bed making whinnying sounds like a stallion in heat. Temple fell in love with Red. In the end Red was murdered, Popeye was executed, and Temple sat calm and serene with her father, Judge Drake, in the Luxembourg Gardens in Paris. Faulkner always insisted that the story was basely conceived and his worst novel. He made furious and costly attempts to improve it just before it was printed. Whatever its provenance, *Sanctuary* stands as a marvelously successful conflation of bizarre sex, hard liquor, and the cultural chasm that separated the higher and lower orders of society.

Faulkner's novels often began either as short stories or with characters in short stories who became leading characters in subsequent novels. During the summer of 1931, when he was having no luck selling his stories, he began casting about desperately and again picked up a story begun earlier concerning Thomas Sutpen. About the same time, he featured Flem Snopes in a tale he called "Centaur in Brass." Most significantly near term, he began a story about a minister named Gail Hightower who was obsessed with his paternal past. This story he called "Dark House," but in August of that year he changed the title to "Light in August." Within a year this work would evolve into a complex of interrelated stories and be published as a whole piece, the second of his three great novels. He was now consciously the master artist. There was no spontaneous exploding of the story on the page before him as with *The Sound and the Fury,* no sudden ecstasy. It was rather, he said, a process of carefully "choosing among possibilities and probabilities" as he pressed the words out before him.[37] It was his most reworked story to date, revealing a capacity for discovering, testing, and developing as he labored.

In September Faulkner sold a short story to *Harper's* for $500. In addition, his publishers Cape and Smith brought out a collection of his stories called *These 13.* The first printing of nearly two thousand copies sold out within a month. In October, he sold two more stories to the magazines.

The years of work were paying off now, still not so much in fortune as in fame. Late in 1930, Sinclair Lewis, in his speech accepting the Nobel Prize for Literature, had mentioned Faulkner as one of the several leading American writers. In April, Bennett Cerf, the genial, sociable, sophisticated cofounder of Random House, indicated that he would like to have Faulkner on the list of authors he published. In September, Faulkner was invited as one of the rising young stars to join thirty-four other authors at a Conference of Southern Writers in late October at the University of Virginia in Charlottesville. His publisher offered to buy the train ticket and give him $100 for expenses. Faulkner accepted the invitation, but he warned his hosts that he would be like the hound dog from the country that comes into town with its owner. The owner parks the wagon on the square, and the hound dog immediately takes refuge under the wagon. "He might be cajoled or scared out for a distance, but first thing you know he has scuttled back under the wagon, maybe he growls at you a little. Well, that's me."[38]

And so it was; except that alcohol was the wagon under which William Faulkner attempted to hide. When a reporter met him as he arrived at the Monticello Hotel, the first thing Faulkner said was, "Know where I can get a drink?" Taken to the SAE fraternity house, he soon had a large glass of whisky in his hand.[39] The next morning, two young men who were to escort him to the inaugural session found him sitting on the curb in front of the hotel with a fruit jar of bootleg whiskey beside him. At the opening meeting, Ellen Glasgow, beautiful and brilliant in her early fifties, gave a mostly extemporaneous discourse in which she re-sounded a favorite theme. "Because you are not only Southern writers, but world writers," she declared, "you bring to our literature the diversity which is life, not the standardization which is death." Elaborating, she distinguished between "the truth of life, the truth of history, and truth of fiction."[40] During most of Glasgow's talk Faulkner leaned forward with his elbows on his knees and held his head in his hands. He would raise his head at appropriate times and say, "I agree, I agree."[41] Historians present, however, were not so yielding. Ulrich B. Phillips, the Georgia-born Yale professor who was then undisputed dean of Southern historians, leapt into the breach in the cause of his muse. He suspected, perhaps, an unflattering association between Glasgow's use of the word "standardization" and the discipline of his profession.[42]

The talk moved on through subjects and speakers relatively peacefully until the youthful North Carolina Pulitzer prize-winning playwright Paul Green ran athwart the Nashville agrarians, present in the persons of Allen Tate and Donald Davidson. Green argued that the Machine Age would do no harm to the creative mind. The Nashvillians took vigorous exception, whereupon Green went wild and declared that "any little runt who is driving a high-powered car at sixty miles an hour is going toward God."[43] Definitely, these people were speaking William Faulkner's language, and he would resonate in one way or another with all of them in his future fiction. In the conference, however, he offered no statement of substance that was recorded, and he appeared only "spasmodically," even though he was "of considerable interest to all as an important if elusive light on the Mississippi horizon."[44] Allen Tate remembered him principally for repeatedly saying "yes ma'am, I want a little drink" and regurgitating on his wife's new dress.[45]

Later, when Paul Green came to the hotel to drive Faulkner to another session, he appeared wearing what Green took to be an aviator's cap from the World War. Faulkner explained the garment without explaining why he had chosen that occasion to wear it. He had been in the Royal Air Force, he said. Decades later Estelle said that he had flown to Charlottesville for the conference in his own plane, and that he had even shown her the field on which he landed.[46] At that time, of course, he had no plane and had not learned to fly. That afternoon, the two young men came for Bill again. One of them was Lambert Davis, who would make a brilliant record as the head of the University of North Carolina Press. They were going to palatial Castle Hill, a private estate, for a reception. Shortly, Faulkner posed the relevant question. "Can we get a drink at Castle Hill?" Once there, he went about "wild-eyed and tie askew," wanting everyone to meet his "little friend," Lambert Davis. Then he disappeared upstairs and had to be chased down and brought to meet the hostess.[47]

Sherwood Anderson attended the conference and afterward described it in a letter to his mother-in-law. "Bill Faulkner had arrived and got drunk," he wrote. "From time to time he appeared, got drunk again immediately, & disappeared. He kept asking everyone for drinks. If they didn't give him any, he drank his own."[48]

In Charlottesville, Sherwood had warned Bill about fame. "They'll make an ass of him if they can, prying into him, boosting him—then dropping him for another new man," he had told Faulkner. "There's the difficulty," he said, "to ride through that and forget it."[49]

Faulkner's publisher, Harrison Smith, met him in Charlottesville, and he, too, was anxious about Faulkner's future. Smith was worried, first because his firm was in financial trouble in the second year of a deepening worldwide depression, and, next, because other publishers were ambitious to steal away his leading writer. His idea was to bring Faulkner on to New York, but to keep him close to himself. Paul Green offered them a ride to the city in his car, and they accepted. Under way, the hound was more relaxed. He told his fellow travelers that when people accused him of being heavily influenced by James Joyce, he always responded that he had never read Joyce. Then he recited easily from memory one of his favorite Joyce poems.[50]

When Faulkner arrived in New York, Smith found that his caution was more than justified. Random House, Knopf, and the Viking Press were all after Faulkner. In the crisis Smith provided funds for a young friend of Green's from Chapel Hill, Milton Abernathy, to escort the writer, now drinking heavily again, on a sea voyage to Jacksonville, Florida. From there, the pair entrained to Chapel Hill, where, among other things, Faulkner attended a class on campus in creative writing. It was all a rather drunken and improbable odyssey.[51]

Shortly, Faulkner returned to New York, and in the city the circus began again. "I have been meeting people and being called on all day," he wrote to Estelle. "And I have taken in about $300.00 since I got here. It's just like I was some strange and valuable beast, and I believe I can make $1,000.00 more in a month."[52] At lunch on November 5 he granted permission to Princeton professor Maurice Coindreau to translate several of his works into French. It was the beginning of a long association that did much to make him a literary giant in France well before he became such in America.[53] Within two weeks, Faulkner understood that he was to be given a contract for $10,000 to write a movie for Tallulah Bankhead, a very Southern and aristocratic actress whose father was a senator from Alabama. He was also, he said, writing a short story for *Cosmopolitan* and rendering a stage version of *Sanctuary* that would begin rehearsals within two weeks. "I have created quite a sensation," he declared to Estelle. "I have had luncheons in my honor by magazine editors every day for a week now, besides evening parties, or people who want to see what I look like. In fact, I have learned with astonishment that I am now the most important figure in American Letters. That is, I have the best future. Even Sinclair Lewis and Dreiser make engagements to see me, and Mencken is coming all the way up from Baltimore to see me on Wednesday. I'm glad I'm level-headed, not very vain. But I don't think it has gone to my head." Then he added a highly significant fact. "Anyway," he said, "I'm writing."[54]

For Faulkner, work was always salvation, and it was true that he was not a vain person in any conventional sense. But in New York, with the drinking and the celebration, it was as if he were in one of those World War I planes spinning downward, frame shuddering and wires screaming more and more shrilly as the machine plunged toward earth. Estelle was frightened for him and came to New York, anemic, tired, distraught as she was.

Faulkner met a host of famous writers, including Lillian Hellman and her companion, Dashiell Hammett, an ex–Pinkerton detective who had written *The Maltese Falcon.* Hammett was almost as good at drinking as Faulkner. They talked literature and drank for days on end. On one occasion the two badgered Bennett Cerf into taking them to a party given by Alfred Knopf's wife, Knopf being out of the city at the time. The two arrived after an afternoon of boozing. They were polite, but continued to drink, undaunted by a list of distinguished guests that included author Willa Cather. Finally, Hammett slipped from the couch to the floor and lay there. Faulkner rose to take his leave only to sink to the floor and pass out also. Hammett was taken to another room to recover, Faulkner got up to say his goodbyes, but collapsed to the floor again. Finally, Ben Wasson, always a good friend to Faulkner in trying situations, managed Bill's departure for him.[55]

Shortly thereafter, Cerf also gave a party to which he invited Faulkner and his friendly rival, publisher Alfred Knopf. Knopf scoured New York for copies of Faulkner's books and, at the party, asked for the author's signature in each. Faulkner refused, explaining that autographs were a part of "his stock in trade" and he couldn't afford to give them away freely. Cerf and Knopf were appalled, but then Cerf persuaded Faulkner to give Knopf a single signature. Turning generous, Faulkner let the famous publisher pick which volume he was to sign.[56]

Estelle was in no condition, either physically or emotionally, to help William Faulkner in the big city. She took to the social life and the drinking quickly. At a party in his high rise apartment overlooking Central Park, Bennett Cerf saw her standing at the window looking at the scene. "When I see all this beauty," she said, "I feel just like throwing myself out the window." Gently Cerf led her away from the window, assuring her that she didn't really intend what she said. "What do you mean?" Estelle protested. "Of course I do."[57] On another occasion, after Dorothy Parker took Estelle on a shopping tour, the two returned to the Faulkners' room in the Algonquin Hotel. Shortly Estelle became hysterical, ripping her dress, and trying to jump out the window. Later, Marc Connelly thought that Estelle suffered from "some kind of slips of mental process, of thinking, and so on." He once saw William Faulkner catch one of these slips at the beginning. Very coolly, Bill slapped Estelle in the face hard, whereupon she quickly regained her balance and went on. It was all as if nothing had happened.[58]

By mid-December, the Faulkners were home again, and life was much more manageable. Faulkner set immediately to work.[59] By mid-February, 1932, he had finished the manuscript for *Light in August.* By mid-March, revising in his usual fashion as he typed up the handwritten draft, he had completed another draft and mailed it off. He was overdrawn for $500 at the bank, merchants were reluctant to accept his checks, and one storeowner instructed his clerks not to "let that Faulkner boy charge anything in the store." At one point, he had to ask his Uncle John for a $5 loan.[60]

Faulkner haunted the post office, hoping for a royalty check. It was a hope that faded rapidly as the house of Cape and Smith went into bankruptcy owing him royalties of $4,000. Lamentably, when his books were at last making a modest income, his publishers failed. Harrison Smith was a very wealthy man through inheritance, but invested virtually none of his own money in his publishing ventures. Nor was he generous with William Faulkner.[61] He slid out of the failed company and formed another with a junior partner named Robert Haas. Remarkably, Faulkner continued with Smith in the new firm. Smith and Haas were to publish *Light in August* and had given Faulkner some small advances, but it would be almost a year before any substantial return could be expected from the book. Faulkner instructed Ben Wasson, now acting as his agent in New York, to attempt to sell serial rights to the novel to one of the leading magazines for $5,000, provided that they would not cut a word. There were no buyers.[62]

Then, suddenly, the prospect of financial relief appeared. There had been talk of screenwriting jobs for him during his New York visit in the fall. Now in the spring he received a substantial offer. MGM would pay him $500 a week for six weeks in Hollywood. Movies were just then getting into the business of developing sound tracks with their films, and filmmakers were hiring writers of all kinds for high salaries. Most major authors did some time in the film studios in the 1930s. Hollywood wanted them for their talents, but there was also a special rivalry among the film companies to lay claim to the names of the most famous.

In April, Faulkner received a contract to begin work in May.[63] MGM sent him a train ticket and an advance. When he showed the check to his father, Murry was incredulous. "Is it legal?" he asked.[64]

Hollywood

On Saturday, May 7, 1932, Faulkner appeared at the Metro-Goldwyn-Mayer studios in Culver City, California, for his first meeting with head writer Sam Marx. Often in encountering new people Faulkner slipped into his wounded flyer persona. This time he improved on all previous performances. He arrived with a scalp wound open and bleeding. Everyone was solicitous, but Faulkner waved them away and dabbed at the cut with a blood-soaked handkerchief. His story was that he had been hit by a cab in New Orleans while changing trains. If so, he must have been in a sad state for the nearly two-day journey to California. It was obvious that he had been drinking.

Faulkner declared that he wanted to go to work right away. When Marx told Faulkner he was going to put him on a Wallace Beery film, Faulkner asked, "Who's he?" In truth, he was not a movie fan, and knew very little about the film world. He immediately proved his ignorance by countering the prospective assignment with the suggestion that he had an idea for a Mickey Mouse cartoon. Then he learned that Mickey Mouse belonged to Walt Disney not MGM, and was led into a projection room to see Wallace Beery in his most recent success, *The Champ*. The film had hardly begun before Faulkner left, and he did not reappear until Monday, May 16, nine days later. He told Marx that he had been wandering in Death Valley. Privately, he confessed that he had been scared by the "hullabaloo" and fled.[65]

Reinstated, Faulkner went to work, and on June 2 mailed Estelle $100.[66] Very soon director Howard Hawks asked for and got his services. Hawks had made *Dawn Patrol* with Clark Gable, and had risen to become one of the most highly respected filmmakers in Hollywood. Born in 1896, he had gone to Phillips Exeter in preparation for entering Cornell University. Hawks had been an army flyer and race car driver before coming to Hollywood. He admired fine literature, and he was passionate about making superb movies. Irving Thalberg, the brilliant young director of production at MGM, recognized Hawks's talent and gave him free rein, including permission to buy for $2,200 the film rights to Faulkner's story "Turn About" and to use Faulkner as a writer on the script.[67]

From the first, Hawks and Faulkner got along famously. Hawks loathed chatting, and he liked for his women to come from old Southern families.[68] Both men liked to hunt and drink, and occasionally they would drive over the mountains into the Imperial Valley. According to a story often told, on at least one occasion Clark Gable came along on such a trip. Hawks and Faulkner began to talk books while the actor listened. Finally, Gable joined in by asking Faulkner who he thought were the best modern writers.

> "Ernest Hemingway, Willa Cather, Thomas Mann, John Dos Passos, and myself," Faulkner answered.
>
> "Oh," the actor said after a moment, "do you write, Mr. Faulkner?"
>
> "Yes," Faulkner answered, then asked: "What do you do, Mr. Gable?"[69]

It is barely possible that, at that moment, Faulkner did not know what Mr. Gable did; it is almost certain that he didn't care. It is equally certain, however, that he came to appreciate Clark Gable as a drinking partner. Mrs. Hawks, "Slim," remembered one trip about 1942 in which she and the three men drove to southernmost California on a dove shooting excursion. On the late night trip back, Faulkner and Gable sat in the back seat of the station wagon and drank steadily. Home again, Gable might have stopped, but Faulkner continued to drink for days afterward and finally had to be hospitalized.[70]

In August, Faulkner's work in California was interrupted. On August 7, 1932, his father died of heart failure, suddenly but not unexpectedly. Murry had been in declining health for some two years. During the same time, ironically, Maud seemed to become stronger. She would out-live Murry by almost thirty years. On the 10th, Faulkner was home. He was filled with a sense of duty to his mother, and a bit anxious about his capacity to fulfill that duty.[71] "Dad left mother solvent for only about 1 year," he wrote Ben Wasson. "Then it is me."[72]

There was death for the Falkner clan in Oxford that summer, but there was also life. Before Bill returned to Hollywood to finish out his work for Hawks, Estelle was pregnant again. In early October he was in California for a three-week stint, having brought Maud and Dean along for the ride. Hawks suggested that he stay longer and make some more money, but Faulkner had heard that Paramount studios was going to pick up its option to buy film rights to *Sanctuary.* This would bring him a bonanza of something over $5,000 after commissions. For Faulkner, it meant that he could go home. Happily he gathered up his family and headed for Oxford.

Light in August was officially published on October 9, 1932. Essentially, it was a story about identity—framed provocatively in terms of displaced persons in a culture that set an exceedingly high premium upon everyone having a place and staying in it according to race, sex, and class. At one level, Faulkner's first great novel, *The Sound and the Fury,* was a story about people who had lost grip on their sex roles as assigned. *Light in August* was a novel about a number of people who had lost their holds on their roles as to race, or sex, or both. Lena Grove was a young woman who had somehow failed to learn the skip-rope lesson. She got pregnant before she got married and set out on a journey to find the man who ought to have been the husband and father. Joe Christmas was a child born of a white mother but who could never know his race because no one really knew whether his father was black or white. A score of other characters lost their places too—including Percy Grimm, a national guard captain and total soldier who, nevertheless, was born too late to participate in combat in World War I; Joanna Burden who was born and lived virtually all of her life in the South but whose culture was wholly Northern; and Gail Hightower who could never be the man that either his father or his grandfather was. In the end Joe Christmas was sacrificed, and his death represents something of an atonement for the social sins of others. One feels that he found his place in dying for their salvation, and in the new dispensation life was once more finding order and security. Yoknapatawpha was saved, born again.

Absalom, Absalom!

A DIFFICULT BEGINNING

Light in August was, perhaps, the most coolly written of Faulkner's three great novels. *The Sound and the Fury* had been most hotly written. *Absalom, Absalom!* (1936) would be wrought in an agony springing from the circumstances of his personal life. In the summer of 1933 he wrote an introduction for a Random House edition of *The Sound and the Fury* in which he looked back over his professional life. He had learned something about writing with his first novel, *Soldier's Pay,* he said, but in doing *The Sound and the Fury* he learned to use all the great writing that he had read "in a series of delayed repercussions like summer thunder. I discovered the Flauberts and Dostoevskys and Conrads whose books I have read ten years ago." He added that he had read nothing since and seemed to have learned nothing. With that writing in 1928, the chrysalis, the mutation, had occurred; the caterpillar became the butterfly; the bright genius of his art was born. It drew upon all that had gone before, but it was new in the world, unique, individual, particular. He had hoped to find rapture again with *Light in August,* the kind of "explosion" of words by whole pages. But no. "I was now aware before each word was written down just what the people would do, I was deliberately choosing among possibilities and probabilities of behavior and weighing and measuring each choice by the scale of the Jameses and Conrads and Balzacs."[73]

Four years would pass before *Absalom, Absalom!* was printed. In between, Faulkner led a tortured life. It was a world of his own creation, however much he might rave about the injustices imposed upon him by others. Among the many complaints that he made, the note most often sounded was his need of money. In the mid-1930s he repeatedly bombarded his agent in New York, Morton Goldman, with frantic requests. Aiming a story at *Cosmopolitan* in 1934, he urged Goldman to "please get the money as soon as possible." "Ask them to please let us have it quick," he begged. "I always need money bad, but this time I am desperate . . ."[74]

Some of this desperation sprang from the needs of the Falkner clan, but much of it came from his marriage to Estelle. Had he not married, he would probably have continued as before—in the house of his father, and then, after Murry's death, in the house of his mother. Had he married a woman with money or a profession or a very modest material appetite, he still could have had Rowan Oak and a comfortable life style. But with Estelle there came large problems about money. Estelle had been reared to live as if she were wealthy. Cornell Franklin had no difficulty maintaining that standard and relished it himself. Her taste for the good life did not die with her divorce.

Socially, the Oldhams had tended to look down on the Falkners, but while some Falkners like Bill's Uncle John continued to prosper, the material condition of the Oldhams declined. During the 1920s and 1930s, Major Oldham's business ventures collapsed one after another. Dorothy Oldham later declared that the critical point in the decline was the failure of the gravel pit in Iuka, an event occasioned, she explained, by the dishonesty of his partners. Finally, in December, 1931, the bank foreclosed on one of his loans and sold his Oxford Beverage Company.[75] In the crisis, the Major's law practice afforded no relief. "Lem Oldham never tried a case," John W.T. Falkner had said in his usual blunt style, "he wouldn't know how."[76] Lem's own explanation of his absence from the courtroom was reported by another Oxford lawyer. "Oh, well," Lem would say, "we've got plenty of fellows who can do the menial work." This lawyer asserted that, indeed, he himself did some of Lem's "menial" courtroom work—and didn't get paid.[77]

When the Republicans were in power and the Major held a federal appointment, the Oldhams could maintain an air of affluence. Perhaps the last capital in that account was spent in May, 1930, when Lida Oldham was slated to become the mistress of the university post office, Bill Falkner's old job.[78] In the late 1920s, Lida also gave piano lessons in her home.

In the early 1930s, Bill felt he had to put Lida on his dependents' list at $100 a month. Soon, just as he worried about taxes and insurance every year in regard both to Rowan Oak and his mother's house, he also felt the need to find such money for the Oldham house should it be necessary.

Meanwhile, Dorothy Oldham had come home to stay. She had graduated from the university in 1926 and took a job teaching history in the public school at Water Valley, some twenty miles south of Oxford. Unhappy with her position she returned to Oxford and took her master's degree in history at Ole Miss in 1930. During the academic year 1930–1931, she taught in the Mississippi College for Women in Columbus.[79] Thereafter, for many years she lived in the house on South Lamar Street.

During the 1930s, Malcolm was also living in the Oldham household. He was a frail, delicate child, and the Oldhams felt that life in Rowan Oak—at first with no plumbing, no heat, and no electricity—was simply too debilitating for him. Moreover, he seemed to fill the void left by the death in 1916 of Ned, the Oldham's only son. "Mac," as Malcolm was called, was apparently the darling of his grandparents and his unmarried aunt in the big house on South Lamar. But the glitter in that house was gone, and so too the money. Major Oldham, as custodian for Malcolm and Victoria, received monthly checks from their father for their support. It seems that little, if any, of this money found its way to Rowan Oak. Indeed, family and acquaintances generally agreed that this was the money on which the Oldhams primarily lived for a number of years. Sallie Murry was not alone in coming to the conclusion that Lem was a "deadbeat."[80]

When *Light in August* was published in October, 1932, Estelle knew that she was pregnant again. Unlike Alabama, this baby went full term and was born on June 24, 1933.[81] She turned out to be a very healthy, hearty, even-tempered, outdoors child. She would need to be. If the infant had been a boy, they planned to name him "Bill." Estelle rued the fact that the child was not a boy, but Bill assured her that there were too many Falkner boys anyway. He was clearly delighted with the baby girl, and they decided to name her "Jill." During Faulkner's first visits to "little Miss Jill" in the hospital, he expressed his pride by wearing his RAF uniform.[82]

William Faulkner adored his daughter. In a sense, she was the sister, the female part, the Caddy, he never had. Jill became one of the constants in his life, a force that worked to hold together a personality often in danger of disintegration. Jill represented a tremendous deepening of the commitment to family, clan, and community that he had made four years before when he married Estelle. She tied him to the world with bonds that he often hated but could not break. Jill was his flesh and blood, and his future. In Hollywood in the summer of 1934, his letters home dripped with affection not only for Jill, but for her mother and her half brother and sister.[83] On her side, Jill would prove by her actions her love for her father, but she was, after all, another person—and separate. Of necessity, she built a life of her own. Moreover, from the first she seemed more Oldham than Falkner, just as her father at first seemed more Butler than Falkner. In time, each would mark his or her difference by a change in name, one by a shift in spelling, the other by marriage. Furthermore, Jill's marriage was exactly the kind of which the Oldhams would approve.

During the year of Jill's birth, 1933, Faulkner was not yet writing his next great novel. He was writing short stories, rather desperately hoping to make several hundred dollars out of each venture.[84] Elements in the stories prefigured the Snopes trilogy, his novel *Requiem for a Nun,* and *Absalom, Absalom!,* but mostly his talent was hobbled by the recurrent need for immediate cash, the necessity of working in Hollywood, his attempts to make Rowan Oak physically more liveable, and the realization of a passion he had long held. At last, he had learned to fly.[85]

In February, 1933, he began to take flying lessons at the Memphis airport from Vernon Omlie, a superb pilot who had flown during the war. Faulkner continued to offer the story that he had lost his nerve for flying after crashing while in the RAF and wanted to redeem himself. Omlie found him a slow student, but after seventeen hours of instruction he finally soloed. Thereafter, Faulkner was frequently in the air—sometimes two or three times a week. In the fall he paid $6,000 for a very large and powerful cabin cruiser, a Waco.[86] It was Hollywood money, some of it earned while working on scripts at home in Oxford. On the weekends he and Estelle would take the baby and go to Memphis. Checking in at the elegant Peabody Hotel, they would visit with Aunt Bama, other relatives and friends, and fly. On one of these occasions, at Estelle's insistence, Faulkner took her to meet Miss Reba, a real-life Mulberry Street madam. Estelle was disappointed. Instead of dash and flash, she saw a rotund, beer-drinking, rather shoddy woman whose conversation was amazingly less than interesting.[87]

One wonders that Faulkner could complain about his own lack of funds or Estelle's extravagance when he could pay $6,000 for an airplane without visible reluctance. It was fortunate for his hobby that he owned his own plane because he might have had trouble renting one. Straining to be generous about William Faulkner as a pilot, it must be said that he was not good at it. His brother Johncy bragged on Bill's navigational skills as if avoiding mention of his talents as a flyer. Faulkner himself confessed that he preferred flying high and straight. Another amateur with whom he frequently flew said that Faulkner did the navigating, disliked acrobatics, and liked smooth flight.[88] Difficulties arose when he attempted to land. Damaged landing gear, shredded wing tips, and inelegant bouncing were his lot. Once in Batesville he even managed to flip an airplane headfirst onto its back. On another occasion Bill and a friend almost slammed into a fence because Bill inadvertently had his foot resting on the brake while they were trying to gain speed for takeoff.[89]

Even so, the game was worth the candle to Faulkner for many reasons, not the least of which was that it gave him a license to engage in "hangar flying" with other aviators. The amount of time spent in the air was small compared to the time spent talking about flying and telling flying stories in the small lounges that were often tucked into the corners of hangars. It gave him a special entree, too, into a grand airshow at the New Orleans airport in February, 1934. He went with his friend Vernon Omlie. There he met the wing walkers, the parachute jumpers, and the pilots who performed amazing and daring aerial aerobatics. He watched the races as pilots zoomed their "crates" around tall towers, painted in checkerboard patterns, called "pylons." He saw these people as gypsies of the modern machine age, alienated by choice from orthodox society and finding ecstasy in the power of their machines to defy gravity and the pedestrian life of those who lived only on the ground. He saw, too, that these people sometimes came crashing down. Later he learned what was apparent to an objective observer: that in these decades almost everyone who flew frequently enough did come crashing down. Even Omlie, widely known as a safe and conservative pilot, was killed while he was a passenger with another flyer. Late in 1934 Faulkner put his images of these people into a short novel entitled *Pylon.* It was written quickly and, for a Faulkner book, it was relatively successful financially.

The tragedy built into flying came home to Faulkner in 1935 with devastating effect. Dean Faulkner had always idolized his oldest brother, and they came to be very close while they lived together in their father's house on the campus. Dean began his college career in the Engineering School, but switched his major to English and aspired to be a writer like Bill. Apparently, Dean had a Butler body. He was short, weighed about 135 pounds and was well muscled. He had a marvelous sense of coordination—attributes that made him a star on the Ole Miss baseball team. Like his brother, he was not a classroom scholar and he was in his mid-twenties before he ended his studies. His father got him a succession of jobs, but something always seemed to go wrong. After Murry died, Dean lived with Maud in the little house on South Street. Again like Bill, he was unlucky in love. The mother of one sweetheart ended that relationship, and Dean and Maud slipped into roles of interdependence that alarmed Bill. Dean grew a thin mustache and added a "u" to his name.

In the crisis, Bill moved to help his brother. He arranged for Dean to take flying lessons from Omlie. Dean took to flying immediately and entered into a partnership with his teacher. Soon he was flying freight and charter passengers, giving lessons himself, and taking part in country airshows, sometimes joined in these by brother Bill. Outgoing, totally likeable, he attracted the attention of a young woman named Louise Hale. In September, 1934, Dean and Louise married. Totally supportive, Faulkner transferred ownership of the Waco to Dean.[90]

In November, 1935, Dean Faulkner was one of several pilots involved in an airshow at the field in Pontotoc. Louise was several months pregnant. A large part of the income for such pilots came from taking local people up for rides. Dean was up with three young farmers, presumably on a jaunt to look at their farms from the air. One of these men, possibly, had had some flying lessons and, apparently, was given control of the aircraft. Suddenly the plane fell into a spin and plunged 4,000 feet, striking the earth with such force as to plow a hole several feet into the ground. All four men were killed, their bodies horribly mangled.

Faulkner took the telephone call in Oxford. He, Louise, and Maud headed for the airfield. Learning how appalling the scene was before they arrived, Bill turned and drove Maud and Louise back to Oxford. He made arrangements for someone to stay with them in Maud's house,[91] secured a photograph of Dean, and drove to Pontotoc. Using the photograph, he and an undertaker spent the night putting Dean's face together as best they could.[92] Bill was sure that Maud would insist on seeing her son one last time. In the end, they did not open the casket, and buried it in the Falkner plot in St. Peter's.[93] Faulkner wrote out the inscription for the stone: "I bare him on Eagle's Wings and brought him unto me." His name was inscribed "Dean Swift Falkner."[94] Bill moved into the little house on South Street with Maud and Louise. In the evening he would draw Louise a bath and bring her a glass of warm milk.[95] He stayed with them for several weeks, writing at night while they slept. Once he broke down and became hysterical. Louise took him into a bedroom because there were visitors.[96] "I've ruined your life," he said to her, and choked back the tears. For years, he had nightmares about the crash.[97] In the crisis Bill had acted well as the head of the family. But now he had another dependent, Louise, and still another, the baby, who would be named Dean, was on the way.

Writing Absalom, Absalom!

Absalom, Absalom!, like many of Faulkner's novels, began to take solid form in his mind first as a short story. In the spring of 1931, even before he began the work that would become *Light in August,* he wrote a story, "Evangeline," that began with a stranger's visit to a decaying country mansion. The story behind that scene was told to the stranger by a tiny, twisted, aging mulatto woman. It involved a Colonel Sutpen whose son Henry killed his sister's would-be lover, Bon, for a mysterious reason. The reason, finally revealed, was miscegenation. Bon had a trace of African ancestry.

"Evangeline" never sold, but Faulkner picked up the tale again in the fall of 1933 when he wrote another story that he called "Wash." Wash Jones was a poor white who cared for the Colonel's plantation while he was away at war. Desperate for a male heir after his return, Sutpen at age sixty seduced Wash's fifteen-year-old granddaughter, Millie. When she bore a baby girl rather than a boy, Sutpen rejected her. Wash cut Sutpen down with a scythe. When the posse appeared, he killed his granddaughter and her child. Then, he charged into the guns of the posse with the scythe and was shot dead. *Harper's* bought "Wash" for $350 in November.

Early in 1934, Faulkner took up the story again. After several tries, he came to use Quentin Compson as the narrator, telling the story to Shreve, his Canadian suitemate at Harvard. From that point on, while he did not work steadily and exclusively at the story, he could not leave it alone. He knew he had a novel, and he thought he could deliver it in the fall of 1934. He wrote to his publisher:

> The one I am writing now will be called *Dark House* or something of that nature. It is the more or less violent breakup of a household or family from 1860 to about 1910. It is not as heavy as it sounds. The story is an anecdote which happened about 1910 and which explains the story. It occurred during and right after the Civil War; the climax is another anecdote which happened about 1910 and which explains the story. Roughly, the theme is a man who outraged the land, and the land then turned and destroyed the man's family. Quentin Compson, of *The Sound and the Fury,* tells it, or ties it together, he is the protagonist so that it is not complete apocrypha. I use him because it is just before he is to commit suicide because of his sister, and I use his bitterness which he has projected on the South in the form of hatred of it and its people to get more out of the story itself than a historical novel would be. To keep the hoop skirts and plug hats out, you might say.[98]

During the summer of 1933 when Faulkner was writing his introduction to the Random House edition of *The Sound and the Fury,* he was acutely conscious of the tendency of Southern writers either "to draw a savage indictment of the contemporary scene or to escape from it into a make-believe region of swords and magnolias and mockingbirds which perhaps never existed anywhere."[99] Writers appeared either to love the South or hate it. Looking at his own career, he thought that "I seem to have tried both of the courses."[100] There were no hoop skirts in *Light in August,* and the writer would view hoop skirts—that is, pretensions to gentility in the ante-bellum mode—in *Absalom, Absalom!* with a very jaundiced eye. Faulkner would do something loosely and vaguely like hoop skirts as he romanticized the adventures of Bayard and Ringo, white and black teenagers in the midst of the Civil War in northern Mississippi, but more and more he emerged as a profound critic of the South, and particularly of the strict roles it prescribed as to sex, race, and class.

Ironically, at the same time that he was writing *Absalom, Absalom!* in 1934, the hoop skirt story of the modern age already existed in manuscript form in Atlanta. It was a massive document written by a young woman named Margaret Mitchell. Like Faulkner, she was a Southerner in her mid-thirties and highly critical of the world to which she was born. Interestingly, she had produced this manuscript mostly between 1926 and 1929, the very years in which Faulkner had come to full maturity as a writer. Unlike him, she was not at all sure she would ever publish her story about a young woman whom she at first called Pansy O'Hara and later renamed Scarlett. So dubious was Mitchell of her work that, at the time Faulkner was beginning *Absalom, Absalom!,* she was using a part of the manuscript as a substitute for the missing leg of an old couch that sat in her apartment just off Peachtree Street in Atlanta. In 1935 a Macmillan editor would virtually wrench the manuscript from her reluctant hands, and, in the fall of 1936, it would be published as *Gone With the Wind.* Millions of people read it, erroneously in the view of the author, as a hoop skirt story lamenting the loss of the grand Old South. However interpreted by readers, perhaps more than any other single book in the mid-twentieth century, it determined what people worldwide would think was the true story of the Old South and its evolution through the Civil War and into Reconstruction. Thereafter, in America and elsewhere, Faulkner's work and his life inevitably would be perceived amid a consciousness of those images. The translation of the book into a movie in 1939 amplified that effect.[101]

All during the spring and summer of 1934, Faulkner kept working on *Absalom, Absalom!* There were interruptions from family, flying, and the necessity he felt repeatedly of taking time out to attempt another quick and saleable short story. On March 30, 1935, however, he took up the novel in earnest again. He had a new title, *Absalom, Absalom!,* drawn from the biblical story of King David's beloved son who took up arms against his father. Absalom's forces were defeated by those of David, who had instructed his officers to crush the rebellion but save his son. After defeat, fleeing from the victors on horseback, Absalom was caught by his long and beautiful hair in the branches of a tree. David's men found him hanging. Still hot from the battle, they forgot their orders and speared him to death. When the news was carried to David, he cried, "Oh, Absalom, my Absalom!" It was a marvelously fitting title because the central power in the story was not a dark house, but the relationship between a father and his son, one white and the other mulatto.[102]

In the spring and summer Faulkner worked furiously at the manuscript. He was into the practice now of mailing chapters to his editor, Hal Smith, as he finished them. When Smith returned Chapter I with the comment, "This is damned confusing," Faulkner revised to make it more clear, then did the same for Chapter II. In the summer he pressed on through the third and fourth chapters while his money problems mounted. He attempted to concoct some short stories to sell, but had only minor success. He began to get headaches. In July he estimated he would need $2,000 before September 1 or face legal bankruptcy.[103] By mid-September, he was not bankrupt, but he was deeper in debt to merchants than ever before—some $1,700 worth. In addition he was trying to give Maud Falkner and Lida Oldham $100 a month each, and faced the necessity of paying tax and insurance bills on all three houses.

In September he went to New York determined to get a better financial arrangement from Smith or find another publisher. It ended with Smith—still unwilling to tap his own substantial resources—advancing him just enough to get by. Even so, Faulkner agreed that if an eight-week contract could be secured for him in Hollywood, he would pay the publisher back out of his salary.[104] Home from New York, he plunged into the writing and was driving hard when Dean was killed. Devastated as he was by that event, he took his work with him when he went to his mother's house to stay with Maud and Louise. During his nights there he launched into Chapter VII (which begins with a consideration of Thomas Sutpen's "innocence"), writing on the dining room table. Relief finally came in the form of another offer from Howard Hawks. On December 16, 1935, he was in Hollywood again to begin four weeks of work at $1,000 a week. Before the month was out, he had found a lover.

Meta

It is probably totally relevant that Meta Doherty was born and spent a portion of her life on a plantation in Tunica County, Mississippi. Tunica is at the northern tip of the Delta, just south of Memphis. Very early in her life she moved to Memphis. Indeed, the census of 1910 shows her there at age two with her father, Clark, age 23, and her mother, Beulah, age 20. Clark Doherty worked in the cotton business on his own account. They lived in a rented house, but employed a 60-year-old black woman, a widow with no children, as their "servant." As a young woman Meta developed considerable talent as a musician and generated an ambition to become a concert pianist. She married a young man named Carpenter and with him went to California where he hoped to become a commercial pilot. They grew apart and divorced.[105]

In December, 1935, at twenty-eight, Meta was working as Howard Hawks's secretary, and it was in Hawks's outer office that Bill found her. Her appearance was not unlike that of Estelle as a young woman. "I knew without undue vanity," she later asserted, "that I was pretty enough, with blond hair that fell in a straight sweep to my shoulders, with a ninety-two pound body as lean and as lithe as a ballerina's, and with a waist that was a handspan around."[106] Contemporaries agreed that Meta was very attractive—lovely eyes and complexion, about Faulkner's own height with a nice figure. Moreover, she was a kind person—gentle in voice and manner, bright, alert, and positive. She was somewhat aloof from, perhaps even superior to, mainstream Hollywood.[107] In 1935 Meta was living in the Studio Club, a rather famous residence for unmarried young women who worked in the film industry. There was no man in her life. The unmarried men she met she found either shallow and dull, or homosexual.

Meta felt that Faulkner was attracted to her at first sight. Soon he asked her to dinner. She knew he was a married man and declined. Bill persisted and

Meta was driven to appeal to Hawks to intervene. Still, it was Meta who was assigned to type up the work that Faulkner did for the studio, and his handwriting was almost indecipherable. He helped her with the translations, standing solicitously over her, addressing her as "ma'am" and "Miss Meta," always the Mississippi gentleman.

Proximity and persistence did what nothing else had done. Meta finally agreed to go to dinner with him. Bill called for her, and took her to a good restaurant. He asked her all about herself, then told her about Dean's death. Afterward they strolled along Hollywood Boulevard, the dapper little man, the thin girl. In a bookstore he bought a copy of *Sanctuary,* inscribed it, and gave it to her. The next night he bought her an expensive dinner in a celebrity restaurant. This time he pulled out all the stops, telling Meta the wounded flyer story, ending with the silver plate in his head. Every night thereafter they went out to dinner together. He talked, sang, and recited poetry. He also showed her a picture of Jill, revealed his worry about her safety when Estelle was drinking, and declared that he and Estelle no longer had sex together. Meta felt Bill's desire, and one night after dinner they went to his hotel and made love, he with a passion, a fury almost, that far exceeded her own.[108]

Faulkner's life was becoming tremendously fragmented. He would rise early and work on *Absalom, Absalom!,* go to the studio for a full day's labor, and then meet Meta. Through it all he was drinking more.[109] When a fellow writer asked him anxiously how he could continue drinking so much and not eat, he answered that "there's a lot of nourishment in an acre of corn."[110] On January 7, 1936, he was taken off pay for "illness." Meta drove him to the train station and saw him off for Mississippi.

At home, he rallied to complete the manuscript for *Absalom, Absalom!* on the last day of January. In his usual fashion, he would now rewrite the whole thing on the typewriter, revising and smoothing as he went. But then he began to drink heavily again. He went for a visit at the hunting lodge of Helen Baird and her husband, but forgot to take his manuscript with him.[111] Back home, he gave himself over totally to drinking. Twelve-year-old Malcolm sat up with him at night, but Faulkner's debilitation was so great that the family finally had to put him into a sanatorium in Byhalia, a village some twenty miles southeast of Memphis.

Like so many Falkner men, Bill had a large tolerance for alcohol. He could drink and still work, and now and again, he could drink for two or three days on end, collapse, recover, and work again. But now, at age thirty-eight, he was gradually losing resiliency, and the physical complications associated with heavy drinking were beginning to take their toll. Henceforth, the pattern was recurrent. There would be pressure on him—something he did not want to do. He would grow restless, and, as Jill recalled the sequence years later, one morning he would be quiet. Then "all of a sudden he would start on his poem that heralded one of these bouts coming on: 'When daisies pied and violets blue . . . ,' and you knew that the next day he'd be drinking."[112] Others noticed that at these times he would drum his fingers on a table or some other surface.

All of this is ordinary to students of alcoholism, but it is acutely distressing to adult friends and relatives who must live through the cycles, and it is absolutely devastating to children. Especially awful is the loving parent becoming—Jekyll and Hyde fashion—a monster. Usually, if the person has a basically strong physical constitution and the first deep collapse occurs in his or her mid-thirties, those concerned can look forward to twenty or thirty years of running the cycle again and again. Eventually, resulting complications kill the victim. Finally, family and friends realize too that there is a certain amount of bodily chemistry involved, that the difficulty is, in part, a physical problem and beyond perfect solution by sheer power of will. It is a problem that must be lived with. But very often the chemistry is mixed in very complex ways with the psychology of the individual. In Faulkner's case one might argue plausibly that the trouble was essentially more mental than chemical. Certainly, not every Falkner was born an alcoholic, and, apparently, no Butlers were.

Faulkner recuperated relatively rapidly from this episode in the winter of 1936. By the end of February he was in Hollywood again, earning $1,000 a week, seeing Meta, and living in the Beverly Hills Hotel. He conveyed in letters to Oxford the warmth he failed to show in person. "I wish I was at home," he wrote, "still in the kitchen with my family around me and my hand full of Old Maid cards."[113] He hoped to head east in a few weeks, and to meet Estelle in New Orleans for two weeks of vacation.[114] Before the month was out, however, he was planning a long stay in Hollywood. He had signed a contract for six months to begin on August 1. In late April, Bill wrote to Estelle that he was working hard, had his weight down to a comfortable 140 pounds, and felt much better. In mid-May he reported that he hoped to leave for Oxford by June 1. "Damn this being an orphan," he declared.[115] During these same weeks, friends would see Bill and Meta walking hand-in-hand along Hollywood Boulevard.[116]

If Meta Carpenter could have seen those letters to Estelle, she might have doubted her own sanity. Faulkner's behavior during the first few weeks they had been together and the sentiments that he expressed so copiously to her while he was in Mississippi convinced Meta that he was deeply in love with her. With his return to Hollywood, she had the unspoken proofs.[117] Forty years later, in 1976, with the aid of a professional writer, Meta published an account of her long-running romance with William Faulkner. Marvelously, she entitled her book *A Loving Gentleman: The Love Story of William Faulkner and Meta Carpenter*. It was a lengthy, detailed, and seemingly candid account. Also, it verged on the strident, as if the author were insistent upon being heard at last.[118]

Indeed Meta's story was late in coming to the surface. There had long been a rumor of a Hollywood "scriptgirl" with suggestions akin to those that go with traveling salesmen and working women. Soon after Faulkner died in 1962, the

The Marble Man

William Faulkner's great-grandfather William C. Falkner (1825–1889). A businessman rather than a slaveholding planter in antebellum Mississippi, Confederate colonel and drop-out warrior, town merchant, commercial farmer, speculator, writer, railroad president and incipient robber baron, he was loved and hated in roughly equal parts. Shortly before he was shot and killed by an erstwhile business associate, he began the process of having his statue carved in Carrara marble. Probably, he envisioned himself thus immortalized on the town square. Instead, the eight-foot statue came to rest on a fourteen-foot pedestal next to his grave in the town cemetery, where it remains today. *Note:* The tips of three fingers of the Colonel's left hand were shot away in the Mexican War, not, perhaps, in valiant service. The fingers of the right hand of The Marble Man were shot away by a person or persons unknown soon after the statue was erected in the Ripley Town Cemetery. (Photograph by Tommy Covington)

Falkner Forebears

UPPER LEFT: Colonel Falkner as he appeared in 1884 in his book describing his travels in Europe during the previous year with his teenage daughter Effie. *(Courtesy Ripley Public Library Collection)*

UPPER RIGHT AND LOWER LEFT: The Colonel's son, John Wesley Thompson Falkner (1848–1922), who in 1885 moved from Ripley to Oxford, where he prospered as a lawyer and businessman. He also rose to eminence as a civic, social, and political leader. (Courtesy Cofield Collection)

LOWER RIGHT: The Colonel's grandson and William Faulkner's father, Murry Cuthbert Falkner (1869–1932), who wanted to run the railroad his father sold in 1902, who entered the livery stable business just as the automobile appeared, and ended his working life as an appointed official on the staff of the University of Mississippi where his father sat as a trustee. (Courtesy Cofield Collection)

The Fannie Forrest Falkner Dogan Family, c. 1910

Family tradition holds that Fannie Forrest Falkner (c. 1864–1929) was Colonel Falkner's daughter by the slave Emeline (1837–1896). Emeline's descendants understand that the Colonel sent Fannie to Rust College, perhaps the most prestigious school for African Americans in Mississippi. She married fellow student Matthew W. Dogan, who became president of Wiley College in Marshall, Texas. Here on the steps of the president's house are: daughter Clara, President Dogan, Lucile, Blanche *(at center),* Ruth, Matthew, Jr., and Fannie. Blanche lives with her daughter Alfreda in Maryland and will be ninety on June 25, 1993. *(Courtesy Fannie Dogan descendants)*

Maud Butler, c. 1879

William Faulkner's mother, Maud Butler (1871–1960), at about age eight. Her grandfather, Charles George Butler, was the first sheriff of Lafayette County, surveyed and laid out the town of Oxford, bought a goodly portion of the land he surveyed, and built the hotel that long occupied the western half of the north side of the town square. He died in 1855, but his wife Burlina managed very well until Union soldiers burned the hotel in 1864. After the war, the Butlers gradually lost most of their wealth, but for a dozen years Maud's father, Charles Edward Butler, earned a good living as town marshal and tax collector. About Christmastime, 1887, "Charlie" Butler ran away and never returned. With him went a substantial portion of the town's annual revenue. *(Courtesy Cofield Collection)*

A Storybook Childhood

UPPER: "Pony Boys" and cousin Sallie Murry Wilkins in front of the Falkners' first residence in Oxford, c. 1904. *Mounted:* Willie. *Third step, seated:* Sallie Murry and Murry Charles or "Jack." *Bottom step:* John Wesley Thompson or "Johncy." *(Courtesy Cofield Collection)*
LOWER: The jail in Oxford. A favored setting for Faulkner stories. Usually the jailor and his family lived downstairs and the prisoners upstairs. On the night of September 8, 1908, Nelse Patton, a black man accused of murdering a white woman, was taken from here by a mob of some two thousand men led by ex-United States Senator William V. Sullivan and lynched on the town square nearby. Faulkner, by now called "Billy," was almost eleven and lived within a few hundred yards of the jail and the square. *(Courtesy Cofield Collection)*

The Falkner Boys, c. 1910

Billy

Jack Johncy

Dean

(Courtesy Cofield Collection)

Youth

ABOVE: Estelle Oldham (1897–1972) was pictured here in the 1913 yearbook of the University of Mississippi. She was not then a student, but appeared as the sponsor of graduating senior Cornell Franklin, whom she would marry five years later. Estelle was the love of William's youth. She first married Cornell, an older and richer man, and then married William. *(Courtesy Cofield Collection)*

BELOW: William, 1914. *(Courtesy Cofield Collection)*

A Flying Faulkner, 1918

William Faulkner, probably December, 1918, in the uniform of a flying officer of the Royal Air Force. This was his first major work of fiction. He was in the R.A.F., but he was not an officer and he did not fly. He added a "u" to his name and affected the manners of an English gentleman for the role. *(Courtesy Cofield Collection)*

Portrait of the Artist, 1925

Paris, Notre Dame in the background, 1925, the artist as a self-confident young man. "I have finished the most beautiful story in the world," he wrote to his great aunt Alabama McLean. "And the hand doesn't hold blood to improve on it." Genius was about to appear. *(Photograph by Odiorne)*

Mississippi in Asia, c. 1926

Estelle and daughter Victoria in Shanghai, c. 1926. Cornell was rapidly becoming one of the leading men in the International Settlement there, and his marriage was rapidly failing. In 1927 Estelle came home with Victoria and her son Malcolm, age three. In 1929 she married William. *(Courtesy Cofield Collection)*

Famous Author, 1931

This is William Faulkner in 1931, the year, perhaps, in which he was most sanguine about his life and work. He was thirty-three, two years married to Estelle, and a year into making Rowan Oak his home. He had published artistically successful novels in 1929 and 1930, and *Sanctuary,* just out, promised to be a financial success. This picture was taken by Oxford photographer J. R. Cofield at the request of the national press, which was very much interested in the man who had written a notorious novel in which a seventeen-year-old Ole Miss co-ed named Temple Drake was raped with a corn cob by an impotent gangster named Popeye. Often very willing to pose for the camera, he sits here irritated, sullen, and smoking. (Photograph by J. R. Cofield)

Rowan Oak, 1931

UPPER: An exterior view of Rowan Oak photographed by Memphis reporter Marshall Smith in August, 1931. The opening scene in this book occurred on the day this picture was taken. *(Courtesy Cofield Collection)*

LOWER: William and Estelle in the parlor of the antebellum "mansion" that he bought in 1930, began to renovate, and named "Rowan Oak." After an initial visit, one longtime Faulkner friend wrote to his wife that "the rooms are bare and what they do contain is rickety, tasteless, ordinary." *(Courtesy Cofield Collection)*

A Worried Man, 1942

Summer, 1942, age forty-four. The years of genius have passed. He will never again write a great novel. He is broke, and he had difficulty staying sober for an interview that might have secured for him a commission in the military. In desperation he has signed a contract to return to Hollywood as a writer at a small fraction of his top salary in the 1930s. This means leaving Jill, his beloved nine-year-old daughter, and his home, Rowan Oak. Within months he will resume his affair with Meta Carpenter, an assistant to producer Howard Hawks. In a sense, he is dying, an uncounted casualty in the Hollywood War. (Photograph by J. R. Cofield)

Family Group, 1955

Faulkner's family in June, 1955. *Left to right:* Malcolm Franklin, Estelle's son; Gloria Franklin, Malcolm's wife; Suzanne Falkner, wife of William's brother Jack; Paul D. Summers, Jr., Jill's husband; Jill; William; Estelle; Jack; Alabama Leroy McLean, William's great aunt.

Faulkner was in Memphis to promote Howard Hawks's film *Land of the Pharaohs,* starring Elizabeth Taylor. He hated such occasions while Estelle loved them. He hated this one especially because it exposed him to interviews in which he was forced to respond to very harsh public criticism in Memphis and Mississippi for his liberal stand on civil rights. Within a year he would abandon that struggle and begin to write again. *(Courtesy Cofield Collection)*

Queen of the Cotillion, 1956

Faulkner Hughes, Queen of the Me-De-So Cotillion, Baltimore, Maryland, 1956. Colonel Falkner, The Marble Man, was reputedly her great-grandfather too. Her grandmother was Fannie Falkner. Her mother, Blanche, married a Baltimore lawyer, W. A. C. Hughes, himself the son of a Methodist bishop, and thus moved into the African-American elite in that city. *(Courtesy Alfreda Hughes)*

The Gentleman Rider, 1961

When J. R. Cofield made this portrait in Oxford in January, 1961, Faulkner was in the process—thus late in life—of leaving Mississippi to make his permanent home in Virginia. Jill, her husband, and their three small boys had already settled there near Charlottesville. "Will" Faulkner had fallen in love with fox hunting in the Virginia style. When he was admitted to a club, the Farmington Hunt, he hastened to acquire its elegant habit, including the pink coat with the Belgian blue collar. He died in July, 1962, but had he lived surely we would now have a series of stories framed by the image he created here. Already, he was generating another fiction that brilliantly married life and art. *(Photograph by J. R. Cofield)* family authorized a biography by family friend and literary scholar Joseph Blotner. Meta, however, steadily refused to be interviewed by Professor Blotner.[119] In 1966, Estelle asked if during his research he had met a girl in Hollywood whose name she could not recall. "Meta?" Blotner asked, and Estelle said yes.[120] Ironically, Meta's image appeared in 1974 in Blotner's Faulkner biography in a group picture along with Bill, Ben Wasson, and Dorothy Parker. At the time, they were guests at the Hollywood home of writer Marc Connelly. In that offering Meta was identified as "Mrs. Ernest Pascal." No one has yet identified a real Mrs. Pascal, and it sounds exactly like a name that a teasing, slightly malicious Faulkner would make up and feed to a believing audience. Through her lawyers, Meta threatened to sue if a correction was not made.[121] Rather clearly, Meta felt she had been pushed unfairly into obscurity, and she set out to change that by writing her own book.[122]

Meta Carpenter, particularly during the spring of 1936, was close to Faulkner in a way that no other adult person ever was. Physical debilitation hampered subsequent relationships across the sex line, and masculine etiquette limited his intimacy with such good friends as Phil Stone and Ben Wasson, though these men knew him in ways that his family never knew him. The family, of course, always presumed that they knew him best, while in reality they knew only a part of him. Like every man everywhere, especially the white Southern man born into the elite—or near elite—of his generation, Bill Faulkner had grave difficulty understanding himself. But Faulkner was peculiarly inept at self-understanding and suffered in his relations with the world accordingly.

What Meta brought that apparently no one else ever brought or, perhaps, could bring to her relations with Bill was a physical intimacy that was unencumbered and the rich emotions that attach only to that state. She was not married to Bill Faulkner, she bore no children by him, or anyone, and she was not his blood kin nor small town childhood sweetheart. There were no institutions that insisted she had to love this man, and continue to love him regardless of circumstances. The love she gave was given—and apparently freely given—from within herself.

Why Meta?

It was no accident that William Faulkner in California pursued a woman from the South, and better yet from Delta plantation Mississippi and Memphis. In a sense, Bill knew Meta before she was born.[123] She spoke his language. For that reason she was extraordinarily desirable and for that reason too she was also more attainable. She was Southern as he was Southern, but she was also female and offered the promise of a consummation long sought.[124] To possess Meta was to possess and realize the other part of himself so long denied. She was his little sister lover who offered not death but life. Helen Baird had never even come close to such a rendering, and Estelle—seemingly wrist-cutting, self-drowning, window-jumping Estelle, already with two children when he married her and a body threatening death if she attempted a third—was such a fragment of life herself.

The realization came to him at thirty-eight that he might yet live a full life with Meta—this man who had thought he would die before he was thirty, who was dying in his thirties, and whose youngest brother had just died. The drowning dying man could grab the straw because Meta was there, and, offering herself, spoke the language he spoke and was within reach and alone—manless. Faulkner, inept and awkward, persisted in daring with Meta where he had not dared with other women in something of the same way that Joe Christmas had dared with Bobbie Allen in his novel *Light in August:* "It was because of her smallness that he even attempted her, as if her smallness should have or might have protected her from the roving and predatory eyes of most men, leaving his chances better. If she had been a big woman he would not have dared. He would have thought, 'It won't be of any use. She will already have a fellow, a man.'"[125] Meta was there, and alone.

Hence Bill's assault on Meta's affections. His attentions to her amounted to a crowding, rushing attack.[126] Persuading her that he was a wounded flyer, he preyed upon her sympathy. One night after they had become lovers, Meta, on arriving home, was startled to find Bill thrashing about and screaming in bed. "Come get me," he cried, "the jerries are going to get me." He was having a nightmare, he said. He had dreamed that he was in his plane over France during the war and the Germans were shooting him down. We don't know whether to believe that Bill was actually having such a nightmare, or assume that he was simply acting again, but Meta believed. Forty years later, when she published her book *A Loving Gentleman,* she still believed that he had been a flyer who was wounded in France.[127]

Faulkner prevailed with Meta, in part, because he was famous. He was acknowledged as one of America's great writers. He had power now that gave a presence to his body heretofore lacking. Thus Bill Faulkner, not by faith alone, nor by the sacraments, but by his works had become a man in his own eyes—worked his way up from the "Little Billy" who had sat in the salons of Memphis brothels drinking beer while other men went upstairs, sitting proximate to and not partaking of that brief shallow imitation of life that went on above his head with women who, Phil Stone said, looked like nothing so much as middle-aged Baptist Sunday school teachers, who in reality served up a female body with much the same spirit and implication that Faulkner's character Bobbie, a waitress in a side street cafe, served up a hamburger. Because that was a part of it also. In spite of his locker room language with men, not just any female body would do for William Faulkner, not just sex would do, there had to be love too, romance and flowers in the field, a union of body and soul.

Meta was the missing self, the other half across the sex line, an octave higher than Estelle had been. She was the female personification of the ideal, "the one fair woman," as Meta herself phrased it, that every young man in the Western World who drank at the fountain of nineteenth-century romanticism believed was his and had been reserved—almost destined—for him and himself alone, a virgin. Having been married, the presumption was that Meta was not, in fact, a virgin. But clearly there was no other man. Deliberately, she chose that there would be no other man. If Meta had not hied herself literally to a nunnery, in Hollywood she had at least taken refuge—strapped on whatever belt of feminine chastity might be donned in that steamy cinematic sex capital of America by retreating into the all-woman Studio Club.

Meta had abstained, and Faulkner rushed—with unseemly haste, perhaps—to assure her that he too, though married, was semi-virginal. "Listen to me," he said to Meta, "you have to know this. When Jill was born, from that time on, Estelle and I have not had anything to do with each other as man and woman. Soon as she could, she moved upstairs at Rowan Oak to a room of her own. I swear to you, Meta, we have not had male-female sex since then. Estelle goes to her bed at night, I go to mine."[128] It seems that Faulkner had caught in his own life the vision of something that might be called "renewable virginity." Abstention restores purity, and prolonged abstention restores virginity. The question becomes, why did he need such a strange idea?

"Pappy liked ladies, like women, plain and simple," Jill would later say. The truth was that he liked some women, not all women or even all "ladies," and as life went on he was especially melting to some pretty young women, usually rather naive and vulnerable. Jill also said that Faulkner's belle ideal was the lady Maud, and that all other women, presumably even including her mother Estelle, were always secondary. There is an essential truth in that. Even so, Bill might visit his mother every day that he was in Oxford, but she could hardly be the lover for whom he yearned. Maud would have to be translated in his mind into another order. She was obviously a nineteenth-century Southern lady. It was unthinkable that she had sex before marriage, that she would ever divorce her husband, or initiate a sexual experience in or out of marriage, or smoke in public, or drink any but very modest amounts if at all.

Estelle, on the other hand, was a new woman of the twentieth century. There were not many of them in the South, but among the well-to-do, the well educated and well traveled, and in the big cities, it was conceivable that a woman could not only think about these things but do them as well. In Atlanta, for example, Margaret Mitchell, born in 1900, was wrestling with exactly these problems, and while she never totally solved them—and hence springs much of the tension in *Gone With the Wind*—she did much better than Estelle. She had her fling and then she conformed, at first well enough with an older man for husband and without children, and finally marvelously with her great novel. As a belle at Ole Miss, Estelle had had her fling too, but fell hard and fractured badly. It seemed that she could never be put together again. If Faulkner were to find a lady and a lover in one person, he would have to look elsewhere.

Faulkner needed ladyhood.[129] He needed the courage, the durability, the quiet strength of the ideal lady that Maud clearly represented. But, seemingly, he also needed the body of a woman. He wanted that without inhibition, without restraint, without fear of pregnancy and possible death, without, in a sense, responsibility. It was as if he could not believe his good luck in having found a physically willing Meta, a lovely, mature woman who seemed, miraculously, never to get pregnant. "In the act of love," she recalled, "Bill, the restrained remote man by day, was seized with a consuming sexual urgency. Desire and sensation shook him as a storm wind buffets a stout tree." She reconstructed Faulkner's explanation of his performance. "I've always been afraid of going out of control I get so carried away," she remembered his saying. "I'm not myself anymore; I'm somebody else. There was a time I worried about myself with women a whole lot. I still do in fact."[130] If we can believe her report and his words, it sounds very much as if Faulkner was, indeed, discovering another self in his relations with Meta. One suspects that, essentially, it was an experience new to him, and that, in fact, he was not worried about himself with women nearly as much as he worried about himself *without* women.

As Faulkner became more comfortable with Meta, he seemed to relax and grow playful. Once, before making love in a beach cottage at the Miramar Hotel, he scattered flower petals on the bed. Sometimes he told Meta bawdy stories and then kissed her blushing cheeks. One day, after she had read his uncensored edition of *Lady Chatterley's Lover,* in which the lovers gave names to their private parts, "he touched himself and with a sly smile announced: 'Mr. Bowen.'" Meta suppressed a laugh. "Not John Thomas but Mr. Bowen," he said. "And not Lady Jane," he said, touching Meta, "but Mrs. Bowen."[131] Curiously, he thus chose to use the name of his aristocratic Oxford kinsfolk, the name that he might have translated into Benbow in his stories.

With Meta, Faulkner let fly a high capacity for the erotic. He gave her a copy of his book of poetry *A Green Bough* (1933) in which he had written:

> Meta
> Bill
> Meta
> who soft keeps for him his loves long girl's body sweet to fuck

He also gave Meta a series of drawings depicting the two of them making love.[132] Meta deposited these drawings in the Berg Collection in the New York Public Library with instructions that they could not be opened for scholarly use until the year 2039. It does not take much imagination, however, to guess their essentially orthodox essence. Moreover, Carvel Collins, a Faulkner scholar and Faulkner friend who saw those and other drawings inspired by Meta, has given us hints. Apparently, one set cartooned the love cycle, the last frame depicting the deflated male and captioned, "That's all."[133]

In Meta, it appears that Faulkner at age thirty-eight had at last found the sexual companion he had long sought. The marble faun unfroze, the mosaic, seemingly set in stone, moved, and William Faulkner melted into the role not merely of faun, but of satyr with pointed ears, cloven hooves, and large, satiable, but renewable lust. Also, it seemed that he would make of Meta a nymphet. "I was confounded by his need to turn me into a sweet, tremulous girl," she related.[134] He did so again and again, delighting in his capacity to make her blush and giggle, and then making love in that furious way.

To Meta, Faulkner argued the case for the faun and physical love. "It is hard on a man like me to be without a woman that way," he declared. The faun, of course, could not go commercial. "I don't bed down with whores," he declared. "Not here, not in Oxford, not anywhere."[135] One would be surprised to find prostitutes very available in Oxford in the 1930s; moreover, these words seemed to erase his boast that he had once spent his vacation in a brothel and give the lie to a lusty image he labored hard to project to his masculine friends.

Speaking with deliberate extravagance, one might say that Faulkner wanted only to bed down with virgins and, paradoxically, for them to remain virginal even after the bedding was done. With Meta he found, for the first time in his life, a woman whose face, form, and character could carry his own projections of purity and, at the same time, could and would meet his physical desires. Even at twenty-eight she offered a sort of boarding school beauty, and yet she was also sufficiently mature to accept Faulkner's extraordinary ardor. With Meta, he found that he could have his cake and eat it too; he had found someone who could be both virginal and endlessly sexual.

To move one step further: In Meta he found a match, a woman who would blush and giggle like a girl at his lusty allusions, and yet slip easily with him into satyristic excursions. Meta was, in fine, a "renewable virgin." In that respect, she paralleled Faulkner himself. He, too, had renewed his virginity after Jill's birth, and he had maintained his virginity against the allegedly easy resort of bedding down with whores. Faulkner's idyll was made possible by Meta's nature, a nature that led her to indulge him and seduce him almost totally. She was, apparently, warm and giving, and she was also deeply and sensually sexual. With Meta, he could achieve a consummation without breaking the vase. Her purity, in effect, mirrored his purity. The "little death," *la petite morte,* that followed love making was not terminal. With this oarsman, he could row across the River Styx, and then row back again.

~

The picture of life in Oxford that Faulkner painted for Meta was very different from one in which he sat about in the kitchen in Rowan Oak playing Old Maid. On one occasion, he said, he had found Estelle lying drunk on the floor while little Jill was crying for her "Pappy." Estelle was often furious with him, and her fury manifested itself in action. On one occasion, she threw the manuscript of *Light in August* out the window of the moving car. Faulkner had to stop, get out, walk back, and gather up the scattered sheets of his work. One morning at Rowan Oak, they emerged from a bedroom with scratches on their faces. Even without the actual violence, the picture of his married life that Bill painted for Meta amounted to a nearly perfect hell. Estelle drank heavily and threatened disaster. "She'd holler and scream and carry on," he declared. He was glad to be away from those awful quarrels with Estelle. They "skinned me alive," he said.[136] Increasingly often, Faulkner was putting distance between himself and Estelle by visits to New York and Hollywood. Another kind of distance was suggested in the mood of the letters he wrote to her. Into the summer of 1934 he might address her as "Sweetheart" or "Dear Love," and sign himself Bill or Billy. In 1936, there were letters with no salutations and no signatures at all—only the blunt, brief message.[137] Finally, Meta understood from Faulkner that "he could not complete the act of love after the first years of marriage with his drunken, quarrelsome wife." He was celibate, but Meta surmised that he "suppressed a raging sexuality" and turned it into his writing.[138]

Sometime during that late winter or spring of 1936, Faulkner arranged for his good friend Ben Wasson to meet Meta at Howard Hawks's house. As they drove away, Bill declared to Ben: "That's the girl I'm in love with. Can't get her out of my mind or system. And don't want to. You don't know what a wonderful person she is." Then he told Ben about Meta. "She's brought me peace of mind," he concluded. "I think I want to marry Meta."[139] Rather clearly, Meta wanted to marry Faulkner. She was ready, she later said, to take him as he was. She could accept his withdrawals, his commitment to his work, his shell ("carapace" she called it) that could cut him off from the very people to whom he was closest. She could also accept that strange special mode of inarticulateness that allowed him to tell Ben Wasson that he loved her, but could not say it to her himself—other than in letters, or in French, or by his actions.

In June, 1936, Faulkner was at home in Oxford and he seemed willing to force a showdown. He found that Estelle had charged some $1,000 worth of goods in Memphis and Oxford stores, including some overstuffed furniture and a radio, "the latter of which I had expressly forbidden to be brought into the house." Not only did Faulkner with self-confessed "sadistic pleasure" eject from the house "pneumatic divans and Cab Calloways," he also "advertised" Estelle. He published ads in Memphis and Oxford newspapers announcing that he would not be responsible for the debts of "Mrs. William Faulkner or Mrs. Estelle Oldham Faulkner."[140]

Advertising Estelle was about the worst thing that Faulkner could do to the socially proud and materially embattled Oldhams. Probably prodded by the Oldham ladies, Lida and Dot, the Major summoned Bill to his office and gave him a dressing down. Faulkner capitulated and canceled further publication of the ad. Several days later when reporters arrived at Rowan Oak to catch the scandalous news, they found a happy family scene in which William and Estelle were arranging a birthday party for their three-year-old daughter Jill. *Time* magazine reprinted the ad in its "People" column. But Faulkner denied "any family ruckus" and explained that "it's just a matter of protection until I pay my back debts."[141]

It was probably in these weeks that Faulkner tested the idea of divorce from Estelle. He came to understand that in a divorce Estelle was almost certain to get custody of Jill. The circumstances led him to do a rather curious thing. He bought a new Ford phaeton (an open car) and on July 15, he, Estelle, and Jill headed west with two black servants: Jack Oliver, a jack of all trades, did the driving, and their cook, Narcissus McEwen, worked as maid. In California they took a house in Santa Monica near the beach.[142] It was a pleasant place with a view of the mountains from the dining room and of the sea from rooms upstairs, but Estelle missed her "sure-enough silver." Every afternoon she took Jill to the beach where the child played in the sand and talked about "Buddy," as Malcolm was sometimes called.[143]

As soon as he could manage it, Bill was seeing Meta again and making love. It was an awkward arrangement, to say the least, and it soon grew worse. Faulkner called Ben Wasson and invited him to dinner at the new house. He asked him to bring Meta, posing as her suitor. The pair was to be picked up and brought over by Jerry, a young man from the studio office, presumably providing even more camouflage. He wanted Meta to meet Estelle, Bill said, and this was the only way he could think of to do it. The meeting and the dinner proceeded smoothly. Estelle and Meta chatted amiably about Southern things, Narcissus cooked and Jack served the meal. Everyone drank moderately and said good night graciously.[144] However, early the next morning, Ben's phone rang. It was Estelle and she was furious. "You didn't fool me for a second, you and Billy. I know that the person you brought to my house last night is Billy's girl out here and not your girl at all!" Poor Ben was caught and could hardly respond. After Estelle hung up, Faulkner called Ben to apologize. "Ain't there something you can do to get her off my back?" he pleaded. "Get her a lover, anything, so she'll leave me alone."[145] This, seven years into marriage.

There was nothing to be done. Estelle was adamant against divorce. Not only would she take Jill, she also promised she would impoverish Faulkner and drag his name through the mud. Meta was torn. She was still sleeping with Faulkner, grabbing him away from Estelle for odd hours. Sometimes when Estelle was drinking, Faulkner would bring Jill, and the three of them would go to the beach together.

Also Meta had met another man. A concert pianist, tall, handsome, and very much in love with her. His name was Wolfgang Rebner, he was German and from a wealthy family. They shared a passion for music. Rebner proposed, and Meta could not say yes. Bill offered her no hope, and yet would not let her go. Faulkner's life was growing more terribly fragmented. He was finishing the final rewriting of *Absalom.* He was working at the studio and making a lot of money, but barely tolerating the work. He was trying desperately to hold Meta and cope with Estelle. Meanwhile, Estelle had slipped into Hollywood social life. Clark Gable came by for drinks, she became special friends with Ronald Colman and his wife, and Faulkner's writer friend Joel Sayre also came frequently. Estelle played "Just a Song at Twilight" for Joel on her rented piano. Often the Faulkners and Meta would be at the same party, and Faulkner persuaded Meta to have them all visit the Studio Club, where again, the two women chatted amiably. Through these weeks, Bill was drinking heavily. He was telling Meta that all he could offer her was undying love, and she was concluding that undying love was not enough. Rebner was pressing his suit, and that fall Meta accepted his proposal.[146]

Trying to achieve some insulation from Faulkner, Meta invited her aunt to come stay with her. Two days before her marriage, she kissed her fiancé at her door about midnight and he left. A few minutes later, Bill knocked. His face was bloody from scratches. He and Estelle had been at a party, he said. Estelle had passed out, revived, and he had taken her home. They had quarreled over Meta, and Estelle had attacked him. He wished Meta happiness, but he would not let her out of his life, he said.[147] In mid-October she had received 300 pages that were to be included in a special edition of *Absalom* with his signature. On the first page he wrote, "and this is number one, and it is inscribed to Meta Carpenter, wherever she may be."[148]

Absalom, Absalom! was published on October 26, 1936. Fortunately for the author, Bennett Cerf and Random House had bought out Smith and Haas, and this book was offered with more publicity than any of his previous works. By mid-November a third printing had produced 10,000 copies. Clifton Fadiman in the *New Yorker* called it "boring," and *Time* magazine's reviewer pronounced it unreadable.[149] Cerf, however, was not dismayed. He had never thought Faulkner would be a financial success for Random House, and he continued to be a staunch supporter of Faulkner's art.

Faulkner had first thought he might ask $100,000 for the film rights to *Absalom,* then offered it to his studio for $50,000—precisely the amount that Margaret Mitchell was getting for *Gone With the Wind* just at that time.[150] "It's about miscegenation," he said. The studio didn't take it. Interracial mixing was not a popular or a saleable subject. Furthermore, irredeemably failed families and dissolving fortunes were not welcome themes in the midst of the Great Depression.

Next, Faulkner began to work on the book that would become *The Unvanquished,* featuring the two teenagers, Bayard Sartoris and Ringo. It was a relatively comfortable, adventurous story, already published in part in the *Saturday Evening Post,* and easily saleable. Its very title was what America needed to hear as the awful depression seemed never to end.

Bill's problems with Estelle continued, and so too hers with him. One morning his friend at the studio, Joel Sayre, noticed marks on his face. Concerned, he asked what had happened. "I was just sitting there, reading *Time* magazine," Bill replied, "when Estelle came at me with a croquet mallet."[151] In the spring of 1937, Faulkner's old friend from New Orleans days, Bill Spratling, came for a visit. They had a few drinks and sat down at the dinner table. Faulkner's face fell forward into his plate and lay there. "I guess I'll have to put him back into the booby hatch again," Estelle sighed. She showed Spratling bruises on her arms. The next day Spratling visited Faulkner at the sanatorium and saw the bars on the windows.[152] At the studio, there would be periods lasting several days in which Faulkner did no work at all and would be taken off the payroll. He had begun the cycle again.

The chaos abated in late May when Estelle took Jill and went home.[153] Cho Cho, who had turned eighteen in February, 1937, had married an attractive young man named Claude Selby. The couple lived at Rowan Oak and would have a baby in September.[154] Understandably, Cho Cho had always felt especially close to "Billy," and she had lived in Rowan Oak from the beginning. She was fourteen when Jill was born. At that point Faulkner became "Pappy," and Cho Cho was sent off to a boarding school in Holly Springs. In the summer of 1936, she was left at home alone when everyone else got into the new car and headed for California. In the fall, she entered Ole Miss as a freshman and met Claude, a student in the School of Law.[155] In the spring of 1937, she was at Rowan Oak, waiting for her baby, while Bill was alone again in California. He would come home in the late afternoons to an empty house and find Jill's "little toys scattered about." He had tied one of her "little scuffed shoes" to the head of his bed. Forlorn, he wrote to Cho Cho asking her to "'take care of my little baby."[156]

Home Again

In August, 1937, after a year in the Golden Land, Faulkner had had enough. He and Ben Wasson drove the Ford home. Oliver and Narcissus had decided to stay in California. Faulkner began the trip with a bottle of bourbon, and he continued to drink as they headed east. In the southwestern desert they passed a group of Indians on the side of the road. "This was theirs," Faulkner said with a sweep of his hand over the landscape. "All of it. This whole country. We took it from them and shoved them off onto reservations. I reckon it's bad enough the way we treat the black folks. But they're like children and need looking after, expect to be looked after. Oh, hell, I don't know any answers for other people. I can't take care of my own problems."[157] Travel, slow travel, the kind where the rubber meets the road over long distances, does seem to promote perspective.

In many ways, Hollywood as Hollywood was simply another disaster in Faulkner's life. It affected his writing, but there is no sign that it added anything really substantial to his talent, and it certainly sponged up his diminishing energies. On the other hand, it brought him Meta and Meta brought him something in life that he had never had before and would never have again. In a sense, through Meta he had one more thrust toward, not happiness, but fullness, maturity. This manifested itself in his writings, first in the novel that he started almost as soon as he arrived in Oxford.

The Wild Palms began as a story about a man and a woman who gave up society and the world for the great passion that they had between them. It was, in a major way, a story of the road that Meta and Bill had not taken. Charlotte Rittenmeyer was the wife of a New Orleans stockbroker with two children who resisted the closing down of her life to conventionality by fleeing with Harry Wilbourne, a young medical intern who financed their flight with money from a wallet that he found in the street. They surrendered all of the assurances that are given by the institutions of life—marriage, parenthood, profession, social reputation—for deeply passionate love.

Well into the writing, Faulkner came to feel that he needed another story to serve as "counterpoint." He had used the same word to describe how he had come to write the Jason portion in *The Sound and the Fury* after writing the Quentin section. Thus he wove into the book the story of a convict, never named, whom he called "the tall man." Foolishly in love and a true romantic, the tall man had bungled a train robbery and been sentenced to Parchman for life. During the great flood of 1927, a decade before Charlotte and John began their adventure together, he and other prisoners were set to work in the emergency. The convict was given a skiff and told to go rescue a pregnant woman stranded in a tree and a man perched atop a cottonhouse. He found the woman and started to go back. Caught in the intricate and confusing currents set up by a river now scores of miles wide, the couple rowed, drifted, and were swept over vast distances before they finally landed on an Indian mound along with a host of fugitive animals, a Mount Ararat to Noah's Ark. There the convict delivered the woman's baby, a child conceived by another man, severing the umbilical cord with the jagged top of a tin can. Finding the authorities again, the convict said: "Yonder's your boat, and here's the woman. But I never did find that bastard on the cottonhouse." (278) The tall man's story ended with the convict back in Parchman refusing parole. It could have been an allegory of Faulkner's own life.

Charlotte's and Harry's romance ended in a beachhouse in midwinter in Pascagoula with the winds and rain whipping those tough little palms in the yard. Harry fumbled an abortion, and Charlotte and the baby both died. Harry was sentenced to fifty years in prison—in essence, life, like the convict. He refused the offer of a cyanide pill from Charlotte's husband with the thought: "Yes . . . between grief and nothing I will take grief." (234) These were the very words that Bill had said to Meta after her marriage to Wolfgang Rebner. It was another way of saying it is better to have loved—lived—and risked the loss than never to have lived at all. Faulkner felt that this was "the theme of the whole book, the convict story being just counterpoint to sharpen it."[158]

Hollywood had given him Meta. It also put him for a time safely beyond the threat of bankruptcy. During 1937 he had earned $21,650 from the studios, a vast amount of money in the midst of the Great Depression. There was no good reason why he should not have been financially secure well before that. Indeed, even by the end of 1932, he had already earned a considerable amount of Hollywood money in weekly wages, and he had sold film rights to *Sanctuary* and *Turn About* for some $9,000.

However, Faulkner felt that he had to take on an amazing array of dependents. He supported, in whole or in part, Estelle, Jill, his mother, Cho Cho, and Lida Oldham (whose husband, the Major, would live into 1945). Faulkner also helped his brother Dean for a number of years before he began to earn a living flying, and Dean's wife and child after Dean's death. Bill Faulkner had hardly arrived home in late summer 1937 before he became a surrogate father yet again. Vickie gave birth to her daughter, Victoria Hamilton Selby, on September 22 at the Oxford hospital.[159] The father, Claude Selby, was very young, thin of body, and not strong. Soon he was gone, deserting his teenage wife and infant child. Vickie later said that Bill was the only one who kept her alive at that point. They worked crossword puzzles together in the evenings and he read to her from *A Shropshire Lad* and from Keats. After a time, Judge Franklin invited her to visit with him in Shanghai—where there was plenty of room in his spacious, column-fronted, Southern-style mansion.[160] In time, Vickie was divorced and in 1940 married William Fielden, an American who had come to China as a very young man and worked his way up in the British-American Tobacco Company in Shanghai. Vickie brought her husband to Rowan Oak for the first time in January, 1942. Lamentably, when they arrived, they found both her stepfather and her mother deep in their cups.[161]

Faulkner also had black dependents. Given the society of those times, there had to be at least one black servant at Rowan Oak. Usually, there were several, some of whom lived in the yard. However, not even Faulkner's long list of dependents totally explains his almost constant state of penury.

Ironically Faulkner the writer understood Southern regional economics very well, but he was nearly totally inept in handling financial matters in his personal life. It was only in the 1950s when his income rose to many times that of the average American that he passed beyond the point of being sorely embarrassed by, indeed desperate about debts that he could not pay. Even when he seemed safely beyond that point, he continued to be haunted by fear of bankruptcy and behaved about money in ways that made him seem terribly cheap.

Several weeks after Faulkner returned to Oxford from California, he felt the need to go to New York to finalize the writing of *The Unvanquished.* It was the restlessness again, and it was followed by heavy drinking. In New York he saw Meta, and met her husband, Wolfgang Rebner. She had gone to Germany with Wolfgang, whose Jewish family, already under the Nazi thumb, would lose several members in the concentration camps. Meta and Wolfgang barely managed to flee with their lives, and now lived in New York in deepening poverty, failing health, and fading dreams of his brilliant career in music. The old feelings between Meta and Bill resurged, but Meta was married. For several days after the meeting, no one heard from Bill. His friend Jim Devine persuaded the manager of the hotel to let him into Bill's room. The place was strewn with empty liquor bottles. Bill was lying on the bathroom floor with a very deep burn across his lower back. In bed and recovering, he told them that he had been sitting on the toilet when he fainted and fell onto a steam pipe. Friends called Sherwood Anderson to the scene where he understood that Bill had been drunk for a week. "Bill had been wandering—nude—about the hotel corridors," Anderson reported.[162] Bennett Cerf persuaded Devine to take Faulkner to Oxford where, as usual, he began a slow and painful recuperation.[163]

Back home again, Faulkner acquired more real estate. In February, 1938, he purchased another section of Bailey's woods. The added acreage would give Rowan Oak more of the isolation that he cherished. In the same month he netted $19,000 from the sale of film rights to *The Unvanquished,* just published.[164] Most vitally, he bought a rather run-down 320-acre farm some seventeen miles northeast of Oxford in Beat Two—an area known as Woodson's Ridge. It was the farm upon which the shrewd banker Joe Parks had been reared. Parks had bought Bill's father's North Street house, squeezed his grandfather out of the bank, and acquired Lem Oldham's hotel on the square. Neither of Faulkner's ventures was costly in those depressed times. He paid $2,500 for the farm, of which only $500 was required at closing. He bought the farm from a governmental agency, the Federal Land Bank, no doubt through his Uncle John who managed local business for the bank.[165]

Immediately, Faulkner filled his farm with black tenants and rescued his brother Johncy from the relative poverty of life as a flyer by making him manager. Johncy and Uncle John recommended that the farm be turned to cattle raising, a wise move that nearly the whole of the cotton South made over the next twenty years. Faulkner insisted, however, on creating several tenant farms combined with, of all things, a horse farm. They compromised on tenants and a mule farm in a time when tractors were displacing mules. Faulkner named the place Greenfield Farm.[166] Thereafter, for more than a dozen years, he frequently slid into the persona of the plain Mississippi farmer, and lost a lot of money in playing the part. But, clearly, he was happy with his farm.

One of the tenants at Greenfield was Ned Barnett, an older black man whom family and local lore asserted had been a slave of the Old Colonel's in Ripley and had served four generations of Falkners.[167] Faulkner's nephew Jimmy declared that Ned had been in the family for generations, and his stepson Malcolm improved on the story by describing him as "a runaway slave" who had attached himself to the Colonel and stayed with him through his campaigns during the Civil War. He was, Malcolm thought, "a colored butler of the traditional manner."[168] Estelle recalled that he wore a tie even when he went to milk the cows. Ned was famous in the family for wearing a frock coat that, reputedly, had belonged to the Old Colonel. One of the family stories about Ned related that every year after the crops were in the ground at Greenfield and there was still much hoeing and hard work to do, Ned would approach Faulkner saying that he felt he would die before the crops were harvested and he wanted to die in Ripley. Invariably, Faulkner would buy his unfinished crop as well as his unfinished work at a good price, only to have Ned return the next year for a repeat performance.

Ned—in his seventies—was not the only elderly black in the South in the 1930s and 1940s playing the part of the faithful old family servant. For many with only meager resources it was virtually the only way to survive. Also William Faulkner was not the only white person buying the act, usually eagerly. There was a lot of satisfaction in taking care of one black person, or even several black persons, and somehow walling out feelings of responsibility for the plight of the masses. Paternalism was neither necessarily difficult nor expensive. On one occasion when Faulkner expected to be away during the Christmas season, he asked Malcolm to do the honors for him. If it was "not too much trouble," he wrote, Malcolm should acquire "a supply of cheap fruit, candy etc. for the farm if Renzi comes in." He should also get "a cheap pint [of] whisky and [a] pound [of] cheap tobacco for Payne." Faulkner concluded that "if they were not negroes and old friends I would not bother you."[169]

Family legends grow easily—and interestingly. Uncle Ned, almost surely, was never even a slave, and certainly he was never a slave of the Old Colonel. He was probably born in August, 1865, just after slavery ended. That was indeed the month and year of birth he gave the census taker in 1900, and it squares with the ages he gave to census takers before and after.[170] He often described vividly the burning of Ripley by Union soldiers, but again he wasn't even born at that time. It is fairly easy to trace Ned in the census records. By 1870, apparently, his mother had died, and he, at age five, lived in Tippah County with his father Aaron, a tenant farmer, and seven siblings ranging in age from eighteen-year-old "Elick" down to Molley, age two. By the time he was sixteen Ned lived in Tippah County's Beat Two and was apprenticed to a farmer who was not a Falkner.[171] In 1882, at age seventeen, he married nineteen-year-old Eliza Childers. At thirty-five in 1900 he was a tenant farmer in Tippah County with a wife and no children.[172] In 1910 he still described himself as a farmer, but he lived in the village of Ripley. Indeed, he lived only a few doors away from Emeline Falkner's house, then occupied by her daughter,

Delia Prince. Delia's son George lived next to Ned, and another son, Arthur (who was probably named after his uncle, Arthur Falkner) lived two doors beyond Ned.[173]

Without doubt, Ned Barnett knew the "shadow family" Falkners well, but how he came to be William Faulkner's tenant and butler in the later 1930s and during the 1940s is problematical. J.W.T. Falkner left Tippah County in 1885, the Old Colonel died in 1889, and while the Murry Falkners were living in Ripley, Ned was farming. Apparently, he somehow came to William first as simply a tenant on his Lafayette County farm, then migrated into his Oxford household as a servant, eventually living in one of the buildings behind the big house. As he approached his eightieth birthday in 1945, it seems that Ned played the role of the faithful old family retainer to perfection, in a significant way taking the place of Mammy Callie who died in 1940. Asked by white folks how it felt to be freed, Ned developed an ingenious answer: "I wouldn't let them free me," he said.[174]

This is not to say that there was raw hypocrisy in the Ned story, nor in the familial legends about Faulkner servants. Mammy Callie lived in a tiny house behind Rowan Oak. When she was sick Estelle and William sometimes joined in her nursing, and when she passed away, they had a service in the parlor and Faulkner spoke the eulogy. Later he placed a small stone on her grave that read "Mammy"—"Her white children bless her."[175] In his will in 1940, Faulkner made elaborate arrangements for Ned to be settled on his own acreage on Greenfield and to be buried, where he declared he wanted to be, back in Ripley.[176]

In 1947, Ned Barnett died. Faulkner journeyed to Ripley to speak at Ned's burial in the town cemetery proximate to "his old Master, Colonel Falkner."[177] Diligent search, however, reveals no stone, not even one so modest as graces the grave of Mammie Callie in Oxford. The remains of some of the "other Falk-ners" were already there, and on that occasion William Faulkner must have walked close by these stones, including that of "Mrs. Emeline Lacy Falkner." Subsequently, Estelle and William cleared out the cedar chest in Ned's room—finding a four-year-old birthday cake that Estelle had made for him and various pieces of discarded Falkner clothing reaching back, allegedly, for generations. Malcolm was there, he said, and saw both his mother and stepfather cry.[178]

~

The Wild Palms appeared in January, 1939, and in the same month William Faulkner's face appeared on the cover of *Time* magazine. Inside, the write-up labored to inject a lot of Southern aristocratic color into his life by depicting the Old Colonel as a plantation owner, duelist, valiant Confederate officer, and postwar railroad builder. It declared, erroneously, that the family wealth had declined precipitously with the death of the Colonel and implied that it had totally evaporated with Murry. It painted William Faulkner as a conservative

Southern Democrat and aristocrat, a landlord with black tenants, and a husband and father living in a plantation mansion called Rowan Oak.[179] Coming forth in the midst of America's love affair with *Gone With the Wind,* both as book (1936) and film (1939), there was a rising tendency, it seems, to cast Faulkner as a character in a "Tara" play—to see him, indeed, as a loyal heir to a hoop skirt and magnolia tradition of the grand Old South. Apparently, there was also a rising inclination to read his fiction as a description and apologia for, if not, indeed, a laudation of that South rather than for what it actually was—a profound indictment of the legend.

In November, 1938, after completing *The Wild Palms,* Faulkner had picked up again the saga of the Snopes family that he had begun a dozen years before. *The Sound and the Fury* and *Absalom, Absalom!* had been about the decline of the aristocracy; the Snopes tale would be about the rise of the dirt farmers, the "poor whites," centering in the person of Flem Snopes. By mid-December he was well into the first of three volumes.[180] Initially called *The Peasants,* it would become *The Hamlet.* In addition to Flem Snopes and Eula Varner (the superbly ripe young daughter of the shrewdest peasant of them all, Will Varner), he had discovered a man "he fell in love with" in V.K. Ratliff. V.K.—called by his initials in the Southern mode—was of the peasantry, and a sewing machine salesman who made his rounds in three counties that included Yoknapatawpha. He circulated in this way with a little doll house in the back of his buckboard containing his demonstration sewing machine. Equally comfortable with the women in the country-side interested in his machine and the lounging men at the country stores, V.K. gathered all the news and gave out all the news, always searching for the essential and useful truth in the facts, and always working quietly, wisely, effectively for the good of the community. As V.K. began to perceive the soulless acquisitiveness of Flem and the threat he posed, he commenced a prolonged crusade to save society from this quintessential form of redneck rapacity.

In a large way, *The Wild Palms* marked an ending of agony, and now *The Hamlet* signalled a new and happier beginning. Faulkner was churning out rivers of words and he relished his work. Sending off some of the pages to Random House in the spring of 1939, he added a line to an accompanying letter. "I am the best in America, by God," he exclaimed.[181] By the end of the year, he was finishing the typescript for the first volume. He had arrived at a set of titles for the trilogy. They would be called *The Hamlet, The Town,* and *The Mansion.*[182] It was a perfect progression to trace the career of Flem Snopes and all those whose lives he touched. *The Hamlet* was published on April 1, 1940, and within a month had sold almost 7,000 copies. By June, *The Hamlet* had earned its author about $2,700, whereas *Absalom,* after almost four years, had earned only about $3,000. Faulkner's new book was a financial marvel compared to earlier performances, but it barely got him out of debt to his publishers.

Meanwhile, he was again falling into debt to merchants in Oxford and

Memphis. In March, 1939, he had scraped together $6,000 to lend to financially distressed Phil Stone—mostly by borrowing on his personal insurance policy. As he explained to Robert Haas of Random House, there was "never any question of mine and thine between us when either had it."[183] By December, 1939, the pressure was so great that he had broken off his more serious writing to "boil the pot" again and try for some saleable short stories. As usual when he tried hardest at this, he failed. His publishers were very sympathetic to Faulkner in his plight and more helpful than the sales of his books warranted, but the relief they could afford was marginal. In the spring he was desperate, and poured out his frustrations in a letter to Haas.

> Every so often, in spite of judgment and all else, I take these fits of sort of raging and impotent exasperation at this really quite alarming paradox which my life reveals. Beginning at the age of thirty I, an artist, a sincere one and of the first class, who should be free even of his own economic responsibilities and with no moral conscience at all, began to become the sole, principal and partial support—food, shelter, heat, clothes, medicine, kotex, school fees, toilet paper and picture shows—of my mother . . . brother and his wife and two sons, another brother's widow and child, a wife of my own and two step children, my own child; I inherited my father's debts and his dependents, white and black without inheriting yet from anyone one inch of land or one stick of furniture or one cent of money; the only thing I ever got for nothing, after the first pair of long pants I received (cost $7.50) was the $300.00 O. Henry prize last year. I bought without help from anyone the house I live in and all the furniture; I bought my farm the same way. I am 42 years old and I have already paid for four funerals and will certainly pay for one more and in all likelihood two more beside that, provided none of the people in mine or my wife's family my superior in age outlive me, before I ever come to my own.[184]

Obviously, there was much omitted from the plaint, including the fact that at age thirty he was actually still living in his father's house and eating at his mother's table—room and board free. Also, he omitted the fact that he was in trouble, in part, because he still had not paid about $1,100 in federal and California state income taxes on sizeable movie monies received in 1937 and 1938. He never mentioned, too, that in Hollywood it was Meta who paid the rent on a bungalow so that they could be alone and who accepted his explanation that he could not take her to the better restaurants because he could not afford it.[185] Even so, the lament stands as a poignant statement of how he felt at this point in his life. In August, he sold two stories, again in the usual spurt of good fortune, for a total of $1,400. But by January, 1941, he did not have $15 to pay the electric bill and Neilson's Department Store was dunning him aggressively and embarrassingly.[186]

In the crisis, he tried a stratagem that had worked modestly for him before. He began to put together a book of short stories. In the process he developed the character Ike McCaslin. Born in 1869 the last son of the slaveholding, landholding aristocracy, Ike became the protégé of Sam Fathers, part black and part Indian, a chief and a great woodsman and hunter. Ike came to reject his heritage as landlord over tenants on the McCaslin estate in favor of staying close to the unspoiled earth and to nature in a shrinking but still huge wilderness along the river in Yoknapatawpha County. As Faulkner labored on the book, he integrated stories previously conceived and finally added what is one of the great works in American literature—a novella, *The Bear.* By December, he sensed that it was a work of which he would be proud. He slowed down; it needed, he said, "careful writing and rewriting to get it exactly right."[187] In May, 1942, Random House published the book as *Go Down Moses.* It was, as Faulkner saw it, a book about the "relationship between white and negro races here," and he dedicated it to "Mammy Caroline Barr."[188]

A Hollywood War

Meanwhile, Faulkner had watched the rise of fascism in Europe with increasing alarm. Not a political person, he nevertheless signed a statement by writers against the Franco regime in Spain. At home, he hated the New Deal, but he was not deeply philosophical in his opposition, and he had no respect for the Republicans on the other side. He simply thought that the various programs, instead of offering relief to distressed farmers and workers, undermined independence and encouraged idleness. His most vitriolic diatribes came out in short stories, especially in those he wrote for popular audiences, and these he wrote when he was desperate for money. Constantly, he referred to these writings as "trash."

As the German armies swept across France in May, 1940, Faulkner's concern became acute. He got out his old RAF uniform and put it on. He told Haas that he was proud that he could still button up the tunic, but knew that he "would last about two minutes in combat."[189] He busied himself in the local effort to establish a civilian air patrol and a watch system for enemy aircraft.[190] After Pearl Harbor, however, Faulkner was exceedingly eager to get into active service. In spite of his status as a celebrity, he was discouraged by authorities on all sides. In the spring of 1942, he went to Washington for an interview with the Navy Department. With difficulty he stopped drinking before the event, but the Navy quickly declined his offer of aid as a flyer, as did the Army Air Force.[191]

Meanwhile, he was growing more and more frantic about his finances. He borrowed from banks on anticipated royalties and mortgaged one by one the animals at Greenfield Farm. He wrote short stories one after another; one out of six sold. His new agent, Harold Ober, very generously advanced him money; Random House did as much as a modicum of business sense allowed. He was sending off stories that were obscure at points or suffered from outright omissions. He revised "The Bear" for *Post* from memory because he had not kept a copy. "I am in a situation where I will take almost anything for it or almost anything else I have or can write," he told Ober. He owed everyone, including $600 due the grocer.[192]

Frustrated, he repeated his jeremiad against those he regarded as dependents. For ten years he had carried a load no artist should have to bear, he lamented, "oldest son to widowed mothers and inept brothers and nephews and wives and other female connections and their children, most of whom I don't like and with none of whom I have anything in common, even to make conversation about." If he thought it hurt his work, he would take his hat and walk out. War was appealing to men, he concluded, because "it's the only condition under which a man who is not a scoundrel can escape for a while from his female kin."[193]

The objective observer and some of the kinfolk alluded to would not have agreed that Faulkner's depiction was totally accurate. He did own 320-acre Greenfield Farm, Phil Stone was working to repay his loan, and Faulkner himself had bragged two years before that with the 35 acres at Rowan Oak he was the largest landowner in the town of Oxford.[194] Again, it was the self-generated lack of cash and self-perceived poverty that took into account only what the author chose. Buying the Waco for $6,000, advertising Estelle, entertaining Meta in California on the cheap while earning a thousand dollars a week—all of these were parts of that piece.

By the summer of 1942, Faulkner saw financial disaster closing in. "I have 60c in my pocket, and that is literally all," he wrote Bennett Cerf. Hollywood was an answer, and friends and agents were busy attempting to arrange something for him.[195] Because of his drinking, the studios were less than enthusiastic. However, Warner Brothers was a possibility. It was a giant machine, producing films for the most popular market, and Jack Warner, in particular, gained a sense of power by hiring famous American authors. Unfortunately, he took a perverse pride in paying them as little as possible. Warner was a friend of Cerf, who was very supportive of Faulkner, and a deal was struck. It was arranged that Faulkner would go to Warner Brothers for twenty-six weeks at $300 a week, a fourth of his previous highest salary but $200 more than he said he would take. The Warners shrewdly gave themselves some seven years worth of options on the use of Faulkner's talents in filmmaking.[196] Faulkner hardly paused to read the contract, and later he would bitterly regret his haste.

Bill Faulkner had not let Meta Carpenter go, and Hollywood meant Meta again. In March, 1940, he had given her $150 to finance a trip to visit her parents in Arizona with instructions to go by way of New Orleans.[197] Faulkner took her off the train in southwestern Mississippi and drove in the night through a torrential rain to New Orleans. Meta was ill and feverish, and her marriage with Rebner was dissolving. They checked into a hotel in the Quarter and made love again in that furious way. Subsequently, Meta and Wolfgang tried hard but unsuccessfully to save their marriage. Finally divorced, Meta returned to Hollywood and began to earn a very creditable reputation as a script supervisor. When she came home just at dark one Saturday evening in the summer of 1942, she found Bill sitting on her doorstep, suitcase at his feet. They became lovers again, but he would not move in with her.[198]

Faulkner spent a total of two out of the next three years in Hollywood. At first, he worked on "The De Gaulle Story," a propaganda piece exalting the continuing resistance of the French to the German occupation. After several months of intensive labor on his part, the whole picture was scrapped for political reasons.[199] Now and again the work would be comfortable enough, especially when Howard Hawks asked for and secured his services. Faulkner got prime credit for adapting Hemingway's *To Have and Have Not* for the screen. This project, his greatest success as a screenwriter, also brought him a new friend. The man was a short, balding, middle-aged actor. He came from Broadway to Hollywood and made his name at first as a villain. It was Humphrey Bogart. Faulkner said to another friend, Ruth Ford, a Mississippi "old grad" and rising young actress, that Bogie's new leading lady and girlfriend was "like a young colt." She was nineteen-year-old Lauren Bacall. Faulkner got along well with Bogart, and with another actor (and songwriter) in the film, Hoagy Carmichael. In these years, Faulkner was hyper but unfocused, a loaded gun wanting to shoot. He strove—almost too hard—to please the studio, and thought fondly of getting into the war by ferrying bombers from American factories to Britain.[200] Whenever he could, he got a leave and went home, and in 1944 he brought Estelle and Jill to Hollywood for the summer. For Meta it was too much, and she attempted to break off their relationship. When Estelle and Jill went east, however, the affair began again, and with full strength.[201]

In June, 1945, Faulkner returned to Hollywood for another term of his contract with Warner Brothers. By that time, his pay was up to $500 a week, but $50 went to the agent who got him the job. He was bitterly unhappy and verging on another collapse. The farm, Rowan Oak, and the family needed him, he declared.[202] By then, Faulkner felt he had some serious writing to do, and he yearned to do it. In the summer of 1943 he had begun to think of an anti-war story about a corporal in World War I who, amid the carnage, leads a nonviolent mutiny that spreads through the army. In time it becomes clear that the corporal was something like Christ come to earth again, and the story ends with his execution arranged by the Generalissimo, who was actually his father. It was another curious Faulkner mutation; the man who had tried so hard to get into two great wars suddenly becoming pacifist at the very height of the second war. Faulkner fell in love with this soldier story.[203] He would work at it for eleven years and in 1954 it became *A Fable,* the book he long thought would be the great novel of his career.

In September, 1945, Faulkner left filmland for good; all subsequent returns were very brief and extremely lucrative. The parting was amicable, and for a couple of years was viewed on both sides as temporary rather than terminal. In truth, Sam Warner had used William Faulkner about as well as he could be used in film writing. Faulkner earned his pay, but he had not distinguished himself. Film executives saw him as "a quietly unhappy man." One of his supervisors commented, in recommending an easy release, that "he had been uncomplainingly turning out scripts which nearly any Hollywood writer could have written."[204] Simultaneously, the war ended, and it seemed that everyone was going home.

Something else vital to Faulkner's career was stirring during the war. As early as February, 1944, Malcolm Cowley, writer and literary critic, had been interested in doing an essay on Faulkner and his work. He was appalled by literary America's neglect of the author. Surprisingly, Faulkner was receptive and helpful, perhaps because he was mellowing a bit and recognized that Cowley was a superbly talented person.[205] As Cowley's piece neared completion, Faulkner read a portion and applauded with his highest accolade. "It was all right," he declared. In any of his books, he said, he was "trying peculiarly to tell a story, in the most effective way I can think of, the most moving, the most exhaustive." More important, he continued, "I am telling the same story over and over, which is myself and the world." Finally, he was attempting to do that in one sentence, "on one pinhead." The South was not very important to him, he said, he just happened to know it, and "life is a phenomenon, but not a novelty, the same frantic steeplechase toward nothing everywhere and man stinks the same stink no matter where in time."[206]

In the summer of 1945 Cowley was back again with the idea of collecting elements of Faulkner's work into a single volume. On one side he reminded the author that of all his books only *Sanctuary* was still in print, and on the other he repeated what Jean Paul Sartre had told him: "For the young people of France, Faulkner is a god." Perhaps a bit love-starved after years of literary disappreciation in America and aggravated by financial privation at home, Faulkner took the bait with enthusiasm and was steadily helpful.[207] When Cowley's *The Portable Faulkner* came from the Viking Press in April, 1946, Faulkner was ecstatic. "By God, I didn't know myself what I had tried to do, and how much I had succeeded," he raved.[208] Neither did America, nor would it for some years yet to come. But, quite literally, Cowley's book put Faulkner into the hands of tens of thousands of Americans; it was at last the real beginning of a popular appreciation of his work.

At Rowan Oak after the war, *A Fable* proceeded slowly and painfully. In his mind it was his magnum opus, and Faulkner was "weighing every word." He was able to survive financially only by the faithful support of Random House, a fact that bothered him more and more and raised the threat of his having to return to Hollywood. Now and again he would break off from the really important work, as he saw his novel, and try to boil the short story pot again.

One of the characters he had developed in several of these stories was Lucas Beauchamp (often pronounced "Beechum"), a lightly colored great-grandson of the slaveholding L.Q.C. McCaslin. Lucas grew into a proud rebel whom society pressed to live as a black man but who steadily, adamantly refused "to be a nigger." In January, 1948, Faulkner started a short story about Lucas, and in February it was rapidly becoming a short novel.[209]

Intruder in the Dust, as the novel was called, is at one level a fascinating detective story in which the author was again a master at withholding information to build suspense. Lucas was jailed for allegedly killing a white man, and he called upon sixteen-year-old Chick Mallison to summon his uncle, lawyer Gavin Stevens, to his defense. Proudly Lucas refused to beg his own innocence, but he gave Chick and Gavin the prescription to prove it—exhume the body. Assisted by his friend Aleck Sander, the son of the Mallison's cook, and Miss Habersham, an elderly maiden lady of the impoverished aristocracy, Chick dug up the grave of the murdered man—hence the "intruder" in the title. They finally got Gavin Stevens and Sheriff Hampton into the action, the true killer was found, and Lucas was saved. Gavin ended the story by asserting that blacks have a world and whites have a world, and the "homogeneity" and integrity of each must be saved. But it was the white people of the South who must do justice to the black, he insisted. It could not be compelled by the North.

Race

THE FIRE THIS TIME

All of this came just as the Civil Rights movement in America was on the rise. It was advanced, on one side, by the rising power of black people and their leaders. It was spurred, on the other, by obvious national necessities first during World War II when manpower was in critically short supply, and after the war by the awareness of some of America's leaders that they were in a competition with the Russians for the allegiance of the "colored" peoples of the Third World. In 1946 President Harry Truman was clearly leading the executive branch of the Federal government down the road toward full civil equality for black Americans, and Southern politicians such as J. Strom Thurmond of South Carolina were already leading much of the South toward rebellion in what would become the "Dixiecrat" party in 1948.

Very soon, Faulkner found himself under severe fire from both the North and the South. Many Northerners were offended by his saying that the North had to keep hands off of race relations in the South. They felt that the South within itself did not have the means of redemption from racial sin. Southern whites were offended by his saying that black people are not simply an inferior branch of humanity, that they were often as moral, courageous, feeling, and intelligent as the best of the whites.

Faulkner's Uncle John caught accurately the mood of the Southern white response when someone suggested to him that he was the model for the character Gavin Stevens in *Intruder in the Dust.* "Me, that nigger lovin' Stevens? Naw, I don't read Billy's books much. But he can write them if he wants to. I guess he makes money at it—writing those dirty books for Yankees."[210] In calling for the white South to do justice to black people, *Intruder* marked Faulkner as a pioneer in the Civil Rights movement in the South, albeit an almost unwitting one.

He came to that end—like many other Southerners who came out of privileged backgrounds—by a path that was obvious and ordinary. As professed paternalists they came into regular and intimate contact with the few black people who worked in their kitchens and yards. The level of human interaction ran high and somehow *some*—not all, perhaps only a few—such whites came to understand that black people are people too. With Faulkner surely it began with Mammy Callie, Ned Barnett, and all those other blacks who lived so close to him during his life. Somehow he refused to stereotype all black people as Sambos. Even as he was writing and rewriting the Dilsey section in *The Sound and the Fury* twenty years before, he moved her speech away from heavy dialect. Four years later with Joe Christmas, he got closer to the heart of the problem of race. If, indeed, blackness and whiteness is a matter of black and white genes, black blood and white blood, what does it mean if in one body the black blood and the white blood are inextricably mixed? For a hundred years dominant Southern whites had solved that problem quickly by embracing the "one drop rule," that is, one drop of black blood makes a person all black, hence mulattoness ostensibly means nothing at all. With Joe Christmas, Faulkner raised the stakes—what if someone doesn't know himself whether he has that drop, whether or not he is a "Negro" at all? What then?

It was a devastating question for a society desperate for the vindication of its racial order, but it was also a real one. There were people in the South who were black cultured but whose black blood was invisible. Some of these did not know with certainty that they did indeed have black blood. They only knew that they were born and reared as if they were black. Indeed, in Oxford there was a man, William Robert Boles, who ran a shoe repair shop just off the square. For years white people thought he was white until suddenly and shockingly, in their view of the event, he married a black woman. One tradition asserted that "Rob" Boles was Faulkner's cousin. Indeed, his birthdate, 1878, and Charlie Butler's history renders that assertion at least plausible. However, there is another tradition that makes Rob the son of another white man.[211]

All during his life, Faulkner would occasionally fall into some round and rhetorical slur against blacks. But he was not a bigot, and he hated bigotry—perhaps in large measure because he felt himself such an outsider, such a ready target for the bully boys at home and abroad. In the summer of 1943 he had a jarring experience that touched him deeply and brought forth a passionate expression of his feelings about America and blacks and Jews. One of the partners in Random House was Bob Haas, an early and generous supporter of the almost always dollarless Faulkner. In the summer of 1943 Haas's son, who flew torpedo planes off carriers in the Pacific, went down at sea and was lost. Faulkner wrote a grief-stricken letter of sympathy to his friend that began "Bob, dear boy."[212] Haas's daughter, age twenty or so, continued flying bombers from America to England to replace the vast numbers shot down over Europe.

Faulkner wrote to Malcolm, who was training to be a combat medic in the army, telling him about the Haases. "All Jews," he said, and declared his readiness to fight bigotry at home as well as abroad: "I just hope I don't run into some hundred percent American Legionnaire until I feel better." In the same letter he talked about the irony that an all-black fighter squadron had flown a successful combat mission in North Africa on the very same day that twenty black people had been killed in a race riot in Detroit in which the police joined the mob. "A change will come out of this war," he declared. "If it doesn't, if the politicians and people who run this country are not forced to make good the shibboleths they glibly talk about freedom, liberty, human rights, then you young men who live through it will have wasted your precious time, and those who don't live through it will have died in vain."[213] William Faulkner was no liberal, but no liberal could have said it so well.

Intruder, published in 1948, got more attention than any book of Faulkner's since *Sanctuary,* and, for a Faulkner book, it sold well. More important both for his fame and his fortune, MGM bought the film rights for $50,000, of which Faulkner received $40,000 after commissions.[214] This bonanza along with other earnings kept him solvent well into 1951—even after he had bought a new Ford stationwagon, a tractor, and put a new roof on Rowan Oak. It also meant that he would now get back to writing *A Fable*—that is, after all the excitement was over that came with the filming of the movie and having its first showing right there in Oxford.[215]

Intruder in the form of film brought a Faulkner story—and Faulkner himself—to mass America. *Life* wanted to get Malcolm Cowley to do an in-depth article on the author such as he had done on Hemingway—with a similar run of interesting pictures. Faulkner said "no" from the start. Even after Cowley had nursed him through one of his collapses at his Connecticut home, he said no again, and explained: "It is my aim, and every effort bent, that the sum and history of my life, which in the same sentence is my obit and epitaph too, shall be them both: He made the books and he died."[216]

At last Faulkner was also beginning to get attention in more intellectually exalted circles in America. In 1942, Yale University Library offered the first major exhibit of Faulkner materials.[217] In the summer of 1948, Professor Carvel Collins came to Oxford gathering information to conduct a Faulkner seminar at Harvard University that fall.[218] A prestigious publication, *College English,* included an article on his work. In the latter process, Faulkner at last acted to kill one of the myths about himself that he had created. In what amounted to a postscript on his response to the author of the article's request for biographical information, he wrote: "I'm proud to have belonged to RAF even obscurely. But had no combat service nor wound."[219]

In 1949, Faulkner was voted the Nobel Prize for literature, but the vote came after much wrangling and too late for a consummation in that year. The proceedings, of course, were secret, but rumors floated about. In April, 1950, he was awarded the once-every-five-years Howells Medal of the American Academy of Arts and Letters. He accepted the medal but he declined to be present at the ceremony. "I am a farmer this time of year," he explained to fellow writer Mark Van Doren. "Up until he sells his crops, no Mississippi farmer has the time or money either to travel anywhere on."[220] It was another Faulkner persona—that of the plain farmer—not real of course, but this one had more substance than some of the others.

Clearly Faulkner was enjoying Greenfield Farm. He now had a black man, Renzi, managing the place, brother Johncy having entered the Navy during the war. Increasingly, he involved himself in the operation of the farm. Sometimes he would take Ned and go to the weekly Monday stock sales, where Jill said they "unfailingly traded down." Her father, she declared, was "a born sucker." He would buy "blind mules, crazy dogs, anything, always seeing in the animal some fine quality others had missed."[221]

Indeed, there was a relatively agrarian phase of his life between 1938 and the early 1950s that might be called his "Greenfield years." He had a cottage built on the farm for what was now his small family—Jill, Estelle, and himself. Victoria went wherever her husband Bill Fielden went, usually abroad following the tobacco business. Malcolm had become a medic in the Army during the war, attended Ole Miss afterwards, then went to China to visit his father in 1947, and married. At the farm Faulkner seemed at ease. Jill remembered those times with pleasure. They would go out especially for Fourth of July barbecues (to which local whites—"the plain folk"—were invited) and to deliver Christmas gifts. The place had a "commissary" that served as a store for several black tenant families and some of the neighbors too, white and black. Faulkner loved pulling down the ledgers off a shelf and writing in them such things as "debit Renzi, 1 can peaches." Jill liked to sit on the high steps leading to the front porch, eating cheese, crackers, and "sourdines," as black folks called them. Inside it was dark and smelled of cheese. There was a counter on the right, in front of shelves. On the other side, along the wall, Jill recalled "barrels of pickles, herring, etc. . . ."[222]

After the war, there were periods when Faulkner would visit the farm several times a week, presuming to give orders and occasionally actually working at some of the tasks with his own two hands. It was like renewing Rowan Oak had been. After a morning of writing, it was very satisfying to go into the out-of-doors and do physical work, the results of which could be felt and seen and talked about while leaning against the fence.

The Nobel Prize

On November 10, 1950, a Swedish journalist telephoned Rowan Oak to tell Faulkner that he had won the 1949 Nobel Prize for literature. The author responded graciously, and the reporter went on to ask if he were looking forward to his trip to Stockholm to receive the award. "I won't be able to come to receive the prize myself," he announced. Then he explained. "It's too far away. I am a farmer down here and I can't get away." The Associated Press commissioned local newspaperman Phil Mullen to interview the winner, and Faulkner reluctantly granted the interview. Later he dropped by Mullen's office to read the draft of the write up. He asked for and got only one change, but it was a giant one. "Change that to I was a member of the RAF," he requested in regard to his war record. "I did not see any service." Earlier, in 1946, when he found that Cowley had included four pages of biography in his introduction to *The Portable Faulkner,* Faulkner objected. When Cowley argued that it was all relevant, including the fact that his plane had been damaged in combat, Faulkner became even more insistent. "You're going to bugger up a fine dignified distinguished book with that war business," he declared.[223] Clearly, Faulkner was protecting his work now, even at the cost of bringing into question his previous veracity.

Faulkner's family had to struggle to keep him in the house to take the call from Sweden that would make the announcement official. When the call came he was gracious enough again, but as soon as he could he left Rowan Oak. He went away on the traditional November hunt having informed the Nobel Prize officials by mail that he would not be present at the ceremony. In the hunting camp he drank, developed a bad cold, and had to be brought home. By that time Estelle had matured the winning strategy. Jill wanted to go to Stockholm, she said, and Faulkner capitulated. Pulling Faulkner back from the beginning of a collapse was a major undertaking. It was achieved in Oxford and held through a visit to New York and the early receptions in Stockholm. Finally, in the late afternoon of Saturday, December 10, a small man, straight-backed and stiff in a rented tuxedo, marched to the microphone and made his 550-word speech.

Like most Nobel Prize speakers, Faulkner felt the need to talk about important things. The age of the atom bomb had just dawned, and the mushroom cloud hung over the spirit of the earth. The temptation of young writers would be to center on the threat of devastation, he said, but he urged transcendence. Much better, he insisted, to focus on those ideal and lasting virtues by which mankind not only endured but prevailed. The eternal verities were courage and compassion, humility and pride, love and honor. Man contesting with himself in the pursuit of virtue was the true story to tell—the story of the human heart in conflict with itself. In the contest, he insisted, man would not only endure, he would prevail.[224]

Between the heavy Southern accent, the rapid delivery, and a too-distant microphone, virtually no one heard the speech, but it caused a sensation when it appeared in print the next day. Mankind wanted very much to endure and prevail, and it thirsted for the assurance that Faulkner gave. Personally, the speech marked an end to one period of Faulkner's life, and the beginning of another—and final—phase. In taking the Nobel Prize, Faulkner joined the global community. However much he might want to keep his life private, however much he might succeed at that within the confines of Rowan Oak, he was now famous as a citizen of the world. He was, virtually, catapulted out of Oxford, out of the South, and into the world at large. Sometimes he liked it, often he hated it, but for the next dozen years, William Faulkner was a public man. Toward the end, he would try one more withdrawal and one last persona.

EIGHT

The Search
1950–1956

One way, among others, of interpreting the last dozen years of Faulkner's life is this: He was striving to make his life whole—often in great desperation and confusion and at first unsuccessfully. In the culture to which he was born, the road to maturity for an individual was clearly marked. First would come love, marriage, and sex; then family, clan, and community. In his youth, Faulkner had somehow missed the road at a critical turn. During the years from 1950 into 1956, he would try to take a firm hold on one piece or another in the progression, only to find rocks crumbling and turning to sand in his grasp. In the last half-dozen years of his life, from 1956 to 1962, he effected a very large and relatively successful transformation that had much to do with his dissolving, rather shockingly this late in life, his Mississippi roots and beginning again in Virginia.

Faulkner entered these last years with a marriage and a family that was in shambles. He further sorely taxed both by his relentless and destructive pursuit of a young woman, Joan Williams. During the process, Estelle virtually collapsed, and Jill resorted to flight and marriage. Increasingly, Faulkner alienated himself from members of his clan and community. Racked by repeated alcoholic episodes, his body at last began to deteriorate rapidly. Only Maud, in her eighties now, remained constant and uncritical in support of her Billy.

Professionally, during the early 1950s Faulkner was convinced that he was writing the great American novel. Yet, when *A Fable* was done in 1954, he sensed that it was a failure. Centered not in the South (as were eighteen of his nineteen novels), but rather in the trenches in France during World War I, the story was designed to exalt peace and the human virtues. Even as his work faltered, however, his fame reached a new high plateau—he had indeed become a citizen of the global community. He moved into the real world and, to an astonishing degree, became an unprivate man as never before. He made speeches and accepted interviews. He visited, traveled, and talked to groups large and small. He journeyed abroad for the United States Department of State and moved vigorously into the fight for justice for black people in the South. Over several years, he became sadly—even bitterly—disappointed with the results of his efforts and withdrew. Finally, in 1956, he found relief by taking up his writing again. Thereafter, until the end, he wrote about the South.

Joan

At the very time that Faulkner was signaling his entrance into the world by traveling to Stockholm to take his Nobel Prize in person, he was involved in another highly frustrating relationship with a young woman. It had begun during the summer of 1949 after a good year for Faulkner, a time when he began to feel himself in command of himself and his surroundings. At last, by the summer of 1948 he had money in the bank. He used part of it to acquire a sailboat and cruise about on Lake Sardis. Created by a huge earthen dam across the Tallahatchie River north and west of Oxford, this was one New Deal project to which Faulkner offered not the slightest objection. Also he participated in the November hunt and bought himself a back-vented corduroy coat such as Malcolm Cowley had (back-vented for comfort while straddling his horse). Further, he was looking for an annuity for his old age into which he could put some money so that "my friends and kinfolks don't or can't borrow it."[1] He had even gained in respect locally when parts of *Intruder* were filmed in and near Oxford and when the finished film premiered there.

But there was no woman, no lover in his life, and Bill Faulkner was starving again. Back in December, 1946, he had written to Cowley that he needed "a new young woman." A year or so later, he had "Buzz" Bezzerides and his wife as house guests at Rowan Oak. They occupied the bedroom next to the one in which Bill and Estelle slept. About two or three o'clock in the morning Buzz heard Estelle's voice in a vicious, fierce whisper, "Don't touch me, Bill. I don't want you to touch me. Don't you touch me." After a moment, Buzz heard "that sharp, intense striking of a hand against flesh." Then silence. Buzz thought that Bill had slapped Estelle's face. Next they were "aware of a sexual encounter on the other side of the door." The following morning at breakfast, Estelle "was cheerful as she could possibly be."[2]

About this same time Faulkner was making a special effort to get the New York address of Ruth Ford, the beautiful actress and graduate of Ole Miss whom he had known in Hollywood during the war.[3] Ruth was divorced and living with her little daughter Shelley. She would come home from the studio, and Bill would be there playing with Shelley. Ruth would bathe, dress, and go out for a date. When she returned, he would still be there. It was a curious performance, explained in part perhaps by a passage from his Elmer story written some twenty years before. Faulkner had Elmer give up on the possibility of seducing women. "He believes now that they just elect you when they happen to be in the right mood and you happen to be handy."[4] Bill, obviously, was making himself handy. Eventually, he cemented a long-running and close relationship with Miss Ford by giving her certain exclusive rights to his play *Requiem for a Nun.* It seemed to be again an attempt on his part to be so giving to an attractive young woman that she could not fail to be giving in return. And again, it was fatuous and futile. Miss Ford soon married and was devoted to her husband, actor Zachary Scott. Eventually, the gift turned sour and embarrassing. In matters of sex, Bill seemed a very slow learner. In February, 1949, when MGM was filming *Intruder* in Oxford, he rued that he was "no longer young enough to cope with all of the local girls who are ready and eager to glide into camera focus on their backs."[5] It was Faulkner as would-be satyr again. Looking for a nymph.

Joan Williams was the woman who came into his life in the late summer of 1949. Joan, like Meta, was a Memphian. She had attended the Hutchinson School for Girls and then took a year at Southwestern (now Rhodes) in Memphis, a Presbyterian-affiliated and very prestigious college in the mid-South. Then she moved on to Chevy Chase College in Maryland.[6] When she first met Faulkner in August, 1949, she had just finished her junior year at still another school, Bard College in New York. At twenty, she was an attractive girl with red hair, freckles, and brown-green eyes. An aspiring writer, she had won one of *Mademoiselle*'s prizes for college writers, and her story would soon be published. It was a highly significant achievement; it meant that she had talent and potential as a writer.

Through a cousin who lived in Oxford, Joan met Faulkner in the yard at Rowan Oak. She was passionate about writing, she had read *The Sound and the Fury,* and she was thrilled. It was a brief encounter in which she did not get out of the car. Too shy even to speak to Faulkner at the chance meeting, she wrote him a letter as soon as she returned to Memphis. She wanted to write, she explained, but her parents were very much against it. Could she see him to talk about it? Faulkner was taken by Joan, apparently from the first meeting, and invited her to write out her questions and mail them to him.[7] Back at Bard she did so, and his reply gave her a shock. "These are the wrong questions," he said. "A woman must ask these of a man while they are lying in bed together." Faulkner had continued the sentence with heavy-handed sexual suggestion. "Not the first time," he had written, "but after several, and when they are lying at peace or at least quiet or maybe on the edge of sleep so you'll have to wait, even to ask them." He went on to say that in his thoughts she was associated with the painter Bougereau. In *Elmer,* as we noted, he had evoked Bougereau's painting of a slightly resistant satyr being drawn away to a tryst by four nymphs young and nude.[8] He had torn up an earlier, even steamier draft of his letter to Joan for fear that it would be seen by someone else.

At fifty-two, Faulkner was running the pattern he had run since adolescence. He was attempting, clumsily, to seduce with words. As usual, he could hardly believe that the words would not work. What he seemed to want was a young girl, or someone who looked like a young girl, responding to his passion body and soul. Helen Baird had wanted no part of it. It is unclear what Estelle wanted, but in the end somebody in the Oldham family wanted marriage and a consequent heavy commitment. That too was a large part of what Meta Carpenter wanted. What Joan wanted, and wanted desperately, was a career as a writer, and obviously it was a goal that William Faulkner could help her achieve. Also she needed emotional support. She had long felt, as she said, unloved and misunderstood at home.[9] Her parents, on the other hand, were anxious about the future well-being of their daughter.

Faulkner came to Memphis to visit Joan during her Christmas vacation. They met in the morning at the bus station. He asked her to take him to the Peabody Hotel, his favorite in Memphis, to leave some typing with a stenographer—this from a person who always did his own typing. Joan didn't know what to do with the man. She put him in the family car and drove him around for hours in freezing weather. Finally, she parked on a bluff overlooking the river. When he put his hand on her arm, she drew back. Cold and confused, she brought him home to meet her mother.[10] Faulkner felt her need of his help, both as a writer and as a surrogate father. Several times, he had said that he did not want their meeting to be "shabby" or leave a "bad taste in the mouth." He wanted, of course, rose petals in the bed again.

Faulkner sensed the girl's vulnerability and moved quickly to make the most of it. Joan had written that she wanted to see him. "I want to see you, too," he answered on December 29. "One day about last October I discovered suddenly that I wanted to see you, very nearly came up East last fall with that purpose."[11] Amazing thoughts from a man who had merely glimpsed a young woman in a car, had no conversation, no voice from her at all, and thought her smallish, slightly plump, and twenty.[12]

Memphis had not worked as a trysting place, but Oxford and vicinity would not do either. By New Year's Eve, Bill had made fantastically elaborate arrangements for a rendezvous. He would meet her at the bus stop at Sardis, a village thirty miles to the west of Oxford. He would be there at 12:00 noon on Tuesday, January 3, and wait until she arrived from Memphis on a bus at either 12:00, 1:30, or 3:30. Then they would drive to Lake Sardis, take a skiff out to a houseboat he co-owned, and settle in. If she could not come, she should call him person to person. "If I sound funny over [the] telephone, you can sift out the trash," he said. "I'll understand your message no matter how I sound."[13] The rendezvous occurred, but, ironically, Estelle joined them, bringing a picnic lunch. Joan remembered her as terribly polite, thin, and frail. Joan's aunt, who knew the Faulkners, advised Joan to "stay away from those drunks."[14]

Joan returned to school, and Bill wrote that it was hard for him to write her, "because as soon as I look at the blank sheet of paper, I want to write you a love letter on it."[15] Within days, he was planning to come see her, fitting his visits in with her need to do schoolwork. She agreed and explained that her awkward behavior in Memphis was caused by her being sick. Bill said no matter: "I would be the sickness too, and the air you breathe, the clothes you wear, the bed you sleep in, all the thinking and feeling that goes on behind your eyes." He wanted three days alone with her "by the ocean all bleak and winter and cold, beyond a window." Soon, however, he had "another brainstorm." She would meet him at the train station in Washington and share his roomette in an overnight trip to New York.[16]

In the end, Faulkner trained to New York alone, and checked into the Algonquin, his favorite hotel. He took Joan to the Haas's apartment for a party in his honor. There was a tense moment on the way up in the elevator in which Bill, apparently, hoped for a firm embrace and a passionate kiss. However, the elevator rose without event, and at the party Joan was the perfect twenty-one-year-old girl, calling him Mr. Faulkner.[17] There was a lot of visiting between the two in the city and at Bard, and Faulkner set her to work as his apprentice on a stage play for *Requiem for a Nun.* Shortly, he had promoted her to being "collaborator" on his play.[18]

Joan could not surrender the relationship, and yet she was embarrassed too. She said that his expression of love, which became increasingly insistent, "doesn't make me too happy"; what she wanted was friendship.[19] In the spring she suggested a writer's colony where she and other young writers would sit at his feet. He thought Taos for two in New Mexico might suit better.[20] She wanted his kiss only on the cheek. He replied that "I can kiss my own nieces and daughters on the cheek."[21]

By the end of March, 1950, Bill was plotting to have Joan visit Rowan Oak during her spring holiday. He made up an elaborate gameplan they would follow to "ride roughshod," as he worded it, over Estelle. "I won't tell lies, but say no more than I have to." The centerpiece of the deception was their collaboration on the play.[22] Joan visited at Rowan Oak, but after her return to Bard Faulkner suspected that Estelle was intercepting Joan's letters to him.[23]

As Joan approached graduation in June, Bill activated his New York friends to find a job for her. That would be the instrument, the "club," she would need to free herself from family and pressures to marry in Memphis. "You can begin to see now how it is almost impossible for a middle class Southerner to be anything else but a middle class Southerner; how you have to fight your family for every inch of art you ever gain—at the very time when the whole tribe of them [are] hanging like so many buzzards over every penny you earn by it." He had suffered, he declared, "but I was a better man than they were."[24] Even so,

he was depressed and needy. "I'm lost now, Joan," he said, "I'm unhappy."[25]

It was a pitiful situation, and it got worse. Joan did not get a job in New York, but rather came home to Memphis. Estelle had "intercepted" a letter from Joan and was furious. "I had to stall on the phone the other night because she put in that call," Bill explained to Joan in mid-July. "I didn't even know it until the phone rang and she refused to answer it, told me to; I had no idea anyone had put in a call. I only learned after that she had called before, talked to you and your mother." He planned to see Joan in a few days. "When I come up, I probably won't let her know I have gone anywhere," he said, "I will just disappear for the day." Joan should write him setting a date for his visit to Memphis. "Address Holston, Gen. Del."[26]

Bill's worst fear was soon realized. Estelle called Joan and arranged a meeting at the Black Cat Restaurant in the Peabody. At first the conversation was cordial, then Estelle asked her accusingly if she wanted to marry her husband. Astonished, Joan simply said "No."[27] Back in Oxford, Estelle telephoned Joan's parents to complain and began to intercept Bill's mail. On one occasion he took the phone apart to prevent Estelle's calling the Williams's house in Memphis, and he attempted to achieve privacy by having Joan mail letters to him at the general delivery window in the post office at specific times. Incredibly, at one point Bill allegedly instructed Joan to address her letters to "Quentin Compson," but soon he settled on the less conspicuous name "Holston."

More incredibly, in early August he was planning to have Joan down to Rowan Oak for a visit, ostensibly to work on the play. If Estelle was caught "at the right time, things will be pleasant if not too prolonged." Otherwise, it would be merely "unpleasant, disgusting, like having to watch an ill-behaved child."[28] Joan's mother also entered the fray. She told Bill "in so many words," he reported to Joan, "calm enough, no hesitation, that she did not believe you could write a play."[29]

In the fall, Joan took a job in Memphis, a dull one.[30] Bill continued attempts to entice her down for a night at Rowan Oak, or for a sail (even to bring young friends from Memphis with her if she liked), or to rendezvous with him in Jackson.[31] Nothing worked and the play, of course, did not get written. They seldom met, and the meetings were marked by long periods of silence.[32] He burned Joan's letters after reading them, and his to her often went very romantic, recalling moments together the previous winter. "We need 2nd Ave., a Berkshire hill, something like that—snow, a little boot of a bug trying to go somewhere in the snow, God knows where or why, snow in your hair and not making any noise at all like your face, lips, so that even the snow smells like a young girl, woman. You fell down and then I fell down, remember? And the cold windy street and Haas's elevator, and how scared you were, and that evening you spent acting like an extremely well-bred, well-behaved child? Hello, Joan, Miss Williams, sweet love. I didn't even have a chance to tell you what a pretty girl-white white—slip, isn't that it?—you had on that day."[33] And again, "every letter from you is a violet and everytime I think of you is one, the color of your eyes, your hair, the shape of your mouth, the shape (imagined) of your body under your clothes, girl woman of course but not screaming at you as most are . . ."[34]

A week later, on Friday, November 10, the telephone at Rowan Oak rang again. It was the Nobel Prize. Faulkner had been hearing rumors for years about his candidacy.[35] Now it came at a time when his work often faltered, his domestic life was a wreck, and he had endured a year of frustration in his love affair with Joan. She wired him congratulations on Saturday, and two letters from her only reached him on Thursday. "I love you too," he replied.[36] He left for the annual hunt the next day, began to drink heavily, became ill, and had to be brought home.

Recovering a week later, he wrote to Joan. "All this fuss and hurrah can't mustnt matter to us," he insisted. "Have wanted to call you, see you, but your name came up once and all the old stink started again." He was leaving for Stockholm. "I don't know when I will see you, but you are the one I never stopped thinking about. You are the girl's body I lie in bed beside before I go to sleep. I know every sweet red hair and sweet curve of it." On Wednesday, December 6, Bill and Jill left for Stockholm.[37]

Saturday evening, he and Jill were at a dinner in Stockholm given in his honor by his Swedish publisher. The house was beautifully situated, overlooking the passage between the sea and the harbor at Stockholm. There he met Else Jonsson, a woman who would become, briefly, his lover. Else's husband had died recently. He had been a journalist in New York between 1942 and 1946 and had come to Oxford to see the American writer he so much admired. Probably, it was he who did most in Sweden to advance Faulkner's candidacy for the Nobel Prize. Else was "tall, statuesque, full-faced [and] vivacious—a beauty," Joseph Blotner wrote when he met her in 1964. She had been in her mid-thirties when she first met Faulkner and the mother of a four-year-old girl, Helen.[38]

Else arrived at the party a bit late and found Faulkner standing alone among the shy Swedish guests. "Like a second hostess I went directly to him," she later recalled. She felt that she knew Faulkner through her husband, and that he knew her. He said something like, "It must have been difficult for you"—as if he had heard of her recent loss. Then he said, "I have known you all my life." Else nodded, feeling it was true.

They sat down to dinner. The host made a toast to Else's husband, and Faulkner then seemed to realize fully who she was. At the table with a dozen or so guests, they talked about oyster fishing, and Faulkner told about doing so on the Gulf shores. One of the ladies asked eagerly if he had ever found a pearl in an oyster. "No," he said, "but there will always be a pearl waiting for me."[39] Else remembered that "after dinner I went and sat down next to Bill on the sofa as naturally as if we had been friends for life."[40]

On Sunday, Else was in the audience when the prize was awarded. Faulkner's speech was inaudible, she said. Even so, "when receiving the prize from the king, he was the most elegant of them all, very graceful indeed, almost pirouetting while making several elegant bows." That evening after the grand dinner in the Town Hall, she "found Bill looking for me." He was "trotting up and down in the gallery where dinner was served." He needed assurance from her, she thought; anxiously he asked whether he had done all right.[41]

On the next day, they had lunch. She suggested that Jill join them, but Faulkner said no. Afterward they walked through the cold gray winter day to Else's apartment. Shortly, Else's little daughter Helen came in, delighted to find her mother at home early, "greeting us in a shrill voice (or so it seemed to Bill)." Else concluded that they had "tried breathlessly to keep up to our life-long friendship, but the time was heartbreakingly short."[42]

Bill and Jill flew from Stockholm to Paris, then home. In February, 1951, Faulkner went to Hollywood for seven weeks of work with Howard Hawks. He attempted to get Joan Williams to go with him, telling her that she was not writing as well as she liked because she was frozen up inside and he wanted to cure her—presumably by the warmth of his lovemaking. "I don't think you are a frigid woman," he wrote. Joan declined his offer. Meanwhile, Faulkner had also written to Meta of his coming. He called her from the Los Angeles airport, and she joined him in his room at the Beverly-Carlton. They made love, and while she dressed to leave, he inscribed a copy of his latest book for her: "This is for my beloved," he wrote.[43] Rather clearly, Faulkner was in dire need of feminine attention, starving again and desperate. Also he had been nearly broke. Meta was with him almost every night and every weekend. When she took him to the airport seven weeks after his arrival, he was $14,000 richer, and he would never see Meta again.

Amazingly, Faulkner was also attempting simultaneously to develop an affair with Else Jonsson. Acting secretly to deceive his family, he induced Random House to make a display of sponsoring a trip to France so that he could do research for *A Fable*. He imposed on Saxe Commins, his Random House editor and close friend, to book a flight for him for April 15, 1951. In addition, Saxe was instructed to reserve one room in the Leutetia Hotel and another in a more obscure hotel nearby. Finally, he asked Saxe to send him a letter concerning the trip "which I can use at home here to make the business look businesslike." His European visit was brief. Else did join him in Paris, but he would be home again before May.[44]

In America, Faulkner continued to pursue Joan Williams. Joan had left

Memphis and was seeking to make her way as a writer in New York. In June Faulkner gave the keynote address—in four and one-half minutes—to Jill's graduating class in Oxford, and he also finished writing the book *Requiem for a Nun.* Then he turned to the failing business of attempting to convert the book into a play. That effort had been the cover for his early attempt at romance with Joan; now it brought him closer to the beautiful actress Ruth Ford.

After graduating from the University of Mississippi, Ruth became an actress in both Hollywood and New York. In New York, Bill often visited her apartment. Ruth's husband, actor Zachary Scott, declared that Ruth and Bill were "sympatico." By way of explanation he said that the three of them were perfectly content to sit in silence together for thirty minutes. Once he came home to find Ruth sitting on the sofa doing something and Bill was sitting there too.

"What are you doing, Bill," he asked.

"I'm just sitting here loving Ruth," Bill replied.[45]

It developed that Faulkner had no talent for writing plays, and the script that emerged was the work of several people and of dubious value. He had promised the part of Temple Drake exclusively, and apparently perpetually, to Ruth Ford. It was, he thought, "her last—best—chance to make tops as an actress."[46] When the play had an invitation to run in Paris during the spring if someone put up $15,000, Faulkner seriously considered the possibility, and finally did offer $2,000 in support of the unlikely project. That venture failed, but Bill traveled to France in May, 1952, anyway and was joined again by Else Jonsson. Faulkner was scheduled to participate in an international writers' congress in Paris. However, as his various commitments to appear came due, he began to drink. He was also in pain from injuries to his spine incurred over the years. Bill was hospitalized and Else returned to Sweden. He recovered sufficiently to fly to England to visit friends. In a London hotel his back pain was so severe that he almost drowned in the bathtub. Desperate, he called Else and flew to Oslo, where they met. They stayed in a hotel and Else arranged for treatments by a "creepy," as she said, but highly recommended masseur. The therapy worked.

A decade later, Joseph Blotner talked with Else about the Oslo rendezvous and her relationship with Bill. Bill was very honest with her, she said, he never asked her to wait for him—presumably for divorce and marriage. "It was my own decision," she declared, "to take this unhappy genius, this former household god, as a lover." Bill was contented with the arrangement, only he asked that she "some day tell Helen about us."[47] Helen, Else's daughter, was five or six years old at the time.

Back home Faulkner found no such happiness in his involvement with Joan Williams. In June, 1952, he arranged to sell for $500 a story that they had done together, but he gave her all the money and all the credit.[48] Between them, apparently, there still was no physical consummation.

In the summer of 1952, as he approached age fifty-five, Faulkner was reaching a crisis. "For the first time in my life," he wrote Saxe Commins, "I am completely bored, fed up." He was not working. "I think now I may, to save my soul, something of peace, contentment, save the work at least, quit the whole thing, give it all to them, leave and be done with it." He felt he was "really sick," and might need to get away, "almost vanish," to get well and "get to work again." He felt that he still wanted "what I have always wanted: to be free; probably until now I have still believed that somehow, in some way, someday I would be free again; now at last I have begun to realize that perhaps I will not." Either he must act "or—in spirit—die." He was not quite there yet, but he might have to act soon and suffer the "scorn and opprobrium" involved because "I have already sacrificed too much . . . to try to be a good artist, to boggle at a little more in order to still try to be one."[49]

William Faulkner was in distress. There was his bad back and recurrent physical pain, and there was Joan. Joan was home in Memphis that summer. The messy business of meeting in Memphis and dodging about was simply too demeaning. An alternative arrangement proved no better. One day Joan took a bus to a neighboring Mississippi town, Holly Springs, and Faulkner drove up from Oxford. They found a wooded area near a lake where they could be alone, but again she refused intimacy. Returning to Oxford, Bill had a flat tire, and the next day his back still hurt from the bending and lifting necessary to change it. But the real pain, he wrote to Joan, was "the unhappiness from yesterday, very unhappy, but after all they are your mouth and your bottom and yours the right to say no about them and anyone that don't like it should better go back where he come from and maybe stay there."[50] It was the Faulkner crudity again, the recurrent me-first lack of sensitivity. But he did reach the right conclusion.

Almost twenty years later, in 1971, Joan published her second novel, *The Wintering*. It was a virtually undisguised account of her involvement with Faulkner. In one episode, probably derived from that meeting in 1952, the fictional couple—Amy Howard and Jeff Almoner—met on a hot summer day in a town halfway between their homes—probably Holly Springs. She had taken the bus from Delton (Memphis), wearing sunglasses. He had driven up from his small Mississippi town, having told his wife he was going fishing. They drove about, got lost, finally found a lake, picnicked out of a basket he had brought, and drank beer. He wanted to make love, she could not. Indeed, she could hardly bear his touch, and could not bear at all the image of being caught in the woods making love, "an old man and a young girl." They parted, frustrated and confused.[51]

Briefly, sometime that summer—three years after their first meeting—they finally became lovers. It was an abortive affair from which Joan emerged frightened and Faulkner not satisfied. He wrote her four letters in one day and several in the next few days. Seemingly, he had pushed too hard. Distressed, he used lines used before. Between grief and nothing, he said, he would take grief. He needed some one to write for.[52] And so on. Vintage Faulkner. Within weeks, he was writing Meta and saying how much he would like two weeks with her, lying on the beach with the sun on his back.[53]

Health

In August, 1952, Estelle had to be hospitalized in Memphis to end an alcoholic episode. In the spring of that same year, even as Faulkner was thinking of investing $15,000 in the Paris production of *Requiem for a Nun,* he had taken steps to see that Estelle got no funds out of Random House while he made his European trip. She was getting to know Saxe Commins and his wife Dorothy well, and Bill feared that she would use that friendship to tap his royalty flow. "In ten minutes, she can have you believing that black is white," he warned Saxe. "Of course, in eleven minutes you know better, but sometimes its too late then. So don't ever send her any money, no matter what tale she tells you, no matter how plausible." Saxe should either say such drafts were not allowed, or simply show her Bill's letter.[54]

In the summer of 1952, Faulkner was worrying about money again, and he resented bitterly, as he said, "seeing what remains of life going to support parasites who do not even have the grace to be sycophants."[55] He contemplated flight to Mexico, an alternative already realized by his old friend Bill Spratling.[56] In October, his drinking reached the point where a desperate Estelle persuaded Saxe Commins to come to Rowan Oak to help nurse him.

Saxe was deeply distressed as he witnessed firsthand Faulkner's tragedy.[57] "I found Bill completely deteriorated in mind and body," he wrote to his wife at home. "He mumbles incoherently and is totally incapable of controlling his bodily functions. He pleads piteously for beer all the time and mumbles deliriously." Saxe was appalled. "This is more than a case of acute alcoholism," he concluded. "It is a complete disintegration of a man." Rowan Oak, as Saxe saw it, was a parallel case. "It is a rambling Southern mansion, deteriorated like its owner, built in 1838 and not much improved since." He contrasted the mansion with the Commins's neat, small house in Princeton. "The rooms are bare and what they do contain is rickety, tasteless, ordinary."[58] Finally, Faulkner suffered a convulsive seizure and had to be hospitalized in Memphis.

In Memphis doctors discovered that five vertebrae in Faulkner's lower back had been fractured, perhaps in a tumble down the stairs in 1946 during one of his drinking spells, perhaps in a fall from a horse during the previous spring. By then horses had replaced flying as his passion, perhaps in significant measure because it was an avocation that he could share with Jill.[59] But also he had to give up flying after an incident in which he and his nephew Jimmy were approaching the Oxford airport for a landing with Bill at the controls. Jimmy, a veteran Marine pilot, seeing that they were coming in short and about to crash into a grove of trees, took over and landed safely. Bill had been drinking. Before Faulkner left the hospital, he suffered another seizure, and after he came home in late October he fell down the stairs yet again.

Faulkner, now sober, had hardly settled in at Rowan Oak before Estelle began to drink heavily. She had read Joan Williams's letters to Bill while he was "hors de combat," he told Saxe. Divorce might have helped, but Bill felt he could not do that to Jill. Estelle, on her side, felt that "Estelle Faulkner, without Bill & Jill *would* be a total nonentity."[60]

In the fall, Joan returned to New York to take a job with *Look* magazine, and Bill, having tasted love in the woods, kept up a barrage of letters—insistent, pleading, intimate. In November, 1952, he was desperate for a change. He went north to Princeton where he first visited Saxe and then moved into the elegant Princeton Inn to work. Joan visited him from time to time. Astonishingly, perhaps desperately, he directed Saxe to deliver to Joan, as her property, the manuscript for *The Sound and the Fury* at any time she wanted it.[61] Again they made love and again bad feelings resulted. Faulkner began to drink heavily and ended in the hospital. Out again, he made at least several visits to a psychiatrist Joan herself had seen. Probably this physician gave him a series of electroshock treatments, with little or no effect. Faulkner only remembered being shocked by the bill and protesting it.[62]

Back in Oxford for Christmas he yearned to be with Joan again, "to talk fantasy and nonsense and good sense and truth to a beloved face, eyes, mouth, bitten-off finger-ends, to drink and eat with equals, to believe in the same things."[63] And yet, the relationship was fraught with dangers—which he caught marvelously in a dream as the new year began:

> I dreamed about us last night. It seems I had an apartment in Princeton, we had spent the weekend and we were giving a party Sunday afternoon, you were hostess and suddenly we decided you had to have a new dress, then we were in New York, trying to buy the dress in time to get back for the party; the dress was something between gold and rust-color, it shimmered; I snapped you up into it in the shop and then we were running, hurrying back to Penn station not to miss the party, you holding the skirt of the dress up like an apron with three or four bottles of champagne and tins of pate and caviar in it, and a cop trotting along with us saying "If she dont put her dress down I'll have to arrest you" and me saying we'll have to get to Princeton because they're going to give you the Nobel prize this afternoon. The cop said, "for what?" and I said "For her novel. Here it is. I'm trying to finish it and think of a title for it." Then Lois, the Frenchman from the Princeton Inn, ran up and took the manuscript and said, "I'll finish it. You help Miss Williams." So I gave him the manuscript and then you and I were in a bar, you looking all flushed and pink and tender and shimmering and beautiful and telling me something, a blue streak, and I said "We must get on to Princeton" and you said "Of course we must. But I can make the bell stop ringing. If we come in like this, they will all know." And I said "Know what?" only it had begun to fade, your face, fad-

> ing, still smiling a little, and me trying to hold on to the dream, knowing by then it was a dream, still saying No no no, wait, wait and you saying Yes bill yes bill I know I know it's all right it's all right and I said Joan Joan not goodbye and you said It's all right, Bill. I know, I know. Not goodbye.[64]

In February, 1953, it was discovered that Faulkner had had spells of complete forgetting, and he had sessions with another New York psychiatrist. This man began by probing Billy's feelings about his mother, only to meet a stony silence. The psychiatrist concluded that Faulkner had not had enough love from his mother. He was always looking for affection. He had a capacity for making women feel sorry for him, and he was not reluctant to use it for his needs, the doctor said. The affair with Joan was necessary to him, she was dependent on him, in part a daughter. Still, Faulkner had "a very strong streak of conventional morality," and he would not "divorce because of what he owed his wife too." The psychiatrist found Faulkner anxious to talk about his personal problems. He felt that he had an intense emotional responsiveness. "Yet this responsiveness never overflowed into facial expression." The "moustache helped to conceal emotions," he thought. Alcohol was a "tranquilizer," he concluded.[65] Several people close to Faulkner agreed with his stepson Malcolm who said, simply, that when Faulkner was pushed he hit the bottle.[66]

Faulkner was again outraged at the bill, $450 for nine sessions, of which Faulkner only remembered three, and two of those, he insisted, were social calls made at the physician's invitation. During this phase of his life, Faulkner would engage in a kind of steady guerilla warfare against the medical profession, not so much against the men as against their fees, which he considered vastly excessive.

Meanwhile, he was keeping Else Jonsson apprised of his situation. In the spring of 1952 during his European trip, she and he both saw, he wrote, that "my nature had changed."[67] Once in Paris and twice since he returned he had awakened in a hospital with no idea how he got there. Faulkner thought that it had all begun with a skull injury from a fall off a horse. An examination, however, revealed that "there is no skull injury." According to the doctor the tests showed that a lobe or part of his brain was "hypersensitive to intoxication."

"Alcohol?" Faulkner asked.

"Alcohol is one of them," the physician replied. Other catalysts were "worry, unhappiness, any form of mental unease." Subtly, the doctor suggested that he stop drinking for several months and run the tests again. "He said that my brain is still normal, but it is near the borderline of abnormality. Which I knew myself; this behavior is not like me."[68] But, of course, it was like him—and had been for nearly twenty years; the difference was that William Faulkner was getting older and his body was losing some of its remarkable resiliency.

Very soon Faulkner was forced to pay attention to his wife and daughter. In the spring of 1953, Estelle's condition grew critical. Her sight became blurred. Later in the year she had an auto accident that she failed to report, and Phil Stone had to intervene to save Estelle's driver's license from revocation.[69]

Faulkner had taken an apartment in Princeton in February, 1953, in order to work and be close to Joan, but had to rush home in April because Estelle was taken to the hospital hemorrhaging internally. "We knew she was sick," Phil Stone wrote, "but we didn't pay any attention to it because we took it for granted that she was probably getting off a drunk." Estelle recovered rapidly and was able, in June, to take a pleasant trip to Massachusetts to see Jill graduate from college at the top of her class. Again, Faulkner gave the commencement address at Jill's graduation.[70]

All during 1953, Bill's relations with Joan were not working. She was depressed; he was depressed, drinking, and trying to work. In the summer he proposed that they go to Paris, Mexico, or even New England and work. He had the engine of his car overhauled and two tires recapped in preparation for their trip. Rumor had it that Joan was coming south for a prolonged visit. Estelle and Jill felt keen embarrassment and planned to take evasive action in order to be where Bill and Joan were not. They had hoped that Bill would "take off" so that they would be spared his unhappy presence.[71] Soon mother and daughter, themselves, fled to Mexico where Jill went to school for a time in Mexico City. Faulkner stayed home alone, still drinking, and writing. At last, his "big book," *A Fable,* was moving.[72]

During this time, Ben Wasson, now living in Greenville, received a surprise visit from his old-time friend. Bill was well advanced in the usual drinking cycle. Bern Keating and his wife Franke, a young Greenville couple, kept Faulkner in their house overnight. During the night, Faulkner fell, cut his head, and bled profusely. The next day they helped Ben bring him back to Rowan Oak. Faulkner sobered up for dinner, but then began drinking heavily. They left the following day, but Ben and Franke, worried about Bill, came back. They found him comatose on the couch, fully dressed and in a bad state of neglect. Two empty bottles sat on the floor nearby. Franke was wild at the servants who lived in the yard and were supposed to take care of him. "I could just kill them," she raged. "I could just shoot every one of them." Instead she went out to the cabin and told them off. Malcolm Franklin arrived, and Ben and Franke went home to Greenville.

Anxious, Ben returned to Rowan Oak once again. This time he found that Faulkner had rolled off the couch onto the floor, and was lying there, still unwashed, physically wasted. While he was attempting to clean Bill, the phone rang. He explained to the caller, a young woman, that Mr. Faulkner couldn't come to the phone.

"Oh," she said. "Just tell him Joan telephoned."

Bill had awakened. "Who was it?" he asked.

"She said to tell you Joan called. That was all."

"God. Godamighty," Faulkner exclaimed and dropped off to sleep. Malcolm appeared then, "kind, gentle Malcolm," as Ben Wasson said.[73] On this occasion the cycle ended in a Memphis hospital. Faulkner came home, but soon began drinking again and finished in Wright's sanatorium in Byhalia. Later he explained to Malcolm that his writing had run dry, "which may have been partly responsible for my—and your—trouble." He sent love to "Mac" and his wife Gloria. "I think often of Ria's kindness and good sense," he concluded, signing himself as "Pappy."[74]

In October, Faulkner recovered sufficiently to drive to New York with Joan, but he was still so ill that she had to do some of the driving. In New York their affair entered its final dissolution. Already, in September, she had begun to see Ezra Bowen, the son of writer Catherine Drinker Bowen, and the young man she would marry. She suggested that physical differences between Bill and herself because of age made their connection impossible. Joan had raised that idea early and often in their relationship, and it seemed to be one that Faulkner found deeply disturbing.[75] This was almost the opposite of the message that he received from Meta, and it must have given the parsimonious Faulkner some satisfaction just then to send Meta $150 in answer to her plea for a loan. She was out of a job and broke. Faulkner was still not willing to end the affair with Joan, and turned philosophic in a letter to her telling her how, in having the affair, she had done something "fine and brave and generous." Then, a few days later he turned surly and sour. "You take too much, and are willing to give too little," he scolded, and immediately denied the accusation that he was peeved because she would not sleep with him every time they were together. "People have attributes like animals," he continued, "you are a mixture of cat and mule and possum—the cat's secretiveness and self-centeredness, the mule's stubbornness to get what it wants no matter who or what suffers, the possum's nature of playing dead—running into sleep or its pretense—whenever it is faced with a situation which it thinks it is not going to like." Joan appropriated Faulkner's animal analogies for her novel, *The Wintering*. However, in the story she made the girl secretive like a cat, and the man stubborn like a mule. "Wasn't I persistent?" Almoner asked and smiled.[76] Faulkner was mad at Joan because she would not be cornered. Ironically, others might have said of him precisely what he said of Joan.

Apparently, Joan, not yet twenty-three, invited him to drop by her apartment for a coffee and an amicable ending. Bill was furious. "I won't stop in," he declared. "I think that two people drawn together as we were and held together for four years by whatever it was we had, knew—love, sympathy, understanding, trust, belief—deserve a better period than a cup of coffee—not to end like two high school sweethearts breaking up over a coca-cola in a corner drugstore."[77] Seemingly, a man in his fifties who pursues a girl in her teens ought not to be greatly surprised at the suggestion of such an ending. Joan was obviously bothered by Faulkner's age, and inevitably she had been attracted to a succession of younger men. Bill retaliated finally with an assault on her young friends. "These people you like and live among don't want the responsibility of creating," he charged. They were sophomoric and parasitic. "They go through the motions of art—talking about what they are going to do over drinks, even defacing paper and canvas when necessary, in order to escape the responsibility of living."[78]

Faulkner faced an end of his affair with Joan Williams in November, 1953. In the same month, he came to the end of a much older affair, the writing of *A Fable*. He was free, and his friend Howard Hawks again appeared to fill his time and give him money.[79] Hawks had persuaded Jack Warner to let him do a film to be called "Land of the Pharaohs" with Elizabeth Taylor as his star. Faulkner was to be one of the writers and would receive not only a salary but a share in the earnings. The only artistry in the project was the highly saleable filmmaking talent that Hawks brought. Elizabeth Taylor and William Faulkner were there because they were famous. Before he left for Europe where they would begin to put the film together, Faulkner went to dinner at the Commins's in Princeton. Albert Einstein was there, but found himself unable to engage Faulkner in conversation.

On Monday evening, November 30, Random House editor Bob Linscott and his future wife Elizabeth took Bill to the airport to catch his Paris flight. Elizabeth later recalled that he didn't want to leave the girl in whom he was then interested. "He expected her to meet him that night for a farewell," she remembered. "We all waited and waited for her, but the time came for his plane and she did not call or come. And Bill left."[80]

Faulkner had written his mother about the European trip, declaring that he didn't want to go, but owed it to Hawks and he would get $15,000 besides. As usual, the letter began "Dear Moms" and ended "Billy." Just before the flight he wrote again: "On the way today. Will write you. I love you."[81]

Hawks and Harry Kurnitz, the veteran writer whom Hawks had hired to back Faulkner up, met Faulkner's plane in Paris. Apparently, he wasn't on it. Later he appeared at their hotel room door between two gendarmes. He was far into the drinking cycle again, and he would repeat the cycle several times before he came home in mid-April. He was in no condition, of course, to work on the film. In one draft of the script, he had the high priest grab the pharaoh's arm whereupon that haughty potentate ordered, "Leave go of my arm."[82] Kurnitz greatly admired Faulkner's work, and gracefully stepped into the breach even though Faulkner got screen credit.

There was a lot of moving around the glamour spots of Europe before Hawks and Faulkner went to Egypt for the actual filming. In Stresa, on Lake Maggiore in northern Italy, the Hawks party stayed in a "palace" owned by a rich Egyptian. They shared St. Moritz, the wintering place of the elite in Switzerland, with King Farouk of Egypt, Gregory Peck, and a host of other famous people. "I don't like it," Billy wrote Maud. "I love you all and miss you all. Want very bad to see Missy and little Jimmy and Dean and Vicki and all my children."[83] In Stresa, he began, in his usually overly elaborate fashion, to arrange a rendezvous with Else Jonsson. He wrote to a mutual friend in Paris,

Monique Salomon, "I write Else tonight, asking her to write me a letter care of you." He wanted Monique to act as a communications agent so that "we will know as soon as possible when we can meet." Finally, however, Bill simply flew to Stockholm and spent the New Year season with Else. "I remember we went to a party on New Year's Eve," Else recalled, "and that he left in a day or two—the last time I met him."[84]

Indeed, already Faulkner had found a new love. At a Christmas Eve party in St. Moritz, he had met Jean Babette Stein, the attractive, fine-featured, dark-haired daughter of the founder of the Music Corporation of America. She was nineteen, shy, and excited at meeting the Nobel Prize–winning author. He responded immediately, went with her to a midnight mass and walked her to her hotel.[85] The love cycle had begun again and Faulkner invested heavily.

After Stockholm, Faulkner had visited for a while at the country estate of his English publisher. Then he returned to St. Moritz to work.[86] In mid-January, Bill flew to Paris to see Jean again.[87] She was studying at the Sorbonne and staying at her Uncle David's luxurious apartment near the Etoile.[88] Then he flew to Rome where Hawks was casting.[89] He settled in at the Albergo Palazzo & Ambasciatori where everything that was superbly fashionable was in walking distance on the Via Veneto. Soon Jean came down for a visit.

In mid-February, 1954, the company relocated in Egypt. Hawks allowed Faulkner to transit by way of Paris.[90] In Egypt when Hawks and Kurnitz met Faulkner's arriving flight, so too did an ambulance. Their head writer had collapsed on the plane, and barely did better on the ground during the next several weeks.[91] In Cairo, Faulkner decided that Jean had followed him about Europe, and he expected her to appear in Egypt any day. When Saxe wrote him about Joan Williams's marriage to Ezra Bowen, Faulkner replied flatly that she had already told him. If she were happy, he declared without modesty, "I am the best friend Bowen ever had." Indeed, he had concluded that his proper relation to Joan was that of father to daughter. Then he rushed on to tell Saxe about Jean. No more talk of "grief or nothing." This time he had evaded both horns of the dilemma. Because there was Jean, there would be no grief. "She has none of the emotional conventional confusion which poor Joan had. This one is so uninhibited that she frightens me a little," he crowed. "She is charming, delightful, completely transparent, completely trustful," he declared. "I will not hurt her for any price. She doesn't want anything of me—only to love me, be in love."[92] Meanwhile, Faulkner's daughter was also in love. Estelle was ecstatic.

Estelle

At this point, Estelle, it seems, was simply trying to survive with as much grace and dignity as possible. She thought that Bill still loved her—even though he was now making explicit statements to the contrary—and seemed somehow to have faith in that love. Most of all, apparently, she was trying to protect Jill. In achieving all three goals, she had to deal with Bill Faulkner and his amorous ambitions elsewhere. In that realm her powers were limited but palpable. He dreaded both her verbal assaults and earnest pleas, and he built elaborate and clumsy structures to mask his would-be red-hot affairs. Estelle, in part at least, to gain his attention and to insist upon his honoring the marital bond, ran up bills, drank excessively, and finally even managed to enter the hospital hemorrhaging in an alarming way. In April, 1953, the latter event had brought him home post haste from his Princeton apartment and Joan. He had joined Jill first in a vigil at the hospital and then in nursing Estelle at Rowan Oak.[93] He'd done his duty as a husband, but it had ruined his spring.

With Jill permanently home from college in June, Estelle seemed gradually to gain strength. They hoped that Bill, "Pappy" as they often called him, would simply go away somewhere with Joan. In the fall of 1953, mother and daughter went to Mexico. When they returned, Faulkner flew off to Europe and Egypt with Howard Hawks. Back home in Oxford, Jill worked on the *Oxford Eagle* and took courses at the university.[94] Estelle contemplated divorce.

Estelle's information on her husband's love life in the spring of 1954 was sadly dated. She understood that Bill had secured a job for Joan working abroad on Hawks's new film project. She had not yet even heard the name Jean Stein. Poor Saxe Commins, who had suffered a heart attack, knew all because both Bill and Estelle insisted on telling him everything. In February, he had to reject as gently as he could Estelle's plea that he pay out of Faulkner's funds a two-year-old bill at Levy's Department Store in Memphis.[95] Next, Estelle raised the idea of divorce as a serious possibility and earnestly sought his advice. For four years, she said, Bill had been home but little and much of that time was marred by drunkenness. Then, more recently, he had told Jill about Joan. "Jill (she will tell you this very frankly) and I are happier and *more at ease* when Bill is away—Since his unfortunate disclosure to Jill about his current affair—she hasn't felt too secure around him—As for me—I'd do anything for peace—and my own sense of *doing the right thing*—"[96]

Soon she gave Saxe her version of the affair with Joan. At Easter, 1950, Bill had told Jill and Estelle that Joan would be collaborating with him on the *Requiem* play. He visited her at Bard and in Memphis, and she visited Rowan Oak once. Eventually, "we found how deeply involved they were—Billy is completely enamored, and Joan professes her love in no uncertain terms—*Bill had Malcolm open and read her letters to him*—and Mac, shocked, gave them to me." After Jill knew about Joan, Faulkner "chided Jill for not having ambitions like Joan, and several other comparisons that aren't worth mentioning—." Jill, Estelle thought, would survive emotionally in spite of it all. "Jill worshipped him—still does," and would manage because "she was young and resilient."

Actually Bill's was the desperate case, she said, and out of their love for each other she could contemplate divorce for his good.[97] Within days, Estelle was also sympathetic to Joan's feelings, and within a few days more Jill showed her an announcement of Joan's wedding. Estelle was glad "the child had found a congenial, nice man to love and marry." Wisely, she recognized that Jill, Bill, and she were still in a "sad state."[98] Within weeks, Jill was ready to announce her own engagement, and Estelle was barely able to delay Jill's announcement of that event until she could secure her father's consent.[99] That came when Bill, sick with an ulcerated stomach, arrived home from Europe.[100] Jill would marry in August, and Estelle would enter a final and relatively happy phase in her existence.

Jill

Jill Faulkner had not had an easy life. She loved each of her parents dearly and faithfully did her duty toward them, but neither could be depended upon as a ready reservoir of love and protection. Physically and emotionally, it seemed that her mother was barely surviving. Her father was often away, and when he was home, he was often drinking or working. There were good times, even great times, of course, and Faulkner sometimes simply melted at the thought of his only child. "Jill is 9 tomorrow," he wrote to a family friend in 1942 and raised the fond image of his daughter in his mind as "fat and fair and full of greens." But recurrently came the disappointment, and recurrently the falling sky and feelings of desertion and aloneness.[101]

Jill, of course, carried it all in her deepest memories. She recalled being in California when she was four. She remembered being at the beach in her red bathing suit and swimming with her father. There were times, perhaps, when Meta was also there. The house in Santa Monica she remembered as big and gloomy, walls of heavy fieldstone, brownish grey. Returning to Rowan Oak, she always had her pony or horse, and other animals about. One of her earliest memories is of being pulled from beneath a horse near the barn at Rowan Oak.[102] Uncle Ned was a "squealer," she said. He would tell on her in a sanctimonious way, and called her "Miss Baby Doll," which she detested. During the war years, as a preadolescent, she spent alternate Saturday nights with her grandmothers. Lida would have her practicing piano in the icy music room, teeth chattering as she struggled not to strike a false note and offend the listening ear. Major Oldham's room was the scene for hot oatmeal on Sunday mornings. Sometimes she would see him strolling down the street in a white suit, sporting a cane. She thought herself much like Miss Maud, who told folks what they wanted to hear and did exactly what she liked.[103]

Bill Faulkner was an anomaly in Oxford, and his difference brought difficulties to his daughter. All through grammar school she could not explain his occupation. "What does your father do?" she was asked. "Nothing," she replied.[104] In the fourth or fifth grade she was helping another girl fill out a form all students were asked to complete. The girl's father was an undertaker, but she wanted to write "mortician." They found, however, that they couldn't spell the word, and both had to leave the space for father's occupation blank.[105]

Most devastating, of course, was the drinking and the fighting. Even as a child, Jill learned well the phases of the drinking cycle. Once, when she was twelve, she saw it coming and begged him to stop. "Think of me," she pled. "Nobody remembers Shakespeare's children," he replied and she never forgot that hurt so cuttingly inflicted by her father.[106] Sometimes both parents would be drinking at the same time and collapsed in their separate beds.[107] Often when both parents were drunk, the servants fled, leaving her alone with them. There seemed to her no one to go to, and relatives and friends usually avoided Rowan Oak on such occasions. Indeed, Sallie Murry said that "you would never know if you went down there what kind of fix things would be in." Also, Jill did not want people to know they were drinking again, so would not ask for help. There were times, however, when she was glad they drank a lot because the arguing would stop. "They were just at each other," she said.[108] As an adolescent, Jill "ached for mediocrity"—and presumably sobriety—in her father, but he insisted that she was lucky to be his daughter. Occasionally, Malcolm, ten years older than Jill, would come and help, and sometimes the servants would stay. Worst of all, however, Jill would occasionally have her teenage friends in for a visit only to be dismayed by the sight of one or both parents falling over the edge.[109] Everybody in the family came to know very well the road to the sanatorium in Byhalia.

Jill also had to cope with the philandering. She had known Meta since she was three years old, and could not have been unaware of the fights between her parents that sprang from that source. In all of this, understandably, she was especially sympathetic with her mother. For Estelle, life at Rowan Oak was dull. Worse, it was she who had to meet the town and cope with the unpaid bills and the rumors that flew of Billy's infidelity. Jill said that Estelle's mother, Lida, had told Estelle that because she wasn't pretty, she had to be charming. She had cultivated that grace, but her charm had lost its effect on William Faulkner. "Given his independent personality," Jill concluded, "he shouldn't have burdened himself with a family."[110]

At last, Jill found a significant liberation. In September, 1951, she entered Pine Manor Junior College in Wellesley, Massachusetts. Frequently, perhaps as often as twice a month, Jill had had the same dream. Within twenty-four hours her legs were going to give out or be cut off. She would never walk again. Both parents were standing there looking over her. She had to decide with which parent she would spend the rest of her life. Then she realized that really neither of them cared about her. Many years later, she recalled that there were times when she was simply busy hating both of them. In college and on her own for the first time in her life, Jill was understandably ecstatic. She made the dean's list in the first and each ensuing semester, and she loved her riding classes. She was sure that she would never go back to Rowan Oak to live.[111]

By the spring of 1954 Jill had met a young army officer, a West Pointer and a veteran of the Korean War. When friends had told Paul Summers that Jill was William Faulkner's daughter, he had asked, "Who's he?" Hearing this, Jill instantly responded, "He's for me." And so he was. Almost as soon as they met, she later declared, she knew what she was going to do. With Paul, she felt, she would find love and security.[112]

Jill and Paul were married at St. Peter's Episcopal Church in Oxford on August 21, the father of the bride very proud in his cutaway coat and doing all of the honors in a grand and gentlemanly style. At the reception in the yard at Rowan Oak, guests were served by red-coated waiters brought in from the Peabody in Memphis. Faulkner was positively beaming. "Isn't Jill the perfect virgin?" he exclaimed to fellow writer Shelby Foote. During the proceedings, Jill would not look at her father, who was already sliding into the drinking cycle.

On the next day, Estelle fell off her chair at lunch, and Saxe Commins that afternoon found Bill nude in his bed, by then drinking heavily. Saxe held his hand and stroked his brow. "Come on, Bill. Come on, old dear," he said, "we've been through this before." Later that afternoon Bill, still undressed, came into the room where Dorothy Commins was. "That woman stole my $50," he exclaimed. Bill left and came back holding up his trousers, showing the pockets turned inside out. "See," he said. Estelle, obviously, had needed some cash.[113] Apparently, Bill and Estelle's daughter had made a wise move.

Jill and her husband went off on their honeymoon, then settled in Charlottesville, Virginia, where Paul entered the university's School of Law. Jill had effected nearly the perfect marriage that the Oldhams would have wanted for a daughter. Paul's uncle, A. Burks Summers, was well-to-do and very well connected. Paul's aunt, Helen Summers, invented the Lincoln Day dollar box supper as a democratic device for raising money for the Republican party. Also, she would chair Eisenhower's Inaugural Festival Committee in 1957. A. Burks Summers was a financier and big game hunter who became Eisenhower's ambassador to Luxembourg in 1960.[114]

Faulkner had dedicated *A Fable,* which was published on August 2, "To my daughter Jill." Youth, however, was undeceived. Jill came to describe the dedication as a "big play" by her father. She herself would have valued more greatly a real display of familial responsibility in previous years. However, she did achieve one true victory at this point. She had persuaded her father to open a bank account for Estelle in Oxford, and she wrote to ensure that he had done so.

"I'm so very happy now," she said. "I want your help in making Mama happy. . . . Please, Pappy, I'm depending on you to do everything possible to give Mama happiness." She concluded, "I'm afraid she feels I'm more or less lost to her."[115] Seemingly, Faulkner did improve in his consideration for Estelle. In the fall he supplied $3,000 for Estelle to journey to Manila to visit her daughter, Victoria, and Victoria's husband Bill Fielden.[116]

Clearly Faulkner was relieved to have Jill well married and on her way. He confessed to Jimmy Faulkner that he had been fearful that she was essentially an Oldham. "The Oldhams are very unstable people," he declared. "I've been watching Jill carefully for a long time now, and she hasn't got any of the Oldham characteristics."[117] For Faulkner, Jill's marriage had to mean, in a substantial degree, that he was relieved of family. Now he did, indeed, belong to the world.

Fame

A Fable was widely reviewed. The reviews fit a pattern that had become predictable for Faulkner books. They seemed to say that this was a confused work by a great writer.[118] This was part of a large and curious phenomenon in which no one appeared to consider how and why Faulkner came to be recognized as a great writer. None of his books had ever been met by a flood of rave reviews and an eager market. It was almost as if his increasingly lengthy string of awards and honors, not his actual writings, had made him a "great writer." Indeed, his honors and awards were rising in number. He had won the William Dean Howells medal from the American Academy of Arts and Letters in 1950, the Nobel Prize for Literature in 1950, and the French Legion of Honor in 1951. Now, in spite of the reviews, *A Fable* was about to win both the National Book Award and the Pulitzer Prize for literature. Even at the time he took the Nobel Prize, the number of copies of Faulkner's books in circulation was approaching the three million mark—in part because of the postwar miracle of publishing in paperback form. In terms of raw fame, he had been featured in *Life* magazine, and, on the very day that *A Fable* was published, *Newsweek* carried his image on its cover. At last, literary Americans at large began to reflect the high esteem for Faulkner's work exhibited by literary Europeans.

Officials in the United States Department of State understood well Faulkner's appeal in foreign parts, and they took advantage of it immediately after he was featured in *Newsweek*. Robert Frost was about to attend an international writers' conference in São Paulo, Brazil, as a part of the celebration of that country's four hundredth anniversary. The State Department asked Faulkner to join with Frost in representing the United States on the occasion. Faulkner readily agreed and left on August 6. During a one-day stay in Lima,

Peru, he attended several functions and declared proudly that he had voted for Adlai Stevenson in 1952, a declaration of uncertain relevance in the circumstances. He was drinking when he arrived in São Paulo and continued to drink. A visit to a physician got him on track again. Among other statements, in his talks he said that the most pressing problem for the world was the race problem. He made several appearances and left a fine impression, but one of the people he didn't meet was, surprisingly, Robert Frost. During a brief visit in Venezuela on the return trip, he spoke in a highly complimentary way about the South American people and won more applause.[119] On August 16, he was home again, and soon informed the State Department that he was available for future such assignments.[120] The diplomats realized that they had found a patriot.

In July, 1955, again sponsored by the State Department, Faulkner ventured forth to attend a conference of about fifty professors of Japanese and American literature in Nagano, Japan. A decade before America had dropped the first atom bomb on Japan and then occupied the country militarily. From 1950 to 1953, the Americans had fought the Korean War out of Japan, and now Japan, though demilitarized by treaty, was emerging as America's strong ally in the Orient. Faulkner flew first to Los Angeles. He was within minutes by car of a visit to Meta but excused himself from seeing her on the flimsy excuse that he did not think the authorities would allow him to break his journey. In Japan, the first two days after his arrival were crowded with events. On the second day, he pled illness as the reason for his absence from a luncheon in his honor attended by 170 persons. That afternoon, at a reception at the residence of the ambassador, he stood with his back to the wall, drink in hand. That night he had to be taken from his room for emergency medical treatment. The ambassador was livid with anger and ready to send him packing, but two young men in the embassy, Lew Schmidt and Leon Picon, promised the ambassador their resignations if they did not make a success of the venture. Hearing this the next morning, Faulkner rallied. "The U.S. government commissioned me to do a job and I'll do it," he told one of them stoutly.

Over the next twenty days, with the remarkably sensitive help of Picon, Faulkner turned in a performance that amounted to a minor triumph in international relations. Always complimentary of the Japanese, always modest about America, he wooed them and won. Affection for Faulkner ran very high. One Japanese author said that Faulkner even looked Japanese. One suspects that they were witnessing a by-now familiar Faulkner trait. He was taking on yet another persona, he was indeed becoming Japanese. But he was also playing the role of great writer and American representative. At the conference of professors at Nagano, he broke a conversational freeze by asking the older professors to encourage the younger professors to speak, after which questions and comments flowed freely. During one three-day period, he met some 500 leaders in Japanese thought and media, taking questions, giving answers, and talking about the similarity of Japan and the South in matters of family, military defeat, and occupation by a conquering army. As he proceeded, he came to be very good at the business, recognizing the themes that concerned the Japanese and developing answers that he repeated with increasing ease. He learned how to speak directly to individuals in the crowd and talk directly into the microphone.

Picon had noticed that Faulkner did best when there were attractive young women about. He arranged for one of his staff, Kyoko Sakairi, to be present at gatherings, and at Nagano he added to the party a twenty-four-year-old teaching assistant from Hiroshima Women's College, Midori Sasaki. In the end, Faulkner was thinking of providing Midori financial aid to study in America. Subsequently, in 1957, she received $490 from the Faulkner Fund to help her attend the University of North Carolina in Chapel Hill.[121]

Faulkner had arranged with the State Department for this to be a trip around the world.[122] He went from Japan to the Philippines, where he visited Victoria and Bill Fielden.[123] From there he flew to Rome, where Jean Stein met him at the airport. After a ten-day respite, he was official again and rapidly losing effectiveness. American diplomats in Italy attempted to paint his visit as the cultural event of the summer, but without success. Next he went to Paris, where he divided his time between official duties and personal pleasures. In particular he spent time with Jean Stein, who gave parties for him in her uncle's elegant apartment. At one dinner party, Tennessee Williams was almost gushing in expressing his appreciation of Faulkner and his work. Williams later told Hemingway of the encounter. "Those terrible, distraught eyes," he said. "They moved me to tears."[124] Another guest, Monique Lange, heard Tennessee Williams ask Faulkner a question about Southern blacks. Faulkner would not answer. Indeed, he remained silent for most of the evening. When Monique asked Faulkner's permission to join some of the other guests in going to another party, Faulkner laughed and said: "Go with your queers."[125]

By then, Faulkner was losing strength and drinking more. At one large official party, his handler put him against a wall in the garden with a drink in his hand, hoping that Faulkner could cope with meeting and talking with a few selected persons brought forth individually. When he introduced Albert Camus, whose work Faulkner greatly admired and who had called Faulkner the greatest writer in the world, Faulkner simply shook his hand and did not speak. Camus courteously withdrew.[126] The triumph so visible in Japan, dwindled in Paris and turned to dust. Faulkner finished his tour with a visit to England and Iceland, and returned home.

Serious disintegration had set in at Rowan Oak. Jill, now expecting a baby, was there in late August, 1955. She tried to reach her father by writing him in New York. Malcolm was in a bad way, she said. It seemed to be schizophrenia, and the doctors were urging psychiatric treatment. Mac himself wanted to put Estelle in a hospital, but no one else did. In early September, Jill wrote Faulkner in France. She explained that she had not come to Rowan Oak to keep Estelle from drinking, as he apparently understood, but was rather seeking a rest. Estelle, she said, had joined Alcoholics Anonymous and needed their encouragement, understanding, and love.[127] With the arrival of a grandchild and rising sobriety, domestic life for the Faulkners was about to undergo a significant mutation.

Ambassador

In the spring of 1956 Faulkner accepted an invitation from President Eisenhower to serve as the head of the writers' group in the "People to People Program." This was to be a private organization initiated by the White House to carry to people behind the Iron Curtain the message that the American way of life was better. Faulkner explained his acceptance of the improbable appointment by saying that "when your President asks you to do something, you do it."

Fortunately, his friends at Random House volunteered to serve as his staff, and late in November got together a meeting of a score of writers in New York. Predictably, everyone had his or her own idea. William Carlos Williams argued that a good case for America as a free country might well be made by freeing the poet and writer Ezra Pound from St. Elizabeth's Hospital, a federal institution near Washington. American authorities had found it more convenient to treat him as an insane person than to try him for treason for his opposition to their war with the Axis powers. In reality, Pound's critique was hardly more radical than some voiced in America, but, unfortunately for his freedom, he had announced his during the conflict in radio talks broadcast from Italy. Saul Bellow, who would receive the Nobel Prize for Literature in 1976, argued strenuously against the freeing of Pound, tying what he felt was Pound's anti-Semitism to the holocaust.

During the meeting, Faulkner sat in a chair a bit removed from the others, an enormous old-fashioned glass filled with Jack Daniels in his hand, seeming to agree with most of the others and offering his own proposal. He would bring 10,000 of our enemies to this country every year, he declared, and put them to work, perhaps in automobile factories. Then, as they left the country, he would take back all of the things they had bought on the installment plan. Poet Donald Hall caught the image beautifully: "a small, tidy, delicate, aloof, stern, rigid, stony figure sitting in his chair rather away from the rest of the people—delicate and stony at the same time . . .—that small aloof figure sitting in his chair rather away from the rest of the people—holding that enormous glass from which he frequently took a long sip, and that quiet, mellow, bourbonny voice coming out with its absurd proposals."

Later, in a meeting of the executive committee, John Steinbeck declared that raising the issue of freeing Pound would only make everybody mad. "Yes, yes," Faulkner replied, and then, pointing to the secretary, ordered, "take this down young lady." The government of Sweden had given the chairman of this committee its greatest award, he said, and "the government of the United States keeps its best poet in jail." Happily for the cause of serene politics, that quote did not find print.[128]

By then, of course, Faulkner was hating the whole enterprise, and he was withdrawing. He now found it insulting that the president was calling writers together to do collectively what they had spent all their working lives doing individually—communicating the essence of American culture. Later that year at a meeting of the chairmen of the various sections of the program and their staff members, Faulkner attended with his chief aide, Harvey Breit, literary critic and bookman. They sat near the back of the room. Shortly after the general chairman, Charles Wilson (retired head of General Electric), started the proceedings, Faulkner whispered to Breit, "Let's get out of here," and they left.[129] In effect, Saxe Commins and Random House finished the job and closed down the shop for him.[130] Subsequently, Faulkner made brief trips for the State Department to Greece, Venezuela, and to Denver, Colorado, for a UNESCO conference.[131] But, essentially, after February, 1957, the United States government had to get along without William Faulkner.

Race

Faulkner's writing brought him increasing fame. During the war he had become conscious of a need to use his fame for the good of humanity. After the war, his efforts in this direction fell primarily on two fronts—representing America abroad and participating in the Civil Rights movement at home.

During and after the war, Faulkner's concern over the abuse of blacks by whites in the South grew. It emerged most explicitly, even didactically, in *Intruder in the Dust* (1948). White Southerners must themselves do justice to the Negro, he lectured, and the North must allow them freedom to do so. Especially after 1950, Faulkner's fame and his expressed opinions made him a focal point, a lightning rod for things racial. When he chose to speak, he was noted, quoted, and used—very often not as he would have liked. There was a pattern in the process that directly reflected the broad history of the civil rights controversy in America.

During the war, America needed the full support of all its people. It could hardly afford to have the 10 percent of the population that was black resistant or even apathetic to the war effort. Black leadership was sensitive to the possibility of using their advantage to promote the realization of the civil rights of their people and did so. There might have been a reaction in white America immediately after the war and a reduction again of the Negro, as there had been after World War I, but America now found itself rolling out of a hot war and into a cold one.

Once into it, the Cold War seemed even more dangerous to the nation's freedom, and the world's freedom, than had the war against the Axis powers. In a sense, along with "free" world leadership, America had inherited the results of crumbling imperialism. The so-called "Third World" nations were on the rise, and their populations were vastly "colored." Russia offered an ideology, Communism, that was ostensibly anti-imperialist and aracial. Given the open nature of American society and the limited capacity of its central government for shaping popular thinking into new forms, the rendering of an aracial America could not be an easy task. As president of the United States, Harry Truman could desegregate the armed forces and establish a commission that would declare that we must have civil rights for all of our citizens. He could propose, as he did in 1948, a comprehensive program of legislation from Congress to promote that end. But Congress might choose not to act on the program, which was in fact the case. The result was drift. There was no clear national policy and no program for the creation of a racially egalitarian America. Eisenhower, coming to the presidency in 1953, did not recognize race relations as a very serious problem; and the South—the heartland of race in America where a scant two generations before 90 percent of *all* American blacks had lived, and more than half still lived—did not at first feel vastly threatened by outside interference in matters of race.

All of this changed suddenly and radically in May, 1954, when the United States Supreme Court handed down its decision in the Brown case that the public schools in America must be desegregated. The Court declared that it would elaborate a year later on how its decision was to be implemented. This was a grace period in which the white South could conceivably make up its mind to accept the law of the land and spend time contemplating means of compliance. Instead, Southerners waited anxiously, sometimes with thoughts that the whole thing might simply blow over. In May, 1955, the Court announced that the district courts, that is the local federal courts, would implement the decision. Individuals were to bring suits in those courts to secure justice case by case. Southerners breathed a sigh of relief. They felt that in the South federal judges, jurors, and prosecutors—all white—would not be very harsh on their fellow white Southerners. Very soon, however, it became clear that federal judges in the South would, indeed, enforce desegregation. It was then that the white South went wild, virtually all of it, but in the lower South, where the ratio of blacks to whites was highest, it went wildest. Mississippi with about 40 percent had the greatest proportion of black people, but Louisiana, Alabama, Georgia, and South Carolina were close, and east Texas, east Arkansas, west Tennessee, north Florida, and eastern portions of North Carolina, Virginia, and Maryland were not far behind. The flames were fanned by a general belief that efforts by Southern blacks to achieve desegregation were instigated if not led by outsiders and Communist agents.

Faulkner's involvement mirrored the escalation. In February, 1956, the color question was foremost in his mind, and it brought him into the world in a degree and in ways unmatched in his life before or after. He thought that outside forces made desegregation inevitable, and it was far better that Southern whites do it themselves—out of simple expediency if not morality. World wide, the Communists were winning and America needed to act. "There are seventeen million Negroes," he declared. "Let us have them on our side, rather than on that of Russia."[132]

In the early 1950s, Faulkner commented on specific racial events on two occasions. In March, 1950, he drew criticism when he protested against the acquittal by a Mississippi jury of a white man charged with the murder of three black children.[133] That reaction was mild compared with one that came a year later when he protested the conviction and sentencing to death of Willie McGee, a Laurel, Mississippi, black man accused of raping a white woman. In this case, a group of Southern white women associated with a civil rights organization elicited from Faulkner a very strong statement against McGee's execution. Journalist friends persuaded him to tone down his statement to say that it was not proved that the encounter was unwilling on the part of the woman and to stress the idea that there were liberals who would simply use McGee as a martyr.[134] The local district attorney in the case joined the subsequent hue and cry against Faulkner by charging, in essence, that he was either a fool or "has aligned himself with the Communists."[135]

In the spring of 1955, Faulkner's involvement in the civil rights struggle heated up as he engaged in an exchange of public letters printed in the Memphis *Commercial Appeal.* It began when one writer charged that Memphis blacks were so shiftless that they would not close up the rat holes in their houses. Faulkner's spirited response drew immediate fire, and very soon the discussion shifted to the issue of segregation in the schools. Faulkner attacked the dual system as expensive and inefficient. Mississippi schools, he declared, were not good enough for either whites or blacks.[136] This drew a flood of replies, including one from his own brother, Johncy, a letter that was supported privately by their brother Jack, again an agent of the FBI after military service in World War II. Johncy's position was clear: he would stand in the schoolhouse door with a gun if anyone attempted to integrate Oxford's school. Both he and his wife had joined the local White Citizens' Council, a grassroots, South-wide organization dedicated to the preservation of segregation.[137] Still Faulkner continued the attack with two more letters and now the fire on him became extremely heavy.[138] While he was visiting Memphis in June to promote Howard Hawks's film *Land of the Pharaohs,* reporters asked him questions about the race issue. Desegregation, he replied, was simply a common sense solution to an obvious problem. Opposing it, he said, was "like living in Alaska and saying you don't like snow."[139] He was feeling intense pressure now from his family, his neighbors, and the white people of Mississippi. "I can see the possible time when I shall have to leave my native state," he confided to his Swedish friend Else Jonsson, "something as the Jew had to flee from Germany during Hitler."[140]

In the summer, Faulkner left for his tour around the world. A part of his mission, of course, was to explain the race problem in America and to give what assurance he could that it was on the way to a full and fair settlement. In Japan he added another thought to his interpretation of racial strife in the South. The race problem sprang not so much from "racial" and political reasons as economic, he said. The hardworking Negro might "take the white man's economy away from him."[141] Even so, he told his Japanese audience, Americans had to face reality and practice freedom at home if they were going to talk about it abroad.

The race problem in America next found Faulkner in Rome. The United Press called him to get his response to the murder of Emmett Till near Greenwood, Mississippi. Till was a black teenager from Chicago visiting relatives in Mississippi that summer. Allegedly, he whistled at and made some comment to a white woman. Relatives of the woman's husband kidnapped and murdered the boy. Faulkner's statement was very strong. "If we in America have reached that point in our desperate culture when we must murder children, no matter for what reason or what color," he declared, "we don't deserve to survive, and probably won't."[142] The reaction to his comment at home in Mississippi was totally predictable.

Back in America in October, 1955, Faulkner found that Jill had come to Oxford from Charlottesville to care for Estelle, who had been hospitalized with an ulcer. Estelle had recovered, and was now attending meetings of Alcoholics Anonymous. Further, Faulkner had hardly unpacked in New York before he received news that Maud had had a stroke and was in the hospital. Things had stabilized by the time he arrived home, and in November he joined battle on the race issue again. At the invitation of Ole Miss Professor James Silver, he took part in a panel discussion on the race question at the meeting of the Southern Historical Association at the Peabody Hotel in Memphis.[143] He reiterated his interpretation of the economic basis of Southern racism and declared that all America would soon have to make the choice between being slave and being free. There followed a heated exchange between panel and floor, and the whole affair was very closely reported by the press.[144]

Now Faulkner felt the fire hotter than ever before. The kindest thing he heard in Mississippi was that he had made an honest mistake. On the other side hate mail flowed in and, in the wee hours of the night, phone calls. Jean Stein was in the Delta just then with a friend of hers who was tutoring an actress attempting to acquire a Southern accent for her part in the film *Baby Doll.* "I get so much threatening fan mail, so many nut angry telephone calls at 2 and 3 am from that country," Faulkner told Jean, "that maybe I'll come over to the Delta to test them." Soon he wrote out a prefatory statement for a pamphlet containing, along with other material, his Memphis speech. The speakers and publishers, he said, would accept the verbal assaults and "the risk of violence" that would follow their actions because they refused to sit silently by while the South ruined itself again over the Negro question.[145]

While Jean was in Mississippi with the movie people making *Baby Doll,* Ben Wasson arranged to take her over to Rowan Oak for a visit. Allegedly, Jean said something to the effect that she was going to scratch Estelle's eyes out. Ben hastily arranged to fill in a group around Jean and get her out of Rowan Oak before the combat could begin. Even so, he thought she was attempting "to linger to the end and make a scene."[146] There was no love lost between Ben and Jean. He thought she had turned Bill against him. In fact, Jean did not have a good opinion of Ben. She had met Ben and Hodding Carter, Sr., in Greenville. Carter she regarded highly. Ben she thought old, very effeminate, and homosexual—attributes she obviously disdained.[147]

After Jean and her friends had visited Rowan Oak, Faulkner guided her on a tour through the Delta, to Vicksburg, and then New Orleans. Finally, of course, he took her to the beaches of Pascagoula and showed her the scenes of his youth. As they were walking along the beach, they approached a small, solitary figure. Amazingly, it was Helen Baird, widowed now, and ill. They talked briefly and Helen reported the meeting to a friend. "He had some young girl with him," she said. "But you have to expect that."[148]

Indeed, with Jean Stein, Bill Faulkner at last found his match across the sex line. She was highly intelligent, beautiful, and very tough. She produced an interview with Faulkner that stands probably as the best. While it is in the usual format of question and immediate response, actually she worked it out carefully over some time. Faulkner, himself, helped with the fine-tuning and polishing. Jean offered it to the prestigious *Paris Review,* but only on the condition that the board of directors make her an editor on the magazine. They did.[149]

Jean was also wealthy and, even though still young, very influential. She had an elegant apartment at 2 Sutton Place high above the East River to which she would invite famous and powerful people—such as Adlai Stevenson. Faulkner could be seen at parties there, sitting in a corner, watching. He was also sometimes seen at her uncle David Stein's apartment near the Arc de Triomphe in Paris with painters, musicians, and tennis players of the international set. Every Tuesday, the salon occurred, candles burning everywhere. In the library there were two panels of fake book spines, hiding the large liquor bar. Jean's uncle, after all, was the European manager for the Music Corporation of America. Faulkner once met a Russian émigré painter there, a sometimes lover of Marie Ford Noailies, who almost broke Faulkner's fingers with a handshake. Faulkner "shrieked." The man later gained notice by splitting a vein or an artery, then painting with his blood on a wall until he died.[150]

George Plimpton, editor and writer, knew Jean well. He thought that she was devoted to Bill and gave him a child-like worship. They would stroll in the Luxembourg Gardens, he recalled, hand in hand. Dorothy Parker was once at a party in New York at which Bill arrived a bit tardily. Jean rushed to him exclaiming "My King!" and threw her arms around him. Shelby Foote recalled that she once sent Bill a bouquet of violets for St. Valentine's Day.[151] Violets had been the special symbol of love between Bill and Joan, each flower, apparently, standing for a kiss. Plimpton felt that Jean's devotion to creative people—artists and writers—sprang from a reaction against her father. Jules Stein began life in South Bend, Indiana, became a leading ophthalmologist, and founded the Music Corporation of America. Jules was a genius at using artistic talent in a hard-nosed business-like fashion. Late in life he turned much of his fortune and great organizing skills into establishing a foundation that has saved the sight of tens of thousands of people.[152]

In 1964, Jean herself told Joseph Blotner that she felt toward Faulkner as one would feel toward a father. He was responsible, she said, for whatever fundamental ideas she had about standards and values. Obviously, she added, there were other components in the relationship.[153] Bill and Jean continued to be close during 1954, 1955, and into 1956.[154] Approaching sixty, however, it seems that the fires of physical passion in Faulkner burned lower. In some respects he was also simply mellowing. "No, I shant shoot a deer," he wrote Jean on the eve of the November hunt. "I don't want to shoot deer, just to pursue them on a horse." He discovered that he did not like "to kill anything anymore" and would probably give his guns away. Now the feeling had special poignancy. "Because every time I see something tameless and passionate with motion, speed, life, being alive, I see your young passionate living shape."[155]

Jean Stein seemed to be a strong, self-confident person who could both give and take without counting. Precisely because it was not one-sided, it was possibly the closest Bill Faulkner ever came to a healthy relationship across the sex line. Even so, it was the curious conjunction again—a young woman just entering adulthood with this aging and often ailing man. Coming late in life, it would be his last. Jean supported Bill in many ways, but her efforts in his behalf in the crisis of race in the South were nothing less than heroic.

In February, 1956, Faulkner's concern about the race question passed into frenzy. The cause was that a federal judge had ordered the University of Alabama to admit a black student named Autherine Lucy by March 5 or face the consequences. She was to appear in person at the university on February 29 to forward the process. Faulkner was frantic at the thought that Alabamans would kill Miss Lucy before they would admit her to their most venerated school, and the ultimate result would be the sending into the South again of federal troops.[156] In his view, the nation was rushing toward disaster; the solution was to slow things down and give Southerners more time to adjust to the situation. To get his message out, Faulkner needed exposure at the national level. His agent, Harold Ober, managed to sell one of his pieces, "A Letter to the North," to *Life* for publication on March 5. It was a plea to the immediate integrationists to "go slow now" and give the white South an opportunity to move upon its own initiative.[157]

Life had at first indicated publication in late February, but Faulkner felt he must state his case much earlier than that. Ober cast hurriedly about. An attempt to make contact with Edward R. Murrow, the dean of American newscasters, failed.[158] But an offer of an interview with Russell Howe, a correspondent for the London *Sunday Times,* did come. The interview would be published in the *Times* and in the very respectable American journal, the *Reporter.* On February 21, Faulkner met Howe in Saxe Commins's office in New York. Feeling tremendous pressure, he had been drinking heavily.[159] As the interview proceeded, Faulkner painted an increasingly dire picture of the consequences of forcing integration upon the South, and ended, seemingly, by totally losing judgment. Miss Lucy would be killed, he predicted, troops would be sent, "and we'll be back at 1860." He hoped that there would be a middle road that he could walk, he said. "But if it came to fighting I'd fight for Mississippi against the United States even if it meant going out into the street and shooting Negroes."[160] It was, to say the least, a startling announcement.

On the next day, Faulkner was to have lunch with Joan Williams. He called that morning and canceled the appointment. A year later he told her he had collapsed after heavy drinking. He said that he "woke up in an apartment not mine," called her, and woke up again two days later. He was revived by friends barely in time for an appearance on the "Tex and Jinx" talk show.[161] Access, apparently, was arranged through Jean Stein's influence.[162] Jean had been with him both before and after his meeting with Russell Howe.[163] Faulkner was privately interviewed by a member of the Tex and Jinx staff in preparation for the interview on the air, and notes from that discussion survive. Desperately searching for some saving formula, Faulkner argued primarily that if blacks could receive a good education in their own schools, the current crisis would pass in five years. In a hundred years he thought full integration could be achieved, and in three hundred years, blacks would be totally assimilated into the white race. Asked what the South feared, he answered that they have to raise cotton and fear that advancement might leave blacks economically dissatisfied. Asked if the Mississippi White Citizens' Council wanted to get rid of blacks, he answered that it "is made up of white men, and white men from the Red Neck group, and they say that if you don't wipe out the negro he will soon be in bed with your daughter. The Red Neck feels that the negro may become the equal of the white man."

The interviewer pressed Faulkner on his seeming switch from liberal to conservative, and mentioned the Till case. Faulkner explained his move as expedient. He was maintaining communication with fellow Southern whites. "The Till boy got himself into a fix, and he almost got what he deserved," he said. "But even so you don't murder a child." The interviewer then offered his impression that "if he had been an adult instead of a child you would have condoned it." Faulkner responded: "It depends—if he had been an adult and behaved even more offensively . . . but you don't murder a child."[164] Another shocking statement.

Seemingly, not many people noticed the Tex and Jinx interview, but the Howe interview came out in print on March 22, and thereafter Faulkner had more national attention than he could well handle. The media highlighted his seeming willingness to shoot down black people in the streets. Chafing under coverage of the furor by *Time* and *Newsweek*, he intimated that he was not responsible for what he had said because he was drunk, and his interviewer was blameable for not adjusting his report accordingly. "They are statements which no sober man would make, nor, it seems to me, any sane man believe," he declared defensively. They were, he said, foolish and dangerous.[165] Howe answered a week later, refusing the implication that his journalism was somehow defective, and that he should have saved Faulkner from himself.[166] Simultaneously, Faulkner very wisely declined a challenge from the eighty-eight-year-old founder of the NAACP, W.E.B. Du Bois, to a debate on the subject of desegregation in Mississippi.[167] He had long believed that the NAACP did not understand Mississippi and its blacks and hence had nothing to offer to a solution.[168]

Anyone sympathetic to Faulkner and listening to his statements during these months would have been dismayed and embarrassed for him. What, indeed, did he think he was doing? At times, when he argued that the Negro deserved justice and would not wait, he sounded as if he were for immediate integration. Then he was talking about distinctly separated and upgraded black schools, integration a hundred years later, and in three hundred years total assimilation by miscegenation.[169] Finally, he lost all credibility. If pushed, and even though the white South was wrong, he said, he would join his fellow white Southerners in shooting down blacks in the streets. Scattered, chaotic as it seemed, there was a reasonable progression in Faulkner's public stands. He advised both Northerners and African Americans to go slow, but as it became clear that neither could or would go slow enough to please Southern whites, he moved from a moderately liberal to a radically conservative posture.

Under pressure, he had fallen into cycles of heavy drinking again. He was failing in the role of artist as savant, a capability he so much admired—indeed, idolized—in several French writers and wanted to emulate. Actually, he was becoming ridiculous, a fact that could not have been lost on him. In March, 1956, he encountered two small boys in Bailey's Woods. One boy asked him what made him so different. Faulkner suggested that the boy ask some folks what they thought and report back. Then he would tell him whether they were right or not. Meeting the boy a few days later, Faulkner asked him what he had found out. The boy had asked two people, he said, "and all I could find out was that you're a Nigger-lover." Faulkner seemed hurt, his eyes became moist. "Well," he said, "I guess that's better than being a fascist."[170] On Sunday, March 18, Faulkner began to vomit blood, passed out completely, and had to be taken to a Memphis hospital. An ulcer was suspected, but none found.[171] Autherine Lucy did enter the University of Alabama. After three days of rioting, however, state police removed her. She accused the university of conspiring with the rioters, and the board of trustees then expelled her.

By June, 1956, Faulkner was responding only sporadically in matters of race, even though powerful pieces written earlier continued to appear. In one instance, he cooperated with Mississippi moderates who hoped to forward the cause by issuing a lampooning magazine they called the *Southern Reposure*. In the first and only issue, they made good use of a vulnerable target, Senator James O. Eastland—even then, as thirty years later, a senator from Mississippi. Faulkner proudly sent copies to friends in New York. Soon, *Ebony* asked him to comment on his interview in the *Reporter*. In his reply, Faulkner advised black leaders to go slow. They must show "inflexible and unviolent flexibility" such as was being shown in the bus boycott then in progress in Montgomery, Alabama. He did not mention its leader, Martin Luther King, Jr. The essential thought was to wear down white resistance peaceably. Presuming to speak as if he were black, he said: "We must learn to deserve equality so that we can hold and keep it after we get it. We must learn the responsibility, the responsibility of equality."[172] Understandably, black leaders might have been offended by his patronizing tone and by his implication that they were not yet responsible and did not yet deserve equality. Further, they might see some hypocrisy in his advice concerning "unviolent flexibility" when he had envisioned circumstances in which he would shoot down black people in the streets. During the crisis over the integration of Central High School in Little Rock, Arkansas, in 1957, he declared that Americans were now forced to recognize "the fact that white people and Negroes do not like and trust each other, and perhaps never can."[173]

Faulkner's last major effort in the field of race relations came in 1958 when he attempted to use his position as Writer-in-Residence in the University of Virginia to persuade the oldest and presumably the wisest of Southern states to lead the way to racial justice. He made the strong argument that America could not survive in peace in a largely hostile world "with ten percent of its population arbitrarily unassimilated."[174] He appealed to the reputed paternalism of the Virginians. The blacks were lacking because of white neglect, and the whites must now repair the damage. They "must teach the Negro the responsibility of personal morality and rectitude—either by taking him into our white schools, or giving him white teachers in his own schools until we have taught the teachers of his own race to teach and train him in these hard and unpleasant habits." Strangely, he went so far as to suggest that the key tenet of white racism was true—that culture was the direct result of heritage, that it was in the genes, and white genes were the only ones that counted. "His tragedy may be that so far he is competent for equality only in the ratio of his white blood," he declared.[175]

Faulkner seemed unaware or unimpressed by the fact that other able persons had previously tried unsuccessfully for racial sanity in Virginia. Most signally, Johns Hopkins professor C. Vann Woodward, the leading Southern historian, had spoken at the university in the fall of 1954 after the Brown decision had been rendered in May. He had called upon Southerners of both the conservative and radical political traditions to use the particular good that was in each of their pasts to work toward an equitable racial order. Early in 1955, Professor Woodward's plea was published as *The Strange Career of Jim Crow,* a book that became, as Martin Luther King declared, the historical Bible of the Civil Rights movement. Virginia had not responded to that appeal with any greater wisdom than other Southern states. On the contrary, the state had decided upon "massive resistance" and "interposition" to preserve the racial status quo. White Virginians, these doctrines declared, would simply be unanimous in resisting the integration of their schools, and they would interpose the considerable resources of state government to block moves by the federal government against its citizens.

Generally over the half-dozen years after 1956 Faulkner's interest in the race problem diminished greatly. It was as if he wanted simply to be free of it all. In the summer of 1957, someone sent him a statement by Norman Mailer that white men resisted integration because they feared the sexual potency of black men. Faulkner responded tersely that he had never heard a man say that before, only "ladies, Northern or middle western ladies, usually 40 or 50 years of age," and suggested that Mailer needed a psychiatrist.[176]

Actually, in the nation at large during several of these years, the question of integration was not much pressed. After a flurry of activity that came with the Supreme Court's pronouncements in 1954 and 1955, Congress proved unable to act, and President Eisenhower was simply not much concerned with matters of race. In 1957, he did send troops to Little Rock, Arkansas, but he did so primarily to assert the supremacy of federal authority and the certainty that America would have law and order rather than to integrate that city's Central High School. In truth, as a result of the Brown decision, only about 10 percent of the school districts in the South were voluntarily integrated. These were mostly in the fringe areas of the upper and western South where the black population amounted to about 10 percent or less of the total and integration posed virtually no threat to white dominance. In 1960, the race question heated up as black leadership launched the sit-in movement to desegregate all public facilities. In 1964, several years of concerted and massive action by black Americans plus their liberal white allies, plus the full support of Presidents Kennedy and Johnson would result in federal legislation opening all public accommodations to all people. But in 1962, when Faulkner died, segregation in the South remained largely intact, and for several years he had made no significant public pronouncement on the race problem.

~

The history of Faulkner's participation in the Civil Rights movement is full of contradiction and confusion. Taken altogether, the thrust of his fiction was powerfully liberal and, clearly, he was a pioneer. In the 1920s white writers almost invariably created individual black characters who were cardboard figures, stereotypes who spoke in a heavy artificial dialect charming to whites. In 1929, Faulkner introduced Dilsey Gibson. In early drafts of the manuscript, Dilsey spoke in dialect in the usual mode. In later drafts, the dialect faded as Dilsey became a whole person, totally admirable, believable, and black. Twenty years later, just as the Civil Rights movement was beginning, he created Lucas Beauchamp as an individual of great "personal morality and rectitude" whose superb sense of his own humanity caused him to "refuse to be a nigger" and put his life in jeopardy in a society in which white supremacy ruled. In real life, at the close of the war Faulkner had helped a local black school teacher, Joe Brown, in his efforts to write poetry and was very encouraging to Richard Wright—black, Mississippi-born, and author of *Native Son* and *Black Boy.*[177]

In *Intruder in the Dust,* Faulkner also insisted that there was a valid and beautiful black culture that stemmed from the "homogeneity" of black people. Their blood lines and their lives, like that of whites, had been kept largely among themselves, and they should continue in that vein as they demanded full justice from whites. In pressing this view, Faulkner was reaching twenty years ahead to the essential point of the "Black Soul" movement of the late 1960s that "Black Is Beautiful." He was also reaching back in time, as did the Soul Movement itself. In 1903, W.E.B. Du Bois had said much the same thing in his book *The Souls of Black Folk,* and in doing so Du Bois drew from a deep well of Western philosophy that insisted that each of the world's great peoples has a soul, a spirit, a Volksgeist given to them by God that will be realized through striving and over many generations of time.

In the South in the turn-of-the-century years, there was a highly influential element among the white elite that drew from that same well to say about the essence of whiteness precisely what Du Bois was saying about blackness. This idea of "white soul" was one of several major currents of Southern thinking that was very much alive during Faulkner's childhood and early youth and one that wove itself loosely but vitally into his work. However, as a system of thought, it had virtually died by the mid-1920s and was lost to written history.

Early on in his public pronouncements on race, Faulkner seemed to hold to the idea that black culture was by nature essentially separate and beautiful. Integration, he said, probably did not mean to black people what white people thought it meant, specifically that blacks intended to push themselves rudely and totally in upon whites and produce a mongrel mix. Later, he apparently thought that black culture was essentially bad and would have to be dissolved. At times he seemed to think that the bad in black culture was the "mark of oppression," that is, the result of abuse by whites over the centuries. At other times, he hinted that the bad was not induced but innate, a function of inheritance.

Faulkner's varying conceptions of the basic nature of black culture produced his varying conceptions of what white people should do about race relations. If black culture was innately good, then white people had only to give blacks resources and room to realize that goodness. If black culture was bad because of environment, then whites must change that environment. If the badness was innate, then only assimilation, a total mixing of blood over the generations, even centuries, would suffice. Apparently, Faulkner never dealt with the logical conclusion implicit in that latter vein of thinking—that such mixing would inevitably degrade white culture. That final thought, of course, was at the heart of white resistance to integration.

Initially, Faulkner had faith that the white South would come nobly to the cause of racial justice; he and others had only to say the words and point the way. Thus, the North must leave the matter totally in the hands of Southern whites. Slowly, in 1955 and 1956, he learned the bitter truth that Southern whites were not going to pick up that cross. On the contrary, it became increasingly clear that when push came to shove many were fully prepared to shoot blacks and defy the Yankees. Nothing he did seemed to move his fellow whites one jot, and neither blacks nor Northerners were willing to wait. In the end, he did what some Southerners who were progressive in matters of race in such circumstances have always done: he abandoned the cause and blamed the blacks. At a party given in his honor in Princeton in 1958, soon after his Virginia speech declaring the necessity of whites uplifting blacks, physicist J. Robert Oppenheimer attempted to engage him in friendly conversation. Faulkner already had decided that he could not talk to people of Oppenheimer's intellectual caliber and wanted desperately to avoid this conversation. Oppenheimer commented that he had recently seen one of his stories dramatized on television and wondered what the author thought about that medium. Faulkner managed to end the conversation in his characteristic fashion. "Television," he declared, "is for niggers."[178]

~

In race relations Faulkner's confusion mirrored the confusion of the South as a whole over the centuries. At one time or another, he advocated every major position that Southern whites had taken in that long and too often sad history. Ironically, the very thing that gave him great power as a writer, an empathy, an imaginative capacity to live more or less fully the lives of others—black and white, male and female, rich and poor—rendered him ridiculous in public life. Empathy simply erased consistency. Fortunately, even as his failure as artist-savant was being hammered into his consciousness, he was turning again to his writing.[179] By June, 1956, he was picking up the cross not of blackness, but of whiteness and white "homogeneity." He was going back to the Snopes trilogy—and the plain folk of the white South.[180] That story was, itself, about to undergo a curious and fundamental mutation.

Class

Faulkner's four great novels, *The Sound and the Fury, Light in August, Absalom, Absalom!,* and *Go Down Moses,* brilliantly interweave themes of race and sex. The Snopes trilogy very nearly omits race and instead develops the lives of individual characters in an almost all-white world. It especially centers upon two themes: one, relations between men and women as they progress from childhood through adult life, and, two, a struggle for dominance in the community between an element of poor whites and the higher orders of Southern society. In the sexual sphere, individual characters struggled with their culture's dictate that they progress along a continuum from love, sex, and marriage through family, clan, and community.

Faulkner published the first volume of the Snopes trilogy in 1940 as *The Hamlet.* In this story, the protagonist was Flem Snopes, a poor white, who led his clan in gradually, insidiously taking over the rural empire built by the shrewd peasant Will Varner in and around Frenchman's Bend. Varner, in turn, had assumed an hegemony that had been exercised in antebellum years by a large landowner and slaveholder, an "aristocrat," who vanished leaving only a decaying mansion and the idea, vague and perhaps even mistaken, that he was a Frenchman. In the story, sex is most eminently represented by Varner's daughter Eula, the essence, as Faulkner wrote, of "mammalian ripeness." Eula became pregnant by a young man who fled. Snopes used the situation to marry the sixteen-year-old girl and hence win control of more of the Varner estate. V.K. Ratliff, in spirit Will Varner's best and truest heir, attempted unsuccessfully to counter Flem's aggressions and save the community. At the end of the novel, Flem took his bride and her child to the town of Jefferson where his ambitions assumed larger scope.

In December, 1955, even as Faulkner was reading hate mail and listening to those menacing late-night voices on his telephone, he had taken up the Snopes story where he had left it some sixteen years before. He was beginning the book that he would call *The Town.* Early in 1956, he was obsessed with the imminent dangers that he saw in race relations, but in late March, after his disastrous interview with Russell Howe, he was back with Flem and Eula and the story again. All during the spring and summer, while he was being called a "nigger lover" in Oxford, he pushed the story along, showing some of the discipline of earlier years. In late August, he finished the manuscript and he loved it. "It breaks my heart," he wrote Jean Stein. "I wrote one scene and almost cried. I thought it was just a funny book but I was wrong."[181]

In *The Town,* published in 1957, the year in which Faulkner turned sixty, Flem used Eula's long-running affair with Manfred de Spain, the bachelor mayor and bank president, to gain power in Jefferson. Soon he was appointed supervisor of the town's coal-fired, steam-driven electrical power plant. Like Charlie Butler, Flem was paid $50 a month by the town, and also like Charlie he appropriated some of the town's resources for his own use. Within the first twenty pages, Faulkner was well into a story in which Flem used two black firemen, Tom Tom Bird and Tomey's Turl Beauchamp, to steal brass from the town's power plant. He finished that tale on page twenty-nine and thereafter black people virtually disappeared from the Snopes saga. In Jefferson, Gavin Stevens, lawyer and aristocrat, elected himself the defender of Eula's purity, and he joined V.K. in his attempt to save the community from Flem's avaricious grasp. In the process of developing these themes, strange and striking mutations occurred in Faulkner's work.

In the *The Hamlet,* Eula had been passive, un-self-moving, almost bovine before and after that single fevered evening in which she conceived her child, Linda. In *The Town* she was a mature woman, but no less seductive. She was intelligent, totally aware, thoughtful, and perfectly articulate. She thought, and she acted on her own motives. It became clear that Gavin's defense of her virtue was not only fatuous but unwelcome. In time, Gavin transferred his defense of female purity to her much more vulnerable teenage daughter Linda. Faulkner thought the end of his novel in which Eula died and Linda went away was "very moving," and he was especially proud of the two women he had created.[182] In the sequel, *The Mansion* (1959), Gavin found that Linda was far ahead of him in dealing with the realities of this world. Belatedly, he sensed that there was mighty little that he could do to preserve the purity of women, and at age fifty-one, almost as a confession of his inadequacies, he married a widow with two grown children and settled down in her ancestral plantation house, expensively renovated, ready-made.

There was also a striking mutation in the character attributed to Snopesism between the 1940 and the 1957 versions. In *The Hamlet,* the Snopeses represent a class of poor whites rising to usurp the positions of the peasantry and the old aristocracy and dominate the community. In *The Town* and *The Mansion,* Gavin and V.K. learned that not every Snopes was, in fact, a Snopes. Linda, of course, bore the Snopes name but carried no Snopes genes. More vitally, they found that some adults who were genuinely Snopes by blood, birth, and rearing, were not Snopes in thought or behavior. They were forced to conclude that Snopesism was a set of values, an idea. Being a Snopes was a matter of neither nature nor nurture. A Snopes by name might well possess genteel values, and an aristocrat by birth, like Jason Compson, could be a Snopes in essence. Indeed, in an early version of the Snopes story written in the 1920s, Faulkner had made Flem Snopes the son of an aristocrat and a poor white. At the end of the trilogy, completed in 1959, Flem was met and defeated, not by the peasant V.K. Ratliff and the aristocrat Gavin Stevens, but rather by characters who were Snopeses themselves by name or blood. Furthermore, there are Snopeses among the characters Faulkner created to lead the South to a better life. Compared with earlier works, *The Mansion* ends in a mood that is strikingly optimistic.

As manifested in *The Town* and *The Mansion,* published in 1957 and 1959, Faulkner had made a highly significant travel in his view of race and class in Southern society. To an extent that is almost shocking, he had dismissed blacks and erased the class line he had earlier drawn so strongly. Now the South would be saved, if it were saved at all, not through a Dilsey Gibson as in 1929, or by a model of human strength and admirable pride represented by Lucas Beauchamp in 1948. Instead, virtuous white people of all classes would form the vanguard, and the rest would follow. All white, it appeared, was ultimately all right. That light—that faith in the mass of white folk—flickered again small and bright in his fiction at the very end, but in his personal life it died quickly during his Virginia years.

NINE

The Virginia Years
1956–1962

Loosely quoting Sir Francis Bacon, Faulkner once said to Jill that when one has children, "one has given hostage to fortune."[1] By early 1956, he might have added that in his own case, he willingly paid the ransom.

Engagement

In the spring of 1956 Jill and her husband Paul Summers were living at Fox Haven Farm near Charlottesville while Paul attended the School of Law. She was pregnant, and as the expected day approached, Bill and Estelle packed their station wagon and drove north. Estelle stayed with Jill while Bill trained on to New York. On April 15, 1956, Jill bore a son, Paul D. Summers, III, and the delighted grandfather came down for a visit. During his stay, Frederick L. Gwynn of the Department of English and his departmental chairman Floyd Stovall came calling with an offer to Faulkner to come to the University of Virginia for the spring semester of 1957 as writer in residence. Rather surprisingly, Faulkner readily agreed.[2] He spoke more easily in public now, but one suspects that the prime mover in this instance was the prospect of being close to his grandson.

Soon Faulkner went back to Rowan Oak, where he worked on *The Town* during the rest of the spring and summer. In the fall he took on the People to People assignment while he was busy typing and revising his manuscript. By mid-February, 1957, Faulkner and Estelle had moved into a rented house on Rugby Road only a twenty-minute walk from campus, and Faulkner held a press conference that inaugurated his appearances in the university. A reporter asked him why he accepted the appointment. "It was because I like your country," Faulkner replied in a line that sounds very much like the one he learned to use during his visits abroad for the Department of State. "I like Virginia, and I like Virginians." So far, so good, but then he took a Faulknerian leap. "Because Virginians are snobs," he said, "and I like snobs. A snob has to spend so much time being a snob that he has little left to meddle with you, and so it's very pleasant here." Needless to say, these few lines brought him some tense encounters and interesting mail. "I didn't mean any harm by that," he told one colleague ruefully, apparently just after extracting from his mailbox the latest batch of missiles from irate Virginians.[3]

Faulkner found life in Charlottesville highly congenial. To begin with, he cut away much of the baggage of his Mississippi past. No one there called him "little Billy" or even "Billy," no hint of Count No-Count, and no history of past due bills and charges that in his writing he had slandered his land and his people for profit. His primary association was with "The University" in a university town and, most particularly, with the English department. On campus and off they recognized and valued him for what he clearly was, one of the several most talented writers in America and in the world. His poses, his pretensions, even his rudeness were taken as attributes of genius, not only to be accepted but even collected and treasured as evidence of Charlottesville's proximity to greatness. It was the kind of thing that surely could never have happened to William Faulkner in and about Oxford, Mississippi.

Within the University of Virginia his way was smoothed with remarkable success by a committee of three—the two men who recruited him and Joseph Blotner, a thirty-six-year-old English professor who would become the first to write a Faulkner biography that, as history, rose significantly above hearsay. It happened that Gwynn and Blotner had both flown in the military during World War II, personal experiences that endeared them to Faulkner. During that semester Faulkner talked to twenty-four separate groups and met students and faculty during weekly office hours. After office hours, usually, he would walk down the hall to "the Squadron Room," as Gwynn's office came to be called, for coffee with Gwynn and Blotner.[4]

Off campus, Faulkner's major interest was horseback riding. Jill had been a horse girl, of course, and this part of Virginia was horse country. Frequently she rode at Grover Vandevender's 500-acre horse farm and riding school. Grover was a few years older than Faulkner. He was a large, florid, open man who had spent most of his life jumping horses and mending his broken bones. As so often happens with horse people after some years, he could read the weather in his aching body. Faulkner became good friends with Grover, and Grover soon taught him enough so that Faulkner could take Grover's horse Sweet William over the jumps. To hold his back in place during these ventures, Faulkner wore a special belt. Grover was also a leading spirit in the "Farmington Hunt," a club that gathered frequently to follow the hounds and the fox. It was an elaborate ritual with bright jackets, round-sounding horns, hunters' shouts, baying hounds, and swarms of running horses gliding over the rolling Virginia countryside. Annually, the Episcopal priest in full vestments blessed the hounds while the hunters watched. It was precisely the kind of heady ritual that Faulkner loved.[5]

Charlottesville had another institution that Faulkner not so much loved as needed. It was the site of the university's School of Medicine and afforded excellent medical facilities. In early February, 1957, Faulkner had gone up to New York where he had learned that Jean Stein was ending their affair. Truman Capote, who knew Jean very well and thought that Faulkner was "madly in love" with her, saw Bill in Robert Linscott's Random House office sobbing over his loss.[6] On coming to the offices on Tuesday morning, February 5, Saxe Commins learned from Linscott "that last night despondent over the break with S. and the fruitlessness of his work with the People to People program, B. began to drink." Saxe, "acutely aware of the fibrillation in my heart and my gastric spasms" and worried about the effects of stress, nevertheless went across the street to Bill's hotel and persuaded the maid to let him into his room. "I found B. stark naked, his clothes scattered all over the floor and on it an empty gin bottle, an empty whiskey flask and an empty wine bottle," Saxe declared, describing the episode in notes written at the time. "He began at once to plead with me for a drink and I became adamant."

"He said, 'I warn you. If you don't get me a drink it will be the end of our friendship.'"

"I am still, three hours later, holding out."

"At noon, S. phoned and I had to say Bill was in deep slumber and couldn't answer the phone. He compounded the lie by shaking his head in approval."

By late afternoon, Saxe, suffering from his heart condition, felt he needed the doctor as much as did his friend. "Certainly it must occur to Bill, besotted as he is, that I am under great tension and in pain, worried about the erratic behavior of my heart and never sure of its willingness to do its job." Celebrity physician Dr. Gilbert arrived, prescribed an ounce of whiskey every three hours as less dangerous than the seconal Bill was using, and left. He affirmed that Jean Stein's decision to end their affair had precipitated the bout. Saxe's pulse climbed to 130. He went out for a pint of Old Granddad as prescribed, and was "welcomed on my return with an ecstatic smile." Bill drank half the bottle in an hour and passed out. The ordeal continued for another day, then Dr. Gilbert brought in a 220-pound male nurse, who, on Friday afternoon, put Bill on the train for Charlottesville. He arrived in a comatose state and was hospitalized. A frantic Estelle called Saxe the next morning. "She wanted to know what set off this deterioration. She wondered whether it was J.S. and I had to say it probably was."[7]

In early April, all parties repeated the performance. When Bill did not appear for a dinner date with Jean, she called Dr. Gilbert, who called Random House. Saxe found Bill in a "semi-comatose state, begging for brandy." Again they packed Bill off on the train for Charlottesville. And again, Bill was sent to the hospital. This time, he joined his stepson Malcolm, already there with the same complaint.[8]

The Franklins

With Jill's marriage, the arrival of a grandson in April, 1956, and the move to Virginia, Estelle had entered a new and relatively happy phase in her life. Victoria (Cho Cho), her eldest child, had married William Fielden before the war and thereafter lived with him in various parts of the world where he was engaged in the international tobacco trade. By 1956, Victoria's daughter, Vicki, was a student in Jill's old school, Pine Manor, in Massachusetts.[9]

Malcolm, however, had fallen upon difficult times, and Estelle was worried about him. After the war Faulkner objected to Mac's attending the University of Mississippi, saying that if he had any sense he would not need to. At Ole Miss, Malcolm met Gloria Moss, and in 1947 they married in China, where he was staying with his father. Faulkner had sent Mac to China, in part to separate him from Gloria and avoid marriage. Never strong, Mac seemed to have been shattered by his experience as an Army medic in Europe during the war.[10] Returning home from the Orient, he took his degree in biology in 1949 and entered graduate school. Mac was becoming an expert on the nervous system of snakes. Gloria also entered graduate school and rivaled her husband as a student. Later, Malcolm said she was "a competitor, a destroyer."[11]

In September, 1954, Gloria and Mac had a son, Mark. From New York, Faulkner wrote congratulations. "We have needed another boy close to Rowan Oak . . . ," he declared, "and you two have done the job."[12] Apparently, Estelle felt the need of also having her only son close to home. Before her departure for Manila that fall, she insisted that Malcolm and Gloria come to Rowan Oak for dinner every evening. "Mama claimed she wouldn't eat unless we came down there every night to eat with her," Gloria wrote to friends, "and with me still being tired from carrying the 25 extra pounds for the length of time I did." Furthermore, Estelle seemed to think that "Pappy" should come to Gloria's house every evening for dinner for several months while Estelle was gone. "I don't think I'm selfish in wanting my husband and my baby completely to myself for just a little while," she protested.[13] In March, 1955, when Estelle returned from her trip around the world, she rued that Victoria and Malcolm could not change personalities. "Cho-Cho had so much ambition and force, and Malcolm has an excellent mind, utterly devoid of any desire for material advancement," she declared.[14]

That spring, Estelle and Bill worked about the house and grounds at Rowan Oak, getting ready for a summer visit from Jill and her family. Life there had not been so pleasant for years.[15] Estelle had stopped drinking. Even though she had a serious bout with ulcers in August, 1955, by January, 1956, she was visiting in Charlottesville, happily excited and "beside" herself in anticipation of the birth of Jill's first child.[16] Estelle's father, Lem Oldham, had died in 1945, and Lida passed away on March 10, 1956, after a long illness. "I loved Mama dearly," Estelle wrote Saxe. A week later, Bill started drinking. He was in the midst of the uproar caused by the Howe interview on race relations. On the first day of the binge, Bill and Estelle drove around Lake Sardis, and home again. On the long drive, Bill told her about his affair with Jean Stein. In November, Estelle wrote at length to Saxe, saying, "I have changed." She had stood all the difficulties of the past eighteen months without "one drink and feel capable of dealing with whatever comes with some poise and dignity," she said. The acid test of her strength was Jean.

> I know, as you must, that Bill feels some sort of compulsion to be attached to some young woman at all times—it's Bill—at long last I am sensible enough to concede him the right to do as he pleases, and without recrimination.

Estelle suddenly felt sorry for Bill and wished "he could know without words between us, that it's not very important after all." Her single fear was "that Jill might hear of this attachment—She adores Bill, is a puritanical little monogamist, and was so hurt by the Joan affair." Bill was better now, she said. "Actually, Bill and I have lived more amicably, and with better understanding the past year than ever before—" She thought it might have to do with her changed behavior and the fact that she was not upset by the Jean Stein affair.[17]

Faulkner himself was indeed changing. At one point, Estelle offered him a divorce. She was, as she said, "tired of being the poor deceived wife in the background." Bill wouldn't even discuss the possibility. Interestingly, just at this time, Bill rushed to assume the defender role in regard to Estelle. He was incensed by an anonymous man who telephoned Estelle from New York and offered to tell her about the Stein affair for $500. He ordered Saxe to find out who the caller was, and declared, "I will attend to him."[18] Two years before, Faulkner had advised Saxe Commins to "give the Franklins up as a lost cause." Now Bill himself assisted the Franklins. He helped Estelle "no end" in getting Malcolm, much debilitated "both mentally and physically," to enter a sanatorium in Richmond. Malcolm's own father, Cornell Franklin, then living in Virginia near Washington, seemingly was no help in the crisis. "Judge Franklin is more than useless," Estelle concluded.[19] Faulkner helped, but he resented having to stand in the place of Mac's natural father. "I have to take care of him and he's not even my son," he fumed to a colleague as they walked along Rugby Road.[20]

Malcolm was, in truth, in dire straits. Estelle explained to Charlottesville friends that he had made "an unfortunate marriage."[21] His wife Gloria had divorced him and immediately married another man, apparently without warning Malcolm of the prospective marriage beforehand. He had verged on violence, burned his snake collection, and taken to drink. Estelle had brought him to Virginia in the spring of 1957, then carried him back to Rowan Oak. Faulkner was definitely not very understanding or sympathetic with his stepson. "He does nothing at all, will not go to work, stays in bed all day long until his mother makes him get up, then sits around in a sullen, surly, moody way, saying nothing for days." He would go neither to a hospital nor a psychiatrist. Faulkner thought he had given up and never would be better.[22] Malcolm, obviously, was suffering from severe depression.

Soon Malcolm took a job with the university's Medical School in Jackson. He had very supportive friends in Jackson and seemed to do better. Then he received an unsigned letter from Oxford insisting that self-respect and family honor required that he straighten up. Apparently Malcolm concluded that family and personal honor demanded manly and violent action against the man who had taken his wife. He telephoned Gloria's husband in New Orleans and challenged him to a duel with pistols. Appalled by his own foolishness, he blacked out for a time and then fell into a deep depression.

Mac's good friend, Johnette Tracy, wrote a protest to Faulkner, whom Malcolm thought had written the unsigned letter. Faulkner replied, explaining what had happened. Dorothy Oldham had written the letter and Estelle had added a note. He and Estelle approved of Dorothy's action and mailed the letter without any signatures assuming Malcolm would know who were the authors. Faulkner thought Dot had a right to remonstrate with her nephew and that the letter would put some spine into Malcolm. However, he said, he himself would not have written such a letter. The trouble with Malcolm, he declared, was that "he had been babied too much in his life."[23] Johnette smoothed things over as best she could. It helped Malcolm to know Faulkner had not and would not have written the letter, she concluded, but most of all he needed "a little honest love and affection."[24] In May, 1957, Faulkner and Estelle were back at Rowan Oak where Dot Oldham was keeping "the negroes working."[25]

~

Dot, too, had not had an easy life. During the 1930s and 1940s, the Oldham family's material fortunes suffered a steady decline even though Dot and her parents continued to live in the house on South Lamar. As the Oldham family fell on hard times, Dot turned bitter and antagonistic toward Bill. She once referred to him as "that bum my sister married."[26] Also, Victoria and she were constantly at loggerheads. In 1936, Dot told the high school principal that if Vickie's diploma were made out as Victoria Faulkner she would not be allowed to attend graduation. Vickie said that if it were *not* made out that way *she* would not attend. Vickie doubted that Dot read Bill's books. All Dot read, she said, was the Bible.[27] Indeed, in religion—unlike Estelle who became Episcopalian—Dot remained staunchly Presbyterian, and—at least in that she did not marry—staunchly Oldham.[28]

Bill as an adolescent and young man had been almost worshipful of the Oldhams. He would romantically kiss "Miss Lida's hand" and drive the Major about in his automobile.[29] "He would pick up things for Mr. Oldham," Dot later recalled, "with the tacit understanding that there would never be any change." Dot as a girl had enjoyed Bill's attention. When she was an adolescent he helped her with her golf game and was generally attentive.[30] However, when Estelle came home from China and Bill was too much in the Major's house and yard, apparently it was Dorothy who became most deeply angry. At the age of twenty-three in 1929, it was she who brought Bill to account and with her own physical presence delivered and sealed the marriage.[31]

Bill soon felt that he had to support the Oldhams materially—as well as the Franklin children and the Falkners—and he resented it bitterly. He would complain to Maud during those daily visits, and Maud would relay those complaints to Sallie Murry. Estelle was using his credit in Memphis to buy things for the Oldhams. The Major kept the $200 a month support that Cornell Franklin sent for the children, and later the $25 a month that came for Cho Cho's baby Vicki. Finally, Bill was so mad at Lem that he got drunk and refused to attend his funeral in 1945. Sallie Murry recalled that at one time the first floor of the Oldham house on South Lamar was bare of furniture, and that finally Dot was there with nothing but the gas, the other utilities having been turned off.[32]

After her mother died Dot moved into a hotel. Tiring of that, she thought of an apartment, but Bill said "if you go into an apartment after you have had your three drinks, you won't know which door to go in." She stayed at Rowan Oak for a time, then moved to a little house off South Lamar on what had been the Oldham lots in Oxford. "She's on the land she was born on," Bill said as tears rolled down his face.[33] Bill was recurrently loyal to Dot, and by his will attempted to make sure that she had a permanent home at Rowan Oak—a refuge she jealously guarded until her death. Indeed, Dot sometimes seemed to see herself as mistress there. Once when Ben Wasson came to call, Dot gave him such a cold reception at the door that repairs were not made for a number of years.[34]

In the fall of 1957, Faulkner agreed to return to Virginia as writer in residence during the following spring semester. In November, he and Estelle visited Charlottesville for a couple of weeks. He attended a football game against South Carolina and during halftime was interviewed by announcer "Bullet Bill" Dudley, once a star on the Cavalier team. Bullet Bill introduced Faulkner as the man who had won the "Mobile Prize for Literature" and the conversation continued amiably in that vein for several minutes. Clearly, at age sixty, we have a mellowing, a changing Faulkner. He was more at ease now, and so was Estelle.[35]

In January, 1958, Faulkner and Estelle settled in Charlottesville in a rented house near the campus, and Faulkner took up a routine much like the year before. He had begun to bring his writing to the campus with him. When no students appeared during office hours, he would pull out the current pages for his manuscript of *The Mansion* and work. During the semester, he gave a talk to the English Club in which he drew upon his experience in the People to People program to stress the danger he saw in the "almost universal will to regimentation." He had only recently begun to read contemporary books again, he said, and he thought the character Holden Caulfield in *The Catcher in the Rye* caught modern life just so when the author said of Holden: "His tragedy was that when he attempted to enter the human race, there was no human race there."[36]

In the summer and on into the fall of 1958, Faulkner was back at Rowan Oak and working on his novel. Saxe Commins died of a heart attack in July, and Faulkner found a new and excellent editor in Albert Erskine. In September, Estelle returned to Charlottesville to help Jill, who was expecting her second baby. The child arrived on December 2, 1958. Jill and Paul named him William Cuthbert Faulkner Summers. Faulkner liked the whole name and insisted upon it in spite of the Cuthbert that he had always considered "sissy."[37] Cuthbert was a name, of course, in the Word family line; hence this child carried in his name an unwitting recognition of the feminine family heritage.

By this time, Faulkner and Estelle had rented a house a few miles west of Charlottesville near the Farmington Country Club. Faulkner frequently attended club events as a guest. He had also made friends with members of another hunt club in the area, the Keswick, and was invited by that club to the annual "Blessing of the Hounds." As a guest he now rode frequently with both clubs, elegantly attired in his riding gear—puffed breeches, bright shiny high black boots, and black hat sitting levelly on his head. He delighted in the ceremony. He would approach the Master of the Hunt, doff his hat, and with relished deference say, "Good morning, Master." He was especially gratified that Alexander Rives, the ex-master of the Keswick Hunt, had twice allowed him to ride his Virginia champion hunter, Wedgewood.[38] Jill felt that her father showed signs that converts often show—he was more ardent about the hunt than many people who were born to it. He was, however, not a good rider. Indeed, one close friend described him as a "terrible" rider. People usually saw considerable daylight between his seat and his saddle on the jumps, and the impact when those two elements met again must have distressed his friable spine. But on he rode, sometimes through rain and snow, and sometimes alone, unaware that others had already turned their horses toward home.[39]

In mid-March, 1959, he suffered a fall. He was riding a jumper he had bought in Virginia, a very large, strong horse, appropriately named Powerhouse. The horse was a gelding, but the castration was not totally effective. Powerhouse could mount a mare, and steadily sought to do so, though he could not fertilize to make a foal. Faulkner was amused by the circumstances.[40]

Faulkner explained the fall to Albert Erskine. "What happened was," he said, "I was going too fast in wet ground and turned the horse too quick to face a fence and threw him down myself." Faulkner managed to wrench his body clear of the falling horse, but landed with his full weight on his right shoulder. In the hospital, they found that he had shattered his collarbone.[41] Plastered, bandaged, and with his coat thrown over his shoulders he returned to the farm, mounted, and rode again. At last, he was accumulating real and very visible wounds by his valor as a horseman to supplant the mythic wounds he had generated for himself as a flyer. The shoulder seemed to mend nicely, but something else was wrong.[42]

During the next few weeks, back in Oxford, Faulkner suffered so terribly with his spine that he went to see Dr. Felix Linder, a childhood friend and now a retired physician who lived a half-mile down Taylor Road from Rowan Oak. At one point, the pain was so great and persistent that tears came to his eyes. Linder gave him some relief by strapping him up, but Faulkner refused a prescription for drugs to lessen his pain. In mid-May, against all advice and good sense, he was riding again and took another fall. He had been riding down Old Taylor Road when, just in front of Linder's house, his horse suddenly spooked, throwing Faulkner onto the pavement. He landed flat on his back. The Linders saw him and brought him home. X-ray photographs revealed that he had smashed another vertebra, if not in the fall just taken, then in some previous one. Now, his lower spine was apparently a mass of fractures, old and new.[43]

Estelle, too, came within a hair of physical disaster. Malcolm had become a technician at the Medical Center in Jackson, but it was not a happy situation and he was drinking. During the summer of 1959, Estelle and Dot drove the station wagon down to see him. Mac was driving one Saturday night with Estelle, Dot, and his friend Miss Elna Du Bose. He stopped at an intersection to let a train pass, but then the brakes gave way. The car rolled into the moving train and was dragged eighty-eight feet. Estelle was severely frightened by the accident, but suffered only minor cuts and bruises.[44]

~

For more than two years Estelle and Bill Faulkner had been moving back and forth between Oxford and Charlottesville. In the summer of 1959, they made a very important commitment. They bought a house at 917 Rugby Road in Charlottesville which they had rented during their first semester in the university.[45] Soon, higher administration in the university decided not to bring Faulkner back as writer in residence for the spring semester, and they did not accede to a suggestion from Faulkner that they give him a permanent appointment. There was some concern that his drinking might embarrass Mr. Jefferson's University. However, Faulkner had an influential and admiring friend in Linton Massey, a gentleman scholar and a well-to-do member of the Keswick Club, whose estate sometimes hosted club events. Massey had begun to collect Faulkner materials back in the 1930s, long before he knew the author. At his suggestion, the university library appointed Faulkner a consultant in contemporary literature and gave him a study on the fifth floor of its building.[46]

Faulkner was in Charlottesville in November, 1959, when *The Mansion* was published. The critics were getting his range a bit better than in previous years. Seemingly, they had re-read his earlier works. They conceded that he was indeed a master writer—or had been. But now they declared that the passion was not there as before. Granville Hicks probably said it best. This book was like the others since 1948, he said, "one feels in them strength of will and mastery of technique rather than the irresistible creative power that surged forth so miraculously in the earlier work."[47] It was a judgment that Faulkner himself had made when he had taken up the Snopes story again almost four years before. "I still have the feeling that I am written out though, and all remaining is the craftsmanship, no force, no fire."[48] That fall, Faulkner was in the saddle more days than not and enjoyed a celebratory Christmas with his family and friends in Oxford. By mid-February he was back in Charlottesville, after having suffered another collapse and another trip to Byhalia to dry out—this time accompanied by his brother Johncy as a patient affected by the same malady.[49]

Faulkner and Estelle both came back to Oxford in June, 1960. Faulkner fell into a relatively relaxed routine of riding, seeing to the upkeep of Rowan Oak and the farm, and sometimes sailing on Lake Sardis in a boat he had bought some years before. As always when he was home, he went to see Maud every day. The tie between mother and son had held firm over time, over distance, and against all obstacles. During his travels, Maud had once sent a message after him. "This is a nice one," she wrote:

"May the wind be at your back,
May the road rise up to meet you,
And may God always hold you in
the palm of his hand."
I love you.
Moms[50]

Often now Billy's visits to his mother occurred in the hospital. Maud was eighty-eight, and her health was in decline. As Faulkner told a friend, "She keeps getting smaller and smaller and smaller." To entertain her, he began to make up a fairy tale about heaven, much as he had done for children in years long gone. At one point, Maud asked, "Will I have to see your father there?" Faulkner replied: "No, not if you don't want to." Maud was relieved. "That's good," she said, "I never did like him."[51]

In October, 1960, Maud suffered a stroke and was taken to the hospital unconscious. She had made Sallie Murry promise that she would not be tied to medical support systems and these were removed. She lived for almost a week, and then passed quietly away. She had asked not to be embalmed and to be buried in a wooden casket. "I want to get back to earth as fast as I can," she explained to Jimmy. Billy picked out the casket and the family held the funeral at home.[52] Afterward they buried her in the Falkner plot in St. Peter's Cemetery. Billy was not insistent, but he preferred that the gravestone read:

Maud Butler
1871–1960
Wife of
Murry C. Falkner

In effect, Maud would have been billed as a Butler before she became a Falkner. The family, however, decided to add Falkner to Maud's maiden name in this fashion:

Maud Butler
Falkner
November 27, 1871
October 16, 1960
Wife of
Murry C. Falkner[53]

Dean's body lay at Maud's feet and Murry's above her head. In the Butler plot, on a slight rise a hundred feet to the east, rested the earthly remains of Maud's mother, Leila, buried more than fifty years before, and on Leila's left was the empty space, where, presumably, her father, Charlie Butler, should have come to rest.[54]

Maud's death marked a significant ending for Faulkner in Oxford and in Mississippi. Already he had a house in Virginia, and soon he would have a home there—professionally as well as personally. Indeed, it appears that he was about to change the setting of his novels from Mississippi to Virginia. Bill told physician and fellow rider Harry Hyer that he was going to write a book about fox hunting. It would be an allegorical novel. Harry asked if he would be in it. Bill replied that if he was, he would not recognize himself.[55] By the end of October, Faulkner and Estelle were back in Charlottesville. During the summer, Floyd Stovall, the chairman of the English department, had discovered a solution to the problem of finding Faulkner a permanent place in the university. He was made a lecturer, an appointment that officially could be made only for a year, but which in practice could be, and was, made perpetual.[56]

Faulkner also succeeded in effecting another permanent appointment, and one that was at least equally if not more pleasing to him. Not long after he had begun riding with Grover and others, he met Mrs. Julio Saurez Galban at a cocktail party. She had been born in a small Alabama town, became a nurse, and married wealthy Mr. Julio Galban, the master of one of the more magnificent estates, Gallison Hall. She asked why Faulkner was not riding with her club, the Farmington, and he answered, "I haven't been invited." To this broad hint, Mrs. Galban replied, "I'll arrange that." Back in Mississippi, he soon had the application in his hand. He appreciated the honor, he said in a note added to the completed application, and he was "looking forward to seeing all the Virginians who have made us so welcome."[57] He was admitted to the club at first as an out-of-town member, but then in the fall of 1960, Dr. E.D. Vere Nicoll, an English-born physician and one of the Masters of the Hunt, told him that "we would consider it an honor if you would wear the buttons and colors of the Farmington Hunt." Clearly delighted, Faulkner asked cautiously what that meant. "Oh," Nicoll replied, "it means that you wear a pink coat and top hat every Saturday when we hunt," indicating thus that full admission had been granted. Faulkner promptly sent off for the scarlet coat with a Belgian blue collar that was the elegant symbol of club membership.[58]

The costume was terrifically important to him. He wrote to Jimmy that he "must have the pink coat etc. by Thanksgiving." He urged his nephew to send his "*top boots,*" which were "in the closet by the office at home, the closet where the guns stay." He was very careful that Jimmy get the right items. "The boots are black with tan tops. They have rolled newspaper stuck in them for boot trees. Jack Beauchamp may have a pair like them in the same closet. Mine are the newer pair with newspaper rolled up in them." And then in a p.s., "Vicky will be home Wed. I asked her to send the boots, but you please check too in case she forgets." Finally, Faulkner also drew a picture of the boots. They would have been small; he wore a size 6½. "Bill" Faulkner in Virginia was ecstatic. "Fox hunting is fine here, country is beautiful," he enthused to Albert Erskine. "I have been awarded a pink coat, a splendor worthy of being photographed in."[59]

The Last Persona

Bill Faulkner never lost his amazing capacity for mingling fact and fiction in accounts of his own life.[60] In 1951, rather astoundingly for so private a person and such a clever deceiver, he was planning to write his memoirs. But then, as if he could not stand the bare truth, he quickly withdrew from such a clear commitment to bold fact. "That is, it will be a book in the shape of a biography but actually about half fiction," he wrote Bob Haas. It would be of novel length, but more like short stories, "based on actual happenings but 'improved' where fiction would help."[61]

He never wrote the book, but in 1954 he published an article entitled "Mississippi" in *Holiday* magazine that was a fruition of the idea. The depiction of himself in this rendition was extremely and unconscionably self-flattering—if one liked the rather arrogant and supercilious person described. It was for

Faulkner an unusual, strange, and very revealing performance. Estelle thought it "explains the two Bills—He is definitely so dual I think—Perhaps artists need be."[62]

The article was Mississippi's deep history and richly varied geography interwoven with his own life and ancestry in a kind of walk around the state. It was offered as fact but full of fiction. He dropped the wounded pilot, but he made himself, as a young man, the captain of a bootlegger's powerboat off the Mississippi coast and an all-around hell-raiser. Then he pictured himself in middle age as the dutiful paternal patriarch, inheriting and honorably meeting obligations to blacks begun by his slaveholding great-grandfather. The implication was that Caroline Barr and Ned Barnett had been born in the Old Colonel's yard and served the family happily and faithfully down through the generations.

Added, too, was a story of sailing in his boat on Lake Sardis with several young men, including one who was the "son of an absconded banker." This lad's "father had vanished recently somewhere in the West out of the ruins of a bank of which he had been prophet."[63] It was a shade of Charlie Butler, even to a paralleling of wording in "absconded marshal" and "absconded banker." Even if Faulkner himself never read those words about his grandfather in the town minutes, he could not have escaped the knowledge, however vague, that they were there—indelibly inked in the heavy and slightly molding tome in the office of the town clerk, lodged during his last years in the large red brick building on the square that he saw almost every day. In Oxford, Estelle felt the effect of Bill's banker story. She reported to friends that "the mother of the 'son-of-the-absconded-banker' cut me dead in our local supermarket."[64]

In January, 1961, Faulkner was constructing his last persona. He went to the studio of Oxford photographer J.R. Cofield. Dressed in his riding costume as a member of the Farmington Hunt, he posed for several portraits. In perhaps the most interesting of these, the body is at ease in the riding habit—the puffed white breeches, dark pink coat, white scarf tied like a cravat and stuck with a pin, and high crowned hat. His right hand grasps firmly the handle of a riding crop, the knuckles protruding under the taut leather glove. The gesture seems to say that I have a whip and I know how to use it. The other end of the staff of the crop rests lightly across his raised left knee under the gloved left hand, open and relaxed. His chin is tilted upward, again comfortably, but with a self-conscious hauteur. The thick salt and pepper mustache, drooping at the ends, hides his lips.

The most striking thing in the photograph are Faulkner's eyes. They gaze evenly off to the right, and they seem not to be looking at anything at all. That blank brown gaze shatters the image of the cool aristocrat, and floods the viewer's feelings with confusion. What does this man mean? What does he want me to think of him? If I did not know that this was William Faulkner, I might indeed guess that the subject is a gentleman rider, or, perhaps, he is a Hollywood actor playing the part of a gentleman rider, or he might even be the ringmaster in a circus. The portrait could be taken as real and serious, or perhaps it is simply an honest, playful, and delightful "let's pretend."

Surely, in Faulkner's mind it is an offering of himself as he would like to be seen—as the gentleman rider—and in that sense it is very much like the marble man offered atop the pedestal at his great-grandfather's grave in Ripley. Yet, the two men were fundamentally and essentially different. William C. Falkner, Colonel Falkner, the great-grandfather, could never imagine that the world would not take him as he took himself; William Cuthbert Faulkner could never imagine that they would take him as he was—hence the fabrications. In the portrait, William Faulkner, the writer, seems to shout in a voice almost strident, "Hey, look at me! Aren't I admirable?" In another voice, almost plaintive, he seems to be begging for attention, for respect, and, if you can possibly manage it, please, some admiration. All together, he seems to say, "You wouldn't buy this, would you? You wouldn't believe this, would you?" It is a hard sell, and a soft sell, and a plea. After the sitting, he had Cofield mail out ten copies of the portrait as soon as completed. Interestingly, four copies went to his publishers at home and abroad, one each to Jill and Dot, and perhaps one to Else Jonsson in Sweden.[65]

What Faulkner was doing in these Virginia years, of course, was constructing yet another persona—one that might indeed be accurately labeled "the gentleman rider." This would be his last and, perhaps, the most comfortable of all. Its essence is aristocratic, and it carries intimations of the cavalier riding loyally for the Stuart kings, of the 19th-century gentry ruling the English countryside, and of the Randolphs, Fitzhughs, and Lees—the First Families of Virginia and, hence, of America—great landowners and large slaveholders distinctly above yet respected by the mass of yeomanry. This man is both in the world—and above it. Faulkner was still elaborating on that persona when he died, and the portrait—loosely like that of Dorian Gray—is not the end. One might say of it and of Faulkner at this stage in his life very much what he said of Flem Snopes and the water tower containing the stolen brass in Jefferson. "It was not a monument; it was a footprint. A monument only says *At least I got this far* while a footprint says *This is where I was when I moved again.*"[66]

The gentleman rider was very different from the bohemian writer that Faulkner had played in his twenties, but it was radically different from the image of the working farmer that he had so often played during the preceding two decades. He had entered the farmer persona in earnest in 1938 when he bought Greenfield Farm out in Beat Two. Actually, Greenfield became a 320-acre plot that included several farms each tenanted by a black family, a central farm that specialized in raising livestock and feed, and a commissary or store. There were years in which Faulkner spent a goodly portion of his waking hours on the farm. Obviously, he liked to drive out into Beat Two after finishing his early morning stint of writing, hear reports and give orders, sometimes drive the tractor, and occasionally actually put a hand to the physical labor of planting and harvesting. Most of all, it seems, Faulkner relished writing in the commissary ledgers, making entries recording the sale to tenants of corn meal, sugar, and such against the day when the crops would be harvested, sold, and "settling up" time would come. At first, Johncy lived there and managed the place for him. Later a black man named Renzi was his manager.

Beat Two was notorious in Lafayette County for the fierce independence of its white farmers. They were a proud, hard-working, common-sensical, usually poor, and sometimes violent people who frequently came into conflict with the town-dwelling authorities. In 1938 and 1939, Faulkner fell in love with his role as a working farmer, and he came to identify deeply with these "plain folk" of the South. "These are my kind of people," he said to his mother. The people out in Beat Two were very much in his mind as he got into writing the first volume of the Snopes trilogy in those years. It was then that he created his beloved V.K. Ratliff, a man squarely out of the plain farmer tradition, a person of high intelligence, deep morality, and great wisdom who had capacities both for seeing the world as it is and for working effectively toward making it what it ought to be. He also elaborated his depiction of the hardy peasantry as represented by Varners, McCallums, Armstids, Bookrights, and Tulls. And, finally, he began to evolve the story of the Snopeses, first conceived a dozen years before.

The Snopeses were people who had begun somewhere in the middling range of the Southern social order before the Civil War. By the turn of the century, however, they were being ground down from farm owning to farm tenanting for a share of the crop, heading toward farm laboring, working sporadically for whatever they could get, drifting, and wintering on sufferance in outbuildings. In the case of Ab Snopes, Flem's father, it was a powerlessness that he countered with a tactic that slaves had favored—the threat to burn the master's barn under the cover of darkness. Arson, it seems, has always been a favored form of retaliation by the powerless of the world. One might begin with the master's barn, and end with the master's house—in extreme cases, at night with the master and his family sleeping in the house. A wise owner would never push his laborers over the edge.

In reality, the people in Beat Two that Faulkner so loved were the direct descendants of what Vanderbilt University historian Frank W. Owsley described as "the plain folk of the Old South." During the last generation of slavery, they had shared generally in the prosperity of the cotton economy. During the war they had supplied, either willingly or by draft, the great majority of the soldiers in the rank and file of the Confederate armies. In the decades after the war, however, they found it increasingly difficult to maintain their middling status in the economy. While the whole of the white South was reduced considerably in the decades after the war, a minority of these yeoman folk lost out altogether, first by losing their farms, then by losing out as tenants for good farms, then by losing out in the competition to tenant any farms at all and becoming day laborers (the worst case scenario), as such to be used to advantage cheaply when needed and discarded when not. In all of this, after 1865, they faced effective competition from black farmers, who at least had the advantage of seeing themselves as rising up from slavery rather than heading down toward it.

Historically, two things were happening to produce this sad state. First, the South had lost power politically by attempting a rebellion and losing. Economic reduction was one of the prices it had to pay as a result of its miscalculation. Secondly, the Industrial Revolution was in full swing, and it fell to the lot of the South to produce raw materials cheaply, especially cotton, for that system while paying dearly to consume its finished products. In the new order, industrial and commercial elements were several steps ahead of farmers everywhere in controlling production and prices. In the turn-of-the-century years, large combinations such as U.S. Steel, Standard Oil, American Tobacco, and several large railroad corporations were able to balance out supply and demand to promote their own interests while farmers perennially produced all that soil, climate, and unrelenting labor could yield regardless of price. In the 1880s, they attempted to organize Farmers Alliances to gain some control over their economic lives both as to production and consumption. These failed dismally and in 1892 they formed the so-called Populist Party in an effort to achieve by political action what they could not do by economic means. That, too, foundered after the elections of 1896, but there were politicians like James K. Vardaman who carried forward the Populist purpose under the Democratic name. At last, in an American prosperity derived from World War I, 1914–1918, they achieved a modicum of success.

By the time Faulkner was a young man in the 1920s, these plain folk had moved into the third postwar generation. The early twenties brought economic reversal and a deep and dispiriting agricultural depression, well before the general depression ushered in by the crash of 1929. The result of this was a wave of migration by Southern whites to the towns and cities, a forced dislocation that still reverberates through Southern culture. When the Great Depression came to the South in the 1930s, it was not news; it was simply more of the same and deeper. Apparently, Faulkner never used the term "depression" in his fiction, and properly so. Nor did he call the New Deal by name, probably because he so hated it for undermining, as he saw it, the individuality and the freedom of his plain folk by its various "doles."

During the war Faulkner was much in Hollywood and not much on the farm. But once he returned, he took it up with rising passion, often offering the necessities of farm life as an excuse for not doing all sorts of things he did not want to do.

He loved to paint idyllic pictures of himself on his farm. In August, 1951, he did so in a letter to Else Jonsson, his Swedish friend and, briefly, lover. "This is the beginning of harvest," he began.

> We are harvesting hay, for horses and cattle. It is very hot, with thunder storms about, which may descend at any time. So you watch the sky, the weather, you gamble on weather, because the hay must not become wet between cutting and the barns . . . So you try to guess three days ahead, lay off a section of the grass, which is clover, bean vines, etc., decide on a certain portion which you can risk, then mow it, with a tractor and a mower blade, my tractor driver, a Negro, running the machine, I watching, until he had cut what I decided to risk, the cut grass lies on the ground through one day of sunlight, then on the third day we have the full crew—the baling machine, which is run by the tractor, a broad raking thing drawn by two mules, another raking machine run from a jeep, which I drive, and five men to put the grass into the baling machine, take out the finished bales, load them onto a wagon in the hot sun, temperature about 95—all chaff and dust and sweat, until sundown, then I come back to the house, have a shower and a drink, and sit in the twilight with another drink until supper, then bed in the heat full of the sounds of bugs, until daylight, when I get up again and go back to another section of grass, to guess again whether I can cut it before it rains or not. Then, when the hay is off the ground, the field, the earth is plowed and more seed is sown for grazing for the cattle during the winter months.[67]

Unfortunately, all too often the idyll was rudely broken by crop failure and more bills to be paid out of his income from writing.[68]

On one occasion in the late 1940s, screenwriter Buzz Bezzerides visited Greenfield with Faulkner. Bill discovered that some of his corn crop had not sprouted. He thought the seed had been wormy and went to the seed store. A half-dozen farmers sitting in a circle passing the time of day listened while he explained his problem to the storekeeper. "Well try again, Bill," was the teasing, condescending answer. Buzz felt that they were contemptuous of him, this city boy playing at farming.[69] In the middle 1950s Faulkner's interest in his farm began to fade. In 1954 and in some subsequent years, he leased all or portions of Greenfield, but there were years in which he did nothing at all with it.[70] In truth, the whole system of tenantry was rapidly dissolving as technology took over. Farming became a matter of internal combustion engines, rural electrification, the farm owner and his family as labor and management all in one. And finance. The farm owner ran his own machinery, and often he drove to town either in his pickup truck or his Cadillac (later his Mercedes or Volvo) to talk to his banker and take out loans in ever increasing amounts. New farmhouses were built in front of or beside the "old family place," and very often they were made of bricks in the ranchhouse style, with wide paved drives, large carports, sometimes swimming pools, and a boat on a trailer somewhere in the yard. In the fields the tenant houses weathered and rotted, sagging and collapsing, rusting tin roofs, windows empty and eyeless. Farming rapidly became "agribusiness." It was totally appropriate that Faulkner moved Flem into town for the second volume of his trilogy, and in the third made him the president of a bank and his house a mansion. By the time Faulkner published *The Mansion* in 1959, he himself had deserted the role of plain farmer.

~

The gentleman rider in Virginia rode to the hounds and hunted the fox in a mode that was a far cry from the hunts that Faulkner knew in the Big Woods of the Tallahatchie bottoms or the Delta swamps. In the Mississippi hunt, horses, like mules, were strictly utilitarian, and the hunters often stood all day stationed in one place like soldiers in trenches, waiting for the prey to draw near. They killed to eat; and there were no women. Mississippi hunts were not socially egalitarian: generals, majors, and judges did not lose their titles in the cane brakes. But also those hunts were not socially exclusive. Bankers and lawyers joined men who were paid by the week or the day and all shared the chores of camp life. Faulkner, himself, had donned the burlap sack as apron and washed pots, pans, and dirty dishes in a tub. The contrast is dramatic between that Faulkner and the Faulkner in the pink riding coat with "the Belgian blue collar" firmly grasping his whip.

Isaac McCaslin's hunt in the Big Woods was even more vastly different from the Virginia hunt. In *The Bear,* Ike first could not, and then would not, kill Old Ben. In the end the Bear was killed by the hand of Boon Hogganbeck, a man who was almost as much bear as the Bear himself. In the Virginia hunts they did kill the fox—a few each year to "blood the young dogs" as they were careful to say, but torn to death by hounds while a score of people on horseback raced to watch.[71] It was inconsistent in Faulkner that he could idealize the one and do the other, but it is more relevant to his greatness as a writer that he could do both and *be* both in different times. That quality gave him a combination of range and depth that brought tremendous power to his fiction. A monolithic, a consistent, coherent worldview would not have killed his genius, but it would have severely limited its power. One of his gifts, perhaps his greatest gift, was that there was no certain Faulkner, nor even a given sequence of Faulkners. It was endless Faulkner. He could be almost anything, take almost any view within the compass afforded him by his culture. In successive phases of his life, he tried very nearly all of them.

The persona of gentleman rider might well be seen as a continuation and an extension of Faulkner's first deep role—that of the wounded flyer. Both were vaguely aristocratic, and there was an essential similarity between the man with his flying machine and the man with his horse. Both attempted to assert mastery over awesome power that gave amplitude to themselves. More important, that power was dangerous, capricious, and liable to go out of control for no discernible reason—with hardly a second's warning and with devastating and often fatal results. Even the most skillful were always at risk, as Dean Faulkner's death clearly testified. Inevitably, people who rode horses for any length of time would suffer falls and injuries, just as surely as would a young flyer on the Western Front in the Great War. The committed rider would acquire broken bones and stiff legs that he exhibited like so many badges certifying courage. The great difference for Faulkner this time was that they could not suddenly end the war on him and thus deny him the opportunity to prove that he was not only as courageous as most men but more so. "Even at 62," he boasted to Joan Williams, "I can still go harder and further and longer than some of the others."[72]

Amazingly, the Virginia persona picked up again, and in full force, the stories and persona of the adventurous pilot. One new friend understood that Faulkner had battled headwinds for several days on one occasion to fly all the way from Memphis to New York and that he had crashed his private airplane "all over the country," always in some comic manner. He told Grover Vandevender, and others, that in 1931 he had flown himself to the Southern Literary Conference and landed on his farm, then the Dixie Flying Field. The most striking story he saved for David C. Yalden-Thomson, descendant of Highland Scots, philosophy professor, and fellow rider. He described in vivid detail a scene at his airdrome in France during World War I. Periodically, the commandant, to hone up the fighting skills of support personnel—mechanics, cooks, etc.—would divide them into two teams and stage a battle on the field, the men armed with pans, umbrellas, pillows, and such. On one occasion General Pershing arrived at the height of combat to find the air full of feathers. "This caused him great joy to remember," David noted.[73] Again, William Faulkner was very convincing as actor as well as storyteller.

Faulkner elaborated the Virginia persona deftly. He told Virginians that his four main blood lines were Falconer, Murry, McAlpin, and Cameron. He even went so far as to secure a length of McAlpin tartan, intending to have kilts made for his little grandsons, a suit for Jill, and a smoking jacket for himself. The package of cloth, Estelle said, never got opened. Even so Faulkner repeatedly mentioned his McAlpin blood to hunt club members. In all of this Faulkner seems to have appropriated Yalden-Thomson's background and made it his own. All four of his great-grandfathers were Highland Scots, Faulkner said, and he was full of tales about these tough and violent people sortieing into the wide world in Kiplingesque fashion.[74]

Joseph Blotner, understandably, was later perplexed as he attempted to sort out Bill's ancestry for his biography. He wondered if some of these names came by way of the Butler line, which he could barely push back beyond the names of Maud's parents.[75] William himself, looking back to his ancestors, gave the Old Colonel more attention and greater reverence than ever before. He told David Yalden-Thomson that his great-grandfather was a lieutenant general in the war between the states, and that he had raised and commanded a division. John Y. Murry, his other Ripley great-grandfather, he said, wore a kilt with a clan weave and sat in the chimney knitting. His aunt, he stated, still had the claymore (a short Scottish sword) that her grandfather Murry had from his grandfather who had carried it at the battle of Culloden (in which the Highland Scots in 1745 were trounced for supporting Bonnie Prince Charles, the Stuart pretender). Sallie Murry scoffed and said William was a "dreamer up" of all this Scotch ancestry. John Murry was a leading doctor and Mason and had no time for such frivolity as knitting. But again, David was convinced. "At bottom," he said, "I always thought that Faulkner saw himself as a highlander living in exile in Mississippi."[76] In Virginia, Faulkner also altered his name again. He conveyed the idea that he was called "Will" by his friends—not Billy or even Bill.[77]

Transition

During the late 1950s William Faulkner was in a great transition. It involved the new persona and the physical move from Mississippi to Virginia, but it was also much more. He was withdrawing from a whole range of activities that had made up his earlier life. He deserted images of rough and ready Mississippi maleness and of the patriotic American faithfully serving his government, only grudgingly maintained his membership in the elite of the literary world, and shifted radically the base of his personal involvements with women, blacks, and the plain folk of the New South.

In the middle 1950s he ceased to participate in the late November hunts in the Delta, but continued to send money to support that proud and dying venture. In the spring of 1962, apparently forgetting his earlier attitude that when your president asks you to do something you do it, he refused to have dinner at the White House with President John F. Kennedy and some fifty American winners of the Nobel Prize. Rather gratuitously, he explained his absence with an insult. "I'm too old at my age to travel that far to eat with strangers," he said. Estelle, who had to send the "regrets," would have liked rather to go.[78] A month later, however, Faulkner was not too old to travel to New York to take the Gold Medal from the National Institute of Arts and Letters. The medal, a high honor conferred on writers by other writers, was presented to him by another great American author also from Mississippi, Eudora Welty. With an unfailing ear for the spoken word and crucial lines, Welty caught his mood perfectly. "When is it gonna be over?" he kept leaning over and asking her as they sat side by side on the stage in front of a thousand people.[79]

It is highly significant that in the last half-dozen years of Faulkner's life there were no young women in the manner of Meta Carpenter, Joan Williams, and Jean Stein. In late 1954 Joan had signaled dramatically the end of their tortured affair by marrying, and Jean Stein was not very visible after 1957. This last involvement began with—and always rested upon—hero worship by a young woman, and her good feelings must have been increasingly taxed by his drinking episodes. She was marvelously supportive of him, but inevitably she was soon attracted and married to a younger man.

Whatever it was, his connection with Jean lasted only three years. The affair with Joan Williams, made of hope and pain in roughly equal parts, was thick and frustrating and lasted roughly twice as long. Faulkner's involvement with Meta was made lopsided by her giving and his taking, but at its best, always briefly and sporadically, it was about as total as two people ever achieve. The relationship did have striking durability, lasting some fifteen years. It ended after a few brief trysts in the Hollywood Beverly-Carlton in 1951, though they corresponded from time to time thereafter.[80]

Like dying echoes, Faulkner encountered both Jean and Joan during his New York trip in the spring of 1962. He had lunch with Jean, now Mrs. William vanden Heuvel, on the day after he took the Gold Medal at the Institute.[81] Ironically, Joan participated in the ceremony itself, receiving recognition for her novel, *The Morning and the Evening.* As Joan went onto the stage to take her award, she detected no sign of recognition from Faulkner. In fact, she thought he was asleep.[82]

Five years before, Joan had sent him stories to read, and he had revved up his romantic engine again. "I haven't got over you yet and you probably know it," he said. "Women are usually quite aware of the men who love them, so I thought maybe you were dodging me."[83] In November, 1960, he wrote Joan a letter but "decided not to send it for a while, if at all maybe."[84] The fire was only a flicker by then, almost a memory of desire. About the same time, he read the manuscript for Joan's novel and pronounced it "all right"—his highest compliment.[85] He had said the same to Eudora Welty back in 1943. He had just read *The Robber Bridegroom* and *The Gilded Six Bits.* "You are doing fine," he wrote from Hollywood, "you are doing all right." He addressed her as "Welty," much as he addressed his friend Phil as "Stone."[86] Faulkner wasn't lying to Joan; he believed in her talent, and he had tutored her superbly: "Any good story can be told in one sentence," he had written her in one lesson a decade before. The loneliness of a child, he declared in another typical lesson, "should be a catalyst, which does something to the rage of the universal passion of the human heart, the adult world, of which it—the child—is only an observer yet. You don't want to write just 'charming' things." He was full of wise generalizations. "The first sentence should . . . ," and so on.[87]

Estelle's acceptance of her husband as he was seemed to grow as the couple moved toward making a new home for themselves in Virginia.[88] A part of that, surely, was the fact that the marriage for which she had been bred all of her young life was finally coming into being. She was now moving into a social setting in which substantial material wherewithal was assured, and her charm, her accomplishments in cuisine, music, and small talk, and her love of grand houses, fine clothes, and a gracious manner could have full play. At another level, too, she now had grandchildren by a daughter who fully understood the pain that she had gone through in her marriage and sympathized with her. Even her drinking in these Virginia years was under control—a phenomenon always a minor miracle.

Faulkner's reform in the sexual realm might have been forced upon him by physical as well as by social circumstances. It might be relevant that Flem Snopes was not depicted as sexually impotent in *The Hamlet* written in the later 1930s, and that he was explicitly declared so in *The Town,* which Faulkner wrote almost totally in 1956.

In matters of race and class, obviously Faulkner simply decided to cut himself loose from previous allegiances. When Paul Pollard, a black man who had worked for him in Charlottesville, wrote to ask Faulkner to buy a lifetime membership in the NAACP for him, Faulkner curtly refused. He thought that the NAACP, seeking to join all black people together in the demand for full civil rights, was in error. "As I see it, if the people of your race are to have equality and justice as human beings in our culture, the majority of them have got to be changed completely from the way they now act," he declared. "Since they are a minority, they must behave better than white people. . . . If the individual Negro does not do this by getting himself educated and trained in responsibility and morality, there will be more and more trouble between the two races."[89]

In these last years Faulkner was hardly more generous to the plain folk of the South—the middling elements to which a large majority of Southern whites had always belonged. Indeed, in his mind, he joined the two together and they spelled trouble. In the spring of 1962, drifting along on a houseboat on a lake with two Oxford friends, the conversation turned to a discussion of the admission of a young black man, James Meredith, into the university in the fall. If there was trouble, Faulkner said, it would come "because of the people out in Beat Two who never went to the University or never intended to send their children to the University." The discussion then turned to consider the probable actions of the reigning governor, Ross Barnett, a man who had sworn to uphold segregation at any price. One of the men asked how Barnett had come to be elected anyway. Faulkner, scanning the shoreline casually through a set of binoculars, answered. "Eighty-two Beat Twos," he said.[90] It was the rednecks of the eighty-two counties of Mississippi who would cause the trouble, he was saying. It was not true, of course. Faulkner had seen the readiness for violence against blacks in his own family in Beat One. Meredith did come to Ole Miss that fall, and within days the campus resembled nothing so much as a bombed-out city in Europe after World War II. The violence left one person dead and numerous injured. The war on the campus was between the authorities trying to keep the peace and raging white Mississippians of all classes. No one who knew anything could believe that it was all a redneck, Beat Two, affair.

By this time, race relations in the South were slipping out of white control. Blacks, especially young blacks under the leadership of the Reverend Martin Luther King, Jr., were moving into a mode of non-violent demonstrations, declaring unmistakably that they would wait no longer for justice to be done. It was a program that refuted directly the Booker T. Washington approach that urged each black person to raise himself by his own bootstraps, and it almost totally eclipsed the gradualist, legalistic approach of the NAACP. The new movement came squarely out of the black churches as they had evolved over the generations, and King's organization, the Southern Christian Leadership Conference, growing out of the Montgomery bus boycott, was distinctly the dominant force in black America. Faulkner, with amazing sensitivity, had caught the first wave in his early writings. King, himself, might have preached such a sermon as the Reverend Sheegog preached in Dilsey Gibson's church on Easter Sunday, 1928, and in 1960 rebels were as assertive of their equality, even in jail, as Lucas Beauchamp was in Faulkner's fiction in 1948. They refused to be "niggers" anymore. On the other side, white Mississippi had organized itself to resist integration, officially in the government and unofficially in the host of voluntary associations called White Citizens' Councils.

In the crisis, the federal government was moving, but it was not yet beyond the kind of commitment that President Eisenhower had made simply to maintain law and order, whatever that law might be. They were willing to treat the symptom rather than the disease. The Kennedy administration had hardly arrived in the White House in 1961 before a ragtag army of Cubans in exile sponsored by the American government made a disastrous attempt to invade Cuba at the Bay of Pigs and overthrow Fidel Castro. Shortly, the Kennedys would regain their balance and come about to take leading roles in the Civil Rights movement, but they had not yet made that full turn when Faulkner died.

Faulkner's response to the realities in race relations was perfectly reflective of the history of the South. In the years of his childhood, when race problems rose some Southern whites attempted to quiet things by preaching the obligation of the whites to do justice to black people, paternalistically, as a matter of honor. When that failed and majority white sentiment turned toward violence and lynching, some of those who had been foremost in pleading the cause of black people turned to say that only black people could solve black problems, and that the lower elements of the white world—the rednecks, crackers, and grits—would simply have to suffer from their own ignorance until sheer pain caused them to gain a measure of wisdom. Meanwhile, they would say, I do perfect justice to individual black people in my own life. My skirts are clean, and I am busy with other, more important concerns.

Family

Looking at Faulkner's self-inspired portrait as the gentleman rider, one senses that he or she is looking at a shell. "Carapace," Meta had called it, suggesting some kind of particularly hard-shelled crustacean, and she wisely declined to attempt penetration. On the other side, Jill thought that she was seeing another Faulkner in these last years, one less remote and self-centered. "Pappy really changed," she said. "He became so much easier for everyone to live with—not just family, but everybody . . . he was a different man. . . . He was enjoying life." Rightly or wrongly, she tied the change to what she thought was the end of his life as a writer. "I don't think he was being driven as much as he had been . . . he had in a sense finished the creative side of his life and wanted to have something else." It was only in those years, she came to think, that she really knew him and he knew her.[91]

Jill, herself, had found love, marriage, sex, family, clan, and community in the sequentially progressive formula classically prescribed by her culture. Moving now with the flow of her own life, she seemed better able to accept the fame, the true greatness of her father as a writer. Her life in Virginia bespoke her arrival as an independent adult. An acquaintance caught the scene beautifully in a Charlottesville drugstore. Two teenage girls were drinking sodas, gazing out the window at people passing along the sidewalk, when Faulkner appeared.

One said, "Look there."

"Who's that?"

"You mean you don't know who that is?"

"No, I don't know who that is."

"Why, that's Jill Summers's father."[92]

William Faulkner had come to Virginia most of all because Jill and her children were there. Through Jill, he was finding much that had eluded him as a young man. Thus late in life, in a sense, he was finding what he needed by working the sequence backward. He was finding community, a small community in which he had a place, and working backward through clan and family, to marriage and love. By determinedly being herself, Jill gave her father that chance to begin again. It is probably true that she, at least, came to know him better than ever in those years—whoever he was.

Without doubt William Faulkner's change had something to do with the arrival of his grandsons. When he had made application for membership in the Farmington Hunt, he wrote in the names of his two grandsons in the space provided for "Junior Riders." They were still years away from riding, he admitted, "but I hope my association with the Farmington Hunt will last even longer than that."[93] He was proud of Jill's "2 little demon boys," proud, too, that one was "named William C.F. Summers, for me."[94] When he came back to Charlottesville after Maud's death, Faulkner was a moving spirit in the organization of the Buck Mountain Riding Club, one of the principal purposes of which was the education of young riders. The club held shows to raise money, and it built a "hut" to center its activities. Faulkner would ride with children all morning and all afternoon with a group of adults whom fellow rider and surgeon Euclid M. Hanbury, Jr., would call a "band of brothers." Faulkner kept the minutes for the club meetings, as he had sometimes done in the commissary ledger at Greenfield, rendering the proceedings in words written in that tiny, almost indecipherable series of vertical dashes that was his script.[95] All this was his rapport with children coming out again, the truly golden thread that ran through the fabric of his life, paradoxically some sort of essential affinity he had with innocence.

The tie with Jill and family was made all the more firm in the spring of 1961 when Jill gave birth to a third son. Like Maud, she had borne three sons in a row and fast. Estelle was there before, during, and after each event. Faulkner adored the children, and it seemed that he could be with them endlessly and easily. Proudly he exhibited three-year-old Will's learning skills to a friend. No doubt having done this before, he stationed Will in front of himself and demanded: "What's your name?" The child looked up at his grandfather and answered stoutly, "Will Faulkner." He looked very much like Faulkner, and he could have been another "Little Breeches" character out of his grandfather's fiction.[96]

Faulkner now also had surrogate teenage daughters whom he adored, Cho Cho's daughter Vicki, and Dean, the daughter of his dead brother. Now and again one of the girls would disappear for a couple of days. Once he sent Vicki a telegram: "Have tried to contact you day and night for two days. You know what I will have to tell your parents." On another occasion, his message to Dean, lost somewhere in Greenwich Village for two days, was succinct. "Come out of the Village," he ordered. Faulkner sent Dean to school in Switzerland and talked with her about spending a whole day and a night in the Sistine Chapel like one romantic seventeen-year-old to another.[97]

Jill might have thought that her father's creative life was substantially over. He himself sometimes said *The Mansion* would be the end. In fact, however, it was in the last year of his life that he wrote what is arguably one of his best works and certainly one of his most charming stories. It came to be called *The Reivers*. In an interview, he said the title came from an old Highland Scotch word for robbers.[98] The book began with the line: "Grandfather said": The grandfather is Lucius Quintus Cincinnatus Priest and he is telling the story of his own coming of age as an eleven-year-old Mississippian early in the twentieth century. Lucius, of course, could have been William Faulkner in that summer of 1909 in which he, too, was eleven and moving into a period of critical change. The grandchildren listening could have been his own. In the story Lucius joins with his forty-year-old friend Boon Hogganbeck to "borrow" Lucius's grandfather's car, a racy Winton Flyer, and head for Memphis. As in *The Bear,* Boon is fractionally Indian, unsophisticated, illiterate, a very spontaneous, natural man of great physical strength. Enroute they discover the elderly but spry black servant, Uncle Ned, stowed away under a rug in the back of the car. Ned, too, is up for adventure.

In Memphis, they checked in at Miss Reba's brothel where Boon wanted to see his favorite young woman, Corrie, a large, gentle country girl. Physically, Corrie was blooming, volumptous, primal and mammalian, Eula Varner in a lower octave. Soon they learned that Uncle Ned had traded the car for a race horse, and further that the horse had been stolen. Unperturbed, Uncle Ned had a solution. They would race the horse and win back the car. Evil was revealed to Lucius in many ways, but in the end, the forces of good triumphed and they won the horse race. Boon married Corrie and they had a child whom they named Lucius Priest Hogganbeck. Lucius had passed through his initiation and entered into society as a young adult; he had lost his innocence to gain a knowledge of good and evil—of courage and compassion, of greed and cruelty—that will allow him to live in the world as a gentleman with honor. Faulkner mailed off his manuscript in August, 1961.

That autumn he and Estelle were back in Virginia in a cottage on the farm Paul and Jill had bought. It was almost too good. "I live up to my arse in delightful family," he wrote his editor, "and I may want a holiday, at the Algonquin."[99] Through the following winter, he made minor changes in *The Reivers.* In the spring of 1962, he began to make the move toward an end he so clearly wanted. In Virginia, he had found a 250-acre estate called Red Acres for sale. The asking price was $200,000, but he was determined to buy it at any cost. To his friend Linton Massey, he declared, "I want Red Acres."[100]

Community at Last

What Faulkner was doing, it seems, was attempting to build for himself a place in a community that would give him a sense of being, of wholeness. During roughly the first half of his life he had accepted, even eagerly embraced his displacement from Oxford society—an expatriate at home. With marriage to Estelle he committed himself, apparently, to full though belated entry into that social universe. In the same instant that he moved from bachelor to husband, he moved to the fatherhood of Cho Cho and Malcolm, and soon there was Alabama and Jill. Establishing a household in a rented flat and then at Rowan Oak meant that he had to go into the world and earn money, and that he had to deal in a responsible way with the institutions in his community—financial, educational, medical, religious, and social. Soon, with the death of his father, he moved on to accept his role as the head of the Murry Falkner clan, including, as he saw it, full support for his mother, the partial support of two of his brothers and their families, and a small host of domestic servants. He also moved to assist the Oldhams.

At the beginning of the year 1929 he had been thirty-one years old, living comfortably in his father's house on campus; three years later he was offering himself as the head of the Murry Falkner clan and struggling under financial burdens that were almost unbearable—even with his Hollywood income. Contrary to Maud's dictum, her son complained bitterly and explained endlessly. In his view, great chunks of his life seemed soon to crumble and wash away. He was vastly undervalued in his own home town. Members of the clan that he helped appeared to him not only ungrateful but insulting. Estelle was dissolving in alcohol and sporadic violence, for which, usually, he saw no reason. Sex between them became impossible. Still she would not give him a divorce without taking Jill and throwing him into bankruptcy. Through all of this his writing was losing power, though, taken all together, it was winning him rising fame. Finally, it earned him the Nobel Prize—a resounding symbol of the high esteem in which he was held not in Oxford, not in Mississippi, not in the South, and not even in America, but in the world.

With the prize he made a giant leap into the international community: he came to see himself as transcending all of the provincialities of home and becoming a champion of universal human values. He accepted speaking engagements and traveled for the State Department literally around the world. Inevitably, his involvement in world affairs brought him squarely up against the race question. Speaking abroad at the invitation of his government, it became fairly easy to take the simple, high moral ground of equality and accept the hearty applause that followed.

Back home in the South and in Mississippi, it was a different matter. He grossly misjudged the real difficulty of the race problem in the South and in America. When the intractability of the problem began to manifest itself to him in massive and unmistakable ways, he faltered, began to drink, and finally turned and fled. As he moved into the late 1950s and shifted his thoughts toward a new home in Virginia, he was very ready to surrender his affection for the plain white folk of the South along with his sympathy for blacks. Increasingly, he caught the vision of a William Faulkner truly valued and happy in a very tight, all white, male-dominated, elitist, small world in Virginia.

In his last years Faulkner often talked about "breaking the pencil" and ceasing to write. *The Reivers* showed that he was still a powerful storyteller and that, at least sometimes, he could do the work comfortably. Had he lived, there would have been more stories surely, and, inevitably, they would have reflected the persona of the gentleman rider, perhaps a Gavin Stevens character raised to a more steady effectuality. In Virginia, he was also adding another string to his literary bow. He was doing something that he had always eschewed and perhaps even despised—he was talking "literature." For the first time in years he was admitting to having read contemporary writers, making evaluations, and talking about them with other students of literature. He was, after all, now a member of the faculty of Mr. Jefferson's University, and he took his appointment seriously. The university was important to Faulkner's new sense of place. His appointment gave him institutional status and a special prestige. Moreover, there were individuals in the Department of English who protected him from assaults by the Lilliputians, supported him in scholarly and academic ways, and in whom he had great personal confidence. Professors Gwynn and Blotner had flown in the military, and there was a lot of security for Faulkner in "the squadron room" and "squadron parties," where the flyers gathered with their wives. Blotner sometimes called him "Chief," and an expansive Faulkner once performed the drill "the changing of the guard" for his sometime military friends.[101]

In particular, he came to depend heavily on Joseph Blotner. A measure of that dependency was taken when Faulkner rued that he would have to "swot up" an acceptance speech for the National Institute's Gold Medal. Joe offered to try a draft. Bill immediately accepted and used Joe's draft to launch his own.[102] He was getting older, he tired more easily now, and he did need help from time to time. His faith in Joseph Blotner was not misplaced. After Faulkner's death, Professor Blotner set to work to produce, in 1974, a massive two thousand–page biography of his friend. It was an early and excellent effort, but its very existence soon drew a horde of new information, some of it shocking, to the surface. Blotner responded in 1984 with a revision that smoothly married the new to the old, generally with great fairness to the subject of the biography. Faulkner could hardly have left his reputation as a writer and as a man in better hands.

Most of all in Virginia, Faulkner was finding a role for himself as a gentleman rider. His membership in the Farmington Hunt Club gave him entree into the whole round of hunt clubs in the region, and, through these, into powerful social circles in the area. Some of these people knew his writings, a few knew them well. Essentially, they knew him as one of the few American writers ever to win a Nobel Prize, and they valued him instantly for that. The prize, in short, brought him admission into the local social pyramid at the top.

In Mississippi he had carried a sense of his immediate family as fallen. The old Colonel had achieved ostensible greatness and the young Colonel had built upon that base. Murry had let it slip away and Uncle John exhibited Snopesean qualities in spite of his good birth. These were misperceptions, but, in effect, real enough for Billy Faulkner. And God only knows what feelings lay behind his deep silence about the Butlers. Beneath it all, Faulkner could never surrender his own high sense of self esteem, but he was somehow compelled to give to the little world of Oxford what he thought it demanded—a dandy, a bum, a Count No-Count, a scalawag, and a "nigger-lover." Going to Virginia was slipping the anchor and sailing away, leaving the dead weight of all that dreary past where it belonged, at the bottom of the Mississippi social sea. The timing of the move and the prospect of its totality had a lot to do with Maud's death in October, 1960. He was free at last, and in Virginia no one knew about the Billy Falkner who had been—the "Little Billy" who was odd in the streets and would not go upstairs with the prostitutes in the brothels.

In curious ways, Faulkner's move from Mississippi to Virginia was not unlike Thomas Sutpen's move from Virginia to Mississippi. Faulkner in his own eyes was a self-made man, a poor boy who made good. But unlike Sutpen he did not leave his fortune in New Orleans or any place else when he made that final new beginning. His fortune was the Nobel Prize, followed by other prizes, recognition in the national media, fame, and—at last—a royalty flow that was rapidly rising to relatively astronomical figures. In January, 1959, he had $45,000 in his account at Random House and $128,000 due to come in over the next few years from movie and television sales.[103] In a sense, Faulkner brought his Sutpen's Hundred with him to Virginia—intact and growing.

Still, again like Sutpen, Faulkner was a novice, a "convert" as Jill had worded it, referring to the Virginia cult of sophisticated riders of hunters and jumpers. He had jumped horses in Mississippi, but it was a sort of self-taught barnyard jumping. In Virginia it was very different, and again he had a protector and a friend in Grover Vandevender who taught Faulkner as well as he could the more refined style practiced in the Virginia hunts. In a way Grover did for William Faulkner what General Compson had tried to do for Thomas Sutpen. He attempted to teach him not just the obvious form, but the subtleties that gave life to form. Faulkner picked up the form very well. He was an eager, intelligent student who loved the language that he had heretofore heard only from afar. He learned the manners, relished the costume, and doubtlessly was soon using the words, phrases, and body language to which he had not been born. It was as if he were an actor who had discovered by chance not only a part he could easily play, but had also found the theater, the stage, and the play already produced and actually even in performance of which it was constituent. He had only to walk on the stage, speak his lines, make his gestures, and join a company already comfortable, practiced, successful, and lauded—if only because the actors and actresses themselves were the primary audience. For Faulkner, it must have been something close to nirvana, miraculously found, late in life.

Faulkner's move to Virginia had something in it of Sutpen, but it had more of his own great-grandfather's move to Mississippi. William C. Falkner had wanted to join a Mississippi community at the top, to be an easy member of the ruling elite, an aristocrat. In his last years William Faulkner came to identify deeply with that first Mississippi Falkner, and he tended to transform him into an image of greatness that the first Falkner's contemporaries did not see. In reality, Bill Faulkner knew better. As a youth, he once confessed, he had felt the effects of Ripley's negative sentiments about Colonel Falkner. Now in his mind, however, he seemed to raise him up as a giant on the new-found Mississippi earth. Early in 1958, as his Virginia connection was growing distinctly thicker, he had traveled to the cemetery in Ripley with his friend A.B. Cullen, the "cement man," to clean up the Falkner plot. During that visit he had made some attempt to have the shot-away fingers of the outstretched right hand restored.[104] More than thirty years later nothing had come of that. The stubs are still there, rather pitifully pleading.

Then, as now, there were monuments to other Falkners in the black section of the cemetery, those of the mulatto Falkners, a stone's throw away from the marble man. William Faulkner must have known the graves—seen the Falkner name repeated and pondered. Moreover, some of the fifteen children of Delia, Hellen, and Arthur were still alive and visible. Their parents had been undeniably the Colonel's slaves, the slaves in his back yard, terrifically intimate with him in their infancy and childhood. These three and sister Fannie were seen as mulattoes, whereas Uncle Ned and Mammy Callie, claimed connections, were always seen as "black." All during William's life, the Emeline Falkner "family place" was on the lot just north of the African church in Ripley. Indeed, the mound of red, fresh-turned earth must have still been visible on Emeline's grave in 1899 when Billy Falkner came to live there in the second year of his life. Delia died in 1918 just before William left for Canada, but Hellen continued to live in the house next door. She was almost exactly the age of Mammy Callie, and died in the same year, 1940. Her son Falkner Edgerton outlived William Faulkner, whose age was nearly identical, by three years. It is a striking fact that the Colonel's real slaves and their progeny were all about, but William chose to lavish his attention first on Mammie Callie, then on Uncle Ned, neither of whom, even remotely, had been Falkner slaves. Reputedly, William buried Ned in the same cemetery with the other Falkners—though no stone is now visible there.

In a sense, when Faulkner moved to Virginia and joined the Farmington Hunt he was moving to a frontier, like the Colonel. There were Virginians from the old families in the Farmington Hunt and other clubs, but the clubs were also peopled by newcomers like Faulkner—by, in a sense, rebels and expatriates from their natal societies. Some of these people were wealthy and brought their "Sutpen's Hundred" in the forms of stocks and bonds and investments. Many were physicians in an era in America when becoming a medical doctor was the quickest and surest road to minor wealth and high, if only local, prestige. It was a time when art in medicine was on the decline, and science—the certainty of cure and, hence, the justifiability of high fees—was on the rise. It was the age of the abbreviated office visit and the costly miracle drug. The American Medical Association had fought off "socialized medicine" unlike their colleagues in Great Britain, Canada, and elsewhere in the industrialized world, and tens of thousands of physicians were generating extremely high incomes year by year. To avoid what seemed a horrendous income tax rate, many of them took advantage of the special benefits that were allowed to farmers by buying country estates and stocking them with cattle—and horses. An animal farm did not require a great amount of hired labor and might in time produce profit and a very comfortable place of retirement. Thus the Farmington Hunt had a fair share of men who were undeniably the masters of their worlds—strong, self-assured, generally intelligent educated men who sometimes had attractive young wives. The hard-knuckled right hand in the soft leather glove firmly grasping the whip while the left rested loose and relaxed was the perfect image these men had of themselves—tough but fair, realists born to command in difficult situations.

Taken altogether, these were new people to that land, not an indigenous aristocracy—more Sutpen than Sartoris or even Compson. The broader community might scoff at their pretensions and evidence disrespect, as it had for Thomas Sutpen and the Old Colonel, but behind the fences and hedges of the clubs, behind the high-walled houses on the great estates, and in the leathered offices and vast hospitals where wealth (acquired or inherited) and well-to-do physicians held undisputed sway, these slights might hardly be felt. They were people who could buy the insulation that allowed them to have, unchallenged and almost unalloyed, a good opinion of themselves. It is easy to understand how Faulkner might find community there.

Dying

There was a flaw in Faulkner's grand design. The rub was, simply, that the gentleman rider was a poor rider, and his persistence in the role at the hazard of his life reflected a much deeper flaw in his character. He could understand the realities in a given situation nearly perfectly, and he could write them brilliantly into his fiction, but in his personal life he was often sadly unable to bring his behavior up to the level of his understanding.

Jumping horses, like flying airplanes, was an exhilarating and very dangerous proceeding. Both made the heart race and the adrenaline flow. Flying was a matter of marrying mind, body, and machine. But there was a mystery in the marriage, and people seemed either born to fly or not. Jumping horses combines mind, body, and animal, but one of the things about which there was no mystery was that horses that jumped had to be large to do the task and the people who rode them had to have some combination of weight and strength to control the animal. Recurrently, Faulkner was among the walking wounded. Typing a letter to a friend, he apologized for his sloppiness. "Was fox hunting today," he explained, "and the horse and I went through a thicket in high gear and a twig caught me in the left eye and it's watering and sight not too good."[105]

Faulkner might possibly have managed the jumpers and hunters fifteen or twenty years before, but he was now in his sixties, and he was always relatively slight in body. Taking a horse, a hunter, over the jumps was also a matter of skill, and there were fundamentals that one could learn and practice. Other riders noticed Faulkner's apparent disregard for the basics. He rode with his toes out instead of tucked in close to the animal; he took the jumps with his knees spread wide instead of viced to the horse. All too often his friends saw too much daylight between his seat and his saddle as he took Powerhouse over a hurdle. Every time he came down, it was a trauma of some kind to his already tortured spine. One of his fellow club members, David Yalden-Thomson, explained the situation vividly. "He was so slight, so *light,* that no decent-sized hunter was really in his control once it was out of the canter," he said. "He would come swishing by one, face set, lips grim, completely out of control of his animal. Then a little later he would come up beside one, and if he'd brushed you or bumped you, he would just grunt, 'Sorry.'" Yalden-Thomson concluded that "one suspected a very self-destructive streak."[106]

The philosopher was right, there was a self-destructive streak, but that was only a part of it. Like everyone, Faulkner knew the paradox that living is dying, but he thought about it more deeply than most. Clearly, he hated his own death; and he was not inventing devices that would kill him.

When Ernest Hemingway put a double-barreled shotgun to his temple and pulled both triggers in July, 1961, Faulkner brooded about it for several days. There was no love lost between the two men. They were conscious rivals, and Hemingway had taken a Nobel Prize soon after Faulkner. In 1956 he wrote that some of Faulkner's stuff was good, but "I think he is a no good son of a bitch myself." Also, he thought that Faulkner had lost his touch. "His last book *A Fable* isn't pure shit," he declared. "It's unpure diluted shit . . ."[107] Faulkner, on his side, thought that Hemingway revealed himself in part by overplaying the part of the virile male. In the end he decided that Hemingway took the easy way out and that it was unmanly of him to do so. Strangely, he tied Hemingway's suicide to sex and marriage. "It's bad when a man does something like that," he said. "It's like saying death is better than living with my wife." He paused and continued, "Hemingway's mistake is that he thought he had to marry all of them."[108] Obviously, that was an error that Will Faulkner had not made.

Faulkner's commitment was to live a full life. He did it sometimes in trivial but revealing ways. One friend noted that he always drove his second serve at tennis just as hard as his first, scorning the safe lob that would keep him in play. He also did it in major ways, as with flying and jumping horses, at the risk of the death he hated. He seemed to come very close to the mark when he said several times that between grief and nothing, he would take grief. He was talking then about the grief that came from disappointment in love. Repeatedly he had striven to achieve that consummation, a more perfect communion with the other half of humanity—the female half, the sister-self—that was him too—

and he had repeatedly failed. Accepting grief meant that he refused to decline the challenge of life, refused the nothing of a living death. In the last half-dozen years of his life, he was relatively free of the need to grieve over the loss of "tremulous" girls, and pain replaced grief as the symbol of life. Between pain and nothing, he would take pain.

In the later 1950s he nearly ceased the search for love, and he entered whole-heartedly into the rider role. He was an inept rider as he was ultimately an inept lover, but he was ever-ready to remount again and suffer the consequent painful injuries. He deliberately chose to live with the pain; he refused medication that would have alleviated his suffering. To tranquilize away the pain with drugs would have been an acceptance of death in life, of nothingness. Pain, like grief, meant that he had tried, and that he accepted responsibility for his failure. It implied courage, endurance, and hope, and it suggested that he would try again. Curiously, his pain symbolized a will not only to meet the challenges of life, but to conquer and prevail. It was, in effect, a strenuous vote for life over death.

Faulkner knew his danger. At a party after one hunt, an acquaintance expressed conversational surprise that he should bother with real horses when he had such magnificent horses inside his head. She asked him if he liked horses. "I'm scared to death of horses, that's why I can't leave them alone," he answered in that soft, quick, almost nervous way of speaking that he sometimes had.[109]

On Saturday, December 16, 1961, Faulkner took yet another fall from his horse, remounted, and finished the hunt. On Monday he entered the hospital, and soon Dr. Nicoll recorded that he was suffering from pain in his lower back and "acute alcoholic intoxication." He indicated that Faulkner "said he had injured this part of his spine in the first World War." X-rays revealed "some irregularity of the bodies of the dorsal vertebrae but no evidence of acute trauma is seen."[110] Another medical professor, astonishingly, found that a part of Faulkner's spinal difficulty came simply from arthritis.[111]

By this time the connection between Professor Blotner and the Faulkners had become deeply personal. On Thursday at 10:15 A.M., Jill called to ask Joe to go to the hospital to be with Bill until Estelle came to take him home. Joe was there as Estelle and an attendant helped Bill into his pajamas. Joe noted that he had a sturdy build but "a strange sort of humped back." Joe and the woman attendant waited with Bill in the room while Estelle drove the car around to the door.

"Is he your son?" she asked Faulkner. Faulkner was silent for a moment.

"He is more or less my son," he said. "He's my spiritual son. He loves me better than he does his father."

Estelle returned. They walked Bill to the car and settled him in the front seat. He looked at Joe through the open window, tired, pale, trench coat over pajamas, and said in his soft voice, "Come out soon, Joe, I need you."

Three days later, on the day before Christmas, Faulkner was again admitted to the Tucker Hospital in Richmond, having, the report said, "self-administered alcohol for pain." He was attended by the senior partner, Dr. James Asa Shield, who, Blotner observed, "radiates authority." Dr. Shield was a master at the Deep Run Hunt and had sometimes ridden with both Faulkner and Dr. Nicoll, the referring physician. Like Dr. Nicoll, Dr. Shield was amazed to find Faulkner actually in very good shape for his age and habits and discovered no basis for acute pain. Dried out thoroughly—the Tucker was a "cold turkey" institution—Faulkner was discharged on December 29.[112]

Early in 1962, Faulkner took two more terrible falls. On January 2, he was out on another of his Virginia horses, Fenceman, when the animal stepped into a groundhog hole and threw its rider headfirst onto the frozen ground. In this spill, Faulkner damaged his left eye, cracked several teeth, and probably suffered a mild concussion. He did not even remember falling, he said. Still, a general physical examination revealed no serious problem, and that still remarkably tough body recovered yet again.[113] Late in the month, he and Estelle were back in Oxford, he shooting quail and riding horses. He had broken a tooth that anchored a bridge. He had four teeth pulled, and a new bridge made. "I feel now like I've got a mouse trap in my mouth," he joked to Joseph Blotner. "It don't hurt Jack Daniel though, thank God."[114]

Also in Mississippi, Faulkner was rapidly closing out accounts as he and Estelle made their final preparations for the permanent move to Virginia. Greenfield Farm would be sold or leased and Dorothy Oldham was to manage Rowan Oak for them. A few years before, Faulkner had declared his intention that Jill inherit one-half of Rowan Oak from him and Victoria the other half from Estelle. Malcolm and Aunt Dot would always have a home there. Dot needed that, he declared, because she "has nothing, though that is nobody's fault but hers." Malcolm was not included in ownership because he "has already been taken care of by his Franklin kin, which Sister was not, and I don't like that."[115]

Finally, he had to pay his respects to Phil Stone. Phil saw Bill on the street a few days after his arrival. "He looks to me like he has aged about five years since I saw him a few months ago," he said.[116] Apparently, however, the old friends did not speak to each other just then. Faulkner had to visit the reception area in Phil's office downtown three times before Phil, apparently reluctantly, came out and talked briefly with him.[117] Phil had long felt, of course, that he had given Bill his real start as a writer and that his contribution was not fully recognized and appreciated.[118] Bill, on his side, had dedicated the Snopes trilogy to Phil in spite of being miffed that Phil had gathered up "all of the odds and ends of mine he had in his possession and sold it to a Texas university." He concluded that he would never see the $6,000 he had lent Phil twenty years before.[119]

Early on Sunday, June 17, Faulkner rode down Old Taylor Road on

Stonewall, another large horse that he had himself found during a buying trip in Oklahoma. The horse had proved highly fractious, and Faulkner was determined to train him. At the bottom of the hill, Stonewall suddenly arched his back and sent Faulkner sailing through the air. He landed in a sitting position on the bank at the side of the road. He couldn't get up. Stonewall came over and nuzzled him, but Faulkner was not able to reach the reins to pull himself up. Stonewall was heading for the barn at Rowan Oak when the cook saw the animal loping across the yard. She called Estelle and everyone went looking for the rider. Estelle found Bill walking painfully up the road toward home. There, he mounted Stonewall again and took him over the jumps he had erected on the grounds. Then he went down the road to get Felix Linder to look at him. He was bruised but apparently had suffered no severe new injuries. When he told Felix that he had remounted and taken Stonewall over the hurdles, Felix was exasperated. "You were a fool to do that," he scolded. "You could have killed yourself."

"You don't think I'd let that damned horse conquer me, do you?" Faulkner replied. "I had to conquer him." Later that day, he and Estelle went out for a drink at a friend's house. Faulkner was walking with a cane and joking about Stonewall. "Now I know why I was able to get him so cheap," he said.[120]

During the following week, Faulkner suffered severe and unrelenting pain in his lower back. His spirit began to flag. Once he walked slowly down to Felix's house. Felix was sitting on the porch and they talked.

"Felix," Faulkner said, "I don't want to die."

Felix responded as best he could and offered to give him something for his pain. "I could do that," he said. "I'll be glad to."

"That ain't what I want," Faulkner said and walked away.[121]

At the end of June, Faulkner made the last of the financial arrangements that would ensure that he could buy Red Acres. He thought he could do it "solo," but his new friend and staunch supporter, Linton Massey, would provide whatever additional financing might be needed.[122] By now Faulkner had tens of thousands of dollars in his account with his publisher, and the inflow of royalties was, at last, large and constant. In early July, in spite of the pain in his back, he could still walk downtown for mail and other minor chores and go out for dinner at his favorite restaurant, The Mansion. Predictably, he had begun to drink again. On Independence Day morning, Jimmy found him still in bed when he should have been at breakfast. On July 5 the pain had become almost unbearable, and he was drinking more. He was about to enter the cycle again, and Jimmy and Estelle decided to take him to Byhalia. When Jimmy broached the subject to Bill, he found that Faulkner, for the first time ever, was very willing to go. Getting ready, he saw that his uncle was disoriented and sometimes incoherent.

They checked him into Wright's Sanatorium in Byhalia at six that evening.

The physician on duty examined him and found no special difficulty. Before they left, Jimmy went to Faulkner's bedside.

"Brother Will," he said. Faulkner looked at him, his eyes knowing and alert now. "When you're ready to come home, let me know and I'll come for you."

"Yes, Jim, I will," he said.

About 1:30 the next morning, Friday, July 6, Faulkner stirred and sat up on the side of his bed. Before the nurse could reach him, he groaned and fell over. He had suffered a heart attack. When the doctor arrived minutes later, he was dead.[123]

~

The news came to Oxford in the middle of the night, and Jimmy Faulkner took charge. Estelle and Dot were in shock and so afraid that the press would find that he died at Byhalia that they could hardly think of anything else.[124] Faulkner had said that he wanted a funeral like Maud's.[125] At the funeral home in the early hours of Friday morning, Jimmy chose a wooden casket in the same plain style. Later, as Sallie Murry, Dot Oldham, and Ella Somerville looked at him in the casket in the parlor at Rowan Oak, they thought that something was not right. Sallie Murry as usual had a strong opinion. "I have never seen such a cheap sleazy casket in all my life," she said. Ella put it into language that Faulkner would have enjoyed. He looked "all squinched up in there," she said. Sallie Murry went upstairs and asked Estelle if she didn't want a better coffin. Estelle thought so, but would leave it to Jimmy. When Jimmy arrived at Rowan Oak later in the morning, he found that Dot had already sent Bill and the coffin back across town to the undertaker's. Jimmy's anger flared, but his brother Chooky persuaded him to be calm. Jimmy drove to the funeral home again and chose another, more expensive casket, but one still made of wood—cypress. That day, Faulkner's body made yet another transit across the town square. He would have liked that scene too. The slow moving, softly bouncing, rubber-tired hack half-circling the square and heading south.[126]

During the remainder of Friday and on through Saturday morning, Faulkner's body lay in the parlor at Rowan Oak while the clan gathered, joined by Faulkner's friends, old and new. At two o'clock, the priest from Estelle's church, St. Peter's, started the service. Finally, Jack, Johncy, Jimmy, and Chooky—brothers and nephews—carried the coffin from the hearth to the front porch. The procession of cars, led by the hearse, rolled slowly down the drive between the lines of century-old cedars, passed through the gates and into the town, following the pattern of streets laid down by his great-grandfather Butler sixty years before he was born.[127]

Joseph Blotner rode in the second vehicle with a driver, the Episcopal priest, and Phil Stone. The man who would work hard to define what William Faulkner had been was riding with the man who thought he had done most to make him what he was. Blotner's impression of Stone was vivid. "Tall and thin, with a fringe of silver hair combed over his high-domed skull, Stone seemed in constant movement, chattering incessantly as they moved up South Lamar and on into the square." They bore to the right around the courthouse, that hub of Lafayette County where Faulkner's great-grandfather had sat as the first sheriff and his grandfather Charlie Butler had served as bailiff. Standing on the sidewalks and courthouse grounds, people followed the procession with their eyes, silent and solemn. The hearse moved on around the circle, passing the site where the Butler Hotel had burned and Burlina Butler had fled barely with the clothes on her back and within sight of the spot on which Charlie Butler had shot Sam Thompson to death. Then they came to North Lamar, completing another arc in the circle of the square that Bill Faulkner had begun to travel almost sixty years before when his grandfather had picked up Maud and the boys at the train station and driven them home.[128]

Several blocks northeast of the courthouse was St. Peter's Cemetery containing the Falkner family plot. There was space for a grave there, next to his grandfather. Jack Falkner would fill that place in 1973. There was another space, probably large enough for a casket, between Dean and the grave of an infant, perhaps Faulkner's own daughter Alabama. Had Bill been buried in the Falkner plot, however, Estelle could not have been buried at his side. Faulkner was not buried there, and hence he was not buried in old St. Peter's where the highest ground was occupied by the first and most eminent settlers—the Thompsons, Sheegogs, Pegueses, Howrys, and August Baldwin Longstreet and his son-in-law Lucius Quintus Cincinnatus Lamar and their families. The Butlers were there too, on the high ground, next door so to speak, to the Thompson clan, some of whom occupied the central and distinctly separate plot in the acreage that Jacob Thompson had donated for the cemetery. Newcomers like the Falkners and Oldhams had plots in the old cemetery, but both were slightly below the highest ground, and ruled away from it by access roads.

Hastily a plot had been obtained in the new part of the cemetery. It was a few hundred feet to the north of the Falkner graves, beyond a knoll and out of sight.[129] Eventually a family marker would be erected and a marble copse put around the plot that would also hold the remains of Malcolm Franklin, who died in Charleston, South Carolina, in 1977, and those of Estelle, who died in 1972. The earthly remains of both Bill and Estelle lie beneath flat marble slabs facing east toward the rising sun, poised for the resurrection. Faulkner is to Estelle's right, on the uphill side. In summer the plot is shaded by a large, spreading, broad-leafed oak. The plot is at the base of a steep decline. The copse on the side of the hill is higher than the rest, designed to hold back and divert the water that rushes down the hill with each rain, bringing with it particles of that rich red earth. In time, the raised copse proved inadequate, and a thick, rough-sawn piece of Mississippi lumber was fixed to raise the dam higher. Still, that was not enough, and another board was added. In the summer of 1987 it was apparent that this, too, was not enough. The fine-washed red Mississippi sand overflows copse and boards, chokes the grass beyond, fills and spreads, swirling and neat across the flat memorial plate of white marble, partially covering the stone, promising to cover it all. Estelle's stone, inches away, stands clean and clear.

ESTELLE OLDHAM FAULKNER

BORN FEBRUARY 10, 1897

DIED MAY 11, 1972

On Faulkner's side, one can sometimes see how visitors have brushed the sand away from the foot of his stone to read the inscription beneath his name:

BELOVED

GO WITH GOD

Faulkner would have relished all that—the fine cut stone over cypress box and body leaching back to earth, the washing sand and brushing it away to read the words that would be covered again . . . finally forever.

PART THREE

The Writing

A Faulknerian Universe

Faulkner's writings, like the Bible, are voluminous and often cryptic. If one reads selectively, one can offer a wide variety of plausible interpretations of his work. If one takes his work as a whole, it is difficult to make any assertion at all that will not justly bring down upon one's head some of that vast band of dedicated, brilliant, and virtually lifelong professional Faulkner scholars. Nevertheless, it seems not only useful but necessary for those of us who are new to the study to attempt some broad interpretation by which to organize that great body of writing—however tentatively arrived at and however tenuously held. Moreover, Faulkner himself gave us materials to work with; he did have a "worldview," one that he developed early in life and adhered to in his work with amazing consistency.

It might be helpful to schematize a Faulknerian universe in which his fictional characters live and move within a space defined by two connected continuums. One continuum stretches between extremes that might be labeled perfect idealism and perfect realism. As used here, idealism is best associated with Plato's philosophy as it was classically stated in what has come to be called "The Allegory of the Cave." Plato said that our knowledge of what is real comes to us in this fashion: It is as if all our lives we have lived in a cave, so chained and blindered that all we see is the back wall of the cave. Above and behind us is a parapet, a sort of walkway upon which various forms come and go. Outside the cave there is a source of light, like the sun. Light comes in through the mouth of the cave, passes around those forms and makes shadows on the back wall. All that we have ever known are those shadows, and we naturally think they are the whole of reality. In actuality, the shadows are merely manifestations of reality. Essence, truth, being—the really IS—lies in the form on the parapet and the light that gives it life. Shadows are vital to our lives because they constitute our only clues to reality, but we must never mistake the shadow for the essence. The summary line for Platonic idealism is: Reality—truth, being, essence—exists in the idea of the thing rather than in the thing itself.

For the idealist, the man-made things that we see about us are only reflections of reality. For examples, the Southerner's columned mansion, the New Yorker's high-rise apartment building, and the Native American's teepee are simply individualized manifestations of the idea of house, of man-made shelter. At another level, institutions such as governments, families, or churches also represent human attempts to realize the ideal. Finally, there are visions of manhood, womanhood, love, honor, courage, and so on that people strive to achieve, but again each is simply pursuing his or her version of the ideal. The idealist must forever study the shadows. He—or she—must strive to perceive and realize ideals never perfectly seen.

Almost certainly, Faulkner knew the allegory of the cave and probably he came to that knowledge early. In the last generation of slavery, Southerners imported massive doses of European idealism, resurgent in the post-Napoleonic decades, and wove them thoroughly into their thinking and institutions. John Keats's *Ode on a Grecian Urn* was squarely out of that tradition and was probably the single most favored poem in the antebellum South. The experiences of Civil War and Reconstruction certainly dampened Southern idealism, but clearly in the succeeding decades it was rising again, evolving, and finally flourishing. Indeed, idealism (and a concomitant romanticism) became one of the great tools by which the New South in the turn-of-the-century years levered up the Old South and made it beautiful. True slavery, ideal slavery, the real slavery, Southerners argued, was paternalistic and marvelously good for its time. In addition, the Confederacy, Robert E. Lee, and even the common soldiers acting intuitively (now raised in stone on the courthouse square) had stood for such ideals as freedom, honor, duty, courage, and loyalty. As a youth, Faulkner consumed large dishes of idealism in Oxford's public schools and social life, and more subtle offerings elsewhere. Apparently, he relished that food.

At the other end of the continuum is a perfect realism. The primary concern of the realist is with manifestations rather than ideas. He or she treats the shadows as if they were real. The house, the family, the government in which one must live day by day do exist, and it is perilous to act as if they were not real. Using recent parlance, the summary line for realism might be roughly stated as: What you see is what you get.

Southern thinking sometimes ran in realistic veins. In fact, during the era of the American Revolution the South was fully in the mainstream of realism as the Western world moved to new heights in that mode in the age of the Enlightenment. For instance, Thomas Jefferson's draft of the Declaration of Independence was rather purely a study in realism. Indeed, it asserted explicitly that what you see is what you get. "We hold these truths to be self-evident," it commenced. Realism faded rapidly in the South in the early decades of the nineteenth century, but it was always there, latent and potentially dominant.

Individuals and whole societies in the Western world have never, of course, been perfectly idealistic or perfectly realistic. Invariably, they contain elements of each. One might borrow from the Eastern concept of yin-yang and say that each of the halves into which the whole is divided contains the seed of its opposite. To be one is, inevitably, to imply the other. The worldview of the individual—and the definition of himself or herself in the world—becomes a matter of priority, of giving primacy to one of two parts in a whole system with some consciousness always of the way not taken. Thus, the idealist has awareness of what is, but her thinking and behavior center primarily upon those ultimate truths—upon what *ought,* ideally, to be. The idealist sees herself in a grand flux that includes past, present, and future, and she tends to be contemplative, and cautious. The realist is primarily concerned with the truth as visible here and now, and she pours her energies into dealing with those manifestations as if they were true. She strives to achieve immediate outcomes that are tangible and palpable.

If this construct of a metaphysical universe seems simplex, it needs to be. William Faulkner was a genius, but he was not deeply schooled or very sophisticated. He really did drop out of school after the seventh grade if not before, and he never took college seriously. Yet he was a voracious reader and intense observer, he had an amazingly quick and retentive mind, and he had a few superb teachers.

Maud Butler was a reader, and she instilled in each of her sons a love of the written word. More significantly, in the summer of 1914, Bill began his four-year, personally tailored tutorial with Phil Stone. It was from Stone, essentially, that Faulkner derived his worldview, one that was reflective of Phil's education and intellectual preferences. Both men were passionate about language and literature. Phil studied Greek for seven years straight, knew Latin well, and took courses in German and French. Faulkner did French. Phil swept through the whole literature of Western culture, but he dwelt upon poetry, especially the romantic poetry of the nineteenth century. Bill followed suit, and also came to rest with the Romantics. Both men acquired a detailed knowledge of Civil War military history, a nodding acquaintance with the arts, and eschewed, totally in Bill's case, science and mathematics. At the time Faulkner went to Canada in 1918 he had acquired a good liberal arts education, second hand as it were, from Yale and the University of Mississippi.

After the war, as a student at the University of Mississippi, enrolled or not, Bill continued the process, adding to his experience practice in writing, drawing, and the theater. Living and working on campus until 1925, when he was twenty-seven, he had an almost ideal setting to mature fully whatever worldview he had earlier embraced. New Orleans opened other areas of learning, and Sherwood Anderson raised the image of a specific professional goal—to be a writer. His European months added more weight and velocity to a vector already set. By the time he returned to live in Oxford in 1927, Faulkner was ripe to bursting, pregnant with a vision of life that would explode with words written on paper in 1928 and become *The Sound and the Fury.*

This work, this story, *was* himself and all that he had been. It was right and he knew it. It was exceedingly complex in language and suggestion, but it hung upon a spare and elegant frame, as did all the works that followed. It had to be so, because it was all the frame he knew, the only metaphysical ordering he knew. It is good, perhaps, that he refused to converse with Oppenheimer and other heavy intellectuals, that he spent the most creative years of his life as the "dog under the wagon." If he had "known" more, probably, he could not have written so well.

~

The other continuum in Faulkner's writings lies between extremes in which man lives in a state of nature on one side and in modern society on the other. It too draws from the common fount of Western thinking, and is vaguely suggestive of the fourth-century Pelagian heresy that denied original sin and the early nineteenth-century pastoral romanticism notably represented by the French writer François Chateaubriand. Again it is a simple idea, specifically that humanity in the natural setting is good. For Faulkner, man and social organization in a state of nature are perfectly organic—that is, all parts (individuals and associations, male and female, the entire environment) ultimately function smoothly, harmoniously together. There is birth and death and even violence, but all of these are functions of ongoing life. In nature the ideal and the real are one—what Is *is* what Ought To Be—sun, shadow, and form all merge.

Faulkner's fictional county, Yoknapatawpha, provides a perfect stage upon which to play out the drama of man's emergence from nature—from the Garden of Eden—into the modern world. In the 1790s, Yoknapatawpha, like the real Union, Tippah, and Lafayette Counties in which Faulkner was born and lived most of his life, was very sparsely settled by Native Americans, a few whites, and even fewer blacks. Soon modernity began to creep in, signaled most eminently by the claim of certain individuals that they owned this or that portion of the earth. With the institution of slavery, they added a special sin, an idea that some people could own other people as well as the land. During the last generation of slavery, in and after the 1830s, the Cotton Kingdom came to northeastern Mississippi like the Snake in the Garden. It was then that Mississippi society, Southern society, as Faulkner drew it in his fiction, crystallized. Then and afterward, it preferred to think of itself as organic, as having achieved some God-given, naturally harmonious order that sang with the universe. In reality, the South had married the sin of slavery—and race—and all the evils material and spiritual that sprang therefrom.

Faulkner demurred from the great consensus on the unflawed South. His work was, essentially, an exhaustive critique of Southern society and a thorough cataloguing of its failure to bring the human values inherent in man, evident in the natural setting, into the modern world. If he knew the writings of Jean Jacques Rousseau, he would have applauded wholeheartedly his famous line: "Man was born free and is everywhere in chains . . ." His objective as critic was, of course, not to damn the South but to save it. Faulkner argued that the modern Southern order was not natural or harmonious, either in slave times or since. Values had been diminished, obscured, and all but lost: sex roles, race roles, and—to use a convenient term he wisely never used—"class" roles had been misconstrued. Institutions had been created (religious, economic, social, and political) that were incongruent with or even hostile to the "eternal verities." The result was that individual Southerners often found themselves off balance and at war within themselves between their concern for what Is and what Ought To Be. Faulkner neatly caught the essence of those struggles when he said, in his Nobel Prize speech, that the true story of man was that of "the human heart in conflict with itself."

The relationship between an ideal-real continuum and a nature-society continuum might be schematized in the following fashion:

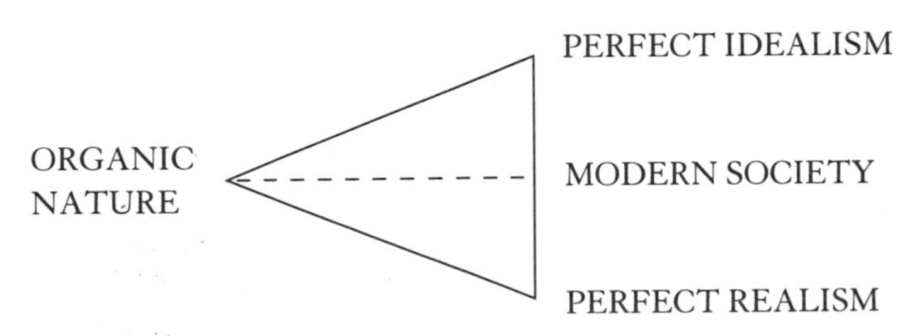

Faulkner's characters all live and move within the triangular space thus established.

To begin with, all children of all times are born innocent, natural, with their capacities for realizing the virtues intact. Immediately, however, their worldview is impacted by mothers, fathers, siblings, and the broad social and physical environment (the history) into which they happen to be born. As children and adolescents, they are readied for entrance into society as adult persons. Often, the debut commences with romantic love, which, in happy circumstances, progresses through courtship to marriage.

Some of Faulkner's fictional children, like Lena Grove and Mink Snopes, were born in modern times but in rural and relatively natural settings and later moved out of those virtual gardens into the world as adults. Thomas Sutpen was born in 1807, about a hundred years before Lena, and was at first reared high in the mountains of western Virginia, virtually a garden. There the definition of private property was what a man could hold in his hands and carry on his back. Sutpen never imagined before he came down from that land of liberty so close to the heavens into the land of plantations and slaves that "there was a country all divided and fixed and neat with a people living on it all divided and fixed and neat because of what color their skins happened to be and what they happened to own." (*Absalom,* 221) Other characters, like Quentin and Jason Compson, were born into a family and a social world already vastly removed from the Garden. Even so, they too must pass from innocence to knowledge.

~

The Compsons illustrate well the working of the ideal-real continuum in the schematic. Quentin was given almost totally to idealism. He was so consumed by his passion for what ought to be that at age twenty he was unable to deal with the impurities of this earthly world and had to leave it. Jason, on the other hand, saw himself as a perfect realist. Clearly, he believed that one got what one saw. He took great pride in his imagined capacity for recognizing hard facts, reaching conclusions, and acting effectively. He was quick to generalize from his observations, to establish rules by which he could live. For instance, he had not the slightest doubt about his keen understanding of womanhood. "Once a bitch, always a bitch, what I say" was how he began his monologue in *The Sound and the Fury* and thus from his first words revealed himself.

However, because Jason so poorly understood and appreciated the unseen realities, especially those of the human spirit, he fell into error repeatedly and with results that were disastrous for his own interests. Again and again, he leapt to conclusions that seemed to be true given the visible evidence, only to discover that he had sorely misjudged the situation. Then he must scurry about, frantically trying to save himself. On one occasion he attempted to use his superior size and strength to extract information on the whereabouts of his runaway niece from a seemingly frail little old man chopping vegetables in the galley of a carnival train. "An old man," he thought, "and not as big as I am." He grabbed the man roughly, firing questions at him in a menacing, bullying tone. However, the man proved to be stronger than Jason had imagined and very spirited. Shortly Jason found himself forced to switch from offense to defense as his intended victim became a furious, hatchet-wielding, would-be murderer of the wounded, bleeding, and scrambling Jason. (*Sound,* 386–88)

Jason was simply incapable of understanding that not all things were palpable, that you do not always get what you see. He was unable to transcend immediate time and place. As an extreme realist, to make sense out of life and act rationally he was forced constantly to recast his universe. He lived precariously minute by minute by man-made time, by the clock—and essentially fixed in the same place, the town where he was born. Increasingly, he was isolated, trapped within his own skin by his own choices, a one-man family living in a one-man apartment, with, finally, a one-man business. He was alive only in the body. Spiritually, he was dead by his own hand just as his brother Quentin was dead physically by his own hand. Jason's working life was bounded by the grading and weighing, the buying and selling of cotton. He assumed that there were really categories of cotton that were classifiable as "middling" or "fair," or "fair to middling" instead of just "cotton," counting imaginary pounds and ounces, dollars and cents in the same way that he counted minutes and hours, taking them as if they were really real. His life was directed, progressive, active—sometimes furiously so—but it was also circular, repetitive, and ultimately meaningless. His seed was cast stillborn, dying fruitless in the body of a Memphis prostitute who came to Jefferson periodically to lend the slightest semblance of love and a pitiful fragment of domesticity to a barren existence. Jason's whole life involved sex without love, body without soul; it was growing shadow and diminishing essence. When Jason died, so too did the Compson name—the sole symbol of Compsonness.

Quentin, unlike his brother, had attempted to free himself from man-made time. He was obsessed by the higher natural truths manifested in sun and shadow. The sun is spirit, the shadow is body. His section opened with the early morning sun casting the shadow of a window sash on the curtain of his Harvard college room. "And then I was in time again," he said. (93) Beginning on the day in which he would end his life, he twisted the hands off the watch passed down to him from his grandfather. The watch still ran, ticking away without readable result. Quentin dressed in his new suit and left the building. "I stepped into sunlight finding my shadow again," he said. "I walked down the steps just ahead of it," he declared, as if the shadow—a representation of himself made on earth by the sun—were something potentially separable from himself, a manifestation of his physical existence that he might lose. (101) Near noon, when the sun would be directly overhead and he might cast no shadow, he got aboard a trolley car, any trolley car, the roof of which could shield him from the sun. "You can feel noon," he mused as he rode. He wondered if even miners in caves in the bowels of the earth feel it. "Then it was past," he said. "I got off and stood in my shadow and after a while a car came along and I got on." It was as if his shadow was one of the last threads tying him to earthly reality; it established his existence. Having secured his shadow again, he went back to the point where he had been just before noon and boarded a streetcar that would take him away from "the sweat" (the commerce and industry of Boston), and back to nature in the countryside. (129–30) Early that evening, he died in the dark, with no sun and no shadow, forever free of body and out of man-made time. (222)

The challenge to the child becoming an adult, whether one was literally emerging from the Garden like Thomas Sutpen, or born into a modern family already out of the Garden like the Compson children, was both to know the real world and to transcend it—to walk the middle line in the schematic, the line between the ideal and the real. Dilsey Gibson did it. Somehow, she had achieved and continued to maintain a superb balance between an awareness of what is and a concern for what ought to be. She was totally undeceived by appearances. Dilsey's kitchen clock had only one hand. It struck five times and Dilsey said with no hesitation, "Eight o'clock." (341–42) She understood time, and she understood that the Compson family was falling into dissolution. She, herself, met every real situation as best she could with the resources available to her—poor as they were—but she never lost her vision of what ought to be, nor her capacity for communicating that vision to individual Compsons or to her own children and grandchildren. Dilsey beautifully married body and soul in her own life, and she radiated wholeness. In a sense, she was a living saint, Christ again on earth. Easter is her day.

The prime mover in the transition of the people of Yoknapatawpha County and the South from a state of nature to a modern society was the Industrial Revolution. At first, as we have seen, the cotton South participated directly in that great world process and in the last decade before the Civil War prospered mightily through the institution of plantation slavery. Through his ancestors, Faulkner himself was close to the process. After the war, the South was greatly reduced in economic and political power. Over the decades cotton production in Latin America, Egypt, and India increased tremendously, and the South found itself reduced, very much like a "third world" country, to subordination to the industrial North. Faulkner's characters after the war lived in a colonial culture. Economically, labor was plentiful, wages were low, manufactured goods were high, and cash money always scarce enough to make borrowed money very costly. The white South was severely defeated in war, the country was occupied by an alien army, and a generalized sense of powerlessness permeated the land. Inevitably, Southerners suffered self-doubt and self-hate and consequently a tendency—always resisted if not ultimately successfully—to tear their people, their families, and themselves apart. In fiction the Compsons certainly did so; in real life, elements of the Butler clan tended to do so. Certainly Charlie Butler stole the town's money and deserted his wife and children. The Falkners, on the other hand, endured and sometimes prevailed by doing whatever needed to be done in the circumstances—whether it was Colonel Falkner using convict labor to complete his railroad line and in the process killing one of the convicts who attempted to escape, or John Falkner, Jr.'s putting his father-in-law into the "Big Place" in the 1920s in an attempt to run it as a boarding house and, when that failed, cutting the ancestral mansion up into apartments to rent and selling the corner lot for a gas station.

Historically, in the postwar South those who did best in terms of money and power somehow cut through to make a connection with the North. Jason well understood that he could not prosper in a grand way in cotton speculation without getting information directly from the North where the market was made. He paid $10 a month to an advisory service in New York to keep him informed by telegraph of the situation on the cotton exchange. "I know I'm right," he told a drummer acquaintance over a Coke at the drug store. "It's a sucker game, unless a man gets inside information from somebody who knows what's going on." On that day trading in the cotton market in New York began at ten o'clock. Jason was alert to the time, waiting for it. "Then it struck ten," he said. "I went up to the telegraph office. It opened a little, just like they said. I went into the corner and took out the telegram again, just to be sure." (238–39) In the end Jason found that he could not know enough fast enough to act effectively. He was powerless very much because he was not at the seat of power. If Jason had been born into the Compson family three generations before, his story would have been vastly different. He would have been a planter and a great slaveholder. It is easy to imagine Jason as a "lord of the lash," and one has no doubt that he would have made slavery pay very well—psychologically and sexually as well as materially. He would have had the power to get very nearly what he saw. As a person Jason would have been no less despicable, but in a slaveholding society he would have commanded respect because he would have functioned successfully in the system. As it happened, he ended a marginal figure, a cotton broker in a little Mississippi town, squeezing out what he could between the powerful industrialists in the textile world and the nearly powerless farmers who lived around him. In view of the alternatives in that time and place—either joining the Yankees by becoming their paid agent or extracting such profits as he could out of tenants and neighbors, blacks and dirt-farming whites—Jason's father's decision simply to withdraw becomes comprehensible.

William Faulkner was born into and reared among an imperialized people, a people much reduced in power from what had been the case within living memory. In writing about their plight, he met the plight of the imperialized people of the world, the people whose land had been raped and labor taken to supply raw materials for the factories of the industrial powers. Faulkner was highly critical of that process and its results in Mississippi. He once declared his amazement that God had done so much for Mississippi and man so little. Not many fellow Mississippians in his lifetime would have agreed. What Faulkner would have called the rape of the land, they would have called progress. For most Mississippians the reduction and even destruction of the wilderness was, indeed, wholly laudable. Sawmills and cotton gins, roads and trains, hamlets, towns, and mansions, banks and even factories were good things and much to be desired. In drawing out a contrast between the good in organic nature and the bad in modern Southern society, Faulkner was not likely to get much audience or appreciation in Mississippi—or in the South in general.

~

In regard to the other axis, in working incisively at the tension between idealism and realism, Faulkner compelled attention because he was probing at the very core of culture in Mississippi, in the South, and, indeed, in the Western world. Broadly speaking, the tension between the ideal and the real, between the furies on the one hand and Apollonian calculation on the other, is the force that keeps Western civilization vital. For us in the West, it is simultaneously our joy and our burden, our cross and our misery. As a whole civilization over successive eras, we have tended to oscillate from one extreme to the other, yawing out and achieving disaster, but never quite destruction, almost as if the disease itself creates the fever than kills the virus.

For the individual at a given moment in the process, there is a paradox. To perceive the ideal and move toward it is, like Quentin, to leave this apparent world. To know this world and move too fully in it is, like Jason, to suppress too much of the spiritual qualities in humanity and to doom oneself to chase frantically after an ever-shifting social and material universe. In his own life, Faulkner knew the paradox intimately, and it runs through the weave of his writings to the very end like some dark and somber thread. For Faulkner virginity symbolized the ideal: the virginity of women, the virginity of men, the virginity of the earth. To possess the woman, the man, the earth was inevitably to violate their purity, to reduce, ruin, and dissolve them.

Faulkner's great power as a writer was that he pressed in on the very core of Western civilization, working at this grand paradox that gives it, and each of us who belong to it, both life and death and gives each in tension and, often, in pain. The paradox—to pluck the rose and yet have it live—lies at the root of the problem of the human heart in conflict with itself. We want to devour this world and everything in it, appetite without end, and yet we want it to remain untouched. We want to re-form the whole surface of the earth—level mountains, raise swamps, and hold the beaches rigid against the waves—and use everything just as we please. Yet we want the earth to remain pristine and pure—clean air, clear water, and virgin land. We want to be increasingly wealthy, to possess everything, and yet we want there to be no poor. We want to have sex to the exhaustion of desire, and yet we want the objects of our passion to be, to have been, and to remain virginal, untouched. We want, simultaneously, to marry lust and innocence, glands and heart. And, of course, this cannot be. To move, to act, to do and be anything at all, it seems that we must put at risk the purity of the earth and all that exists thereon. Such is the human condition.

"Did you ever have a sister?" demanded the desperate Quentin. "Did you?" (199, 206)

TEN

Sex in the Sylvan Setting

Most of all in his writings, William Faulkner dwelt on the tensions that work between men and women—a theme central, of course, in every culture. What should a woman be, what should a man be, and what should they be together? In the South, that universal tension was terribly heightened by the impact of race and class.

Faulkner was born into a Southern world that had a vision of itself as an organic society with a place for everyone and everyone, hopefully, in his or her place. In regard to gender roles, the Victorian order in the South was exceedingly clear. Women should be pious and pure, domestic and submissive. Men should be protectors. Like knights of old slaying dragons, they should protect their ladies physically. Also they should be the material protectors, the providers who "bring home the bacon" day by day for the comfortable support of their families.

In the Victorian mind, God had so arranged the world that there was one certain woman ideally created for every man and one man for every woman. When they found one another they would recognize their destiny instantly and intuitively. There would be a sequence—rituals of recognition, love, courtship, engagement, and marriage. Before marriage the woman would be a virgin. After marriage would come sex and then children. Children represented the perfection of familyhood. Children heightened domestic bliss and insured the perpetuity of the family. They also formed a blood union of the families of the parents and hence solidified the ties of clan that had begun with marriage. Family and clan necessarily led to community.

In the progression of love, marriage, and sex; family, clan, and community, marriage was crucial. It was the wide gate through which boys and girls became adults and entered society. The gate was not easily missed in the Southern world. All arrows pointed that way. To not marry, for both men and women, was to live one's life in an incomplete state, more or less tangential to the social circle. In the turn-of-the-century South, Victorian ideals held sway, and few men or women died without having been married. Fewer still failed to make an earnest attempt to be married.

Searching for the Perfect Couple

Faulkner was profoundly critical of the sex roles prescribed by the Southern social order. Repeatedly he measured the distance between what society insisted was the ordinary and ideal progression and what actually happened. Arrayed below are, arguably, the most important characters in Faulkner's depiction of Southern culture. Excluding some black characters, not one of these persons enjoyed the happy progression that Southern society envisioned.

	Women	*Men*
Sartoris 1929	Narcissa Benbow	Horace Benbow
	Belle Mitchell	Bayard Sartoris
Sound 1929	Caddy Compson	Quentin Compson
	Dilsey Gibson	Jason Compson
	Mrs. Caroline Compson	Benjy Compson
		Mr. Jason Compson
Dying 1930	Addie Bundren	Anse Bundren
	Dewey Dell Bundren	Jewel Bundren
		Darl Bundren
		Cash Bundren
Sanctuary 1931	Temple Drake	Popeye
Light 1932	Lena Grove	Joe Christmas
	Bobbie Allen	Lucas Burch
	Joanna Burden	Simon McEachern
		Gail Hightower
		Byron Bunch
		Percy Grimm
		Doc Hines
Absalom 1936	Rosa Coldfield	Thomas Sutpen
	Ellen Coldfield	Henry Sutpen
	Judith Sutpen	Charles Bon
	Clytie Sutpen	Shreve McKenzie

	Women	Men
Wild 1939	Charlotte Rittenmeyer	Harry Wilbourne The Tall Convict
Hamlet 1940	Eula Varner Mrs. Varner Yettie Snopes	Will Varner Jody Varner Flem Snopes V.K. Ratliff Labove Ike Snopes Mink Snopes Jack Houston
Bear 1942		Ike McCaslin Sam Fathers Boon Hogganbeck Buck McCaslin Buddy McCaslin
Intruder 1948	Miss Habersham	Lucas Beauchamp Charles (Chick) Mallison
Requiem 1951	Nancy Mannigoe	Gavin Stevens
Town 1957	Linda Snopes Maggie Mallison	Manfred de Spain Montgomery Ward Snopes
Mansion 1959		Wall Street Snopes Joe Goodyhay
Reivers 1962	Everbe Corinthia	Lucius Q.C. Priest Uncle Ned

Specifically, if one looks at the crucial stage in the progression, marriage, one finds among the leading characters no reasonably perfect union—nor even, one might add, a reasonably happy couple outside of marriage. Now and again, Faulkner gives us the promise of a happy union, only to pull the token back. In 1932 in *Light in August,* he introduced V.K. Surratt comfortably settled in bed with his wife telling her about Lena and Byron between episodes of making love. When V.K. comes on stage again as a major character in 1940, his family name had shifted to Ratliff, and he was and always had been a bachelor.

At first glance Will Varner and his wife appear to be an ideal couple, each playing to the hilt the gender role prescribed. But then contradictions appear. They had sixteen children, and only two had stayed in the proximity of Frenchmen's Bend, and those two are still living in the same house with their parents.

One understands more fully the defection of the Varner children while observing the couple's response to Eula's unwed pregnancy. Preparing to marry Eula off to Flem Snopes, Will Varner berated his bachelor son Jody, who wanted to defend the family's reputation by doing violence to the malefactor. "Hell and damnation," Will exclaimed, "all of this hullabaloo and uproar because one confounded running bitch finally foxed herself. What did you expect—that she would spend the rest of her life just running water through it!" (*Hamlet,* 143–44) Mrs. Varner, for her part, was ready to quiet Jody with a stick of stove wood to the head. "I'll fix him," she cried. "I'll fix both of them. Turning up pregnant and yelling and cursing here in the house when I am trying to take a nap." (142)

With Faulkner, seemingly golden marriages turned to dross upon examination. That perfect child, Charles E. (Chick) Mallison, appeared to be born to storybook parents. His father was the intelligent, very responsible, settled owner of a hardware store. His mother, Maggie Mallison, was the daughter of the most eminent local judge. She was intelligent, sensitive, attractive, and a leading matron in the community. Chick was an only child, and Maggie seemed the perfect mother. But then one gradually understands the depth of her devotion to her twin brother, Gavin Stevens, who lived with the couple for several decades. Maggie spent much of her energy attempting to save her brother from the rather disastrous effects of his inability to rise through the love stage in the passage to adulthood. Specifically, she labored mightily to pump him up to some kind of performance in dealing with his lust for Eula Varner, and then a dozen years later on the same stage with the same scenery attempted somehow to mediate her middle-aging and bachelor brother to some sort of mature sexual relation with Eula's teenage daughter. The result was a rather strange family in which the son developed far more intimacy with his uncle and his uncle's bachelor buddy, V.K., than he did with his own father. It was as if when Mr. Mallison married Maggie he became not so much husband as orphan.

If intelligence, courage, and evenness of temper counts, Charles appeared to mature beautifully under the tutelage of his mother, her brother, and V.K., but when last seen in 1959 he was about forty years old and still unmarried. Moreover, there was no hint of either love or sex ever having entered his life. So far as we know, his foot had never found the first rung of the sexual and social ladder. He had learned from his uncle only to be a faithful spectator looking carefully and curiously in on other people's lives, and his greatest consummations were to encapsulate this or that life experience in so many words—to extract essence from appearance and control it by verbal devices. Faulkner added a characteristically deft stroke when he made Chick a bombardier in Europe during World War II. Chick observed the war from on high and, no doubt, studied the earth through a kind of telescope that was known as a Norden bombsight. He did not shoot shells in manly defiance of gravity as did the artillery; he simply dropped bombs and bombs of their own weight found earth again. Eventually, he was shot down and observed the rest of the conflict as a rather contented and passive prisoner of war, looking up instead of down.

~

Faulkner's major characters lived and moved upon a marital and sexual landscape that was in shambles. It was littered with the fragments left by a destructive social order—love without consummation, sex without love or marriage, adultery, rape, attempted rape, rape with an inanimate object, rape using another male, incest, miscegenation, prostitution, homosexuality, androgyny, bestiality, voyeurism, nymphomania, pedophilia, necrophilia, impotence, and, finally, frigidity, both male and female. Moreover, sex of any kind was very often associated directly with physical violence. Sometimes it was sex with violence; sometimes, curiously, it was violence instead of sex. Further, Faulkner's fiction is not at all lacking in characters who are sadistic, masochistic, or both. Often enough, sex relates race and violence. Small wonder that Faulkner's neighbors in Oxford asked how he could write "that stuff," or that many American readers pronounced him outrageous.

When love, sex, and marriage did go well with Faulkner's characters, it often happened in a sylvan setting. The woods are nature, and in nature all is well. When his couples moved out of the woods and into modern society, unions were taxed and broken. Very often the trail of dying love ran congruently with the travel of what Faulkner brilliantly called "the slain wood" as it moved from the forest through sawmills, to planing mills, and into houses and mansions. In the process, the wood lost touch with the ground. Divorced from the earth by brick foundations and man-set stones, wooden structures rose higher and higher. High-rising houses become symbols of man's overweening pride, and of his willingness to do violence not only to nature but to his fellow men and women. In Faulkner's universe, it becomes virtually impossible to live in a mansion and enjoy the happy fruits of love, marriage, sex, family, and clan. It is an irony that he himself, like some of his Falkner ancestors, could neither be comfortable with nor without a "Villa," a "Big Place," a Rowan Oak or Red Acres. Within a decade of acquiring his big house, he recognized his danger and bought Greenfield Farm and Bailey's Woods as if to root himself in nature again. Almost to the end he attempted to continue his annual November visits to the "Big Woods" in the Tallahatchie bottoms.

Mink and Yettie

Faulkner's potentially most perfect couple began their union in the deep woods. The man was Mink Snopes, at first very unsympathetically portrayed by Faulkner in *The Hamlet* in 1940. During his early life, Mink had lived on a dozen different tenant farms as his father moved from one to another. Then suddenly, about the turn of the century when he was twenty-three, Mink felt the need to leave and strike out for the sea. He had never seen the sea and did not know where it was, but he headed in the right direction, south, toward the Gulf of Mexico. Days later, almost there, and after walking for twenty-four hours without food, he found himself in the midst of a great forest as night fell. Then he saw a light. It was a lumber camp, literally carved out of the woods. Approaching, he saw a young woman of striking physique standing in the light of an open doorway while the workers called to each other, busily closing down the operation for the night. "Those hard loud manshouts and cries seemed to rise toward her like a roaring incense," Faulkner wrote. (235–36) The woman was Yettie.

Yettie's mother had died in childbirth. She was the only daughter of a wildcatting lumberman, "a roaring man of about fifty" who was no taller than Mink, "with strong, short iron-gray hair and a large prominent belly." In real life, Yettie's father could have been Charlie Butler. The man had leased convicts to take the "virgin timber" from the tract. He built a rough settlement deep in the woods—plank and canvas barracks for the men, a kitchen, and a house for himself and his mistress. The latter was "a magnificent quadroon woman most of whose teeth were gold." She superintended the cooking for the camp. For his daughter Yettie, the father had attached to his house a separate room with a separate entrance.

Mink took a job as an axe man, and he soon learned why Yettie had a separate entrance. On his first day in the woods, he turned from his work to see her "sitting on a big, rangy, well-kept horse behind and above him, in overalls, looking at him not brazenly and speculatively, but intently and boldly, as a bold and successful man would." He saw in her "the habit of success—that perfect marriage of will and ability with a single undiffused object—which set her not as a feminine garment but as one as masculine as the overalls and her height and size and the short hair; he saw her not as a nympholet but the confident lord of a harem."

So it was. Day by day, Yettie would send the mulatto woman or the foreman to one man after another with orders for the man to come to her. Soon Mink was summoned, and responding he felt he had entered "not the hot and quenchless bed of a barren and lecherous woman but the fierce simple cave of a lioness." They met "early one afternoon, the hot sun of July falling through the shadeless and even curtainless windows open to all outdoors, upon a bed made by hand of six-inch unplaned timbers cross-braced with light steel cables, yet which nevertheless would advance in short steady skidding jerks across the floor like a light and ill-balanced rocking chair."

Mink would have many passions in his life thereafter, but only one woman. Of all the men, only Mink was jealous of her, and jealous forever of the dozens of men who had preceded him with her. "He had been bred by generations to believe invincibly that to every man, whatever his past actions, whatever depths he might have reached, there was reserved one virgin, at least for him to marry;

one maidenhead, if only for him to deflower and destroy." (236–37) Mink soon discovered that he had not will enough to leave Yettie to continue his journey to the sea.

Five months later, Yettie's father went bankrupt. The camp was struck, and Mink and Yettie were married. They went back to the country from which he had come and rented a small farm on shares, and the next year another. They had no children and Yettie expected none. "I've had a hundred men, but I never had a wasp before," she said. "That stuff comes out of you is rank poison. It's too hot. It burns itself and my seed both up. It'll never make a kid." But in three years it did, and two years later it made another. The children shackled her, and she signaled her acquiescence by letting her dark hair grow long and dyeing it blond. In camp she had used the razors of the men to keep her hair "man-short." (238–39)

When they had first begun to farm, Mink had almost all of the pay he had earned at the lumber camp. But that went, and over the years they were made poorer and poorer, until he didn't have the tools, or the animals, or the fertilizer—anything more than his hands and that small, wiry, virtually inexhaustible body—to fight the capricious climate and a merciless marketplace to make a farm go. Mink was not lazy, nor unintelligent, nor uncaring. He simply was born into an economy that afforded him increasingly less chance of making a living for himself and his family. In the crisis he was failed by both community and clan. Finally, to save his honor—his sense of himself as a man and person, a human being—he sacrificed his wife and children, his freedom, and would have sacrificed his life. He killed his arrogant neighbor Jack Houston in the only way he could, from ambush, with a rusty old shotgun that ought not to have worked. Even as he pulled the trigger he knew that he had no resources upon which to flee, and nothing to live on if he stayed.

Instinctively, Yettie knew what he had done. When he came home after killing Houston, she confronted him. She was leaving but not going far, she said, because when they hung him she was going to be where she could see it. As she talked, he stood up, "small, almost a half head shorter than she, barefoot, moving toward her, not fast, sidling a little, his head bent and apparently not even looking at her as she stood . . . the bleached hair darkening again at the roots since it had been a year now since there had been any money to buy more dye." He slapped her. She didn't flinch or blink. "You damned little murdering bastard," she said. He slapped her again, bringing blood, and again, patiently, wearily. "Go," he said. "Go, go." He followed her into the house, watching her body in the lamp light. "It's like drink. It's like dope to me," he said, and he thought how between them were the nameless and numberless men she had known. They were a part of his past too, "as if he and not she had been their prone recipient." (221) Yettie went to Frenchmen's Bend and that night began to tell people that Mink had not killed Houston—even before anyone knew that Houston had been killed. She was taken into Will Varner's house, where she worked, and soon came to possess a ten dollar bill that she tried to give to Mink. He refused the profferred note.

372

"Did you sell Will something for it, or did you just take it out of his pants while he was asleep?" Mink challenged. "Or was it Jody?"

"What if I did?" Yettie said. "What if I can sell enough more of it tonight to get ten more?" (240) She begged him to stay in the woods, wanting him to take flight. He tore himself away from her, and when she tried to stop him he found a stick, raised it, and moved wearily toward her. She turned and left. Mink went back into the country, was arrested and held in the county jail. Later, Yettie came to Jefferson to be near him. V.K. Ratliff took Yettie and the two children into his home. She worked in a shabby boarding house. Sometimes on Sunday afternoons V.K. would see her and the children going or coming through the jailhouse gate. She and the children were there where none of the other Snopes kin appeared. Mink went to Parchman on a life sentence. Still Yettie wrote to him. She wanted to come and bring the children to see him. Mink would not allow it. Now, he was living only to get free to avenge his honor by killing Flem, his kinsman, who had broken the laws of clan.

Ike

In a wrenching parody of the ideal, Faulkner did create one perfect Victorian couple. The male was ecstatically in love with the female. Quite literally, it was a pastoral romance. At dawn he would wait for her by the stream in the meadow, lying in the grass, knowing that she would come that way. "Then he would hear her and he would lie drenched in the wet grass, serene and one and indivisible in joy," the water-laden air that touched her also touched him "and shaped them both somewhere in immediate time, already married." As she approached, "he would lie amid the waking instant of earth's teeming life, the motionless fronds of water-heavy grasses stooping into the mist before his face in black fixed curves, along each parabola of which the marching drops held in minute magnification the dawn's rosy miniatures, smelling and even tasting the rich, slow warm barn-reek, the flowing immemorial female, hearing the slow planting and the plopping suck of each deliberate cloven mud-spreading hoof, invisible still in the mist loud with its hymneal choristers." (*Hamlet,* 165)

The beloved was a cow. The lover was Ike Snopes in *The Hamlet,* an idiot, adult in age but a child in mind. He could almost say his name, "Ike H-mope." Ike was heavy, with very thick thighs that might have been meant for a woman. He lived with Mrs. Littlejohn who ran the boardinghouse in Frenchmen's Bend. She had taught him to sweep the rooms and make the beds. But once he saw Jack Houston's cow, he knew love. He would rise before dawn and go out into the pasture by the stream. She would come to drink in the early morning. "Then he would see her: the bright thin horns of morning, of sun, would blow the mist away and reveal her, planted, blond, dew-pearled, standing in the parted water of the ford, blowing into the water the thick, warm, heavy, milk-laden breath; and lying in the drenched grasses, his eyes now blind with sun, he would wallow faintly from thigh to thigh, making a faint, hoarse moaning sound. Because he cannot make one with her through the day's morning and noon and evening." At first, Ike's love was unrequited. "She raised her head and looked at him and scrambled up the further bank." He followed her home and "into the shed, speaking to her again, murmurous, drooling, and touched her with his hand." He awoke lying on his back her still kicking the plank wall by his head. Jack Houston rescued him and drove him away like some firm but understanding father protecting his daughter. (165–68)

The lovers were separated but love went on. Later, when Ike was making beds and sweeping floors upstairs in Mrs. Littlejohn's boardinghouse, he looked out the window and saw smoke in the distance. It was a grass fire in Houston's pasture. He knew immediately that his beloved was in danger. He ran more than three miles to the pasture and saw the smoke beyond the creek. "He made the hoarse, aghast sound again and ran down the hill and through the now-dry grass in which at dawn he had lain, and to the creek, the ford. He did not hesitate. He ran full-tilt off the bank and onto the rimpled stream, continuing to run even after he began to fall, plunging face-down into the water, completely submerged, and rose, streaming, knee-deep, bellowing." Struggling on, "he actually heard the cow's voice, faint and terrified, from beyond the smokepall on the other hill." He ran into the smoke toward the voice. He heard rapid hoofbeats and a screaming horse charging toward him. He fell sprawling and "the wind, the dragon-reek, blasted at him . . . as the maddened horse soared over his prone body and vanished."

He passed through the smoke and fire, hopping now to save his feet from the hot, scorching earth, to come to the side of his beloved standing on the bank above the creek. The horse charged at them, and in the rush all fell into the ravine. The horse scrambled up and ran down the ditch, while he, "lying beneath the struggling and bellowing cow, received the violent relaxing of her fear constricted bowels." She tried, "as though in a blind paroxysm of shame, to escape not him alone but the very scene of the outragement of privacy where she had been sprung suddenly upon and without warning from the dark and betrayed and outraged by her own treacherous biological inheritance, he following again, speaking to her, trying to tell her how this violation of her maiden's delicacy is no shame, since such is the iron imperishable warp of the fabric of love." Finally, away from the fire, she drank and accepted his touch. "She does not even stop drinking: his hand has lain on her flank for a second or two before she lifts her dripping muzzle and looks back at him, once more maiden meditant, shamefree." (168–75)

Houston came and took the cow home. Thereafter, Isaac stole the animal away from the shed where she had been comfortably housed by Houston and her chastity guarded. He led her some distance away, to a woods where they made a nest. He left the nest nightly to steal cattle feed from a neighboring barn. When he returned with the food, they would feast together out of the same bag. He milked her until she was comfortable, and at evening they lay down together, she "the mammalian attar." (175–86) For the lovers there was "no distance in either space or geography" because they were together and no time other than sun and moon and stars. However, the feed bag leaked, and the lovers were traced and found. Houston gave Isaac the cow, which then came to stay in the barn behind the boardinghouse. (186–96)

If it had not happened before in the woods, the marriage was consummated in the barn. After an absence, V.K. Ratliff returned to the hamlet to find that Lancelot "Lump" Snopes had removed a board from the barn wall so that the men, the idlers in the hamlet, could watch the recurrent act of love. Curious, V.K. looked too, "and it was as though it were himself inside the stall with the cow, looking out of the blasted tongueless face at the row of faces watching him who had been given the wordless passions but not the specious words." V.K. drove the men away and returned the board to its place, saying, "this here engagement is completed." (196)

V.K. called the Snopes clan together to do its duty. Folklore dictated that they must buy and slaughter the animal, cook a portion and feed it to the offending man, and he would be cured. This was done with Eck Snopes, a Snopes of surprising decency, doing the buying. (197–204)

In the next year V.K. returned to Frenchman's Bend. Hanging up his harness in Mrs. Littlejohn's barn, he found Ike sitting in one of the stalls, "the drooling mouth slacking and emitting a sound, hoarse, abject, not loud." Ratliff saw that he held on his overalled knees the wooden effigy of a cow. Eck told him that he had bought the wooden cow for Ike. "I felt sorry for him," he explained. "I thought maybe any time he would happen to start thinking, that ere toy one would give him something to think about." (266–67) Ike thus has his ideal fixed in wood, and one might well say of him: "Forever wilt thou love, and she be fair." His love will remain unplucked and pure.

In the story of Ike and the cow, Faulkner gave us a nearly perfect parody of the Victorian and Southern model for love, marriage, and sex. Ike played his role with marvelous fidelity. His love for the cow was all-consuming and all-giving—it was total, and she the one female in the universe for him. He fulfilled perfectly the two parts of the Southern male role—he protected his love from deadly physical peril, and he became the material provider. While one might wonder if the cow could be pious, one could hardly imagine her as impious or challenge her purity, domesticity, and ultimate submissiveness—all within the limits of her nature. In the South, an idiot was sometimes referred to as "natural." Ike was a natural man with "no muscular and spiritual reluctance to overcome" in pursuing his passion for his loved one. Indeed, during the period in which he and she had lived in a state of nature, the process of love, courtship, engagement, and marriage had gone beautifully, rhapsodically. It was only when the couple was brought into the man-made world, into barns and stalls, and Lump Snopes had led others in voyeuristically projecting evil upon them that corruption entered. It was V.K., acting as one of the community, who came, who saw, and said, "We cannot live like this."

Androgyny

Again and again in his writings, Faulkner seems to make the point that sex or gender roles in Southern culture were vastly exaggerated. Society required men to be much too masculine, and women too feminine. By nature, men and women were different, but not nearly so different as the social order prescribed. The result was that society itself caused great confusion and frustration in matters of love, sex, and marriage.

Often Faulkner made this point by creating women like Yettie who had "male qualities," and men like Ike who had "female qualities." The idea reached its ultimate expression in the highly admirable character V.K. Ratliff. V.K.'s maleness is beyond question. He went into the world, made money, and fought valiantly to protect the weak and helpless. He had no difficulty relating to men lounging on the front porches of country stores, nor even in telling them lusty stories. At one point, sitting with the men on the porch of Varner's store, he was overheard saying: "Now as the feller unbuttoned one gallus of his overalls . . ." And yet if piety means affinity with goodness, and purity means a moral state that makes such piety possible, he ranked high in these prescribed categories of feminine excellence also. Most obviously, V.K. was amazingly domestic. Gradually one learns that he maintained a small neat house, that he was an excellent cook and a superb seamstress. His very livelihood was tied to "women's work," as the phrase went then. He chose to be a sewing machine salesman and circulated through three counties in his buckboard drawn by two horses whom he fondly called "rabbits." In the back of his buckboard he carried a sort of little girl's doll house with door and windows in which he kept his demonstrator sewing machine. V.K. could often be seen in front of a farmhouse, surrounded by women as he stood at the back of his wagon deftly demonstrating his machine. At the same time, he was gathering and distributing local news—"gossiping"—with the ladies. V.K. had a special rapport with women. We learn relatively late in the Snopes trilogy that he knew, intimately, Eula Varner Snopes, that paragon of womanhood, and that she knew him as well if not better than did his closest male friend Gavin Stevens.

Like Eula and unlike Gavin, V.K. was born and reared close to the land and later came to live in the town. He dealt easily with both the country farm folk and the people in the hamlet and the town. Rooted in the soil, he nevertheless, moved with intelligence and balance into the modern world. He sold machines that were made by machines in factories; he was totally comfortable as a commercial agent of the industrial revolution and dealt easily and very successfully in matters of money, banking, and credit. Few people who have ever sewn by hand for more than an hour would argue against a machine that drives a needle.

In our schematic, V.K. is a person who came out of the garden into the modern world and maintained a capacity for balance in his judgments between what is and what ought to be. He accepted feelings, emotions, and intuition as ways of knowing truth that transcended facts, but he also watched the world, reasoned, and gave weight to what he saw. Finally, he acted, he moved, he did things. "Feeling knows before knowing does," Faulkner might have written of him in one of his opaque modes.

V.K. had a distinctly male body. He was sexually aware, joyous, almost lusty, but he had no lover. In the mutation from V.K. Surratt in 1932 to V.K. Ratliff in 1940, Faulkner took away his wife, and it was almost as if V.K. married himself. He existed in some state beyond priesthood in which his male and female parts had come to some plan of union, like monk and nun conjoined. V.K. was physically male, and his purpose may have been to seed the earth by his acts and bring forth good in the human universe in which he moved. Perhaps, for him that mission was love enough, marriage enough, family enough, and the fruition was consummation too.

V.K.'s intimacy with Eula was natural. He was her father's real heir who improved upon the legacy. Both Will Varner and V.K. were superbly wise and able, but whereas Will turned his talents to self-indulgence, and taking all he could get, V.K. served his community and gave as he received. Most of all, V.K. fit Eula because in the Faulknerian universe they were one: she was a natural woman as he was a natural man. Eula moved only when she needed to move. In her early life she could live as if in a cocoon because her father, and her mother, and local society had made things that way. She responded in almost animal (one is tempted to say bovine) fashion. Let there be no useless motion, no panic or hysteria; hers was the poise of the well-fed lioness. When the time was ripe, when need stirred within her, she turned to the male among males who had fought his way to her side and in the midst of fury and violence, with surging blood and rising heat, conceived and gave life. Then, she was quiet again, non-moving, non-seeking, beyond need.

We don't know that Eula ever knew love for anyone other than her daughter Linda. Certainly, McCarron's love for Eula, if it existed at all, was not sufficient to prevent his desertion of her. His feeling for Eula, whatever it was, was hardly greater than his love of competing with other men for a goal that, in one sense, dissolved with the getting. In her early life, Eula apparently skipped love, found sex naturally, and then married virtually by no act of her own. She had willed sex, and out of that will and act came Linda and, hence, love and family. Because she was a Varner and had married Flem, she had clan and a place in the community, but these were not things that she valued for herself. Again, later in life, she moved in the social world only when there was something substantial to move for.

There was no man to match Eula's mountains. Her relation with Manfred de Spain was undefined. In the end she surely loved Linda over Manfred, and his love of her had in it an unhealthy measure of the simple male competitiveness that had marked that of McCarron. Probably, Eula and Manfred's meetings were less frequent and even more physically satisfying than the people of Jefferson liked to believe. Possibly, they came together and made love during those times when Eula took Linda off to the spas—the Garden again—in summers. Men had great difficulty with Eula's sexuality; she had none. As she said to Gavin when she offered herself to him: "You just are, and you need, and you must, and so you do, that's all." (*Town,* 94) In effect, the world fabricated a man for Eula out of the parts of men around her. She had total love and devotion from Gavin and sex from Manfred. She was married to Flem, and had a child by McCarron. All of these things were less than fulfilling for her. Ultimately, there was Linda and love, and Linda's existence forced her to join the community and seek security for Linda. "Marry her, Gavin," she pled, she to whom marriage had been less than a fig. (332) In the end, Eula killed herself attempting again to save Linda's future in the community. Thus her mother would be labeled a suicide rather than a whore. At a deeper level, Eula killed herself because all of the men in her life were tried and found wanting. They gave her only fragments, mere pieces. V.K. was her soul-mate and his pronouncement on her suicide rings truest of all. "Maybe, she was bored," he said. (358)

Desperate Searches

Marriage, as I have said, was the wide gate to which all arrows pointed the young. It was important to men, but it was vital to women. For a time after the Civil War, filling the prescription was more difficult because there were many more women of marriageable age than men. In reality as in fiction, there were many Miss Rosa Coldfields who passed through life as spinsters however much they might have yearned to marry. In the crisis some women of the elite married beneath their station—taking to husband the real-life equivalents of characters Will Benteen and Tom Slattery in *Gone With the Wind.* Now and again, white women willingly took black lovers and sometimes married black men, most likely men of light color and material substance. In his fiction, Faulkner has no willing sexual union much less marriage between a white woman and a man known unarguably to be black.

In the 1880s sex ratios among Southern whites were heading toward even and again, as earlier in the century, it was becoming unthinkable that a woman would not marry. Generally speaking in the South in the 19th century and on into the 20th century, the pressure upon a woman to marry and stay married was so great that even a bad marriage was better than no marriage at all. The result, ironically, was that it became a whispered truism that the happiest state of all for a woman was widowhood. There is a double irony in the fact that in most Southern states laws of inheritance worked in such a way as to make the widow of a man of property who had no children the most fortunate, the most independent, of all. To marry and have the wealthy husband die childless was the perfect evasion, the end-around-run to the goal line with a minimum of bruises and scratches. In his early writing, Faulkner gave us several men who had survived their wives (widowers), but he gave us no major characters who were widows. The widows came late and were interconnected. Linda whom Gavin loves is a widow, and so too is Mellisandra Backus, the woman he marries.

By the turn-of-the-century years, when Faulkner's own parents married, marriage for every one was again not only demographically possible but socially mandatory. During the next generation, however, things began to change. In the nation at large women were entering a new age in which they were voting, smoking, and drinking in public. Furthermore, they sometimes cursed in private and had affairs. Also they wore pants, shorter dresses, and bathing suits that revealed so much more of themselves in body and spirit than had the attire of their Victorian mothers. It was the age of the flapper and the liberated woman, and some women took up careers by choice rather than necessity. Even in the South, some women refused marriage and got away with it.

In Faulkner's own clan, his sister-in-law, Dorothy Oldham, did not marry and became the curator of the Mississippi Collection in the library of the university. On the other hand, Dorothy's older sister, Estelle, was clearly in no state to make up her mind about marriage in April, 1918, but was, in effect, given no choice. Moreover she yielded to a union that was arranged by her mother and the mother of the groom. She had her first child at virtually the first possible moment. That marriage ended after nearly a decade of cruel and inhuman punishment on all sides. But Estelle had hardly finished that drill before she was pressed into another marriage, again, apparently, at the insistence of her mother and quondam mother-in-law. Not only insistent but active in the process was her very determined and assertive sister Dorothy. Alas, once more the result was less than happy.

Estelle's experience reflected that of Faulkner's leading fictional women. Some raced forward and leapt at love, the first rung in the social ladder. Others rose step by step only to be stymied, slip back, or fall off altogether. Still others skipped whole rungs or attempted to catapult themselves to attain some higher point in the progression.

Of all these women, Caddy Compson, Faulkner's own darling and original inspiration for *The Sound and the Fury,* is perhaps the most appealing and the most tragic in her searching. She is beautiful and natural in spite of her parents. If the system is fair and just, it ought to work for her. At seventeen she finds firm footing on the first rung. She falls in love with Dalton Ames, a brown-faced, khaki-clad, sharp-shooting, Rhett Butler, knowing man of the world. Quentin confronts Dalton and tries to warn him off. He fails miserably, Dalton leaves and Caddy arrives. She attempts to help her brother in his crisis by describing what love is.

> do you love him Caddy
> do I what
> she looked at me then everything emptied out of her eyes and they looked like the eyes in the statues blank and unseeing and serene
> put your hand against my throat
> she took my hand and held it flat against her throat
> now say his name
> Dalton Ames
> I felt the first surge of blood there it surged in strong accelerating beats
> say it again
> her face looked off into the trees where the
> sun slanted and where the bird
> say it again
> Dalton Ames
> her blood surged steadily beating and beating against my hand (203)

A heart-rending scene in which love is literally made palpable. In a sylvan setting. Caddy became pregnant and Dalton disappeared. Mrs. Compson took Caddy to one of the spas (the Garden, yet again) where a courtship began that ended with her marrying Herbert Head. The baby arrived, Head realized he was not the father and cast Caddy and the baby out. Caddy left her daughter, Quentin, in Jefferson and went into the world, a fallen woman and an outcast. In the 1920s she was married to a minor magnate in the film industry in Hollywood, and, when last seen in 1943, she was in Europe, riding in a sports car with a staff general in the German army. Caddy traded her goodness, her elegance, and her beauty for the semblance of place in other worlds, other communities.

Joanna Burden, like every other major character in *Light in August,* was a displaced person. She was unique among women, however, in that she began with community and late in her life tried desperately to press back and downward into love, sex, and family. Her community was a peculiar one. Though born in the South, "when she spoke even now, after forty years, among the slurred consonants and the flat vowels of the land where her life had been cast, New England talked as plainly as it did in the speech of her kin who had never left New Hampshire and whom she had seen perhaps three times in her life." (*Light,* 227) She was New England cultured and white in the middle of the black belt South. Using her considerable wealth as something of a dowry, she had married herself to black educational communities, affixing herself to that world by the bequests that she made to a dozen black colleges, filling her life by doling out advice to students, faculty, and staff; attached to Jefferson and the county only by the house in which she lived and the soil that held the dusting remains of her kinfolk.

Joe Christmas came late to Joanna's life, and with him, first sex. Sex was forced, but, strangely, it was not rape. "It was as if he struggled physically with another man for an object of no actual value to either, and for which they struggled on principle alone," said Faulkner. Joe mused, "My God, it was like I was the woman and she was the man." When he went to her again, she was unresisting and he was furious. He tore at her clothes, saying, "I'll show you! I'll show the bitch!" She seemed to help him strip her by small movements, but "the body might have been the body of a dead woman." Even after a year of this, "it was as though he entered by stealth to despoil her virginity each time anew." Each night he was "faced again with the necessity to despoil again that which he had already despoiled—or never had and never would." (221–23)

Then, one day he came to his cabin behind her house to find her sitting on his cot, looking as he had not seen her look before. "She's trying to be a woman and she don't know how," he thought. (227) Joanna told him the story of her life and that of the Burden clan, revealing all, like a lover in courtship, and she tried to get him to talk about himself and his family. This began a second phase in their relationship—it was love. He would go to her at night, and she would insist on recounting every detail of her day and ask about his. He watched her "pass through every avatar of a woman in love." She fabricated "fits of jealous rage," and sex between them found a new and lusty passion. She "had an avidity for the forbidden word symbols; an insatiable appetite for the sound of them on his tongue and on her own." She secreted messages for him in a hollow fencepost, and made him find her hidden "in closets, in empty rooms, waiting, panting, her eyes in the dark glowing like the eyes of cats." Sometimes she made him seek her "beneath certain shrubs about the grounds, where he would find her naked, or with her clothing half torn to ribbons upon her, in the wild throes of nymphomania," posing erotically, hands wild, and breathing: "Negro! Negro! Negro!" (242–45) Joanna had done love and sex; next she would do family.

In the third phase Joanna grew fat and declared that she was "with child." It was December and roughly the same time that Lena Grove was becoming pregnant by Lucas Burch. Now they always met in the bedroom "as though they were married." (249) Joe thought she would say marriage, but she never did—and purposefully so. Instead, she said to herself: "A full measure. Even to a bastard negro child. I would like to see father's and Calvin's faces." (251) Every evening now Joe prepared himself "like a bridegroom" and went to her without haste, thinking "we got all night." He expected her to be eager, but she put aside his hand "with the firmness of a man." (253) She wanted him to take over her business affairs and her mission to black people, to join her in the community that she had created. She began to pray, telling God what they had done, using the sexual words that they had spoken to each other so furiously—now calmly, dispassionately, as if she were talking about two other people. Again and again she attempted to make Joe join her in prayer, and he repeatedly refused. Ultimately she decided that if they cannot pray, then they must die.

Between Caddy attempting to climb from the bottom and Joanna starting at the top, there were a wide variety of performances on the social ladder among Faulkner's women. Rosa Coldfield was desperately in love with Thomas Sutpen, but when Sutpen suggested sex and family before marriage, she was outraged and love turned to hate. Bobbie Allen was stalled on sex, whatever might have been her early history and her, seemingly, first experiences of love with Joe Christmas. A life lost in fighting for democratic ideals in Spain deprived Linda Snopes of a beautiful marriage with Barton Kohl and, presumably, subsequent sex and family. Ellen Coldfield got up to familyhood and tried to move on to clan and community, only to find it all dissolving about her, as had Thomas Sutpen's first wife, Eulalie. From girlhood, Lucy Pate set her sights upon becoming the wife of Jack Houston. With almost frightening single-mindedness she achieved that goal in spite of Houston's desperate attempts at flight and evasion—suggestive of Faulkner's own resistance to marriage. In the end, Lucy was killed by Houston's stallion (an avatar of the strong, willful, violent male) while she was searching the stallion's stall for a hen's egg, unmistakably the symbol for the next stage of her ascent.

Faulkner's men also have difficulty with the ladder, and especially with marriage. It is deeply revealing that roughly half of his major male characters (who are about twice as numerous as major female characters) are bachelors. Roughly half of these are strenuously, determinedly, sometimes violently unmarried. In addition, Houston and Hightower were widowers who showed no signs of remarrying, and Ike McCaslin had, in effect, set his wife aside, virtually unilaterally annulled his marriage, and returned to a state of confirmed bachelorhood, a wilderness priesthood.

Unmarried men were not unusual in the South in which Faulkner lived, but Faulkner's universe brilliantly reflected the real ambivalence that existed among Southern men, at least of his generation, toward the institution of marriage. Love was fine, children were fine, and maybe even sex was fine. But marriage was a frightful institution in the Faulknerian universe, and most of the men who gave themselves to it were men whom their wives might have done better without—notably Simon McEachern, Gail Hightower, Doc Hines, Jack Houston, Flem Snopes, and Thomas Sutpen.

Surrogates for Sex in Marriage

382 In Faulkner's universe, the sexual landscape, like the marital landscape, was in terrific disarray. Sometimes sex is conspicuous by its absence, sometimes horribly confused with violence, and characters evince a rather awful tendency to pursue surrogates for sex in the married state through prostitution, incest, homosexuality, and, most of all, miscegenation.

Historians have sometimes argued that white men in the South painted themselves into a sexual corner. In the middle years of the nineteenth century they took advantage of black women and so pedestalized white women as to render physical and sexual relations with their wives unusually difficult. The southern wife was pious and pure, the angel, the conduit with God, and accessible physically only for procreation. For men to press themselves upon their wives beyond that point was to yield to lust, but to abstain was to breed frustration. In *Gone With the Wind,* for example, Ashley Wilkes resisted the seductive wiles of Scarlett O'Hara with great difficulty and frustration. On the other side, Ashley did not abstain from sex with his wife Melanie—a paragon of piety and purity—even though he understood that another pregnancy would endanger her life. Apparently, Ashley chose the moral moment for sex, and Melanie paid the price by dying in childbirth. Margaret Mitchell did well when she created Melanie Wilkes and her husband as characters and juxtaposed them to Scarlett, who never totally emerged from adolescent confusion, and a very mature Rhett, who properly valued both love and sex.

Miscegenation

Slavery provided a possible sexual solution for Southern white men; it provided everywhere a class of women who were theirs for the buying. Moreover, myth held that black women were naturally lusty, earthy creatures (like Faulkner's Yettie or Eula) for whom there could be no violation. Indeed in the Old South, a man with money, any man, could buy a very desirable woman who happened to be a slave, and he could do with her as he pleased. Local society might censure him for some acts—if it knew—but the law did not. In law, there was no such thing as the rape of a slave by her master, even if the slave were still a child.

The trade in desirable slave women might not have been general or vast, but it was certainly conspicuous. There was, in fact, a market that dealt in "fancy girls." A fancy girl was a female slave, relatively young, who had some talent in the domestic arts, such as fine sewing, who might have musical ability, who could converse with intelligence and perhaps even refinement, and, above all, who possessed a considerable measure of feminine beauty. So often beauty in the eyes of the whites meant lightness of color and distinctly Caucasian features.

As slavery proceeded over the generations, so too did the mixing of the races and, probably, most whites who mixed with blacks did so with slaves who were already light in color. In the last generation of slavery, there were some slaves who were indistinguishable from people who called themselves white.

The trade in fancy girls probably reached its peak in New Orleans in the 1850s. There the price of such a slave might be double that of a "prime" male slave and might reach several thousand dollars. In New Orleans in 1851, a Swedish traveler, Fredrika Bremer, visited a slave market in the French Exchange in the St. Louis Hotel that specialized in "superior-looking girls, varying from mulatto to octoroon." She saw one after another mount the block to be sold in a setting of classical arches, columns, and variegated marble floors under a graceful rotunda.[1] It was no coincidence that Faulkner in his story *The Bear* sent Carothers McCaslin to New Orleans in 1807 to buy the slave girl Eunice, an octoroon Faulkner once said. McCaslin was then a vigorous man of thirty-five whose wife had given birth in the mid-1790s to a girl, then in 1799 to the twins Buck and Buddy, and then no more. Appearances suggest that McCaslin bought himself a beautiful concubine, and he knew exactly where to go to make the purchase.

Historically, domestic servants tended to be of mixed blood. White people who could afford to use slaves as house servants fathered—and sometimes mothered—children by these servants who were by blood and appearance much more Caucasian than they were African. These children were reared with an intimate knowledge of the culture of the white elite, and sometimes they were so favored by the white parent as to gain a concerted education in that culture. The slave South was full of stories in which certain men in planter families habitually crossed the race line for sex and fathered a sequence of children who were simultaneously black and white. Lucas Beauchamp was perfectly historical for provenance, and so too was Clytie. Charles Bon was more than historical, but the exaggerated circumstances in which he existed highlighted the deep tragedy of the plight of the real-life child of mixed blood and elite education.

Almost every community had a planter family in which the men were mavericks and not only had a sequence of mulatto children, but also refused to ignore their progeny and rather sought to protect them. Consider this letter, written in the 1850s by an aging father to his most trusted son. The father was a planter and large slaveholder, a famous and highly cultured man, and for a time a leading Southern senator. It was a letter that Carothers McCaslin might well have written. It explains to the son why he will receive a special bequest at his father's death:

> In the Last Will I made I left to you, over & above my other children, Sally Johnson the mother of Louisa & all the children of both. Sally says Henderson is my child. It is probable, but I do not believe it. Yet act on her's rather than my opinion. Louisa's first child may be mine. I think not. Her second I believe is mine. Take care of her

> other children who are both of your blood and not of mine & of Henderson. The services of the rest will I think compensate for indulgence to these. I cannot free these people & send them North. It would be cruelty to them. Nor would I like that any but my own blood should own as Slaves my own blood or Louisa. I leave them to your charge, believing that you will best appreciate & most independently carry out my wishes in regard to them. Do not let Louisa or any of my children or probable children be the Slaves of Strangers. Slavery in the family will be their happiest earthly condition.[2]

While Louisa appears not to have been his daughter by Sally, Louisa is certainly Sally's daughter and the planter had sex with both mother and daughter over an extended period of time. He thinks it probable that he had a child by the mother and seems even more certain that he had a child by the daughter. Louisa's other two children are not of his blood but are of the blood of his son, meaning that the son, or, more likely, the male kin of the planter's wife, had sex with Louisa and had children by her. An endlessly tangled web, indeed.

In slavery miscegenation by masters happened in some fashion everywhere. It wreaked havoc with the emotions of individual men and women, and tore rudely the ideal fabric of marriage and community in Southern culture. Had Thomas Sutpen visited even briefly this slaveholder in the late 1850s on his "Hundred," his lordly Carolina estate, had he met the mistress and her children, he might have said this is the grand design realized. Had he proceeded to study Louisa's and Sally's children, he would have recognized their paternity, and he might have understood that in that Southern social world forms were not always pure and some transgressions were tolerated—even if grudgingly so. If he had traveled about a bit more in the old southeast, where the races had been mixing long before anyone even thought of Mississippi, where there were planter families that had a trace of African blood from that antiquity and yet moved well enough among the social elite, he might have learned even more. Local people usually knew of the trace, and it did count, but in the ordinary processes of life, wealth and culture seemed to override a slight taint of African ancestry. In real life, almost surely, Thomas Sutpen could have publicly recognized Charles Bon as his son and had the essence of his Grand Design too. In the real world, Bon could have married white and eventually graced Sutpen's Hundred as its master.

Historically considered, blood connections between the black elite and the white elite existed often enough in the New South as well as the Old. During the Civil Rights movement, one of the first black students to apply and seriously contest for admission to one of the great state universities of the South was blood kin to a trustee who sat on the board that fought against admission. While not bruited about, knowledge of such ties was generally a part of community lore. One can only wonder about the Faulkners and specifically about William. He never openly recognized his mulatto kin, but in March, 1956, when he was abandoning his campaign for racial sanity in the South and vomiting blood in Oxford, his second cousin Faulkner Hughes was preparing to reign as Queen at the annual cotillion of the Me-De-So Club in Baltimore.

Not all of the people who mixed, of course, were of the elite class. In the antebellum period, overseers had access to black women. Slave owners might demand abstinence of their overseers and generally did so, but they were ultimately powerless to enforce the demand hour by hour. They were also somewhat powerless to prevent white relatives and neighbors, slaveholders and nonslaveholders, from having sexual encounters with their slaves. This was especially true in the country where the woods were thick and satyrs might play. Abolitionists had a point when they insisted that slavery was one great brothel. It was less than a perfect analogy because it ignored the question of volition on the part of the alleged prostitutes. Overwhelming evidence indicates that these liaisons began with rape—not love or even, in one sense or another, money.

Also not all of the whites who mixed were males, and not all white women who mixed were of the lower orders. White women on the plantations did have sex with male slaves. Seemingly, mixing was done much less frequently by women than by men, and for good reasons. Maternity is obvious; paternity sometimes obscure. Furthermore, women were generally dependent, and the sanctions that could be brought against them very severe. White women who crossed the race line for physical intimacy often did so for love, for the high passion that a Victorian education had taught them was the most sublime expression of humanity. For example, there was a case in South Carolina in the last years of slavery in which the teenage daughter of a planter family became pregnant and had a mulatto child. She had fallen in love with the young slave who served as a driver and frequently drove the daughter about in the family carriage. After the birth, the young woman announced her love for the slave and kept both the slave and the baby. The baby became a man and a large landowner in the post-Reconstruction era. Between his lightness of color and his wealth the color line was almost lost. Such women might step eagerly up to love, and they might pass lustily on to sex, and even into family with surprising comfort; but there could be no marriage and the children born to the union were bound to suffer a more or less taxing indeterminacy. Excepting the special case of Joanna Burden, Faulkner's major women, unlike his major men, never had either love or sex across the race line. It was one of several things that did exist in Southern culture that he simply ruled out of his fiction.

Joseph Blotner often had a late afternoon drink with Bill and Estelle while they sat on the terrace at the Blotner house in Virginia. On one such occasion, New Jersey born and bred Joe asked Bill if "colored men" were not attracted to white women. "No," Bill said quickly and firmly. "They like their own kind." The next question might well have asked: "Are white women not attracted to 'colored men?' " Historically, the answer is a resounding "Yes." Consider, for example, this comment in a letter written in 1874 by an upcountry South Carolina farmer to his brother in Alabama: "My dear Brother as you have made several Enquiries of me and desireing me to answer them I will attempt and endeavor to do So to the best information that I have on the Various Subjects alluded to by you the first Interrogatory is Relative to John H. Lipscomb's daughter haveing Negro Children, I am forced to answer in the affirmative no doubt but she has had two; and no hopes of her Stopping."[3]

Emancipation profoundly changed sexual relations between blacks and whites in the South. In freedom, black men and women laid claim to power over their own bodies. In particular, they pledged themselves to familyhood, and they possessed enough freedom to make good the pledge. Scattered but fairly persuasive evidence indicates that the birth of "new issue" mulattoes, that is those born of one white and one "Negro" parent, were few and far between after 1865. Interracial mixing never ceased, of course, any more than human nature changed. In every community there was the notorious case, the maverick who made bold sexually across the race line. But such cases were rare, and there were laws against cohabitation, seduction, and adultery that could be and sometimes were applied to errant males by a white-ruled world that had never been perfectly at ease with race mixing and now was dead set against it.

Prostitution

With emancipation, the sexual escape hatch by way of race was practically closed, but Southern women remained pedestalized. Prostitution was another way in which white men might spare their wives the "indignity" of a lusty sex life. Prostitution existed in the Old South, and after the Civil War it flourished. Well into the twentieth century, every city of any size had its brothels, and the larger the city the more brothels there were and the more openly they operated. New Orleans and Memphis spawned whole sections (Storyville and the environs of Beale and Mulberry Streets south of the Peabody hotel) that were given over to "the sporting life." In towns and villages there were often women like Bobbie Allen, who sold sex without the benefit of house and madam. As we have seen, the town minutes of Oxford in the early 1880s reveal a striking tolerance of streetwalkers at the same time that they exhibited unrelenting hostility to those whistling boys who were called "mackerel."

One cannot avoid being impressed by the significant place that brothels occupied in Faulkner's own life and imagination. Recurrently plagued by deep feelings of inferiority, desperately searching for assurance that he was a sexual creature of some magnitude, he found in the brothels of Memphis an oasis. It is possible that "Little Billy" never went upstairs, that it was enough simply to be proximate to sex, and that he had rehearsed carefully his lines to explain the abstinence that his friends might have marked as peculiar behavior. "No thanks, Ma'am, I'm on my vacation," he said. It was almost as if the crooked hand had found, ready-made, the crooked glove that gave it cover and comfort.

Interestingly, Faulkner's comrade and mentor Phil Stone apparently suffered no such ambiguity. Brilliant, dapper, balding, a talking machine, Phil went into the brothels and, it is said, never took off his hat. Indeed, one is struck by the casualness with which the men of Oxford's elite patronized the brothels in Memphis. Apparently, they might drop over to a Mulberry Street house for a drink while waiting for a train at the railway station nearby. Even the seemingly staid Lemuel Oldham did so, and a lawyer friend might decide casually to go upstairs with one of the girls while others in the party had their drinks.

Sex was one thing, marriage another. Phil, like Faulkner, had great trouble integrating love, marriage, and sex, and it seems that he struggled with the classic male affliction of regarding all women as either ladies or whores. He was middle-aged when he married. Faulkner was in his thirties when he married, and fairly soon he wanted to divorce his wife. Marriage was all right, he seemed to think, but some men were not made for marriage, and very few could stand an unadulterated marriage. The system, apparently, was too tight for human endurance.

Incest

If a man were "shy," if he had trouble relating across the sex line, the trouble might be abated by mating with someone he knew well, and what female might he know better than his sister, mother, daughter, or cousin? The court records of Tippah and Lafayette counties often carried charges of incest, and Faulkner gives us one striking instance in his fiction. In 1810 Eunice, the slave that Carothers McCaslin had bought in New Orleans in 1807, gave birth to the child Tomasina. "Tomey" was the daughter of Carothers. Shortly before her birth, perhaps after learning that Eunice was pregnant, he caused Eunice to be married to his slave Thucydus. In December, 1832, Eunice drowned herself upon learning that Tomey was pregnant by Carothers, her own father. (*Bear,* 63–66) Carothers, for all his mastery over land and men both black and white, was a man who had serious problems with women. He bought himself a surrogate wife, then probably married her to a black man he owned so that his child by her would have an ostensibly legitimate father. Subsequently, it seems, he abstained from sex for a couple of decades (because we hear of his fathering no other children) and finally had sex with his daughter. His daughter died in childbirth and he abstained for the remainder of his life. Carothers McCaslin was a powerful man, but he was also a sexual cripple who attempted at first to make himself whole through slavery and miscegenation, and then by incest.

Faulkner's fiction is fraught with potential incest between brother and sister. In particular, it filled his early work. In "Elmer," the novel that he was writing in 1925 and never published, the pre-adolescent Elmer slept in the same bed with his older sister Jo Addie. Elmer had strong but diffused sexual feelings for his sister who was both "Dianalike" and resembled his mother.[4] In the draft of *Mosquitoes* that Faulkner sent to his publishers in 1926, eighteen-year-old Patricia Robyn, called "Pat," crawled into bed with her older brother and nuzzled him about the neck and face. She bit his ear, and he kicked her out.[5] The most powerful and complicated case of incestuous feelings involved Quentin Compson. Quentin loved Caddy and wanted to possess her to the exclusion of all others, but yet he wanted her to remain pure and untouched. Incest is also a major theme in *Absalom, Absalom!,* but there Charles Bon used it as a threat in his attempt to get his father to recognize him. If Charles Bon had committed the act it would have been done not for love and not for physical gratification but as retribution for the sins of his father.

In the nineteenth-century South there was a curious form of near-incest in which sets of brothers and sisters married one another. In Faulkner's own ancestry, his granduncle William R. Butler married Anna Eliza Bowen, the sister of his good friend and Ole Miss classmate William Bolivar Bowen who, in turn, married William Butler's sister Emily. Indeed the marriage records of Lafayette and Tippah counties are surprisingly full of such things. The court records indicate that now and again folks went a bit too far in marrying their cousins. In some states, marrying a "first cousin" was incest by law. However re-marriages after the death of spouses produced children in ambiguous states of cousinness. Sometimes, it seems, some Southerners took the "kissing cousin" license too far, and Southern courts felt compelled to haul couples already married and settled into households before the bar and charge them with incest.

Homosexuality

An obvious surrogate for sex in the socially prescribed pattern was homosexuality. Again, one sees the theme most clearly in Faulkner's early writing. As a preadolescent, Elmer had "developed a fine sexless passion" for his teacher, a woman. "But this year he was ravished away from that constancy by a boy, a young beast as beautiful to him as a god, and as cruel." That ended when the boy came upon Elmer on the playground one day and tripped him "violently to earth."[6] Later Elmer the painter handled tubes of paint pigment erotically, and entered a relationship with a handsome Italian man whom he had encountered in jail, suggestive of the experience of Faulkner's friend Bill Spratling in a Genoese prison.

Faulkner never published "Elmer," but he wrote a short story, probably early in 1926 and eventually called "Divorce in Naples," that might have been derived from the nexus that produced "Elmer." In this story a Greek sailor, a large dark man, and another sailor, a slight, blond boy of eighteen from Philadelphia, became lovers. The ship docked in Naples and the boy had sex with a prostitute and confessed the affair to his lover. One senses that this was the beginning of the end of the affair, that the boy was transiting to a heterosexual mode.

In *Mosquitoes,* curiously, not only was Patricia physically intimate with her brother, she also felt a deep attraction for Jenny, a "voluptuous shop girl" whom she invited to a party aboard a yacht on Lake Pontchartrain. Pat, who had a boy's body and a unisexual nickname, got into a bunk bed with Jenny who was sleeping nude. "She slowly stroked the back of her hand along the swell of Jenny's flank."[7] The sequel has survived only in typescript, the publisher having deleted a portion of the original manuscript before publishing the book. Jenny drowsily turned and kissed Pat. "Jenny made again her drowsy moaning sound, and without seeming to move at all she came to the other with a boneless enveloping movement, turning her head until their mouths touched. Immediately Jenny went lax, yet she still seemed to envelop the other, holding their bodies together with her mouth."[8] Pat reacted by violently spitting and declared that that is not the way nice people kiss. She was about to demonstrate that operation when an older woman in the party, Mrs. Wiseman, barged into the cabin and disrupted proceedings, "staring at them with a dark intent speculation."[9] Later, in a passage that was printed, Mrs. Wiseman was also attracted to Jenny. "She raised Jenny's face," Faulkner wrote, "and kissed her on the mouth."[10] "Elmer" was never printed, and Faulkner's publisher cut the strongest passages from the "Lesbian" scene from *Mosquitoes.* Thereafter, themes of homosexuality in Faulkner's writing are sometimes powerful but always muted. For example, one senses that Joe Christmas (appearing in print in 1932) brought handsome, almost beautiful Lucas Burch into his cabin for reasons that transcended mere mercantile convenience but were subconscious. Also, Henry Sutpen (appearing in 1936) loved his half-brother Charles Bon and wanted his sister to marry Charles even if it meant incest and, perhaps, because it did mean incest. After *Absalom,* the writing of which ended as Faulkner's affair with Meta rose in intensity, the theme of homosexuality in his work faded practically into nonexistence.

Interestingly, in all of the early stories touching the matter of homosexuality, the protagonist was actually a young person searching for his or her sexuality. These characters were experimenting, and they seem to be heading toward heterosexual personalities. Again, Faulkner could also be saying that the vast difference between men and women projected by society is not natural, not real, that the sort of quest in which late adolescent Patricia Robyn was engaged is the difficult but ordinary search for a sexual self that every human must make.

Violence *vice* Sex

There is in every culture, perhaps, a tendency to weave together sex and violence. In the South because race came to be so thoroughly mixed with sex, and because slavery and race were themselves deeply and inextricably mixed with violence, sex has had a particular aura of violence. For Southern white men, violence as a surrogate for sex—violence instead of sex—was one way of avoiding both sex and marriage and hence, as some men feared, the loss of one's sense of self and power.

There is something in this species of violence vaguely suggestive of the sacrificial lamb, or better, the sacrificial goat. Because the danger of loss of self in sex is so great—the implication of escalating and engrossing commitment so awesome, so beyond one's clear and comfortable powers—some ritual sacrifice must be made to honor and meet the mystery. Young men who hovered about Eula on Sundays were so stirred and yet so stymied that they could think of nothing to do afterward but go down by the creek and furiously bruise and bloody one another with their fists. Gavin Stevens in Eula's later life suffered the same fate. Hot, frustrated, and desperate he forced Manfred to fight and to spill his blood to such an extent that Manfred appealed to the men around them to "hold him until I can get away." A generation later, Gavin had learned only slightly more grace when Linda's would-be lover, a Golden Gloves boxer, served as an unwitting Abraham to the lamb-like Gavin. And, of course, Quentin got from super-masculine Gerald Bland, also a boxer, the bloodying in New England that he was not able to get from Dalton Ames in Jefferson.

The Faulkner story that deals most brilliantly with the theme of violence instead of sex is that of Labove, the schoolmaster in Frenchman's Bend. Labove was a large, raw-boned country boy who labored on a farm and worked in a sawmill to earn enough money to attend a summer session at the University of Mississippi. His ambition was to become a school teacher. At Ole Miss the football coach discovered his talent for cool and deliberate violence, and persuaded him to become a full-time student. Labove soon saw a wider world and resolved to take his bachelor's and law degrees, practice law, and eventually become the governor of the state. He was progressing steadily in his plan until he met Eula Varner. He had taught school in Frenchman's Bend only a term before Jody brought eight-year-old Eula to his door.

"No. No. Not here," Labove cried to himself. "Don't leave her here."

But Eula was there, with "that face eight years old and a body of fourteen with the female shape of twenty." (*Hamlet* 113) Labove had told himself that he would quit teaching when he got his degrees and passed the bar. Yet he did not. Instead, he attended the graduation ceremonies at the university and then went straight to a brothel in Memphis. "At least it wont be my virginity that she is going to scorn," he told himself. (117) The next morning he borrowed stationery from the prostitute with whom he had spent the night to write to Will Varner, a trustee, that he would take the school again next year. He considered only briefly the possibility of waiting until Eula came of age and marrying her.

"He did not want a wife at all, certainly not yet and probably not ever," he thought. "He just wanted her one time as a man with a gangrened hand or foot thirsts after the axe stroke which will leave him comparatively whole." (118)

At school again, he would wait every day until the students left so that he could go to the place where Eula had sat. He would "lay his hand on the wooden plank still warm from the effect of her sitting or even kneel and lay his face to the plank, wallowing his face against it, embracing the hard unsentient wood, until the heat was gone." Labove was mad and he knew it. "There would be times now when he did not even want to make love to her but wanted to hurt her, see blood spring and run, watch that serene face warp to the indelible mark of terror and agony beneath his own." He would cast out that image, and immediately another would come to him in which their positions would be reversed. "It would now be himself importunate and prostrate before that face which, even though but fourteen years old, postulated a weary knowledge which he would never attain, a surfeit, a glut of all perverse experience." (119)

Labove continued in this way until one day Eula came back after school to claim her forgotten schoolbag. At a glance, she saw what he had been doing. Rising, he moved toward her, saying, "Don't be afraid."

"Afraid?" she said. "Of what?' "

"That's it," he said. "That's the trouble. You are not afraid. That's what you have got to learn. That's one thing I am going to teach you, anyway." Labove "moved as quickly as ruthlessly as if she had a football or as if he had the ball and she stood between him and the final white line which he hated and must reach." He held her hard but loosely while she struggled. He felt and delighted in her strength.

"That's it," he said. "Fight it. Fight it. That's what it is; a man and a woman fighting each other. The hating. To kill, only to do it in such a way that the other will have to know forever afterward he or she is dead." Eula fought. She caught him under the chin with the thrust of an elbow. As he reeled back she caught him squarely in the face with a full-armed blow that sent him sprawling into the furniture and onto the floor. Eula stood over him.

"Stop pawing me," she said. "You old headless horseman Ichabod Crane." Then she went out the door. Moments later, she marched back in, grabbed her satchel, and left again.

Getting up, Labove prepared to fight Jody who would surely come to avenge his sister. Labove relished the idea. "It would not be penetration, true enough, but it would be the same flesh, the same warm living flesh in which the same blood ran, under impact at least—a paroxysm, an orgasm of sorts, a katharsis, anyway—something." As he waited, he thought that he wanted someone to get hurt, "that was exactly what he wanted: for somebody to get hurt, and then he asked himself quietly, Who? and he answered himself; I don't know. I don't care." Educated in the classics as he was, Labove should have bought a goat, or a bull, or a sheep and made a sacrifice. But instead he waited until finally he decided Jody had not come because he wanted witnesses and thus would meet him at the store. He went to the store, only to find Jody totally unaware of the role assigned to him. Returning to the school he padlocked the door, drove a nail in the wall, and hung the key on it. Then he left Frenchman's Bend, never to be heard from again. (120–26)

Anyone familiar with all-white football in the black belt South in Faulkner's day will recognize the pure genius that he showed in making Labove a football player. A decade later, Tennessee Williams hewed close to the same mark in *Cat on a Hot Tin Roof* when he cast Chip as a onetime football star at Ole Miss who was having grave difficulties in relating sexually with his wife Maggie. Hollywood did fine work in the story by having Paul Newman play Chip and silk-slip–clad Elizabeth Taylor portray a sultry and frustrated Maggie.

Further, anyone familiar with white men lynching black men in the South in the turn-of-the-century years will recognize a syndrome suggesting that the culture was sometimes given to violence instead of sex. Sometimes it simply wanted "somebody to get hurt" and when it asked itself who, the answer came back: "I don't know; I don't care." In essence, any black person would do, in effect standing in for any man who raped white women—or would if he could. Albert Bushnell Hart, the Harvard historian, caught something of this truth in 1908 while traveling in Mississippi. During an interview with a young white man, he asked about lynching. "You don't understand how we feel down here," the man explained. "When there is a row, we feel like killing a nigger whether he has done anything or not."[11]

Violence and Sex

The white culture into which William Faulkner was born in 1897 had mixed and horribly confused race, sex, and violence. By the 1930s, the race element was very much muted, but in fiction the mixing of sex and violence continued—for instance, in the famous "rape scene" in *Gone With the Wind.* Faulkner had sounded that note in the mid-1920s in writing *Mosquitoes.* In one draft of his manuscript he said that Pete, the dark, Italian-American lover of "the voluptuous shopgirl" Jenny, had hit her once. "She had rather liked it . . ."[12]

On the other side, Southern society at large in the 1920s and 1930s was in a romantic mood, and it insisted that the South was a land of moonlight and magnolias, of sweethearts and gentle lovers. When Faulkner wrote *Sanctuary* early in 1929, he wove together themes of sex and violence to argue in compelling fashion that reality offered evidence to the contrary. One does not have to go among the blacks, it argued, to find sex and violence. Indeed, the purest of the pure in Southern white culture, an upper class young white girl, Temple Drake, can wade right in and find the water fine. In the story Gowan Stevens, a gentleman of the first order and a heavy drinker, stupidly delivered Ole Miss co-ed Temple Drake into the hands of bootlegging gangsters. Temple was about to be raped in a corn crib by a feebleminded member of the gang when a

Memphis hood called Popeye shot the man squarely between the eyes in front of the terrified Temple and then raped her with a corn cob. Subsequently, Popeye imprisoned Temple in a Memphis brothel and imported one of his henchmen, Red, to rape Temple while he watched standing at the foot of the bed making noises like a wild stallion. Popeye, as it happened, was impotent. In time, Temple came to love Red, but the story ended with both Popeye and Red dead and Temple rescued. In the final scene, she sits serenely in the Luxembourg Gardens in Paris watching the passing world. Most people read the novel as dealing with the evil in man. Revealingly, Faulkner maintained that it was a story about how impervious women are to evil, a striking commentary in view of the fact that he began the writing in January, 1929, and finished on May 25, the very eve of his marriage to Estelle.

Virginity

An obvious escape from sex was virginity. In Faulkner's lifetime, Southern society invested heavily in controlling the virginity of its women, and only lightly in controlling the virginity of its men. When girls and boys came of age in the South, as elsewhere, they were pressed to undertake the rites of passage to adulthood. They were called upon to embrace their sex, male or female, in accordance with strictly marked gender lines, to then act upon it, and progress up the social ladder. The loss of virginity—first sex—was a great transition in that process. It was a onetime event, and it happened in a certain moment in one's entire lifetime. For the male, only he could say that such a moment had or had not occurred in the past. For a female the presence or absence of virginity was a physical fact, a check point usually susceptible to verification and hence to social control. Excluding physical difficulties, a woman who had sex frequently over even a short period of time would soon demonstrate her loss of virginity by visible pregnancy. For that event to occur out of wedlock—as it did with Caddy, Lena, and Eula—was probably the most awful of social sins in the South. Thus Southern society made a pressure point out of the moment when a woman lost her virginity. When it happened, how it happened, and who it happened with were special concerns in a Southern community.

A golden thread in Faulkner's life and work, and a paradox, was that in his fiction he strenuously rejected virginity as specially significant while in his personal life he, in effect, valued the Southern prescription for virginity before marriage—however tortured, tattered, and torn he might be by that stance. The manner in which Faulkner offered his case in his writings is curious and revealing. He offered us a broad array of virgins in his fiction, but they are mostly men. Only three of his major women are apparent virgins, and all three appear in *Absalom, Absalom!* Judith and Clytie were very much vestal virgins in Thomas Sutpen's temple. Rosa Coldfield devoted her purity to Sutpen in a very different, almost equal and opposite, mode. Three of his leading women are outright prostitutes—Bobbie Allen, Corrie in *The Reivers,* and Nancy Mannigoe in *Requiem for a Nun.* Most significantly, his three great female white characters, his finest women: Caddy, Eula, and Lena, have no difficulty at all with virginity, either as an idea or a physical fact.

Mr. Compson once told Quentin that "it was men invented virginity, not women." (96) One might have added that in Faulkner's fictional world they invented it for practice by themselves. A half-dozen of Faulkner's leading men were clearly virgins and another half-dozen were probably so. Quentin Compson, Byron Bunch (until Lena moved him), and Gavin Stevens (at least up to the time of his marriage to Melisandre Backus) were virtually stymied by their obsession with romantic ideals. Each was so awed by his potential for destructive action across the sex line that he virtually neutered himself. Flem and Popeye were nearly the opposite of Faulkner's prostitutes; they were impotent. Jason had Benjy castrated and finally incarcerated to de-sex him. Percy Grimm, Henry Sutpen, V.K. Ratliff, Charles Mallison, Jody Varner, Uncle Buddy, and the tall convict in *The Wild Palms* apparently passed through life as virgins, and Simon McEachern perhaps did so. While Faulkner does not tell us explicitly, he added an interesting thread to the web when he painted married men like Flem certainly and Gail Hightower probably as virgins not only before marriage but after. Moreover, almost all of his married men were faithful to their wives while married women often were not. Eula had Manfred, Mrs. Bundren had the preacher, and Mrs. Hightower found her lovers in Memphis hotels.

In Faulkner's fiction, the loss of virginity symbolized a necessary movement from the ideal to the real, from feelings and emotions to action, not only in sex but in the whole broad world. In the metaphor of the Grecian urn, if the maiden loses her virginity, then the man and the maiden have moved and shattered the urn. Thus, the ideal is lost beyond recall. The story of *The Bear* conveyed this idea superbly. To kill the Bear was to surrender forever the heart-thumping high life of the chase. Ike McCaslin lived for the chase but dreaded its consummation. For Ike, the ideal would be to continue the chase forever. It is unrequited love kept unrequited. After one confrontation with the Bear, Sam in effect said to Ike: "You had the gun and you didn't shoot." (Much the same might be said of Gavin after his confrontation with Eula in his office.) Later when he was a young man, Ike argued the case for idealism with Cass Edmonds in Cass's library. To illustrate his argument, he pulled down from the shelf a copy of "Ode on a Grecian Urn" and read from it: "Forever wilt thou love And she be fair . . ."

In *The Town* Faulkner repeated the *Ode* theme with an ingenious twist. After Eula's death, Gavin seized the privilege to preside over the carving of Eula's face for a marble medallion that would be fixed to a monument over her grave. Using a picture and drawings, he worked meticulously with artisans in

Italy by telegram and letter to get the piece right. At last it was finished and at last he had Eula just where he wanted her, frozen in marble—inviolate. Henceforth the urn could not be shattered, his love would never be possessed by anyone. Gavin had his ikon in the stone medallion, just as the idiot Ike Snopes had his in the wooden cow. Further, just as Ike McCaslin had resisted the big death of the Bear, Gavin was then safely beyond the threat of the "little death" of consummation with Eula. He could make of her in his mind whatever he wanted, and never again, terrified, be forced by her to shout at her, "Don't touch me!" (*Town,* 94)

Even so, Gavin was tested in the flesh again when Linda, Eula's reincarnation in her daughter, came home from the Spanish Civil War. Telling him that she loved him, she said, "You can _ _ _ _ me." Gavin blushed at the word frankly spoken. He obfuscated and thrashed about in masterly confusion before coming up with the line that he wrote for her to read—she had lost all hearing—and by which he excused himself: "because we are the 2 in all the world who can love each other without having to." (*Mansion* 238–39) A very poor response from the man who had presumed to teach Linda both real passion and romantic ideals (which she found in the Communist cause) and had sent her to Greenwich Village to meet a whole man, Barton Kohl, who took her off to the war that killed him and exploded a bomb in her face. Gavin thus responded to Linda, who had been blasted away from all sound by that bomb, who from that moment had lost all feeling in her face, whose face, immobilized, had been frozen like that of her mother on the obelisk in the town cemetery, and whose voice, as Chick Mallison said, was "dry, lifeless, dead. That was it: dead." (217) Linda's face had in essence joined that of her mother on the monument, and Gavin again had—to quote the *Ode* once more—his "bride of silence."

It is curious indeed that in his fiction Faulkner so roundly cursed virginity before marriage while in his personal life he both cursed and honored it. He seemed to count his own virginity as a burden and searched desperately for some way to rid himself of it. Yet, when he had the opportunity in the brothels, he seemed stoutly to resist the loss. Possibly, he was still a virgin into the 1920s. Accepting the analogy might require a leap of the imagination, but Billy Faulkner sitting in the parlor of a Memphis whorehouse was, in the context of his whole life, not vastly removed from the lover on the Grecian urn. Labove went to a Memphis brothel so that he would not be a virgin when the really great moment with Eula came, but Faulkner went and remained a virgin. Strangely, he seemed somehow to find a measure of relief in being proximate to where sex was happening, but also in abstinence, in preserving his innocence, in preserving his difference from some of his closest friends. The yearning was there—the ridiculous leaning of the body forward like some Vaudeville comedian with shoes nailed to the floor—but he could not take the step that would satisfy the demand of gravity. Soon after he met Meta in December, 1935, he told her that he did not go with prostitutes, and, in spite of all his dissembling, one is inclined to believe it, even in Europe where prostitution was quite different from and more comfortable than that at home. In the late 1930s he wrote to Meta that he needed a girl, a "spittoon" with whom to have sex. But it didn't work, he said, because he "simply didn't rise." The spittoon image suggested that he thought of sex as a process by which he would be relieved of waste material, the "gangrened hand or foot," almost the opposite of the romanticism with which he invested the same act with Meta.

Faulkner apparently held a dichotomous view of women. It was the idea usual among men in Western civilization, so common as to be trite and boring were it not so fundamentally vicious. Women were either whores or angels. However much Faulkner might be drawn to company with so-called whores, in his own life he always went with the so-called angels. Particularly was this so after he married Estelle and demonstrably ceased to be a virgin himself. Meta was virginal in appearance when she first met Faulkner, and both Joan Williams and Jean Stein had the virginal quality of youth when he first met them. They were still in their teens when he was a man in his fifties. It was in the midst of his involvement with these two women that Jill married. As noted, at the wedding reception, standing in the yard at Rowan Oak and gazing fondly at the bride dressed all in white, Faulkner exclaimed exultantly to his friend Shelby Foote: "Isn't Jill the perfect virgin!" In Faulkner's eyes Jill was indeed the perfect, the ideal virgin, and his mother Maud was the paragon of what followed marriage and sex—the perfect lady. It was unthinkable to him that either of these women might have had sex before marriage, or be pregnant out of wedlock, or have a lover as well as a husband. These were the two women he most admired in his life, yet there is no totally clear celebration of either woman, or the perceived values of either woman, in his fiction.

In adolescence, Estelle was Faulkner's first lady. But then the angel took flight. Helen Baird combined the innocence of the waif, the girl-child, with the promise of a lusty sexual partner. No clinging vine, he could see in her the potentially uninhibited, free-swinging bohemian artist. Yet when he met Helen he was already almost thirty and had acquired virtually no skill in courtship. He seemed to think that proximity, romantic poses, and simple persistence would turn the trick. But Helen was too wise, and he was cast reeling back to Estelle again.

Estelle was human and no angel. She said rather proudly to Mary Holland that in China she had not sat quietly at home while Cornell pursued his amorous adventures elsewhere. If the Wasson story of the embrace in the music room of the Oldham house was true, she was not, indeed, a model of perfect fidelity in that first marriage. Estelle was pinned by circumstances to Oxford during her separation before divorce, and proximity and persistence finally yielded results for William Faulkner. Estelle's family was deeply disturbed by appearances. Estelle, it seemed, was unraveling. Faulkner married Estelle to repair the damage he felt he had done, to put her back on the pedestal again, to make the shattered vase whole. He was determined at first to make the marriage work. However, it was a humpty-dumpty enterprise, as his mother Maud thought. It was poor judgment and a bad move. It was no favor to Estelle, and it meant decades of seldom relieved misery for himself. Objectively, Faulkner needed no such commitment (as he later declared), and in 1929 he had already escaped it years beyond the ordinary. At bottom he was not made for marriage and fidelity. In his heart of hearts, he himself was the marble faun. He wanted to love forever and she be fair. In reality, he would have a sequence of lovers, and each would be, in some sense, virginal, and, as Meta well said, "tremulous."

In the Faulknerian universe, the preservation of virginity has implications along the two axes. By abstention, one refuses to ascend the ladder of social commitment. No sex means no family, no marriage, minimal clan, and minimal involvement in the community. Abstention curbs commitments, limits one's liabilities, preserves independence, and promotes individuality. In some degree, to remain virginal is to stay in the Garden, and that, in turn, implies avoiding the tension that is involved in the polarity between the ideal and the real. In the social world virginity in childhood is not a problem, of course, but as one comes of age one is hard pressed by society to accept his or her gender role and act upon it. To act is to become an adult, to come out of the Garden and into society, to lose innocence, gain knowledge, and accept responsibility for one's own actions.

In his writing, Faulkner arrived at two solutions as to how a person might enter the world and yet remain virgin. One solution was to keep the character natural. In nature, there was no rape, no violation as to sex and purity, no loss in the loss of virginity. There would come a moment in life, and the action would flow. For Faulkner's great women, Caddy, Lena, and Eula, and for Yettie too, virginity was a non-issue. As if to underscore their naturalness, each of these women ended her virginity in a "sylvan setting." Sex in the natural setting was inherently good and the loss of virginity there could not be bad.

Faulkner also offered another—rather revolutionary—solution to the problem of lost purity. Virginity might be lost, but also it might be regained over time by abstinence in an appropriate spirit and manner. In Faulkner's writing, as in moments in his life, there was a curious idea that we might call "renewable virginity."

Lena Grove illustrates the idea well. In the eyes of the community she was a fallen woman. But because of her very nature, she could not be lessened by sex before marriage. Forever would Lena love, and yet be fair. Her own clear purity redeems her, first, in the eyes of Byron Bunch. Lena is a virgin with child, and Byron is virgin too. Together they can begin again and nothing, absolutely nothing, is lost. Faulkner played that story in his own life. Estelle had been married and had children. Then came separation, presumably abstinence, and at last Faulkner, with courtship, marriage, and family again. Even as he was 398 writing about Lena in 1931 and 1932, he was married to a renewable virgin. Faulkner repeated the game with Meta and did something of the same thing himself when he swore to Meta early in their relationship that he had not had sex with Estelle since Jill's birth well over a year before.

Purity, virtue, and virginity could be regained—we could go back into the Garden and begin again. Especially might men do so with a woman like Lena—or like Meta in real life. With a good woman, a man can move out of the Garden and into the modern world without losing the true values that are our salvation—love and honor, pride and pity, compassion and courage, hope and endurance. A woman, presumably, can do the same with a good man.

The most curious of all of Faulkner's renewable virgins is Quentin Compson. Quentin first gave himself the impossible task of preserving Caddy's virginity as if his own purity were at stake. When that was lost he took on the even greater task of preserving the purity of all womanhood and, seemingly, of the whole world. During a picnic party in the countryside near Cambridge, his mission brought him to confront the arch spoiler Gerald Bland. Quentin stared at Bland while he listened to him brag about making a date with a girl and gloating about how hurt she must have felt when he did not appear. Quentin suddenly jumped up and shouted, "Did you ever have a sister, did you?" and hit him.

Quentin had just been flashing back in his mind to how he had wanted to hit Dalton Ames and drive him away from Caddy, whose virginity Ames had recently despoiled. Instead of hitting Ames, "He had fainted just like a girl." (*Sound,* 201) Bland boxed Quentin bloody, and he retreated out of sight to a watering trough to wash away the blood. His friends Shreave and Spoade attempted to help him. Several times Quentin rued that he did not have another handkerchief to wipe all the blood away. Especially, he seemed to want to clean his vest. Quentin wanted to apologize to the group, but he refused to be seen by them with blood still showing on his clothes, his "new suit." Back in his Harvard room alone, Quentin washed himself, combed his hair, brushed his teeth, and finally even brushed his hat. He packed away his bloody clothes and put on fresh ones. But he kept the vest. It seemed special raiment to him, like the chasuble of the priest. He used gasoline to clean the blood from that garment and hung it on a chair in front of a lamp to dry. Later he donned the vest. "In the mirror the stain didn't show." (222) It was as if Quentin was the virgin and the blood that he spilt during the fight was virgin's blood. Bland was the symbol of maleness: selfish, imperious, and impervious to the destruction he caused. "I'm sorry I didn't bleed on him a little at least," Quentin rued. (205) To dissolve and wash away the blood, to remove the stain, seemed somehow to restore virginity for Quentin. Thus purified, he could calmly relieve himself of this earthly existence.

Renewable virginity is a strange idea, but it was one that William Faulkner would use again and again both in his life and in his writing until the very end.

ELEVEN

Community

In the Faulknerian universe there is no problem with community in nature. Difficulties multiply as man moves out of nature, as he seeks to dominate and, indeed, destroy the natural order. In Yoknapatawpha it began with the Indians who imagined erroneously that they owned the land and sold it to the white men. Then the white men divided all the land neatly into squares, which they proceeded to sell and buy among themselves as if they really owned those fragments of earth. Furthermore, white men bought slaves to work the soil and thus increased their sins with the idea that they could actually own certain human beings and buy and sell them just as they did plots of land.

The Slain Wood

In the modern world, the prime mover in the process was the industrial revolution and its technological, commercial, and financial concomitants. This ogre reached into Mississippi to pick the fleecy staple, of course, but Faulkner preferred to dwell upon the fashion in which the monster devoured the woods. His stories are replete with trees and forests and the sawmills that tore them violently away. Again and again, he traced the story of—as he so eloquently called it—"the slain wood." Very often his characters suffered the fate of the wood. Cut away from their roots, torn and shaped by machines, they met the plight of life in the modern world. Thus, Mink Snopes, as innocent and as natural as the animal for which he was named, found love and total passion with Yettie in the deep woods. Their meeting, symbolically, commenced in the very midst of the slaughter of the wilderness, and it ended in a dilapidated, clapboard tenant shack, the result of systematic exploitation built into the modern industrial order. The exploitative material order so reduced Mink, so imperiled his humanity, self-respect, and manhood, that his love for the marvelously feral and faithful Yettie could not endure "out of the garden."

400

In *Light in August* Lena Grove (as in a grove of trees and, specifically, as in The Grove which is the centerpiece of the campus at Ole Miss) also came off the land. She came from a farm to live at Doane's Mill. The mill was a sawmill. Lena, Faulkner's most angelic woman, was seduced by a sawdust Casanova, a rootless man, already stripped of family, clan, and community. His very work was the rape of the woods and his avocation was the more subtle outrage of women. Lucas loves and leaves, just as the sawmill cuts and goes. "It had been there seven years," Faulkner said of the mill, "and in seven more years it would destroy all of the timber within its reach." Then some pieces of machinery would be moved to another virgin site and other pieces left to dissolve, "gutted boilers lifting their rusting and unsmoking stacks with an air stubborn, baffled and bemused upon a stumppocked scene of profound and peaceful desolation, unplowed, untilled, gutting slowly into red and choked ravines beneath the long quiet rains of autumn and the galloping fury of vernal equinoxes." (*Light,* 2–3) Later, Lena met Byron, who worked in a planing mill in the town of Jefferson. Jefferson was more "civilized" and the planing mill, appropriately, took rough-cut boards from the crude milling operations in the countryside and "dressed" them, that is smoothed them into the lumber that would be used to build, among other things, homes for families. Byron's Saturday afternoon work consisted of carefully loading the smooth boards into box cars for shipment to towns and cities like Memphis, New Orleans, and Chicago. Byron Bunch loved Lena in the grand style of the Romantic Era that Lord Byron exalted in his poetry; he was brave knight to her fair lady. Much of Byron's life outside of work came to be dedicated to smoothing Lena's way to house and home, to a husband for herself and a father for her child, in short, to familyhood.

Some men, greedy and careless, used the wood to raise houses higher and higher from the earth. In Faulkner's writings second stories and attics usually supported the play of human vices rather than virtues. Often, the Compsons, Coldfields, and Sutpens were at their worst upstairs rather than down. More careful people, people who sought balance and avoided excesses of greed and acquisitiveness, lived in small houses close to the earth. Dilsey, V.K., and Lena all lived close to the ground. Byron Bunch, coming into the world again with Lena, moved from the second story of Mrs. Beard's boarding house into a small tent in the field within calling distance of the cabin of his beloved Lena. Now, redemptively, he slept on the ground. Buck and Buddy McCaslin refused to live in the mansion their father had built with slave labor. Wisely, they put the slaves in the mansion, while they lived in a cabin built by themselves, not out of boards, of course, but of logs. Paradoxically, even Flem Snopes seemed reluctant to live too high above the earth. When he first moved to Jefferson he lived in a tent, then for some years in a small one-story house. Later, when Flem acquired the de Spain mansion, he sat in a downstairs parlor where he dared raise his feet only so high on a step fixed to the fireplace mantel. In Faulknerian fiction, a high house often went before a great fall. Sometimes the fall was by fire, a signal of light and smoke that raised a warning in the sky for all to see. Ironically, Faulkner himself suffered great anxieties to acquire and maintain his family in a mansion, and he located his own bedroom on the second floor. Later, he added a room on the first floor that he used for his work.

In his writing Faulkner seemed to assert that anyone who defied gravity in any way and attempted to raise himself physically from the earth was liable to be brought low and suffer a humiliating fate. Imperious Jack Houston was shot ignominiously off his high horse by a rusty old shotgun held by little Mink Snopes. Joanna's high-held head was cut away from her body and rolled on the ground while her high house burned. Gail Hightower, willfully down from the tower himself, watched as Byron, made prideful by his new-found mission for Lena, held himself erect as he approached Hightower's house. "He watches quietly the puny, unhorsed figure moving with the precarious and meretricious cleverness of animals balanced on their hinder legs; that cleverness of which man animal is so fatuously proud and which constantly betrays him by means of natural laws like gravity." (*Light,* 70)

Southern whites, of course, saw no rape of nature in clearing the land nor any fundamental flaw in their organization of society. They saw themselves as having discovered in an organic society, almost miraculously, God's plan for social salvation. It was only when individuals resisted roles clearly assigned by race, gender, or "class" that trouble came. In the 1920s and 1930s, after three generations of greater and lesser disasters, the South felt that it was finally getting people into their proper places again. God was in heaven and all was right with the world. In truth, the South had probably never been so much together as it then was. Southerners imagined an Old South of moonlight and magnolias, cotton fields, faithful old family servants, and Mount Vernon mansions. That had been lost, but nobly lost, in the War for Southern Independence. The Old South had gone with the wind, but the values of the Old South, the true values of soul and spirit, were not lost but risen, and now joined the necessities of the modern world to make a New South that married the spirit of the old to the material accomplishments of the New. By this marriage, Southern society, in its own eyes, was superior to all others. It was whole, it was organic and ongoing.

Southern culture developed ingenious devices for preserving its image of itself as a whole, harmonious organism. One of these was an amazing capacity for not seeing what was clearly before its eyes. An obvious and striking example was the fact that it could look at people who had a drop or two of black blood—who were clearly more white than most "white" people—and call them unblinkingly "black." Faulkner understood quite well the capacity of the

Southern community for not seeing, and he related that phenomenon in the story of Hightower's wife and her persistent adultery in Memphis hotels. As that woman persisted in violating her role, the community commenced the process of transforming her into a non-being. "And even the neighbors on either side would no longer see her about the house," Faulkner said. "And soon it was as though she were not there; as though everyone had agreed that she was not there, that the minister did not even have a wife." (*Light,* 61) In the end the minister's wife got the message. She either jumped or got herself pushed out of the window of an upper-story room in a Memphis hotel. Gail Hightower, in fact, then had no wife. In the South, often, wishing does make it so.

Faulkner knew, too, that Southern communities had a way of dealing with individuals who persistently refused to perform in assigned roles and who would neither go away nor self-destruct. That response might be called the "pearl effect." Supposedly, the pearl begins with a grain of sand that invades the oyster's shell and irritates the animal within. The oyster responds by lacquering over the particle until it becomes a marvelously smooth, lustrous ball. What begins as an irritation ends as a gem—and a perpetual union.

Faulkner ran this process, too, in the Hightower story. At first the community attempted to ignore the minister's disturbing behavior. But when Hightower persisted, they tried to expel him. Unknown persons seized him, took him to the woods, tied him to a tree, and whipped him. They threatened his life if he did not leave. Hightower, of course, could not leave the scene of his grandfather's death. Further, he refused to name his assailants, and, thus ironically, married himself to the community even more firmly. "He would neither tell nor depart," Faulkner said. "Then all of a sudden the whole thing seemed to blow away, like an evil wind. It was as though the town realised at last that he would be a part of its life until he died, and that they might as well become reconciled. As though, Byron thought, the entire affair had been a lot of people performing a play and that now and at last they had all played out the parts which had been allotted them and now they could quietly live with one another." (*Light,* 67) Hightower had become simply another "character" in the community of Jefferson, accepted like the town drunk, the village idiot, womanizer, bootlegger, or the well-dressed ne'er-do-well who might be called "Count No-Count."

"Seeming will make it so," Southerners might have sung. Indeed, one could almost say that Southern communities valued appearances, "what ought to be," even more than realities. In that relatively closed world, if a certain appearance could be made to persist and if all could simply agree that the appearance was real, in time the appearance did, in effect, become real. In the South, when a community agreed upon a certain appearance, for instance, that "our blacks are good blacks" and well taken care of by us, they were exceedingly intolerant of anyone who presumed otherwise—most of all if the naysayers were other Southern whites.

Again the Hightower story illustrates the point. When the Memphis reporters came to Jefferson to find out about this minister whose wife had just died in such a newsworthy way, the congregation went to the church on Sunday morning apparently laboring hard to believe that nothing had happened. "The old ladies and some of the old men were already in the church, horrified and outraged, not so much about the Memphis business as about the presence of the reporters." (62) They, themselves, might sense a problem, but they definitely did not want outsiders telling them that there was a problem. If necessary, they were even prepared to ignore the death of the minister's wife in disgraceful circumstances.

If I were pressed to chose one word that comes closest to capturing the essential nature of Southern culture, that word would be "placeness." There is a place for everything and every person, and everyone and everything ought to be in its place. There is also placeness in time—a time for certain words to be spoken, certain gestures to be made, and certain rituals to be performed. Placeness is a quality in every culture, but in the South, because of the necessity of keeping blacks in their place, that quality is vastly exaggerated.

Faulkner caught this passion for placeness beautifully in the closing scene of *The Sound and the Fury.* Benjy was a natural person, and he was supremely sensitive to disruptions in the natural order. He loved goodness ("Caddy smelled like trees"), but when there were bad feelings in the air, when things were out of order, Benjy knew it and he raised the alarm unmistakably and immediately in the form of a high, wailing cry. Benjy's mother, née Caroline Maury, had married above her place in the social hierarchy when she wed Jason Compson. Perhaps for that reason, appearances were vitally important to her, and she persisted in insisting that all things be seen and labelled in certain ways. Hence when Benjamin as a small child was found to be an idiot, Mrs. Compson changed his name from Maury to Benjamin. "No Maury ever . . . ," she would say. After Mr. Compson died, she insisted that Jason be labelled the head of the house in spite of his obvious lack of moral and practical qualifications for the task. Indeed, Mrs. Compson passed on her passion for appearances to Jason—who was ruthless in his determination to make other members of the family behave in certain ways.

One of the rituals in the Compson household was that every Sunday afternoon, Benjamin, sitting in the back seat of the family surrey with a flower held in both hands, would be driven to the cemetery to visit the Compson graves. Ordinarily, it was Dilsey's son T.P. who hitched the old horse Queenie to the surrey and did the driving. But on Easter Sunday, 1928, T.P. was away and Dilsey allowed her grandson Luster, a sometimes foolish lad, to take up the task. Luster drove off with Benjy sitting on the back seat holding the flower, "his eyes serene and ineffable." Approaching the town square Luster wanted to make a smart show for the black people standing about. He whipped Queenie into a trot with his switch and turned left at the Confederate monument that stood on the south side of the square. T.P. had always turned right to circle the square en route to the cemetery. "For an instant Ben sat in an utter hiatus. Then he bellowed. Bellow upon bellow, his voice mounted, with scarce interval for breath. There was more than astonishment in it, it was horror; shock; agony eyeless, tongueless; just sound."

Jason suddenly appeared, bounding across the square from the hardware store in which he worked. He leapt into the driver's seat, pushing Luster aside, sawing and whipping Queenie around to pass to the right around the monument. Then he pulled Queenie to a halt, turned, and hit Luster on the head with his fist. "Don't you know better than to take him to the left?" he cried. Driving again, Luster proceeded around the square, and Ben grew quiet as "facade flowed smoothly once more from left back over his shoulder. . . . The broken flower drooped over Ben's fist and his eyes were empty and blue and serene again as cornice and facade flowed smoothly once more from left to right; post and tree, window and doorway, and signboard, each in its ordered place." (396–401) It was totally fitting that the last word in *The Sound and the Fury* was "place."

Redemption: The Organic Society

The Compson children, like all other Southern white children of their generation, were born into a world they never made. They were born into a culture already severely damaged by its history—by slavery, bloody civil war and defeat, and by a vast reduction in wealth and spirit. Some families bravely began again and transcended disasters. The Compson children, however, came to a family unable or unwilling to meet the challenges of modern life. Before the war, in the last decades of slavery, Southern culture had gone awry and prescribed roles of gender, race, and social position that were contrary to nature and ultimately untenable. Alienation from the natural virtues continued after the war, aggravated by the reduction, the colonialization, of the South by the North. In the three decades that followed the publication of *The Sound and the Fury,* Faulkner offered three sets of solutions to the problem of how Southern culture might regain the virtues natural to man. The first solution—faith in the recuperative powers of the organic society—appeared in *Light in August* in 1932.

Light in August is the Faulkner book that is most about the organic society.

Ironically, it depicts the organic society in terms of people who have fallen out of that order. Lena Grove, Gail Hightower, Byron Bunch, Joe Christmas, Doc Hines, Simon McEachern, Bobbie Allen, Lucas Burch, and Percy Grimm are all displaced persons, and the book is about how they all, in one way or another, come to find place again as if moved by some unseen force, an invisible Player in a game with real but unwritten rules and unseen squares on a board.

Lena, the leading woman, is a person displaced by a single unthinking act. After eight years of living in the lean-to attached to her brother's house, she opened the window for the first time. "She had not opened it a dozen times before she discovered that she should not have opened it at all." (3) She found love and soon was pregnant. Lucas, the man, fled, promising to send for her when he got a job and resettled. Six months later, her brother noted her condition and called her a whore. She held to the faith that Lucas would send for her. Two weeks later, during the night, she went through the opened window one last time and headed west, seeking Lucas. After four weeks of traveling, she arrived in Jefferson. Behind her, Lena's journey "is a peaceful corridor paved with the unflagging and tranquil faith and peopled with kind and nameless faces and voices." (4) This is the organic society in motion as it ought to be, slow and steady as a mother's heartbeat, working its will through the people who sit quietly talking on their front porches in towns and villages on August nights, who move about in fields and farm kitchens in the still cool early mornings, the people who pass along the road in wagons giving Lena rides to hamlets with names like Pocahontas and Frenchman's Bend. Like ten thousand tiny hairs, their words and acts brushed Lena into place again, and she, with total faith in the goodness of humanity declared: "Folks have been kind. Folks have been right kind." (10) Lena had faith that "when a little chap" came into the world, his father would be there. Her faith was honored most essentially in the person of wifeless, childless Byron Bunch, who flowed into Lena's life as if also pushed along by some gentle but purposeful and powerful force.

Joe Christmas was the ultimate in displaced persons. He was the son of an errant Southern white girl and a carnival man of darker hue, perhaps a Mexican. His father might have been partially black, or he might not have been black at all. The crucial factor was that neither Joe nor anyone else could ever know with certainty whether he was black or white in a society in which everything began with that definition. Joe was intelligent and handsome. He was physically strong, mentally tough, and fearless in the face of violence. Yet his strengths only gave power to his indirection. Joe Christmas careened through life, disastrously, destructively, half out of control, a tortured mind and a tortured body tragically vulnerable to the use that other people would make of them. Yet Joe would not simply destroy himself and cease to be. He struggled to breathe, to act, to exist. Like some Flying Dutchman, he roved the world, searching for a haven of rest and peace. Seeing people in Jefferson sitting and talking quietly on their front porches on a summer's night, he said, "That's all I wanted." (108) In that strictly biracial universe of the early twentieth-century South, he was led in his search to flash alternately white and black—a brilliant indetermination that attracted literally scores of disordered people to him, seeking to use him to make themselves seem whole. They rooted him out of his hideaways and chased him flapping from one color to the other and back again. Finally, Joe found place and peace in an astounding way.

At one level Joe's story was simply another tale of one man's search for identity. But Faulkner raised the stakes in the old game to a new and terrific height by taking a man who did not know and could never know his color and setting him down in that Southern social universe where color was vitally important. Joe's not knowing his color was tragic, not ever being able to know was tragedy doubled; not ever being able to know in a universe in which everyone else knew his and her own color—even inevitably knew because it was prescribed by the community to which he or she had been born and in which he or she lived—was tragedy squared.

In the South everyone knew his color and, hence, his place. On that Southern stage all actors were either white or black. They lived in two very real, very separate, and yet interwoven worlds. Southern infants spilled onto the boards with lines already spoken, gestures already made, feelings already felt. The child had only to note his nose and follow its color. In part, belonging was made easy because it was made compulsory. For practically everyone, there was no such thing as defining oneself independently of the community, no such thing as living there and opting out of the role prescribed. Individuals would indeed slip from time to time, but the organic society would nudge them back again, sweeping them along and into the current. Like Lena Grove, one needed, finally, only simple faith and physical persistence to find oneself comfortably again a part of the great social symphony.

Doc Hines killed Joe's father and allowed his mother to die in childbirth. Then he took the child away from the place of his birth and deposited him on the doorstep of the all-white orphanage where he worked. The baby was found and brought into the orphanage during a Christmas party. The young women named him Christmas, and Doc Hines gave him the name Joe. For five years Doc tended the boiler in the orphanage. When the children came out in the yard to play, Doc sat in the doorway of the boiler room, steadily watching Joe. Over the years the children sensed that Joe was somehow vitally different. His skin was parchment colored, and they concluded that he was black. They began to call him "nigger."

When Joe was five he suffered the trauma that would mark his life as a man among women. For almost a year he had been creeping into the dietitian's room during rest period and stealing a taste of her toothpaste. One day he heard her and her lover approaching. He hid behind the curtain that closed off a corner of her room. While the couple had intercourse—she very frightened of being discovered and he very insistent—Joe nervously ate toothpaste. Finally, he threw up. "Well, here I am," he said to himself. The curtain flew back, and the dietitian jerked Joe to his feet, limp and glassy eyed. "You little rat," the woman hissed. "Spying on me! You little nigger bastard!" (114) In the days that followed, Joe waited for the punishment that never came. Instead, the dietitian attempted to bribe him with a silver dollar, an effort that he did not understand at all. Nearly insane with feelings of guilt, frightened and furious, she told the matron that Joe was black and must be transferred to a black orphanage. Surprisingly, the matron refused that option and ordered the dietitian to search the files for someone to adopt Joe. She chose Simon McEachern, a farmer with a wife and no children.

Joe was brought before McEachern in the matron's office. McEachern was middle-aged, thick-bodied, and bearded. He wore a black suit and polished black shoes, planted squarely side by side. He held his black hat in "a blunt clean hand." Joe felt the man stare at him, cold, intent, "yet not deliberately harsh," as if he were a horse or second hand plow, "convinced beforehand that he would see flaws, convinced beforehand that he would buy." McEachern skirmished, asked about Joe's parents, and the matron refused information. "It's no matter," he said. "He will grow up to fear God and abhor idleness and vanity despite his origins." (133–34)

It was no accident that McEachern was there. Probably, he had been attempting to adopt a child for some time and had been refused. The dietitian delivered Joe to him, and he had a use for the child. McEachern was a Presbyterian and a deep Calvinist. He was convinced of his sainthood, his election for salvation in a world full of sinners predestined for damnation. The true Calvinist must enforce saintly living upon sinners as a part of his covenant with God. The reader might guess that McEachern had so alienated himself from his community by his self-righteousness that he had not been able previously to enforce saintly behavior on anyone. Joe would be his captive sinner, and a means by which he would fulfill his covenant with God.

McEachern brought Joe to a small, stark world filled with hard work, rigid discipline, and the forms of piety. Mrs. McEachern tried to make him the child she apparently never had and an ally in rebellion against her husband, offering him, among other things, food as a bribe. Joe would have none of that. Women, food, and sex had become mixed in his mind with confusion and chaos. McEachern had given him, at least, a world of order, predictability, and hence a feeling that he had some power over his life in the world.

Race and sex were inextricably joined in Southern culture, and to suffer confusion about one was inevitably to suffer confusion about the other. Joe was not born with difficulties in matters of gender. In the orphanage when he was about three years old there was a girl of twelve named Alice. He had allowed

Alice to mother him, to wash his face, dress him, and comb his hair. When she was adopted, Joe remembered that she came to him in the middle of the night to say goodbye. Alice was the last woman he felt wholly good about. (127–28) When he was fourteen, he went with four other farm boys to a deserted sawmill shed where one of the older boys had arranged for them to meet a black girl. When his turn came, Joe went into the darkened shed. He was seized "by a terrible haste. There was something in him trying to get out, like when he used to think of toothpaste." When he found the girl in the dark, he suddenly went wild, kicking her, pulling her up, and hitting at her. The other boys rushed in and "fell upon him, swarming, grappling, fumbling, he striking back, his breath hissing with rage and despair." They bore him down, "yet he still struggled, fighting, weeping. There was no She at all now. They just fought; it was as if a wind had blown among them, hard and clean." Violence *vice* sex. They pinned him to the ground and still he would not give up. Finally, they sprang away and ran. They waited for him outside, but he turned homeward without speaking. One of them called quietly, gently, across the distance, "See you tomorrow at church, Joe." (146–48)

Then Joe was seventeen, and he saw Bobbie Allen. Bobbie was a waitress in a backstreet restaurant in Jefferson. She was also a prostitute, brought to the town from Memphis by Max and Mame, the couple who ran the restaurant. Bobbie was over thirty, "slight, almost childlike," a face with button eyes, "always downlooking." She had a man's name and a man's hands even as she went about the women's work of serving food. Ingeniously, Faulkner was weaving a fourth theme—food—more and more clearly in with themes of race, sex, and violence. Joe was fascinated with Bobbie from first sight, but it was only because she was so small, so totally unthreatening, that he dared approach her. She was surprised and flattered by his attention. "Well, say." (172)

Soon after he became eighteen they made a date to meet at the streetcorner after she finished work. Joe slipped out of the window of his upstairs room and slid down a rope, passing McEachern's bedroom window. He met Bobbie only to find that she was having her period. Frustrated, confused, he slapped her. Fleeing, he entered the woods on the edge of town. He was outraged by the uncertainty, the lack of control and chaos brought into the world by women. In the woods he imagined that he saw a row of "suavely shaped urns in the moonlight, blanched. And not one was perfect. Each one was cracked and from each crack there issued something liquid, death colored, and foul!" (177–78) He leaned against a tree and vomited.

A week later he met Bobbie again. Taking her arm, he drew her down the road toward the woods he had entered the week before. As they crossed a fence, her dress caught on a barb. He tore it free and, still pulling her, crossed a newly plowed field in which plants had just begun to grow. They entered the woods—nature, the Garden again. "She let herself be half carried and half dragged among the growing plants in the field, the furrows, and into the woods, the trees." (178)

Thus Joe knew love, and first experienced sex in the sylvan setting. For a month it went on in that way, and it was good. Then Joe came to the house in Jefferson in which Bobbie lived with Max and Mame. They were in her room when Max and Mame entered, and as they talked Joe felt the scorn of the Memphis couple for his country ignorance. When they left, Joe said, "Let's go."

"Go?" she said. "Go where?" She began ripping off her clothes, flinging them down.

"Here?" he said, unbelieving. "In here?"

In the bare room, lit by a bare bulb suspended from the ceiling by a wire, he first clearly saw a naked woman. In the woods he had loved Bobbie, and, it seemed she had loved him. In the house, amid the slain wood, love changed. That night, lying in bed, caressing her flank, Joe confessed.

"I think I got some nigger blood in me," he said. "I don't know. I believe I have."

"You're lying," she declared.

"All right," he said.

"I don't believe it," she said.

"All right," he said again. (184–85)

Thereafter, Joe fell into a maelstrom of corruption that whirled around Bobbie and her Memphis friends. He drank, smoked, lied, gambled, stole, and called Bobbie his whore to other men. Finally, caught at a country dance by McEachern, he showered a chair down on his adopted father's head and left him for dead. Joe and Bobbie fled separately. He found her back in her room with Max, Mame, and one of the Memphis hoodlums. Bobbie was furious.

"Bastard! Son of a bitch!" she shouted at him. "Getting me into a jam, that always treated you like you were a white man. A white man!" Joe was amazed. "Why, I committed murder for her," he said to himself. "I even stole for her." Then she seemed to blow out of his life like a scrap of paper in a high wind. He began to move menacingly toward her as if he still held the piece of chair like a club.

"He told me himself he was a nigger!" Bobbie screamed. "The son of a bitch! Me f___ing for nothing a nigger son of a bitch that would get me in a jam with the clodhopper police. At a clodhopper dance!" (204)

The men knocked Joe to the floor where he lay fully conscious but unmoving. Mame stuck a bill in his pocket and they left. Joe rose, found his way to the front yard, and entered "the street which was to run for fifteen years." (210)

Joe roamed south as far as Mexico, then North to Detroit and Chicago. Always there were the cities, and the mean streets where he went to the whorehouses. If he had money he paid, if he did not, he told them he was a Negro and either they threw him out or beat him up. Once he rose and told the woman he was black. "You are?" she said without interest. "I thought maybe you were just another wop or something." Then she looked at his face and grew frightened. "What about it? You look all right," she said. "You ought to seen the shine I turned out just before your turn came." She watched him, becoming very still. "Say, what do you think this dump is, anyhow? The Ritz Hotel?" It took two policemen to restrain him, and they thought at first the woman was dead. (211–12)

He was sick for two years after that. He had not known that there were white women who would willingly take black men. Before he had teased white men into calling him black and then fought them. Now he fought black men who called him white. In Chicago and then in Detroit he lived with black people, and for a time lived with a very dark woman as if married. He would lie beside her at night while she slept, breathing deeply, "trying to breathe into himself the dark odor, the dark and inscrutable thinking and being of negroes, with each suspiration trying to expel from himself the white blood and the white way of thinking and being. And all the while his nostrils at the odor which he was trying to make his own would whiten and tauten, his whole being writhe and strain with physical outrage and spiritual denial." (212) Finally, one day the street became a country road on the outskirts of Jefferson, Mississippi.

Again Joe would be used, and again by a woman, Joanna Burden. His life with Joanna was a three-year confusion of race, sex, food, and violence. It was a replay of the chaos that women represented to him, compounded by Joanna's own multiple displacements. At first, he built a small universe with Joanna—the cabin with his cot, his dinner every evening on the kitchen table, sex in her bedroom, and, subsequently, the straight line two-mile path that he wore in walking to and from his job shoveling sawdust into an incinerator at the planing mill in Jefferson. It was a strange place, but it was a place. He had ceased to run, though he told himself repeatedly to put his razor in his pocket and go. Sometime in the early spring before that fateful August he brought Lucas Burch to live with him in the cabin. Joanna said: "You didn't have to do that." (255) He didn't have to bring a man into his life, she meant, to keep her out of the cabin. The liquor business, the hijacking, changing bottles for money, buying a new car with the proceeds; all this was the old familiar comfortable corruption. It was all male and very manageable compared to his life with Joanna.

"I'll go tomorrow," he kept saying to himself, and yet he did not go. (252) Joanna, who could be many things, carried in herself the promise of wholeness for Joe. She might be the woman who would make him whole and give him a place in life . . . and peace. Finally, however, Joanna decided that Joe must join her in purity, piety, and the mission to black folks. She no longer set out food for him in the kitchen. Joe would pass by the barren table and think: "My God. When have I sat down in peace to eat." (263) He would mount the stairs to find her door shut and hear her praying. He would not listen or leave, but wait until she opened the door. He would not sit now, but talked while standing. The thread of communication had become very thin. But it was the only thread, the last thread that kept Joe tied to the world of humanity.

Earlier, Joe had gone into the woods, built a fire and sat by a spring. He carried a detective magazine. He read the magazine page by page, word by word, to the very end and burned it. He went to his cache of whiskey and poured it all into the ground. Neither the words or the whiskey meant anything to him anymore. He was slipping away from the world of humankind, losing communication. Now it was only he and Joanna, and Joanna was fading. One evening she summoned him by note. When he went to her for the last time, she was sitting up in bed, her arms folded under a shawl. When he would not kneel and pray, she pulled an old and very large pistol from under her shawl, pointed it at his chest and pulled the trigger. Joe saw the shadow of the gun on the wall. The hammer flicked away and the firing pin struck the first of two rounds in the cylinder, but the gun failed to fire. (267) Joe drew the razor across Joanna's throat. This was his last communication with her, and it was total.

Joe went into the woods, the wilderness, and when Friday came he went straight to Mottstown. At a barber shop, he cleansed himself much as had both Quentin and Eula before their deaths. Then he walked about town until someone recognized him. Thereafter, Faulkner wove elements of Christ's crucifixion into his story of Joe Christmas. Lucas, like Judas to Jesus, witnessed against him in hope of getting the thousand-dollar reward. Hightower, like Peter, at first denied him. The national guard captain, Percy Grimm, like the Roman centurion for Christ, administered the coup de grâce that made a merciful end to his earthly life. Percy, the perfectly responsive, almost mechanical, superbly effective instrument of the will of the community ("the Player") chased Joe with the instincts of an unerring hunter. Joe resisted death, almost as if he were saying one last time, Father-let-this-cup-pass-me-by. He ran to Hightower's house and entered the back door. He met Hightower in the hallway, beat him down with his manacled hands, and plunged on. Grimm and three men rushed in and pulled the bleeding Hightower to his feet. Grimm shouted, "Which room, old man?"

> "Men! Listen to me," cried Hightower. "He was here that night. He was with me the night of the murder. I swear to God."
>
> "Jesus Christ!" Grimm shouted, his young voice clear and outraged, like that of a young priest. "Has every preacher and old maid in Jefferson taken their pants down to the yellowbellied son of a bitch?"

Grimm ran toward the kitchen where Christmas had turned a table on its edge in a corner. He waited behind it, his two hands visible at the top, holding it in place. The wooden table had become his cross. Grimm crashed into the room, "already firing, almost before he could have seen the table overturned and standing on its edge across the corner of the room, and the bright and glittering hands of the man who crouched behind it, resting upon the upper edge." Grimm shot five times from a pistol that might have carried as many as ten rounds. Later, someone "covered all five shots with a folded handkerchief." (438–39) Like Christ, Joe suffered five wounds.

Grimm flung the table aside. When the other men entered the room, they saw him crouched over the body. Then they saw what he was doing. Grimm sprang back, flinging the bloody butcher knife behind him. "Now you'll let white women alone," he cried, "even in hell." Joe lay with eyes empty. "For a long moment he looked up at them with peaceful and unfathomable and unbearable eyes. Then his face, body, all, seemed to collapse, to fall in upon itself, and from out the slashed garments about his hips and loins the pent black blood seemed to rush like a released breath." (439-40)

Joe died for the multiple sins of man. He was sacrificed for the ignorance, the innocence of the people in the community in which he had lived for three years. He served to bring relief to all those people who were displaced in their ideas about race and sex—the men who came to look at Joanna's body "who believed aloud that it was an anonymous negro crime committed not by a negro but by Negro and who knew, believed, and hoped that she had been ravished too; at least once before her throat was cut and at least once afterward." People who had never even seen Joanna Burden were outraged, people who would despise her had they known her, the volunteer firemen, who had deserted their counters and desks, swung down from their fire engine and were shown several different places where the sheet had lain, "and some of them with pistols already in their pockets began to canvass about for someone to crucify." (271–72) Thus all the sins and all the fears of punishments for sins were projected upon Joe and he was sacrificed.

Joe was both crucified and lynched. In reality, in the Southern world to which William Faulkner was born there was no vast difference between the two. Both were done by whites to blacks for the sake of preserving the moral order. Percy was the perfect tool of the society and his thought was clear. His idea, his words, were quite simple and direct. "We got to preserve order," he said. (427) Joe was lynched as black men had been lynched during the years of Faulkner's youth, not in confusion and chaos, but with clear and passionate purpose. It was done by men who saw their duty, and it was approved by a society that required action. It happened in communities that felt themselves in danger of losing moral virtue. It was no comfort to black people in America, but symbolically the lynchers were lynching themselves. The lynched were essentially Christ figures—as the eminent contemporary black leader W.E.B. Du Bois wisely saw—dying for the myriad sins of others. It was as if the evil in man had found focus and body, and a physical act, a ritual, that people surely had the power to perform, would restore balance and virtue.

Thus Joe, the most displaced of persons, in the end found place as the sacrificial lamb. It was he who by his sacrifice atoned for the ignorance and confusion of those around him. He, like Lena, had served to bring displaced persons back into the world, into the community, into a harmonious organic society. Lena was moved by faith; Joe by the simple instinct for life over death. Ultimately he found his place as savior, and as savior he was raceless, and, by Grimm's hand, sexless too.

Redemption: Back to Nature

One might argue that *Light in August* is the most optimistic of Faulkner's great books. Certainly, it outranks *The Sound and the Fury* and *Absalom, Absalom!* in that respect. The explanation for the difference, perhaps, lies in Faulkner's personal life. In 1931 and 1932 while he was writing the book he was just gaining national reputation as a talented novelist. At last *Sanctuary* had brought him popular attention. He had become the master of Rowan Oak, his father had died recently, and he had become the head of the Falkner clan. He was thirty-five, physically fit, and Estelle was pregnant with his first child. For a time it must have seemed to him that he could live in the world with a substantial measure of contentment and still maintain his life as a writing artist. It is a novel full of ironies in which disasters, even such a great disaster as Joe encountered, turned into triumph. It was an indictment of Southern culture and particularly of the race and sex roles that were assigned to individuals. Yet the overall statement was that the organic society did work.

Faulkner's own life over the next several years might have argued to him that such optimism was unwarranted, that Southern society as it then existed was terrifically flawed and the best solution for the individual was escape. Indeed, three of his white characters in *The Sound and the Fury* had escaped, but not necessarily to a better world. Caddy went to Hollywood and Europe, Quentin to Harvard and death, and the girl Quentin to an unknown but predictably awful end with the carnival man. In his writing in the decade after 1932 Faulkner developed other escapes; most notably he seemed to advocate a return to nature.

Faulkner early evolved a symbology in which buildings stood for artificial, man-made institutions and the "outdoors" stood for the natural order. In his stories, doors and door frames, windows and window frames became especially important. His characters were forever looking in or looking out, crawling in or crawling out of windows. They passed in and out of doors, faced closed doors and locked doors, and plunged through, paused, rested, or sat in doorways. Very often to go into a house or building was to attempt to enter the modern world and deal with it on its own terms, to go out was to abandon that effort and seek salvation in nature. Stairs, porches, chimneys, and attics also had easily understood meanings.

Faulkner's writings are filled with houses: cabins, the modest homes of farmers and tenant farmers, the shacks of poor whites, the houses of town folks, and the mansions of the more affluent. He also does much with institutional houses, the places where the displaced might find more or less sheltering homes—boarding houses, brothels (whorehouses, houses of prostitution), and jails (jailhouses and prisons). All these he treated with a sympathy that is striking. Especially did he write kindly about the people who ran such institutions—the Mrs. Beards and Littlejohns of the boarding houses, the Miss Rebas of the brothels, and the jailors and wardens of the jails and prisons. Similarly, courthouses along with sheriffs, judges, and lawyers came off quite well. Colleges, universities, and professors get slight but sympathetic treatments. Public schools and professional teachers are underrepresented and sometimes, but seldom, elicit sympathy, while modern hospitals, nurses, and doctors are all but ignored. The signal exception was Harry Wilbourne, the intern in *The Wild Palms,* who ended by botching an abortion that killed both his lover and his child. Faulkner gives us close details of banks, drugstores, barbershops, and other business establishments, but he gave us, essentially, no factories, no factory workers, and no factory owners at all. Understandably, he rejected and ignored in his fiction what he rejected and ignored in his personal life.

By 1942 when he published the novella *The Bear* as a part of a series of connected stories he titled *Go Down Moses,* Faulkner seemed to argue that man's best chance for earthly salvation, of again finding and embracing the primal human virtues, was a return to nature.

The Bear is Old Ben, who has been the reigning creature in the Big Bottom through the middle decades of the nineteenth century. To the farmers living around the bottom he has been a rogue, killing and eating their animals. He was indestuctible, breaking up traps set for him, absorbing and carrying over the years the bullets they had shot into him. He was too big and too smart to be brought down, living almost too long, "solitary, indomitable, and alone: widowered childless and absolved of mortality—old Priam reft of his old wife and outlived all his sons." (*Moses,* 193–94)

The Big Bottom was more than a hundred square miles stretching along the Tallahatchie River. When the story opened in 1883, it was still a wilderness, the earth as God made it, as yet largely unspoiled by man. Major de Spain bought the Bottom from Thomas Sutpen soon after the Civil War, and he had begun logging operations on its edges. Every fall and summer, the Major took a hunting party into the Bottom for two weeks. The hunters included General Compson, the Major's Civil War commander; Walter Ewell, a yeoman farmer and crack shot; Ash, the aging black cook; and "Cass" Edmonds, the great-grandson and heir to the lands of Carothers McCaslin. The wise old hunter in the party was Sam Fathers, the son of a black slave mother and the Chickasaw chief who was her owner. About the year 1809 Sam was traded with his mother to Carothers McCaslin for a gelding pony. Also in the party was Boon Hogganbeck, one-fourth Indian, the grandson of a Chickasaw squaw. He was middle-aged, six-four in height, large-headed, ruddy-faced, with "the mind of a child, the heart of a horse, and little hard shoe-button eyes without depth or meanness or generosity or viciousness or gentleness or anything else." (227) Boon was about as close to the Bear himself as human flesh ever became. Finally, there was Tennie's Jim, a lightly colored young man of twenty-two who was mostly white. His grandfather and his great-grandfather were not only white but the same man, again Carothers McCaslin.

Thus Faulkner made up a party of men whose blood represented the mixing of not two races but of three, men whose ancestry was not only both black and white, but white and Indian, and Indian and black. If American Indians indeed migrated from the Orient in pre-history, then the party represented all of the races of the earth. Further, the Indian blood in the party represented both that of the aristocrat, a chief, and that of the commoner, a squaw. Ash, apparently, was purely black, and the other men were purely white but came from different strata in that society. The party joined youth and age, and town and country. There were no women in the group, but the story was profoundly sexual.

In November, 1877, Isaac McCaslin, age ten, joined the hunt. Ike was the grandson of Carothers McCaslin and the ward of McCaslin "Cass" Edmonds. Sam became the boy's mentor, and the boy was an eager and extremely able student. In the following summer, Ike went into the woods alone, wanting to see the Bear, not to kill it. He took only a watch and a compass, leaving his gun behind because Sam told him that he had to choose between the gun and seeing the Bear. Deep into the woods by mid-day, he felt that to see the Bear he would also have to strip himself of watch and compass—metaphorically of time and space. He did so and moved on, tried to circle to return to where he had left those instruments and found himself lost. Just as he realized that he was totally lost, he saw the Bear's fresh prints in the ground, looked up, and saw the Bear himself. The Bear gazed at Ike for several moments. Then it moved away, turned to look back at him again, and was gone. "It faded, sank back into the wilderness without motion as he had watched a fish, a huge old bass, sink back into the dark depths of its pool and vanish without any movement of its fins." (209)

Later, Ike killed a deer and Sam marked his face with the hot blood as a sign of his admission into the fraternity of hunters. Soon, he knew that he could find Old Ben any time he wanted. Once he even encountered the Bear so closely that he could smell him and he did not shoot. Neither did Sam who stood behind him. They knew that Old Ben would be killed some day, and it should be they who brought about his death at the end of a chase. For the Bear to be killed, they had to have a dog that was big enough and smart enough to hold him at bay until the men could come up.

The dog was Lion. Sam had captured him after neighboring farmers had complained of their livestock being attacked and eaten—they thought by a panther, or a bear. It was Lion, a ninety-pound dog, gun-metal blue with hot, yellow eyes. Sam alternately starved and fed the dog until he was master. Then he married Lion to Boon. "It was as if Lion were a woman—or perhaps Boon was the woman. That was more like it, the big grave, sleepy-seeming dog which, as Sam Fathers said, cared about no man and no thing: and the violent, insensitive, hard-faced man with his touch of remote Indian blood and the mind almost of a child." In camp next fall, the hunters discovered that Boon slept with Lion in his bed. On the next day, Boon and Lion jumped the Bear who swam the river and finally lost them after a twenty-mile chase. A year later, Lion finally brought Old Ben to bay and General Compson got in two shots and drew blood before Ben broke off the engagement and ran. Lion gave chase and stopped the Bear again. Boon, riding a one-eyed mule who somehow wasn't frightened by the smell of wild blood, caught up while the dogs held the Bear at bay. He pumped five shots at Ben without hitting him once. The Bear killed a hound with one swipe of its paw, turned, and made for the river. Lion, Boon, and the one-eyed mule gave chase again, working down one side of the river and up the other. At last they struck the trail where the Bear had turned into the woods away from the river, but dark came on and Boon had to drag Lion back to camp, fighting him, as he said, "hand to hand." Boon left Lion with Sam and came to his room alone. "I ain't fit to sleep with him," he explained. (226)

Next year, they remained in camp into early December, waiting for the weather to clear so that Lion and Ben could run the race again. General Compson insisted that Ike ride Katie, the one-eyed, spookless mule. As the party prepared to enter the woods, Lion looked at Ike "across the trivial uproar of the hounds, out of the yellow eyes as depthless as Boon's, as free as Boon's of meanness or generosity or gentleness or viciousness." (238) Almost immediately, the dogs found the Bear. Lion lept at him. Old Ben raked Lion aside with one great sweep of his paw and waded into the hounds. He killed one with a single blow, then cut, and ran. Now it was bear and hounds, mules, horses, and men strung out, racing through the woods, yelping and yelling. Then it was Ike and Sam alone on mules galloping behind the dogs, through a cane brake and up onto the bluff above the river. They met Boon running along the bluff. "He went straight across," Boon cried, swinging himself up on the mule behind Ike. They plunged down the bank and into the river, swimming the mule, Boon on one side, Ike on the other. Sam was behind them and the river was full of dogs. Ike heard the Major whooping on the bank behind him and looked back to see Tennie's Jim dive his horse down the bank and into the water.

The dogs swam faster than the others and were scrambling up the bank on the far side before the mules found footing. Ike got a leg over Katie's back and came out of the water riding. Boon, running alongside, grabbed a stirrup. They crested the bank and crashed through the undergrowth toward the baying dogs. They found Old Ben reared on hind legs, back to a tree, the dogs swirling around as Lion leapt and sunk his teeth in Ben's throat. Ben grabbed Lion in both arms. Ike dismounted, raised and cocked his gun. The Bear raked at Lion's belly with both claws. Boon shouted something at Ike, ran through the dogs, and jumped on the Bear's back. Ike saw his left arm go under Ben's throat and the glint of his knife in his right hand as it rose and fell. All three crashed to the ground, and when the Bear rose Boon was still on his back working the knife. The Bear turned and carrying both man and dog took two or three more steps toward the woods before he fell, crashing to the earth so hard that the whole fused mass of beasts and man seemed to bounce once and then lie still.

Ike and Tennie's Jim ran to Boon. He was kneeling, quite calm now, at the Bear's head. Boon's left ear was shredded; blood running down his face and thinning in the light rain. His boot was ripped open from knee to instep. Lion was barely alive, his belly torn open, entrails spilling out. Boon sent Tennie's Jim for a boat they had seen a hundred yards down river, and then they saw Sam Fathers lying face down in the mud. They turned him over. His eyes were open; there was no wound, no mark on his body. He said something in the Indian tongue. They could hear Tennie's Jim and the Major calling back and forth across the water, the voices carrying in the still, thick air, round and ringing, heard dully like sound through heavy iron. Tennie's Jim came up, and they carried Sam down to the skiff. Boon wrapped Lion in his coat and brought him to the boat. They hitched the Bear's body to the one-eyed mule and pulled it to the bank and rolled it too into the boat. Ike and Boon rowed them all across the quiet, smooth, yellow river in the drizzling light, while Tennie's Jim swam the horse and two mules back. Again the river joins all in its ceaseless flow—white, black, and red; mules and mare, animals and men. First, in the hot and running fury of the chase, and then in the peace of consummation.

Lion died that night. Boon buried him in the woods. The Major broke camp and moved out. Boon, Ike, and Tennie's Jim stayed to take care of Sam. Cass McCaslin and the Major returned at daybreak several days later to find Boon and Ike squatting between Lion's grave and a platform made of saplings raised head high. It supported a blanket-wrapped bundle. This was in fact the manner of a Chickasaw burial. Boon confronted them defiantly with his rifle. Cass had to take the rifle away from Boon who glared wildly at the two men.

> "This is the way he wanted it," Boon cried. "He told us. He told us exactly how to do it. And by God you ain't going to move him." McCaslin snicked the five bullets out of Boon's gun.
>
> "Did you kill him, Boon?" he asked
>
> "No!" Boon said. "No!"

> "Tell the truth," McCaslin demanded. "I would have done it if he had asked me to." Then the boy moved. He was between them, facing McCaslin. The water felt as if it had burst and sprung not from his eyes alone but from his whole face, like sweat.
>
> "Leave him alone!" he cried. "Goddamn it! Leave him alone!" (253–54)

In a sense, *The Bear* contained the sum of all that Faulkner had said before and was the apogee of his art. In several score pages Faulkner carried us back into the Garden and made all things right by making all things one. Sometimes contradictory, sometimes mysterious, sometimes violent, the natural order is nevertheless whole and harmonious. Figures move, consummation is achieved, the vase breaks, and yet nothing is violated, nothing is lost. Nature just is, and it does—ultimately timeless and placeless, without watch or compass.

Faulkner caught the image beautifully in a scene in which Ike and his much older cousin Carothers McCaslin talk in the plantation commissary of an evening. Carothers asked why Ike didn't shoot the Bear. Ike, by then a young man, pulled down a book and read out the stanzas of "Ode on a Grecian Urn."

> She cannot fade . . .
> Forever wilt thou love and she be fair.

"Truth is one. It doesn't change," Ike declared. "It covers all things which touch the heart—honor and pride and pity and justice and courage and love . . . They all touch the heart, and what the heart holds becomes truth, as far as we know truth." (296–97) Ike, like Quentin, was a nearly perfect idealist, and he, too, could not live in the modern world.

Ike learned true values in nature, but in subsequent stories when he attempted to move into contemporary society with those values—by becoming a carpenter like the young Jesus, by marrying and hence commencing to take membership in the community—the venture failed. Soon, Ike renounced the heritage of lands and tenants that would come from his father and returned to the Big Woods to live. The implication was that one cannot live morally in modern society. Better to live alone—wifeless, childless, but a friend of man, of hunters and seekers—in the Garden. In his own life in those years, William Faulkner was doing something of the same. He had bought Greenfield, and he was buying more of Bailey's Woods to isolate Rowan Oak from the world. He had retreated from Hollywood and Meta, and he was becoming notorious in his obsession with privacy. He was, in a real sense, alone in his Garden.

Redemption: Individual Saviors

In *The Sound and the Fury,* Faulkner offered modern man little or no hope. Three years later in *Light in August,* he offered hope in the form of mysteriously redemptive qualities contained in the organic society. In 1942 in *The Bear,* the individual must save himself by somehow returning to the wilderness. Thereafter, Faulkner saw salvation as coming from certain strong individuals in society who would save not only themselves, but elements of Southern society as well.

Intruder in the Dust, published in 1948, was Faulkner's first substantial publication after *Go Down Moses.* In this story it was sixteen-year-old Chick Mallison who saved Lucas Beauchamp when he was accused of killing a white man. Chick was called into service by Lucas himself on the strength of a gentlemanly debt owed to him by the boy. Chick, in turn, enlisted the aid of Aleck Sander, the son of the family cook and his black counterpart. Miss Habersham, an elderly white woman of the old aristocracy who maintained a high sense of right and duty in material circumstances much reduced, insisted on joining the rescue party. In slavery, her family had owned Lucas's wife. Together the trio dug up a grave and put in motion a chain of events that brought Sheriff Hampton and lawyer Gavin Stevens into the effort to save Lucas. The first three were moved by personal loyalties and an instinctive recognition of proper moral values; the latter were moved by duty and some sense of responsibility for maintaining a moral order and due process of law. Old Ephraim, Aleck Sander's grandfather, stated the situation with perfect succinctness. If you wanted something done, he said, "get the womens and childrens at it" because the men are too bound up by "the rules and cases." (*Intruder,* 112)

Having declared through Ephraim that lawyers are too bound up in the rules to be initially effective, Faulkner moved on in *Requiem for a Nun* in 1951 to have lawyer Gavin Stevens save Nancy Mannigoe from execution for infanticide. Nancy, an ex-prostitute and generally fallen person, smothered Temple Drake's baby to death in an attempt to stop Temple from running away with a hoodlum she knew from her days in a Memphis brothel and thus rescue the remnants of the family that Temple had begun. *Requiem* was not one of Faulkner's most successful stories. His next significant novel was *A Fable* (1954). Faulkner thought this would be his magnum opus. In this story the savior was Jesus Christ come to earth again in the person of a corporal in the French army during World War I. The corporal organized a mutiny among the soldiers. After the mutiny failed, the corporal was literally crucified on the orders of the generalissimo who was actually his father and thus, in reality, God. Again, this novel has seldom been acclaimed as a success.

In *The Town* (1957) and *The Mansion* (1959), the second and third volumes of the Snopes trilogy, Faulkner educed at least four individuals who would labor successfully to save their communities and, by extension, Southern society. Colonel Devries worked in politics, Reverend Goodyhay in religion, Wall Snopes in business, and V.K. Ratliff became a moral and social activist at large. All of the latter day saints were men.

Colonel Devries

During World War II Colonel Devries had led black troops in combat and won the Congressional Medal of Honor. He was still a young man when he came home in 1945 and ran against the wily redneck state senator Clarence Snopes for a seat in the United States House of Representatives. Clarence had begun in politics with the blessings of Will Varner, but he had progressed rapidly by double crossing both the Ku Klux Klan and the sprinkling of liberal-minded voters in Yoknapatawpha County. Clarence quickly got the upper hand on Devries by dwelling on his seeming eagerness to command black troops and probable credentials as a "nigger-lover." Clarence seemed to have won the nomination in the all-white Democratic primary before the campaign even started. "You see. You can't beat him," said Gavin, already surrendering. (*Mansion,* 295–312)

Then came the annual picnic at Varner's Mill where all of the candidates for office made speeches. Clarence was standing and talking to voters and admirers when he suddenly noticed that the legs of his pants were getting wet. He looked down to see several dogs urinating on him while others were preparing to do the same. He fled to a vehicle and home. Clarence did not return to the hustings; indeed he announced his retirement from politics. Eventually we find that it was V.K. who arranged that outcome. He had organized the Colonel's twin nephews to rake weeds soaked with canine urine gently across Clarence's pants legs. The dogs followed naturally. V.K. then offered the case to Uncle Billy Varner, who promptly deposed Clarence. "I ain't going to have Beat Two and Frenchman's Bend represented nowhere by nobody that ere a son-a-bitching dog that happens by cant tell from a fence post," he declared. The Colonel, of course, won the race. (312–19)

Reverend Goodyhay

Also in *The Mansion* Faulkner introduced the Reverend Joe Goodyhay, a Marine sergeant who returned from the South Pacific divinely called to build a pure and simple Christian community among people who had been desolated in one way or another by the war. Goodyhay had been on a landing craft with his platoon when the bomb hit. The other men jumped over the side, but he stayed, attempting to save one of the men caught in the boat's lines. He had already given himself up for drowned, floating at the bottom of the ocean, when Jesus appeared and, speaking in the language of the military, ordered him to rise up, fall in, and go into the world. Like Colonel Devries, he won a medal for his bravery. Mink, after his release from Parchman, encountered Goodyhay in the Delta near Memphis.

Reverend Goodyhay was a lean, swift-moving man in his mid-thirties. His wife had run off with a potato chip salesman during the war. He was a highly energetic, no-nonsense, in-the-world person. He gathered about him a congregation of people who had suffered deep personal losses during the conflict. They were fragments of family, clan, and community, the human remnants of the war, the flotsam and jetsam left after the storm. They were hard-working, humane, and generous. In the back yard of the simple frame house in which he lived, Goodyhay collected lumber from dismantled houses with which to build a chapel. He and his helpers were sorting out doors and door frames, windows and window frames, heavy timbers for sills, studs, and rafters, and boards for walls. The lumber was like the people. Goodyhay was hoping that a master carpenter would come and help them put it all together, but they continued to labor, not waiting for that event. Mink helped with the work. "Save all the sound pieces," he was told. "Don't split the nails out, pull them out." While Mink was there, the congregation began to lay the foundations for the chapel next to a "willow grown bayou." Apparently, however, the owner reneged on a promise to give this land as a building site. The Reverend raced off in his truck. He returned, and they carried the materials to another site out of the Delta and nearer to Memphis. It was "a dump, a jumbled plain of rusted automobile bodies and boilers and gin machinery and brick and concrete rubble." Clearly Goodyhay's mission was to bring redemption to a modern world in shambles. He would retrieve the "slain wood" of man's folly and build a temple by work and faith near the nerve center of material corruption in the mid-South, Memphis.

On Sunday morning, Mink went to the worship service, temporarily housed in an abandoned black schoolhouse. Goodyhay's message was clear and simple: that everyone must make his own salvation—come, as he said, "hell and high water." The congregation persuaded him to tell his story yet again, as they always did, of the drowning, and Jesus, and the call. This was a litany that repeatedly moved the little congregation. "Tell it again, Joe," they said. "Go on. Tell it again." Goodyhay ended the service with his usual plain and simple prayer. "Save us, Christ," he said, "the poor sons of bitches." Obviously this was the kind of religion that Faulkner appreciated. In this sphere, as in politics, he apparently hoped for a moral regeneration to emerge spontaneously from the trials and tribulations that men and women had endured during World War II. (265–82)

Wall Street Snopes

Devries and Goodyhay are characters who come on very late and briefly in Faulkner's writings; his agent for economic salvation, Wall Street Snopes, had appeared in 1931 as a small boy in the story "The Spotted Horses."[1] Wall, as he came to be called, was the son of Eck Snopes. Eck was so decent that V.K. and Gavin both refused to believe that his mother had not lapsed in marital fidelity at the time of his conception. Eck was the large, generous, and simple man who had paid for Ike Snopes's cow and then bought him a toy wooden cow for consolation after her slaughter. Finally he had been blown to invisibility when he took a lamp into an empty gas tank searching for a lost child. Wall was only sixteen then, but he became the man in the family for his mother and ten-year-old brother, Admiral Dewey. Wall had been twelve when the family moved to town. He insisted on going to school, beginning with kindergarten, and over the months and years very nearly caught up with his age group. At the same time he began working in a grocery store, rising at 4:30 every morning to sweep the floor and build a fire. His mother bought a half-interest in the store with the thousand dollars the gas company gave her after her husband's death. Three years later, Wall had bought out his partner. (*Town,* 126–29)

At nineteen, just before he graduated, Wall proposed marriage to his second grade teacher, Miss Vaiden Wyott. "Miz Vaiden" had been the first person really to recognize Wall's character and talents, and she had given him encouragement just when he needed it. She was ten years his senior. Tearfully and gently she refused his proposal, and later, considerately and quietly, moved to another state. Soon Wall married a local farm girl, a small, thin, feisty woman whose capacities and ambition matched Wall's. Faulkner never gave a name to Wall's wife, but in size, looks, and manner she might have resembled Maud Butler in her youth. Together, the young couple built up the store until a crisis came. Wall overstocked and was forced to ask the bank for a loan to refinance his inventory. Flem Snopes, who had already tried to buy into the store, blocked the loan, hoping to force Wall to sell him a share of the business. Refused at the bank, Wall was heading for Flem's house when his wife caught up with him. With curses and tears and railing against the Snopes clan, she persuaded Wall not to yield to Flem. Secretly, V.K. became Wall's financial angel, Wall insisting on making him a partner rather than simply taking a loan. Thereafter Wall expanded his store and shortly turned it into a self-service facility with a parking lot to accommodate the automobiles that everyone seemed to have acquired.

In time, Wall began to sell goods at low prices to other local merchants out of his warehouse, which he stocked using credit supplied by the big wholesalers in Memphis rather than local banks. The result was that everyone was served material goods in the most economical way. Eventually, Wall expanded his operations to other towns, closely assisted by his wife and brother Dewey. He developed a chain of grocery stores, and finally made the necessary move to Memphis, the economic center for a vast hinterland of towns, hamlets, and farms and the heart of materialism. When we last see Wall he had expanded his operations into three states, not only getting wealthy himself, but spreading a spirit of humanitarian, social-serving free enterprise like contagious goodness. Wall's story argued for a tough individualism, but this individual was able to meet the large and real necessities of the modern world and yet maintain the ideal values. By his example and by his wise leadership, Wall was going to make economic life right for everyone. He had, after all, already taken Memphis by storm, and one could easily predict that he would not stop there.

V.K.

Will Varner was the shrewd peasant who inherited the dominance of the evaporated aristocracy of Frenchman's Bend in the post-Reconstruction decades. Both V.K. Ratliff and Flem Snopes were his spiritual sons who would contend for dominance in the early decades of the twentieth century, first in the country and then in the broader sphere represented by the town.

Since the middle of the 1920s Flem Snopes had stood in Faulkner's mind as the symbol for the corruption of community, clan, and family in the modern world. Flem himself was moved not so much by simple materialism as by a ruthless drive for possession and control that led him to exploit the desires and needs of others. Indeed, it was as if the money that Flem acquired disappeared into a black hole rather than being invested in ways that created jobs, products, and a real improvement in the quality of life in the community—the "good capitalism" that resulted from Wall's business operations. Flem was simply a negative force in material life wherever he was.

Flem was heir to Will Varner, but whereas Will's drive for money and power was open and his cheating was obvious, traditional, and even expected, Flem's was insidious and his manipulation of people so adept that he did not even need to cheat. Lazy, self-indulgent Will Varner joined Flem instead of fighting him. He arranged Eula's marriage to Flem, and rode before the wind—just as he had joined the Yankees as landlord and storekeeper instead of fighting them. He "willed" himself to become the master of his locale, shrewdly and patiently, dealing with exterior forces as he must. By the time Flem had gained significant power in Jefferson, Will apparently had regained control of Frenchman's Bend and Beat Two.

V.K. Ratliff was also Will's heir—and son—in spirit if not in flesh. But he was the good son who opposed Flem. In *The Hamlet* V.K. managed only a stand-off with Flem in a complicated affair involving the buying and selling of a herd of goats. At the end of that novel V.K.'s own hatred and, perhaps, greed led him to a humiliating defeat by Flem in buying from him the decaying plantation of the original Frenchman. Flem had acquired the manor house from Will Varner as a part of his reward for marrying an already pregnant Eula. The story was a marvelous play of symbols.

In *The Town* (1957) Flem moved on to Jefferson, and V.K. again emerged as the man to challenge his rising power. In that effort he gained a devoted, idealistic, but slow-learning ally in Gavin Stevens. V.K. was, par excellence, the moral, thinking, active agent of the community. He maintained, as he grew older, an almost perfect balance between idealism and realism. Realistically, he accepted modernity—including technology. In the 1920s he retired his horses and wagon and bought himself a Model T Ford which he converted to a pickup truck by cutting out some parts and welding in others. He kept the little house with the sewing machine inside, and it rode about in the truck bed. Next, he changed to sell a new product—radios. Finally, he had taken on the selling of yet another and even more modern machine. When we last saw V.K., there was a tiny television antenna mounted on the top of the doll house!

Radios and televisions were perfect devices for V.K. because he was the arch communicator wherever he was. He gathered, interpreted, and disseminated the news in the community with high fidelity and total integrity. Like such real-life communicators as Walter Cronkite and Edward R. Murrow, he enjoyed tremendous respect and deep confidence from his fellow citizens. Men, women, and children were all drawn to him. The mysterious Eula confided in him, and even Flem talked to him with remarkable ease. Recurrently Gavin—who usually felt that he knew and could understand very nearly everything, repeated evidence to the contrary notwithstanding—was amazed by V.K.'s knowledge. On one occasion Gavin was exasperated by V.K.'s exhibiting yet again that he knew more about women than did Gavin. "So would you mind telling me how the hell you learned?" he exclaimed.

"Maybe by listening," V.K. replied quietly. (229)

In Faulkner's fiction, V.K. eventually became the key character to bridge the gap between the mass of common white people and the persisting aristocracy. In effect, he worked to marry the two together in an all-white communion. Faulkner illustrated V.K.'s cohesive function by describing his efforts to learn and use the language of the elite. Originally, V.K. said "sho" for sure, "hisself" for himself, "ever night" for every night, "drug" for dragged, and "outen" for out of, and so on. After he began to associate with the aristocracy in the town, he studied their language. Especially close to Gavin Stevens and Chick Mallison, he began to use his new tongue with them. Finally, Chick objected strenuously and insisted that V.K. reform himself back to the original. "When you say 'taken'," he declared, "it sounds a heap more took than just 'took,' just like 'drug' sounds a heap more dragged than just 'dragged.' " (*Town,* 261) "A heap more" was probably a phrase that Chick as a child had learned from V.K.; Gavin would have said "much more."

V.K. represented the souls of white folk. In the promotion of the common good, he was a fine tactician and a superb strategist. It was he who moved in precisely the best time, place, and manner with Wall Snopes and Colonel Devries to empower these characters to do good. He was, in a sense, the philosopher king. He pursued knowledge of the facts, but he was undeceived by them. He preferred the truth to the facts. "Between what did happen and what ought to happened," he said as he pieced out a story of Eula's conception of Linda with McCarron, "I dont never have trouble picking ought." In that particular case, he finally decided with a perfect sense of the essence of things, that it was all of the men of Yoknapatawpha County who "seeded them loins." (*Town,* 100)

By joining V.K. to Gavin, Faulkner had, in effect, allied the plain folk of the

South to the best of the persisting aristocracy. Furthermore, the best qualities of the plain folk, personified by V.K., Wall, and Goodyhay, took the lead, and Faulkner seemed to be saying that this was as it should have been. The peasantry, the plain folk of the Old South brought into the New, carried the genius that would be salvation. It was heavily Hegelian—thesis, antithesis, and synthesis as thesis again—and Volksgeistian. Homogeneity, the souls of white folk conjoined, was the answer. In his last book, *The Reivers,* he would pull that chip back from the center of the table and put it into his pocket again.

Flem

At the same time that Faulkner was thus mustering the forces of good in his fiction, he was also creating an amazing implosion of evil in the person of Flem Snopes. Flem himself had early sown the seeds of his own destruction by violating the laws of family and clan. He had deliberately prolonged his stay in Texas until his cousin Mink was tried and sent to the state penitentiary at Parchman. Flem, like Mink, was fully conscious of the fact that only he among all the Snopes clan might have the power to save him. Later, knowing that Mink would attempt to kill him when released, Flem sent Montgomery Ward Snopes, another kinsman, to Parchman as a convict to entice Mink into an escape effort organized to fail and add twenty years to his sentence. Flem had cleverly framed Montgomery Ward to achieve his incarceration. By that maneuver he had also rid the town of a Snopes who was an embarrassment to his own ambition. Flem had learned that to get more power, he must seem to be a respectable part of the community, and so too must his kinfolk. He had learned that in a Southern community seeming to be was at least as important as being. "I'm interested in Jefferson," he replied when prodded as to his motives in thus dispatching Montgomery Ward by an as yet uncomprehending Gavin. "We got to live here," he said. (*Town,* 176) As Flem gained power, he carefully changed houses, furniture, and his clothes to match his new position in the hierarchy. His concern for appearances actually changed his behavior in significant ways, and sometimes for the common good. It was almost as if the organic society, even in a case so dire as that of Flem Snopes, still had the mysterious power to heal its own lesions and survive.

After Linda returned from Europe, it gradually became clear that she knew that Flem had, in effect, killed her mother by his scheme to gain control of the bank. She arranged to set Mink free to do the justice that ought to be done. Gavin thought that he had arranged matters so that Mink, after thirty-six years in Parchman, would be freed and leave the state. V.K. learned that he was free and not leaving the state simply by using the telephone to talk to the warden, a modern style of communication that apparently had not occurred to Gavin. V.K. and Gavin tried hard to intercept Mink, and they warned Flem of his danger. Flem refused to flee or hire guards. Instead he waited in the parlor of his mansion, his foot only so high on the leg of the mantelpiece. When Mink entered the room, Flem swung about to face him—and the gun. But he made no effort to save himself. He sat for several moments while the gun misfired and Mink nervously cocked it again. He was still not moving when it fired.

Gavin puzzled aloud why Flem made no move to help himself. It was V.K. who answered. It was the game of "Give me leave," he said, a game that country boys played in which one would say "Gimme lief" to another, then back off and hit him with a stick or a rock. The hit boy would then return the favor in the same way. Ratliff explained:

> "—Flem had had his lief fair and square like the rule said, so there wasn't nothing for him to do but jest set there, since he had likely found out years back when she finally turned up here again even outen a communist war, that he had already lost—"
>
> "Stop it!" Stevens said. "Don't say it!"
>
> "—and now it was her lief and so suppose—"
>
> "No!" Stevens said. "No!" But Ratliff continued.
>
> "—she knowed all the time what was going to happen when he got out, that not only she knowed but Flem did too—"
>
> "I won't believe it!" Stevens said. "I won't! I can't believe it," he said. "Don't you see I cannot?" (*Mansion,* 429–31)

Gavin, the idealist and romantic, the Galahad without horse or lance, always had trouble with unpleasant realities, especially when they ran counter to his image of the woman he loved. V.K. accepted realities and responded accordingly. In effect, Faulkner was saying that Flem first abused the idea of family and then of clan, and that it was Linda as family and Mink as clan who brought him to his just and natural end, a result that redounded to benefit everyone. Most importantly, Flem himself recognized his sins and waited quietly for justice to be done. Belatedly, even Flem proved himself essentially a social being, respecting the feelings and rights of others to fair play and yielding with amazing grace to the capacity of the organic society for self-righting. In the end, even Flem had soul. If the worst of us ultimately possesses some fragment, some modicum of moral virtue, Faulkner seemed to say, are we not all saved? Might not we all together endure and prevail?

The Garden

Recapitulation: Out of the Garden

At the time that Faulkner finished *The Mansion,* he seemed to be positing a saving force in the South—a sort of Volksgeistian impetus—that sprang ultimately and principally from the mass of white people themselves. There was an innate goodness in white folk of all classes that manifested itself in the rise of such leaders as Wall Snopes, Goodyhay, Devries, and V.K. Ratliff. Thus led and organized Southerners might move into the modern world without a total and permanent eclipse in their vision of the eternal verities. There had been no such optimism in *The Sound and the Fury.* The saving grace in that story, if there was one, was Dilsey. It was almost as if the white aristocracy from the golden age of the antebellum South had somehow passed on the torch of truth to Dilsey and she carried it forward as they stumbled and fell. The light that Dilsey shone burned brightly, but, when Dilsey was last seen, the hand that held it was faltering out of simple age.

Light in August, published three years after *Fury,* drew a curious optimism from a land in desolation. Lena's faith and Joe Christmas's dogged persistence combined to produce an end that offered hope. Somehow, the story seemed to promise that those ten thousand tiny hairs of the organic society would brush everyone into place and harmony. Perhaps at no other time in the middle years of his adult life was Faulkner himself so contented as when he wrote *Light in August.* Thereafter, his descent into misery was rapid and fairly total. By the end of the decade, the best he could suggest for the truly moral individual was a renunciation of the world and a return to the wilderness with Ike McCaslin. A weak but liveable alternative, paradoxically, was "jail." The tall convict in *The Wild Palms* found relative peace and harmony in Parchman penitentiary—in effect, a prison farm, a community of men living in a strict order, almost like monks working in a lush and fertile garden on the flat lands of the Delta. Jail, like the Big Woods, was at least a place where men would be safe from women and other chaotic social forces. The tall convict and his chains grew friends, very much as Joe Christmas as a boy had a certain rapport with Simon McEachern, his chain and his jailor. There were enclaves in society—retreats, seclusions, isolations—that afforded ways of surviving in a confused and unjust world.

Even while Faulkner was writing *The Wild Palms* and *Go Down Moses,* he reached out into Beat Two to purchase his farm, Greenfield. Thus, at the end of the Great Depression he was physically among the plain white farmers of Lafayette County as never before. All of his life, of course, he had seen them in town on Saturdays and on Court Days attending to business. Beginning signally with *The Hamlet* in 1940, he brought them to the fore. In Flem he saw the worst of whiteness emerging in the country, eating up the land like so many locusts, and heading for town. At the same time, he brought forth a fundamentally good peasantry led by the highly effective Will Varner and the highly moral V.K. Ratliff. As the story proceeded in *The Town* and *The Mansion,* Will Varner reclaimed the countryside from Flem, and V.K. joined with the aristocrat Gavin Stevens in attempting to counter Flem in town. In the end, of course, Flem was stopped by the fragment of decency still within him that respected the rules of his people, and by the willingness of his own family and clan to do the thing that ought to be done.

At the time that Faulkner ended the Snopes trilogy, his person and his thoughts were already very much in Virginia, following his rather late acceptance of marriage, family, clan, and community. It was almost as if he could then safely leave Mississippi to V.K. and Gavin, to the white folk of the deep South, commoners and aristocrats, now joined together in a sort of white communion. Thus ended what we might call "the Greenfield phase" of Faulkner's work, the portion in which he adored in greater or lesser degree the plain folk of the South. Across the race line, black folks had all but disappeared from his writing by the late 1950s. They had also disappeared from his life. Having made his move in civil rights and met frustration, he all but abandoned the cause. He was disappointed with black people, and in the early 1960s, he was rapidly becoming disappointed with the mass of white folks too. As racial issues rapidly heated up again in and after 1960, he saw no V.K. Ratliffs to move the white mass toward moral responsibility. Indeed, in Mississippi in Governor Ross Barnett he saw the opposite—a bad Snopes triumphant in politics. The death of his mother in 1960 constituted another and very strong endorsement of his license to leave Mississippi and live in Virginia. It was a license that he was in the process of finalizing when he began to write *The Reivers.*

The Reivers

The Reivers was a pulling back of the idea that the plain whites were going to save Southern humanity. The future lay primarily with Lucius Quintus Cincinnatus Priest, an eleven-year-old son of the aristocracy. He "makes his manners" like a gentleman, and he was a gentleman, with values bred into him over the generations. One of his companions was the very physical, exceedingly natural, child-man Boon Hogganbeck. Boon was one-quarter Indian, but not of the chiefly sort, and three-quarters plain white. He had never been a farmer and, perhaps, he was even "poor white." He was a simple man with a stout spirit and a great heart. It was he who had killed the Bear. He would do right when properly led. Interestingly, the third character in the trio was black and older. Uncle Ned knew the world well and moved in it courageously, aware of the perils, but willing to face them and gamble on his knowledge and wits to bring himself and his friends safely through. Ned was the faithful old family servant leavened by an admirable streak of independence. Philosophically, he was a male Dilsey. He knew where things were and where they ought to be. He was also mischievous, an adventurer, almost a hipster-trickster taken out of black mythology. He could gamble with the devil and win.

Boon initiated the action when he was moved by an ardent desire to visit the Memphis prostitute whom he loved. His employer was Lucius's grandfather. When the grandfather went away for a weekend, Boon seduced Lucius into helping him borrow, use, actually steal his grandfather's automobile, a Winton Flyer, by teaching him to drive the fascinating machine. Enroute to Memphis, Lucius and Boon discovered Ned hiding under a rug in the backseat. Boon was irate, but Ned replied: "I wants a trip too," he said. "Hee, hee, hee." (*Reivers,* 70) In Memphis, Ned escalated the problem to sublime heights by trading off the car which he did not own for a race horse that the traders did not own.

In the process of resolving the difficulty, Lucius worked his way through the rites of passage to manhood. It was highly significant that Lucius went to Memphis to become a man. He did not go into the Big Woods as did Ike McCaslin in *The Bear.* In Faulkner's fiction Memphis was the heart of corruption, the amalgamated Sodom and Gomorrah of the mid-South, the very symbol and substance of the evils of modernity. It was the place where several decades later, if one reads *The Mansion,* Wall Snopes would arrive to begin a moral regeneration of the economic structure of the South and where Reverend Goodyhay would appear at the gate like Paul at Corinth. Indeed, Lucius himself would preach the Gospel of his story two generations later to his own grandchildren.

In *The Reivers,* Lucius came down from the height of the family mansion in Jefferson to pass through the slough of Hell Creek Bottom and Hurricane Creek into Memphis where he was housed in the attic of a brothel. In the brothel he encountered two diamonds in the rough—the madam, Miss Reba, and her maid, the gold-toothed Minnie, both of whom were straightforward, wise, generous, and superbly worldly people. More importantly, he also met there Boon's love, Miss Corrie. Corrie was one of Miss Reba's girls. She was a large, gentle, Junoesque young woman from rural Arkansas. Staying in the attic with Lucius was Miss Corrie's fifteen-year-old brother, Otis, a sort of diminutive Popeye, an incipient gangster, and an instrument of evil. Back in Arkansas, Otis had sold peeks through knotholes in the wall of their shack while Corrie sold sex as required by her guardian, a foul woman who used Corrie shamelessly as soon as she was barely of an age to be prostituted. Lucius took offense at Otis's attempts to further denigrate his own sister in the brothel and the two boys fought in the attic. Otis drew a knife that Lucius took from him but suffered a cut in the hand in the process. No Ike McCaslin as deerslayer here, and no Sam Fathers—half Indian and all chief—to paint his face in blood. Instead there was Miss Corrie to wash away his own blood and bind up his wound. And there was Boon to announce Lucius's maturity:

> "Eleven years old, and already cut in a whorehouse brawl," he said. Then he declared Lucius licensed to preach, teach, and lead.
>
> "I wish I had knowed you thirty years ago," he said: "With you to learn me when I was eleven years old, maybe this time I'd a had some sense too." (159)

The scene of action next shifted to the village of Parsham some twenty miles to the east where the horse race took place. As they were managing step by step to prepare for the race, the party had to fend off a large, bullying, and abusive deputy sheriff who was determined to take advantage of his badge to have his way with Corrie, preferably over Boon's dead body. Miss Reba finally succeeded in driving the deputy sheriff away, and Lucius rode the horse to victory under the astute management of Uncle Ned. They reclaimed the car and returned to Jefferson.

Lucius labored to absorb his experiences and they seemed beyond bearing—what he had done, what he had not done, and what he had learned of injustice and misery in the world. He wanted to forget it all, but his grandfather said he must learn to live with it. "A gentleman can live through anything," his grandfather said. "A gentleman accepts the responsibility of his actions and bears the burden of their consequences, even when he did not himself instigate them but only acquiesces to them, didn't say No though he knew he should." Lucius, overwhelmed, cried while his grandfather held him.

> "There," he said at last. "That should have emptied the cistern. Now go wash your face. A gentleman cries too, but he always washes his face." (302–3)

Boon and Corrie married, and we discover, astonished, that Corrie's real name is Everbe Corinthia. Everbe, "ever-be" (or, perhaps, "Eve-be") suggests the primal woman, the first mother of the everlasting earth. Corinthia, perhaps, suggests Corinth where St. Paul came to live and preach to the Greeks in a city that had been famous for centuries for the marvelous qualities of its prostitutes—women who served the goddess Isis. Again, Faulkner was enriching a character with allusions to classical and Biblical traditions.

Boon and Everbe Corinthia soon produced a son, a child one-eighth Indian and seven-eighths "redneck," who would carry an aristocratic name.

> "What are you going to call it?" asked Lucius.
> "Not it," Everbe replied. "Him. Can't you guess?"
> "What?" Lucius asked again.
> "His name is Lucius Priest Hogganbeck," she said. (305)

Curiously, Faulkner had ended his first Yoknapatawpha novel in much the same way that he ended his last. Narcissa Benbow had married and given birth to Bayard Sartoris's son. At first it seemed that he would be named John, one of the Sartoris names that recurrently carried arrogance and death. On the last page, Narcissa changed this child's destiny:

> "He isn't John," she said. "He's Benbow Sartoris."
> "What?"
> "His name is Benbow Sartoris." (*Sartoris,* 380)

Those words in *The Reivers* were the very last words that Faulkner wrote for print. Lucius Priest was a priest who was to carry into the world the message of the moral responsibility of the individual for his acts. His message, like his name, could be passed on to future generations. Lucius Priest and men of his quality would lead, and others would accept and follow. Thus, William Faulkner might have charged his own grandsons to carry that message, the sons of his beloved daughter Jill. A good woman, a natural woman like Everbe, can be the symbol and the means of salvation. Virtue, she illustrates, can be regenerated out of vice; virginity, paradoxically, can be regained. The Garden is never irrevocably lost.

~

Faulkner's solution for the plight of the South often seems thin and at times even fatuous. Phil Stone was given to hyperbole, but he was pointing in the right direction when in 1955 he evaluated Bill's solution to the desegregation crisis in the schools. Bill "did not quite finish the eighth grade and never got a degree from any school," Phil observed, and yet "I have no doubt that he is very likely to come forward with a plan to perfect the whole school system, but any

Falkner, not just Bill, would within three days present to God a plan for the reorganization of Heaven."[1] Behind it all, perhaps, was Bill's need, his passion, to be thought worthy, to be valued.

Very definitely, Faulkner's genius as a social commentator on the South was not exhibited in his solutions; it was in his criticism—neither systematic, comprehensive, nor factually informed. His sense of the sins of the South was "heart-felt." It sprang from the land and culture that gave him life. His erstwhile friend and mentor Sherwood Anderson caught it well back in the mid-1930s. Thomas Wolfe and William Faulkner, he said, "may write of terrible happenings, but you feel always an inside sympathy with the fact of life itself."[2] Anderson declared that there was, indeed, a fundamental problem with the region. "It lies in that South I am always speaking about, the terrible South that Stark Young and his sort ignore . . . the beaten, ignorant, Bible-ridden, white South. Faulkner occasionally really touches it. It has yet to be paid for."[3]

Faulkner did best when he wrote about the unatoned sins of his natal region, but he himself relished most that he wrote about the universals of human existence. In Virginia in 1957, he said that he could easily move to New England or any other place and write about the people there. "People are about the same anywhere," he declared, "and that's what I am most interested in."[4] He liked Joan's first novel, he said to her, because it was "not regional nor topical, but universal." "Go on," he insisted, "the more you write, the more you will learn how to express, milk dry, the love and hatred you have to feel, not for man in his behavior, but for man in his condition."[5]

The Garden Again

In his last years, Faulkner seemed to be saying that there would ever be the earth, with which, in the end, we all would merge and find eternal being. Resist, fight as we would, all that we could do to violate the earth would come to naught and we would be ashes and dust. There would come a time when the sun would rise daily on rusting television towers and rounding pyramids. Rains would fall, rivers rise and run, and winds, tides, tornadoes, hurricanes, earthquakes, and volcanoes run their courses and do their work. Summer and fall, winter and spring, hot and cold, would all flow in the sequence that we know. But we would have passed, you and I. And perhaps in time so would we all, all humanity, every last person, and the earth would be green again, pristine again, the Garden beyond man and woman, without Adam and without Eve. The Earth, Faulkner seemed to say, is the ultimately renewable virgin.

In this mood, Faulkner had ended the Snopes trilogy. Mink had satisfied his honor by taking his fair shot at Flem. He was leaving. But Mink was sixty-three then, roughly Faulkner's own age as he was writing the story, and he needed to rest. He took refuge in the earthen cellar beneath the collapsed house where he had last lived as a tenant farmer. He felt that if he lay on the bare ground, the earth might claim him while he slept. Mink mused: "The ground itself never let a man forget it was there waiting, pulling gently and without no hurry at him between every step, saying, Come on, lay down: I aint going to hurt you." So Mink gathered some old boards to make a kind of platform to lie on "to defend himself from the ground in case he dropped off to sleep." (*Mansion,* 434) The earth was always pulling, tugging at him, he thinks. "A man had to spend not just all his life but all the time of Man too guarding against it; even back when they said man lived in caves, he would raise up a bank of dirt to at least keep him that far off the ground while he slept, until he invented wood floors to protect him and at last beds too, raising the floors storey by storey until they would be laying a hundred and even a thousand feet up in the air to be safe from the earth." (435)

In the early morning hours, V.K. and Gavin found Mink at the old farm, and they set him in motion again, walking west—the small, slight figure. Toward dawn, after Mink had traveled a while, he lay down, now on the bare earth, and he felt the gentle tug. "Only he located the right stars at that moment, he was not laying exactly right since a man must face the east to lay down, walk west but when you lay down, face the exact east," he said to himself and shifted. "He was exactly right and he was free now." He closed his eyes and pretended to sleep. He thought about "the ground already full of the folks that had the trouble but were free now." Soon, he would be "himself among them, equal to any, good as any, brave as any, being inextricable from, anonymous with all of them; the beautiful, the splendid, the proud and the brave, right on up to the very top itself among the shining phantoms and dreams which are the mile stones of the long human recording—Helen and the bishops, the kings and the unhomed angels, the scornful and graceless seraphim." (435–36) So, also, with William Faulkner, whose remains now lie at rest in St. Peter's Cemetery amid the Falkners and Butlers, the Thompsons, Lamars, and Sheegogs, and the Oldhams too. All are one, lined and rowed, facing east, toward the morning sun.

Acknowledgments

Inevitably, the stories of the lives of great achievers are told and retold—"the lives of the saints," as it were. Every generation in every culture, it seems, feels a need to have a story of the lives of its notable producers—generals and statesmen, artists and writers—as well as their works. So too with William Faulkner. His works, the stories he wrote, will inevitably be complemented by the story of his life, told and retold according to the evolving needs of successive ages. And each time, there is both joy and pain in the telling and the hearing. To some degree, the pain comes from reducing a life to a string of words that can never quite be fair. In a great degree, however, the pain comes to the still living, those who were there and who struggle now to make their lives one with their past and whole.

I am indebted to literally hundreds of students, colleagues, and archivists for what is done here:

I began the study during the spring of 1982 while at the Charles Warren Center at Harvard University. During the previous fall, I had offered an undergraduate seminar in the college on "William Faulkner and Southern History." In that process I felt acutely the need for a concise history of the man and his culture to complement the fiction that my students were reading. One Friday during the spring semester, I mailed off the manuscript for a book, *The Crucible of Race,* upon which I had worked for eighteen years. On Monday, I began to write this one. It was a desultory effort for some four years during which I completed *The Crucible of Race* as a book (1984) and then produced an abridgment, *A Rage for Order* (1986).

I had taught the Faulkner undergraduate seminar in Chapel Hill for several years before the Harvard venture. Afterward, I have done so regularly. I also took opportunities, in 1984, to offer the course at Millsaps College in Jackson, Mississippi, and Rhodes College in Memphis, both of which got me into Faulkner territory in a most intimate fashion. This study draws heavily on those experiences.

In the summer of 1986, I began the research for this book in earnest. Almost immediately, I learned that, except for Joseph Blotner's biographies, published in 1974 and 1984, nearly all of what was known of Faulkner's ancestry and some of his biography was based on hearsay, stories repeated again and again over the decades and accepted. As usual, the oral history was shaped most of all by the survivors—those who lived longest and told the final tale. Much of the story had an Oldham cast to it, Dot living to 1968 and Estelle to 1972. Phil Stone, being accessible to interested persons during Faulkner's lifetime, also influenced the tradition; as did Bill's brothers Johncy and Jack, primarily by each publishing a book of reminiscences on the Falkners after Bill's death in 1962.

As a historian, I was first struck by the almost total neglect in accounts of Faulkner's ancestry of the maternal line, the Butlers. It soon became clear that even when the Butlers were mentioned briefly, there was considerable confusion as to who they were and where they came from. Next, I was amazed at how "The Old Colonel," William C. Falkner in Ripley, had been miscast. He was not a slaveholding planter as usually imagined, but rather, essentially, a town-dwelling businessman, and his real reputation was made only after the war, even more precisely, one might say, after Reconstruction. On the Faulkner side, maternal lines had again been neglected—the Word connection for example, almost totally.

Faulkner's ancestry proved to be a marvelous device for getting into the texture of culture in northeastern Mississippi—and the South—from the 1830s to the present. Somewhere in the clan virtually every facet of that vast history is demonstrated—often dramatically, as in the case of Emeline Falkner. The story of Faulkner's ancestors is, in effect, the real Yoknapatawpha County, the culture that made William Faulkner, and is totally complementary to the one that he made in his fiction.

This is micro history, not a history of grand aggregates. Finding traces of the hundreds of individuals involved in these stories required kinds of research I had never done before, and I made up the program as I went along. The courthouses in Oxford and Ripley proved to be gold mines of information in which the clerks and their staffs were steadily and cordially helpful. I am especially indebted to Danny Shackleford, Clerk of the Chancery Court of Tippah County, and his staff in this way. Probably the most helpful archivist of all was Tommy Covington, the amazingly knowledgeable, warmly congenial head of the Ripley Public Library.

The reader will see in the notes the dozen or so archives in which I worked, but I would like to express particularly my appreciation to the archivists in the special collections libraries of the University of Virginia, the Mississippi Department of Archives and History, the University of Mississippi, and Tulane University. Also, the main branch of the Memphis Public Library is wonderfully rich in Southern and mid-South materials, including a large and easily useable collection of census materials, all of which is managed by a very expert and efficient staff. As a scholar I am in their debt, and as a person and a scholar I am deeply in the debt of Betty Carter Woodson of Memphis, a kind and gracious lady who gave me a base of operations in Faulkner country, a very comfortable "home away from home," and shared with me the excitement of the hunt. Further, I am very grateful to Professor Robert C. Kenzer and Carol Kenzer for locating and transcribing for me information contained in the R. G. Dun and Company records in the Baker Library in Harvard University. I want specially to thank Louis Daniel Brodsky and Robert Hamblin for allowing me access to the superb collection of Faulkner material they maintain in the Kent Library at Southeast Missouri State University at Cape Girardeau. In that collection I met Joseph Blotner through his papers, and I came to appreciate more deeply the vast and excellent labor he had done in opening this field of scholarship.

My friend and colleague Frank Ryan read the manuscript and offered a host of perceptive comments. With me as usual from the very beginning to the very end was Rosalie I. Radcliffe who repeatedly lends me the use of her superb talent in the English language. Of my student assistants, five did long and highly intelligent labor on the manuscripts—Donna Shaw, Lisa Angel, Mitzi Plummer, Mary Michaels Orr, and Arati Korwar. They are, virtually, my partners in this venture. The Lineberger family not only supported my Chair in the Humanities at the University of North Carolina, but also a portion of the cost of researching and writing the manuscript.

At Oxford University Press, Sheldon Meyer and Leona Capeless guided the ship through the narrow and swift-watered straits of modern-day publishing with stout courage and steady hands. Rebecca Schneider was my editor, at once keenly attentive to detail and highly sensitive to the large moral issues involved in Faulkner's writings, life, and culture.

Finally, the National Endowment for the Humanities gave the project a great thrust forward with a grant that allowed me to devote an entire year, 1987–1988, to research and writing. This was followed by several weeks at the Bellagio Study and Conference Center on Lake Como in Italy. It was in this marvelous setting, afforded by the Rockefeller Foundation, that the final conceptualization of this book took place.

Notes

Though Parts I and II share sources, for Part I, Ancestry, the most important sources are located in Mississippi. In the notes these are indicated as follows:

RPL—Ripley Public Library in Ripley, Mississippi. Tommy Covington, the librarian, has collected a vast amount of highly valuable material relating to Ripley and Tippah County, the original family seat of the Falkners in Mississippi. Among these are numerous extracts made from primary sources (for instance, from the U.S. Census, state tax lists, and local newspapers) and arranged in forms easily useable by the researcher.

TCCH—Tippah County Courthouse in Ripley, Mississippi. In Mississippi, court records are divided between the Chancery Court, which deals with matters of property, and the Circuit Court, which deals with criminal matters. There is a clerk for each branch and each maintains an archive. In the notes that follow, ChC after the symbol for the courthouse indicates the archive of the chancery clerk, and CC that of the circuit court. Thus, TCCH-ChC or TCCH-CC. In the Tippah County Courthouse, there is also a storage area in what had been the balcony of the courtroom. Thus, TCCH (attic).

LCCH—Lafayette County Courthouse in Oxford, Mississippi. Lafayette County (Oxford) was the original home in Mississippi of the Butlers, William Faulkner's maternal ancestors. There is an abundance of information in the courthouse, dating from the 1830s to the present, concerning the Butlers and the culture of which they were a part. There is a special storage area for archival material on the third floor, some of which is held in a locked vault.

UMASC—University of Mississippi, Archives and Special Collections, John Davis Williams Library. Because Oxford is the site of the state university, the town is well represented in its Special Collections. For example, the minute book of the local Masonic lodge is held there and the university has made a concerted effort to collect Faulkner material.

TM—Town Minutes of Oxford. These are contained in a single volume held in the vault of the Town Clerk.

MDAH—Mississippi Department of Archives and History, Jackson. Especially valuable here are microfilms of the records of Confederate soldiers serving from Mississippi. The Archives also have the United States Census for the state along with indexes (the latter being practically a necessity in locating a large number of individuals over a number of decades), materials gathered by the WPA in the 1930s for a history of each county, and various state records.

For Part II, Biography, there are two collections that are most useful. These are:

FCVA—William Faulkner Foundation Collection, Special Collections, Alderman Library, The University of Virginia, Charlottesville. This collection is especially rich in correspondence between Faulkner and his friends and publishers. It also contains materials relating to his RAF service and the history of the Falkner clan in the mid-nineteenth century.

BC—The Louis Daniel Brodsky Collection in the Kent Library at Southeastern Missouri State University at Cape Girardeau. The Brodsky Collection contains numerous autographed volumes of Faulkner books, a rich array of photographs, correspondence with friends, and a vast number of items relating to the author that appeared in the media during the course of his life.

BP—Within the Brodsky Collection are the Blotner Papers containing letters and copies of letters and notes of interviews and other materials that Professor Joseph Blotner used in writing both his 1974 and 1984 biographies of Faulkner. These materials were gathered over a span of twenty years during which Professor Blotner became something of a lightning rod attracting new information concerning the famous writer, some of which was highly charged. Invaluable are his detailed notes of literally hundreds of interviews (indicated in notes as "I") which he conducted with people who knew Faulkner, many of them intimately, and voluminous correspondence with some of these and others not interviewed. Professor Blotner used much of this material in his biographies, of course, but some he did not use and some might be used in a different fashion given another and later perspective.

There are other Faulkner collections at leading universities in the United States. Those at Yale, Princeton, and Texas are primarily of interest to literary scholars. However, the William B. Wisdom Collection of William Faulkner in the Howard-Tilton Memorial Library at Tulane University in New Orleans is especially valuable to the historian because it contains material relating to Helen Baird.

Newspaper sources for both Part I and Part II are abundant. Especially useful are:

TRA—The Ripley Advertiser. The most complete collection is in the Ripley Public Library.

TOE—The Oxford Eagle. The most complete collection is in the John Davis Williams Library at the University of Mississippi.

Some published works have been most useful and frequently cited. The symbols for these are:

BW—Ben Wasson. *Count-no-Count, Flashbacks to Faulkner.* Jackson: University Press of Mississippi, 1983.

Duclos—Donald Philip Duclos. "Son of Sorrow: The Life, Works and Influence of William C. Falkner, 1825–1889." Ph.D. diss., University of Michigan, 1962.

FIU—Faulkner in the University. Eds. Frederick L. Gwynn and Joseph Blotner. Charlottesville: University of Virginia Press, 1959.

JB—Joseph Blotner. *William Faulkner: A Biography.* New York: Random House, 1984. The two-volume 1974 edition will be cited as JB (1974).

LIG—Lion in the Garden: Interviews with William Faulkner, 1926–1962. Eds. James B. Meriwether and Michael Millgate. New York: Random House, 1968.

LG—Meta Carpenter Wilde. *A Loving Gentleman: The Love Story of William Faulkner and Meta Carpenter.* New York: Simon and Schuster, 1976.

MBB—John Faulkner. *My Brother Bill: An Affectionate Reminiscence.* New York: Trident Press, 1963.

PSO—Susan Snell. *Phil Stone of Oxford: A Vicarious Life.* Athens: University of Georgia Press, 1991. PSY will refer to Susan Snell's dissertation: "Phil Stone of Yoknapatawpha." Ph.D. diss., University of North Carolina, 1978.

SLWF—Selected Letters of William Faulkner. Ed. Joseph Blotner. New York: Random House, 1977.

In the notes, symbols will stand for individuals as follows:

BW—Ben Wasson
Dot—Dorothy Oldham
E—Estelle Oldham
EJ—Else Jonsson
HB—Helen Baird
JB—Joseph Blotner
Jill—Jill Faulkner Summers
JS—Jean Stein
JW—Joan Williams
JWTF—John Wesley Thompson Falkner
MF—Maud (Butler) Falkner
MCF—Murry Charles "Jack" Falkner
PS—Philip Avery Stone
SC—Saxe Commins
SM—Sallie Murry Wilkins
WF—William Faulkner
WS—William Spratling

The symbol I stands for interview and is especially useful in relation to the Blotner Papers.

Unless otherwise noted all references to the United States Census in the antebellum period are taken from schedules entitled "Free Inhabitants."

Approximate dates are in parentheses. Faulkner frequently did not date his letters, but might give the day of the week. Post-marked envelopes saved with their contents, plus evidence in the texts of the letters themselves, makes constructed dates for nearly all citations fairly accurate.

OUT OF THE GARDEN

1. Theodore Karl, a highly perceptive reader of Faulkner's life and works, argued persuasively in 1989 that *Sanctuary* is one of Faulkner's most serious works. Theodore R. Karl, *William Faulkner: American Writer, A Biography* (NY: Nicolson, 1989), 371–74.

2. Marshall J. Smith, "Faulkner of Mississippi," *Bookman* (Dec., 1931): 411–17.

3. Lavou Rascoe, "Interview with William Faulkner," *Western Review* 15 (Summer, 1951): 300–304.

PART I

ONE

1. Grant Foreman, *Indian Removal: The Emigration of the Five Civilized Tribes of Indians* (Norman: University of Oklahoma Press, 1932), 22–29.

2. LCCH, Circuit Court Records Room, "Court Cost Account Book, March 1858–August 68," p. 155.

3. Some family members gave Clark as William's middle name. BP, I, SM, n.d.; I, MCF, Mar. 31, 1965. However, no signature has been found in which he himself used that name instead of the initial "C."

4. BP, I, Judge J.W.T. Falkner with Robert Coughlan, n.d.

5. *The Heritage of Surry County,* ed. Hester Bartlett Jackson (Winston-Salem, NC: Hunter, 1983), 1: 183–84; Franklin E. Moak, "William Joseph Faulkner," in *The Forkner Clan—Forkner/Fortner/Faulkner,* comp. Mona Forkner Paulas (Baltimore, MD, 1981), 1: 26–36.

6. U.S. Census, 1860, Mississippi, Tippah County (North), households #1326, #1343; MDAH, Confederate Soldiers Serving from Mississippi (microfilm), James W. Falkner, 269, rolls 2 and 115.

7. RPL, "A Genealogy of the Word Family Written by James Word, December 23, 1882," via Eleanor D. MacDonald, Farmington, NM.

8. FCVA, ms. indictment of John Wesley Thompson, October term, 1834, Habersham County, Georgia.

9. FCVA, Justianna D. Thompson to John Wesley Thompson, Oct. 12, 1834.

10. FCVA, ms. Justianna D. Word poem, May 1, 1824.

11. RPL, James Word Genealogy.

12. Pontotoc County Courthouse, Circuit Court, "State Docket for Pontotoc County, 1837" [actually, May, 1837, into March, 1847]; MDAH, Personal Tax Rolls, Tippah County, 1837.

13. RPL, "Tippah County, Mississippi, Census of 1841–1845," pp. 7, 14, 22; "Tax Lists 1838, 1839, 1856"; "U.S. Census, 1840, Mississippi, Tippah County," p. 29. The contents of these first two citations were extracted from original documents, collated alphabetically, typed, and deposited in the Ripley Public Library.

14. RPL, extracts, state census, 1841–1845, pp. 1, 14; MDAH, Personal Tax Rolls, Tippah County, 1841.

15. TCCH (attic), "Record Book—Circuit Court—Sept 1852–Sept 1853," p. 608; U.S. Census, 1860, MS, Tippah, household #1326.

16. *TRA,* Jan. 17, 1846.

17. MDAH, WPA Source Material for Mississippi History—Tippah County, Roll #A784, pp. 17–18; Duclos, 34–47; *Aberdeen Southern Tribune,* June 26, 1845; *TRA,* Jan. 17, 31, 1846; *Holly Springs Guard,* Nov. 6, 1845, Jan. 9, 1846; *Jackson Clarion,* Nov. 28, 1889.

18. MDAH, Compiled Service Records of Volunteer Soldiers who served during the Mexican War in Organizations from Mississippi, 2nd Mississippi Volunteers; *TRA,* Apr. 30, 1887; RPL, James Word Genealogy.

19. MDAH, Service Records, Mexican War, 2nd Mississippi Volunteers, William C. Falkner; Duclos, 49–67; J.W.T. Falkner gravestone, St. Peter's Cemetery, Oxford, Mississippi. In Appendix A, pp. 414–28, Duclos rendered copies of relevent documents from Falkner's military file in the National Archives.

20. TCCH-ChC, book labeled "Administration Chancery Record 1846–1849," pp. 81–83; James Spight gravestone, Town Cemetery, Ripley; MDAH, Confederate Soldiers, 2nd Mississippi Volunteers, Lazarus Pearce.

21. TCCH-ChC, "Administration Chancery Record 1846–1849," pp. 317–18, 415–18.

22. TCCH-ChC, Deed Book H, p. 502; Book I, p. 222.

23. TCCH-ChC, "Administration Chancery Record 1846–1849," p. 83.

24. TCCH-ChC, Deed Book H, pp. 502, 503.

25. TCCH-ChC, Deed Book J, p. 86.

26. Jane Isbell Haynes, *William Faulkner, His Tippah County Heritage: Lands, Houses, and Businesses, Ripley, Mississippi* (Columbia, SC: Seajay Press, 1985), 61–71.

27. MDAH, Mexican War, 2nd Mississippi Volunteers; *Biographical Directory of the American Congress* (Washington: U.S. Government Printing Office, 1971), 1122; Haynes, *William Faulkner,* 61, 62, 67, 70, 77, 82.

28. Duclos, 71–74, 77, 78.

29. TCCH (attic), "Record Book," (typed label added: "Execution Docket-Circuit Court Sept 1850–____1852"), cases #3326–3333.

30. TCCH-CC, "Minutes of the Circuit Court, 1851, Book 2," pp. 404–7; "Circuit Court Record Book March 1851 to Sept 1854," pp. 36, 65.

31. Duclos, 76–77.

32. Haynes, *William Faulkner,* 20–23; Andrew Brown, *History of Tippah County, Mississippi: The First Century* (Ripley: The Tippah County Historical and Genealogical Society, 1976), 80, 83; Duclos, 82–85, citing *Memphis Appeal* reprinted in *TRA,* Apr. 16, 1881; *TRA,* Apr. 30, 1881.

33. *Biographical Directory,* 1122.

34. Duclos, 52–58.

35. Ibid., 58–63, 414–28.

36. BP, I, SM, n.d.

37. U.S. Census, 1850, MS, Tippah, e.d. 2, hh. #21; RPL, extracts, "1850 Slave Schedule of Tippah County, Mississippi," p. 9; Duclos, 76.

38. Lafayette County Library, Oxford, booklet, "Pontotoc County Pioneers, 1849–1856," vol.1, no. 2 (Summer, 1980), publ. by Hazel Bass Neet, p. 63; from Pontotoc Marriage Records, p. 199.

39. U.S. Census, 1850, MS, Tippah, e.d. 2, hh. #220; *Ripley Southern Sentinel,* Mar. 8, 1894; Dunbar Rowland, *History of Mississippi, the Heart of the South* (Chicago-Jackson: S.J. Clarke, 1925), 3: 557–58; Duclos, 185.

40. *TRA,* May 15, 1886.

41. U.S. Census, 1850, MS, Tippah, Schedule of Slave Inhabitants, W.C. Falkner holding.

42. Mississippi, vol. 20, p. 225, R. G. Dun & Co. Collection, Baker Library, Harvard University Graduate School of Business Administration. Cited hereafter as R. G. Dun & Co. Collection.

43. U.S. Census, 1860, MS, Tippah, Town of Ripley, Schedule of Slave Inhabitants, p. 12 and passim.

44. FCVA, bill of sale, F.T. Leak to J.W. Thompson, Jan. [2?], 1852.

45. Joel Williamson, *New People: Miscegenation and Mulattoes in the United States* (New York: Free Press, 1980), 44–54.

46. U.S. Census, 1860, MS, Tippah (North), Town of Ripley, p. 200, hh. #1477; *Historical and Current Catalogue, University of Mississippi, 1849–1899, 1898–1899* (Jackson, Mississippi: *Clarion-Ledger* Printer, 1899), 82, 91.

47. TCCH-CC, "Judge's Docket, Circuit Court, March term, 1860–February term, 1867," p. 43 (entry July 31, 1860); MDAH, Confederate Soldiers (microfilm), 1st Mississippi, 269, roll 115.

48. U.S. Census, 1860, MS, Tippah (North), hhs. #1411, 1415.

49. Haynes, *William Faulkner,* 20; Brown, *History of Tippah,* 83; Duclos, 86, 88.

50. Duclos, 6.

51. Mississippi, vol. 20, p. 225, R. G. Dun & Co. Collection.

52. FCVA, bill of sale, Mar. 21, 1857.
53. TCCH-ChC, "Administration Chancery Record 1846–1849," pp. 82–83.
54. TCCH-ChC, "Admin's—Chancery Court, 1855," pp. 116–17.
55. TCCH-ChC, "Minutes Probate Court, 1851," pp. 413, 432, 438, 452, 476.
56. FCVA, bill of sale, Jan. 2, 1858.
57. RPL, extracts, "1850 Slave Schedule of Tippah County Mississippi," pp. 9, 30; U.S. Census, 1860, MS, Tippah, Town of Ripley, Schedule of Slave Inhabitants, p. 12.
58. RPL, Falkner Scrapbook, clipping from *The Ripley Enterprise,* May 5, 1910.
59. TCCH (attic), "Record Book—Circuit Court, Sept. 1852–Sept. 1853," case #4076, pp. 407–9.
60. TCCH (attic), "Circuit Court Record Book, Sept. 1851–Sept, 1852," case #3615, pp. 35–37.
61. TCCH (attic), "State Docket No. 1—Circuit Court (1859–1877)," case #1960, p. 68.
62. TCCH (attic), "State Docket No. 1—Circuit Court (1859–1877)," p. 13.
63. TCCH-CC, "Circuit Ct, Execution Docket, 1859–67," p. 330, case #7486.
64. LCCH-CC, "State Docket. November Term 1837–October 1857," cases #593, 778.
65. TCCH, various record books.
66. Mattie Russell, "Land Speculation in Tippah County, 1836–1861" (Master's thesis, University of Mississippi, 1940), 15–16, 44–45.
67. LCCH-ChC, Deed Book H, pp. 27, 28, 29.
68. Mississippi, vol. 20, p. 225, R. G. Dun & Co. Collection.
69. Ibid., vol. 20, p. 221.
70. Ibid., vol. 1, p. 534 (reports dated Jan. 20, 1848 to Nov. 1, 1858).
71. Ibid., vol. 1, p. 535.
72. Duclos, p. 12; Alexander L. Bondurant, "William C. Falkner, Novelist," *Publications of the Mississippi Historical Society* 3 (1900): 116–17, 123; *TRA,* Nov. 15, 1855; *Men of Mark in Mississippi;* MDAH, Fontaine Letters; Brown, *History of Tippah,* 74.
73. RPL, ms. journal, "The Sons of Temperance, Ripley Division, No. 75, Mississippi Sons of Temperance," pp. 10, 12, 13.
74. *Heritage of Surry County,* 1: 183–84.
75. RPL, extracts, "1850 Slave Schedule," pp. 18, 6, 12, 11, 5.
76. Ibid., 14.
77. Haynes, *William Faulkner,* 75– 76.
78. RPL, extracts, "1850 Slave Schedule," p. 29.
79. RPL, "Notes on Ripley," compiled by Tommy Covington for the first annual Faulkner Conference, Note #3. See also: Russell, "Land Speculation," p. 72; TCCH (attic), "Record Book—Circuit Court, Sept 1852–Sept 1853," p. 26; "Circuit Court—Execution Docket, 1855–1857," pp. 578–79.
80. RPL, Covington, Note #5; TCCH (attic), "Circuit Court—Execution Docket, 1855–1857," p. 561; Dunbar Rowland, *Military History of Mississippi, 1803–1898* (repr. 1908 edition, Spartanburg, SC: Reprint Co., 1978), 307.
81. Pontotoc County Courthouse, Circuit Court, "State Docket for Pontotoc County 1837," "General Index," case #28, Nov., 1836; ms., biographical sketch of T.J. Word, in possession of Professor William Powell, Chapel Hill, NC.
82. TCCH-ChC, Deed Book I, pp. 137, 151; Book J, p. 560.
83. *Oxford Organizer,* May 4, 11, 18, 1850.
84. Powell, sketch of Word, p. 4.

85. Mississippi, vol. 2, pp. 239, 254, R. G. Dun & Co. Collection.

86. By way of comparison, at the same time his uncle John had $8,000 in real and $15,485 in personal property. U.S. Census, 1860, MS, Tippah (North), Town of Ripley, p. 200, hh. #1326; p. 203, hh. #1343.

87. MDAH, Personal Tax Rolls, Tippah County (microfilm roll #363), 1861.

88. U.S. Census, 1860, MS, Tippah (North), hhs. #1626, 1643.

TWO

1. *The War of the Rebellion: A Compilation of the Official Records of the Union and Confederate Armies* (Washington, DC: U.S. Government Printing Office, 1880–1901), Ser. I, vol. 2, pp. 868–69.

2. *War of the Rebellion,* Ser.I, vol. 2, pp. 470, 473, 474, 483, 490, 570.

3. MDAH, Vairin (A.L.P.) diary, p. 77; *Biographical and Historical Memoirs of Mississippi* (Cheogis Godspeed, 1981), 2: 850–52.

4. Duclos, 124–46.

5. Ibid., 151–54.

6. BP, notes of an interview with Mrs. Thompson, Memphis, ca. 1890; Duclos, pp. 156–57.

7. *War of the Rebellion,* Ser. I, vol. 17, Pt. I, p. 42. See also p. 40.

8. *War of the Rebellion,* Ser. I, vol. 17, Pt. I, pp. 138, 149–50, 490–91; Pt. II, pp. 40–43.

9. *War of the Rebellion,* Ser. I, vol. 17, Pt. I, pp. 552, 557.

10. MDAH, Confederate Soldiers Serving from Mississippi, 269, roll 33; Duclos, 178.

11. Dunbar Rowland, *Military History of Mississippi, 1803–1898* (repr. 1908 edition; Spartanburg, SC: Reprint Co., 1978), 34; Duclos, 129–82 passim; *Biographical Directory of the American Congress* (Washington: U.S. Government Printing Office, 1971), 1122.

12. Duclos, 180–81; MDAH, Confederate Soldiers, Index, Stricklin's Company, Ashcroft's Battalion, Eleventh Mississippi Cavalry, 269, rolls 24, 44; Rowland, *Military History,* 526–27.

13. Pontotoc Public Library, WPA Sources, Pontotoc County History, Part I, pp. 392, 394.

14. Pontotoc Town Hall, plat of Pontotoc; Pontotoc County Courthouse, Chancery Clerk's Office, "Deed Record," book 16, p. 349; TCCH-ChC, Deed Book U, pp. 565, 566; RPL, James Word Genealogy.

15. TCCH-ChC, Deed Book U, pp. 565, 566, 567, 617; Deed Book V, pp. 18, 90, 98, 222, 223, 279, 347, 584, 585, 682; Pontotoc County Courthouse, Chancery, "Deed Record," book 17 (Feb. 19, 1867), pp. 191–92.

16. TCCH-ChC, Deed Book V, p. 303; Duclos, 185–86, 193–94; *TRA,* Sept. 24, 1881; Aug. 12, 1882; Sept. 12, 1885.

17. TCCH (attic), "State Docket No. 1—Circuit Court (1859–1877)," p. 91 et seq.

18. MDAH, Confederate Soldiers, 269, rolls 115, 2.

19. RPL, Falkner Scrapbook, letter, Dennis Daugherty to Tippah County Historical and Genealogical Society, Feb. 5, 1986.

20. MDAH, Confederate Soldiers, 2nd Mississippi.

21. U.S. Census, 1860, MS, Tippah (North), p. 204, hh. #1357; MDAH, Confederate Soldiers, 2nd Mississippi.

22. Rowland, *Military History,* 40–48; RPL, James Word Genealogy; TCCH-ChC,

Record Book D, pp. 423–24; U.S. Census, 1850, MS, Tippah, third division, hh. #180; RPL, extracts, "1850 Slave Schedule, Tippah County, Mississippi," p. 15; U.S. Census, 1860, MS, Tippah (North), p. 21, hh. #148.

23. MDAH, Confederate Soldiers, 2nd Mississippi; Vairin, diary, 29.

24. MDAH, Confederate Soldiers, 2nd Mississippi.

25. Rowland, *Military History,* 48; Vairin, diary, 35, 75; MDAH, Confederate Soldiers, 2nd Mississippi.

26. Vairin, diary, 75.

27. MDAH, Confederate Soldiers, 2nd Mississippi; Rowland, *Military History,* 48–50.

28. For example, see *TRA,* Feb. 19, 1881.

29. MDAH, WPA Source Material for Mississippi History—Tippah County, "Civil War," p. 25

30. Mattie Russell, "Land Speculation in Tippah County, 1836–1861" (Master's thesis, University of Mississippi, 1940), 44, 72, 73; TCCH-ChC, Deed Book #9, pp. 325–26; Andrew Brown, *History of Tippah County, Mississippi: The First Century* (Ripley: The Tippah County Historical and Genealogical Society, 1976), 210–11; *TRA,* Jan. 29, 1881.

31. RPL, William C. Falkner to Ira South, n.d., 1887, Falkner Scrapbook.

32. TCCH (attic), "State Docket No. 1—Circuit Court (1859–1877)," pp. 47 through unnumbered page after p. 119.

33. Mississippi, vol. 2, pp. 239, 254, R. G. Dun & Co. Collection.

34. UMASC, Faulkner Family Collection, William Falkner to John T. Johnson, June 14, 1874.

35. *TRA,* Mar. 20, Apr. 3, 1886.

36. Donald Duclos, interview with John W. T. Falkner, August, 1959, in Duclos, p. 300.

37. *TRA,* Aug. 13, 1887.

38. Brown, *History of Tippah,* 279–82.

39. *TRA,* Mar. 20, Apr. 3, July 17, Oct. 13, 1886; Feb. 19, 26, Apr. 23, July 2, 1887.

40. Duclos, 345–46.

41. BP, clipping of a local newspaper, *The Gazette,* and a letter from the finder, "Frank to J.B.," Apr. 14, 1983; Duclos, 345–46.

42. RPL, ms. journal, "The Sons of Temperance," entries, Jan. 16, 30, Feb. 15, 1869.

43. Ibid., entries, Mar. 26, Apr. 17, May 7, June 26, July 9, Sept. 10, 1874; Feb. 19, June 4, 1875. For Henry in Feb., 1874: TCCH (attic), "State Docket No. 2," entry, Feb. 7, 1874; "Judgement Roll, No. 2," (March 1860–Jan. 1888), p. 14, case #2100.

44. Mississippi, vol. 2, p. 255, R. G. Dun & Co. Collection.

45. Brown, *History of Tippah* 72, 111; MDAH, WPA Source Material, Tippah, p. 12; MDAH, Confederate Soldiers, 1st Partisan Rangers; RPL, ms. journal, "The Sons of Temperance," entries, Feb. 20, 27, Mar. 26, 1869; U.S. Census, 1860, MS, Tippah, hh. #1346 (J.E. Rogers); RPL, extracts, U.S. Census, 1870 (for J.E.R. and Charly); U.S. Census, 1880, MS, Tippah, Ripley, hh. #49 (for J.E.R.); Rowland, *Military History,* 397.

46. RPL, ms. journal, "The Sons of Temperance," entries, Mar. 26, Apr. 17, May 7, June 26, July 9, Sept. 10, 1874; Feb. 19, June 4, Nov. 19, 1875.

47. TCCH-CC, "Marriage Record, White," Book 3, p. 308.

48. RPL, extracts, U.S. Census, 1880, 1900; MDAH, WPA, Source Material, Tippah, p. 12; Ripley Town Cemetery; RPL, Noverta Walker Scrapbook.

49. BP, Sallie Burns to Jimmy Faulkner, Nov. 21, 1964.

50. BP, copy, letter, Jimmy Faulkner to Sallie Burns, n.d.

51. Duclos, 345, citing an interview held in Sept. 1959; Duclos, 346.

52. Duclos, 346.

53. William C. Falkner, *The White Rose of Memphis* (New York: Carleton, 1881); *TRA,* Jan. 7, 1882.

54. *TRA,* Aug. 12, 1882; May 5, 19, 26, Oct. 6, 1883, et passim. William C. Falkner, *Rapid Ramblings in Europe* (Philadelphia: Lippincott, 1884).

55. *TRA,* Nov. 15, 1884.

56. *TRA,* Oct. 18, 1884.

57. *TRA,* Feb. 14, Apr. 18, 25, 1885; Aug. 8, 1886.

58. BP, I, SM, Nov. 12, 1966.

59. *TRA,* Oct. 13, 1886; Mar. 19, Sept. 17, 1887; RPL, extracts, "Mississippi Marriage Records, 1843–1925, Reverse," p. 47; *TRA,* Aug. 28, 1889.

60. *Ripley Southern Sentinel,* Aug. 29, 1889.

61. TCCH-ChC, "Minute Book, Chancery Court #3," pp. 234–35, 324–25.

62. *TRA,* Nov. 6, 1889; *Jackson Clarion-Ledger,* Nov. 14, 1889; RPL, Falkner Scrapbook, clipping, Nov. 7, 1889.

63. Duclos, 321; RPL, "Tippah County Circuit Court Records," Issue Docket of the Town of Ripley, 1886, cases #282, 285.

64. Duclos, 321, interview with J.W.T. Falkner, III, Aug., 1959.

65. Duclos, 324–25; *Memphis Appeal,* Nov. 8, 1889; *TRA,* Nov. 6, 1889; BP, Will Tieir to JB., Nov. 5, 1967.

Tieir was twenty in 1889 and had lived next door to the Thurmonds for eleven years prior to the shooting.

66. RPL, Falkner Scrapbook, photostat of the official returns.

67. Duclos, 326.

68. UMASC, Faulkner Family Collection, telegram, "Special to *Avalanche,*" (Memphis), telegrapher's copy, Nov. 5, 1889, by J. Brown.

69. Ibid., telegram, telegrapher's copy, J.J. Anderson to Col. J.W.T. Falkner, Nov. 5, 1889, 8:39 p.m.

70. Ibid., telegram, telegrapher's copy, J.W.T. Falkner to Mrs. John Falkner, Nov. 6, 1889; telegram, telegrapher's copy, J.W.T. Falkner to Col. M.C. Galloway, Nov. 6, 1889.

71. Ibid., telegram, telegrapher's copy, Charles Douglass to the *Avalanche,* "night special," Nov. 7, 1889; RPL, "Marriages and Obituaries Scrapbook," compiled by Belle Godwin, clipping (probably from the *Sentinel*).

72. UMASC, Faulkner Family Collection, telegram, telegrapher's copy, J.W.T. Falkner to Ira D. Oglesby, Nov. 8, 1889.

73. Ibid., telegram, dispatch to the *Avalanche* (Memphis), telegrapher's copy, Feb. 7, 1890.

74. TCCH (attic), "State Docket #3, Circuit Court, Tippah County (1885–1891)," p. 232.

75. *Ripley Southern Sentinal,* Feb. 26, 1891; TCCH (attic), "Minute Book #3, Circuit Court," case #2880, pp. 567, 568, 571, 588, 616, 617, 619, 628.

76. BP, Will Tieir to JB, Nov. 5, 1967.

77. BP, Sallie Burns to Jimmy Faulkner, Nov. 21, 1964.

78. *Ripley Southern Sentinal,* Feb. 26, 1891.

79. BP, Jimmy Faulkner to Sallie Burns, n.d. (ca. Nov. 1964).

80. BP, Sallie Burns to Jimmy Faulkner, Nov. 21, 1964.

81. *Ripley Southern Sentinel,* Oct. 31, 1889.

82. TCCH-ChC, "Will Book I," pp. 155–59; Brown, *History of Tippah,* 293–94, 295.

83. Brown, *History of Tippah,* 301; Duclos, 338–40.

84. Third annual Report of W.C. Falkner's Estate, Nov. 1, 1892.

85. RPL, Falkner Scrapbook, clipping, *Enterprise,* May 5, 1910.

86. U.S. Census, 1870, VA, Caroline, Port Royal Township, hh. #237; 1860, MS, Tippah (South), hh. #511.

87. Humphreys County Courthouse, Annex, Chancery Clerk's Office, "Will and Inventory Book," "H," p. 388 (1855). For 1856, June, see pp. 526, 567. Harris was not cited in 1853 (p. 147) or 1854.

88. TCCH-ChC, "Final Record, Chancery Court, June 1857–Dec. 1860," pp. 409–56.

89. TCCH-ChC, Deed Book S, p. 425; U.S. Census, 1860, MS, Tippah, Schedule of Slave Inhabitants, W.C. Falkner holding, p. 12.

90. I, Elizabeth Rogers, June 25, 1990; I, Forrest Luther, July 5, 1990; Alfreda Hughes-Hightower to Joel Williamson, Nov. 2, 1991; gravestone, Wiley University Cemetery, Marshall, TX.

91. U.S. Census, 1870, MS, Tippah, printed page 152, ms. page 8, Ripley, hhs. #47, 48; 1880, MS, Tippah, Enumeration District 194, page 6.

92. Warmouth T. Gibbs, *President Matthew W. Dogan of Wiley College, A Biography* (n.p., n.d.), passim; I. Garland Penn, "From Bootblack to College President," *Christian Advocate,* Feb. 6, 1930, pp. 148–50.

93. U.S. Census, 1870, MS, Tippah, printed page 152, ms. page 8, Ripley, hhs, #47, 48; RPL, extracts, U.S. Census, 1870, p. 64; I, Elizabeth Rogers, June 25, 1990.

94. U.S. Census, 1880, MS, Tippah, Enumeration District 194, page 6.

95. TCCH-ChC, "Deed Record, Book 7," pp. 309–10; attic storage, packet #2019.

96. U.S. Census, 1880, MS, Tippah, e.d. 194, sheet 4.

97. I, Elizabeth Rogers, June 25, 1990; I, Forrest Luther, July 5, 1990.

98. Fannie Falkner autograph book, in possession of Forrest Luther.

99. *Pontotoc True Democrat,* reprinted in *TRA,* May 15, 1886.

100. Printed program in possession of Forrest Luther.

101. I, Forrest Luther, July 5, 1990; Rust College Catalogue, 1895–96.

102. *Who's Who in Colored America, 1938–40* (Chicago: Marquis, 1951), p. 158.

103. I, Elizabeth Rogers, June 25, 1990; I, Forrest Luther, July 5, 1990

104. I, Forrest Luther, July 5, 1990; Wiley University Cemetery, Marshall, Texas.

105. Issue of the periodical: *Up the Hill,* June, 1956, vol. 9, pp. 30–33, in possession of Forrest Luther.

106. I, Elizabeth Rogers, June 25, 1990.

107. *Ripley Standard,* Oct. 21, 1898.

108. Gravestone, Ripley Town Cemetery.

109. TCCH (attic), packet #2016.

110. *Catalogue, University of Mississippi 1849–1899, 1898–1899,* p. 200.

111. Gravestone, Ripley Town Cemetery.

112. U.S. Census, 1870, MS, Tippah, printed page 149, hhs. #6, 7.

113. U.S. Census, 1880, MS, Tippah, e.d. 194, sheets 4–6.

114. *TRA,* Dec. 12, 1885.

115. *TOE,* Jan. 14, 1886.

116. *TOE,* Sept. 5, 1889.

117. FCVA, "May 1900, 10th Annual Report of Executor—William Clark Falkner Estate, by John W.T. Falkner."

118. *TOE,* Aug. 7, 1902.

119. John Falkner's ventures were often noticed by the press, e.g., *TOE,* Mar. 28, 1901; July 23, 1891.

120. *TOE,* Jan. 18, 1899; *MBB,* p. 13.

121. *Oxford Globe,* Jan. 16, July 19, 1896.

122. *TOE,* Feb. 10, 1898; U.S. Census, 1860, MS, Lafayette, hh. #1358.

123. MDAH, Confederate Soldiers, Co. A, 29th Mississippi Inf., Washington Porter Wilkins, Charles B. Howry; *TOE,* Dec. 7, 1908; Rowland, *Military History,* 108, 272–80.

124. BP, JWTF, Jr., report card, 1908–1909; *TOE,* Aug. 5, 1909.

125. RPL, "A Genealogy of the Word Family Written by James Word, December 23, 1882," supplied by Eleanor D. MacDonald, Farmington, NM.

126. *Catalogue, University of Mississippi,* p. 134.

127. BP, JB to Jimmy Faulkner, Nov. 21, 1966. In 1966, Joseph Blotner found an eyewitness to events surrounding the shooting of Murry Falkner. He was John Henry Anderson, age 85. He was walking home from school and arrived at the scene just as the assault occurred. I, Nov. 19, 1966. See also: Duclos, 349–50.

128. Ibid.

129. BP, I, Jimmy Faulkner, Mar. 17, 1965.

THREE

1. His gravestone in St. Peter's Cemetery in Oxford gives North Carolina as his birthplace. The census of 1850 gives his birthplace as Tennessee. U.S. Census, 1850, MS, Lafayette, hh. #1335. Probably, he was born in North Carolina and moved to Tennessee before taking up residence in Mississippi.

2. MDAH, *Confederate Soldiers Serving from Mississippi* (microfilm), 28th Mississippi Cav., 269, roll 332, William R. Butler. William's military records and the census suggest that he was born in 1830. However, his gravestone gives his birthdate as February 23, 1828.

3. U.S. Census, 1850, MS, Lafayette, hh. #1335.

4. John Cooper Hathorn, *Early Settlers of Lafayette Co., Mississippi: A Period Study of Lafayette County from 1830–1860, with Emphasis on Population Groups* (Oxford: Skipwith Historical and Genealogical Society, Inc., 1980), 30–34.

5. Hathorn, *Early Settlers,* 16.

6. UMASC, Minnie Holt Manuscripts, Polly Comer, slave interview, p. 4.

7. For a general description of the patrol in the South, see: Joel Williamson, *The Crucible of Race: Black-White Relations in the South Since Emancipation* (New York: Oxford University Press, 1984), 18–19.

8. LCCH-CC, "State Docket," November Term 1837–October 1857.

9. Hathorn, *Early Settlers,* 18, 21.

10. Hathorn, *Early Settlers,* 29; LCCH-ChC, Lafayette County Police Record, Book I, 29, 102, 106, 134.

11. Hathorn, *Early Settlers,* 44; LCCH-ChC, Lafayette County Estate Records, Book I.

12. Hathorn, *Early Settlers,* 60–61.

13. MDAH, Personal Tax Rolls (microfilm), roll #339, Lafayette.

14. U.S. Census, 1840, MS, Lafayette; *Oxford Observer,* Sept. 16, 1843.

15. U.S. Census, 1840, MS, Lafayette.

16. St. Peter's Cemetery, Oxford; LCCH-CC, Probate Court Records, Dockets #32, 63, 65; U.S. Census, 1860, MS, Lafayette, p. 205, hh. #1333; NC Tax Roll, Wake County, 1820, North Carolina Room, Wilson Library, UNC.

17. LCCH-CC, "Court Minutes," April 6, 1846–October 1864, p.[1]; also case #856, Oct. 24, 1846, in "Circuit Court Records, April 6, 1846 to May 4, 1850."

18. U.S. Census, 1850, MS, Lafayette, p. 414, hh. #1335; Slave Inhabitants, p. 191.

19. *Oxford Organizer,* June 23, 1849, et. seq.

20. Ibid., June 23, 1849.

21. *Historical and Current Catalogue, University of Mississippi, 1849–1899, 1898–1899* (Jackson, Mississippi: *Clarion-Ledger* Printer, 1899), 31.

22. TCCH-CC, "Marriage Record," July 15, 1850–December 31, 1856, p. 24; *Oxford Organizer,* July 27, 1850.

23. Oxford and Lafayette County Library, *Lafayette County Heritage,* 239.

24. *TOE,* May 14, 1908.

25. *Lafayette County Heritage,* 238–40; MDAH, Confederate Soldiers, 12th Inf.

26. Charles Bowen, "Bowen Family," *Lafayette County Heritage,* 239–40.

27. *Catalogue,* 39.

28. LCCH-CC, "Marriage Record," Jan. 23, 1858–Oct. 6, 1868, p. 33; "Circuit Court Record, 1870–1877" (actually April 30, 1866–May, 1877), p. 83, case #3457.

29. LCCH-ChC, will of Charles G. Butler, Will Book I, pp. 95–96.

30. U.S. Census, 1860, MS, Lafayette, p. 205, hh. #1333.

31. U.S. Census, 1860, MS, Lafayette, Slave Inhabitants, printed page 192.

32. Ibid., p. 205, hh. #1334; Slave Inhabitants, printed page 192.

33. LCCH-ChC, Deed Books, esp. I, J, K, Q, T, W, BB, CC, EE, FF, JJ.

34. LCCH-ChC, Deed Book JJ, p. 540.

35. U.S. Census, 1850, MS, Lafayette, hh. #1580.

36. MDAH, Personal Tax Rolls, roll #339, Lafayette; Confederate Soldiers, 28th Cav.

37. LCCH-CC, "Marriage Record," Jan. 23, 1858–Oct. 6, 1868, p. 33; MDAH, Confederate Soldiers, 29th Inf.; Dunbar Rowland, *Military History of Mississippi,* 1803–1898 (repr. 1908 edition; Spartanburg, SC: Reprint Co., 1978), 290.

38. MDAH, Confederate Soldiers, 29th Inf.

39. MDAH, Confederate Veteran's and Widow's Pension Applications, J.V. Butler, Aug. 3, 1900.

40. TM, pp. 10, 14, 16, passim.

41. Ibid., pp. 18, 34, 37, passim; *Catalogue,* 66.

42. Gravestones, Butler plot, St. Peter's Cemetery, Oxford.

43. U.S. Census, 1860, MS, Lafayette, p. 205, hh. #1333; LCCH-ChC, Deed Book K, p. 437; U.S. Census, 1870, MS, Lafayette, p. 12 (stamped page 610).

44. LCCH-CC, Deed Book K, p. 358.

45. LCCH-CC, Deed Book J, pp. 242–43, 273–74, 290.

46. LCCH-CC, Deed Book Q, p. 549.

47. LCCH-CC, Deed Book J, pp. 241–42; W, pp. 288–89; *Oxford Falcon,* Aug. 28, 1869.

48. Judging from census records and R.G. Dun & Co. reports, Charles was born between June, 1848, and June, 1849.

49. LCCH-CC, "Marriage Record," Jan. 23, 1858–Oct. 6, 1868, p. 304.

50. Gravestone, Butler plot, St. Peter's Cemetery, Oxford; U.S. Census, 1880, MS, Lafayette, p. 166.

51. U.S. Census, 1850, MS, Lafayette, hhs. #22, 528.

52. Gravestones, Butler and Falkner plots, St. Peter's Cemetery, Oxford; LCCH-CC, "Marriage Record," Jan. 23, 1858–Oct. 6, 1868, p. 304.

53. LCCH-CC, packet #1283.

54. U.S. Census 1860, MS, Lafayette, hh. #1323; 1870, stamped p. 610, vis. p. 8; 1850, hh. #396; Mississippi, Lafayette County, vol. 12, p. 366Q, 366R, 366–14, 366–29 R.G. Dun & Co. Collection; MDAH, Personal Tax Rolls, roll #363, Lafayette, 1874, Charles E. Butler.

55. LCCH-ChC, Deed Book T, pp. 29, 95; gravestones, St. Peter's Cemetery, Oxford.

56. TM, 144, Apr. 25, 1876.

57. TM, 112, 122, 155, Apr. 30, 1877, et seq.

58. TM, 128, Apr. 26, 1875; 144, Apr. 25, 1876.

59. TM, 191, June 2, 1879; 226, Jan. 9, 1882; 146, 147, July 31, 1876; passim.

60. TM, 166, Jan. 7, 1878; 174, Aug. 12, 1878; 176, Aug. 16, 1878; 182, Oct. 5, 1878.

61. Gravestone, St. Peter's Cemetery, Oxford; Lafayette County Library, James Henry Hand, *Abstract of Annual Returns, Mississippi Free and Accepted Masons* (New Market, Alabama: Southern Genealogical Services, 1969), 136; UMASC, Record Book, Masonic Lodge, Oxford, Mississippi, entries for July 16, 24, 1878.

62. Ibid., entries for Feb. 18, Mar. 4, Apr. 15, July 1, 1879; Mar. 2, Sept. 7, 1880; Jan. 4, 1881.

63. U.S. Census, 1880, MS, Lafayette, "Town of Oxford," p. 166.

64. Ibid., p. 4; *Lafayette County Heritage,* 239.

65. TM, 208, Aug. 10, 1880.

66. TM, 226, Jan. 9, 1883; 227, Feb. 6, 1882; 228–29, Mar. 6, 1882; 229–30, Apr. 3, 1882.

67. TM, 231, Jan. 1, 1883; 238, Feb. 5, 1883.

68. LCCH-ChC, Deed Book W, pp. 444–45; K, 355; I, 527, 528, 588; K, 358.

69. LCCH-ChC, Deed Book X, p. 358.

70. *TOE,* Feb. 3, 1910.

71. *TOE,* May 17, 1883.

72. Ibid.

73. *TOE,* May 17, 1883; Jan. 14, 1915.

74. *Jackson* (MS) *Clarion,* May 23, 1883.

75. LCCH-CC, third floor vault storage, packet #1870; *Jackson Clarion,* May 23, 1883; "Court State Docket Circuit Court, Lafayette County, Mississippi, March 1872–April 1889" (Hereafter cited as Docket, Circuit Court), May Term, 1883, p. 136, case #1870.

76. *Jackson Clarion,* May 23, 1883.

77. LCCH-CC, "Appeal Bond," packet #1795. All packets from circuit court are in a vault on the third floor of the courthouse.

78. "Bench Warrant," Jan. 23, 1882, packet #1795; U.S. Census, 1880, MS, Lafayette, p. 22.

79. U.S. Census, 1880, MS, Lafayette, e.d. 74, hh. #220; "Bond to Answer in Court," packet #1795.

80. Appeal bonds, Feb. 4, 1882, packets #1795, 1796.

81. Subpoena, Feb. 4, 1882, packet #1795.

82. "Bench Warrant," re: Eudora Watkins, Jan. 3, 1882, endorsed by "C.E. Butler D.S.", packet #1795; "Bond to Answer in Court," Feb. 4, 1882, packet #1795.

83. Subpoena, Feb. 4, 1882, packet #1795; *Oxford Falcon,* passim; TM, May 7, 1883.

84. U.S. Census, 1880, MS, Lafayette, "Town of Oxford," p. 22; deposition by S.M. Thompson, Nov., 1882, packet #1796; BP, I, Ralph S. Muckenfuss, Apr. 9, 1967.

85. LCCH-CC, indictment by the Grand Jury, Circuit Court, Lafayette County, May 3, 1882, packet #1796.

86. TCCH (attic), "State Docket #3, Circuit Court," pp. 3, 8, 12, 37, 83; LCCH-CC, Docket, Circuit Court, pp. 70 (case #1486), 124 (case #1796).

87. TCCH (attic), "Secret Record of Indictments, 1893–190_," pp. 151, 181, 273.

88. Subpoena, Charles E. Butler, Apr. 14, 1882, packet #1796.

89. LCCH-CC, Docket, Circuit Court, p. 124, cases #1795, 1796.

90. LCCH-CC, packets #1795, #1796, passim; LCCH-CC, Docket Book, Oct. 1874–May 1880; TM, p. 168.

91. Samuel M. Thompson, Affidavit, Nov. term, 1882, packet #1796; LCCH-CC, Docket Book, pp. 124, 129, 136.

92. LCCH-CC, Minute Book, B, Lafayette Circuit Court, pp. 387–88, Nov. 17, 1882; subpoena issued Mar. 2, 1883, packet #1795.

93. LCCH-CC, Docket Book, p. 125, case #1808.

94. Affidavit of Samuel M. Thompson, Nov. 14, 1882, packet #1796.

95. LCCH-CC, Docket, Circuit Court, p. 134, case #1857; Minute Book, B, Lafayette Circuit Court, p. 439, May 18, 1883.

96. TM, p. 239, May 7, 1883.

97. LCCH-CC, Docket, Circuit Court, pp. 43, 56, 59, 62, 64, 73, 75; cases #1321, 1362, 1415, 1519. See also: "Circuit Court Record, 1870–1877," p. 157, case #1112 (Oct. 25, 1867); p. 615, #1321; p. 702, #1362; p. 712, #1415; p. 726, #1415; p. 733, #1362; Minute Book, B, Lafayette Circuit Court, p. 34, Dec. 13, 1877.

98. LCCH-CC, Docket, Circuit Court, pp. 73, 75, 81, 92; cases #1520, 1633, 1634.

99. *Catalogue,* 163; U.S. Census, 1880, MS, Lafayette, "Town of Oxford," p. 22; Sullivan gravestone, St. Peter's Cemetery, Oxford; advertisements in various issues, the *Eagle* and the *Globe.*

100. *Jackson Clarion,* May 23, 1883; LCCH-CC, Docket, Circuit Court, pp. 128, 136; case #1685.

101. *TOE,* May 3, 1883; *Oxford Falcon,* Sept. 6, 1866.

102. U.S. Census, 1870, MS, Lafayette, "Town of Oxford," p. 14; *TOE,* May 31, 1883; Rowland, *Military History,* 98–108; Julia Wendel, "Reconstruction in Lafayette County," Publications of the Mississippi Historical Society, 1913, 223–64.

103. LCCH-CC, Docket, Circuit Court, p. 128, case #1685, (Nov., 1882); p. 136, #1685, (May, 1883).

104. MDAH, *Confederate Soldiers,* indexes; S.M. Thompson, 1st Cav.; Herman Wohlleben, 1st Cav.

105. UMASC, Masonic Lodge, Oxford, Record Book, entries, July 16, 1878; July 1, 1879.

106. LCCH-CC, Docket, Circuit Court, p. 142, case #1870.

107. LCCH-CC, bond, May 10, 1883, packet #1870; U.S. Census, 1880, MS, Lafayette, passim.

108. U.S. Census, 1870, MS, Lafayette, p. 8; UMASC, Masonic Lodge, Oxford, Record Book, entries for Feb. 18, 1879, Mar. 2, 1880.

109. LCCH-CC, petition by Charles E. Butler, May 11, 1883, packet #1870.

110. TM, 240, May 7, 1883; 244, Sept. 3, 1883; affidavit, packet #1870.

111. LCCH-CC, affidavit, W.O. Beanland, May 14, 1884, packet #1870; TM, 249, Jan. 7, 1884.

112. Various drafts of charges each marked "refused," and another draft marked "given," LCCH-ChC, packet #1870.

113. LCCH-CC, packet #1870.

114. LCCH-CC, Docket, Circuit Court, p. 137, case #1796.

FOUR

1. *Biographical Directory of the American Congress* (Washington, Government Printing Office: 1971), 1257; U.S. Census, 1850, MS, Lafayette, hh. #1580.

2. UMASC, L.Q.C. Lamar letters, L.Q.C. Lamar to E.D. Clark, July 15, 1881.

3. Ibid., L.Q.C. Lamar to E.D. Clark, May 12, 1882.

4. TM, 231, May 1, 1882; Virginia Lamar gravestone, St. Peter's Cemetery, Oxford; UMASC, L.Q.C. Lamar Letters, L.Q.C. Lamar to E.D. Clark, (Mar. 1) 1885; telegram, Mar. 18, 1885.

5. *Biographical Directory,* 1257.

6. Lafayette County Library, typescript, compiled by the DAR, "Some Early History of Lafayette County, Mississippi," (1922) 53; UMASC, L.Q.C. Lamar Letters, L.Q.C. Lamar to E.D. Clark, May 12, 1882.

7. UMASC, Minutes of the Hermaean Society, Oct. 1, 15, 22, Nov. 5, Dec. 10, 17, 1887; *Historical and Current Catalogue, University of Mississippi, 1849–1899, 1898–1899,* 215.

8. LCCH-ChC, packet #1749.

9. Ibid.

10. TM, 263–74, entries from Jan. 5 to Dec. 14, 1885; LCCH-ChC, Deed Book CC, p. 321.

11. TM, 276, Jan. 4, 1886; *Oxford Globe,* Nov. 26, 1891; U.S. Census, MS, Lafayette, 1860, ca. p. 205, hh. #1340; 1870, p. 12; 1880, p. 4; UMASC, Masonic Lodge, Oxford, Record Book, entries for Mar. 4, 1879, Mar. 2, 1880.

12. TM, 276, Jan. 4; 278, Jan. 8, 1886.

13. TM, 295, June 25, 1886.

14. TM, 301, Sept. 6, 1886.

15. TM, 309, Feb. 25, 1887; 313–14, Apr. 30, 1887; LCCH-CC, "Bar Issue Docket," case #4669, pp. 182, 186, 193, 194, 199, 205, 210 (Nov. 1887–Apr. 1890); TM, 314, Apr. 30, 1887.

16. TM, 320, Sept. 2; 324, Nov. 25; 329, Dec. 30, 1887.

17. TM, 330, Jan. 2, 1888.

18. TM, 332, Jan. 12, 1888.

19. UMASC, Charles Roberts Letters, 1862–1865, Charles Roberts to Mrs. Roberts, July 18, 1864; University Archives, Chancellor's Collection, Bem Price to E. Mayes, Oct. 12, 1887.

20. TM, 332, Jan. 12, 1888.

21. TM, 333–34, Feb. 6, 1888.

22. TM, 334, Feb. 6, 1888.

23. TM, 335, Feb. 9; 336, Feb. 13; 343, Mar. 7, 8, 1888.

24. TM, 344, Mar. 8; 345, Mar. 12, 1888.

25. TM, 350, Apr. 2; 358, June 4, 1888.

26. TM, 359, June 11; 360, June 14, 1888.

27. TM, 360, June 18; 361, June 22, 1888.

28. TM, 268–69, Aug. 7. 1885.

29. UMASC, Chancellor's Papers, lists: "faculty," Dec. 31, 1887; "hands . . .," Mar., 1888.

30. UMASC, "Some Early History of Lafayette County, Mississippi," typescript prepared by the David Reese Chapter (Oxford) DAR, 1922.

454

31. Manuscript notes, Robert Charles Kenzer, " 'We Are All Blessed With Kin': Family, Kinship, and Neighborhood in a Southern Community, 1849–1881" (Ph.D. diss., Harvard University, 1984).

32. LCCH-ChC, Probate Court Records, Wills, Docket #63. Burlina's father might have been Sherwood House, who had been carried on the tax roll in Wake County, North Carolina, in 1820 and buried in the Butler plot in St. Peter's Cemetery after his death in 1841. Possibly, Sherwood House's first name was actually Henry. That of his wife was Nancy. Nancy House (age 71 and North Carolina–born) was living with Burlina in 1860 and was buried alongside Sherwood in 1868. *Journal of North Carolina Genealogy* 9, no. 1 (Spring, 1963), pp. 1083–1099; U.S. Census, 1860, MS, Lafayette, hh. #1333; gravestones, St. Peter's Cemetery, Oxford.

33. BP, I, SM, Aug. 19, 1964; MCF to JB, Aug. 21, 1972.

34. BP, JB to MCF, Aug. 7, 1972; MCF to JB, Aug. 21, 1972.

35. BP, I, Dot, Mar. 21, 1965; I, E, July 26, 1966.

36. LCCH-ChC, Deed Book EE, pp. 161, 454, 479.

37. BP, I, E, July 26, 1966; see also: I, SM, Nov. 14, 1966.

38. Dorothy Zollicoffer Oldham, "Life of Jacob Thompson" (Master's thesis, University of Mississippi, 1930), pp. 4, 40, 121.

39. Oldham, "Jacob Thompson," pp. 4, 40, 121.

40. Oldham, "Jacob Thompson," 1–5. Much of this and the following information is drawn from Oldham's text.

41. Oldham, "Jacob Thompson," 6–25.

42. Gravestones, Thompson plot, St. Peter's Cemetery, Oxford; U.S. Census, 1850, MS, Lafayette, hh. #394.

43. John Cooper Hathorn, *Early Settlers of Lafayette Co., Mississippi: A Period Study of Lafayette County from 1830–1860, with Emphasis on Population Groups* (Oxford: Skipwith Historical and Genealogical Society, Inc., 1980), p. 16; LCCH-ChC, Lafayette County Police Record, Book I, p. 1.

44. Oldham, "Jacob Thompson," 35–36.

45. U.S. Census, 1850, MS, Lafayette, hhs. #394, 395, 396; Slave Schedule, p. 191.

46. Hathorn, *Early Settlers,* 47, 49.

47. Gravestone, Thompson plot, Elmwood Cemetery, Memphis.

48. Gravestones, Thompson plot, Elmwood Cemetery, Memphis.

49. Oldham, "Jacob Thompson," 35–38.

50. Hathorn, *Early Settlers,* 50.

51. *Oxford Organizer,* July 27, 1850.

52. Hathorn, *Early Settlers,* 53–54, 114–32. In 1860, Jacob was the largest producer of cotton in Lafayette County. His mother-in-law Tabitha Jones took fourth place, while his brother-in-law Yancey Wiley took seventh. Adding in his brother William and his other brother-in-law Abner Lewis, the Thompson connection produced 963 bales of cotton in this year, or about 5 percent of the total in the county. Another dozen top producers belonged to the Avent, Bowles, Pegues, Price, and Carter families. Altogether this most productive element in the cotton aristocracy marketed almost 16 percent of Lafayette's crop.

53. Oldham, "Jacob Thompson," 43; DAR, "Some Early History," 54.

54. MDAH, pamphlet, "A History of St. Peter's Episcopal Church, Proto-Cathedral of Mississippi, Commemorating Its One Hundredth Anniversary, Oxford, Mississippi, 1951," "fourth page."

55. Gravestones, Thompson plot, St. Peter's Cemetery, Oxford.

56. U.S. Census, 1860, MS, Lafayette, hhs. #1538, 1568, 1569; Avents buy 1,760 acres in northwest corner of Lafayette County for $13,000, June 15, 1844, LCCH-ChC, Deed Book D, p. 124; LCCH-CC, Marriage Record, Book 1, p. 22.

57. *Historical and Current Catalogue, University of Mississippi, 1849–1899, 1898–1899* (Jackson, Mississippi: *Clarion-Ledger* Printer, 1899), 43; LCCH-CC, Marriage Record, January 23, 1858 to October 6, 1868, p. 109; gravestones, Thompson plot, Elmwood Cemetery, Memphis; James Buchanan, *The Works of James Buchanan,* compiled and edited by John Bassett Moore (Philadelphia: J.B. Lippincott, 1910), vol. 10: 318–20.

58. *Nashville American,* Aug. 29, 1909; Oldham, "Jacob Thompson," 103.

59. Oldham, "Jacob Thompson," 99–113; *Oxford Falcon,* Sept. 6, 1866; LCCH-ChC, codicil to will of Jacob Thompson, Mar. 12, 1885, copy filed in Will Book #2, pp. 23–30.

60. Oldham, "Jacob Thompson," 120–26. See also: *Biographical Directory,* p. 1810.

61. UMASC, WPA interview with Joanna Thompson Isom, n.d. but marginal note indicates 1936, typescript in Minnie B. Holt mss.

62. Ibid.

63. Oldham, "Jacob Thompson," 102–3.

64. U.S. Census, 1850, MS, Lafayette, hh. #396. See also: hhs. #394 and 397; and Slave Schedule for Joneses and Thompsons.

65. U.S. Census, 1860, MS, Lafayette, Slave Schedule, pp. 43–44 (also p. 172).

66. Ibid., 70.

67. LCCH-CC, third floor vault storage, packet #1401, Nov. 14, 1877.

68. *Catalogue, University of Mississippi,* 70; TM, 330, Jan. 2, 1888.

69. MDAH, Jason C. Niles diary (microfilm), Dec. 24, 1887.

70. *TOE,* Feb. 22, 1883; Jan. 12, 1888.

71. *Oxford Globe,* Apr. 27, 1894.

72. Ibid., Nov. 6, 1890; Aug. 9, 1894.

73. Ibid., Apr. 12, 27, 1894.

74. Ibid., Apr. 20, 1894.

75. Ibid., Oct. 31, 1895.

76. Ibid., Dec. 19, 1895; Oct. 28, 1896.

77. Ibid., Mar. 7, 1967.

78. TM, 351, Apr. 2; 357, June 4, 1888.

79. TM, 377, Sept. 28; 378, Oct. 1, 1888.

80. LCCH-ChC, Deed Book X, p. 358; FF, p. 653.

81. TM, 371, Sept. 6, 1888.

82. TCCH-CC, "Bar Issue Docket . . . ," pp. 187, 194, 200 (case #4690).

83. *Oxford Globe,* Apr. 5, 12, 26; Oct. 11, 1888; Apr. 18, 1889.

84. Ibid., Sept. 19, 1889.

85. Mississippi University for Women Library, Columbus, Special Collections, *Fifth Annual Catalogue of the Mississippi Industrial Institute and College for the Education of White Girls of Mississippi,* Session of 1889–1890 (Columbus: College Printing Office, 1890).

86. Ibid., annual *Catalogue,* Sixth through Thirteenth, 1891 through 1898.

87. BP, I, E, July 26, 1966.

88. *Oxford Globe,* July 7, Oct. 6, 1892; July 2, 1891.

89. Ibid., May 16, 1889; Jan. 1, Nov. 26, 1891; July 20, 1893; Aug. 9, 1894.

90. *Oxford Globe,* July 20, 1893.

91. LCCH-ChC, Deed Book JJ, pp. 152, 540.

92. *Oxford Globe,* July 12, 1894; Aug. 3, 1896; Nov. 13, 1890; Sept. 7, 1893; Apr. 12, 1894.

93. Ibid., Apr. 4, 1895.
94. U.S. Census, 1900, MS, Lafayette, "Town of Oxford," hh. #64.
95. *Oxford Globe,* Sept. 24, Dec. 24, 1896.
96. U.S. Census, 1900, MS, Lafayette "Town of Oxford," hhs. #3, 64.
97. Skipwith Society Collection, *Oxford Globe Supplement,* Dec. 6, 1900.
98. *TOE,* June 6, 1896.
99. *TOE,* July 16, 1896.
100. *Oxford Globe,* Jan. 17, July 11, 1895; Jan. 16, 1896.
101. *TOE,* Oct. 1, 1896.
102. *TOE,* Oct. 29, Nov. 12, 1896; *Oxford Globe,* Oct. 29, 1896.

PART II

FIVE

1. *Oxford Globe,* Oct. 29, 1896.
2. Ibid., July 12, 1894; Apr. 4, 1895. See also: U.S. Census, 1900, MS, Lafayette County, "Oxford City," sheet #3, hh. #64. Addie married on July 11, 1894; her baby was born March 20, 1895.
3. *TOE,* May 4, 1899; Feb. 22, 1900.
4. BP, SM to JB, Aug. 10, 1967; RPL, Covington Map.
5. FCVA, WCF to "Aunt Bama," (Sept. 10, 1925).
6. Robert Cantwell, "The Faulkners: Recollections of a Gifted Family," *New World Writing* (New York: New American Library, 1952), 56.
7. *Ripley Southern Sentinel,* Jan. 14, 1901; TCCH-ChC, Deed Book V, p. 691; Book 16, pp. 30–32.
8. *TOE,* June 20, 1901.
9. *TOE,* Oct. 3, 1901.
10. *Ripley Southern Sentinel,* Oct. 17, Nov. 14, Dec. 26, 1901.
11. *TOE,* Mar. 25, May 20, 1902; *Ripley Southern Sentinel,* Mar. 27, 1902.
12. TCCH-ChC, 12th Annual Report, Nov., 1901. Comparable figures are in the 13th Annual Report, Nov., 1902.
13. *MBB,* 13–14; *Ripley Southern Sentinel,* May 22, 1902.
14. *TOE,* Jan. 3, 1889; BP, I, Jimmy Faulkner, Mar. 17, 1965; Murry C. Falkner, *The Falkners of Mississippi: A Memoir* (Baton Rouge: Louisiana State University Press, 1967), 3–4.
15. Falkner, *The Falkners,* 4.
16. BP, Jimmy Faulkner to JB, (Summer, 1972).
17. BP, I, Lily Moore Watson, n.d., 1964.
18. *TOE,* Nov. 20, Dec. 14, 1902.
19. *TOE,* Oct. 2, 1902.
20. *TOE,* Mar. 13, May 9, Aug. 28, 1902.
21. *TOE,* Sept. 15, 1904.
22. BP, I, Sallie Murry Wilkins, Nov. 14, 1966.
23. U.S. Census, 1880, MS, Attala, e.d. 12, sheet 38, lines 30, 32; U.S. Census, 1900, MS, Attala, e.d. 1, sheet 3, hh. #65.
24. U.S. Census, 1900, MS, Attala, e.d. 1, sheet 3, hhs. #64, 65; MDAH, *Confederate Soldiers,* 15th Mississippi; Dunbar Rowland, *History of Mississippi, The Heart of the South* (Jackson: S.J. Clarke, 1925), 4:189–90.
25. U.S. Census, 1880, MS, Attala, e.d. 1, sheet 30, lines 29–35; MDAH, *Confederate*

Soldiers Serving From Mississippi (microfilm), 20th Mississippi, POW Record, roll 22, Chase, Ohio; MDAH, Attala Co., Miss., Cemeteries; Kosciusko City Cemetery, Oldham plots; Rowland, *History of Mississippi,* 4:189–90.

26. *TOE,* Apr. 16, 1903; *MBB,* 88.
27. BP, I, Dr. Ralph S. Muckenfuss, Apr. 9, 1967.
28. Rowland, *History of Mississippi,* 4:189–90.
29. Ibid., 190.
30. *MBB, 88.*
31. U.S. Census, 1910, MS, Lafayette, e.d. 26, sheet 1A, hh. #51.
32. BP, I, E, Aug. __, 1963; Dec. 9, 1964.
33. University of North Carolina–Chapel Hill, Southern Historical Collection, Jason Niles Diaries, pp. 114, 117.
34. Ibid., pp. 114, 117, 189, et passim; *TOE,* July 2, 1891; June 5, 1902.
35. BP, I, E, Aug. __, 1963.
36. LCCH-ChC, Deed Book VV, pp. 391–92, 557; *TOE,* Mar. 9, Nov. 2, 9, 1905; Jan. 4, 1906.
37. BP, I, Taylor H. McElroy, Mar. 23, 1965; I, SM, Nov. 26, 1965; I, Branham Hume, Nov. 23, 1965; I, E, Oct. 27, 1965.
38. BP, I, E, Nov. 28, 1967.
39. *TOE,* Feb. 6, 1902.
40. Falkner, *The Falkners,* 44–47.
41. *TOE,* Jan. 3, 1907.
42. Falkner plot, St. Peter's Cemetery, Oxford; *TOE,* Nov. 21, 1907.
43. BP, I, SM, Aug. 19, 1964; *TOE,* June 6, 1907; Butler plot, St. Peter's Cemetery, Oxford.
44. BP, Jimmy Faulkner to JB, n.d., ("Thursday").
45. LCCH-ChC, Deed Book XX, p. 42; *TOE,* Mar. 25, 1909; BP, SM to JB, Aug. 10, 1967.
46. U.S. Census, 1910, MS, Lafayette, e.d. 26, begins sheet 1A, hhs. #51, 58, 59, 65, 198, 199, 200, 214, 240; *MBB,* 38, 40, 41; Falkner, *The Falkners,* 31; *TOE,* Aug. 13, 1903; June 29, 1911; BP, I, E, Mar. 29, 1967; *Historical and Current Catalogue, University of Mississippi, 1849–1899, 1898–1899,* 162.
47. U.S. Census, 1910, MS, Lafayette, "Part Beat One," hh. #199.
48. BP, I, Earl Warthoam (black blacksmith), Sept. 10, 1964.
49. Falkner, *The Falkners,* 9 10, 12–15, *MBB,* 47–52; U.S. Census, 1910, MS, Lafayette, e.d. 26, sheet 10–10A, hh. #199.
50. Phillip Alexander Bruce, *The Plantation Negro as a Freeman* (New York: Putnam, 1889), 84–85.
51. *Jackson Weekly Clarion-Ledger,* July 30, 1903, in George C. Osborne, "A County Editor Finds Himself & James K. Vardaman Champion Reform," *The Journal of Mississippi History* 8 (Jan., 1946): 85.
52. "Governor Vardaman on the Negro," *Current Literature* 36 (Mar., 1904): 270–71.
53. William F. Holmes, *The White Chief; James K. Vardaman* (Baton Rouge: Louisiana State University Press, 1970), 121–22.
54. Quoted in Joel Williamson, *The Crucible of Race* (New York: Oxford University Press, 1984), 128. For Felton in broad context, see same, pp. 124–130.
55. *Thirty Years of Lynching in the United States, 1889–1918* (New York: NAACP, 1919), 35, 74–79.
56. Much of the following account was taken from the *Jackson Daily Clarion-*

Ledger, Sept. 10, 1908. See also John B. Cullen in collaboration with Floyd C. Watkins, *Old Times in the Faulkner Country* (Chapel Hill: University of North Carolina Press, 1961), 89–98.

57. *Memphis Commercial Appeal,* Sept. 4, 1908.

58. FCVA, WF to Morton Goldman, (Feb. 18, 1935); "Dry September," *Scribner's Magazine* 89 (Jan., 1931): 49–56.

59. *Biographical Directory of the American Congress* (Washington: Government Printing Office, 1971), p. 1775.

60. *Jackson Daily Clarion-Ledger,* Sept. 9, 1908.

61. *TOE,* May 3, 1906; Jan. 27, 1907.

62. *TOE,* Mar. 12, 1908; LCCH-CC, "General Docket, State Cases, March 18, 1893–ca. 1917"; "Court State Docket, Circuit Court, March 1903–September 1909," cases #3198, 3251, 3253–3255.

63. *Jackson Daily Clarion-Ledger,* Sept. 10, 1908.

64. Rowland, *Military History,* 376. Possibly, Edwin was the "idiot" Maud Falkner referred to in an interview with James Dahl in 1953. James Dahl, "A Faulkner Reminiscence: Conversations with Mrs. Maud Falkner," *Journal of Modern Literature* 3, no. 5 (Apr., 1974): 1028.

65. *TOE,* Sept. 24, 1908.

66. BP, I, SM, Jan. 17, 1967.

67. *Thirty Years of Lynching,* 74–79.

68. JB, 122; Eleventh Grade Yearbook Drawings by Faulkner (1913), *Brodsky Collection Guide,* 1, 9–12.

69. WF to Malcolm Cowley, (Dec. 24, 1945), in *SLWF,* 213–14.

70. BP, I, E, July 26, 1966; Apr. 26, 1967; Jimmy Faulkner to JB, (Summer, 1972).

71. U.S. Census, 1910, MS, Lafayette, Oxford City, hhs. #394, 395; LCCH-CC, 3rd floor, packet #1870; *Oxford Independent,* Dec. 24, 1917; Mar. 4, 1918.

72. *TOE,* Mar. 21, June 6, 1918; Jan. 23, Aug. 21, Oct. 24, 1919; May 4, 1920.

73. U.S. Census, 1910, MS, Lafayette, Oxford City, hh. #348; UMASC, "Some Early History of Lafayette County," typescript prepared by the David Reese Chapter (Oxford) DAR in 1922; Butler plot, St. Peter's Cemetery, Oxford.

74. Maud Falkner to J.R. Cofield, reported in JB, 51.

75. For height, see: Robert W. Fogel, "Nutrition and Decline in Mortality Since 1700. . ." Working Paper No. 1402, National Bureau of Economic Research (July 1984), p. 44; *LG,* 264; BP, I, Robert Farley, Apr. 3, 1965.

76. BP, I, Essie Eades, Nov. 24, 1965; I, SM, Nov. 25, 1965; I, Taylor McElroy, Nov. 18, 1967.

77. BP, I, Ralph S. Muckenfuss, Apr. 9, 1967.

78. BP, promoted to 7th in 1911-photocopy, 6th grade report card, 1910–1911.

79. JB, 33–34, 35–36.

80. BP, I, Katrina Carter, Nov. 21, 1965.

81. BP, I, MCF, Mar. 31, 1965.

82. BP, I, Taylor H. McElroy, Mar. 23, Apr. 3, 1965; *MBB,* 85, 87–88, 89.

83. BP, I, E, Feb. __, 1965; I, SM, Nov. 26, 1965; I, E, Aug. __, 1963.

84. BP, I, SM, Nov. 14, 1966; I, Robert Farley, Apr. 3, 1965; I, Mrs. Demarest (Myrtle Ramey), Dec. 30, 1966.

85. BP, I, Robert Farley, Apr. 3, 1965; I, Mrs. Rudolf Weinmann, Feb. 2, 1965; I, SM, Nov. 14, 1966.

86. BP, I, Ralph S. Muckenfuss, Apr. 9, 1967; I, Essie Eades, Nov. 24, 1965. See also: BP, I, BW, Mar. 28, 1965.

87. BP, I, SM, Mar. 22, 1971; Nov. 26, 1965.

88. BP, I, E, Dec. 9, 1964.

89. BP, photocopy of WF's report card for 1910–1911 indicating promotion to the 7th grade in 1911. Yet he was on 6th grade honor roll reported in *TOE,* June 30, 1910.

90. BP, note on SM in a letter to JB, Jan. 18, 1968.

91. BP, I, Ella Somerville, Mar. 22, 1965.

92. BP, I, E, Dec. 9, 1964.

93. BP, I, SM, Mar. 26, 1965; I, Dewey and Felix Linder, Mar. 24, 1965; I, SM, Mar. 19, 1965; I, Mrs. Demarest (Myrtle Ramey), Dec. 30, 1966.

94. *TOE,* Jan. 18, 1912.

95. LCCH-CC, Index Book to Wills, #5326, pp. 3–21.

96. BP, I, SM, Nov. 14, 1966.

97. *TOE,* Mar. 9, 1922.

98. *TOE,* Oct. 14, 1909; July 21, 1910; Nov. 9, 1911; June 13, 1912.

99. LCCH-ChC, Deed Book I, pp. 295, 387; *TOE,* Mar. 7, 1912.

100. *TOE,* Dec. 5, 1912; Nov. 13, 1913.

101. *TOE,* Jan. 22, May 2, 1912; Aug. 7, 1913; LCCH-ChC, Deed Book XX, pp. 295–96, 382.

102. *TOE,* Aug. 15, 1912; Sept. 12, 1912.

103. BP, I, E, Mar. 29, 1967; *TOE,* Dec. 5, 1912.

104. BP, I, Dot, Nov. 14, 1967.

105. BP, I, Mrs. Rudolf Weinmann, Feb. 2, 1965; I, Robert Farley, Apr. 3, 1965.

106. BP, I, Taylor McElroy, Mar. 23, 1965; with a note by JB; clipping, *The Cavalier.*

107. BP, I, Mrs. Rudolf Weinmann, Feb. 2, 1965.

108. *TOE,* Nov. 13, 1913.

109. BP, I, Robert Farley, Apr. 3, 1965.

110. Copy of the Record of Lida Estelle Oldham, Mary Baldwin College, 1913–1914; BP, I, E, Dec. 9, 1964.

111. BP, I, E, Dec. 9, 1964; I, BW, Mar. 28, 1965; I, Mrs. Rudolf Weinmann, Feb. 2, 1965.

112. BP, I, E, Dec. 9, 1964.

113. BP, I, Mrs. Arthur A. Halle, Mar. 17, 1965; I, Mrs. Rudolf Weinmann, Feb. 2, 1965.

114. BP, SM to JB, Jan. 18, 1968; I, SM, n.d.

115. BP, I, SM, Nov. 14, 1966; I, Jimmy Faulkner, Nov. 27, 1965.

116. BP, I, E, Dec. 9, 1964.

117. BP, I, SM, Nov. 15, 1967; I, Taylor McElroy, Nov. 18, 1967; I, E, Dec. 9, 1964.

118. BP, I, E, Dec. 9, 1964; I, Essie Eades, Nov. 24, 1965.

119. BP, I, SM, Nov. 14, 15, 1967. Mrs. Hairston had made an advantageous second marriage, much as had Lida Oldham's mother. The Franklins had first come to Mississippi from New York in the 1830s and settled in Columbus as merchants. The Hairstons came from Virginia in the 1840s and settled in the county as planters. They brought with them literally hundreds of slaves and sufficient funds to buy thousands of acres of semi-developed land. They lost their slaves in the war, but they kept their lands to persist as one of the very richest families in Columbus and environs. U.S. Census, 1850, MS, Lowndes, hhs. #49, 319, 325, 819; 1870, hhs. #475, 476, 460, 481, 750, 768, 799.

120. BP, I, SM, n.d.

121. BP, I, E, Dec. 9, 1964.

122. *TOE,* Apr. 11, 1918; Thomas E. Lamar, "Debts and Credits," *The Faulkner Newsletter and Yoknapatawpha Review* 1 (July–Sept., 1981): 3.

123. *TOE,* Apr. 25, 1918.

124. Ibid.; *MBB,* 134.

125. *Oxford Independent,* Mar. 19, 1915.

126. *TOE,* Apr. 25, 1918.

127. *TOE,* Apr. 25, May 27, 1918.

128. BP, I, SM, Nov. 14, 1967; *TOE,* Feb. 13, 1919.

129. BP, I, MCF, Dec. 2, 1965; I, E, Feb. 23, 1965.

130. Rowland, *History of Mississippi,* 4: 170.

131. BC, Phil Stone to Glenn O. Carey, Apr. 5, 1950; William B. Ferris, Jr., "William Faulkner and Phil Stone," *South Atlantic Quarterly* 67 (Aug., 1969): 538; *PSO,* 18–30, 53–70.

132. *MBB,* 128–29; *Oxford Independent,* Sept. 24, 1915; *TOE,* Sept. 15, 1914; *PSO,* 76–89.

133. BP, I, Robert Farley, Apr. 3, 1965; I, SM, Mar. n.d., 1965.

134. BP, *Greenville* (MS) *Delta Democrat Times,* Sunday, July 15, 1962, p. 20; I, BW, Mar. 28, 1965.

135. BW, 26, 28, 33, 36–37; BP, I, BW, Mar. 28, 1965.

136. BC, *Greenville Delta Democrat Times,* n.d.

137. *TOE,* June 27, 1918.

138. Michael Millgate, "William Faulkner, Cadet," *University of Toronto Quarterly* 35 (Jan., 1966): 117.

139. BC, Phil Stone to Glenn O. Carey, Jan. 21, 1950. See also: Gordon Price-Stephens, "Faulkner and the Royal Air Force," *Mississippi Quarterly* 17 (Summer, 1964): 125–26; *PSO,* 102–6.

140. O.B. Emerson and John Hermann, "William Faulkner and the Falkner Family Name," *Names* 24, no. 8 (Sept., 1986): 255–65.

141. *TOE,* July 4, 1918; Feb. 7, 1918.

142. *TOE,* various issues, March, April, May, June, 1918.

143. Falkner, *The Falkners,* 91–94.

144. *Oxford Independent,* Apr. 15, 1918.

145. Falkner, *The Falkners,* 96–98.

146. *TOE,* Dec. 19, 1918.

147. Falkner, *The Falkners,* 98–102.

148. *TOE,* Dec. 19, 1918.

149. BP, I, MCF, Dec. 2, 1965; I, Jimmy Faulkner, n.d.; *TOE,* Mar. 20, 1919.

150. Falkner, *The Falkners,* passim.

151. FCVA, various papers relating to his membership in Royal Air Force Course 42, 4 School of Aeronautics, University of Toronto.

152. Michael Millgate, "Faulkner in Toronto: A Further Note," *University of Toronto Quarterly* 37 (Jan., 1968): 198

153. Millgate, "William Faulkner, Cadet," 123.

154. Carvel Collins, "Faulkner's War Service and His Fiction," Modern Language Association lecture, New York, Dec. 28, 1966.

155. Millgate, "William Faulkner, Cadet," 123; "Faulkner in Toronto," 198–99.

156. JB (1974), 225; BC, Phil Stone to Robert Daniel, Apr. 6, 1942.

157. Collins, "Faulkner's War Service."

158. FCVA, General Orders concerning Uniforms, Nov. 21, 1918.

159. Falkner, *The Falkners,* 90–91; *MBB,* 139–90; JB (1974), 225.

160. *MBB,* 138–39.

161. FCVA, General Orders concerning Uniforms, Nov. 21, 1918; Honorary Commission, with form dated Nov. 20, 1920.

SIX

1. For an example of acclaim, see: Granville Hicks, "The Past and the Future With William Faulkner," *Bookman* 74 (Sept., 1931):19.

2. A. Wigfall Green, "William Faulkner at Home," *Sewanee Review* 40 (Summer, 1932): 299–300.

3. BW, 32.

4. JB, 79–80.

5. JB, 324.

6. BP, I, Mrs. Julius Friend, Feb. 3, 1965; I, Marc Antony, Feb. 1, 3, 1965.

7. John McClure in *Double Dealer* 7 (Jan.–Feb., 1925).

8. BP, I, Robert Farley, Apr. 3, 1965.

9. BP, I, Katrina Carter, Nov. 21, 1965.

10. BW, 19–20, 24–25.

11. *PSO,* 97–98; BP, I, BW, Nov. 29, 1965.

12. *PSO,* 126–27, 128–30.

13. *PSO,* 127–28.

14. UMASC, Chancellor's Collection, Chancellor (Alfred Hume), University of Mississippi, to Murry Falkner, Nov. 8, 11, 1918; Murry Falkner to "My Dear Chancellor," May 19, 1919.

15. BP, I, MCF, Jan. 18, 1968; SM to JB, Jan. 18, 1968; SM to JB, "Friday morning," n.d.

16. BP, I, MCF, Dec. 2, 1965.

17. BP, Hubert S. Libscomb to JB, Sept. 21, 1965.

18. *New Republic* 20 (Aug. 6, 1919): 24; *TOE,* Nov. 27, 1919.

19. BC, *Ole Miss, 1919–1920* 24: 29, 105, 145, 155, 157, 174.

20. BP, I, Louis Cockran, June 4, 1965; *Mississippian,* Mar. 24, 1920; I, WF, *New York Herald Tribune,* Nov. 14, 1931.

21. *Mississippian,* May 12, 1920.

22. WF, letter to the editor, *Mississippian,* Apr. 7, 1920. For a discussion of Faulkner and the *Mississippian,* see: Carvel Collins, "Introduction" in WF, *Early Prose and Poetry,* ed. Carvel Collins (Boston: Little, Brown, 1962), 13–17.

23. BW, 32.

24. Calvin S. Brown, "Faulkner Manhunts: Fact Into Fiction," *Georgia Review* 20 (Winter, 1966): 388–95.

25. *Mississippian,* Nov. 10, 1920.

26. BW, 49; BW Pamphlet.

27. BP, I, BW, Mar. 25, 1965. See also: BP, I, Ella Somerville, Nov. 18, 1966.

28. *Mississippian,* Feb. 16, 1921.

29. *MBB,* 142; BP, I, Branham Hume, Nov. 23, 1965.

30. BP, I, E, n.d.; also Dec. 13, 1964.

31. *TOE,* Sept. 15, 1921; Stark Young to Eldon J. Hoar, printed in *Stark Young: A Life in the Arts, Letters, 1900–1962,* ed. John Pilkington, (Baton Rouge: Louisiana State University Press, 1975), 2: 1155–56; Stark Young, "New Year's Crow," *New Republic* 83, no. 1206 (Jan. 12, 1938): 283.

32. Michael Millgate, *The Achievement of William Faulkner* (New York: Random House, 1966), 9, citing an interview with Elizabeth Prall by University of Wisconsin Professor Walter B. Rideout; as reported in Rideout letter to Millgate, Dec. 14, 1963; Marshall J. Smith, "Faulkner of Mississippi," *Bookman* 74, no. 4 (Dec., 1931): 416; BP, I, Elizabeth Prall Anderson, Jan. 28–30, 1966.

33. Millgate, *Achievement,* 9; BP, I, Elizabeth Prall Anderson, Jan. 28–30, 1965.

34. *PSO,* 135; "Early Notices of Faulkner by Phil Stone and Louis Cochran," ed. James B. Meriwether, *Mississippi Quarterly* 17 (Summer, 1964): 148–64; BP, I, E, Sept. 9, 1965.

35. BP, I, Branham Hume, Nov. 23, 1965.

36. BP, I, A.P. Hudson, Apr. 4, 1965.

37. Emily Whitehurst Stone, "Faulkner Gets Started," *Texas Quarterly* 8 (Winter, 1965): 146–47.

38. Phil Stone, letter to the editor, *Saturday Review of Literature* 42 (June 27, 1959): 23.

39. BP, I, Mrs. Frank A. Conkling (Eula Dorothy Wilcox), Mar. 16, 1965.

40. *SLWF,* 6, WF to the Four Seas Company, Nov. 23, 1923.

41. BP, I, J.D. Thames, Nov. 29, 1965.

42. FCVA, note, John W.T. Falkner, III, to F, Jan. 26, 1924.

43. Wisdom Collection at Tulane University, *Mayday* (Notre Dame, Ind.: University of Notre Dame Press, 1980), intro. Carvel Collins, p. 15; *PSO,* 359, note 41.

44. BP, I, C.C. Hathorn, Nov. 18, 1967; I, Dot, Nov. 17, 1967; I, R.P. Warren, Jan. 19, 1966.

45. JB, 115.

46. MCF, *The Falkners of Mississippi: A Memoir* (Baton Rouge: Lousiana State University Press, 1967), 111.

47. *TOE,* Jan. 1, 1920.

48. BP, copy, report card, University of Mississippi; I, Jimmy Faulkner, Nov. 14, 1966; I, Taylor McElroy, Nov. 18, 1967.

49. BP, I, SM, Nov. 26, 1965.

50. BP, I, Taylor McElroy, Nov. 18, 1967.

51. PSY, 329; Stone, "Faulkner Gets Started," 142. See also: *PSO,* 360, note 59.

52. BW, 63; BP, I, BW, Mar. 28, 1965.

53. FCVA, typescript.

54. *New Yorker* 46 (Nov. 21, 1970): 50.

55. *Memphis Commercial Appeal,* Dec. 14, 1950.

56. BP, Hubert S. Lipscomb to JB, Sept. 21, 1965.

57. James K. Feibleman, "Literary New Orleans Between Wars," *Southern Review,* n.s., 1 (July, 1965): 705–6.

58. *Double Dealer* 3 (June, 1922): 337.

59. BP, I, Mrs. Julius Friend, Feb. 3, 1965; *FIU,* 230.

60. BP, I, Anita Loos, Apr. 22, 1965; I, Albert Goldstein, Feb. 2, 1965.

61. Hamilton Basso, "William Faulkner: Man and Writer," *Saturday Review of Literature* 45 (July 28, 1962): 11.

62. *TOE,* Dec. 4, 1925.

63. BP, I, Elizabeth Prall Anderson, Jan. 29, 1965.

64. Basso, "William Faulkner," 12; WS, "Chronicle of A Friendship: William Faulkner in New Orleans," *Texas Quarterly* 9 (Spring, 1966): 35.

65. BP, I, Elizabeth Prall Anderson, Jan. 29, 1965; I, JB to MCF, Aug. 5, 1966.

66. WS, "Chronicle," 35; Sherwood Anderson, *We Moderns: Gotham Book Mart,*

1920–1940 (New York: 1940), 29.

67. WF, "Verse Old and Nascent: A Pilgrimage," *Double Dealer* 7 (Apr., 1925): 129–31; *Early Prose and Poetry,* ed. Carvel Collins (Boston: Little, Brown, 1962), 114–18.

68. *Double Dealer* 7 (Jan.–Feb., 1925): 83–84, 102–107; 7 (Apr., 1925): 129–31; *Faulkner Studies* 3 (Winter, 1954): 46–53.

69. WF, *William Faulkner: New Orleans Sketches,* ed. Carvel Collins (New York: Random House, 1968), 55.

70. "And Now What's To Do," *A Faulkner Miscellany,* ed. James B. Meriwether (Jackson: University Press of Mississippi, 1974), 145–48.

71. Jean Stein, "The Art of Fiction," *Paris Review* 3, no. 12 (Spring, 1956): 47.

72. BP, I, Samuel Louis Gilmore, Feb. 3, 1965.

73. BP, I, Harold Levy, Feb. 5, 1965.

74. Sherwood Anderson, "A Meeting South," *Dial* 78 (Apr., 1925): 269–79.

75. BP, I, Keith Temple, Feb. 5, 1965; I, Mrs. Flo Field, Feb. 3, 1965.

76. BP, I, Anita Loos, Apr. 22, 1965.

77. BP, I, Harold Levy, Feb. 5, 1965.

78. BP, I, Mrs. Louis Andrews Fischer, Feb. 2, 1965; Hodding Carter, "The Forgiven Faulkner," *Journal of Inter-American Studies* 7, no. 2 (Apr., 1965): 137–38.

79. BP, I, Anita Loos, Apr. 22, 1965.

80. Sherwood Anderson, "A Meeting South," *Dial* 78 (Apr., 1925): 269–79.

81. Sherwood Anderson to WF, n.d., 1927, *Letters of Sherwood Anderson,* ed. Howard Mumford Jones with Walter B. Rideout (Boston: Little, Brown, 1935), 162–64; Spratling, "Chronicle," 35–36; WF, "Sherwood Anderson: An Appreciation," *Atlantic Monthly* 191 (June, 1953): 27–29.

82. WF, "Sherwood Anderson," 29; BP, I, Elizabeth Prall Anderson, Jan. 29, 1965.

83. Sherwood Anderson to Horace Liveright, June 1, 1925, *Sherwood Anderson, Selected Letters,* ed. Charles E. Modlin (Knoxville: University of Tennessee Press, 1984), 69–70.

84. Louis Kronenberger, "Gambler in Publishing: Horace Liveright," *Atlantic Monthly* 215 (Jan., 1965): 100.

85. Wisdom Collection at Tulane, WF to HB, n.d. (late–1930s); BP, I, WS, Jan. 29–30, 1965.

86. BP, I, Carl and Betty Carmer, Aug. 23, 1965; I, Jim Lyman, June 19, 1965; I, Ann Farnsworth, Mar. 30, 1965.

87. Wisdom Collection, WF to HB, n.d.

88. BP, I, Jim and Helen Baird Lyman, June 19, 1965.

89. BP, I, Carl and Betty Carmer, Aug. 23, 1965.

90. BP, I, Jim and Helen Baird Lyman, June 19, 1965.

91. Wisdom Collection, WF to HB, n.d., (1937).

92. BP, I, Jim and Helen Baird Lyman, June 19, 1965.

93. Wisdom Collection, WF to HB, n.d.

94. WS, "Chronicle," 36.

95. JB, 154–56.

96. WS, "Chronicle," 38; *Sherwood Anderson & Other Famous Creoles* (Austin: University of Texas Press, 1966).

97. BP, I, BW, Mar. 28, 1965.

98. BP, I, Emily Stone, Mar. 27, 1965; WS, "Chronicle," 38; Emily Whitehurst Stone, "How A Writer Finds His Material," *Harper's* 231 (Nov., 1965): 158.

99. FCVA, typescript, *A Portrait of Elmer.* Also: WF, ms. 1, "Elmer" and "A Portrait of Elmer," introduced and arranged by Thomas L. McHaney (New York: Garland, 1987).

100. *SLWF,* 23–25, WF to MF, (Sept. 22, 1925).

101. FCVA, "Elmer" typescript, 110.

102. *SLWF,* 23–25, WF to MF, (Sept. 22, 1925).

103. *SLWF,* 22, WF to MF, Sept 13, 1925.

104. BP, WF to MF, Sept. 10, 1925.

105. BP, I, Helen Baird Lyman, June 19, 1965.

106. BP, I, Douglas Schneider, Jan. n.d., 1965.

107. BP, I, William C. Odiorne, June 7, 1965; I, Joan Williams Bowen, Nov. 15, 1965.

108. BP, William H. Hoffman to JB, Oct. 1, 25, 1965.

109. BP, I, Harold Levy, Feb. 5, 1965; I, William C. Ordione, June 7, 1965; William H. Hoffman to JB, Oct. 1, 1965.

110. FCVA, WF to Mrs. Walter B. McLean, (Sept. 10, 1925). Also: *SLWF,* 17–18, WF to MF, Sept. 6, 1925.

111. *SLWF,* 27–28, WF to MF, Oct. 3, 1925; BP, WF to MF, Sept. 28, (1925).

112. *SLWF,* 29–31, WF to MF, (Oct. 9, 1925).

113. Sherwood Anderson to Horace Liveright, Apr. 19, 1926, *Letters of Sherwood Anderson,* 154–55.

114. *Helen: A Courtship and Mississippi Poems* (New Orleans and Oxford: Tulane University and Yoknapatawpha Press, 1981), intros. Carvel Collins and JB, 19.

115. BP, I, MCF, Mar. 31, 1965; *Helen: A Courtship,* 19; *MBB,* 155.

116. James G. Watson, "Literary Self-Criticism: Faulkner in Fiction on Fiction," *Southern Literary Quarterly* 30 (Fall, 1981): 51.

117. Wisdom Collection, Tulane.

118. WF, "Divorce in Naples," in *Collected Stories of William Faulkner* (New York: Random House, 1950), 879–80.

119. James A. Wobbe, "How Faulkner Wrote Sonnet," *New Orleans Item,* Aug. 29, 1954, p. 18.

120. WF, *Uncollected Stories of William Faulkner,* ed. Joseph Blotner (New York: Random House, 1979), 352–67.

121. FCVA, *Mosquitoes* typescript, reverse, p. 269; Wisdom Collection, "Helen: A Courtship."

122. BP, I, BW, Mar. 28, 1965.

123. BP, I, Marjorie Gumbel, Dec. 28, 1965.

124. Wisdom Collection, WF to HB, n.d. At that point, he was probably writing *Sartoris.*

125. BP, I, Jim and Helen Baird Lyman, June 19, 1965.

126. FCVA, WF to Horace Liveright, (July, 1927).

127. FCVA, WF to Horace Liveright, (Oct. 16, 1927).

128. FCVA, Horace Liveright to WF, (Nov. 25, 1927).

129. William R. Ferris, Jr., "William Faulkner and Phil Stone," *South Atlantic Quarterly* 68 (Autumn, 1969): 540–41. See also: Emily Stone, "Faulkner Gets Started," 144; Introduction to the Modern Library edition of *Sanctuary,* vi; *PSO,* 202.

130. FCVA, WF to Horace Liveright, (Nov. 30, 1927).

131. Kronenberger, "Gambler," 95.

132. "An Introduction," ed. James B. Meriwether, *Southern Review,* n.s., 8 (Autumn, 1972): 709.

133. Leon Howard, "The Composition of *The Sound and The Fury,*" *Missouri Review* 5 (Winter, 1981–1982):115; "An Introduction to *The Sound and the Fury,*" *Mississippi Quarterly* 26 (Summer, 1973): 415; *LIG,* 146–47.

134. BW, 76–77.
135. BW, 76.
136. BP, I, BW, Mar. 28, 1965.
137. BW, 79.
138. BW, 79–81.
139. *TOE,* June 2, 1921.
140. JB, 96–98.
141. BP, I, Ella Somerville, Aug. 18, 1964.
142. BP, I, Eula Dorothy Wilcox, Mar. 16, 1965.
143. BP, I, BW, Nov. 20, 1965; I, Eula Dorothy Wilcox, Mar. 16, 1965; I, WS, Taxco, Mexico, Jan. 28, 29, 30, 1968.
144. BP, I, Eula Dorothy Wilcox, Mar. 16, 1965; I, Sallie M. Crane, Mar. 25, 1965; I, Branham Hume, Nov. 23, 1965.
145. BP, I, Carl and Betty Carmer, Aug. 23, 1965.
146. BP, I, E, n.d.
147. BP, I, Samuel Louis Gilmore, Feb. 3, 1965. Also note by JB.
148. BP, I, Harold Levy, Feb. 5, 1965; I, William H. Hoffman, Oct. 1, 1965.
149. BP, I, E, Feb. 23, 1965.
150. BP, I, Tom Kell, Mar. 30, 1965.
151. Wisdom Collection, WF to HB, n.d. (late 1930s).
152. BP, I, E, Apr. 18, 1968.
153. BP, I, Katrina Carter, Nov. 21, 1965.
154. *TOE,* June 5, 1919.
155. BP, I, Dot, Nov. 14, 1967.
156. Gravestone, Oldham plot, St. Peter's Cemetery, Oxford.
157. *TOE,* Feb. 13, 1919.
158. Wisdom Collection, Estelle (Franklin) to Mary Vic (Mills), n.d., (1919).
159. *TOE,* Oct. 2, 1919.
160. *TOE,* May 12, June 6, Oct. 13, 21, 1921.
161. BP, I, Dot, Nov. 14, 1966; I, E, Feb. 23, 1965.
162. *TOE,* July 8, 1920.
163. *TOE,* June 2, 1920, June 23, 1921.
164. *PSO,* 134–36; BP, I, E, Sept. 9, 1965.
165. *TOE,* Dec. 4, 1924.
166. *TOE,* Mar. 5, 1925.
167. *TOE,* Mar. 17, 1926.
168. *TOE,* July 7, 1926.
169. BP, I, E, n.d., and Aug. n.d., 1963; I, Victoria Fielden, Oct. 27, 1964.
170. *TOE,* Jan. 17, 1927.
171. BP, I, SM, Nov. 23, 1965; Nov. 15, 1967; I, E, n.d.
172. BP, I, SM, Nov. 15, 1967; I, Jimmy Faulkner, Nov. 14, 1966.
173. BP, I, E, n.d., and Aug. n.d., 1963.
174. BP, I, SM, Nov. 15, 1967.
175. JB, 189.
176. BP, I, E, n.d., and Aug. n.d., 1963.
177. *TOE,* Mar. 9, 1927.
178. BP, I, Robert Farley, Apr. 3, 1965.
179. BP, I, E, n.d., 1965.
180. FCVA, ms. "Star Spangled Banner Stuff."

181. *TOE,* June 2, 1927.

182. BC, transcribed copy, WF to Bama McLean, (datelined Oxford, Thursday, probably Sept. 29, 1927).

466

183. FCVA, WF to Horace Liveright, Oct. 15, 1927; Horace Liveright to WF, Oct. 20, 1927.

184. Howard, "Composition," 115.

185. *TOE,* Apr. 5, 19, 1928.

186. BP, I, Jim Meriwether, Jan. 24, 1968; ms. note on typed sheet, "Ole Miss 1916."

187. BP, I, Mac Reed, Nov. 16, 1966.

188. BP, I, Victoria Fielden, Oct. 27, 1964.

189. BP, I, Mrs. Almond Coleman (Louise Hudson), Oct. 10, 1965.

190. BW, 84–89.

191. BP, I, BW, Mar. 28, 1967.

192. BP, I, Owen Crump, June 9, 1966.

193. Introduction to the Modern Library edition of *Sanctuary,* 1964, vi.

194. JB, 239.

195. Ibid., 237.

196. BP, I, SM, Nov. 14, 1967; Mar. 22, 1971.

197. BP, I, SM, Nov. 14, 1967.

198. New York Public Library, Berg Collecion, WF to Harrison Smith, (late May, early June, 1929).

199. BP, I, E, Aug. 22, 1964; I, JW, Aug. 22, 1965.

200. BP, I, E, Summer, 1965; LCCH-CC, Marriage Record Book W, p. 404, June 20, 1929.

201. JB, 240–41.

202. BP, I, Victoria Fielden, Oct. 27, 1964; I, SM, Nov. 14, 1967; I, Mrs. Almond Coleman, Oct. 10, 1967; I, E, Apr. 26, 1967.

203. BP, I, Rosebud and Myrtle Stone, Mar. 30, 1965; I, Mrs. Martin Shepherd, Mar. 31, 1965.

204. BP, I, E, Apr. 26, 1967; I, Victoria Fielden, Oct. 27, 1964.

205. BP, I, Ann Farnsworth, Mar. 30, 1965.

206. BP, I, Mrs. Martin Shepherd, Mar. 31, 1965; I, Tom Kell, Mar. 30, 1965.

207. BP, I, Mrs. Martin Shepherd, Mar. 31, 1965; I, Ann Farnsworth, Mar. 30, 1965.

208. BP, I, MCF, Mar. 31, 1965.

209. BP, clipping (perhaps *The Cavalier*), n.d.

SEVEN

1. Introduction to the Modern Library edition of *Sanctuary,* 1964, vii.
2. FCVA, WF to Mrs. Walter B. McLean, (probably Oct. 1929); BP, I, Howard Duvall, Nov. 17, 1966.
3. *TOE,* Oct. 24, 1929; BP, I, Robert Farley, Apr. 3, 1965.
4. JB, 247– 48; BP, I, SM, Nov. 14, 1966.
5. *TOE,* Dec. 23, 1920; Jan. 6, June 21, 1921.
6. *TOE,* Aug. 21, 1919, et seq.
7. *TOE,* Oct. 3, 1929.
8. *TOE,* Sept. 26, 1929.
9. JB, 248; *PSO,* 203–4.

10. Emily Whitehurst Stone, "Faulkner Gets Started," *Texas Quarterly* 8 (Winter, 1965): 146.

11. *Forum* 83 (Apr., 1930): 233–38.

12. *Saturday Evening Post* 203 (Sept. 6, 1930): 16–17, 78, 82.

13. FCVA, WF to BW, (Spring, 1930).

14. LCCH-ChC, Circuit Court Minutes of the Probate Court, Lafayette County, Apr. 18, 1853–Aug. 7, 1856.

15. BP, copy, deed, Apr. 12, 1930.

16. *TOE,* July 31, 1930; BP, I, Victoria Fielden, Oct. 27, 1964; I, Malcolm Franklin, Sept. 26, 1966.

17. BP, I, MCF, Mar. 31, 1965.

18. LCCH-ChC, Deed Record, Book 97, p. 136 indicates that John's wife, Sue Harkins Falkner, sold the lot to the Standard Oil Company on Dec. 2, 1927, for $5,000; BP, I, SM, Nov. 15, 1967.

19. BP, copy, deed, Apr. 12, 1930.

20. *TOE,* Feb. 14, 1929.

21. *TOE,* June 26, 1930.

22. *TOE,* Sept. 4, 18, 25, 1930; BP, I, Mrs. Byron Gathright, Nov. 27, 1965; *William Faulkner of Oxford,* eds. James W. Webb and A. Wigfall Green (Baton Rouge: Louisiana State University Press, 1965), 91.

23. JB, 266–67.

24. BC, telegram, WF to Mrs. Walter B. McLean, Jan. 19, 1931.

25. BP, SM, Nov. 15, 1967; I, Victoria Fielden, Oct. 27, 1964.

26. BC, telegram, Holland Porter to 'Bama McLean, Jan. 20, 1931.

27. BP, I, SM, Aug. 19, 1965.

28. JB, 273–74.

29. BP, I, Mrs. Demarest, Dec. 30, 1966.

30. BW, 106–8.

31. BP, I, Manuel Komroff, Jan. 22, 1965.

32. BP, I, Paul Green, Oct. 16, 1968.

33. BC, PS to Robert Coughlan, Oct. 10, 1952.

34. William Faulkner Collection, Princeton University, WF to Alfred Dashiell, Feb. 25, 1931.

35. Andrew Scott Berg, *Max Perkins: Editor of Genius* (New York: Dutton, 1978), 226–27.

36. For example, see: Granville Hicks, "The Past and the Future of William Faulkner," *Bookman* 74 (Sept., 1931): 17–24.

37. James B. Meriwether, "Faulkner Lost and Found," *New York Times Book Review* (Nov. 5, 1972): 7.

38. *SLWF,* 51, WF to James Southall Wilson, Sept. 24, 1931.

39. BP, I, Dayton Kohler, Dec. 31, 1964; I, Lewis Mattison, n.d.

40. Donald Davidson, "A Meeting of Southern Writers," *Bookman* 74 (Feb., 1932): 459–96.

41. Emily Clark, "A Week-end at Mr. Jefferson's University," *New York Herald Tribune Books* (Nov. 8, 1931): 1–2; BP, I, Dayton Kohler, Dec. 31, 1964.

42. Josephine Pinckney, "Southern Writers' Congress," *Saturday Review of Literature* 8 (Nov. 7, 1931): 266.

43. Davidson, "A Meeting," 496; Pinckney, "Southern Writers' Congress," 266.

44. Davidson, "A Meeting," 494–97.

45. BP, copy, letter, Allen Tate to Virginia __, Oct. 31, 1931.

46. BP, I, E, n.d. and Aug. n.d., 1963; I, Lee Devin, Aug. 3, 1966; I, Paul Green, Oct. 16, 1968.

47. BP, I, Dayton Kohler, Dec. 31, 1964; I, Mrs. James Southall Wilson, Mar. 9, 1965.

48. Sherwood Anderson to Laura Lou Copenhaver, Oct. 24, 1931, *Letters of Sherwood Anderson,* ed. Howard Mumford Jones (Boston: Little , Brown, 1953), 252.

49. Sherwood Anderson to John Lineaweaver, (Dec. 28, 1931), in *Sherwood Anderson, Selected Letters,* 142–43.

50. JB, 286–87.

51. FCVA, WF to Harrison Smith, (mid-Jan., 1932).

52. *SLWF,* 52–53, WF to E, (Nov. 4, 1931).

53. Maurice Edgar Coindreau, "The Faulkner I Knew," *Shenandoah* 16 (Winter, 1965): 27–35.

54. *SLWF,* 53–54, WF to E, (Nov. 13, 1931).

55. BP, copy, letter, Alfred A. Knopf to JB, Aug. 7, 1968; I, Lillian Hellman, Jan. 17, 1965.

56. BP, copy, letter, Alfred A. Knopf to JB, Aug. 7. 1968; I, Bennett A. Cerf, Sept. 20, 1967.

57. Paul Gardner, "Faulkner Remembered," in *A Faulkner Perspective* (Franklin Center, PA, 1976), 17.

58. Albert Isaac Bezzerides, *William Faulkner: A Life on Paper,* ed. Ann J. Abadie (Jackson: University Press of Mississippi, 1980), 68.

59. FCVA, WF to Harrison Smith, (early Jan., 1932).

60. JB, 303.

61. BP, I, Louise Bonino, Nov. 11, 1964.

62. FCVA, WF to BW, (late Winter, 1932); (Spring, 1932).

63. FCVA, WF to BW, (Apr., 1932).

64. JB, 302–3.

65. *Faulkner's MGM Screenplays,* ed. Bruce F. Kawin (Knoxville: University of Tennessee Press, 1982), xxiii–xxiv; *New York Times,* Dec. 23, 1932.

66. *SLWF,* 64–65, WF to E, (June 2, 1932).

67. FCVA, WF to BW, (Sept. 25, 1932).

68. BP, I, David Hempstead, June 12, 1965.

69. BP, I, Howard Hawks, June 3, 1965; I, Howard Hawks, *La Quinzaine* 32 (July, 1967): 28–29; Kawin, *MGM Screenplays,* xxvi–xxviii.

70. BP, Nancy Keith to JB, Mar. 10, 1966; Slim Keith (Mrs. Kenneth Keith) to JB, (Apr. 15, 1966).

71. Panthea Reid Broughton, "An Interview with Meta Carpenter Wilde," *Southern Review* 18 (Oct., 1982): 788.

72. FCVA, WF to BW, (Sept. 25, 1932).

73. Meriwether, "Faulkner Lost and Found," 7.

74. FCVA, WF to Morton Goldman, (late Winter–early Spring, 1934).

75. BP, I, Dot, Dec. 21, 1966; *TOE,* Dec. 4, 1931.

76. BP, I, SM, n.d.

77. BP, I, Taylor H. McElroy, Mar. 23, 1965.

78. *TOE,* May 22, 1930.

79. BP, in Dot Oldham folder, obituary clipping, Mar. 21, 1965; I, SM, n.d.

80. BP, I, SM, Nov. 23, 1965; I, Victoria Fielden Johnson by Louis Daniel Brodsky,

May 20–24, 1985, et. seq., in Louis Daniel Brodsky, *William Faulkner, Life Glimpses* (Austin: University of Texas Press, 1990), 133, 136, 145, 151–53, 155–56.

81. *TOE,* June 27, 1933.

82. Malcolm Franklin, *Bitterweeds, Life at Rowan Oak with William Faulkner* (Irving, TX: Society for the Study of Traditional Culture, 1977), 46.

83. BP, WF to E, (two letters, July 21, 1934).

84. FCVA, WF to Harrison Smith, (July 20, 1933).

85. FCVA, WF to Morton Goldman, July 29, (1934).

86. BP, I, E.O. Champion, Mar. 22, 1965.

87. BP, I, E, Mar. 2, 1965.

88. BP, I, E.O. Champion, Mar. 22, 23, 1965.

89. BP, I, E.O. Champion, Mar. 23, 1965.

90. BP, I, Louise (Hale) Meadow, Nov. 26, 27, 1965.

91. MCF, *The Falkners of Mississippi: A Memoir* (Baton Rouge: Louisiana State University Press, 1967), 129–32.

92. BP, I, Louise Meadow, Mar. 19, 1965; I, SM, Mar. 19, 1965; I, Nunnally Johnson, Apr. 23, 1965.

93. BP, I, SM, Mar. 19, 1965.

94. Falkner plot, St. Peter's Cemetery, Oxford.

95. BP, I, Louise (Hale) Meadow, Nov. 26, 1965.

96. BP, I, SM, Mar., 1965.

97. BP, I, E, Dec. 9, 1964.

98. FCVA, WF to Harrison Smith, (Feb., 1934).

99. "An Introduction to *The Sound and the Fury,*" *Mississippi Quarterly* 26 (Summer, 1973): 410, 412.

100. Meriwether, "Faulkner Lost and Found," 7.

101. Darden Asbury Pyron, *Southern Daughter: The Life of Margaret Mitchell* (New York: Oxford University Press, 1991), 308–9.

102. *FIU,* 76.

103. FCVA, WF to Morton Goldman, (late July, 1935).

104. *SLWF,* 93, WF to E, (Oct. 5, 1935).

105. *LG,* 17–18; U.S. Census, 1910, TN, Shelby, e.d. 271, sheet 11B, 733 Lucy Avenue extended.

106. *LG,* 27.

107. *LG,* 22.

108. *LG,* 22, 30–41, 47–53, 56–57.

109. *LG,* 65–66.

110. BP, I, David Hempstead, June 15, 1965; JB, 365.

111. Broughton, "An Interview," 777.

112. Abadie, *William Faulkner,* 31–32.

113. *SLWF,* 94–95, WF to E, (Mar. 2, 1936).

114. *SLWF,* 95, WF to E, (Mar. 9, 1936).

115. FCVA, WF to Morton Goldman, (late Mar., 1936); WF to E, (Apr. 28, 1936), Jill Faulkner Summers Private Archive (JFSPA), cited in JB, 368; WF to E, (May 16, 1936), JFSPA, cited in JB, 368.

116. BP, I, David Hempstead, June 6, 1966.

117. Broughton, "An Interview," 788.

118. Meta Carpenter Wilde and Orin Borsten, *A Loving Gentleman: The Love Story of William Faulkner and Meta Carpenter* (New York: Simon and Schuster, 1976).

119. BP, JB to "Buzz" (Albert Isaac Bezzerides), May 27, 1966; JB to "Buzz," May 31, 1980; Broughton, "An Interview," 779–80.

120. BP, I, E, June n.d., 1966.

121. JB (1974), 932; *LG,* 141; BP; JB (1984), photographic insert, correctly captioned, 332–33.

122. Broughton, "An Interview," 779.

123. *LG,* 42.

124. *LG,* 26–27; Broughton, "An Interview," 780, 792.

125. *Light in August,* 161–62.

126. *LG,* 23–24, 47–48, 50.

127. *LG* 45–47; Broughton, "An Interview," 780–81.

128. *LG,* 22, 24, 52.

129. Broughton, "An Interview," 797.

130. *LG,* 62.

131. Ibid.

132. *LG,* 75; Broughton, "An Interview," 781, 782–83.

133. Broughton, "An Interview," 783–84; Carvel Emerson Collins, introduction to *The William B. Wisdom Collection: A Descriptive Catalogue* (New Orleans: Tulane University Libraries, 1980), xvii.

134. *LG,* 77, 81; Broughton, "An Interview," 793.

135. *LG,* 52.

136. JB (1974) 65; *LG,* 142.

137. *SLWF,* 64, 82–83, 94–95, 95.

138. *LG,* 126–27.

139. BW, 141–44.

140. Broughton, "An Interview," 777; *LG,* 103; *Memphis Commercial Appeal,* June 22, 1936; *TOE,* June 25, 1936.

141. JB, 371–72; *Time,* July 6, 1935, p. 36.

142. *LG,* 127–28, 167.

143. BC, Estelle Faulkner to Malcolm and Victoria Franklin, (July 27, 1936).

144. *LG,* 171–75.

145. BW, 149; Broughton, "An Interview," 777, 789–90

146. Broughton, "An Interview," 777, 791.

147. *LG,* 196; Broughton, "An Interview," 790–91.

148. Broughton, "An Interview," 776–801.

149. *New Yorker* 12 (Oct. 31, 1936): 62–64.

150. FCVA, WF to Morton Goldman, Sept. 4, 1936.

151. BP, I, Joel Sayre, Nov. 9, 1964.

152. BP, I, WS, Jan. 28–30, 1965.

153. Broughton, "An Interview," 777.

154. BP, I, E, Oct. 27, 1964; I, Jimmy Faulkner, Nov. 15, 1966.

155. I, Victoria Fielden Johnson by Louis D. Brodsky, in Brodsky, *Life Glimpses,* 132–41.

156. FCVA, WF to Victoria Franklin Selby, n.d., 1937.

157. BW, 156; *SLWF,* 101, WF to E, (July 28, 1937).

158. *SLWF,* 106–7, WF to Robert K. Haas, July 8, 1938.

159. *TOE,* Sept. 23, 1937.

160. BP, I, Victoria Fielden, Oct. 28, 1964; Joel Williamson, private archive, I, Sissy and Mario Prodhon, Sept, 21, 1987; The Prodhons lived in Shanghai between the wars

and knew both Cornell Franklin and William Fielden, the man Vickie subsequently married, very well.

161. BP, I, Victoria Fielden, Oct. 24, 1964.

162. Sherwood Anderson to Laura Copenhaver, (Nov. 11, 1937), in *Sherwood Anderson, Selected Letters,* 213–14.

163. Broughton, "An Interview," 794–96.

164. FCVA, WF to Morton Goldman, Feb. 28, 1938.

165. LCCH-ChC, Deed Record, Book III, pp. 46-47, 79.

166. BP, I, Jimmy Faulkner, Mar. 21, 1965.

167. BP, clipping, *Ripley Southern Sentinel,* July 19, 1962.

168. Franklin, *Bitterweeds,* 114.

169. BP, I, Jimmy Faulkner, Nov. 14, 1966; Wisdom Collection, WF to Malcolm Franklin, (Dec., 1954).

170. RPL, extracts, U.S. Census, 1900, p. 7.

171. RPL, extracts, U.S. Census, 1880, p. 9.

172. TCCH-CC, Marriage Records, Book 2, p. 233; RPL, extracts, U.S. Census, 1900, p. 7.

173. U.S. Census, 1910, MS, Tippah, e.d. 97, "Ripley town," sheets 3–4, hhs. # 57–63.

174. Wisdom Collection, item 3A, quoted by Chancery Judge William Anderson, Tippah County.

175. Gravestone, St. Peter's Cemetery, Oxford; BC, newspaper clipping, *Memphis Commercial Appeal.*

176. BC, will, Mar. 27, 1940.

177. BP, clipping, *Ripley Southern Sentinel,* July 19, 1962, William Anderson, "Comments on William Faulkner and the Faulkner Family."

178. Franklin, *Bitterweeds,* 116.

179. *Time,* Jan. 23, 1939, 45–46, 48.

180. *SLWF,* 107–8, WF to Robert Haas, Dec. 15, 1938.

181. *SLWF,* 113, WF to Robert Haas, Apr. 24, 1939.

182. *SLWF,* 115, WF to SC, (Oct., 1939).

183. *SLWF,* 111, 112–13, 116, WF to Robert Haas, (Mar. 22, 1939), (Mar. 29, 1939), (Dec. 7, 1939).

184. SLWF, 116, 122–23, WF to Robert Haas, (Dec. 7, 1939), (May 3, 1940).

185. *LG,* pp. 60, 63, 64, 136–37.

186. FCVA, WF to Harold Ober, (Aug. 5, 1940), (Jan. 18, 1941).

187. *SLWF,* 146, WF to Robert Haas, Dec. 2, (1941).

188. *SLWF,* 139, WF to Robert Haas, May 1, 1941.

189. *SLWF,* 125, WF to Robert Haas, (May 27, 1940).

190. *SLWF,* 141, WF to Robert Haas, (June 30, 1941).

191. *SLWF,* 152, WF to Bennett Cerf, (June 6, 1942); Wisdom Collection, WF to Mrs. B.I. Wiley, (June 23, 1942).

192. FCVA, WF to Harold Ober, (Nov. 10, 1941), (June 25, 1942).

193. FCVA, WF to Harold Ober, (June 22, 1942).

194. *SLWF,* 127–29, WF to Robert Haas, (June 7, 1940).

195. *SLWF,* 154–55, WF to Bennett Cerf, (June 23, 1942).

196. FCVA, WF to Harold Ober, Aug. 1, 1942.

197. BP, copy, WF to Robert Haas, Mar. 6, 1940.

198. *LG,* 241–42, 276.

199. See introductory essay by Robert W. Hamblin in *Faulkner: A Comprehensive Guide to the Brodsky Collection,* eds. Louis Daniel Brodsky and Robert W. Hamblin, vol. 3, *The de Gaulle Story* (Jackson: University Press of Mississippi, 1984), pp. ix–xxxii.

200. FCVA, WF to Harold Ober, (Jan. 25, 1943).

201. *SLWF,* 181, WF to Mrs. William F. Fielden (Victoria, or "Vickie"), (Apr. 30, 1944); *LG,* 300–3, 307–8.

202. *SLWF,* 194–95, WF to E, (July 26, 1945).

203. *SLWF,* 180, WF to Robert Haas, (Jan. 15, 1944).

204. BC, Finlay McDermid to Steve Trilling, Aug. 31, 1945.

205. *SLWF,* 182, WF to Malcolm Cowley, May 7, (1944).

206. *SLWF,* 184–86, WF to Malcolm Cowley, (end Nov., 1944).

207. *SLWF,* 196–98, 210–11, WF to Malcolm Cowley, (Aug. 16, 1945); WF to Robert Haas, (Dec. 4, 1945).

208. *SLWF,* 233, WF to Malcolm Cowley, (Apr. 23, 1946).

209. FCVA, WF to Harold Ober, Feb. 1, (1948).

210. James Dahl, "A Faulkner Reminiscence: Conversations with Mrs. Maud Falkner," *Journal of Modern Literature* 3 (April 1974): 1029.

211. *PSO,* 122.

212. *SLWF,* 175, WF to Robert Haas, (July 1, 1943).

213. Wisdom Collection, WF to Malcolm Franklin, (July 4, 1943).

214. *SLWF,* 269–70, WF to Bennett Cerf, (July 13, 1948).

215. I, Victoria Fielden Johnson by L.D. Brodsky, in Brodsky, *Life Glimpses,* 157–62.

216. *SLWF,* 285, WF to Malcolm Cowley, (Feb. 11, 1949).

217. BC, Robert Daniel to 'Bama McLean, July 15, 1942.

218. JB, 485.

219. FCVA, WF to Dayton Kohler, Jan. 10, 1950.

220. *SLWF,* 302, WF to Mark Van Doren, Apr. 1, 1950.

221. BP, I, Jill Faulkner Summers, n.d.

222. BP, I, Jill, July 9, 20, 24, 1968.

223. *SLWF,* 219, WF to Malcolm Cowley, (Jan. 21, 1946).

224. *Essays, Speeches, & Public Letters,* ed. James B. Meriwether (New York: Random House, 1966), 119–21.

EIGHT

1. *SLWF,* 292, WF to Robert Haas, July 5, (1949); 281–82, WF to president of the American Academy, Dec. 31, 1948; 277–79, WF to Malcolm Cowley, (Nov. 1, 1948); FCVA, WF to Harold Ober, (July 16, 1948).

2. *SLWF,* 244–45, WF to Malcolm Cowley, (Dec., 1946); I, Albert Isaac Bezzerides, Sept. 2–7, 1983, in Louis Daniel Brodsky, *William Faulkner, Life Glimpses* (Austin: University of Texas Press, 1990), pp. 68–69.

3. FCVA, WF to Harold Ober, (Mar. 24, 1947).

4. BP, I, Ruth Ford, Nov. 13, 1964; FCVA, typescript, "A Portrait of Elmer," p. 4.

5. *SLWF,* 286, WF to Eric J. Divine, (Feb. 23, 1949).

6. Joan Williams, "Twenty Will Not Come Again," *Atlantic Monthly* 145 (May, 1980): 61.

7. BP, I, JW, Nov. 15, 1964; WF to JW, Aug. 31, 1949.

8. Williams, "Twenty," 58–61; BP, WF to JW, Oct. 14, 1949.

9. Williams, "Twenty," 58–59.

10. Ibid., 61–62.
11. FCVA, WF to JW, (Dec. 29, 1949).
12. BP, WF to JW, Oct. 14, 1949.
13. BP, WF to JW, Dec. 31, 1949.
14. BP, I, JW, Aug. 22, 1964.
15. BP, WF to JW, Jan. 7, 1950.
16. BP, WF to JW, Jan. 13, 23, 25, 1950.
17. BP, WF to JW, Mar. 22, Sept. 3, 1950; I, JW, Aug. 22, 1965.
18. FCVA, WF to JW, (Feb. 13, 1950, et seq.); Williams, "Twenty," 63.
19. BP, WF to JW, Feb. 23, 1950.
20. BP, WF to JW, May 9, 1950; I, JW, Apr. 20, 1965.
21. BP, WF to JW, May 9, 1950.
22. BP, WF to JW, Mar. 22, 1950.
23. BP, WF to JW, May 6, 1950.
24. BP, WF to JW, May 9, 1950.
25. BP, WF to JW, May 6, 1950.
26. BP, WF to JW, July 19, 1950; I, JW, Aug. 22, 1965.
27. Williams, "Twenty," 62.
28. BP, WF to JW, Aug. 4, 1950.
29. BP, WF to JW, Aug. 14, 1950.
30. BP, WF to JW, Oct. 3, 1950.
31. BP, WF to JW, Sept. 3, 1950.
32. BP, WF to JW, Oct. 23, 1950.
33. BP, WF to JW, Sept. 3, 1950.
34. BP, WF to JW, Nov. 3, 1950.
35. BP, WF to JW, Feb. 23, 1950.
36. BP, WF to JW, Nov. 15, 1950.
37. BP, WF to JW, Dec. 5, 1950.
38. BP, I, EJ, Mar. 24, 1964; EJ to JB, Sept. 12, 1967.
39. BP, EJ to JB, July 1, 1969.
40. BP, EJ to JB, Sept. 12, 1967.
41. Ibid.
42. Ibid.
43. BP, WF to JW, Jan. 15, 1951; LG, 320.
44. BC, WF to SC, (mid-Feb., late Feb., late Mar.), 1951, telegram, Mar. 29, (two in early Apr.), 1951; Robert K. Haas to WF, Mar. 8, 1951; BP, I, EJ, Mar. 27, 1964.
45. BP, Ruth Ford to JB, July 1, 1973; I, Zachary Scott, Dec. 30, 1964.
46. *SLWF,* 325–26, WF to SC, (Jan., 1952).
47. BP, WF to Monique and Jean Jacques Lange, (June 16, 1952); I, EJ, Mar. 28, May 8, 9, 1964.
48. FCVA, WF to JW, (July 29, 1952).
49. BC, WF to SC, (July 30, 1952).
50. BC, WF to JW, (mid-Aug., 1952); BP, WF to JW, Aug. 4, 1952.
51. Joan Williams, *The Wintering* (New York: Harcourt, 1971), 132– 48.
52. BP, WF to JW, Oct. 18, 1952.
53. *LG,* 323.
54. BC, WF to SC, (early May, 1952).
55. *SLWF,* 339, WF to EJ, (Aug. 19, 1952).
56. BC, WF to SC, (early Sept., Sept. 28, 1952).
57. BC, Personal Narrative, Saxe Commins, Oct. 7–8, 1952.

58. BC, SC to Dorothy Commins, Oct. 8, 1952; SC to Robert Haas and Bennett Cerf, Oct. 8, 1952; Personal Narrative, SC; *SLWF,* 342, WF to EJ, (Oct. 24, 1952).

59. *SLWF,* 334, WF to SC, (June 22, 1952); BP, notebook, M.J.S. Campbell Clinic, Memphis, Sept. 26, 1952, and I, Nov. 14, 1966.

60. BC, WF to SC, Oct. 25, 1952; E to SC, (Oct. 29, 1952); BP, WF to JW, Oct. 24, 1952.

61. BC, signed carbon, WF to SC, (Dec. 9, 1952).

62. BP, I, JW, Aug. 22, 1965; I, Dr. Lever Stewart, Feb. 25, 1966; I, Mrs. Eric P. Mosse and daughter Sybil Taylor, Jan. 21, 1966.

63. BP, WF to JW, Dec. 31, 1952.

64. BP, WF to JW, (Jan. 3, 1952).

65. BP, I, S. Bernard Wortes, Aug. 17, 1965.

66. BP, I, Malcolm Franklin, Sept. 22, 1966.

67. *SLWF,* 346–47, WF to EJ, (Feb. 22, 1953).

68. *SLWF,* 347, WF to EJ, (Mar. 31, 1953).

69. BC, E to Dorothy Commins, (Jan. 8, 1953); PS to George H. Saucier, Oct. 6, 1953.

70. BC, PS to Carvel Collins, (Apr. 20, 1953); WF to SC, (Apr. 24, 1953); E to Dorothy Commins, (June 18, 1953).

71. FCVA, WF to JW, (June 16, 1953); JB, 572; BC, E to Dorothy and Saxe Commins, (July 29, 1953).

72. BC, WF to SC, (Aug. 3, 1953); PS to George S. Saucier, Oct. 6, 1953.

73. BW, 177–89.

74. Wisdom Collection, Tulane University, WF to Malcolm Franklin, (Oct., 1953), in a pamphlet containing William Faulkner's letters to Malcolm Franklin to become an appendix to *Bitterweeds,* published by the Society for the Study of Traditional Culture, Irving, Texas, in 1976.

75. BP, I, JW, Aug. 22, 1965; see also: Williams, *Wintering,* 141–42.

76. BP, WF to JW, (Nov. 21, 1953); Williams, *Wintering,* 279.

77. BC, WF to JW, (Oct., 1953).

78. BP, WF to JW, (Nov. 21, 26, 1953).

79. BC, Howard Hawks to WF, Nov. 16, 1953.

80. BP, Elizabeth Linscott to JB, Oct. 13, 1965.

81. *SLWF,* 355, 357, WF to MF, (Oct. 19, 1953), (Nov. 30, 1953).

82. JB, 583.

83. BP, WF to MF, Dec. 12, 1953, (Dec. 20, 1953); WF to JW, (Dec. 12, 1953).

84. BP, WF to Monique Salomon, (Dec. 21, 1953); EJ to JB, Aug. 17, 1971.

85. BP, I, JS, Sept. 21, 1967.

86. FCVA, WF to JW, (Jan. 11, 1954).

87. BP, Jean Stein vanden Heuvel to JB, Aug. 24, 1969.

88. BP, I, George Plimpton, Feb. 22, 1967.

89. BP, JB to Jean Stein vanden Heuvel, Aug. 1, 1969.

90. BP, Jean Stein vanden Heuvel to JB, Aug. 24, 1969.

91. BP, I, George Garrett, Nov. 7, 1964.

92. BC, WF to SC, Feb. 27, 1954, (Mar. 14, 1954).

93. BC, WF to SC, (Apr. 22, 1953), (Apr. 24, 1953).

94. James Dahl, "A Faulkner Reminiscence: Conversations with Mrs. Maud Falkner," *Journal of Modern Literature* 3, no. 4, (Apr., 1974): 1026–36.

95. BC, E to SC, (Jan. 29, 1954), Feb. 6, 1954.

96. BC, E to SC, (Feb. 11, 1954).

97. BC, E to SC, (Feb. 29 [sic], 1954).

98. BC, E to SC, (Mar., 1954), (Mar. 12. 1954).

99. BC, E to SC, (Apr. 19, 1954).

100. BC, WF to SC, (Apr. 28, 1954).

101. BC, WF to SC, (Apr. 22, 1953); PS to George A. Saucier, Oct. 6, 1953; A.M. Smith to PS, (Oct. 15, 1953); PS to A.M. Smith, (Nov. 25, 1953); BP, I, Jill, July 25, 1968; Wisdom Collection, WF to Mrs. B.I. Wiley, (June 23, 1942).

102. BP, I, Jill, July 8, 9, 1968.

103. BP, I, Jill, Aug. 13, 1968, Aug. 13, 1969.

104. BP, I, Malcolm Franklin, Sept. 26, 1966.

105. BP, I, Jill, Aug. 6, 1968.

106. BP, I, Jill, Aug. 11, 1968.

107. BP, I, James H. Adams, Mar. 26, 1965.

108. BP, SM to JB, Mar. 22, 1971; I, Jill, July 25, 1968.

109. BP, I, Jill, July 25, 1968.

110. Paul Gardner, "Faulkner Remembered," *A Faulkner Perspective* (Franklin Center, PA, 1976): 14–15.

111. BC, WF to SC, Sept. 6, 1951; BP, I, Jill, July 25, 1968; I, E, May 29, 1967; clipping, *TOE,* Feb. 28, 1952.

112. BP, I, Jill, July 25, 1968, Aug. 25, 1969; Jill to WF, Mar. 22, 1954.

113. BP, I, Shelby Foote, Nov. 20, 1965; I, BW, Mar. 28, 1965; I, Dorothy Commins, Aug. 20, 1965; Jane Sanderson, "A Kind of Greatness," *Delta Review* 2 (July–August, 1965): 15–17.

114. BP, clippings, *Washington Post,* June 8, 21, 1961.

115. BC, Jill to WF, (Sept. 20, 1954).

116. BC, WF to SC, (Oct. 26, 1954); Gloria Franklin to Dorothy and Saxe Commins, (Oct. 31, 1964).

117. JB, 577.

118. For example, see: Phillip Blair Rice, "Faulkner's Crucifixion," *Kenyon Review* 16 (Autumn, 1954): 661–70.

119. *SLWF,* 367, WF to Muna Lee, June 26, 1954; BC, Muna Lee to SC, (Sept. 15, 1954).

120. *SLWF,* 369, WF to Harold E. Howland, Aug. 15, 1954; BC, Harold E. Howland to WF, Sept. 2, 1954.

121. JB, 599–608; BP, William Faulkner Prize Interest Fund, Bank of Oxford.

122. *SLWF,* 380–81, WF to Harold E. Howland, May 10, 1955; BP, WF to SC, July 6, 1955.

123. *SLWF,* 385–86, WF to Leon Picon, (Aug. 24, 1955).

124. Kenneth Tynan, "Papa and the Playwright," *Esquire* (May 11, 1963): 1–10.

125. JB, 611.

126. Madeleine Chapsal, "A Lion in the Garden," *Reporter* 13 (Nov. 3, 1955): 40.

127. BP, Jill to WF, Aug. 29, Sept. 7, 1955.

128. BP, I, Donald Hall, Jan. 2, 1968.

129. *SLWF,* 403, WF to Harvey Breit, Sept. 13, 1956; 404, WF to "selected writers," (late Sept., 1956); 407–8, WF to Jean Ennis, Jan. 8, 1957; BP, I, Harvey Breit, Nov. 12, 1964.

130. *SLWF,* 406, WF to SC, (Dec. 10, 1956).

131. *Saturday Review* 42 (Nov. 14, 1959): 21.

132. SLWF, 394–96, WF to David Kirk, Mar. 8, 1956.

133. *Jackson Daily News,* Mar. 27, 1950.

134. *Memphis Commercial Appeal,* Mar. 27, 1951.

135. *Jackson Daily News,* Mar. 29, 1951.

136. *Memphis Commercial Appeal,* Mar. 20, 1955.

137. *Memphis Commercial Appeal,* Mar. 27, 1955; BP, I, MCF, Mar. 31, 1965; I, Albert Erskine, July 23, 1964; BC, PS to MF, Feb. 14, 1958; I, Victoria Fielden Johnson in Brodsky, *Life Glimpses,* 162.

138. *Memphis Commercial Appeal,* Apr. 3, 10, 1955.

139. *Memphis Commercial Appeal,* June 14, 1955.

140. BP, WF to EJ, June 12, 1955.

141. *LIG,* 142–50.

142. JS, "The Art of Fiction," *Paris Review* 3, no. 12 (Spring, 1956): 51.

143. BC, James W. Silver Letters, "To Whom It May Concern," Aug. 21, 1961.

144. *Three Views of the Segregation Decision* (Atlanta: Southern Regional Council, 1956), 9–12.

145. BP, I, BW, Mar. 28, 1965; *SLWF,* 388, WF to JS, (Nov. 28 or 29, 1955); James W. Silver, *Mississippi: The Closed Society* (New York: Harcourt, 1964), xii.

146. BP, I, BW, Mar. 28, 1965.

147. Ibid.; I, JS, Nov. 10, 1964.

148. BP, I, BW, Mar. 30, 1965; BW, *Count-No-Count,* 195–98; BP, I, JS, Nov. 10, 1964; I, Ann Farnsworth, Mar. 30, 1965.

149. BP, I, George Plimpton, Feb. 22, 1967.

150. Ibid.

151. Ibid.; BP, I, Dorothy Parker, Apr. 17, 1965; I, Shelby Foote, Nov. 25, 1967.

152. BP, I, George Plimpton, Feb. 22, 1967; *Who Was Who in America,* 7 (Chicago: Marquis, 1981), 544.

153. BP, I, JS, Nov. 10, 1964.

154. BP, I, Mrs. Sewell Hoggard, Apr. 17, 1965; I, Anthony West, Feb. 24, 1964.

155. BP, excerpt, WF to JS, "Wednesday," (Nov., 1954); JS to JB, Sept. 24, 1969.

156. BP, Memorandum, Harold Ober's office, Feb. 24, 1956; *SLWF,* 396, WF to JS, (Mar. 17, 1956).

157. *Life,* Mar. 5, 1956.

158. BP, Memorandum, "ALD," Feb. 20, 1956.

159. BP, I, JS, Nov. 10, 1964.

160. Russell Warren Howe, "A Talk with William Faulkner," *Reporter* 14 (Mar. 22, 1956):18–28; *LIG,* 262.

161. FCVA, WF to Joan Williams Bowen, Tuesday 12th (Jan., 1957); BP, WF to JW, (June 12, 1956).

162. BP, Memorandum, "ALD," Feb. 20, 1956.

163. BP, JS, "Notes," p. 2125.

164. BP, "Notes of conversation with Mr. Dawson of the Tex and Jinx Program (NBC)," Friday, Feb. 24, 1956.

165. *Reporter,* Apr. 19, 1956; *Time,* Apr. 23, 1956, 12.

166. *Time,* Apr. 23, 1956, 12.

167. *SLWF,* 398, telegram, WF to W.E.B. Du Bois (Apr. 17, 1956), *New York Times,* Apr. 18, 1956.

168. *SLWF,* 396, WF to JS, (Mar. 17, 1956).

169. Howe, "A Talk," 18.

170. BP, I, Clarence Moore, Oct. 31, 1965.

171. *SLWF,* 397, WF to JS, (Mar. 24, 1956).

172. BC, *Southern Reposure,* 1, no. 1 (Summer 1956); FCVA, WF to Allan Morrison, June 23, 1956; *Ebony,* Sept., 1956, 70–73.

173. WF to Editor, *New York Times,* Oct. 7, 1957, printed Oct. 13, 1957.

174. *FIU,* 209–13, 214, 216.

175. JB, 649.

176. WF to Lyle Stuart (Summer, 1957) in Norman Mailer, *Advertisements for Myself* (New York: Putnam, 1959), 332–33.

177. *SLWF,* 201, WF to Richard Wright, (Sept. 11, 1945), *New Letters* 38, (Winter 1971), 128.

178. JB, 656.

179. BC, WF to SC, (Dec., 1955).

180. *SLWF,* 399–400, WF to SC, (early June, 1956).

181. *SLWF,* 402, WF to JS, (Aug. 22, 1956).

182. *SLWF,* 399–400, WF to SC, (early June, 1956).

NINE

1. BP, I, Jill, July 25, 1968.
2. *SLWF,* 406, WF to Floyd Stovall, (Oct. 18, 1956).
3. BP, Memo, D.C. Yalden-Thompson, July 16, 1963; JB, 633–34.
4. JB, 633–34.
5. BP, I, Grover Vandevender and Mrs. Ethel Moore, July 19, 1965.
6. BP, I, Truman Capote, Dec. 29, 1967.
7. BC, Personal Narrative, SC, Feb. 2–10, 1957.
8. BC, Memo, SC, Apr. 2, 1957; JB, 639.
9. BC, E to Dorothy and Saxe Commins, Jan. 5, 1956.
10. I, Victoria Fielden Johnson by L.D. Brodsky, May 20–24, 1985, in Louis Daniel Brodsky, *William Faulkner, Life Glimpses* (Austin: University of Texas Press, 1990), 153–55.
11. BP, I, Malcolm Franklin, Sept. 26, 1966; I, E, Aug. 22, 1964.
12. BC, Telegram, Malcolm Franklin to WF, Sept. 14, 1954; *SLWF,* 370–71, WF to Malcolm and Gloria Franklin, Sept. 21, 1954.
13. BC, Gloria Franklin to Dorothy and Saxe Commins, Nov. 1, 1954.
14. BC, E to SC, Mar. 20, 1955.
15. BC, E to SC, Mar. 20, 1955; E to Dorothy Commins (Mar. 30, 1955); WF to SC, July 6, (1955).
16. BC, E to Dorothy Commins, Aug. 15, 1955; E to Dorothy and Saxe Commins, Jan. 5, 1956.
17. BC, E to SC, Nov. 5, 1956.
18. BC, E to Dorothy and Saxe Commins, Feb. 15, 1957; WF to SC, Jan. 23, 1957.
19. BC, WF to SC, Mar. 16, 1955; E to Dorothy Commins, Apr. 23, 1957; E to Dorothy and Saxe Commins, May 10, 1957.
20. BP, note added by JB to I, Victoria Fielden, Oct. 27, 1964.
21. BP, I, Atch Hench, n.d., regarding Sunday, May 5, 1957.
22. BC, WF to SC, (Oct., 1957); WF to Johnette Tracy (Dec., 1957).
23. BC, WF to Johnette Tracy, (Dec., 1957).
24. BC, Johnette Tracy to James W. Silver, (Dec. 13, 1957).
25. BP, E to Yvonne Blotner, July 8, (1957); BC, WF to Dot, (Nov. 9, 1959).
26. BP, "Dot" notes.

27. BP, I, Victoria Fielden, Oct. 27, 1964.
28. BP, obituary clipping.
29. BP, I, Dot, Mar. 21, 1965.
30. BP, "Dot" notes.
31. BP, SM to JB, Mar. 22, 1971.
32. BP, I, SM, Nov. 23, 1965; SM to JB, Mar. 22, 1971.
33. BP, I, Dot, Nov. 14, 1966.
34. BP, BW to JB, Mar. 14, 1965; JB to BW, Apr. 7, 1965.
35. *SLWF,* 411–12, WF to Floyd Stovall, Sept. 9, 1957; BP, I, Charles McDunn, fall, 1965.
36. JB, 648, 651–52.
37. BC, telegram, WF to Dorothy Commins, July 18, 1958; JB, 659.
38. *SLWF,* 418, WF to Mrs. Julio S. Galban, Jan. 2, 1959; WF to Donald S. Klopfler, (mid-Jan., 1959); WF to William Fielden, (Feb. 1, 1959); BP, I, Doug Nicoll, Feb. 28, 1966.
39. JB, 683; BP, I, Doug Nicoll, Feb. 28, 1966; I, Linton Massey, June 15, 1966; *SLWF,* 418, WF to Mrs. Julio S. Galban, Jan. 2, 1959.
40. BP, I, Harry Hyer, Aug. 7, 1968; I, Grover Vandevender, July 19, 1965 (GV said WF was riding Fenceman not Powerhouse.); I, Molly Nicoll, Feb. 11, 1966.
41. *SLWF,* 429, WF to Albert Erskine, (mid-Apr., 1959); BP, I, E.D. Vere Nicoll, Feb. 28, 1966, record dated Mar. 18, 1959.
42. JB, 665; *SLWF,* 437–38, WF to E.D. Vere Nicoll, Apr. 7, 1959.
43. JB, 666–67; *MBB,* 258.
44. BP, clipping, *Memphis Commercial Appeal,* July 20, 1959; I, Arthur G. Guyton, Oct. 5, 1967.
45. *SLWF,* 437–38, WF to Albert Erskine, (Oct. 15, 1959); BC, E to Dorothy Commins, Nov. 19, 1959.
46. BP, I, Linton Massey, Dec. 19, 1969.
47. *Saturday Review* 42 (Nov., 1959): 21.
48. BC, WF to SC, (Jan., 1956).
49. JB, 676–77; *SLWF,* 440–42, WF to E, (Jan. 20, 1960).
50. JB, 679; BC, MF to WF, (Oct. 11, 1954).
51. JB, 676, 679; BP, Blotner memo, re. Oct. 29, 1960; I, Vickie Fielden and Dean Faulkner, Mar. 18, 1965.
52. BC, PS to Kraig Kloson, Oct. 21, 1960; BP, I, SM, Nov. 26, 1965; I, Jimmy Faulkner, Mar. 22, 1965.
53. BP, WF to Jimmy Faulkner, n.d.; gravestone, St. Peter's Cemetery, Oxford.
54. Gravestones, St. Peter's Cemetery, Oxford.
55. BP, I, Harry Hyer, Aug. 7, 1968.
56. *SLWF,* 446–47, WF to Floyd Stovall, Aug. 25, 1960.
57. BP, Mrs. J.S. Galban to WF, Feb. 4, 1959; WF to Mrs. Julio S. Galban, Feb. 8, 1959; I, Mrs. Julio Saurez-Galban, June 13, 1967.
58. BP, I, Doug Nicoll, Aug. 7, 1968; WF's membership card.
59. BP, WF to Jimmy Faulkner, (Oct. or Nov., 1960); WF to Albert Erskine, (Oct. 30, 1960); SLWF, 368, WF to SC, (July 2 or 9, 1954).
60. For example, see: SLWF, 335–36, WF to Antony Brett James, July 8, 1952.
61. SLWF, 320–21, WF to Robert Haas, Aug. 20, (1951).
62. BC, E to SC, (Mar., 1954).

63. WF, "Mississippi," *Holiday* (Apr., 1954), 34–36.

64. BC, E to Dorothy and SC, Mar. 30, 1954.

65. BP, I, J.R. Cofield, Mar. 25, 1965; Nov. 19, 1966.

66. *The Town,* p. 29. Italics in original.

67. BP, WF to EJ, (Aug. 27, 1951).

68. BC, WF to SC, (Nov. 1, 1952).

69. Brodsky, *Glimpses,* 67, I, Albert Isaac Bezzerides, Sept. 3-7, 1983.

70. SLWF, 345, 364, WF to SC (Jan. 5, 1953); WF to JS, (May 29, 1954); BC, WF to SC, Jan. 5, 1953; LCCH-ChC, Deed Record, Book 134, p. 131.

71. BP, I, Jill, Aug. 13, 1968.

72. SLWF, 372, WF to JS, (mid-Nov., 1954); FCVA, WF to JW, (Nov. 6, 1959).

73. BP, I, Grover Vandevender and Mrs. Ethel Moore, July 19, 1965; I and memo., David C. Yalden-Thompson, July 16, 1963.

74. BP, I, Jean Ennis, Nov. 12, 1964; I, E, Dec. 9, 1964; Blotner memo. of dinner with Alexander and Betty Jo Rives, Nov. 12, 1959.

75. BP, JB to Jimmy Faulkner, July 26, 1966.

76. BP, I, David C. Yalden-Thompson, July 16, 1963; SM to JB, July 29, 1966.

77. BP, I, Mrs. Ev (Evalyn) Galban, June 13, 1967.

78. BC, E to James W. Silver, Apr. 23, 1962.

79. JB, 703–4.

80. *LG,* 321–22.

81. BP, I, JS, Nov. 10, 1964.

82. JB, 704.

83. BC, WF to JW, (Apr. 17, 1957).

84. BC, WF to JW, (Dec. 12, 1960).

85. BC, WF to JW, Jan. 4, (1961).

86. FCVA, WF to Eudora Welty, Apr. 29, (1943).

87. FCVA, WF to JW, (Dec. 20, 1951), (May 7, 1952), (July 3, 1953).

88. BC, E to Dorothy Commins, Apr. 30, (1958).

89. BP, WF to Paul Pollard, Feb. 24, 1960.

90. BP, I, Aubrey Seay, Sept. 11, 1964.

91. BP, I, Jill, July 25, 1968.

92. BP, I, Nancy Bowers, Sept. 28, 1966.

93. *SLWF,* 422–23, WF to Mrs. Julio S. Galban, Feb. 8, 1959.

94. *SLWF,* 438, WF to Bob Haas, (Nov. 9, 1959).

95. BP, E.M. Hanbury, Jr., to JB, Sept. 21, 1967; I, Harry Hyer, Aug. 7, 1968; I, Grover Vandevender and Mrs. Ethel Moore, July 19, 1965.

96. JB, 682.

97. BP, I, Vickie Fielden and Dean Faulkner, Mar. 18, 1965.

98. BC, Simon Claxton, "William Faulkner: An Interview," *The Cate Review,* June, 1962, 3–6, 18–19.

99. BP, WF to Albert Erskine, (Oct. 22, 1961).

100. BP, WF to Linton Massey, June 29, 1962.

101. BP, JB memo, for July 6, 1961.

102. BP, JB memo, May 8, 1961.

103. BP, Robert Haas to WF, Jan. 18, 1959.

104. BP, I, James Faulkner, Mar. 21, 1965.

105. *SLWF,* 424–25, WF to Mauna Lee, Mar. 4, 1959.

106. BP, memo, D.C. Yalden-Thompson, July 16, 1963.

107. BP, Ernest Hemingway to Mr. Rider, July 29, 1965 (copy); see also: Stephen Longstreet to JB, May 14, 1966.

108. JB, 689–90.

109. BP, I, Nancy Bowers, Sept. 28, 1968.

110. BP, Medical Record, Nicoll office, Dec. 19, 1961; I, Leo Falk, Mar. 9, 1966.

111. BP, I, Dr. Lever Stewart, Feb. 25, 1966.

112. BP, I, J.S. Shield, July 21, 1966.

113. BP, I, Leo Falk, Mar. 9, 1966.

114. BP, I, Dr. Abernathy (dentist), Nov. 14, 1965; WF to JB, Jan. 31, 1962.

115. BP, WF to William Fielden, Nov. 7, 1959.

116. BC, PS to Richard P. Adams, June 8, 1862.

117. BC, PS to James B. Meriwether, June 15, 1962.

118. BC, PS to E. Byrne Hackett, June 17, 1931.

119. FCVA, WF to Harold Ober, Feb. 4, 1959.

120. JB, 708–9.

121. BP, I, Drs. Linder, Mar. 24, 1965; I, Aubrey Seay, Sept. 11, 1964; I, Dr. Felix Linder, Aug., n.d., 1964.

122. *SLWF,* 461–63, WF to Linton Massey, (June 29, 1962); telegram, WF to Linton Massey, July 2, 1962.

123. JB, 711–13.

124. BP, SM to JB, Oct. 14, 1970.

125. *MBB,* 6.

126. BP, SM to JB, Oct. 14, 1970; JB, 714–15.

127. JB, 716–17.

128. JB, 717–18; *MBB,* 6–8; William Styron, "As He Lay Dead, A Bitter Grief," *Life,* July 20, 1962, 39–42.

129. *MBB,* 9.

PART III

TEN

1. Fredrika Bremer, *The Hours of the New World: Impressions of America,* trans. Mary Howitt, 3 vols. (London: A. Hall, Virtue, & Co., 1853), 3: 7–11.

2. Quoted in Joel Williamson, *New People: Miscegenation and Mulattoes in the United States* (New York: Free Press, 1980), 55–56.

3. BP, notes, June, 1957; Southern Historical Collection, University of North Carolina—Chapel Hill, Lipscomb Family Papers, Edward Lipscomb to Smith Lipscomb, June 19, 1874.

4. FCVA, typescript, "A Portrait of Elmer."

5. FCVA, typescript, "Mosquitoes," 184.

6. FCVA, typescript, "A Portrait of Elmer."

7. *Mosquitoes,* 147.

8. FCVA, typescript, "Mosquitoes," 205.

9. Ibid., 204–5.

10. Ibid., 204.

11. Albert Bushnell Hart, "The Outcome of the Southern Race Question," *North American Review* 188 (June, 1908): 56.

12. FCVA, typescript, "Mosquitoes," 166.

ELEVEN

1. *Scribner's* 84, no. 6 (June, 1931): 585–97.

THE GARDEN

1. BC, Phil Stone to Dave Womack, Mar. 28, 1955.
2. Sherwood Anderson to Laura Lou Copenhaver, Nov. 9, 1937, *Letters of Sherwood Anderson,* ed. Howard Mumford Jones (Boston: Little, Brown, 1953), 392–93.
3. Sherwood Anderson to Laura Lou Copenhaver, Mar., n.d., 1935, *Letters of Sherwood Anderson,* 310.
4. BP, I, Atch Hench, May 5, 1957.
5. BC, WF to JW, Jan. 4, (1960).

Index

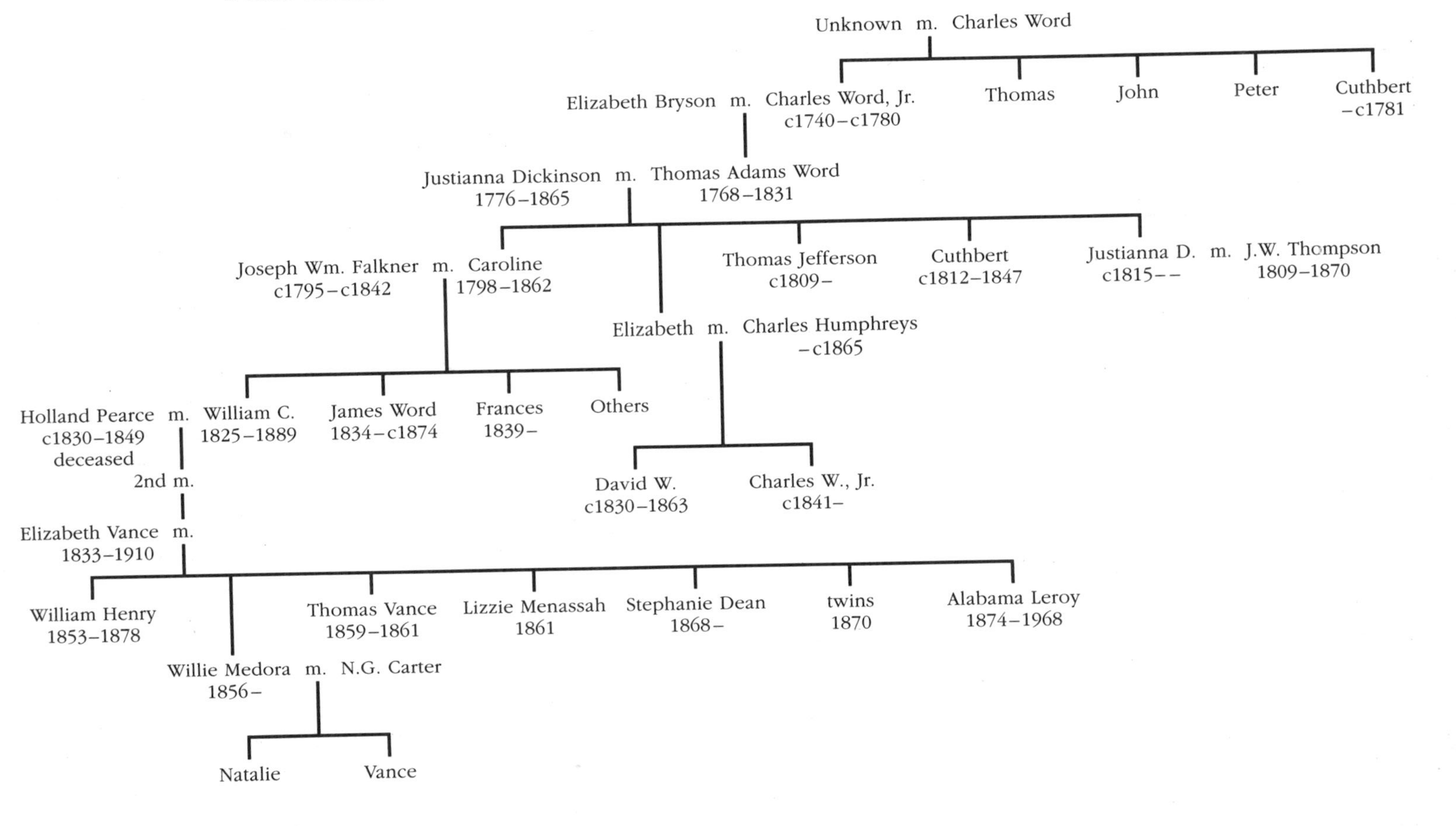
WORD-FALKNER-VANCE
Unknown m. Charles Word
Elizabeth Bryson m. Charles Word, Jr.
c1740–c1780
Thomas
John
Peter
Cuthbert
–c1781
Justianna Dickinson m. Thomas Adams Word
1776–1865
1768–1831
Joseph Wm. Falkner m. Caroline
c1795–c1842
1798–1862
Thomas Jefferson
c1809–
Cuthbert
c1812–1847
Justianna D. m. J.W. Thompson
c1815– –
1809–1870
Elizabeth m. Charles Humphreys
–c1865
Holland Pearce m. William C.
c1830–1849
deceased
1825–1889
James Word
1834–c1874
Frances
1839–
Others
David W.
c1830–1863
Charles W., Jr.
c1841–
2nd m.
Elizabeth Vance m.
1833–1910
William Henry
1853–1878
Thomas Vance
1859–1861
Lizzie Menassah
1861
Stephanie Dean
1868–
twins
1870
Alabama Leroy
1874–1968
Willie Medora m. N.G. Carter
1856–
Natalie
Vance

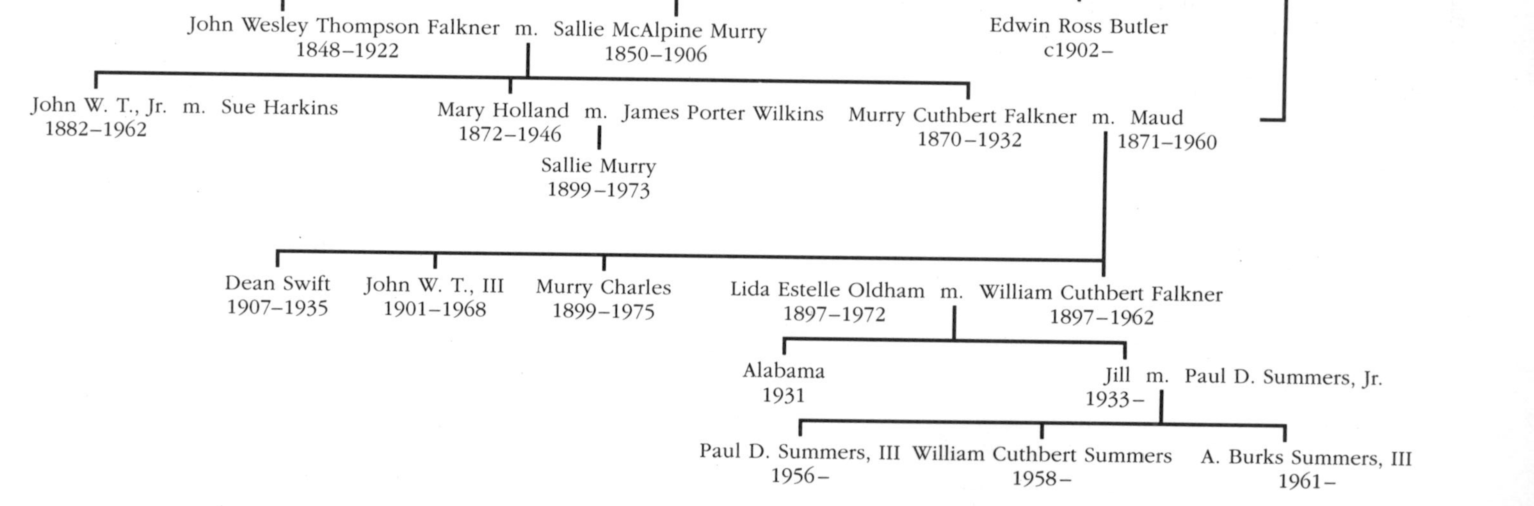

BUTLER – FALKNER
Sherwood Henry House m. Nancy
1784–1841
1789–1868
probable
Charles George Butler m. Burlina W. Butler
1805–1855
1811–1877
William R. m. Anna Elizabeth Bowen
c1830–1868
1832–1858
Emily m. William Bolivar Bowen
1832–1858
1830–1887
S. Henry m. Vermelle Boone
1834–1864
Mary Anne m. Hulsey Edwards
1837–1898
Martha J. m. John H. Nelson
c1840–
1836–1878
Charles Edward m. Leila Dean Swift
1848–
1849–1907
William C. Falkner m. Holland Pearce
1825–1889
c1830–1849
Emily Holcombe m. John Young Murry
Addie Buffaloe m. Sherwood Tate
1870–1949
1869–1930
Edwin Ross Butler
c1902–
John Wesley Thompson Falkner m. Sallie McAlpine Murry
1848–1922
1850–1906
John W. T., Jr. m. Sue Harkins
1882–1962
Mary Holland m. James Porter Wilkins
1872–1946
Sallie Murry
1899–1973
Murry Cuthbert Falkner m. Maud
1870–1932
1871–1960
Dean Swift
1907–1935
John W. T., III
1901–1968
Murry Charles
1899–1975
Lida Estelle Oldham m. William Cuthbert Falkner
1897–1972
1897–1962
Alabama
1931
Jill m. Paul D. Summers, Jr.
1933–
Paul D. Summers, III
1956–
William Cuthbert Summers
1958–
A. Burks Summers, III
1961–

OLDHAM

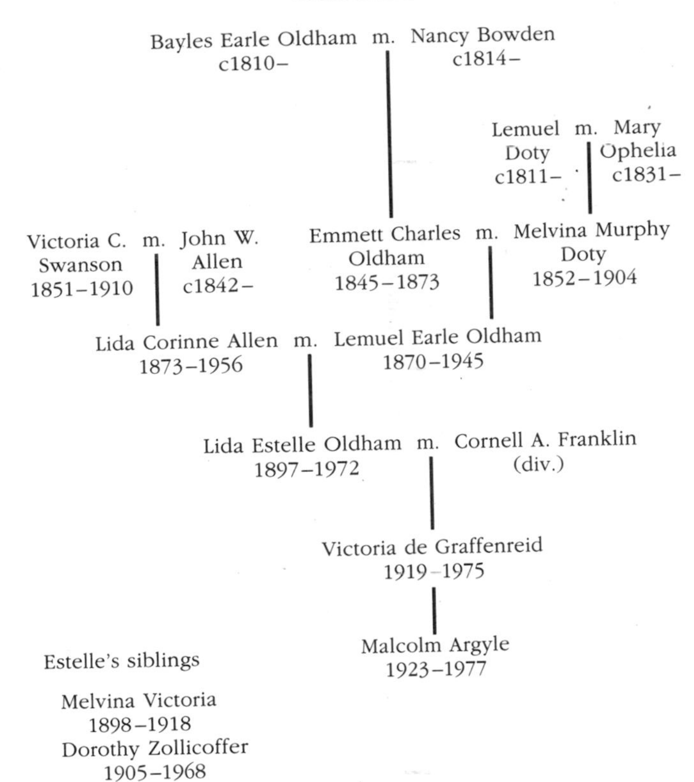
Bayles Earle Oldham m. Nancy Bowden
c1810–
c1814–
Lemuel Doty m. Mary Ophelia
c1811–
c1831–
Victoria C. Swanson m. John W. Allen
1851–1910
c1842–
Emmett Charles Oldham m. Melvina Murphy Doty
1845–1873
1852–1904
Lida Corinne Allen m. Lemuel Earle Oldham
1873–1956
1870–1945
Lida Estelle Oldham m. Cornell A. Franklin (div.)
1897–1972
Victoria de Graffenreid
1919–1975
Malcolm Argyle
1923–1977
Estelle's siblings
Melvina Victoria
1898–1918
Dorothy Zollicoffer
1905–1968
Edward de Graffenreid
1907–1916

EMELINE FALKNER

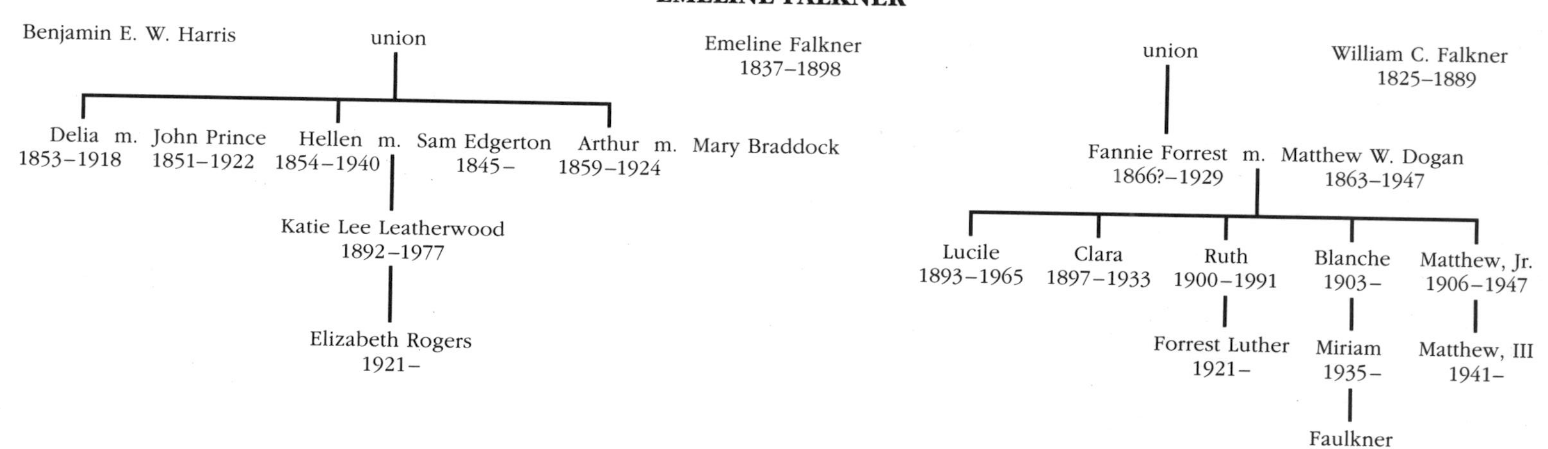